UNIT OPERATIONS - II

FOR
THIRD YEAR DIPLOMA COURSE IN CHEMICAL ENGINEERING/TECHNOLOGY
PETROCHEMICAL AND POLYMER ENGINEERING

K. A. GAVHANE

Vice Principal & Head of Chemical Engg. Dept.
S.E. Society's Satara Polytechnic,
Satara.

N0901

UNIT OPERATIONS - II　　　　　　　　　　　　　　ISBN 978-81-96396-12-1
Twenty Ninth Edition : August 2015
© : Author

The text of this publication, or any part thereof, should not be reproduced or transmitted in any form or stored in any computer storage system or device for distribution including photocopy, recording, taping or information retrieval system or reproduced on any disc, tape, perforated media or other information storage device etc., without the written permission of Author with whom the rights are reserved. Breach of this condition is liable for legal action.

Every effort has been made to avoid errors or omissions in this publication. In spite of this, errors may have crept in. Any mistake, error or discrepancy so noted and shall be brought to our notice shall be taken care of in the next edition. It is notified that neither the publisher nor the author or seller shall be responsible for any damage or loss of action to any one, of any kind, in any manner, therefrom.

Published By :　　　　　　　　　　　　　　　　　　　　　**Printed By :**
NIRALI PRAKASHAN　　　　　　　　　　　　　　　　　　Repro India Ltd,
Abhyudaya Pragati, 1312, Shivaji Nagar,　　　　　　　　　　Mumbai.
Off J.M. Road, PUNE – 411005
Tel - (020) 25512336/37/39, Fax - (020) 25511379
Email : niralipune@pragationline.com

☞ DISTRIBUTION CENTRES

PUNE
Nirali Prakashan : 119, Budhwar Peth, Jogeshwari Mandir Lane, Pune 411002, Maharashtra
Tel : (020) 2445 2044, 66022708, Fax : (020) 2445 1538
Email : bookorder@pragationline.com, niralilocal@pragationline.com

Nirali Prakashan : S. No. 28/27, Dhyari, Near Pari Company, Pune 411041
Tel : (020) 24690204 Fax : (020) 24690316
Email : dhyari@pragationline.com, bookorder@pragationline.com

MUMBAI
Nirali Prakashan : 385, S.V.P. Road, Rasdhara Co-op. Hsg. Society Ltd.,
Girgaum, Mumbai 400004, Maharashtra
Tel : (022) 2385 6339 / 2386 9976, Fax : (022) 2386 9976
Email : niralimumbai@pragationline.com

☞ DISTRIBUTION BRANCHES

JALGAON
Nirali Prakashan : 34, V. V. Golani Market, Navi Peth, Jalgaon 425001,
Maharashtra, Tel : (0257) 222 0395, Mob : 94234 91860

KOLHAPUR
Nirali Prakashan : New Mahadvar Road, Kedar Plaza, 1st Floor Opp. IDBI Bank
Kolhapur 416 012, Maharashtra. Mob : 9850046155

NAGPUR
Pratibha Book Distributors : Above Maratha Mandir, Shop No. 3, First Floor,
Rani Jhanshi Square, Sitabuldi, Nagpur 440012, Maharashtra
Tel : (0712) 254 7129

DELHI
Nirali Prakashan : 4593/21, Basement, Aggarwal Lane 15, Ansari Road, Daryaganj
Near Times of India Building, New Delhi 110002
Mob : 08505972553

BENGALURU
Pragati Book House : House No. 1, Sanjeevappa Lane, Avenue Road Cross,
Opp. Rice Church, Bengaluru – 560002.
Tel : (080) 64513344, 64513355,Mob : 9880582331, 9845021552
Email:bharatsavla@yahoo.com

CHENNAI
Pragati Books : 9/1, Montieth Road, Behind Taas Mahal, Egmore,
Chennai 600008 Tamil Nadu, Tel : (044) 6518 3535,
Mob : 94440 01782 / 98450 21552 / 98805 82331,
Email : bharatsavla@yahoo.com

niralipune@pragationline.com | www.pragationline.com
Also find us on www.facebook.com/niralibooks

PREFACE TO THE TWENTY NINTH EDITION

I am very happy to present this Twenty-ninth edition of the book – **Unit Operations – II** in SI units to students of diploma in chemical engineering and chemical technology.

The subject matter is divided into twelve chapters and sufficient number of illustrative examples are given on each chapter. The entire matter is revised, arranged in a proper order with simplified diagrams, checked thoroughly for corrections and put in a simple language so that the students of diploma in chemical engineering will grasp it very easily.

A lot of additional matter is incorporated wherever necessary so as to make the book more complete.

The topic-Try yourself with answers is included as Appendix – I in this edition which will positively help students to judge the depth of the subject matter. This book is also very much useful for degree students of chemical and petrochemical engineering.

I am very thankful to staff members of chemical engineering departments located throughout the Maharashtra for recommending this book right from the first edition.

I hope positively that students as well as the staff members will appreciate the content of the book.

I would welcome and appreciate suggestions and comments from students and staff members for improving the quality of the book.

PUNE
November 2014

K. A. GAVHANE
kagavhane @ yahoo.in
Mobile : 9850242440

CHAPTER ONE

INTRODUCTION

Chemical Engineering is that branch of engineering which deals with the production of bulk materials from basic raw materials in a most economical and safe way by chemical means.

The profession of chemical engineering deals with the industrial processes in which raw materials are converted or separated into useful products. The treatment of raw materials, chemical transformation proper and separation of the desired product(s) are the usual stages of any chemical manufacturing activity. A chemical engineer converts raw materials into useful finished products of a greater value in an optimal way through processes involving physical and/or chemical (or biochemical) changes.

A chemical engineer is the one who is skilled in development, design, construction, operation and control of industrial plants in which matter undergoes a change. He must choose proper raw materials and must see that the products manufactured by him meet the specifications set by the customers. Chemical engineers work in four main segments of the chemical process industries : research and development, design, manufacturing/production and sales.

The traditional roles of chemical engineers include teaching, research and development, design, production, plant maintenance and trouble shooting, plant management, marketing, entrepreneurship, and consultancy. Chemical engineers play a vital role in the development and production of various essential needs of mankind like food, clothing, housing, health, communication, energy, utilisation of natural resources, and protection of the environment.

Chemical engineers are engaged in the production of fertilizers insecticides, pesticides, food products, drugs and pharmaceuticals, plastics, synthetic fibers, dyes and dye intermediates, paints and lacquers, synthetic fuels, paper, nuclear energy, synthetic rubber, etc.

Chemical process : Every industrial chemical process is designed to produce economically a desired product from given raw materials through a series of steps involving physical or chemical change in the material under consideration. The steps involving certain physical changes are regarded as unit operations; whereas the step(s) involving chemical changes in the material under consideration (i.e. chemical reactions) are regarded as unit process(es). Fig. 1.1 shows a typical chemical process.

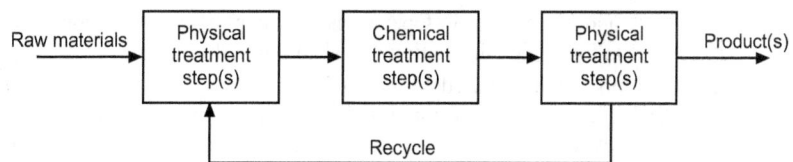

Fig. 1.1 : Typical chemical process

The raw materials undergo physical treatment steps so as to put them in the form in which they can be reacted. Then, they pass through the reactor in which chemical transformation of some or all of raw materials takes place by one or more chemical reactions. The product mixture comprising of products produced and unreacted raw materials undergo further physical treatments - separation, purification to obtain the desired product. So, any chemical process carried out on a commercial scale, can be thought of as the sum of unit operations and unit process(es) performed on the raw materials in a correct sequence from the feed to product end.

UNIT OPERATIONS

The concept of unit operations was introduced by A.D. Little in 1905.

The operations carried out in the process industries involving physical changes in the system under consideration are regarded as unit operations.

Features :

1. These are physical in nature, i.e., changes involved in them are primarily physical.
2. These are common to all types of diverse industries.
3. Individual operations have common techniques and are based on the same scientific principles regardless of the material being processed.
4. They are independent of industries in which they are carried out.
5. Practical methods of carrying them out may be more or less different in different industries.

Hence, the concentration of solutions by evaporation is a unit operation (involving a change in the concentration of the solution) that can be carried out in all types of diverse industries. This operation is basically similar in the handling of sugar or salt, or fruit juices with some differences in the most suitable arrangements.

They are basically used to conduct the physical steps of preparing the reactants, separating and purifying the products, recycling the unconverted reactants and controlling the energy transfer in and out of the chemical reactor.

A physical change resulting in a change in any property of matter occurs by the action of some sort of driving force. The normal driving force in heat flow is temperature difference.

Broadly, unit operations are Mechanical Operations, e.g., size reduction (crushing and grinding), filtration, size separation, etc. Fluid Flow Operations in which the pressure difference as a driving force, Heat Transfer (Operations) in which the temperature difference acts as a driving force and Mass Transfer Operations in which the concentration difference/ gradient acts as a driving force, e.g., distillation, gas absorption, drying, etc.

The theory of unit operations is based on the fundamental laws of physical sciences such as law of conservation of mass, law of conservation of energy, Newton's laws of motion, Ideal gas law, Dalton's law of partial pressure, Newton's law of cooling, Raoult's law, etc.

CLASSIFICATION OF UNIT OPERATIONS

1. Fluid flow : It is concerned with the principles that determine the flow or transportation of any fluid from one point to another.

2. Mechanical operations : These involve size reduction of solids by crushing, grinding, pulverising, etc., mixing, conveying and mechanical separations such as decantation, filtration, settling and sedimentation, screening, flotation, etc.

3. Heat transfer : It deals with the principles that determine the accumulation and transfer of heat energy (thermal energy) from one place to another owing to the existence of a temperature difference. Heat transfer occurs in heating, cooling, phase change, evaporation, drying, distillation, etc. The modes/mechanisms by which heat transfer may occur are conduction, convection and radiation.

4. Mass transfer : It is concerned with the transfer of mass from one phase to another distinct phase. Mass transfer operations depend on molecules diffusing or vaporising from one distinct phase to another and are based on (or they utilise) differences in vapour pressure, solubility, or diffusivity. Molecular diffusion and turbulent/eddy diffusion are the mechanisms of mass transfer. Mass transfer operations include separation techniques like distillation, gas absorption, drying, extraction, crystallisation, etc.

This text covers heat and mass transfer operations - a part portion of the unit operations of chemical engineering.

Unit Systems :

The various systems of units and the basic / fundamental quantities associated with them are given below.

Fundamental Quantity	Unit Systems				Dimension
	SI	MKS	CGS	FPS	
Length	Meter (m)	Meter (m)	Centimeter (cm)	Foot (ft)	L
Mass	Kilogram (kg)	Kilogram (kg)	Gram (g)	Pound (*lb*)	M
Time	Second (s)	Second (s)	Second (s)	Second (s)	θ
Temperature	Kelvin (K)	Celsius (°C)	Celsius (°C)	Fahrenheit (°F)	T

$$°C = \text{degrees Celsius}$$
$$K = \text{Kelvin}$$

Symbolic abbreviations of the units are given in bracket.

The International System of Units abbreviated as SI units has now been adopted throughout the world, in particular, in the field of science and technology.

BASIC SI UNITS

Mass	:	kilogram (kg)
Length	:	meter (m)
Time	:	second (s)
Temperature	:	kelvin (K)
Mole	:	kilogram mole (kmol)
Force	:	newton (N)
Pressure	:	newton / (meter)^2 [N/m^2 = Pa (pascal)]
Energy	:	newton · meter (N.m) = J (joule)
Power	:	newton · meter / second ((N.m)/s = J/s = W)

1. **Pressure :** The units of pressure in SI, MKS and FPS systems are N/m^2 (known as pascal, symbol Pa), kgf/cm^2 and lbf / in^2 (known as psi) respectively.

$$1 \text{ atm} = 760 \text{ torr (or mm Hg)} = 101325 \text{ N/m}^2 \text{ or Pa}$$
$$= 101.325 \text{ kPa} = 1.033 \text{ kgf/cm}^2$$

2. **Work / Energy :** The units of work (energy) in SI, MKS, CGS and FPS systems are joule (J), m.kgf, erg and ft.lbf respectively.

3. **Heat :** The units of heat in SI, MKS, CGS and FPS systems are joule (J), kilocalorie (kcal), calorie (cal) and British thermal unit (Btu) respectively.

$$1 \text{ cal} = 4.187 \text{ J,}$$
$$1 \text{ Btu} = 1055.056 \text{ J}$$

In the SI system, heat flow/heat flux is usually expressed in watts (W).

Some of the prefixes for SI units :

(i) giga (G) — multiply by 10^9
(ii) mega (M) — multiply by 10^6
(iii) kilo (k) — multiply by 10^3
(iv) milli (m) — multiply by 10^{-3}
(v) micro (μ) — multiply by 10^{-6}
(vi) nano (n) — multiply by 10^{-9}

CONVERSION FACTORS TO SI UNITS

To convert from	To	Multiply by
1. Length, L :		
ft	m	0.3048
cm	m	0.01
in	mm	25.4
in	m	0.0254
2. Area, L^2 :		
ft^2	m^2	0.0929
cm^2	m^2	10^{-4}
3. Volume, L^3 :		
ft^3	m^3	0.02832
cm^3	m^3	10^{-6}
l	m^3	10^{-3}
4. Velocity, L/θ :		
ft/s	m/s	0.3048
ft/h	m/s	8.467×10^{-5}
5. Volumetric flow rate, L^3/θ		
ft^2/s	m^3/s	0.02832
ft^3/h	m^3/s	7.867×10^{-6}
l/h	m^3/s	2×10^{-7}
l/s	m^3/s	10^{-3}
6. Mass, M :		
lb	kg	0.4536
t	kg	1000
g	kg	10^{-3}
7. Density, M/L^3 :		
lb/ft^3	kg/m^3	16.019
g/cm^3	$kg/m^3 = g/l$	1000
8. Mass flow rate, M/θ :		
lb/s	kg/s	0.4536
lb/h	kg/s	1.26×10^{-4}
9. Mass flux, mass velocity, $M/L^2\theta$:		
$lb/(ft^2 \cdot h)$	$kg/(m^2 \cdot s)$	1.356×10^{-3}
$g/(cm^2 \cdot s)$	$kg/(m \cdot s)$	10

10. Molar flux, molar mass velocity, mole / $L^2\theta$:		
lbmol / (ft² · h)	kmol / (m² · s)	1.336×10^{-3}
gmol / (cm² · s)	kmol / (m² · s)	10
11. Force, F :		
lbf	N	4.448
kgf	N	9.807
dyn	N	10^{-5}
12. Pressure, F/L² :		
lbf/ft²	N/m² = Pa	47.88
std. atm	N/m² = Pa	1.0325×10^5
std. atm	kPa	101.325
in Hg	N/m² = Pa	3.386
in H₂O	N/m² = Pa	249.1
dyn/cm²	N/m² = Pa	10^{-1}
mmHg	N/m² = Pa	133.3
torr	N/m² = Pa	133.3
bar	N/m² = Pa	10^5
kgf/cm²	N/m² = Pa	9.808×10^4
13. Energy, work, heat, FL :		
cal	N·m = J	4.187
Btu	N·m = J	1055
kcal	N·m = J	4187
erg	N·m = J	10^{-7}
kW·h	N·m = J	3.6×10^6
14. Enthalpy, FL/M :		
Btu/lb	(N.m)/kg = J/kg	2326
cal/g	(N.m)/kg = J/kg	4187
kcal/kg	(N.m)/kg = J/kg	4187
15. Molar enthalpy, FL/mole		
Btu/lbmol	(N.m)/mol = J/mol	2326
cal/gmol	(N.m)/mol = J/mol	4187

16. Heat capacity, specific heat, FL/MT :		
Btu/(lb · °F)	N.m/(kg·K) = J/(kg·K)	4187
cal/(g · °C)	N.m/(kg·K) = J/(kg·K)	4187
17. Molar heat capacity, FL/mole T :		
Btu/(lbmol · °F)	N.m/(kmol·K) = J/(kmol·K)	4187
cal/(gmol · °C)	N.m/(kmol·K) = J/(kmol·K)	4187
18. Energy flux, $FL/L^2\theta$:		
Btu/(ft² · h)	N.m/(m² · s) = W/m²	3.155
cal/(cm² · s)	N.m/(m² · s) = W/m²	4.187×10^4
19. Thermal conductivity, $FL^2/L^2\theta T = FL/L^2\theta\ (T/L)$:		
Btu·ft / (ft² · h · °F)	N.m/(m·s·K) = W/(m·K)	1.7307
kcal·m/(m²·h·°C)	N.m/(m·s·K) = W/(m·K)	1.163
cal·cm/(cm² · s · °C)	N.m/(m·s·K) = W/(m·K)	418.7
20. Heat transfer coefficient, $FL/L^2\theta T$:		
Btu/(ft² · h · °F)	N.m/(m² · s · K) = W/(m²·K)	5.679
cal/(cm² · s · °C)	N.m/(m² · s · K) = W/(m²·K)	4.187×10^4
kcal/(m² · h · °C)	N.m/(m² · s · K) = W/(m²·K)	1.163
21. Power, FL/θ		
(ft·lbf)/s	(N.m)/s = W	1.356
hp	(N.m)/s = W	745.7
Btu/h	(N.m)/s = W	0.2931
kcal/h	(N.m)/s = W	1.163
22. Viscosity, $M/L\theta$		
P (poise ≡ g/(cm.s)	kg/(m.s) = (N.s)/m²	0.10
cP	kg/(m.s) = (N.s)/m² = Pa·s	0.001
lb/(ft.s)	kg/(m.s)	1.488

While writing the units of fundamental or derived quantity, please remember the following :

1. Correct : 10 kgf.m incorrect : 10 kgfm
2. Correct : 10 kg incorrect : 10 kgs ... no plural form of the unit symbol.
3. Correct : 10 cm incorrect : 10 cm.
   ... no period (full stop) at the end of the unit symbol.
4. Correct : 10000 W/(m^2.K) incorrect : 10000 W/m^2·K
5. Correct : 10 kW incorrect : 10 k W

Temperature intervals or differences are related by :

$$1 \text{ deg C} = 1.8 \text{ deg F} = 1 \text{ K}$$
$$20 \text{ deg C} = 20 \text{ K}$$

❏❏❏

CHAPTER TWO

CONDUCTION

Heat transfer deals with the study of rates at which exchange of heat takes place between a hot source and a cold receiver. In process industries there are many operations which involve transfer of energy in the form of heat, e.g., evaporation, distillation, drying, etc. and also chemical reactions carried on a commercial scale take place with evolution or absorption of heat. It is also necessary to prevent the loss of heat from a hot vessel or a pipe system. In all these cases, the major problem is that of transfer of heat at the desired rate. The knowledge of laws of heat transfer, mechanisms of heat transfer and process heat transfer equipments is of great importance from a stand point of controlling the flow of heat in the desired manner.

It is well established fact that if two bodies at different temperatures are brought into thermal contact, heat flows from a body at high temperature to a that at lower temperature (**second law of thermodynamics**). The net flow of heat is always in the direction of temperature decrease. Thus, heat is defined as *a form of energy which is in transit between a hot source and a cold receiver*. The transfer of heat solely depends upon the temperatures of the two bodies/substances/parts of system. In other words, temperature can be termed as the level of thermal (heat) energy, i.e., high temperature of a body is the indication of high level of heat energy content of the body.

Whenever the temperature difference (driving force for heat transfer) exists between two parts of a system, the heat may flow by one or more of the three basic mechanisms, namely, conduction, convection, and radiation. We will first see three modes of heat transfer in brief and then we will consider heat conduction through solids in detail.

Conduction : It is the transfer of heat from one part of a body to the another part of the same body or from one body to another which is in physical contact with it, without appreciable displacement of particles of a body. In metallic solids, thermal conduction results from the motion of unbound electrons. It is restricted to **flow of heat in solids**. Examples of conduction : Heat flow through the brick wall of a furnace, the metal sheet of a boiler and the metal wall of a heat exchanger tube.

Convection : It is the transfer of heat from one point to another point within a fluid (gas or liquid) by mixing of hot and cold portions of the fluid. It is attributed to the macroscopic motion of fluid. Convection is restricted to **flow of heat in fluids** and is closely associated with fluid mechanics. In **natural convection**, the motion of fluid is the result of difference in density of the warmer and cooler fluid elements arising from the temperature difference / gradient in the fluid mass. In **forced convection**, motion of fluid is produced by mechanical means such as : an agitator, a fan or a pump. Examples of heat transfer mainly by convection are : heating of room by means of a steam radiator, heating of water in cooking pans, heat flow to a fluid pumped through a heated pipe.

Radiation : Radiation refers to the transfer of heat energy from one body to another, not in contact with it, by electromagnetic waves through space. Examples of heat transfer by radiation mode are the transfer of heat from the sun to the earth and loss of heat from an unlagged steam pipe.

Conduction can occur in solids, liquids, and gases while convection can occur only in fluids (gas or liquid). Conduction as well as convection occurs only in the presence of material medium whereas radiation can occur even in vacuum and no material medium is required for heat flow by radiation. It is observed that heat flow by conduction is slow, faster by convection and the fastest by radiation mode.

CONDUCTION :

It is our common observation that when some material object is heated at one of its locations, then in a short while its remaining parts also get heated. This shows that heat flows through the material object from a high temperature region to a low temperature region. The flow of heat in this manner is called as heat conduction or simply conduction, wherein the particles of object participate in the process but they do not move bodily from the hot or high temperature region to the cold or low temperature region.

Conduction is the mode of heat transfer in which a material medium transporting the heat remains at rest. The heat conduction occurs by the migration of molecules and more effectively by the collision of the molecules vibrating around relatively fixed positions. In liquids and solids where little or no migration occurs, heat is transferred by the collision of vibrating molecules. [The molecules of a substance are always in a state of vibration. When the substance is heated at one of its locations, the molecules of that location receive energy and they begin to vibrate with larger amplitudes and as a result of increase in their amplitude, they will collide with the neighbouring molecules and in the process they transfer a part of their energy to the neighbouring molecules. This process occurs repeatedly and thus results in heat flow from one molecule to another along the heat flow path i.e. through the substance.]

Conduction refers to *the mode of heat transfer in which the heat flow through the material medium occurs without actual migration of particles of the medium from a region of higher temperature to a region of lower temperature.*

It is a fact that conduction occurs in solids, liquids and gases but pure conduction is found to present only in solids, with gases and liquids it is present with convection, so we will consider here heat conduction in solids for better understanding of conduction mechanism as convection is not present in solids.

In this chapter, we restrict our discussion to **steady state unidirectional heat conduction in solids**.

By *steady state heat flow* we mean that the situation of heat flow in which the temperature at any location along the heat flow path does not vary with time. In other words, it is the heat flow under conditions of constant temperature distribution – temperature is a function of location only i.e. temperature varies with location but not with time. Hence, steady state heat conduction is the heat transfer by conduction under conditions of constant temperature distribution.

By unidirectional or one dimensional heat flow we mean that the flow of heat occurring only in one direction, i.e., along one of the axes of the respective coordinate system used. (For example, say along the x-direction in case of a Cartesian co-ordinate system).

Fourier's Law :

The physical law governing transfer of heat through a uniform material (whenever temperature difference exists) by a conduction mode was given by the French scientist : Joseph Fourier.

Fourier's law states that *the rate of heat flow by conduction through a uniform (fixed) material is directly proportional to the area normal to the direction of the heat flow and the temperature gradient in the direction of the heat flow*.

Mathematically, the Fourier's law of heat conduction for steady state heat flow is given by

$$Q \propto A\,[-dT/dn] \qquad \ldots (2.1)$$
$$Q = -kA\,[dT/dn] \qquad \ldots (2.2)$$

where Q is the rate of heat flow/transfer in watts (W), A is the area normal to the direction of heat flow in m^2, T is the temperature in K, n is the distance measured normal to the surface, i.e., the length of conduction path along the heat flow in m, dT/dn is the rate of change of temperature with distance measured in the direction of heat flow (called as temperature gradient) in K/m. k is a constant of proportionality and is called the thermal conductivity. It is the characteristic property of a material through which heat flows.

The negative sign is incorporated in equation (2.2) because the temperature gradient is negative (since with an increase in n there is a decrease in T, i.e., temperature decreases in the direction of heat flow) and it makes the heat flow positive in the direction of temperature decrease.

The Fourier's law for a steady state unidirectional (say x-direction) heat conduction then becomes

$$Q = -kA\,[dT/dx] \qquad \ldots (2.3)$$
$$q = Q/A = -k\,[dT/dx] \qquad \ldots (2.4)$$

where Q is the rate of heat flow, i.e., heat flow per unit time in W, and q is the heat flux, i.e., rate of heat flow per unit area in W/m^2 in x-direction. In further discussion we will make use of Equation (2.3). The **Fourier's law** [equation (2.3)] is a fundamental differential equation of heat transfer by conduction. It is simply a definition of k.

One Dimensional Steady State conduction :

Steady state heat conduction is a simpler case in the sense that the temperature does not vary with time. T is independent of time and is a function of position in the conducting solid.

One dimensional heat conduction implies that the temperature gradient exists only in one direction which makes the heat flow unidirectional. The cases of heat flow through a slab (plane wall), a circular cylinder, a sphere and long fins can be analysed by a one dimensional steady state conduction. In the discussion to follow we will treat heat flow to be in x-direction only.

In discussion to follow we assume that k does not vary with temperature.

Plane wall (slab) of uniform thickness :

The heat flow through the wall of a stirred tank containing a hot or cold fluid or the wall of a large furnace can be examples of one dimensional heat flow. Consider a plane/flat wall as shown in Fig. 2.1.

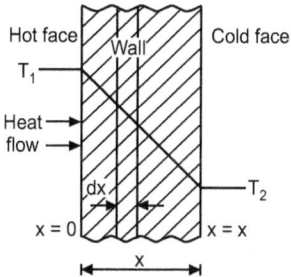

Fig. 2.1 : Conduction through a plane wall

Consider that the wall is made of a material of thermal conductivity k and is of uniform thickness (x) and constant cross-sectional area (A). Assume that k is independent of temperature and the area of wall is very large in comparison with the thickness so that the heat losses from the edges are negligible. A hot face is at temperature T_1 and a cold face is at temperature T_2 and both are isothermal surfaces. The direction of heat flow is perpendicular to the wall and T varies in the direction of x-axis.

As in steady state, there can be neither accumulation nor depletion of heat within a plane wall, Q is constant along the path of heat flow. The usual use of Fourier's law requires that the differential equation (2.3) be integrated over the entire path from x = 0 to x = x (total thickness of the wall) as we normally know temperatures only at the faces.

$$Q = -kA \left[\frac{dT}{dx} \right]$$

$$Q\, dx = -k \cdot A\, dT \qquad \ldots (2.5)$$

The variables in Equation (2.5) are x and T.

$$Q \int_0^x dx = -k \cdot A \int_{T_1}^{T_2} dT \qquad \ldots (2.6)$$

$$Q \cdot x = -kA\, (T_2 - T_1) \qquad \ldots (2.7)$$

Rearranging, we get

$$Q = \frac{kA(T_1 - T_2)}{x} \qquad \ldots (2.8)$$

$$Q = \frac{k \cdot A}{x} \cdot \Delta T \qquad \ldots (2.9)$$

where $\Delta T = (T_1 - T_2)$

$$Q = \frac{\Delta T}{x/kA} = \frac{\Delta T}{R} \qquad \ldots (2.10)$$

where R (= x/kA) is the thermal resistance (of wall material of thickness x), Q is the rate of heat flow and ΔT is the driving force.

Equation (2.10) equates the rate of heat flow to the ratio of driving force to thermal resistance.

The reciprocal of resistance is called the conductance, which for heat conduction is :

$$\text{Conductance} = 1/R = 1/(x/kA) = k \cdot A/x \qquad \ldots (2.11)$$

Both the resistance and conductance depend upon the dimensions of a solid as well as on thermal conductivity, a property of the material.

When k varies linearly with T (Equation 2.12), Equation (2.10) can be used rigorously by taking an average value $\bar{k}$ for k. $\bar{k}$ may be obtained either by using the arithmetic average of the individual values of k at surface temperatures T_1 and T_2 [$\bar{k} = (k_1 + k_2)/2$] or by calculating the arithmetic average of temperatures [$(T_1 + T_2)/2$] and using the value of k at that temperature. One can take linear variation of k with T under integration sign and integrate the equation.

Thermal Conductivity :

The proportionality constant 'k' given in Equation (2.2) is called as the thermal conductivity. It is a characteristic property of the material through which heat is flowing and varies with temperature. It is one of the so called transport properties of the material (like viscosity, μ).

Thermal conductivity is *a measure of ability of a substance to conduct heat*. Larger the value of k, higher will be the amount of heat conducted.

Thermal conductivity is *the quantity of heat passing through a quantity of material of unit thickness with unit heat flow area in unit time when unit temperature difference is maintained across the opposite faces of material.*

If Q is measured in watts (W $\equiv$ J/s), A in m^2, x in m and T in K, then units of k are W/(m·K) in the SI system.

$$Q = -kA\,(dT/dx)$$

$$k = \frac{-Q \cdot dx}{A \cdot dT}, \quad \frac{W \cdot m}{(m^2 \cdot K)}$$

$$= \frac{-Q \cdot dx}{A \cdot dT}, \quad W/(m \cdot K) \equiv J/(s \cdot m \cdot K)$$

Thermal conductivity depends upon the nature of material and its temperature. Thermal conductivities of solids are higher than that of liquids and liquids are having higher thermal conductivities than for gases.

In general, thermal conductivity of gases ranges from 0.006 to 0.6 W/(m·K) while that of liquids ranges from 0.09 to 0.7 W/(m·K). Thermal conductivity of metals varies from 2.3 to 420 W/(m·K). The materials having higher values of thermal conductivity are referred to as **good conductors** of heat, e.g., metals. The best conductor of heat is silver [k = 420 W/(m·K)] followed by red copper [k = 395 W/(m·K)], gold [k = 302 W/(m·K)] and aluminium [k = 210 W/(m·K)]. The materials having low values of thermal conductivity [less than 0.20 W/(m·K)] are called as and used as **heat insulators** to minimise the rate of heat flow. e.g. asbestos, glass wool, cork, etc.

For small temperature ranges, thermal conductivity may be taken as constant but for large temperature ranges, it varies linearly with temperature and the variation of the thermal conductivity with temperature is given by the relationship

$$k = a + bT \qquad \ldots (2.12)$$

where a and b are empirical constants and T is the temperature in K.

Compound resistances in series / Heat conduction through a composite plane wall :

When a wall is formed out of series of layers of different materials, it is called as a **composite wall.**

Consider a flat wall constructed of a series of layers of three different materials as shown in Fig. 2.2. Let k_1, k_2 and k_3 be the thermal conductivities of the materials of which layers are made. Let thicknesses of the layers be x_1, x_2 and x_3 respectively.

Let ΔT_1 be the temperature drop across the first layer, ΔT_2 that across the second layer and ΔT_3 that across/over the third layer. Let ΔT be the temperature drop across the entire composite wall.

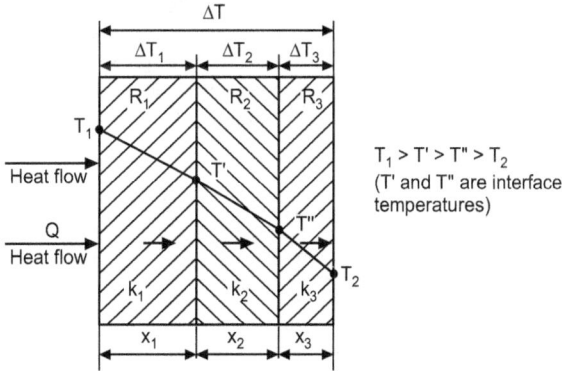

$T_1 > T' > T'' > T_2$
(T' and T" are interface temperatures)

Fig. 2.2 : Conduction through resistances in series

Let T_1, T', T" and T_2 be the temperatures at the faces as shown in Fig. 2.2. T_1 is the temperature of a hot face and T_2 is the temperature of a cold face. Assume further that the layers are in excellent thermal contact.

Furthermore, let the area of the composite wall, at right angles to the plane of illustration, be A.

Overall temperature drop is related to individual temperature drops over layers by equation :

$$\Delta T = \Delta T_1 + \Delta T_2 + \Delta T_3 \qquad \ldots (2.13)$$

It is desired to derive an equation / formula giving the rate of heat flow through a series of resistances.

Rate of heat flow through the layer-1, i.e., through the material of thermal conductivity k_1 is given by

$$Q_1 = \frac{k_1 A}{x_1}(T_1 - T') \qquad \ldots (2.14)$$

$$(T_1 - T') = \frac{Q_1}{(k_1 A/x_1)} \qquad \ldots (2.15)$$

$$\Delta T_1 = T_1 - T' \qquad \ldots (2.16)$$

$$\therefore \quad \Delta T_1 = \frac{Q_1}{(k_1 A/x_1)} \qquad \ldots (2.17)$$

Similarly for layer-2

$$\Delta T_2 = (T' - T'') = \frac{Q_2}{(k_2 A/x_2)} \qquad \ldots (2.18)$$

and for layer-3 :

$$\Delta T_3 = (T'' - T_2) = \frac{Q_3}{(k_3 A/x_3)} \qquad \ldots (2.19)$$

Adding Equations (2.17), (2.18) and (2.19), we get

$$\Delta T_1 + \Delta T_2 + \Delta T_3 = \frac{Q_1}{(k_1 A/x_1)} + \frac{Q_2}{(k_2 A/x_2)} + \frac{Q_3}{(k_3 A/x_3)} = \Delta T \qquad \ldots (2.20)$$

Under steady state conditions of heat flow, all the heat passing through the layer-1 (first resistance) must pass through the layer-2 (second resistance) and in turn pass through the layer-3 (third resistance), therefore Q_1, Q_2 and Q_3 must be equal and can be denoted by Q. Thus, using this fact, Equation (2.20) becomes

$$\frac{Q}{(k_1 A/x_1)} + \frac{Q}{(k_2 A/x_2)} + \frac{Q}{(k_3 A/x_3)} = \Delta T \qquad \ldots (2.21)$$

$$Q\left[\frac{1}{(k_1 A/x_1)} + \frac{1}{(k_2 A/x_2)} + \frac{1}{(k_3 A/x_3)}\right] = \Delta T \qquad \ldots (2.22)$$

$$\therefore \quad Q = \frac{\Delta T}{\left[\dfrac{1}{k_1 A/x_1} + \dfrac{1}{k_2 A/x_2} + \dfrac{1}{k_3 A/x_3}\right]} \qquad \ldots (2.23)$$

$$Q = \frac{\Delta T}{\left[\dfrac{x_1}{k_1 A} + \dfrac{x_2}{k_2 A} + \dfrac{x_3}{k_3 A}\right]} \qquad \ldots (2.24)$$

Let R_1, R_2 and R_3 be the thermal resistances offered by the layer-1, 2 and 3 respectively. R_1, R_2 and R_3 are given as :

$$R_1 = x_1/k_1 A \qquad \ldots (2.25)$$

$$R_2 = x_2/k_2 A \qquad \ldots (2.26)$$

and
$$R_3 = x_3/k_3 A \qquad \ldots (2.27)$$

Equation (2.24) becomes :

$$Q = \frac{\Delta T}{R_1 + R_2 + R_3} \qquad \ldots (2.28)$$

If R is the overall resistance, then for resistances in series, we have :

$$R = R_1 + R_2 + R_3 \qquad \ldots (2.29)$$

Equation (2.28) becomes :

$$Q = \frac{\Delta T}{R} \qquad \ldots (2.30)$$

Equation (2.30) is used to calculate the rate of heat flow as the ratio of overall temperature drop (driving force) to the overall resistance of the composite wall.

Equation (2.30) is the same as the equation for the rate of any process :

$$\text{Rate of transfer process} = \frac{\text{Driving force}}{\text{Resistance}}$$

One can calculate the temperatures at the interfaces of layers of which the wall is made by making use of

$$\frac{\Delta T}{R} = \frac{\Delta T_1}{R_1} = \frac{\Delta T_2}{R_2} = \frac{\Delta T_3}{R_3} \qquad \ldots (2.31)$$

Based upon the thickness and thermal conductivity of the layer, the temperature in that layer may be large or small fraction of the total temperature drop. A thin layer with a low thermal conductivity value may well cause a much larger temperature drop and a steeper thermal gradient than a thick layer having a high thermal conductivity.

Heat flow through a cylinder :

Consider a thick walled hollow cylinder as shown in Fig. 2.3 of inside radius r_1, outside radius r_2 and length L. Let k be the thermal conductivity of the material of cylinder.

Let the temperature of the inside surface be T_1 and that of the outside surface be T_2. Assume that $T_1 > T_2$, therefore heat flows from the inside of the cylinder to the outside. It is desired to calculate the rate of heat flow for this case.

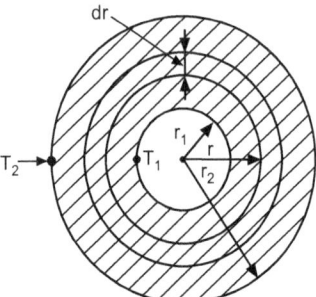

Fig. 2.3 : Heat flow through thick walled cylinder

Consider a very thin cylinder (cylindrical element), concentric with the main cylinder, of radius r, where r is between r_1 and r_2. The thickness of wall of this cylindrical element is dr.

The rate of heat flow at any radius r is given by

$$Q = -k\, 2\pi rL \left(\frac{dT}{dr}\right) \qquad \ldots (2.32)$$

Equation (2.32) is similar to Equation (2.3). Here the area perpendicular to heat flow is $2\pi rL$ and dx of Equation (2.3) is equal to dr.

Rearranging Equation (2.32), we get

$$\frac{dr}{r} = \frac{-k\,(2\pi L)}{Q}\, dT \qquad \ldots (2.33)$$

only variables in Equation (2.33) are r and T (assuming k to be constant).

Integrating Equation (2.33) between the limits gives

when $r = r_1$, $\quad T = T_1$
when $r = r_2$, $\quad T = T_2$

$$\int_{r_1}^{r_2} \frac{dr}{r} = \frac{-k\,(2\pi L)}{Q} \int_{T_1}^{T_2} dT \qquad \ldots (2.34)$$

$$\ln r_2 - \ln r_1 = \frac{-k\,(2\pi L)\,(T_2 - T_1)}{Q} \qquad \ldots (2.35)$$

$$\ln (r_2/r_1) = \frac{k\,(2\pi L)\,(T_1 - T_2)}{Q} \qquad \ldots (2.36)$$

The rate of heat flow through a thick walled cylinder :

$$\therefore \quad Q = \frac{k\,(2\pi L)\,(T_1 - T_2)}{\ln (r_2/r_1)} \qquad \ldots (2.37)$$

Equation (2.3) can be used to calculate the flow of heat through a thick walled cylinder.

It can be put into more convenient form by expressing the rate of heat flow as :

$$Q = \frac{k\,(2\pi r_m L)\,(T_1 - T_2)}{(r_2 - r_1)} \qquad \ldots (2.38)$$

where r_m is the logarithmic mean radius and is given by

$$r_m = \frac{(r_2 - r_1)}{\ln (r_2/r_1)} = \frac{(r_2 - r_1)}{2.303 \log (r_2/r_1)} \qquad \ldots (2.39)$$

$$A_m = 2\pi r_m L \qquad \ldots (2.40)$$

A_m is called the logarithmic mean area.

Equation (2.38) becomes :

$$Q = \frac{k A_m (T_1 - T_2)}{(r_2 - r_1)} \qquad \ldots (2.41)$$

$$Q = \frac{(T_1 - T_2)}{(r_2 - r_1) / k A_m} = \frac{\Delta T}{R}$$

where $\quad R = (r_2 - r_1) / k A_m$

The RHS of Equation (2.39) is known as the logarithmic mean and in the particular case of Equation (2.39), r_m is known as the logarithmic mean radius. It is the radius which when applied to the integrated equation for a flat wall, will give the correct rate of heat flow through a thick-walled cylinder.

The logarithmic mean is less convenient than the arithmetic mean, and the arithmetic mean is used without appreciable error in case of thin-walled cylinders.

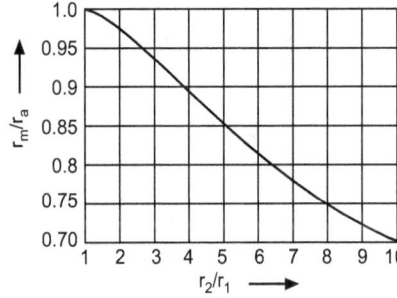

Fig. 2.4 : Relation between logarithmic and arithmetic means

Heat flow through a sphere :

Consider a hollow sphere of inner radius r_1 and outer radius r_2. Let T_1 be the temperature at the inner surface and T_2 be the temperature at the outer surface. Assume that $T_1 > T_2$, so that heat will flow from inside to outside.

Consider a spherical element at any radius r (between r_1 and r_2) of thickness dr.

Then rate of heat flow according to Fourier's law is given as :

$$Q = -k (4\pi r^2) \frac{dT}{dr} \qquad \ldots (2.42)$$

where $\quad A = 4\pi r^2 =$ area of heat transfer

$\quad\quad\quad\quad k =$ thermal conductivity of a material of which sphere is made

Rearranging Equation (2.42), we get

$$\frac{dr}{r^2} = \frac{-4\pi k}{Q} dT \qquad \ldots (2.43)$$

Integrating Equation (2.43) between the limits :
when $\quad r = r_1, \quad T = T_1$
and $\quad r = r_2, \quad T = T_2$

$$\int_{r_1}^{r_2} \frac{dr}{r^2} = \frac{-4\pi k}{Q} \int_{T_1}^{T_2} dT \qquad \ldots (2.44)$$

$$\left[-\frac{1}{r}\right]_{r_1}^{r_2} = \frac{-4\pi k}{Q}(T_1 - T_2) \qquad \ldots (2.45)$$

$$\left[\frac{1}{r_1} - \frac{1}{r_2}\right] = \frac{4\pi k}{Q}(T_1 - T_2) \qquad \ldots (2.46)$$

Rearranging, we get

$$Q = \frac{4\pi k (T_1 - T_2)}{\left[\dfrac{1}{r_1} - \dfrac{1}{r_2}\right]} \qquad \ldots (2.47)$$

$$Q = \frac{4\pi r_1 r_2 k (T_1 - T_2)}{(r_2 - r_1)} \qquad \ldots (2.48)$$

$r_m = \sqrt{r_1 r_2}$ = mean radius which is geometric mean for sphere.

∴ Equation (2.48) becomes :

$$Q = \frac{4\pi r_m^2 k (T_1 - T_2)}{(r_2 - r_1)} \qquad \ldots (2.49)$$

Thermal Insulation :

Process equipments such as a reaction vessel, reboiler, distillation column, evaporator, etc. or a steam pipe will lose heat to the atmosphere by conduction, convection and radiation. In such cases, the conservation of heat that is usually of steam and coal is an economic necessity and therefore some form of lagging should be applied to the hot surfaces. In furnaces, the surface temperature is reduced substantially by making use of a series of insulating bricks that are poor conductors of heat.

Insulation is necessary (i) to prevent an excessive flow of costly heat to the surroundings from process units and pipelines in which heat is generated, stored or conveyed at temperatures above the surrounding temperature, (ii) to prevent an excessive flow of heat from the outside to materials which must be kept at temperatures below that of the surroundings, (iii) to provide for protection of personnel from skin damage through contact with very hot and very cold surfaces (to provide safe environment) and (iv) to provide comfortable/acceptable working environment. The working environment in the viscinity of process units and pipelines carrying hot or cold streams can become uncomfortable and unacceptable, if insulation is not provided. In a chemical plant, steam is transported to process equipments, as per requirement, through steam lines. If the steam lines are not insulated, then the loss of heat from these lines to the ambient air may result in condensation of steam, thus lowering quality of steam and creating operational problems in the equipments in which the steam is admitted.

The important requirements of an insulating material are as follows :
(i) It should have low thermal conductivity.
(ii) It should withstand working temperature range.
(iii) It should have sufficient durability and mechanical strength. This includes resistance to moisture and the chemical environment.
(iv) It should be easy to apply, non-toxic, readily available, inexpensive (low basic material cost, installation cost and maintenance cost).
(v) It should not constitute a fire hazard.

Cork [k = 0.025 W/(m·K)], asbestos (k = 0.10), glass wool (k = 0.024), 85 percent magnesia (k = 0.04) are commonly employed lagging materials in industry. Cork is common in refrigeration plants. 85% magnesia with asbestos, glass wool are widely used for lagging steam pipes. Thin aluminium sheeting is often used to protect the lagging.

The optimum thickness of insulation :

The optimum thickness of an insulation is obtained by a purely economic approach. The greater the thickness, the lower the heat loss and the greater the initial cost of insulation and the greater the annual fixed charges (maintenance and depreciation).

It is obtained by a purely economic approach. Increasing the thickness of an insulation reduces the loss of heat and thus gives saving in operating costs; but at the same time, cost of insulation will increase with thickness. The optimum thickness of an insulation is the one at which the total annual cost (the sum of values of heat lost and annual fixed charges) of the insulation is minimum.

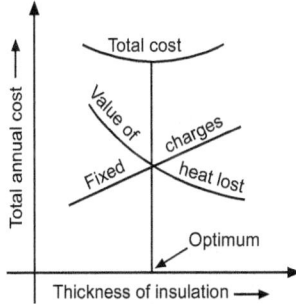

Fig. 2.5 : Optimum thickness of insulation

Note : Discussion on **systems with variable k** and **critical radius of insulation** is given at the end of this chapter.

SOLVED EXAMPLES

Example 2.1 : *Calculate the rate of heat loss Q, through a wall of red brick [k = 0.70 W/(m·K)] 5 m in length, 4 m in height and 250 mm in thickness, if the wall surfaces are maintained at 373 K (100° C) and 303 K (30° C) respectively.*

Solution : Mean area of heat transfer = A = 5 × 4 = 20 m²

Thickness of brick wall = x = 250 mm = 0.25 m

Temperature difference = ΔT = 373 − 303 = 70 K
Thermal conductivity of red brick = k = 0.70 W/(m·K)
The rate of heat loss is :

$$Q = k \cdot A \left[\frac{\Delta T}{x}\right] = 0.70 \times 20 \times \left[\frac{70}{0.25}\right] = \mathbf{3920\ W} \qquad \ldots \text{Ans.}$$

Example 2.2 : *Estimate the heat loss per m^2 of the surface through a brick wall 0.5 m thick when the inner surface is at 400 K (127° C) and the outside surface is at 310 K (37° C). The thermal conductivity of the brick may be taken as 0.7 W/(m·K).*

Solution : $\quad Q = \dfrac{k \cdot A\,(T_1 - T_2)}{x}$

where
$\quad k = 0.7\ W/(m·K)$
$\quad A = 1\ m^2$
$\quad T_1 = 400\ K, \quad T_2 = 310\ K, \quad x = 0.5\ m$

Heat loss per m^2 is, $\quad Q = \dfrac{0.7 \times 1.0 \times (400 - 310)}{0.5} = \mathbf{126\ W} \qquad \ldots \text{Ans.}$

Example 2.3 : *It is necessary to insulate a flat surface so that the rate of heat loss per unit area of this surface does not exceed 450 W/m^2. The temperature difference across the insulating layers is 400 K (127°C). Evaluate the thickness of insulation if (a) the insulation is made of asbestos cement having thermal conductivity of 0.11 W/(m·K), and (b) the insulation is made of fire clay having thermal conductivity of 0.84 W/(m·K).*

Solution : (a) Area of heat transfer = 1 m^2
$\quad Q/A = 450\ W/m^2$
$\quad \Delta T = 400\ K$
$\quad k$ for asbestos $= 0.11\ W/(m·K)$

$$Q = \frac{k \cdot A\,\Delta T}{x} \quad \therefore \quad x = \frac{kA\,\Delta T}{Q}$$

$$x = \frac{0.11 \times 1 \times 400}{450}$$
$$= 0.098\ m$$
$$= 98\ mm$$

Thickness of asbestos cement insulation = **98 mm** ... Ans. (a)

(b) Area of heat transfer = A = 1 m^2
$\quad k$ for fire clay insulation = 0.84 W/(m·K)
$\quad \Delta T = 400\ K$

$$Q = \frac{k \cdot A\,\Delta T}{x}$$

$$x = \frac{0.84 \times 1 \times 400}{450}$$
$$= 0.747\ m$$
$$= 747\ mm$$

Thickness of fire clay insulation = **747 mm** ... Ans. (b)

Example 2.4 : *A steam pipeline, 150/160 mm in diameter, carries steam. The pipeline is lagged with a layer of heat insulating material [k = 0.08 W/(m·K)] of thickness 100 mm. The temperature drops from 392.8 K (119.8 °C) to 313 K (40 °C) across the insulating surface. Determine the rate of heat loss per 1 m length of pipe line.*

Solution :
$$Q = \frac{k \cdot A_m (T_1 - T_2)}{(r_2 - r_1)}$$

r_1 = inside radius of insulation
= 160/2 = 80 mm = 0.08 m
r_2 = outside radius of insulation
= 80 + 100 = 180 mm = 0.18 m
L = length of pipe = 1 m
A_m = $2\pi r_m L$
= $\frac{2\pi (r_2 - r_1) L}{\ln (r_2/r_1)}$ = $\frac{2\pi (0.18 - 0.08) \times 1}{\ln (0.18/0.08)}$ = 0.775 m²

k = 0.08 W/(m·K)
T_1 = 392.8 K, T_2 = 313 K

The rate of heat loss per unit length of pipe is :

$$Q = \frac{0.08 \times 0.775 \times (392.8 - 313)}{(0.18 - 0.08)}$$

= **49.5 W/m** ... **Ans.**

Example 2.5 : *A wall is made of brick of thermal conductivity 1.0 W/(m·K), 230 mm thick. It is lined on the inner face with plaster of thermal conductivity 0.4 W/(m·K) and of thickness 10 mm. If a temperature difference of 30 K is maintained between the two faces, what is the heat flow per unit area of wall ?*

Solution : Let an area of 1 m².

Thermal resistance of brick = $x_1/k_1 A$

$$R_1 = \frac{0.230}{1.0 \times 1.0} = 0.230 \text{ K/W}$$

Thermal resistance of plaster = $R_2 = \frac{x_2}{k_2 A}$

$$= \frac{0.010}{0.4 \times 1.0} = 0.025 \text{ K/W}$$

$$Q = \frac{\Delta T}{R}$$

$$= \frac{\Delta T}{R_1 + R_2}$$

$$= \frac{30}{0.230 + 0.025}$$

= 117.6 W ≡ **117.6 J/s** ... **Ans.**

Example 2.6 : *A steam pipeline, 150/160 mm in diameter, is covered with a layer of insulating material of thickness 50 mm. The temperature inside the pipeline is 393 K (120 °C) and that of the outside surface of insulation is 313 K (40 °C). Calculate the rate of heat loss per 1 m length of pipeline.*

Data : k for pipe is 50 W/(m·K) and k for insulating material is 0.08 W/(m·K).

Solution : Consider 1 m of pipeline.

Thermal resistance offered by wall of pipe $= R_1 = \dfrac{r_2 - r_1}{k_1 A_{m_1}}$

where $r_1 = 150/2 = 75$ mm $= 0.075$ m

$r_2 = 160/2 = 80$ mm $= 0.08$ m

$A_{m_1} = 2\pi r_{m_1} L$

$= \dfrac{2\pi (r_2 - r_1)}{\ln (r_2/r_1)} L$

$= \dfrac{2\pi (0.08 - 0.075)}{\ln (0.08/0.075)} \times 1 = 0.487$ m²

$k_1 = 50$ W/(m·K)

$R_1 = \dfrac{0.08 - 0.075}{50 \times 0.487} = 0.000205$ K/W

$= 2.05 \times 10^{-4}$ K/W

Thermal resistance offered by insulation $= R_2 = \dfrac{r_3 - r_2}{k_2 A_{m_2}}$.

$A_{m_2} = 2\pi r_{m_2} L$

$= \dfrac{2\pi (r_3 - r_2) L}{\ln (r_3/r_2)}$

where $r_3 = r_2 + 50$ mm

$= 80 + 50 = 130$ mm $= 0.13$ m

$A_{m_2} = \dfrac{2\pi (0.13 - 0.08)}{\ln (0.13/0.08)} \times 1$

$A_{m_2} = 0.647$ m²

$k_2 = 0.08$ W/(m·K)

$R_2 = \dfrac{(0.13 - 0.08)}{0.08 \times 0.647} = 0.966$ K/W

Total thermal resistance $= R = R_1 + R_2$

$= 2.05 \times 10^{-4} + 0.966 = 0.9662$ K/W

The rate of heat loss per 1 m of the pipeline

$$Q = \frac{\Delta T}{R}$$

$$= \frac{393 - 313}{0.9662}$$

$$= 82.8 \text{ W/m} \qquad \ldots \text{Ans.}$$

Example 2.7 : *A furnace is constructed with 225 mm thick of fire brick, 120 mm of insulating brick and 225 mm of the building brick. The inside temperature is 1200 K (927 °C) and the outside temperature is 330 K (57 °C). Find the heat loss per unit area and the temperature at the junction of the fire brick and insulating brick.*

Data :   k for fire brick = 1.4 W/(m·K)

            k for insulating brick = 0.2 W/(m·K)

            k for building brick = 0.7 W/(m·K)

Solution : Let area = 1 m²

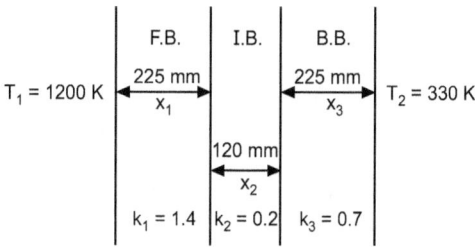

Fig. Ex. 2.7

Let T' and T" be the temperatures at the fire brick / insulating brick and the insulating brick/building brick junctions respectively.

$$\text{Thermal resistance of fire brick} = \frac{x_1}{k_1 A}$$

$$R_1 = \frac{0.225}{1.4 \times 1} = 0.1607 \text{ K/W}$$

$$\text{Thermal resistance of insulating brick} = \frac{x_2}{k_2 A}$$

$$R_2 = \frac{0.120}{0.2 \times 1} = 0.60 \text{ K/W}$$

$$\text{Thermal resistance of building brick} = \frac{x_3}{k_3 A}$$

$$R_3 = \frac{0.225}{0.7 \times 1} = 0.322 \text{ K/W}$$

The heat loss per unit area is

$$Q = \frac{\Delta T}{R}$$

$$= \frac{1200 - 330}{0.1607 + 0.60 + 0.322}$$

$$= \mathbf{803.5 \ W/m^2} \qquad \ldots \text{Ans.}$$

$$\frac{\Delta T \text{ firebrick}}{\Delta T \text{ entire}} = \frac{R_1}{R}$$

$$\frac{1200 - T'}{1200 - 330} = \frac{0.1607}{0.1607 + 0.60 + 0.322}$$

$$T' = \mathbf{1071 \ K \ (798 \ ^oC)} \qquad \ldots \text{Ans.}$$

Similarly, for insulating brick :

$$\frac{(1071 - T'')}{1200 - 330} = \frac{0.60}{0.1607 + 0.6 + 0.322}$$

$$T'' = \mathbf{589 \ K \ (316 \ ^oC)} \qquad \ldots \text{Ans.}$$

Example 2.8 : *A 50 mm diameter pipe of circular cross-section and with walls 3 mm thick is covered with two concentric layers of lagging, the inner layer having a thickness of 25 mm and a thermal conductivity of 0.08 W/(m·K), and the outer layer having a thickness of 40 mm and a thermal conductivity of 0.04 W/(m·K). Estimate the rate of heat loss per metre length of pipe if the temperature inside the pipe is 550 K (277 °C) and the outside surface temperature is 330 K (57 °C). k for pipe is 45 W/(m·K).*

Solution : Consider length of pipe = L = 1 m

Thermal resistance of wall of pipe = $R_1 = \dfrac{r_2 - r_1}{k_1 (2\pi r_{m_1} L)}$

$$r_1 = (50/2) \text{ mm} = 25 \text{ mm} = 0.025 \text{ m}$$

$$r_2 = 25 \text{ mm} + 3 \text{ mm} = 0.028 \text{ m}$$

$$r_{m_1} = (0.028 - 0.025) / \ln (0.028/0.025) = 0.0265 \text{ m}$$

$$k_1 = 45 \text{ W/(m·K)}, \ L = 1 \text{ m}$$

$$R_1 = (0.028 - 0.025)/(45 \times 2\pi \times 0.0265 \times 1)$$

$$= 0.00040 \text{ K/W}$$

For the inner lagging :

$$r_1 = 0.028 \text{ m}$$

$$r_2 = 0.028 + 0.025 = 0.053 \text{ m}$$

and $\quad r_{m_1} = (0.053 - 0.028) / \ln (0.053/0.028) = 0.0392 \text{ m}$

Thermal resistance of the inner lagging = $R_2 = \dfrac{r_2 - r_1}{k_2 (2\pi r_{m_1} L)}$

$$R_2 = \dfrac{0.053 - 0.028}{0.08 \times 2 \times \pi \times 0.0392 \times 1.0} = 1.2688 \text{ K/W}$$

For the outer lagging :

$r_1 = 0.053$ m

$r_2 = 0.053 + 0.040 = 0.093$ m

$r_{m_1} = (0.093 - 0.053) / \ln(0.093/0.053) = 0.0711$ m

Thermal resistance of the outer lagging = $R_3 = \dfrac{r_2 - r_1}{k_3 \, 2\pi r_{m_1} L}$

$$R_3 = \dfrac{0.093 - 0.053}{0.04 \times 2\pi \times 0.0711 \times 1} = 2.2385 \text{ K/W}$$

The rate of heat loss per metre of pipe is

$$Q = \dfrac{\Delta T}{R}$$

$$= \dfrac{550 - 330}{0.0004 + 1.2688 + 2.2385}$$

$$= \mathbf{62.7 \text{ W/m}} \qquad \ldots \text{Ans.}$$

Example 2.9 : *A wall of 0.5 m thickness is constructed using a material having thermal conductivity of 1.4 W/(m·K). The wall is insulated with a material having thermal conductivity of 0.35 W/(m·K) so that heat loss per m² is 1500 W. The inner and outer temperatures are 1273 K (1000 °C) and 373 K (100 °C) respectively. Calculate the thickness of insulation required and temperature of the interface between two layers.*

Solution : Let the thickness of insulation required be x_2 metres.

$T_1 = 1273$ K, $T_2 = 373$ K, $k_1 = 1.4$ W/(m·K), $k_2 = 0.35$ W/(m·K), $x_1 = 0.5$ m

$$\dfrac{Q}{A} = \dfrac{(T_1 - T_2)}{x_1/k_1 + x_2/k_2}$$

$$1500 = \dfrac{(1273 - 373)}{0.5/1.4 + x_2/0.35}$$

Solving we get $x_2 = 0.085$ m = 85 mm

Thickness of insulation required = **85 mm** $\qquad \ldots$ **Ans.**

Let T' be the temperature of interface.

$$\dfrac{Q}{A} = T_1 - T'/(x_1/k_1)$$

$$1500 = (1273 - T')/(0.5/1.4)$$

$$T' = \mathbf{737.3 \text{ K } (464.3 \text{ °C})} \qquad \ldots \textbf{Ans.}$$

Example 2.10 : *A cylindrical tube has inner diameter of 20 mm and outer diameter of 30 mm. Find out the rate of heat flow from tube of length 5 m if inner surface is at 373 K (100° C) and outer surface is at 308 K (35° C). Take the thermal conductivity of tube material as 0.291 W/(m·K).*

Solution : Basis : Tube of length 5 metres.

The equation to be used for calculating the rate of heat flow through the tube (cylinder) is

$$Q = \frac{k \cdot 2\pi r_m L (T_1 - T_2)}{(r_2 - r_1)} \qquad \ldots (A)$$

where,

Thermal conductivity = $k = 0.291$ W/(m·K)

Length = $L = 5$ metres

Inner radius = $r_1 = 10$ mm = 0.01 m

Outside radius = $r_2 = 15$ mm = 0.015 m

Inside temperature = $T_1 = 373$ K

Outside temperature = $T_2 = 308$ K

$$r_m = \text{log mean radius} = \frac{r_2 - r_1}{\ln\left(\frac{r_2}{r_1}\right)}$$

$$= \frac{0.015 - 0.01}{\ln\left(\frac{0.015}{0.01}\right)} = 0.0123 \text{ m}$$

Putting the values of the terms involved in Equation (A), we get

$$Q = \frac{0.291 \times 2\pi (0.0123) \times 5 (373 - 308)}{(0.015 - 0.01)}$$

$$= 1460.8 \text{ W} \equiv \mathbf{1460.8 \text{ J/s}} \qquad \ldots \textbf{Ans.}$$

Example 2.11 : *88 mm O.D. pipe is insulated with a 50 mm thickness of an insulation having a mean thermal conductivity of 0.087 W/(m·K) and 30 mm thickness of an insulation, having mean thermal conductivity of 0.064 W/(m·K). If the temperature of the outer surface of the pipe is 623 K (350 °C) and the temperature of the outer surface of insulation is 313 K (40 °C), calculate the heat loss per metre of pipe.*

Solution : Basis : One metre length of pipe.

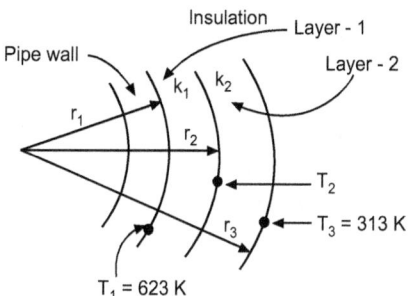

Fig. Ex. 2.11

Refer to Fig. Ex. 2.11

$$r_1 = \frac{88}{2} = 44 \text{ mm} = 0.044 \text{ m}$$

$$r_2 = 44 + 50 = 94 \text{ mm} = 0.094 \text{ m}$$

$$r_3 = 44 + 50 + 30 = 124 \text{ mm} = 0.124 \text{ m}$$

Rate of heat flow through thick-walled cylinder of radii r_1 and r_2 is

$$Q = \frac{k_1 (2\pi r_{m_1} L)(T_1 - T_2)}{(r_2 - r_1)}$$

∴ $$Q = \frac{T_1 - T_2}{\dfrac{r_2 - r_1}{k_1 (2\pi r_{m_1} L)}}$$

Heat loss through combined insulation is given by equation :

$$Q = \frac{(T_1 - T_2)}{\dfrac{(r_2 - r_1)}{k_1 (2\pi r_{m_1} L)}} + \frac{(T_2 - T_3)}{\dfrac{(r_3 - r_2)}{k_2 (2\pi r_{m_2} L)}}$$

or $\Delta T_1 = QR_1, \ \Delta T_2 = QR_2$

$\Delta T = \Delta T_1 + \Delta T_2 = Q[R_1 + R_2]$

$Q = \Delta T \ (= T_1 - T_2)/(R_1 + R_2)$

∴ $$Q = \frac{T_1 - T_3}{\dfrac{r_2 - r_1}{k_1 (2\pi r_{m_1} L)} + \dfrac{r_3 - r_2}{k_2 (2\pi r_{m_2} L)}} \qquad \ldots (A)$$

As $T_1 - T_3 = \Delta T = (T_1 - T_2) + (T_2 - T_3)$

where, ΔT = overall temperature drop

T_1 = temperature at the outer surface of a wall = 623 K

T_3 = temperature at the outer surface of outer insulation = 313 K
k_1 = thermal conductivity of insulation - 1 = 0.087 W/(m·K)
k_2 = thermal conductivity of insulation - 2
     = 0.064 W/(m·K)
L = Length of pipe = 1 metre
r_{m_1} = log mean radius of insulation layer – 1

∴ $r_{m_1} = \dfrac{r_2 - r_1}{\ln\left(\dfrac{r_2}{r_1}\right)}$

$= \dfrac{(0.094 - 0.044)}{\ln\left(\dfrac{0.094}{0.044}\right)} = 0.066 \text{ m}$

r_{m_2} = log mean radius of insulation layer - 2

$r_{m_2} = \dfrac{r_3 - r_2}{\ln\left(\dfrac{r_3}{r_2}\right)} = \dfrac{0.124 - 0.094}{\ln\left(\dfrac{0.124}{0.094}\right)} = 0.1083 \text{ m}$

Putting the values of all parameters in Equation (A), we get
The heat loss per metre of pipe is

$Q = \dfrac{(623 - 313)}{\left(\dfrac{0.05}{0.087 \times 2\pi \times 0.066 \times 1}\right) + \left(\dfrac{0.03}{0.064 \times 2\pi \times 0.1083}\right)}$

Q = **149.4 W/m** ... **Ans.**

Example 2.12 : *A furnace is constructed with 229 mm thick of fire brick, 115 mm of insulation brick and again 229 mm of building brick. The inside temperature is 1223 K (950 ºC) and the temperature at the outermost wall is 323 K (50ºC). The thermal conductivities of fire brick, insulating brick and building brick are 6.05, 0.581 and 2.33 W/(m·K). Find the heat lost per unit area and temperature at the interface.*

Solution :

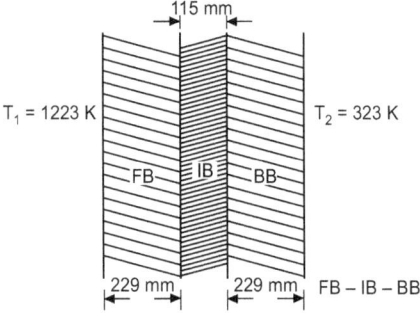

Fig. Ex. 2.12

Assume :

Heat transfer area = A = 1 m²

x_1 = thickness of fire brick = $\frac{229}{1000}$ = 0.229 m

x_2 = thickness of insulating brick = $\frac{115}{1000}$ = 0.115 m

x_3 = thickness of building brick = $\frac{229}{1000}$ = 0.229 m

k_1 = thermal conductivity of fire brick = 6.05 W/(m·K)

k_2 = thermal conductivity of insulating brick = 0.581 W/(m·K)

k_3 = thermal conductivity of building brick = 2.33 W/(m·K)

T_A = temperature at interface between fire brick and insulating brick (K)

T_B = temperature at interface between insulating brick and building brick (K)

T_1 = 1223 K, inside temperature

T_2 = 323 K, outside temperature

Overall temperature drop :

$$\Delta T = 1223 - 323 = 900 \text{ K}$$

$$Q = \frac{\Delta T}{R_1 + R_2 + R_3} = \frac{900}{\left(\frac{x_1}{k_1 A}\right) + \left(\frac{x_2}{k_2 A}\right) + \left(\frac{x_3}{k_3 A}\right)}$$

$$= \frac{900}{\frac{0.229}{6.05 \times 1} + \frac{0.115}{0.581 \times 1} + \frac{0.229}{2.33 \times 1}} = 2694 \text{ W/m}^2$$

∴ $Q_1 = Q = \dfrac{T_1 - T_A}{\dfrac{x_1}{k_1 A}}$

∴ $2694 = \dfrac{1223 - T_A}{\dfrac{0.229}{6.05 \times 1}}$

∴ $1223 - T_A = 102$

∴ $T_A = 1121$ K (848° C)

Similarly,

$$Q_3 = Q = \frac{T_B - T_2}{x_3/k_3 A} = \frac{T_B - 323}{x_3/k_3 A}$$

$$2694 = \frac{T_B - 323}{\frac{0.229}{2.33 \times 1}}$$

∴ T_B = 587.8 K (314.8° C)

Q based on 1 m² surface = 2694 W

Interface temperature

(i) Between FB – IB = **1121 K (848°C)** ... **Ans.**

(ii) Between IB – PB = **587.8 K (314.8°C)** ... **Ans.**

Example 2.13 : *A furnace is constructed with 230 mm thick of fire brick, 115 mm of insulating brick and then 230 mm of building brick. The inside temperature of the furnace is 1213 K (940°C) and the outside temperature is 318 K (45°C). The thermal conductivities of fire brick, insulating brick and building brick are 6.047, 0.581 and 2.33 W/(m·K). Find the heat lost per unit area and the temperature at the interfaces.*

Solution :

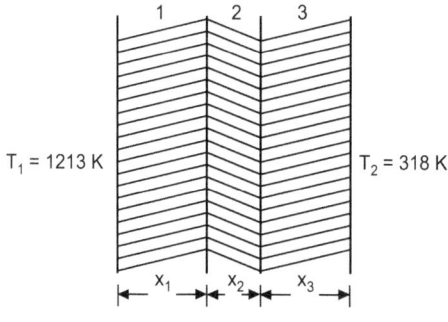

Fig. Ex. 2.13

x_1 = thickness of fire brick layer
      = 230 mm = 0.23 m

x_2 = 115 mm = 0.115 m

x_3 = 230 mm = 0.23 m

Let T_A and T_B be the temperatures at the interfaces between the fire brick-insulating brick and the insulating brick-building brick, respectively.

$$\begin{bmatrix} \text{Heat lost per} \\ \text{unit area} \end{bmatrix} = \frac{Q}{A} = \frac{\Delta T}{x_1/k_1 + x_2/k_2 + x_3/k_3}$$

where, ΔT = 1213 – 318 = 895 K

k_1 = 6.047 W/(m·K) (fire brick)

k_2 = 0.581 W/(m·K) (insulating brick)

k_3 = 2.33 W/(m·K) (building brick)

$$\left[\begin{array}{l}\text{Heat lost per}\\ \text{unit area}\end{array}\right] = \frac{895}{\left(\dfrac{0.23}{6.047}\right) + \left(\dfrac{0.115}{0.581}\right) + \left(\dfrac{0.23}{2.33}\right)}$$

$$= 2674.2 \text{ W} \equiv \mathbf{2674.2 \text{ J/s}} \qquad \text{... Ans.}$$

$$\frac{\Delta T}{R} = \frac{\Delta T_1}{R_1}$$

$$\therefore \quad \frac{\Delta T}{x_1/k_1 A + x_2/k_2 A + x_3/k_3 A} = \frac{\Delta T_A}{x_1/k_1 A}$$

$$\frac{T_1 - T_2}{x_1/k_1 + x_2/k_2 + x_3/k_3} = \frac{T_1 - T_A}{x_1/k_1}$$

$$\frac{1213 - 318}{\left(\dfrac{0.23}{6.047}\right) + \left(\dfrac{0.115}{0.581}\right) + \left(\dfrac{0.23}{2.33}\right)} = \frac{(1213 - T_A)}{\left(\dfrac{0.23}{6.047}\right)}$$

∴ T_A = 1108.5 K (835.5 °C) = temperature at the interface between fire brick and insulating brick.

$$\frac{\Delta T}{R} = \frac{\Delta T_3}{R_3}$$

$$\frac{(T_1 - T_2)}{x_1/k_1 A + x_2/k_2 A + x_3/k_3 A} = \frac{T_B - T_2}{x_3/k_3 A}$$

$$\frac{(T_1 - T_2)}{x_1/k_1 + x_2/k_2 + x_3/k_3} = \frac{T_B - T_2}{x_3/k_3}$$

$$\frac{1213 - 318}{\left(\dfrac{0.23}{6.047}\right) + \left(\dfrac{0.115}{0.581}\right) + \left(\dfrac{0.23}{2.33}\right)} = \frac{T_B - 318}{\left(\dfrac{0.23}{2.33}\right)}$$

∴ T_B = 565 K (292° C) = temperature at the interface between the insulating brick and building brick.

Example 2.14 : *A flat furnace wall is constructed of 45 mm layer of sil-o-cel brick, with a thermal conductivity of 0.138 W/(m·K) backed by a 90 mm layer of common brick of conductivity 1.38 W/(m·K). Calculate the total thermal resistance considering area of wall as 1 sq. meter.*

Solution : Basis : 1 sq.m. of heat transfer area

x_1 = thickness of sil-o-cel brick = 45 mm = 0.045 m

x_2 = thickness of common brick = 90 mm = 0.09 m

k_1 = thermal conductivity of sil-o-cel brick = 0.138 W/(m·K)

k_2 = thermal conductivity of common brick = 1.38 W/(m·K)

A = area of heat transfer = 1 m²

R_1 = thermal resistance of sil-o-cel brick = $\dfrac{x_1}{k_1 A}$

R_2 = thermal resistance of common brick = $\dfrac{x_2}{k_2 A}$

Total resistance = R = $R_1 + R_2$

$$R = \frac{x_1}{k_1 A} + \frac{x_2}{k_2 A} = \frac{0.045}{0.138 \times 1} + \frac{0.09}{1.38 \times 1} = \mathbf{0.391\ K/W} \qquad \text{... Ans.}$$

Example 2.15 : *A cylindrical tube of inside radius r_1 and outside radius r_2 is lagged by insulating material with r_3 as the outer radius of insulation. Derive the expression for rate of heat flow.*

Solution : Consider a cylindrical tube of length 'L' with inside radius r_1 and outside radius r_2. Let thermal conductivity of wall material of the tube be k_1. Assume that the tube is surrounded by an insulation layer so that the radius of the outer layer of insulation be r_3. Let k_2 be the thermal conductivity of insulation. Let T_1, T', T_2 be the temperatures inside the tube, at the interface between the tube and insulation, and at the outer edge of the insulation respectively. Assume that $T_1 > T_2$.

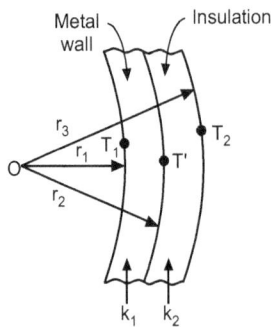

Fig. Ex. 2.15

Consider a small cylindrical element of thickness 'dr' of radius 'r' so that the rate of heat transfer through it is given by :

$$Q = -k \cdot 2\pi r\, L\, (dT/dr) \qquad \text{... (1)}$$

$$\frac{dr}{r} = \frac{-k(2\pi L)}{Q}\, dT \qquad \text{... (2)}$$

For rate of heat transfer (Q_1) through wall of tube, the above equation can be integrated between limits :

$r = r_1$, $T = T_1$ and $r = r_2$, $T = T'$

$$\int_{r_1}^{r_2} \frac{dr}{r} = \frac{-k_1(2\pi L)}{Q_1} \int_{T'}^{T_1} dT \qquad \ldots (3)$$

$$\ln\left(\frac{r_2}{r_1}\right) = \frac{k_1(2\pi L)}{Q_1}(T_1 - T') \qquad \ldots (4)$$

Similarly, the rate of heat transfer (Q_2) through insulation is given by the equation :

$$\ln(r_3/r_2) \approx \frac{k_2(2\pi L)}{Q_2}(T' - T_2) \qquad \ldots (5)$$

Rearranging equations (4) and (5), we get

$$(T_1 - T') = Q_1\left(\frac{\ln(r_2/r_1)}{k_1(2\pi L)}\right) \qquad \ldots (6)$$

$$(T' - T_2) = Q_2\left(\frac{\ln(r_3/r_2)}{k_2(2\pi L)}\right) \qquad \ldots (7)$$

Overall temperature drop $= \Delta T = T_1 - T_2$

$$(T_1 - T_2) = (T_1 - T') - (T' - T_2) \qquad \ldots (8)$$

Putting the values of $(T_1 - T')$ and $(T' - T_2)$ from equations (6) and (7) into equation (8), we get

$$(T_1 - T_2) = Q_1\left[\frac{\ln(r_2/r_1)}{k_1(2\pi L)}\right] + Q_2\left[\frac{\ln(r_3/r_2)}{k_2(2\pi L)}\right] \qquad \ldots (9)$$

At steady state, $Q_1 = Q_2 = Q$ i.e. whatever heat passes through tube must pass through insulation.

$$\therefore \quad (T_1 - T_2) = Q\left[\frac{\ln(r_2/r_1)}{k_1(2\pi L)} + \frac{\ln(r_3/r_2)}{k_2(2\pi L)}\right] \qquad \ldots (10)$$

$$Q = \frac{(T_1 - T_2)}{\left[\frac{\ln(r_2/r_1)}{k_1(2\pi L)} + \frac{\ln(r_3/r_2)}{k_2(2\pi L)}\right]} \qquad \ldots (11)$$

Let r_{m_1} be the log mean radius of tube.

$$r_{m_1} = \frac{r_2 - r_1}{\ln(r_2 - r_1)} \qquad \ldots (12)$$

$$\therefore \quad \ln(r_2/r_1) = \frac{r_2 - r_1}{r_{m_1}} \qquad \ldots (13)$$

Let r_{m_2} be the log mean radius for insulation layer.

$$\therefore \quad r_{m_2} = \frac{r_3 - r_2}{\ln (r_3/r_2)} \quad \ldots (14)$$

$$\therefore \quad \ln (r_3/r_2) = \frac{r_3 - r_2}{r_{m_2}} \quad \ldots (15)$$

Putting the values from equations (13) and (15) of $\ln (r_2/r_1)$ and $\ln (r_3/r_2)$ into equation (11), we get

$$Q = \frac{T_1 - T_2}{\dfrac{(r_2 - r_1)}{k_1 \, 2\pi \, r_{m_1} \, L} + \dfrac{(r_3 - r_2)}{k_2 \, 2\pi \, r_{m_2} \, L}}$$

Example 2.16 : *A flat furnace wall is constructed of 114 mm layer of Sil-o-cel brick, with a thermal conductivity of 0.138 W/(m·K) backed by 229 mm layer of common brick, of conductivity 1.38 W/(m·K). The temperature of inner face of wall is 1033 K (760 °C) and that of the outer face is 349 K (76 °C).*

(a) What is the heat loss through the wall ?

(b) Supposing that the contact between two brick layers is poor and that a 'contact resistance' of 0.09 K/W is present what would be the heat loss ?

Solution : Consider 1 m² of wall (A = 1 m²)

Thermal resistance of Sil-o-cel brick layer $R_1 = x_1/k_1 A$

$$x_1 = 114 \text{ mm} = 0.114 \text{ m}, \quad k_1 = 0.138 \text{ W/(m·K)}$$

$$\therefore \quad R_1 = \frac{0.114}{0.138 \times 1} = 0.826 \text{ K/W}$$

$$x_2 = 229 \text{ mm} = 0.229 \text{ m}, \quad k_1 = 1.38 \text{ W/(m·K)}$$

Thermal resistance of common brick = $R_2 = x_2/k_2 A = \dfrac{0.229}{1.38 \times 1} = 0.166$ K/W

$$\Delta T = 1033 - 349 = 684 \text{ K}$$

Heat loss from 1 m² of wall,

$$Q = \Delta T/(R_1 + R_2) = 684 / (0.826 + 0.166)$$

$$= \mathbf{689.5 \text{ W}} \quad \ldots \textbf{Ans. (a)}$$

Contact resistance = 0.09 K/W

Total resistance = R = $R_1 + R_2$ + Contact resistance

$$= 0.826 + 0.166 + 0.09$$

$$= 1.082 \text{ K/W}$$

Heat loss from 1 m² is

$$Q = \Delta T / R = 684 / 1.082$$

$$= \mathbf{632.2 \text{ W}} \quad \ldots \textbf{Ans. (b)}$$

Example 2.17 : *An ice box has walls constructed of a 10 mm layer of cork-board contained between two wooden walls, each of 20 mm thick. Find the rate of heat removed per unit area if the inner wall surface is kept at 263 K (– 10 °C), while the outer surface temperature is 303 K (30 °C). Find out the zone in the wall where the temperature is 293 K (20 °C).*

Data : *Thermal conductivities of cork-board and wood respectively are 0.041 and 0.105 W/(m·K).*

Solution :

Q = Amount of heat transferred

$$= \frac{\Delta T}{\sum x/kA}$$

$$\frac{Q}{A} = \frac{\Delta T}{\sum x/k} = \frac{\Delta T}{\frac{x_1}{k_1} + \frac{x_2}{k_2} + \frac{x_3}{k_3}}$$

Fig. Ex. 2.17

$\Delta T = T_1 - T_2 = 303 - 263 = 40$ K

$x_1 = 20$ mm $= 0.02$ m (wood wall)

$x_2 = 10$ mm $= 0.01$ m (cork-board)

$x_3 = 20$ mm $= 0.02$ m (wood wall)

$k_1 = k_3 = 0.105$ W/(m·K) (thermal conductivity of wood)

$k_2 = 0.041$ W/(m·K) (thermal conductivity of cork-board)

$$\frac{Q}{A} = \frac{40}{\left(\frac{0.02}{0.105}\right) + \left(\frac{0.01}{0.041}\right) + \left(\frac{0.02}{0.105}\right)} = 64 \text{ W/m}^2$$

Trial-I : Let x be the distance from outside of the outer wooden wall and inside the wooden layer.

$$\frac{\text{Temperature drop upto a distance in x}}{\text{Total temperature drop}} = \frac{R_x}{R}$$

where
R_x = resistance upto a distance x metre

R = total resistance

Let $A = 1 \text{ m}^2$

$$R_x = \frac{x}{0.105 \times 1} = 0.9524 \, x \text{ K/W}$$

$$R = \frac{0.02}{0.105 \times 1} + \frac{0.010}{0.041 \times 1} + \frac{0.02}{0.105 \times 1} = 0.625 \text{ K/W}$$

$$\frac{303 - 293}{40} = \frac{0.9524 \, x}{0.625}$$

Solving, we get

$\qquad x = 0.0164 \text{ m} = \mathbf{16.4 \text{ mm}}$ ... **Ans.**

∴ Temperature of 293 K (20 °C) will be reached at a point 16.4 mm from the outermost wall surface of the ice-box.

Example 2.18 : *A pipe 65 mm outside diameter is lagged with 50 mm layer of asbestos (conductivity = 0.14) and a 40 mm layer of cork [conductivity = 0.035 W/(m·K)]. If the temperature of the outer surface of the pipe is 423 K (150 °C) and the temperature of the outer surface of the cork is 308 K (35 °C), calculate the heat loss per metre of pipe.*

Solution :

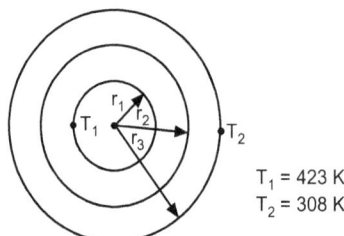

$T_1 = 423$ K
$T_2 = 308$ K

Fig. Ex. 2.18

$r_1 = 65/2 = 32.5$ mm

$r_2 = 32.5 + 50 = 82.5$ mm

$r_3 = 32.5 + 50 + 40 = 122.5$ mm

Let r_{m_1} and r_{m_2} be the log mean radii.

$$r_{m_1} = \frac{r_2 - r_1}{\ln\left(\frac{r_2}{r_1}\right)} = \frac{82.5 - 32.5}{\ln\left(\frac{82.5}{32.5}\right)} = 53.7 \text{ mm} = 0.537 \text{ m}$$

$$r_{m_2} = \frac{r_3 - r_2}{\ln\left(\frac{r_3}{r_2}\right)} = \frac{122.5 - 82.5}{\ln\left(\frac{122.5}{82.5}\right)} = 101.2 \text{ mm} = 0.1012 \text{ m}$$

$r_2 - r_1 = 82.5 - 32.5 = 50 \text{ mm} = 0.05$ m

$r_3 - r_2 = 122.5 - 82.5 = 40 \text{ mm} = 0.04$ m

$$\Delta T = T_1 - T_2 = 423 - 308 = 115 \text{ K}$$
$$k_1 = 0.14 \text{ W/(m·K)}$$
$$k_2 = 0.035 \text{ W/(m·K)}$$
$$Q = \frac{\Delta T}{\sum x/kA}$$
$$Q = \frac{\Delta T}{\dfrac{r_2 - r_1}{k_1 \, 2\pi \, r_{m_1} \, L} + \dfrac{r_3 - r_2}{k_2 \, 2\pi \, r_{m_2} \, L}}$$

Take $L = 1$ m

$$Q = \frac{115}{\dfrac{1}{2\pi}\left[\dfrac{0.05}{0.14 \times 0.0537 \times 1} + \dfrac{0.04}{0.035 \times 0.1012 \times 1}\right]}$$

$$= \mathbf{40.3 \text{ W/m}} \qquad \text{... Ans.}$$

Example 2.19 : *A hollow sphere has an inside surface temperature 573 K (300 °C) and the outside surface temperature 303 K (30 °C). Find the heat loss by conduction for an inside diameter of 50 mm and outside diameter of 150 mm.*

Data : *The thermal conductivity of material is 17.45 W/(m·K).*

Solution : I.D. of sphere = 50 mm

$$r_1 = \frac{50}{2} = 25 \text{ mm} = 0.025 \text{ m}$$

O.D. of sphere = 150 mm

$$r_2 = 75 \text{ mm} = 0.075 \text{ m}$$

$$\frac{Q}{A} = \frac{\Delta T}{(r_2 - r_1)/k}$$

$$A = \sqrt{A_1 A_2} = \sqrt{4\pi r_1^2 \times 4\pi r_2^2}$$

$$A = 4\pi r_1 r_2$$

$$Q = \frac{4\pi r_1 r_2 k \, \Delta T}{(r_2 - r_1)} = \frac{4\pi k \, \Delta T}{\dfrac{1}{r_1} - \dfrac{1}{r_2}}$$

$$= \frac{4 \times \pi \times 17.45 \, (573 - 303)}{\dfrac{1}{0.025} - \dfrac{1}{0.075}} = 2220 \text{ W}$$

∴ Heat loss = Q = **2220 W** ... Ans.

Example 2.20 : *A furnace wall is made up of 230 mm of fire brick, 75 mm of insulating brick and 89 mm of red brick. The temperature at the inner surface of the wall is 1073 K (800°C) and that of the outer surface is 333 K (60°C). Average thermal conductivity values of the three types of bricks i.e. fire brick, insulating brick and the red brick are 1.21, 0.121 and 0.865 W/(m·K) respectively. Calculate the temperatures at the interface between different kinds of bricks.*

Solution :

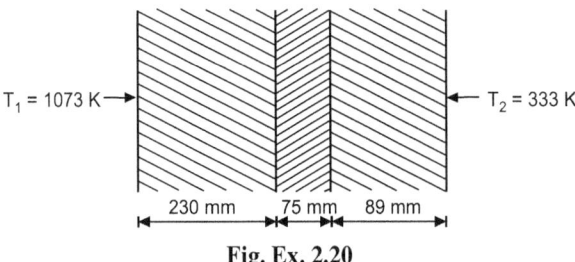

Fig. Ex. 2.20

x_1 = thickness of fire brick = 230 mm = 0.23 m

x_2 = thickness of insulating brick = 75 mm = 0.075 m

x_3 = thickness of red brick = 89 mm = 0.089 m

k_1 = 1.21 W/(m·K)

k_2 = 0.121 W/(m·K)

k_3 = 0.865 W/(m·K)

Let A = 1 m²

$$\sum R = \sum x/kA$$

$$= \frac{x_1}{k_1 A} + \frac{x_2}{k_2 A} + \frac{x_3}{k_3 A}$$

$$= \frac{0.23}{1.21 \times 1} + \frac{0.075}{0.121 \times 1} + \frac{0.089}{0.865 \times 1}$$

$$= 0.19 + 0.62 + 0.103 = 0.913 \text{ K/W}$$

ΔT_1 = temperature drop over fire brick

$$R_1 = x_1/k_1 A = \frac{0.23}{1.21 \times 1} = 0.19 \text{ K/W}$$

$$\frac{\Delta T_1}{\Delta T} = \frac{R_1}{\sum R}$$

$$\Delta T_1 = \Delta T \times \frac{R_1}{\sum R} = (1073 - 333) \times \frac{0.19}{0.913} = 154 \text{ K}$$

Temperature at the interface between fire brick and insulating brick

$$= 1073 - 154 = \textbf{919 K (646°C)} \qquad \text{... Ans.}$$

$$\frac{\Delta T_2}{\Delta T} = \frac{R_2}{\Sigma R}$$

$$R_2 = x_2/k_2 A = \frac{0.075}{0.121 \times 1} = \mathbf{0.62} \qquad \text{... Ans.}$$

$$\Delta T_2 = \Delta T \times \frac{R_2}{\Sigma R} = (1073 - 333) \times \frac{0.62}{0.913} = 502.50 \text{ K}$$

Temperature at the interface between insulating brick and red brick

$$= 919 - 502.5 = \mathbf{416.5 \text{ K} \ (143.5^\circ C)} \qquad \text{... Ans.}$$

So the temperatures of the two interfaces are 919 K and 416.5 K.

Example 2.21 : *A furnace wall made up of steel plate 10 mm thick lined on inside with silica brick 150 mm thick on the outside with magnesite brick 150 mm thick. The temperature on inside edge of the wall is 973 K (700°C) and on the outside is 288 K (15°C). Calculate the quantity of heat passed in watts per m².*

It is required to reduce the heat flow to 1163 W/m² by means of air gap between steel plate and magnesite brick. Estimate the width of this gap. Thermal conductivities in W/(m·K) are 16.86, 1.75, 5.23 and 0.033 respectively for steel, silica brick, magnesite brick and air.

Solution :

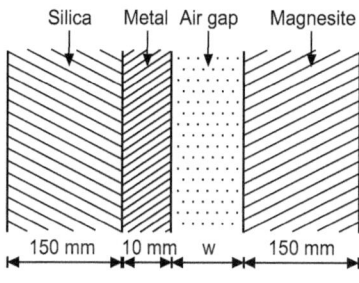

Fig. Ex. 2.21

$$w = \text{proposed air gap, m}$$

$$\begin{bmatrix} \text{Heat loss from} \\ \text{furnace wall} \end{bmatrix} = Q = \frac{\Delta T}{\Sigma R}$$

Let the heat transfer area be A = 1 m²

$$\Sigma R = \Sigma x/kA = \frac{0.15}{1.75 \times 1} + \frac{0.01}{16.86 \times 1} + \frac{0.15}{5.23 \times 1} = 0.1153 \text{ K/W}$$

(in absence of air gap)

Heat loss per m² is :

$$Q = \frac{\Delta T}{\Sigma R} = \frac{973 - 288}{0.1153} = 5941 \text{ W/m}^2$$

Let the new resistance be $\sum R'$ when the heat loss will reduce to 1163 W/m².

$$1163 = \frac{\Delta T}{\sum R'}$$

$$\sum R' = \frac{973 - 288}{1163} = 0.589$$

Let   w = width of air gap

$$\sum R' = \sum R + \frac{w}{k_{air} \times A}$$

$$0.589 = 0.1153 + \frac{w}{0.033 \times 1}$$

$$w = (0.589 - 0.1153) \times 0.033 = 0.0156 \text{ m} = 15.6 \text{ mm}$$

Width of the air gap = **15.6 mm** ... **Ans.**

Example 2.22 : *A 300 mm O.D. pipe is covered with two layers of insulation [k_1 = 0.105 W/(m·K) and k_2 = 0.07 W/(m·K)]. The better insulating material is on the outside and is 40 mm thick. The other insulating material is of 50 mm thickness. The inner and outer surface temperatures of the insulation are 623 K (350º C) and 323 K (50º C). Estimate :*

(a) *Heat loss per metre length.*

(b) *Heat loss per square metre of outer insulation surface.*

(c) *Temperature of the surface between the two layers of insulation.*

Solution : O.D. of pipe = 300 mm

r_1 = 300/2 = 150 mm = 0.15 m

r_2 = 150 + 50 = 200 mm = 0.20 m

r_3 = 200 + 40 = 240 mm = 0.24 m

x_1 = 50 mm = 0.05 m

x_2 = 40 mm = 0.04 m

$$r_{m_1} = \frac{r_2 - r_1}{\ln\left(\frac{r_2}{r_1}\right)} = \frac{0.2 - 0.15}{\ln\left(\frac{0.2}{0.15}\right)} = 0.1738 \text{ m} = 0.174 \text{ m}$$

$$r_{m_2} = \frac{r_3 - r_2}{\ln\left(\frac{r_3}{r_2}\right)} = \frac{(0.24 - 0.20)}{\ln\left(\frac{0.24}{0.20}\right)} = 0.2194 \text{ m} \simeq 0.22 \text{ m}$$

$$R_1 = \frac{x_1}{k_1 A} = \frac{0.05}{0.105 \times \pi \times 0.174 \times L} = \frac{0.827}{L}$$

$$R_2 = \frac{x_2}{k_2 A} = \frac{0.04}{0.07 \times \pi \times 0.22 \times L} = \frac{0.827}{L}$$

(a) Heat loss :

$$Q = \frac{\Delta T}{R_1 + R_2} = \frac{\Delta T}{\frac{0.871}{L} + \frac{0.827}{L}}$$

$$\frac{Q}{L} = \frac{\Delta T}{0.871 + 0.827} = \frac{623 - 323}{1.698} = 176.7 \text{ W/m}$$

$$\frac{Q}{L} = 176.7 \text{ W/m} \qquad \ldots \text{Ans. (a)}$$

(b) Perimeter of outer insulation :

$$= 2\pi \left(\frac{O.D.}{2} + x_1 + x_2\right)$$

$$= 2\pi (0.15 + 0.05 + 0.04) = 1.508 \text{ m}$$

Heat loss per m² of outer insulation surface is :

$$\frac{Q/L}{\text{Perimeter}} = \frac{176.7}{1.508} = 117.2 \text{ W/m}^2 \qquad \ldots \text{Ans. (b)}$$

ΔT_1 = temperature drop over first insulation

R_1 = resistance of first insulation

$$= \frac{x_1}{k_1 A} = \frac{0.871}{L}$$

Similarly, $\quad \sum R = \frac{0.871}{L} + \frac{0.827}{L} = \frac{1.698}{L}$

$$\frac{\Delta T_1}{\Delta T} = \frac{R_1}{\sum R}$$

$$\Delta T_1 = \Delta T \times R_1 / \sum R$$

$$\Delta T_1 = \frac{(623 - 323) \times 0.871}{L \times \frac{1.698}{L}} = 153.9 \text{ K}$$

Temperature of the surface between the two layers of insulations

$$= 623 - 153.9 = 469.1 \text{ K } (196.1° \text{ C}) \qquad \ldots \text{Ans.}$$

Example 2.23 : *Compute the heat loss per m² of surface area for a furnace wall, 300 mm thick. The inner and outer surface temperatures are 593 K (320° C) and 311 K (38° C) respectively. The variation in thermal conductivity (W/(m·K)) with temperature in K is given by the following relation :*

$$k = 0.003 \, T - 10^{-6} \, T^2$$

Solution : $\quad Q = - kA \, dT/dx$

$$k = 0.003 \, T - 1 \times 10^{-6} \, T^2$$

$$Q \int_0^x dx = -A \int_{T_1}^{T_2} (0.003\, T - 10^{-6}\, T^2)\, dT$$

$$Q \cdot x = A \int_{T_2}^{T_1} (0.003\, T - 10^{-6}\, T^2)\, dT$$

$$Q = \frac{A}{x} \left[\frac{0.003}{2} (T_1^2 - T_2^2) - \frac{10^{-6}}{3} (T_1^3 - T_2^3) \right]$$

where, $A = 1\ m^2$
$x = 30\ cm = 0.3\ m$
$T_1 = 593\ K$
$T_2 = 311\ K$

$$Q = \frac{1}{0.3} \left[\frac{0.003}{2} ((593)^2 - (311)^2) - \frac{10^{-6}}{3} ((593)^3 - (311)^3) \right]$$

$= 1274.4\ W$

Heat loss per $1 m^2 =$ **1274.4 W** ... **Ans.**

Example 2.24 : *Calculate the rate of increment of the thickness of ice layer on the lake when the thickness of ice is 200 mm and air temperature 263 K. Thermal conductivity of ice is 1.675 W/(m·K) and density of ice is 900 kg/m³. Take latent heat of ice as 335 kJ/kg. Calculate also the time to double the thickness of ice.*

Solution : Considering conduction through 1 m² area of the slab of ice, heat required to be conducted through ice to increase the layer thickness by x mm is given by

$$= 1 \times \frac{x}{1000} \times 900 \times 335 = 301.5\ x\ kJ$$

Thus, 301.5 x kJ is required to be conducted through 1 m² area of average thickness $0.20 + \frac{x}{1000 \times 2} = (0.20 + 0.0005\,x)$ m in say t hours.

$$\frac{\text{heat to be conducted}}{t} = \frac{-kA\, dT}{dx}$$

heat to be conducted $= 301.5\ x\ kJ = 301.5\ x \times 10^3\ J$

$(-dT) = -(263 - 273) = 10\ K$

$$301.5\ x \times 10^3 = \frac{-kA\, dT}{0.20 + 0.0005x\ m} \times t$$

$$= \frac{1.675 \times 1 \times 10}{0.20 + 0.0005x} \times t$$

when $t = 1\ hr = 3600\ s$

$$301.5\ x \times 10^3 = \frac{1.675 \times 1 \times 10}{0.20 + 0.0005x} \times 3600$$

$x\,(0.20 + 0.0005x) = 0.20$

If x = 1, L.H.S. becomes approximately equal to R.H.S.

$$\begin{bmatrix}\text{Rate of increment} \\ \text{of thickness}\end{bmatrix} = \frac{x}{t} = \frac{1\text{ mm}}{1\text{ h}} = 1\text{ mm/h}$$

Original thickness = 200 mm

$$\begin{bmatrix}\text{Time required to double} \\ \text{the thickness of ice}\end{bmatrix} = \frac{200\text{ mm}}{1\text{ mm/h}} = \mathbf{200\text{ h}} \qquad \ldots \text{ Ans.}$$

Example 2.25 : *The inside and outside temperature of a furnace wall 300 mm thick of refractory brick [k = 1.57 W/(m·K)] are at 1923 K (1650 °C) and 593 K (320 °C) respectively. Find the reduction in heat loss through the wall to be obtained by adding 300 mm thickness of insulating bricks having k = 0.35 W/(m·K) assuming the inside surface temperature of refractory bricks to remain fixed at 1923 K (1650 °C). The temperature of outside surface of the brick may be taken as 300 K (27 °C).*

Solution :

$$Q = \frac{k \cdot A (T_1 - T_2)}{x}$$

where
- $k = 1.57$ W/(m·K)
- $A = 1$ m²
- $x = 300$ mm $= 0.3$ m
- $T_1 = 1923$ K
- $T_2 = 593$ K

$$Q_1 = \frac{1.57 \times 1 \times (1923 - 593)}{0.3} = 6960 \text{ W}$$

$$Q_2 = \frac{A(T_1 - T_2')}{x_1/k_1 + x_2/k_2}$$

- $x_1 = 0.3$ m
- $x_2 = 0.3$ m
- $k_1 = 1.57$ W/(m·K)
- $k_2 = 0.35$ W/(m·K)
- $T_2' = 300$ K
- $T_1 = 1923$ K

$$Q_2 = \frac{1 \times (1923 - 300)}{\frac{0.3}{1.57} + \frac{0.3}{0.35}} = 1548 \text{ W}$$

$$\begin{bmatrix}\text{Reduction in heat} \\ \text{loss per m}^2\end{bmatrix} = Q_1 - Q_2$$

$$= 6960 - 1548 = \mathbf{5412 \text{ W}} \qquad \ldots \text{ Ans.}$$

Example 2.26 : *A cold room has one of the walls which measures 4.6 m × 2.3 m constructed of bricks, 115 mm thick, insulated by cork slabbing 75 mm thick. The cork is protected externally by wood 25 mm thick. Estimate the leakage through the wall per 24 hours if the interior temperature is 271 K and the exterior 291 K. The thermal conductivities of brick, cork and wood are 0.113, 0.005 and 0.021 W/(m·K) respectively.*

Solution : $Q' = \dfrac{A(T_1 - T_2)}{x_1/k_1 + x_2/k_2 + x_3/k_3}$

$A = 4.6 \times 2.3 = 10.58 \text{ m}^2$

$Q' = \dfrac{10.58\,(291 - 271)}{\dfrac{0.115}{0.113} + \dfrac{0.075}{0.005} + \dfrac{0.025}{0.021}} = 12.72 \text{ W}$

Q = Heat leakage per 24 hours

$= 12.27 \times 3600 \times 24 \times 10^{-3}$

$= 1060 \text{ kJ}$ ... **Ans.**

Example 2.27 : *A furnace wall is made up of a steel plate 10 mm thick, lined on inside with silica brick 150 mm thick, and on outside with magnesite bricks 150 mm thick. The temperature on the inside edge of the wall is 973 K (700 °C) and on the outside is 423 K (150 °C). Calculate the quantity of heat passed in W/m² and temperature at the interface of steel and magnesite brick. Thermal conductivity of steel, silica brick and magnesite brick are 16.86, 1.75 and 5.23 W/(m·K) respectively.*

It is required that the heat flow be reduced to 1163 W/m² by means of an air gap between the steel and magnesite brick. Find the width of air gap, if k for air is 0.0337 W/(m·K).

Solution : $Q = \dfrac{(T_1 - T_2)}{\Sigma\, x/kA}$

$\Sigma\, x/kA = \dfrac{x_1}{k_1 A} + \dfrac{x_2}{k_2 A} + \dfrac{x_3}{k_3 A}$

where, $x_1 = 10 \text{ mm} = 0.01 \text{ m}$

$x_2 = 150 \text{ mm} = 0.15 \text{ m}$

$x_3 = 150 \text{ mm} = 0.15 \text{ m}$

$k_1 = 16.86 \text{ W/(m·K)}$

$k_2 = 1.75 \text{ W/(m·K)}$

$k_3 = 5.23 \text{ W/(m·K)}$

Let $A = 1 \text{ m}^2$

$\Sigma\, x/kA = \dfrac{0.010}{16.86 \times 1} + \dfrac{0.15}{1.75 \times 1} + \dfrac{0.15}{5.23 \times 1} = 0.115 \text{ K/W}$

Q = Heat flow $= \dfrac{(973 - 423)}{0.115} = 4782.6 \text{ W/m}^2$

Temperature drop in magnesite bricks

$= \dfrac{Q x_3}{k_3} = 4782.6 \times \dfrac{0.15}{5.23} = 137.2 \text{ K}$

∴ Interface temperature between steel and magnesite brick

$$= 137.2 + 423 = 560.2 \text{ K}$$

$\sum x/k$ with air gap for reducing the heat loss to 1163 per m² is

$$\sum x/k = \frac{1 \times (973 - 423)}{1163} = 0.473$$

∴   x/k for air $= 0.473 - 0.115 = 0.358$

∴ Air gap thickness $= 0.358 \times 0.0337 = 0.01206$ m

$$= 12.06 \text{ mm} \qquad \ldots \text{Ans.}$$

Example 2.28 : *A steam pipe 115 mm outside diameter, is covered with two layers of different materials. The first layer is 50 mm thick and has thermal conductivity of 0.062 W/(m·K). The second layer is 30 mm thick and has a thermal conductivity of 0.872 W/(m·K).*

Outside surface temperature of steam pipe is 508 K (235 °C) and that of the outer surface of lagging is 311 K (38 °C). Calculate the heat loss per metre length of pipe and the temperature between the two layers of insulation.

Solution :
$$Q = \frac{2\pi L (T_1 - T_2)}{\frac{\ln (r_2/r_1)}{k_1} + \frac{\ln (r_3/r_2)}{k_2}}$$

where, $T_1 = 508$ K

$T_2 = 311$ K

$r_1 = 115/2 = 57.5$ mm $= 0.0575$ m

$r_2 = 57.5 + 50 = 107.5$ mm $= 0.1075$ m

$r_3 = 107.5 + 30 = 137.5$ mm $= 0.1375$ m

$k_1 = 0.062$ W/(m·K)

$k_2 = 0.872$ W/(m·K)

Assume $L = 1$ m

∴
$$Q = \frac{2\pi \times 1 (508 - 311)}{\frac{\ln \left(\frac{0.1075}{0.0575}\right)}{0.062} + \frac{\ln \left(\frac{0.1375}{0.1075}\right)}{0.872}}$$

$$= 119.3 \text{ W/m}$$

∴ Heat loss per metre length of pipe

$$Q = 119.3 \text{ W/m} \qquad \ldots \text{Ans.}$$

Let T be the temperature between two layers of insulation.

$$Q = \frac{2\pi L (T_1 - T)}{\frac{\ln (r_2/r_1)}{k_1}}$$

$$119.3 = \frac{2\pi \times 1 \, (508 - T)}{\dfrac{\ln\left(\dfrac{0.1075}{0.0575}\right)}{0.062}}$$

Solving for T, we get

$$T = 316.4 \text{ K } (43.4°C) \quad \text{... Ans.}$$

Example 2.29 : *A steel pipe with an outside diameter of 115 mm and a wall thickness of 5 mm is covered with 50 mm thickness of 85% magnesia. The surface temperature on the inside of the pipe is 423 K (150 °C) and that on the outside of insulation is 305 K (32 °C).*

Calculate :

(i) The heat flow per metre of length.

(ii) The temperature at the outer surface of the steel pipe and

(iii) The conductance of the pipe and insulation based on its inside surface area.

k for steel = 43.03 W/(m·K)

k for insulation = 0.07 W/(m·K)

Solution :
$$Q = \frac{2\pi L \, (T_1 - T_2)}{\dfrac{\sum \ln(r_2/r_1)}{k}}$$

$$= \frac{2\pi L \, (T_1 - T_2)}{\dfrac{\ln(r_2/r_1)}{k_1} + \dfrac{\ln(r_3/r_2)}{k_2}}$$

where, L = 1 m (assume)

T_1 = 423 K

T_2 = 305 K

$r_1 = \dfrac{115 - 2 \times 5}{2} = 52.5$ mm $= 0.0525$ m

$r_2 = \dfrac{115}{2} = 57.5$ mm $= 0.0575$ m

$r_3 = \dfrac{115}{2} + 50 = 107.5$ mm $= 0.1075$ m

Heat loss per metre length of pipe :

$$Q = \frac{2\pi \times 1 \times (423 - 305)}{\dfrac{\ln\left(\dfrac{0.0575}{0.0525}\right)}{43.03} + \dfrac{\ln\left(\dfrac{0.1075}{0.0575}\right)}{0.07}}$$

$$= \mathbf{82.92 \text{ W/m}} \quad \text{... Ans. (a)}$$

Let T be the temperature at the outer surface of steel pipe.

$$Q = \frac{2\pi L (T_1 - T)}{\frac{\ln(r_2/r_1)}{k}}$$

$$82.92 = \frac{2\pi \times 1 \times (423 - T)}{\frac{\ln\left(\frac{0.0575}{0.0525}\right)}{43.03}}$$

Solving for T, we get

$$T = 422.97 \text{ K } (149.97 \text{ °C}) \quad \ldots \text{Ans. (b)}$$

This shows that there is a negligible temperature drop over the steel pipe thickness. Thus, the resistance of the pipe material is negligible as compared with that of the insulation.

As inside diameter is 105 mm, inside area per metre of pipe length is

$$\pi \times 0.105 \times 1 = 0.335 \text{ m}^2$$

Thus, conductance per m length based on the inside area,

$$C = \frac{1}{R} = \frac{Q}{A(T_1 - T_2)}$$

$$= \frac{82.92}{0.335 (423 - 305)} = 2.1 \text{ W/K}$$

$$\therefore \quad C = 2.1 \text{ W/K} \quad \ldots \text{Ans. (c)}$$

Example 2.30 : *A steam pipe 100 mm outside diameter is covered with two layers of insulating material, each 25 mm thick, the thermal conductivity of one being three times that of the other.*

Working from first principles show that the effectivity of the two layers is 15.7% less when the better insulating material is on the inside than when it is on the outside. Assume same overall temperature difference in both the cases.

Solution : Consider a thick cylinder of length L. Let k be the thermal conductivity of cylinder material. Consider element of thickness dr at a radius r concentric with the cylinder. The rate of heat of transfer through elementary layer of thickness dr at radius r is

$$Q = -k \, 2\pi r L \, dT/dr$$

Integrating between limits r_1 and r_2 and T_1 and T_2,

$$Q \int_{r_1}^{r_2} dr\, r = -2\pi L k \int_{T_1}^{T_2} dT$$

$$Q \ln(r_2/r_1) = 2\pi L k (T_1 - T_2)$$

$$Q = \frac{2\pi L\, k\, (T_1 - T_2)}{\ln(r_2/r_1)}$$

$$Q = \frac{2\pi L\, (T_1 - T_2)}{\dfrac{\ln(r_2/r_1)}{k}}$$

For a composite cylinder,

$$Q = \frac{2\pi L\, (T_1 - T_2)}{\sum \dfrac{\ln(r_2/r_1)}{k}}$$

Assume that the conductivity of the better insulating material as k and that of outer as 3 k.

With the better insulating material on the inside,

$$Q_1 = \frac{2\pi L\, (T_1 - T_2)}{\dfrac{\ln(r_2/r_1)}{k} + \dfrac{\ln(r_3/r_2)}{3k}}$$

$r_1 = 100/2 = 50$ mm $= 0.05$ mm
$r_2 = 50 + 25 = 75$ mm $= 0.075$ m
$r_3 = 75 + 25 = 100$ mm $= 0.10$ m

$$Q_1 = \frac{2\pi L\, (T_1 - T_2)}{\dfrac{\ln\left(\dfrac{0.075}{0.050}\right)}{k} + \dfrac{\ln\left(\dfrac{0.10}{0.075}\right)}{3k}}$$

With the better insulating material on the outside,

$$Q_2 = \frac{2\pi L\, (T_1 - T_2)}{\dfrac{\ln(r_2/r_1)}{3k} + \dfrac{\ln(r_3/r_2)}{k}}$$

$$= \frac{2\pi L\, (T_1 - T_2)}{\dfrac{\ln\left(\dfrac{0.075}{0.05}\right)}{3k} + \dfrac{\ln\left(\dfrac{0.10}{0.075}\right)}{k}}$$

$$\therefore \quad \frac{Q_1}{Q_2} = \frac{1/3\, \ln(3/2) + \ln(4/3)}{\ln(3/2) + 1/3\, \ln(4/3)}$$

$$= 0.843 = 1 - 0.157$$

$\therefore$ By putting on the better insulating material inside, the heat conducted is reduced by 15.7% than that conducted by placing it on the outside.

$\therefore \qquad Q_1 = 0.843\, Q_2$

Example 2.31 : *A 165 mm external diameter pipe is lagged with 35 mm thickness of lagging of which thermal conductivity is 0.041 W/(m·K). The lagging outside temperature is 308 K, and brine temperature at a section inside the pipe is 252 K. Find the rising temperature of the brine per metre length at this section, if the brine mass flow is 0.32 kg/s. Specific heat of brine is 3.6 kJ/(kg.K).*

Solution : Neglecting the thermal resistance of pipe,

$$Q = \frac{2\pi L \, k \, (T_1 - T_2)}{\ln (r_2/r_1)}$$

Let
$L = 1 \text{ m}$
$T_1 = 308 \text{ K}$
$T_2 = 252 \text{ K}$
$r_1 = 165 \text{ mm} = 0.165 \text{ m}$
$r_2 = 165 + 2 \times 35 = 235 \text{ mm} = 0.235 \text{ m}$

$$Q = \frac{2\pi \times 1 \times 0.041 \times (308 - 252)}{\ln \left(\frac{0.235}{0.165}\right)}$$

= 40.8 W per metre length of pipe.

Heat gained by the brine = 40.8 W

$\begin{bmatrix} \text{Rise in temperature} \\ \text{of the brine} \end{bmatrix} = \Delta T$

$$\Delta T = \frac{Q}{\dot{m} \cdot C_p}$$

$$= \frac{40.8}{0.32 \times 3.6 \times 10^3} = 0.0354 \text{ K } (0.0354° \text{ C})$$

$\Delta T = \textbf{0.0354 K (0.0354° C)}$ ... **Ans.**

Example 2.32 : *The inside and outside surface of a hollow sphere at $r = r_1$ and $r = r_2$ ($r_1 < r < r_2$) are maintained at temperatures T_1 and T_2 respectively. The thermal conductivity varies with temperature as*

$$k = k_0(1 + \alpha T + \beta T^2)$$

Derive an expression for total heat flow rate Q through the sphere.

Solution : Fourier equation for sphere is given as

$$Q = -kA \frac{dT}{dr}$$

$$\frac{Q}{A} dr = -k \, dT$$

For sphere, $\quad A = 4\pi r^2$

$\quad k = k_0(1 + \alpha T + \beta T^2)$

Putting the values of A and k, we get

$$\frac{Q}{4\pi} \int_{r_1}^{r_2} \frac{dr}{r^2} = -k_0 \int_{T_1}^{T_2} (1 + \alpha T + \beta T^2)\, dT$$

$$\frac{Q}{4\pi} \left[-\frac{1}{r}\right]_{r_1}^{r_2} = k_0 \int_{T_2}^{T_1} (1 + \alpha T + \beta T^2)\, dT$$

$$\frac{-Q}{4\pi}\left[\frac{1}{r_2}-\frac{1}{r_1}\right] = k_0\left[(T_1 - T_2) + \frac{\alpha}{2}(T_1^2 - T_2^2) + \frac{\beta}{3}(T_1^3 - T_2^3)\right]$$

$$\frac{Q(r_2 - r_1)}{4\pi r_2 r_1} = k_0(T_1 - T_2)\left[1 + \frac{\alpha}{2}(T_1 + T_2) + \frac{\beta}{3}(T_1^2 + T_1 T_2 + T_2^2)\right]$$

$$Q = \frac{k_0\, 4\pi\, r_1 r_2 (T_1 - T_2)}{r_2 - r_1}\left[1 + \frac{\alpha}{2}(T_1 - T_2) + \frac{\beta}{3}(T_1^2 + T_1 T_2 + T_2^2)\right]$$

Example 2.33 : *A plane wall with isothermal faces T_1 at $x = 0$ and T_2 at $x = x$ has thermal conductivity $k = k_0(1 + aT)$. Show that the heat conducted through the wall is given by*

$$Q = \frac{k_0 A}{x}\left[1 + \frac{a}{2}(T_1 + T_2)\right](T_1 - T_2)$$

Solution : Fourier's law for heat conduction is

$$Q = -kA\, dT/dx$$

$$Q\, dx = -kA\, dT$$

$$k = k_0(1 + aT)$$

$\therefore \quad Q \int dx = -k_0 A \int (1 + aT)\, dT$

The limits of integration are

$\quad x = 0, \qquad\qquad T = T_1$

$\quad x = x \qquad\qquad T = T_2$

$$Q \int_0^x dx = -k_0 A \int_{T_1}^{T_2} (1 + aT)\, dT$$

$$Q \cdot x = k_0 A \int_{T_2}^{T_1} (1 + aT)\, dT$$

Integrating, we get

$$Q = \frac{k_0 A}{x} \left[(T_1 - T_2) + \frac{a}{2} (T_1^2 - T_2^2) \right]$$

$$Q = \frac{k_0 A}{x} \left[(T_1 - T_2) + \frac{a}{2} (T_1 + T_2)(T_1 - T_2) \right]$$

$$\therefore \quad Q = \frac{k_0 A}{x} \left[1 + \frac{a}{2} (T_1 + T_2) \right] [T_1 - T_2] \quad \text{... Ans.}$$

Example 2.34 : *An exterior wall of house may be approximated by a 100 mm layer of a common brick [k = 0.70 W/(m·K)] followed by a 40 mm layer of gypsum plaster [k = 0.48 W/(m·K)]. What thickness of loosely packed rockwool insulation [k = 0.065 W/(m·K)] should be added to reduce the heat loss through the wall by 25% ?*

Solution : Assume, $A = 1 \text{ m}^2$

$$Q = \frac{\Delta T}{\Sigma x/kA}$$

$$\Sigma x/kA = \frac{x_1}{k_1 A} + \frac{x_2}{k_2 A}$$

where, $x_1 = 100 \text{ mm} = 0.10 \text{ m}$

$x_2 = 40 \text{ mm} = 0.04 \text{ m}$

$k_1 = 0.7 \text{ W/(m·K)}$

$k_2 = 0.48 \text{ W/(m·K)}$

$$\Sigma x/kA = \frac{0.10}{0.7 \times 1} + \frac{0.04}{0.48 \times 1} = 0.226 \text{ K/W}$$

$$\therefore \quad Q = \frac{\Delta T}{0.226} = 4.42 \, \Delta T$$

With rockwool insulation added, the heat flow is 0.75 Q. Heat flow through the new system

$$= 0.75 \, Q = Q'$$

$$Q' = \frac{\Delta T}{\Sigma x/kA}$$

$$Q' = \frac{\Delta T}{x_1/k_1 A + x_2/k_2 A + x_3/k_3 A}$$

where, $x_3 = $ thickness of rockwool insulation in m

$k_3 = 0.065 \text{ W/(m·K)}$

$$Q' = \frac{\Delta T}{\frac{0.10}{0.7 \times 1} + \frac{0.04}{0.48 \times 1} + \frac{x_3}{0.065 \times 1}}$$

But $Q' = 0.75\, Q$

$\therefore \quad 0.75 \times 4.42 \times \Delta T = \dfrac{\Delta T}{0.226 + \dfrac{x_3}{0.065}}$

$0.75 \times 4.42 \left[0.226 + \dfrac{x_3}{0.065} \right] = 1$

$0.7492 + 51\, x_3 = 1$

$x_3 = 4.92 \times 10^{-3}\,\text{m} = \mathbf{4.92\ mm}$ ... **Ans.**

Thickness of rockwool insulation required = **4.92 mm.** ... **Ans.**

Example 2.35 : *A steam pipe, 40 mm outside diameter, is to be insulated by two layers of insulation each 20 mm thick. The material M-1 has conductivity k and the material M-2 has conductivity 3k. Assuming that the inner and outer surface temperatures of composite insulation to be fixed, find which arrangement would give less heat loss rate, M-1 near pipe surface and M-2 as the outer layer or vice versa ? Also calculate the percent reduction in heat loss.*

Solution : (1) Let the layer of material M-1 be nearer to the surface.

$$Q_1 = \dfrac{T_1 - T_2}{\dfrac{\ln r_2/r_1}{2\pi L k_1} + \dfrac{\ln r_3/r_2}{2\pi L k_2}}$$

Here, $k_1 = k$ and $k_2 = 3k$

$r_1 = 40/2 = 20\ \text{mm} = 0.02\ \text{m}$

$r_2 = 20 + 20 = 40\ \text{mm} = 0.04\ \text{m}$

$r_3 = 40 + 20 = 60\ \text{mm} = 0.06\ \text{m}$

T_1 and T_2 be the temperatures at the inner surface of pipe and at the outer surface insulation.

$$Q_1 = \dfrac{T_1 - T_2}{\dfrac{\ln(0.04/0.02)}{2\pi L k} + \dfrac{\ln(0.06/0.04)}{2\pi L \times 3k}}$$

$$Q_1 = \dfrac{T_1 - T_2}{\dfrac{\ln 2}{2\pi k} + \dfrac{\ln 1.5}{6\pi k}}$$

$$= \dfrac{k L (T_1 - T_2)}{0.1318} = 7.59\, kL\, (T_1 - T_2)$$

(2) Let the layer of material M-2 be nearer to the surface.

$$Q_2 = \frac{T_1 - T_2}{\frac{\ln r_2/r_1}{2\pi L k_1} + \frac{\ln r_3/r_2}{2\pi L k_2}}$$

$$= \frac{T_1 - T_2}{\frac{\ln (0.04/0.02)}{2\pi L \times 3k} + \frac{\ln (0.06/0.04)}{2\pi L k}}$$

$$= \frac{kL(T_1 - T_2)}{\frac{\ln 2}{6\pi} + \frac{\ln 1.5}{2\pi}}$$

$$= \frac{kL(T_1 - T_2)}{0.1013} = 9.87\, kL(T_1 - T_2)$$

For any value of k, T_1 and T_2, Q_1 is always less than Q_2.

∴ M-1 near the surface is advisable (i.e. arrangement one will result in less heat loss).

$$\begin{bmatrix}\% \text{ reduction in} \\ \text{heat loss}\end{bmatrix} = \frac{9.87\, kL(T_1 - T_2) - 7.59\, kL(T_1 - T_2)}{9.87\, kL(T_1 - T_2)} \times 100$$

$$= \frac{9.87 - 7.59}{9.87} \times 100$$

$$= 23.1\ \% \qquad \ldots \text{Ans.}$$

Example 2.36 : *A steel pipe [k = 50 W/(m·K)] of 100 mm I.D. and 110 mm O.D. is to be covered with two layers of insulation each having thickness of 50 mm. The thermal conductivity of the first insulation material is 0.06 W/(m·K) and that of second is 0.12 W/(m·K). Estimate the heat loss per 1 m length of pipe when the temperature of the inside tube surface is 523 K (250 ºC) and that of the outer surface of insulation is 323 K (50 ºC).*

If the order of insulation material were reversed, i.e. the insulation with higher value of thermal conductivity was put first, calculate the change in the heat loss with all other conditions kept unchanged. Comment on results.

Solution : $T_1 = 523$ K, $T_2 = 323$ K

$r_1 = 100/2 = 50$ mm $= 0.050$ m, $r_2 = 110/2 = 55$ mm $= 0.055$ m

$r_3 = 55 + 50 = 105$ mm $= 0.105$ m, $r_4 = 105 + 50 = 155$ mm $= 0.155$ m

$k_1 = 50$ W/(m·K), $k_2 = 0.06$ W/(m·K)

$k_3 = 0.12$ W/(m·K)

Case I :

First layer of insulation is of the insulation material having k = 0.06 W/(m·K), i.e., of the material having a lower value of thermal conductivity.

$$\left(\frac{Q}{L}\right)_1 = \frac{2\pi (T_1 - T_2)}{\frac{\ln (r_2/r_1)}{k_1} + \frac{\ln (r_3/r_2)}{k_2} + \frac{\ln (r_4/r_3)}{k_3}}$$

$$= \frac{2\pi (523 - 323)}{\frac{\ln (0.055/0.05)}{50} + \frac{\ln (0.105/0.055)}{0.06} + \frac{\ln (0.155/0.105)}{0.12}}$$

$$= 89.9 \text{ W/m} \qquad \ldots \text{Ans.}$$

Case II :

The insulation material of higher thermal conductivity is put first, i.e., near the pipe surface and the insulation of lower thermal conductivity at the outer layer. In this case, $k_2 = 0.12$ W/(m·K) and $k_3 = 0.06$ W/(m·K).

$$\left(\frac{Q}{L}\right)_2 = \frac{2\pi (523 - 323)}{\frac{\ln (0.055/0.05)}{40} + \frac{\ln (0.105/0.055)}{0.12} + \frac{\ln (0.155/0.105)}{0.06}}$$

$$= 105.75 \text{ W/m} \qquad \ldots \text{Ans.}$$

As $(Q/L)_1$ is less than $(Q/L)_2$, the insulation material having low thermal conductivity should be put first, i.e., near the pipe surface.

With material having low k value :

$$\% \text{ reduction in heat loss} = \frac{105.75 - 89.6}{89.6} \times 100 = 18.02$$

By comparing the results, it is seen that loss of heat is increased by 18.02% by putting insulation material with higher thermal conductivity near the pipe surface. As the purpose of insulation is to reduce the heat loss, it is always better to provide the insulating material with low thermal conductivity on the surface of pipe first i.e. near the pipe surface.

Example 2.37 : *A steam pipe 10 cm O.D. is to be insulated by two layers of insulations each 2.5 cm thick. The material 'A' has conductivity k and the material 'B' has conductivity 3 k. Assuming that the inner and outer temperatures of composite insulation to be fixed, find :*

(i) *Which arrangement would give less heat loss rate, 'A' near the pipe surface and 'B' as outer layer or vice versa ?*

(ii) *What is the percent reduction in heat loss rate ?*

Solution : Let T_1 be the temperature at the outer surface of pipe and T_2 be the temperature at the outer surface of insulation. These temperatures are fixed in both the following cases :

Case I : A near the surface.

Case II : B near the surface.

We have $\quad Q = \dfrac{(T_1 - T_2)}{\dfrac{\ln(r_2/r_1)}{2\pi k_1 L} + \dfrac{\ln(r_3/r_2)}{2\pi k_2 L}}$

Assume $\quad L = 1\ m$

Case I : 'A' near the pipe surface :

r_1 = outer radius of pipe = 100 mm = 0.10 m

r_2 = outer radius of inner insulation (A) = 100 + 25 = 125 mm = 0.125 m

r_3 = outer radius of outer insulation (B) = 125 + 25 = 150 mm = 0.150 m

k_1 = thermal conductivity of 'A' = k, W/(m·K)

k_2 = thermal conductivity of 'B' = 3 k, W/(m·K)

$\therefore\quad Q_1 = \dfrac{(T_1 - T_2)}{\dfrac{\ln(0.125/0.10)}{2\pi \times k \times 1.0} + \dfrac{\ln(0.15/0.125)}{2\pi \times 3k \times 1.0}}$

$Q_1 = \dfrac{\Delta T}{\dfrac{0.0355}{k} + \dfrac{0.0097}{k}}$

$= \dfrac{\Delta T}{0.0452/k} = 22.12\ k\ \Delta T$

Case II : 'B' near the pipe surface :

$Q_2 = \dfrac{(T_1 - T_2)}{\dfrac{\ln(0.125/0.10)}{2\pi \times 3k \times 1.0} + \dfrac{\ln(0.15/0.125)}{2\pi \times k \times 1.0}}$

$Q_2 = \dfrac{\Delta T}{\dfrac{0.012}{k} + \dfrac{0.029}{k}} = \dfrac{\Delta T}{\dfrac{0.041}{k}} = 24.39\ k\ \Delta T$

$Q_1 = 22.12\ k\ \Delta T$ and $Q_2 = 24.39\ k\ \Delta T$ $\therefore$ Q_1 is less than Q_2, i.e., arrangement 'A' near the pipe surface and 'B' as the outer layer gives less heat loss. **... Ans. (i)**

For less heat loss, 'A' near the pipe surface should be used. For reducing the heat loss, the material having low thermal conductivity should be always near the pipe surface.

$\begin{bmatrix} \%\ \text{Reduction in heat loss} \\ \text{(with A near pipe surface)} \end{bmatrix} = \dfrac{24.39\ k\ \Delta T - 22.12\ k\ \Delta T}{22.12\ k\ \Delta T} \times 100 = \mathbf{10.26}$ **... Ans. (ii)**

Example 2.38 : *A wall of a furnace 0.224 m thick is constructed of a material having a thermal conductivity of 1.3 W/(m·K). This will be insulated on the outside with material having an average k of 0.346 W/(m·K) so that the heat loss from the furnace will be equal to or less than 1830 W/m². The inner surface temperature is 1588 K (1315 °C) and the outer 299 K (26 °C). Calculate the thickness of insulation required.*

Solution : $x_1 = 0.224$ m, $k_1 = 1.3$ W/(m·K)

$x_2 = ?$ $k_2 = 0.346$ W/(m·K)

$T_1 = 1588$ K and $T_2 = 299$ K

Q/A = heat loss = 1830 W/m²

We have $\dfrac{Q}{A} = \dfrac{(T_1 - T_2)}{x_1/k_1 + x_2/k_2}$

$1830\,(x_1/k_1 + x_2/k_2) = (1588 - 299)$

$\dfrac{x_1}{k_1} + \dfrac{x_2}{k_2} = 0.7044$

$\dfrac{0.224}{1.3} + \dfrac{x_2}{k_2} = 0.7044$

$x_2/k_2 = 0.5321$

$x_2 = 0.5321\,k_2 = 0.5321 \times 0.346 = 0.184$ m = 184 mm

Thickness of insulation required = **184 mm** ... **Ans.**

Example 2.39 : *An exterior wall of a house may be approximated by a 100 mm layer of common brick followed by a 40 mm layer of gypsum plaster. What thickness of loosely packed rock wool insulation should be added to reduce the heat loss through the wall by 80 percent ?*

Data : *k for common brick = 0.7 W/(m·K)*

k for gypsum layer = 0.48 W/(m·K)

k for rock wool = 0.065 W/(m·K)

Solution : Heat loss is given by

$Q = \Delta T / \sum R$

Q without insulation = $Q = \Delta T / \sum R$

Q with insulation = $Q' = \Delta T / \sum R'$

With rock wool insulation, heat loss is reduced by 80%.

∴ Heat loss with insulation will be 20% of the heat loss without insulation.

$Q' = 0.2,\ Q = 0.2\,\dfrac{\Delta T}{\sum R} = \dfrac{\Delta T}{\sum R'}$

∴ $\dfrac{Q'}{Q} = 0.2 = \dfrac{\sum R}{\sum R'}$

Let $A = 1$ m²

$x_1 = 100$ mm = 0.10 m, $x_2 = 40$ mm = 0.04 m

x_3 = thickness of rock wool insulation

$k_1 = 0.7$ W/(m·K), $k_2 = 0.48$ W/(m·K), $k_3 = 0.065$ W/(m·K)

Brick : $\quad R_1 = x_1/k_1 A = 0.1/0.7 \times 1 = 0.143$ K/W

Plaster : $\quad R_2 = x_2/k_2 A = 0.04/0.48 \times 1 = 0.083$ K/W

$\therefore \quad R = R_1 + R_2 = 0.143 + 0.083 = 0.226$ K/W

Rock wool : $\quad R_3 = x_3/k_3 A = x_3/0.065 \times 1 = 15.4\, x_3$ K/W

$\quad R' = R_1 + R_2 + R_3 = 0.226 + 15.4\, x_3$

$\quad R = $ Resistance without insulation

$\quad R' = $ Resistance with insulation

$\therefore \quad 0.2 = \dfrac{0.226}{0.226 + 15.4\, x_3}$

Solving for x_3, we get

$$x_3 = 0.0587 \text{ m} = 58.7 \text{ mm} \approx 59 \text{ mm}$$

Thickness of rock wool insulation = 59 mm.

Systems with Variable Thermal Conductivity :

Now we will take into account the variation of k with temperature in deriving the desired equations for heat flow.

Plane wall with variable k :

A plane wall of thickness x has one surface at T_1 and the other surface at T_2. If the thermal conductivity of wall varies with temperature as per the following equation :

$k = k_0 (1 + \alpha T)$, derive an expression for the heat flow rate, Q.

Solution : From Fourier's law, we have

$$Q = -kA\, dT/dx$$

$$Q\, dx = kA\, dT$$

but $\quad k = k_0 (1 + \alpha T)$

$\therefore \quad Q\, dx = -k_0 (1 + \alpha T)\, A\, dT$

The boundary conditions are :

at $\quad x = 0, \quad T = T_1$

and at $\quad x = L, \quad T = T_2$

$$Q \int_0^x dx = -k_0 A \int_{T_1}^{T_2} (1 + \alpha T)\, dT = k_0 A \int_{T_2}^{T_1} (1 + \alpha T)\, dT$$

$$Qx = k_0 A \left[T + \dfrac{\alpha}{2} T^2 \right]_{T_2}^{T_1}$$

$$Q = \dfrac{k_0 A}{x} \left[(T_1 - T_2) + \dfrac{\alpha}{2} (T_1^2 - T_2^2) \right]$$

$$Q = \dfrac{k_0 A}{x} (T_1 - T_2) \left[1 + \dfrac{\alpha}{2} (T_1 + T_2) \right] \quad \ldots (2.50)$$

Hollow cylinder with variable k :

The inner and outer surfaces of a hollow cylinder are maintained at uniform temperatures T_1 and T_2 respectively. The cylinder of length L has r_1 and r_2 as the inside and outside radii. The thermal conductivity of the material of cylinder is temperature dependent and given by the equation :

$$k = k_o (1 + \alpha T + \beta T^2)$$

Derive an expression for the rate of heat flow through the cylinder.

Solution : We have

$$Q = -kA \frac{dT}{dr} = -k_o (1 + \alpha T + \beta T^2) A \frac{dT}{dr}$$

The boundary conditions are :

at $r = r_1$, $T = T_1$ and at $r = r_2$, $T = T_2$

$$Q\, dr = -k_o (1 + \alpha T + \beta T^2) \cdot 2\pi r L\, dT$$

$$Q \int_{r_1}^{r_2} \frac{dr}{r} = -k_o \cdot 2\pi L \int_{T_1}^{T_2} (1 + \alpha T + \beta T^2)\, dT$$

$$Q \int_{r_1}^{r_2} \frac{dr}{r} = 2\pi k_o L \int_{T_2}^{T_1} (1 + \alpha T + \beta T^2)\, dT$$

$$Q\, [\ln r]_{r_1}^{r_2} = 2\pi k_o L \left[T + \frac{\alpha}{2} T^2 + \frac{\beta}{3} T^3 \right]_{T_2}^{T_1}$$

$$Q \ln(r_2/r_1) = 2\pi k_o L \left[(T_1 - T_2) + \frac{\alpha}{2}(T_1^2 - T_2^2) + \frac{\beta}{3}(T_1^3 - T_2^3) \right]$$

$$Q = \frac{2\pi k_o L \left[(T_1 - T_2) + \frac{\alpha}{2}(T_1^2 - T_2^2) + \frac{\beta}{3}(T_1^3 - T_2^3) \right]}{\ln(r_2/r_1)}$$

$$Q = \frac{2\pi k_o L\, (T_1 - T_2)\, [1 + \alpha/2\,(T_1 + T_2) + \beta/3\,(T_1^2 + T_1 T_2 + T_2^2)]}{\ln(r_2/r_1)}$$

... (2.51)

Equation (2.51) is the desired expression for the rate of heat flow through a hollow cylinder.

Hollow sphere with variable k :

The inside and outside surfaces of a hollow sphere $a \leq r \leq b$ at $r = a$ and $r = b$ are maintained at temperatures T_1 and T_2 respectively. The thermal conductivity varies with temperature as :

$$k(T) = k_o (1 + \alpha T + \beta T^2)$$

Derive an expression for the heat flow rate Q through the sphere.

Solution : $Q = -kA\ dT/dr = -k\ 4\pi r^2 \dfrac{dT}{dr}$

$\therefore \quad Q \cdot \dfrac{dr}{r^2} = -4\pi k\ dT$

Limits for integration are :

at $r = a$, $T = T_1$ and at $r = b$, $T = T_2$

$$k = k_o(1 + \alpha T + \beta T^2)$$

$\therefore \quad Q \displaystyle\int_a^b \dfrac{dr}{r^2} = -4\pi k_o \displaystyle\int_{T_1}^{T_2} (1 + \alpha T + \beta T^2)\ dT$

$$-Q\left[\dfrac{1}{r}\right]_a^b = 4\pi k_o \left[T + \dfrac{\alpha}{2}T^2 + \dfrac{\beta}{3}T^3\right]_{T_2}^{T_1}$$

$$-Q\left[\dfrac{1}{b} - \dfrac{1}{a}\right] = 4\pi k_o \left[(T_1 - T_2) + \dfrac{\alpha}{2}(T_1^2 - T_2^2) + \dfrac{\beta}{3}(T_1^3 - T_2^3)\right]$$

$$Q\left[\dfrac{1}{a} - \dfrac{1}{b}\right] = 4\pi k_o \left[(T_1 - T_2) + \dfrac{\alpha}{2}(T_1^2 - T_2^2) + \dfrac{\beta}{3}(T_1^3 - T_2^3)\right]$$

$$Q\left[(b - a)/ab\right] = 4\pi k_o \left[(T_1 - T_2) + \dfrac{\alpha}{2}(T_1^2 - T_2^2) + \dfrac{\beta}{3}(T_1^3 - T_2^3)\right]$$

$\therefore \quad Q = \dfrac{4\pi k_o \cdot ab}{(b - a)} \left[(T_1 - T_2) + \dfrac{\alpha}{2}(T_1^2 - T_2^2) + \dfrac{\beta}{3}(T_1^3 - T_2^3)\right]$

$$Q = \dfrac{4\pi k_o\ ab}{(b - a)}(T_1 - T_2)\left[1 + \dfrac{\alpha}{2}(T_1 + T_2) + \dfrac{\beta}{3}(T_1^2 + T_1 T_2 + T_2^2)\right]$$

... (2.52)

Equation (2.52) is the desired expression for the heat flow through a sphere.

Critical Radius of Insulation :

It is always necessary to provide insulation on the external surfaces of pipelines and vessels to reduce the heat loss to the ambient, e.g., steam piping, piping carrying refrigerant, etc. It is natural to expect that greater insulation will result in less heat loss. The following analysis reveals that this may not be always the case.

Consider a long pipe carrying steam at T_i is having inner and outer radii as r_1 and r_2 respectively. It is wrapped with an insulation of thermal conductivity k_2 to a radius r_3. Let h_o be the heat transfer coefficient at the radius r_3. The outer surface is exposed to the convective environment (i.e., ambient) at T_o. Let h_i be the heat transfer coefficient at the inner surface.

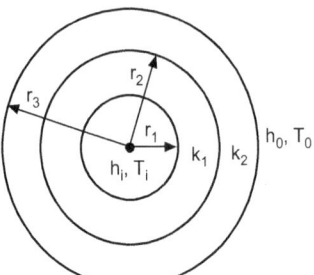

Fig. 2.6 : Insulated steam pipe

The rate of heat transfer is given by :

$$Q = \frac{2\pi L (T_i - T_o)}{\frac{1}{r_1 h_i} + \frac{\ln(r_2/r_1)}{k_1} + \frac{\ln(r_3/r_2)}{k_2} + \frac{1}{r_3 h_o}} \qquad \ldots (2.53)$$

When Q is plotted as a function of r_3, other parameters being held constant, it will pass through a maxima for a certain value of r_3. This value is called as the critical radius.

We have

$$Q = \frac{T_i - T_o}{\frac{1}{2\pi L}\left[\frac{1}{r_1 h_i} + \frac{\ln(r_2/r_1)}{k_1} + \frac{\ln(r_3/r_2)}{k_2} + \frac{1}{r_3 h_o}\right]}$$

$$\Sigma R = \frac{1}{2\pi L}\left[\frac{1}{r_1 h_i} + \frac{\ln(r_2/r_1)}{k_1} + \frac{\ln(r_3/r_2)}{k_2} + \frac{1}{r_3 h_o}\right] \qquad \ldots (2.54)$$

In Equation (2.54), all parameters except the outer radius of insulation are considered as constant because only r_3 depends upon the thickness of the insulation.

The value of critical radius (r_c) that is r_3 is obtained by differentiating ΣR with respect to r_3 and equating to zero, i.e., by minimising the denominator as the numerator is held constant.

$$\frac{d\Sigma R}{dr_3} = 0 = \frac{1}{2\pi L}\left[0 + 0 + \frac{1}{k_2}\cdot\frac{1}{r_3} + \frac{1}{h_o}\left(-\frac{1}{r_3^2}\right)\right]$$

$$\therefore \quad \frac{1}{k_2 r_3} = \frac{1}{h_o r_3^2}$$

$$r_3 = k_2/h_o = r_c \qquad \ldots (2.55)$$

where r_c is critical radius of insulation.

It can be written as :

$$r_c = k_2/h_o = k/h$$

$k = k_2$ = thermal conductivity of insulating material

$h = h_o$ = convective heat transfer coefficient at the outer surface of insulation

For $r_c = k_2/h_o = k/h$, the heat loss is a maximum.

Equation (2.55) expresses the critical radius of insulation concept. If the critical radius of insulation is greater than the outer radius of a pipe (or a container) then the thickness of insulation upto r_c, i.e., adding insulation upto r_c will increase the heat loss from the pipe. The addition of insulation thereafter will reduce the heat loss from the pipe. On the other hand, when the critical radius of insulation is less than or equal to the outer radius of the pipe or container, then the addition of insulation will immediately reduce the heat loss from the pipe.

i.e., if the outer radius of a pipe or a container is greater than r_c (critical radius), then every layer of insulation provided will give reduction in the heat loss (and vice versa upto r_c).

The rate of heat flow, Q is governed by the thermal resistance of an insulation, $\ln (r_3/r_2)/2\pi Lk_2$ and thermal resistance, at the outer surface, $1/2\pi Lr_3 h_o$. The insulation resistance increases with r_3, while the resistance at the outer surface decreases.

Upto the critical radius, the rate of decrease of convective resistance is greater than rate of increase of conduction resistance and the rate of flow of heat to the ambient consequently increases. Beyond the critical radius, rate of increase of the resistance of insulation is greater than the rate of decrease of the resistance at the surface and consequently the rate of heat flow to the ambient, i.e., the heat loss to the ambient decreases.

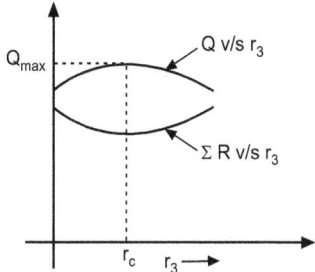

Fig. 2.7 : Variation of Q and $\sum R$ with r_3

Critical radius of insulation : It is the outer radius of insulation at which the rate of heat flow is maximum. It depends upon the thermal conductivity of an insulating material and heat transfer coefficient at the outer surface of insulation.

Example 2.40 : *Calculate the critical radius of insulation for asbestos [k = 0.17 W/(m²·K)] surrounding a pipe and exposed to room air at 293 K (20°C) with h = 3.0 W/(m²·K). Calculate the heat loss from a 473 K (200°C), 50 mm diameter pipe when covered with the critical radius of insulation and without insulation. Would any fibre glass insulation having thermal conductivity of 0.04 W/(m·K) cause decrease in heat transfer ?*

Solution : k = 0.17 W/(m·K) and h = h_o = 3.0 W/(m²·K)

Critical radius = r_c = 0.17/3.0 = 0.0567 m = 56.7 mm

Inside radius of insulation = r_1 = 50/2 = 25 mm = 0.025 m

Heat transfer with insulation :

$$Q/L = \frac{2\pi (T_1 - T_2)}{\frac{\ln (r_c/r_1)}{k} + \frac{1}{r_c h_o}}$$

$$= \frac{2\pi (473 - 293)}{\frac{\ln (0.0567/0.025)}{0.17} + \frac{1}{0.0567 \times 3.0}} = 105.7 \text{ W/m}$$

Without insulation, the convection from the outer surface of pipe is

$$Q/L = h (2\pi r) (T_1 - T_2)$$
$$= 3.0 (2\pi \times 0.025) (473 - 293) = 84.8 \text{ W/m}$$

Increase of heat transfer $= \frac{105.7 - 84.8}{84.8} \times 100 = 24.65\%$

So, addition of 56.7 − 25 = 31.7 mm of insulation actually increase the heat transfer by 24.65%.

Fibre glass insulation, $k = 0.04$ W/(m²·K)

Critical radius of insulation $= r_c = k/h = \frac{0.04}{3.0} = 0.0133$ m

In this case, the value of critical radius (0.0133 m) is less than the outside radius of pipe (0.025 m). So addition of any fibre glass insulation would cause a decrease in the heat transfer.

Critical radius insulation for insulated sphere :

For a sphere, we have :

$$Q = \Delta T / \sum R$$

Let r_1, r_2 be the inside and outside radii of sphere and r_3 be the outer radius of insulation. r_2 is also the inner radius of insulation.

Let k_1 and k_2 be the thermal conductivities of the sphere material and insulation. Let h_i and h_o be the heat transfer coefficients on the inside of the sphere and at the outer surface of the insulation.

Total thermal resistance is given by :

$$\sum R = \frac{1}{4\pi r_1^2 h_i} + \frac{(r_2 - r_1)}{4\pi k_1 r_1 r_2} + \frac{r_3 - r_2}{4\pi k_2 r_2 r_3} + \frac{1}{4\pi r_3^2 \cdot h_o} \quad \ldots (2.56)$$

Differentiating $\sum R$ with respect to r_3 and equating to zero, we get (Equation 2.56).

In the above equation only r_3 depends upon insulation provided, so all other parameters are taken as constant.

$$\frac{d \sum R}{dr_3} = 0 = \frac{-1}{4\pi k_2 r_3^2} - \frac{2}{4\pi h_o r_3^3}$$

$$\therefore \quad r_3 = \frac{2 k_2}{h_o} = r_c$$

∴ Critical radius of insulation for sphere = $r_c = \dfrac{2k_2}{h_o} = \dfrac{2k}{h}$ ... (2.57)

where $k = k_2$ = thermal conductivity of insulating material

and $h = h_o$ = heat transfer coefficient between the outer surface of insulation and ambient.

Example 2.41 : *Derive a relation for the critical radius of insulation for a circular cross-section having radius R and length L.*

Solution : Consider an insulated pipe of length L with R_1 and R_2 as its inside and outside radii respectively. Let R_3 be the outer radius of insulation. Let k_1 and k_2 be the thermal conductivities of pipe material and insulating material respectively. Let h_i and h_o be the heat transfer coefficients on the inside surface of pipe and at the outer surface of insulation. Then

$$Q = \dfrac{(T_1 - T_2)}{\sum R}$$

$$\sum R = \dfrac{1}{2\pi R_1 L h_i} + \dfrac{\ln(R_2/R_1)}{2\pi L k_1} + \dfrac{\ln(R_3/R_2)}{2\pi L k_2} + \dfrac{1}{2\pi R_3 L h_o}$$

Consider all parameters except r_3 as constant, as only r_3 depends upon the insulation provided.

Differentiating $\sum R$ with respect to r_3 and equating to zero, we get

$$\dfrac{d\sum R}{dR_3} = 0 = \dfrac{1}{2\pi k_2 L} \times \dfrac{1}{R_3} + \dfrac{1}{2\pi h_o L} \times \dfrac{-1}{R_3^2}$$

∴ $1/k_2 = 1/h_o R_3$

∴ $R_3 = k_2/h_o = R_c$

∴ Critical radius of insulation = $R_c = k_2/h_o = k/h$

where $k = k_2$ = thermal conductivity of insulating material and $h = h_o$ = convective coefficient on the outer surface of insulation (between the outer surface and the ambient).

Example 2.42 : *A steam pipe with 100 mm I.D. and 110 mm O.D. is covered with an insulating material having thermal conductivity of 1.0 W/(m²·K). The steam temperature is 473 K (200°C) and ambient temperature is 293 K (20°C). Taking the convective heat transfer coefficient between the insulation surface and air as 8.0 W/(m²·K), find the critical radius of insulation. For this value (r_c), calculate the heat loss per metre of pipe and outer surface temperature. Neglect the resistance of pipe wall.*

Solution : Critical radius = r_c = k/h = 1.0/8 = 0.125 m = 125 mm

Neglecting pipe wall resistance, heat loss per 1 m with critical insulation is given as :

$$Q/L = \dfrac{2\pi(T_1 - T_2)}{\dfrac{\ln(r_c/r_1)}{k} + \dfrac{1}{r_c h}}$$

where $R_1 = 473$ K, $T_2 = 293$ K

$r_c = 0.125$ m, $k = 1.0$ W/(m·K)

$h = 8.0$ W/(m²·K)

and r_1 = outer radius of pipe = inner radius of insulation

= 110/2 = 55 mm = 0.055 m

$$\frac{Q}{L} = \frac{2\pi (473 - 293)}{\frac{\ln (0.125/0.055)}{1.0} + \frac{1}{0.125 \times 8}} = 620 \text{ W/m} \quad \ldots \text{Ans.}$$

The outer surface temperature can be determined by the relation

$$\frac{Q}{L} = \frac{2\pi (T - T_2)}{1/r_c\, h}$$

where T is the outer surface temperature

$$620 = \frac{2\pi (T - 293)}{1/(0.125 \times 8)}$$

Solving for T, we get

$T = 391.72$ K (118.72°C) ... Ans.

EXERCISES

1. **Fill in the blanks :**
   (a) Heat flow mechanism through solids is known as .... **Ans.** conduction
   (b) SI units of thermal conductivity are .... **Ans.** W/(m·K)
   (c) Thermal resistance to heat transfer by conduction has units of ... **Ans.** K/W
   (d) Materials having very low thermal conductivity values are called as ....
   Ans. Heat Insulators
   (e) Heat flow by conduction is governed by .... law. **Ans.** Fourier's
   (f) Driving force for heat flow is .... difference. **Ans.** temperature
   (g) SI unit of rate of heat flow is .... **Ans.** watts (W)
   (h) Conduction under condition of constant temperature distribution is called as ..... conduction. **Ans.** steady state
   (i) Thermal conductance is the reciprocal of .... **Ans.** thermal resistance
   (j) For thick-walled cylinder of radii r_1 and r_2, logarithmic mean radius is given by .... **Ans.** $(r_2 - r_1) / \ln (r_2 / r_1)$
   (k) Linear variation of thermal conductivity is given by the expression, k = ...
   Ans. a + bT

2. Derive the expression for heat transfer through furnace wall made of three different materials in series. Assume k_1, k_2 and k_3 to be the thermal conductivities of materials and x_1, x_2 and x_3 the respective thicknesses. Assume hot face and cold face temperatures to be T_1 and T_2 respectively.

3. Derive the expression for heat flow through thick walled cylinder by conduction. Take r_1 and r_2 as the inner and outer radii of cylinder, k as a mean thermal conductivity. Assume T_1 as inside temperature and T_2 as the outside temperature.

4. Derive the expression for heat flow through thick walled cylinder (with r_1 as inside radius and r_2 as outside radius) lagged with a layer of insulation. Take k_1 as thermal conductivity of material and k_2 as thermal conductivity of insulating material. Assume r_3 as the outer radius of insulation, inside temperature T_1 and temperature at outer surface of insulation as T_2.

5. What do you mean by thermal conductivity ? Write in brief on its variation with temperature.

6. The opposite faces of plane wall of thickness, x, are maintained at T_1 and T_2. The variation of thermal conductivity with temperature is given by $k = k_o (1 + bT)$. Derive the expression for heat flow Q through plane wall. Assume that $T_1 > T_2$.

7. Derive a relation for critical radius of insulation for a circular cross-section having length L, r_1 and r_2 as inside and outside radii of pipe and r_3 as outer radius of insulation. k_1 and k_2 be the thermal conductivities of pipe material and insulating material respectively. Inner temperature is T_1 and outer temperature is T_2 ($T_1 > T_2$).

CHAPTER THREE

CONVECTION

A large majority of practical applications of heat transfer in the chemical process industries involve either heat transfer to a fluid or heat transfer from a fluid.

The heat flow mechanism in solids is by conduction; whereas the heat flow mechanism in fluids is due to convection. *Convection* is the transfer of heat from one point to another point within a fluid by mixing of hot and cold portions of the fluid.

Heat transfer by convection occurs as a result of the movement of the fluid on a macroscopic scale in the form of circulating currents. The circulating currents may be set up either by heat transfer process itself or some external agency. It is restricted to the **heat flow in fluids**.

In the case of convective heat transfer, the physical mixing of the hot and cold portions of a fluid is responsible for the flow of heat from one place to another within the fluid.

There are two types of convection.

Convection is classified as :

(i) free or natural convection and **(ii) forced convection**.

When the circulating currents arise from the heat transfer process itself, i.e., from density differences arising in turn due to temperature differences / gradients in a fluid mass, it is called **free** or **natural convection**.

Examples of natural convection :

1. Heating of a vessel containing liquid by means of a gas flame situated underneath.

The liquid at the bottom of the vessel gets heated, expands and rises because its density has become less than that of the remaining liquid. Cold liquid of higher density takes its place and a circulating current is set up.

2. The flow of air across a heated radiator/heat of a room by means of a steam radiator.

When the circulating currents are produced by an external agency such as an agitator in a reaction vessel, pump, fan or blower, the action is called **forced convection**. Here fluid motion is independent of density gradients.

Example of forced convection :

Heat flow to a fluid pumped through a heated pipe.

In general, higher rates of heat transfer are obtained in forced convection as compared to natural convection owing to a greater magnitude of circulation in the forced circulation.

In the case of convective heat transfer taking place from a surface to a fluid, the circulating currents die out in the immediate viscinity of the surface and a film of the fluid, free of turbulence, covers the surface. Through this film heat transfer takes by thermal conduction and, as the thermal conductivity of most fluids is low, the main resistance to heat transfer lies in the film. Therefore, an increase in the velocity of the fluid over the surface results in improved heat transfer mainly because of reduction in the thickness of the film.

If the resistance to heat transfer is considered as lying within the film covering the surface, the rate of heat transfer Q is given by

$$Q = kA \, \Delta T/x$$

The effective thickness x is not generally known and therefore this equation is usually rewritten in the form :

$$Q = hA \, \Delta T$$

This is the basic equation for the rate of heat transfer by convection under steady state conditions, where 'h' is called the film heat transfer coefficient or surface coefficient or simply film coefficient. The value of 'h' depends upon the properties of the fluid within the film region, hence it is called the film heat transfer coefficient. It depends upon the various properties of the fluid, linear dimension of surface and fluid velocity (i.e. the nature of flow).

Numerically, **heat transfer coefficient (h)** is the quantity of heat transferred in a unit time through a unit area at a temperature difference of one degree between the surface and surrounding. h has the units of $W/(m^2 \cdot K)$ in the SI system. The term $1/h$ is called as the **thermal resistance**.

The process of transfer of heat from a hot fluid to a cold fluid through metal wall is very common in the chemical and process industry. The heat transferred may be latent heat of a phase change, e.g., condensation, vaporisation etc.; or may be sensible heat. In all process equipments, e.g., heater, cooler, condenser, reboiler etc. heat is transferred by conduction and convection.

Individual and Overall heat transfer coefficients :

Consider that a hot fluid is flowing through a circular pipe and a cold fluid is flowing on the outside of the pipe. The heat will flow from a hot fluid to a cold fluid through series of resistances. Generally, the velocity of the fluid may be considered to be zero at the solid surface and it rapidly increases as we move away from the wall surface. It is found that even in the turbulent flow, where convective heat flow occurs from a surface to a fluid, the thin film of the fluid free of turbulence (viscous sublayer) exists at the wall surface. This thin film of fluid covering the surface is of great importance in determining the rate of heat transfer as all the heat reaching the bulk of the cold fluid must pass through the film of fluid by conduction. The thermal conductivities of the fluids are very low so that the resistance offered by the film to the heat flow is very large, though the film is thin. Beyond this film, the turbulence existing brings about rapid equalisation of temperature.

The temperature gradients for the situation under consideration are shown in Fig. 3.1. The dotted lines $Y_1 \, Y_2$ and $Z_1 \, Z_2$ represent the boundaries of thin films (hot and cold fluid films). The flow to the left of $Y_1 \, Y_2$ and right of $Z_1 \, Z_2$ is turbulent. The temperature gradient from the bulk of the hot fluid to the metal wall is represented by $T_a \, T' \, T_2$, where T_a is the maximum temperature of the hot fluid, T' is the temperature at the boundary between turbulent and viscous regions and T_2 is the temperature at the actual interface between fluid and solid. Similarly, the temperature gradient in the cold fluid is represented by lines T_3 T" T_b. In heat transfer calculation, for convenience, average temperature of the fluid is usually used rather than the maximum temperature or the temperature at the outer surface of the film. The average temperature (T_1) of the hot fluid is represented by the line marked NN and similarly the average temperature (T_4) of the cold fluid is represented by the line marked MM.

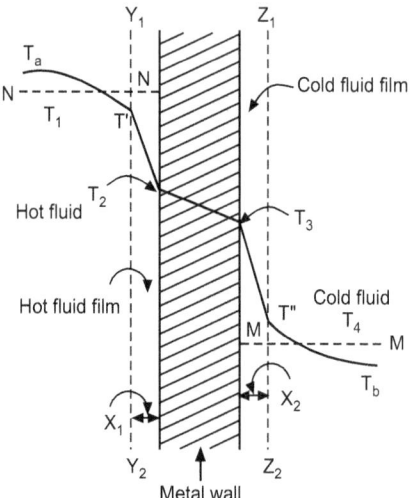

Fig. 3.1 : Temperature gradient in forced convection

The temperature change from T_1 to T_2 is taking place in the hot fluid film of thickness x_1. The rate of heat transfer through this film by conduction is given by :

$$Q = \frac{k_1 A_1 (T_1 - T_2)}{x_1} \qquad \ldots (3.1)$$

The effective film thickness x_1 depends upon the nature of flow and nature of the surface, and is generally not known. Therefore Equation (3.1) is usually rewritten as :

$$Q = h_i A_i (T_1 - T_2) \qquad \ldots (3.2)$$

where h_i is known as the inside heat transfer coefficient or the surface coefficient or the simply film coefficient.

As seen from Equation (3.2), the film coefficient is a measure of the rate of heat transfer for unit temperature difference and unit surface of heat transfer and it indicates the rate or speed of transfer of heat by a fluid having a variety of the physical properties under varying degrees of agitation. In the SI system, it has the units of W/(m²·K).

The overall resistance to heat flow from hot fluid to cold fluid is made up of three resistances in series. They are :

1. Resistance offered by film of hot fluid.
2. Resistance offered by metal wall and
3. Resistance offered by film of cold fluid.

The rate of heat transfer through the metal wall is given by :

$$Q = \frac{kA_w(T_2 - T_3)}{x_w} \quad \ldots (3.3)$$

where
- A_w – log mean area of pipe
- x_w – thickness of pipe wall

and
- k – thermal conductivity of material of pipe.

The rate of heat transfer through the cold fluid film is given by :

$$Q = h_o A_o (T_3 - T_4) \quad \ldots (3.4)$$

where h_o is the outside film coefficient or individual heat transfer coefficient.

Equation (3.2) can be rearranged as :

$$T_1 - T_2 = \frac{Q}{h_i A_i} \quad \ldots (3.5)$$

Similarly, Equations (3.3) and (3.4) can be rearranged as :

$$T_2 - T_3 = \frac{Q}{(kA_w/x_w)} \quad \ldots (3.6)$$

and

$$T_3 - T_4 = \frac{Q}{h_o A_o} \quad \ldots (3.7)$$

Adding Equations (3.5), (3.6) and (3.7), we get

$$(T_1 - T_2) + (T_2 - T_3) + (T_3 - T_4) = Q\left[\frac{1}{h_i A_i} + \frac{1}{(kA_w/x_w)} + \frac{1}{h_o A_o}\right] \quad \ldots (3.8)$$

$$\therefore \quad (T_1 - T_4) = Q\left[\frac{1}{h_i A_i} + \frac{1}{(kA_w/x_w)} + \frac{1}{h_o A_o}\right] \quad \ldots (3.9)$$

where T_1 and T_4 are the average temperatures of the hot and cold fluid respectively. Therefore equations similar to Equation (3.1) in terms of overall heat transfer coefficients can be written as :

$$Q = U_i A_i (T_1 - T_4) \quad \ldots (3.10)$$

or

$$Q = U_o A_o (T_1 - T_4) \quad \ldots (3.11)$$

where U_i and U_o are the overall heat transfer coefficients based on the inside and outside area, respectively.

Equations (3.10) and (3.11) state that *the rate of heat transfer is the product of three factors namely overall heat transfer coefficient, area of heating surface and temperature drop.*

Equation (3.11) can be rearranged as :

$$(T_1 - T_4) = \frac{Q}{U_o A_o} \quad \ldots (3.12)$$

Comparing Equations (3.9) and (3.12), we get,

$$\frac{1}{U_o A_o} = \frac{1}{h_i A_i} + \frac{1}{(kA_w/x_w)} + \frac{1}{h_o A_o} \qquad \ldots (3.13)$$

$$\frac{1}{U_o} = \frac{1}{h_i}\left(\frac{A_o}{A_i}\right) + \frac{x_w}{k}\left(\frac{A_o}{A_w}\right) + \frac{1}{h_o} \qquad \ldots (3.14)$$

where A_o – area of heat transfer based on the outside diameter, i.e., the outside area of the tube

A_i – area of heat transfer based on the inside diameter, i.e., the inside area of the tube.

We have $A_i = \pi D_i L$ (where L is length of pipe)

$A_o = \pi D_o L$

$\therefore \quad \dfrac{A_o}{A_i} = \dfrac{D_o}{D_i} \qquad \ldots (3.15)$

Similarly, $\dfrac{A_o}{A_w} = \dfrac{D_o}{D_w} \qquad \ldots (3.16)$

where D_w = logarithmic mean diameter

$D_w = 2 \cdot r_m$ where r_m – logarithmic mean radius.

Putting the values of area ratios in Equation (3.14), we get

$$\frac{1}{U_o} = \frac{1}{h_i}\left(\frac{D_o}{D_i}\right) + \frac{x_w \cdot D_o}{k D_w} + \frac{1}{h_o} \qquad \ldots (3.17)$$

Similarly,

$$\frac{1}{U_i} = \frac{1}{h_i} + \frac{x_w D_i}{k \cdot D_w} + \frac{1}{h_o}\left(\frac{D_i}{D_o}\right) \qquad \ldots (3.18)$$

For thin walled tubes, the inside and outside radii are not much different from each other, the overall heat transfer coefficient U_o or U_i may be replaced simply by 'U' and is written in terms of h_i, h_o, etc. as :

$$\frac{1}{U} = \frac{1}{h_i} + \frac{x_w}{k} + \frac{1}{h_o} \qquad \ldots (3.19)$$

Or

$$\frac{1}{U} = \frac{1}{h_i} + \frac{1}{(k/x_w)} + \frac{1}{h_o} \qquad \ldots (3.20)$$

Or

$$U = \frac{1}{1/h_i + x_w/k + 1/h_o}$$

When the metal wall resistance is very small in comparison with the resistances of fluid films, then Equation (3.19) reduces to :

$$\frac{1}{U} = \frac{1}{h_o} + \frac{1}{h_i} \qquad \ldots (3.21)$$

$$\frac{1}{U} = \frac{h_o + h_i}{h_i h_o} \qquad \ldots (3.22)$$

Fouling Factor :

When the heat transfer equipment is put into service, after sometime, scale, dirt and other solids deposit on both sides of the pipe wall, providing two more resistances to the heat flow. The added resistances must be taken into account in the calculation of the overall heat transfer coefficient. The additional resistances reduce the original value of U and the required amount of heat is no longer transferred by the original heat transfer surface. Hence, heat transfer equipments are designed by taking into account the deposition of dirt and scale by introducing a resistance R_d known as the fouling factor (it is a thermal resistance due to scale).

Equation (3.19) then becomes

$$\frac{1}{U} = \frac{1}{h_i} + \frac{x_w}{k} + \frac{1}{h_o} + R_d \qquad \ldots (3.23)$$

The overall heat transfer coefficient calculated by taking into account R_d is known as the 'design or dirty overall heat transfer coefficient' and the one calculated without taking into account the term R_d is known as the 'clean overall heat transfer coefficient' – [as given by Equation (3.19)].

The dirty overall coefficient [calculated by Equation (3.23)] is always less than the clean overall coefficient. Fouling factor R_d is composed of R_{di}, the dirt factor for an inner fluid at the inside surface of a pipe and R_{do}, the dirt factor for an outer fluid at the outside surface of the pipe; $R_d = R_{di} + R_{do}$. The dirt or fouling factor R_d has the units of $(m^2 \cdot K)/W$.

Resistance form of overall coefficient :

The reciprocal of an overall heat transfer coefficient is an overall resistance and it may be given by the following equation :

$$\frac{1}{U_o} = \frac{1}{h_i}\left(\frac{D_o}{D_i}\right) + \frac{x_w}{k}\left(\frac{D_o}{D_w}\right) + \frac{1}{h_o} \qquad \ldots (3.24)$$

The individual terms on R.H.S. of the above equation represent the individual resistances of the two fluids and of the metal wall.

The overall temperature drop is proportional to 1/U. Similarly, the individual temperature drops in the two fluids and metal wall are proportional to the respective individual resistances. Therefore,

$$\frac{\Delta T}{1/U_o} = \frac{\Delta T_i}{D_o/D_i h_i} = \frac{\Delta T_w}{(x_w/k)(D_o/D_w)} = \frac{\Delta T_o}{1/h_o} \qquad \ldots (3.25)$$

where, ΔT is the overall temperature drop

ΔT_i is the temperature drop through the inside fluid

ΔT_w is the temperature drop through the metal wall.

ΔT_o is the temperature drop through the outside fluid.

Magnitude of film heat transfer coefficients :

Table 3.1 gives the range of values of the film heat transfer coefficients for various processes of heat transfer.

Table 3.1 : Magnitudes of film heat transfer coefficients (h_i or h_o)

Type of Processes	Range of values of h in W/(m²·K)
No phase change :	
Water (heating or cooling)	300 – 20,000
Gases (heating or cooling)	20 – 300
Air (heating or cooling)	1 – 50
Oils (heating or cooling)	50 – 1500
Organic solvents (heating or cooling)	350 – 3000
Condensing :	
Condensing steam (film-type condensation)	6000 – 20,000
Condensing organic vapours	1000 – 2000
Ammonia	3000 – 6000
Condensing steam (drop-wise condensation)	30,000 – 100,000
Evaporation :	
Water	2000 – 12000
Organic solvents	600 – 2000
Ammonia	1100 – 2300

Table 3.2 gives the range of values of the overall heat transfer coefficients for various fluid systems in a shell and tube equipment.

Table 3.2 : Approximate range of values of overall heat transfer coefficients, U

Hot side (Hot fluid)	Cold side (Cold fluid)	Overall U in W/(m²·K)
Heat exchangers (without phase change) :		
Water	Water	900 – 1700
Gases	Water	20 – 300
Organic solvents	Water	300 – 900
Water	Brine	600 – 1200
Gases	Brine	20 – 300
Heavy organics	Heavy organics	50 – 300
Heaters :		
Steam	Water	1500 – 4000
Steam	Gases	30 – 300
Dowtherm	Gases	20 – 200
Steam	Light oils	300 – 900
Steam	Organic solvents	600 – 1200

… Contd.

Evaporators :		
Steam	Water	2000 – 4000
Steam	Organic solvents	600 – 1200
Steam	Light oils	400 – 1000
Water	Refrigerants	400 – 900
Condensers :		
Steam	Water	2000 – 4000
Saturated organic solvents	Water	600 – 1200
Low boiling hydrocarbons	Water	400 – 1200
Organic solvents with high noncondensable	Water	100 – 500

Classification of individual heat transfer coefficients :

The problem of predicting the rate of heat transfer from one fluid to another through a solid metal wall reduces essentially to the problem of predicting the values of the film coefficients of the fluids involved in the overall process. In practice, we come across a variety of cases and each one must be considered separately. The following classification of cases encountered in practice will be adopted :

(a) Heat transfer to or from fluids inside tubes, without phase change.

(b) Heat transfer to or from fluids outside tubes, without phase change.

(c) Heat transfer from condensing fluids.

(d) Heat transfer to boiling liquids.

Heat transfer to fluids without phase change : In most of the heat exchange applications, heat is transferred between fluid streams without phase change in the fluids. Examples of this type of heat transfer are :

Heat exchange between hot and cooler petroleum streams.

Heat transfer from a stream of hot gas to cooling water.

Cooling of a hot liquid stream by cooling water/air.

In such cases the two streams are separated by a metal wall that constitutes the heat transfer surface. The surface may consist of tubes, or other channels of constant cross section or of flat plates.

A fluid being heated or cooled may be flowing in laminar flow, in turbulent flow or in the transition range between laminar and turbulent.

An equation for predicting the film coefficient or the surface coefficient in any particular case must include all the properties of the fluid and conditions of its flow that effect the problem. In a particular case the factors that might be considered are the diameter of pipe, the velocity of flowing fluid, density, viscosity, thermal conductivity, specific heat of the fluid etc. The dimensional analysis is one of the most useful methods to assemble these factors into an equation. It shows in what relation to each other certain of these variables should appear, and results in arranging them into various dimensionless groups.

It is found that an equation for the film coefficient for heat transfer to or from a flowing fluid without phase change will probably be of the form :

$$N_{Nu} = f\left(N_{Re}, N_{Pr}, N_{Gr}, \frac{L}{D}\right)$$

Application of Dimensional Analysis to heat transfer by convection :

Dimensional analysis is a method of correlating a number of variables into a single equation expressing an effect. When the value of a given particular physical quantity is influenced by a number of variables, then it is impossible to determine their individual effects by the experimental methods. In such cases, a problem can be made more manageable by adopting the method of dimensional analysis wherein the variables are arranged in dimensionless groups which are significantly less than the number of variables. Dimensional analysis finds application in many areas of chemical engineering such as fluid flow, heat transfer, etc.

The rate of heat transfer per unit area depends on the viscosity μ, density ρ, specific heat capacity C_p, thermal conductivity of the fluid k, a linear dimension of the surface l, the velocity of the flowing fluid u, the temperature difference, ΔT, and the product of the thermal expansion coefficient, β and the acceleration due to gravity, g. The relationship between the heat flux and the above cited parameters may be given as

$$\frac{Q}{A} = \alpha \, [u^a \, l^b \, \rho^c \, C_p^d \, \Delta T^e \, (\beta \cdot g)^f \, k^i, \mu^m] \qquad \ldots (3.26)$$

The dimensions of the variables in terms of length L, mass M, time θ, temperature T, and heat H are given as follows :

Q/A	rate of heat transfer per unit area	$H\,L^{-2}\,\theta^{-1}$
u	velocity of the flowing fluid	$L\,\theta^{-1}$
l	linear dimension of the surface	L
μ	viscosity of the flowing fluid	$M\,L^{-1}\,\theta^{-1}$
ρ	density of the flowing fluid	$M\,L^{-3}$
k	thermal conductivity of the flowing fluid	$H\,L^{-1}\,\theta^{-1}\,T^{-1}$
C_p	specific heat of the flowing fluid	$H\,M^{-1}\,T^{-1}$
ΔT	temperature difference	T
$(\beta \cdot g)$	coefficient of thermal expansion times the acceleration due to gravity.	$T^{-1}\,L\,\theta^{-2}$

Substituting the dimensions of each term in Equation (3.26) gives

$$(HL^{-2}\theta^{-1}) = \alpha\,(L\theta^{-1})^a\,(L)^b\,(ML^{-3})^c\,(HM^{-1}T^{-1})^d\,(T)^e\,(T^{-1}L\theta^{-2})^f \times$$
$$\times (HL^{-1}\theta^{-1}T^{-1})^i \times (ML^{-1}\theta^{-1})^m \qquad \ldots (3.27)$$

Equating the indices of the dimensions on each side of Equation (3.27), we get

in length $-2 = a + b - 3c + f - i - m$
in mass $0 = c - d + m$
in time $-1 = -a - 2f - i - m$
in temperature $0 = -d + e - f - i$
in heat $1 = d + i$

There are five equations (in length, mass, time, temperature and heat) and nine variables so that the above equation (3.27) will be rearranged in four dimensionless groups in terms of any three indices. Let us choose a, f and d be the three indices. Thus,

Solving simultaneously :

We have $1 = d + i$
∴ $i = 1 - d$
We have $-1 = -a - 2f - i - m$
∴ $-1 = -a - 2f - (1 - d) - m$
∴ $m = d - a - 2f$
We have $0 = -d + e - f - i$
             $0 = -d + e - f - (1 - d)$
∴ $e = 1 + f$
             $0 = c - d + m$
             $0 = c - d + d - a - 2f$
∴ $c = a + 2f$
             $-2 = a + b - 3c + f - i - m$
             $-2 = a + b - 3(a + 2f) + f - (1 - d) - (d - a - 2f)$
∴ $b = -1 + a + 3f$

Substituting the values of b, c, e, i and m, Equation (3.27) becomes

$$\frac{Q}{A} = \alpha\,[(u)^a\,(l)^{-1+a+3f}\,(\rho)^{a+2f}\,(C_p)^d\,(\Delta T)^{1+f} \times (\beta g)^f\,(k)^{1-d}\,(\mu)^{d-a-2f}] \qquad \ldots (3.28)$$

Collecting the terms, we get

$$\frac{Q}{A} = \alpha\left[\frac{k\,\Delta T}{l}\left(\frac{l u \rho}{\mu}\right)^a \left(\frac{C_p \mu}{k}\right)^d \left(\frac{\beta g\,\Delta T\,l^3\,\rho^2}{\mu^2}\right)^f\right] \qquad \ldots (3.29)$$

$$\frac{Ql}{A\,\Delta T k} = \alpha\left[\left(\frac{l\cdot u\rho}{\mu}\right)^a \left(\frac{C_p\cdot\mu}{k}\right)^d \left(\frac{\beta g\cdot\Delta T\,l^3\cdot\rho^2}{\mu^2}\right)^f\right] \quad \ldots (3.30)$$

$$\frac{hl}{k} = \alpha\left[\left(\frac{l\,u\rho}{\mu}\right)^a \left(\frac{C_p\cdot\mu}{k}\right)^d \left(\frac{\beta g\cdot\Delta T\cdot l^3\cdot\rho^2}{\mu^2}\right)^f\right] \quad \ldots (3.31)$$

As $Q = hA\,\Delta T \quad \therefore \quad Q/A\,\Delta T = h$

If the linear dimension of the surface is D (in the case of pipe), then the above equation becomes

$$\frac{hD}{k} = \alpha\left[\left(\frac{Du\rho}{\mu}\right)^a \left(\frac{C_p\,\mu}{k}\right)^d \left(\frac{\beta\cdot g\,\Delta T\,D^3\,\rho^2}{\mu^2}\right)^f\right] \quad \ldots (3.32)$$

The groups on both the sides of Equation (3.32) are dimensionless

$\dfrac{hl}{k} = \dfrac{hD}{k}$ (for pipe) = Nusselt number, N_{Nu}

$\dfrac{l\,u\,\rho}{\mu} = \dfrac{Du\rho}{\mu}$ (for pipe)

$\phantom{\dfrac{l\,u\,\rho}{\mu}}$ = Reynolds number, N_{Re}

$\dfrac{C_p\,\mu}{k}$ = Prandtl number, N_{Pr}

and $\dfrac{\beta g\cdot\Delta T\,l^3\,\rho^2}{\mu^2} = \dfrac{\beta g\cdot\Delta T\,D^3\,\rho^2}{\mu^2}$ (for pipe)

$\phantom{\dfrac{\beta g\cdot\Delta T\,l^3\,\rho^2}{\mu^2}}$ = Grashof number, N_{Gr}

Physical significance of the groups :

Reynolds number = $\dfrac{\text{Inertia forces}}{\text{Viscous forces}}$

Grashof number = $\dfrac{\text{Buoyancy forces} \times \text{inertia forces}}{(\text{viscous forces})^2}$

Prandtl number = $\dfrac{\text{molecular diffusivity of momentum}}{\text{molecular diffusivity of heat}}$

Nusselt number = $\dfrac{\text{Wall heat transfer rate}}{\text{Heat transfer by conduction}}$

The above relationship given by equation (3.32) can be written as :

$$N_{Nu} = \alpha\,[N_{Re}]^a\,[N_{Pr}]^d\,[N_{Gr}]^f \quad \ldots (3.33)$$

For natural convection where there is a buoyancy effect, N_{Gr} influences the heat transfer characteristic more than N_{Re} so that N_{Nu} is a function of N_{Gr} and N_{Pr}.

For natural convection :

$$N_{Nu} = f\,(N_{Pr},\,N_{Gr}) \quad \ldots (3.34)$$

For forced convection, Reynold's number influences the heat transfer characteristics and the Grashof number may be omitted. Thus, for **forced convection** :

$$N_{Nu} = f(N_{Re}, N_{Pr}) \qquad \ldots (3.35\ a)$$

I. Application of dimensional analysis for a forced convection equation :

To derive a relationship for heat transfer coefficient, h for forced convection heat transfer on the assumption that the coefficient h is a function of the following variables :

- l — linear dimension of the surface
- C_p — specific heat of the fluid
- ρ — density of the fluid
- μ — viscosity of the fluid
- k — thermal conductivity of the fluid

and

- u — velocity of the fluid.

Solution : It is given that h is a function of L, u, ρ, μ, C_p and k. Therefore, we can write :

$$h = f(\rho, u, L, \mu, C_p, k)$$

$$h = A(\rho^a u^b L^c \mu^d C_p^e k^f) \qquad \ldots (3.35\ b)$$

where A, a, b, c, d, e, and f are constants.

Express the energy terms mechanically by dimensions of the variables :

The dimensions of each variable in terms of M, L, T, θ and F are :

Parameter	Units	Fundamental dimensions
h	N·m/(m²·s·K) = W/(m²·K)	FL/L²θT = FL⁻¹θ⁻¹T⁻¹
k	N·m/(m·s·K) = W/(m·K)	FL/LθT = Fθ⁻¹T⁻¹
C_p	N·m/(kg·K) = J/(kg·K)	FL/MT = FLM⁻¹T⁻¹
μ	kg/(m·s)	M/Lθ = ML⁻¹θ⁻¹
u	m/s	L/θ = Lθ⁻¹
l	m	L = L
ρ	kg/m³	M/L³ = ML⁻³

Substituting the dimensions of all parameters in the above equation, we get :

$$FL^{-1}\theta^{-1}T^{-1} = A\,(ML^{-3})^a\,(L\theta^{-1})^b\,(L)^c\,(ML^{-1}\theta^{-1})^d\,(FLM^{-1}T^{-1})^e\,(F\theta^{-1}T^{-1})^f \ldots$$

Equating the indices/powers of M, L, θ, T and F, we get

- Force, F : $1 = e + f$ ... (i)
- Mass, M : $0 = a + d - e$ ... (ii)
- Length, L : $-1 = -3a + b + c - d + e$ ... (iii)
- Temperature, T : $-1 = -e - f$ ... (iv)
- Time, θ : $-1 = -b - d - f$ ... (v)

Let us obtain the values of all constants in terms of a and e.

From equation (i),
$$f = 1 - e$$
From equation (ii),
$$d = e - a$$
From equation (v),
$$-1 = -b - d - f$$
$$b = 1 - d - f = 1 - (e - a) - f$$
$$b = 1 - e + a - f$$
$$b = a + (1 - e) - f = a + f - f$$
$$\therefore \quad b = a$$
From equation (iii),
$$-1 = -3a + b + c - d + e$$
$$c = 3a - b + d - e - 1$$
$$= 3a - a + (e - a) - e - 1$$
$$c = 2a - a - 1 = a - 1$$

Substituting back, Equation (1) becomes
$$h = A\,(\rho)^a\,(u)^a\,(L)^{a-1}\,(\mu)^{e-a}\,(C_p)^e\,(k)^{1-e}$$

Collecting the terms, we get
$$h = A\left(\frac{L u \rho}{\mu}\right)^a \left(\frac{C_p \mu}{k}\right)^e (k/L)$$

$$\therefore \quad \frac{hL}{k} = A\left(\frac{L u \rho}{\mu}\right)^a \left(\frac{C_p \mu}{k}\right)^e \quad \ldots (3.35\ \text{c})$$

In the case of pipe, the linear dimension is D (inside diameter) and the above equation becomes

$$\frac{hD}{k} = A\left(\frac{D u \rho}{\mu}\right)^a \left(\frac{C_p \mu}{k}\right)^e$$

We can obtain the same expression if we express energy terms thermally by the dimensions of the variables.

Equation (3.35 c) is the required relationship; where A, a and e must be evaluated from a minimum of three sets of experimental data.

This equation contains three dimensionless groups/numbers :

(i) Nusselt number, $N_{Nu} = hL/k$

(ii) Reynolds number, $N_{Re} = Lu\rho/\mu$

(iii) Prandtl number, $N_{Pr} = C_p \mu/k$.

Obtain the relationship by expressing energy terms thermally.

Expressing the energy terms thermally by dimensions of the variables :

Parameter	Units	Fundamental dimensions
h	W/(m²·K) = J/(s·m²·K)	$H/\theta L^2 T = H\theta^{-1} L^{-2} T^{-1}$
k	W/(m·K) = J/(s·m·K)	$H/\theta LT = H\theta^{-1} L^{-1} T^{-1}$
C_p	J/(kg·K)	$H/MT = HM^{-1} T^{-1}$
μ	kg/(m·s)	$M/L\theta = ML^{-1} \theta^{-1}$
u	m/s	$L/\theta = L\theta^{-1}$
l	m	$L = L$
ρ	kg/m³	$M/L^3 = ML^{-3}$

Substituting the dimensions of all the parameters, we get

$$H\theta^{-1} L^{-2} T^{-1} = A\,(ML^{-3})^a (L\theta^{-1})^b (L)^c (ML^{-1}\theta^{-1})^d (HM^{-1} T^{-1})^e (H\theta^{-1} L^{-1} T^{-1})^f$$

Equating the indices/powers of M, L, θ, etc.

$$H : \quad 1 = e + f \qquad \ldots (i)$$
$$M : \quad 0 = a + d - e \qquad \ldots (ii)$$
$$L : \quad -2 = -3a + b + c - d - f \qquad \ldots (iii)$$
$$\theta : \quad -1 = -b - d - f \qquad \ldots (iv)$$
$$T : \quad -1 = -e - f \qquad \ldots (v)$$

Obtain the values of all constants in terms of a and e.

From equation (i), $\quad f = 1 - e$
From equation (ii), $\quad d = e - a$
From equation (iv), $\quad b = 1 - d - f = 1 - e + a - 1 + e = a$
From equation (iii), $\quad c = a - 1$

Substituting back values of the indices b, c, d and f in Equation (3.35 b),

$$h = A\,(\rho)^a (u)^a (L)^{a-1} (\mu)^{e-a} (C_p)^e (k)^{1-e}$$

Collecting the terms, we get

$$h = A \left(\frac{Lu\rho}{\mu}\right)^a (C_p \mu/k)^e (k/L)$$

$$\therefore \quad \frac{hL}{k} = A \left(\frac{Lu\rho}{\mu}\right)^a (C_p \mu/k)^e \qquad \ldots (3.35\text{ d})$$

II. Application of dimensional analysis for a natural convection equation :

To derive a relationship for the heat transfer coefficient h for natural convection between a surface and a fluid assuming that the coefficient h is a function of the following variables :

- l — a characteristic linear dimension of the surface,
- ρ — density of the fluid,
- μ — viscosity of the fluid,
- k — thermal conductivity of the fluid,
- C_p — specific heat of the fluid,
- β·g — the product of the acceleration due to gravity and coefficient of cubical expansion of the fluid,
- ΔT — the temperature difference between the fluid and the surface.

Solution : It is given that the coefficient h is a function of l, k, ρ, C_p, μ, βg and ΔT. Therefore, we can write :

$$h = f[l, \rho, \mu, k, C_p, \beta \cdot g, \Delta T]$$

$\therefore \qquad h = \alpha \, [l^a \, \rho^b \, \mu^c \, k^d \, C_p^e \, (\beta g)^f \, (\Delta T)^g]$

The dimensions of each variable in terms of M, L, T, F and θ are :

Parameter	Units	Fundamental dimensions
h	N·m/(m²·s·K) = W/(m²·K)	FL/L²θT = FL⁻¹θ⁻¹T⁻¹
k	N·m/(m·s·K) = W/(m·K)	FL/LθT = Fθ⁻¹T⁻¹
C_p	N·m/(kg·K) = J/(kg·K)	FL/MT = FLM⁻¹T⁻¹
μ	kg/(m·s)	M/Lθ = ML⁻¹θ⁻¹
l	m	L = L
ρ	kg/m³	M/L³ = ML⁻³
βg	m/(s²·K)	L/θ²T = Lθ⁻²T⁻¹
ΔT	K	T = T

Substituting the dimensions of each variable in the above equation, we get :

$$FL^{-1}\theta^{-1}T^{-1} = \alpha \, (L)^a \, (ML^{-3})^b \, (ML^{-1}\theta^{-1})^c \, (F\theta^{-1}T^{-1})^d \, (FLM^{-1}T^{-1})^e \, (L\theta^{-2}T^{-1})^f \times (T)^g$$

Equating the indices/powers :

Force,	F :	$1 = d + e$	... (i)
Mass,	M :	$0 = b + c - e$	... (ii)
Length,	L :	$-1 = a - 3b - c + e + f$	... (iii)
Temperature	T :	$-1 = -d - e - f + g$	... (iv)
Time	θ :	$-1 = -c - d - 2f$	... (v)

Solving in terms of e and f we get from equation (i),

$$d = 1 - e$$

From equation (v),

$$c = 1 - d - 2f, \quad \text{but } d = 1 - e$$

$\therefore \qquad c = 1 - (1 - e) - 2f = e - 2f$

From equation (ii), we have

$$b = -c + e \quad \text{but } c = e - 2f$$

$\therefore \qquad b = -(e - 2f) + e = 2f$

From equation (iii), we have

$$a = -1 + 3b + c - e - f$$
$$a = -1 + 3(2f) + (e - 2f) - e - f = -1 + 3f$$

From equation (iv), we have

$$g = -1 + d + e + f = -1 + 1 + f = f \quad [\text{as } d + e = 1]$$

Substituting back,

$$h = \alpha\, (l)^{-1+3f}\, (\rho)^{2f}\, (\mu)^{e-2f}\, (k)^{1-e}\, (C_p)^e\, (\beta g)^f\, (\Delta T)^f$$

Collecting the terms, we get

$$h = \alpha \left(\frac{C_p \mu}{k}\right)^e \left(\frac{l^3 \rho^2 \beta g\, \Delta T}{\mu^2}\right)^f (k/L)$$

$$\therefore \quad \frac{hL}{k} = \alpha \left(\frac{C_p \mu}{k}\right)^e \left(\frac{l^3 \rho^2 \beta g\, \Delta T}{\mu^2}\right)^f \qquad \ldots (3.35\ e)$$

Equation (3.35 e) is the desired relationship for natural convection.

Here $\dfrac{C_p \mu}{k}$ is the Prandtl number (N_{Pr})

hL/k is the Nusselt number (N_{Nu})

and $\dfrac{l^3 \rho^2 \beta \cdot g\, \Delta T}{\mu^2}$ is the Grashof number (N_{ar})

Empirical equations for calculation of heat transfer coefficients in laminar, turbulent and transition region in forced convection :

[A] Film coefficients-in pipes – Laminar flow :

Heat transfer to laminar flow may be encountered whenever fluids to be heated or cooled are viscous or flow rates are low. In polymer, food or pharmaceutical industry, we may come across a heat exchanger where the flow is in the laminar region ($N_{Re} < 2100$).

For heating or cooling of viscous fluids, an empirical correlation is

$$N_{Nu} = 1.86\, [(N_{Re})(N_{Pr})(D/L)]^{1/3}\, [\mu/\mu_w]^{0.14} \qquad \ldots (3.36)$$

Equation (3.36) is the Sider-Tate equation for the calculation of the heat transfer coefficient for laminar flow of fluids in horizontal tubes or pipes. Equation (3.36) is valid for

$N_{Re} < 2100$ and $(N_{Re}\, N_{Pr},\, D/L) > 100$

where D is the diameter of pipe and L is the length of pipe.

The term $(\mu/\mu_w)^{0.14}$ is called as the Sider-Tate correction. The term (μ/μ_w) is the *ratio of the viscosity of the fluid at the bulk temperature and the viscosity of the fluid at the wall temperature.*

$$\frac{hD}{k} = 1.86 \left[\left(\frac{D u \rho}{\mu}\right)\left(\frac{C_p \mu}{k}\right)\left(\frac{D}{L}\right)\right]^{1/3} \left(\frac{\mu}{\mu_w}\right)^{0.14} \qquad \ldots (3.37)$$

where h is the inside heat transfer coefficient, D is the inside diameter of pipe.

In the above equation all the physical properties of the fluid are taken at the mean bulk temperature of the flowing fluid, i.e., at the arithmetic mean of inlet and outlet temperatures of the fluid flowing through pipe $(T_i + T_o)/2$ and μ_w is evaluated at the average wall temperature.

Graetz number is defined by the following equation :

$$N_{Gz} = \frac{\dot{m} C_p}{kL} \qquad \ldots (3.38)$$

where $\dot{m}$ is the mass flow rate

$$\dot{m} = \rho u A = \frac{\pi}{4} \rho u D^2 \qquad \ldots (3.39)$$

$$N_{Gz} = \frac{\pi}{4} \frac{\rho u C_p D^2}{k L}$$

$$= \frac{\pi}{4} \frac{D u \rho}{\mu} \frac{C_p \mu}{k} \cdot \frac{D}{L}$$

$$= \frac{\pi}{4} N_{Re} \cdot N_{Pr} \cdot \frac{D}{L} \qquad \ldots (3.40)$$

By substituting for $N_{Re} \cdot N_{Pr} \cdot \frac{D}{L}$ from Equation (3.40), Equation (3.36) becomes :

$$N_{Nu} = 1.86 \left[\frac{4}{\pi}(N_{Gz})\right]^{1/3} \times \left(\frac{\mu}{\mu_w}\right)^{0.14}$$

$$N_{Nu} = 2 [N_{Gz}]^{1/3} [\mu/\mu_w]^{0.14} \qquad \ldots (3.41)$$

$$\frac{hD}{k} = 2.0 \left[\frac{\dot{m} C_p}{k L}\right]^{1/3} [\mu/\mu_w]^{0.14} \qquad \ldots (3.42)$$

Equation (3.42) is the Sider-Tate equation for laminar flow/viscous flow in terms of the Graetz number.

The Peclet number is defined as the product of the Reynolds number and the Prandtl number.

$$N_{Pe} = N_{Re} \cdot N_{Pr} = \frac{D u \rho}{\mu} \cdot \frac{C_p \mu}{k} = \frac{D u}{\alpha} \qquad \ldots (3.43)$$

$\alpha = k/\rho C_p$, α is the thermal diffusivity and has units of m²/s.

The choice among these groups is arbitrary.

For thin fluids in laminar flow –

For values of $(N_{Re} \cdot N_{Pr} D/L) > 12$, following empirical equation is applicable :

$$N_{Nu} = 1.62 \left(N_{Re} \cdot N_{Pr} \cdot \frac{D}{L}\right)^{1/3} \qquad \ldots (3.44)$$

Equation (3.44) can be written as

$$N_{Nu} = 1.75 \left(\frac{\dot{m} C_p}{k L}\right)^{1/3} \qquad \ldots (3.45)$$

For viscous liquids in laminar flow, equation (3.42) is applicable in which variation of viscosity with temperature is introduced.

[B] Film coefficients - in pipes – Turbulent flow :

The most important situation in heat transfer is the flow of heat in a stream of fluid in turbulent flow in pipes or tubes. Turbulence is encountered at $N_{Re} > 2100$. As the rate of heat transfer is greater in turbulent flow than in laminar flow, most of the heat transfer equipments are operated in the turbulent range.

The Dittus-Boelter equation for predicting the heat transfer coefficient for turbulent flow in tubes or pipes is :

$$\frac{hD}{k} = 0.023 \left[\frac{Du\rho}{\mu}\right]^{0.8} \left[\frac{C_p\mu}{k}\right]^a \qquad \ldots (3.46)$$

where 'a' has a value of 0.4 for heating and 0.3 for cooling. It is commonly used for water like materials.

Here also the fluid properties are evaluated at the arithmetic mean bulk temperature, i.e., at $(T_i + T_o)/2$ of the flowing fluid. T_i and T_o are the inlet and outlet temperatures.

For heating :

$$N_{Nu} = 0.023 \, [N_{Re}]^{0.8} \, [N_{Pr}]^{0.4} \qquad \ldots (3.47)$$

For cooling :

$$N_{Nu} = 0.023 \, [N_{Re}]^{0.8} \, [N_{Pr}]^{0.3} \qquad \ldots (3.48)$$

Equations (3.47) and (3.48) are valid for Reynolds number greater than 10000 and has been tested for the values of Prandtl number between 0.7 and 160.

For turbulent flow in tubes/pipes, the Sieder-Tate equation that takes into account the variation of the viscosity of the fluid near the wall with thermal gradients is

$$\frac{hD}{k} = 0.023 \left(\frac{Du\rho}{\mu}\right)^{0.8} \left(\frac{C_p\mu}{k}\right)^{1/3} (\mu/\mu_w)^{0.14} \qquad \ldots (3.49)$$

Equation (3.49) is the Sieder-Tate equation.

Equation (3.49) is valid for $N_{Re} > 10,000$ and $0.7 < N_{Pr} < 700$ and $L/D > 60$. $(\mu/\mu_w)^{0.14}$ is called as the Sieder-Tate correction factor.

Here all the fluid properties are taken at the mean bulk temperature, i.e., at $(T_i + T_o)/2$, where T_i is inlet fluid temperature and T_o is the fluid outlet temperature. μ_w is the viscosity of fluid at the wall temperature.

An alternate equation that in many ways is more convenient is the one proposed by Colburn.

In the Colburn equation, the Stanton number (N_{st}) is used instead of the Nusselt number (N_{Nu}) :

$$N_{st} = \frac{h}{C_p \rho u} \qquad \ldots (3.50)$$

It should be noted that :

$$\frac{h}{C_p \rho u} = \frac{hD}{k} \cdot \frac{\mu}{Du\rho} \cdot \frac{k}{C_p \mu} \qquad \ldots (3.51)$$

$$N_{st} = N_{Nu} \cdot N_{Re}^{-1} \cdot N_{Pr}^{-1}$$

$$N_{Nu} = N_{st} \cdot N_{Re} \cdot N_{Pr} \qquad \ldots (3.52)$$

E.M. Sider and C.E. Tate proposed the following empirical equation for predicting the heat transfer coefficient for turbulent flow.

$$N_{Nu} = 0.023 \, (N_{Re})^{0.8} \, (N_{Pr})^{1/3} \, (\mu/\mu_w)^{0.14} \qquad \ldots (3.53)$$

Putting the value of N_{Nu} from equation (3.52) into equation (3.53), we get

$$N_{st} \cdot N_{Re} \cdot N_{Pr} = 0.023 \, (N_{Re})^{0.8} (N_{Pr})^{1/3} (\mu/\mu_w)^{0.14} \qquad \ldots (3.54)$$

$$N_{st} \cdot N_{Pr}^{2/3} \cdot (\mu_w/\mu)^{0.14} = 0.023 \, (N_{Re})^{-0.2} \qquad \ldots (3.55)$$

$$\frac{h}{C_p \rho u} \left(\frac{C_p \mu}{k}\right)^{2/3} \left(\frac{\mu_w}{\mu}\right)^{0.14} = 0.023 \left(\frac{Du\rho}{\mu}\right)^{-0.2} \qquad \ldots (3.56)$$

Equation (3.56) is the Colburn equation.

Turbulent flow of gases :

For heating or cooling of gases in turbulent flow, for which the Prandtl group usually has a value of about 0.74, an empirical correlation is

$$N_{Nu} = 0.02 \, (N_{Re})^{0.8} \qquad \ldots (3.57)$$

For turbulent flow in pipes, the following simplified equations hold in SI units :

1. For air at 1 atm. pressure

$$h = \frac{3.5 \, u^{0.8}}{D^{0.2}} \qquad \ldots (3.58)$$

2. For water in tubes

$$h = 1063 \, (1 + 0.00293 \, T) \, \frac{u^{0.8}}{D^{0.2}} \; W/(m^2 \cdot K) \qquad \ldots (3.59)$$

where T is average bulk temperature in K.

3. For organic liquids :

$$h = 423 \, \frac{u^{0.8}}{D^{0.2}} \qquad \ldots (3.60)$$

Mass velocity is given by equation :

$$G = \dot{m}/A$$
$$= \rho u A/A$$
$$= \rho u, \; kg/(m^2 \cdot s) \qquad \ldots (3.61)$$

So in all the equations involving the Reynolds group, we can write N_{Re} also as:

$$N_{Re} = \frac{Du\rho}{\mu}$$

$$N_{Re} = \frac{DG}{\mu} \qquad \ldots (3.62)$$

In all the equations cited above use the following SI units:

D in m, u in m/s, L in m, G in kg/(m²·s), ρ in kg/m³, C_p in J/(kg·K), μ in P_a·s = kg/(m·s) = (N·s)/m² and k in W/(m·K) + J/(m·s·K) so that unit of h will be W/(m²·K).

Flow in non-circular cross-sections:

To use the Sider-Tate or Colburn equation for cross sections other than circular, it is only necessary to replace the diameter D in both Reynolds and Nusselt numbers by the equivalent diameter, D_e.

$$D_e = 4 \times r_H \qquad \ldots (3.63)$$

$$D_e = \frac{4 \times \text{cross-sectional area}}{\text{wetted perimeter}}$$

e.g. D_e for circular pipe:

$$D_e = \frac{4\,(\pi/4\,D^2)}{\pi D} = D$$

For an annulus of outer diameter D_o and inner diameter D_i

$$D_e = \frac{4\left[\frac{\pi}{4}[D_o^2 - D_i^2]\right]}{\pi D_i} = \frac{D_o^2 - D_i^2}{D_i} \qquad \ldots (3.64)$$

where, D_o = inner diameter of outer pipe (outside diameter of annulus)

D_i = outer diameter of inner pipe (inside diameter of annulus)

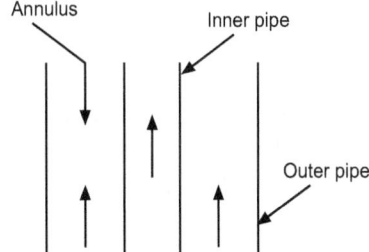

Fig. 3.2 : Double pipe heat exchanger

For duct of rectangular cross-section x by y:

$$D_e = \frac{4xy}{2\,(x+y)} = \frac{2xy}{(x+y)} \qquad \ldots (3.65)$$

The Colburn analogy; Colburn j factor :

For N_{Re} between 5000 – 200000, the friction factor (f) for a smooth pipe is given by the empirical equation given below :

$$f = 0.046 \left(\frac{Du\rho}{\mu}\right)^{-0.2} \quad \ldots (3.66)$$

Comparison of Equation (3.66) with Equation (3.55) for heat transfer in turbulent flow inside a pipe/tube shows that

$$\frac{h}{C_p \rho u}\left(\frac{C_p \mu}{k}\right)^{2/3}\left(\frac{\mu_w}{\mu}\right)^{0.14} \equiv j_H = \frac{f}{2} \quad \ldots (3.67)$$

Equation (3.67) is the Colburn analogy between heat transfer and fluid friction. The factor j_H is called the Colburn j factor. Equation (3.55) can be written in the j-factor form as given below :

$$j_H = 0.023 \, (N_{Re})^{-0.2} \quad \ldots (3.68)$$

For laminar flow region, we have

$$N_{Nu} = 2.0 \left[\frac{\dot{m} C_p}{kL}\right]^{1/3}\left[\frac{\mu}{\mu_w}\right]^{0.14} \quad \ldots (3.69)$$

By use of Equation (3.40), Equation (3.69) becomes :

$$N_{Nu} = 2.0 \left[\frac{\pi}{4}\frac{D}{L} N_{Re} \cdot N_{Pr}\right]^{1/3} [\mu/\mu_w]^{0.14} \quad \ldots (3.70)$$

Multiplying Equation (3.70) by $(1/N_{Re})(1/N_{Pr})$, we get

$$\frac{h}{C_p \rho u}\left(\frac{C_p \mu}{k}\right)^{2/3}\left(\frac{\mu_w}{\mu}\right)^{0.14} = j_H = 1.86\left(\frac{D}{L}\right)^{1/3}\left(\frac{Du\rho}{\mu}\right)^{-2/3} \quad \ldots (3.71)$$

[C] Film coefficients-in pipes - in Transition Region :

Equation (3.37) is valid only for Reynolds numbers less than 2100 and turbulent flow equation for predicting the heat transfer coefficient, i.e., Equation (3.55) is valid only for Reynolds numbers more than 10,000. The range of Reynolds numbers between 2100 and 10000 is called the transition region. For this, no simple equation is applicable and therefore a graphical method is used. The graphical method is based on the graphs of Equations (3.71) [modified form of (3.37)] and (3.68) [modified form of (3.55)] on a common plot of the Colburn j factor v/s N_{Re} at several values of L/D - with L/D as a parameter.

Equation (3.71) shows that for each value of L/D, a logarithmic plot of L.H.S., i.e., j_H v/s N_{Re} gives a straight line with a slope equal to (– 2/3). The lines terminate at $N_{Re} = 2100$.

Equation (3.66) when plotted on the same coordinates gives a straight line with a slope equal to (– 0.20) for $N_{Re} > 10,000$.

The curved lines between $2100 < N_{Re} < 10{,}000$ represent the transition region.

The range of Reynolds number covered in Fig. 3.3 is 10000 to 30000, so Fig. 3.3 is referred in this range. Beyond its lower and upper limits (i.e., $N_{Re} < 1000$ and $N_{Re} > 30000$), Equations (3.37) and (3.55) respectively can be used.

For the transition region, i.e., for $2100 < N_{Re} < 10000$, the following empirical equation can be used for the calculation of heat transfer coefficient.

$$N_{Nu} = 0.116\,[(N_{Re})^{2/3} - 125]\,[N_{Pr}]^{1/3}\left[1 + \left(\frac{D}{L}\right)^{2/3}\right][\mu/\mu_w]^{0.14} \quad \ldots (3.72)$$

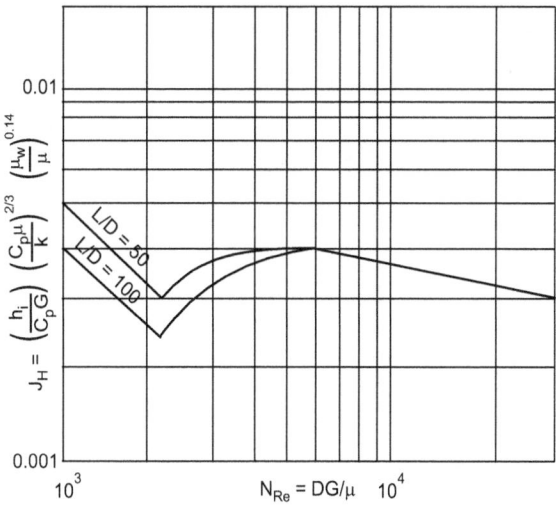

Fig. 3.3 : Tube side heat transfer curves transition range

In Fig. 3.3, j_H is the ordinate and N_{Re} is the abscissa and L/D is a parameter. First of all N_{Re} is evaluated from the data provided and then from Fig. 3.3, j_H is obtained for the corresponding N_{Re} and L/D and in turn, it gives the value of the tube side heat transfer coefficient.

Wilson Plot :

This plot is used for the determination of film heat transfer coefficients.

Consider a shell and tube heat exchanger wherein steam is condensing on the shell side and a cold fluid is flowing through the tubes in the turbulent flow region. The overall heat transfer coefficient is determined by the direct measurements of rate of heat transfer, overall temperature difference and area at various cold fluid velocities. In this case, the condensing steam side coefficient (h_o) remains almost constant and the resistance offered by the metal wall is also constant. Assuming clean tubes, Equation (3.19) reduces to

$$\frac{1}{U} = \frac{1}{h_i} + C \quad \ldots (3.73)$$

where 'C' is a constant.

Equation (3.54) for turbulent flow suggests that :

$$N_{Nu} \propto (N_{Re})^{0.8} \qquad \ldots (3.74)$$

$$\therefore \quad h_i \propto (u)^{0.8} \qquad \ldots (3.75)$$

$$h_i = a\,(u)^{0.8} \qquad \ldots (3.76)$$

Equation (3.73) then becomes :

$$\frac{1}{U} = \frac{1}{a\,(u)^{0.8}} + C \qquad \ldots (3.77)$$

where 'u' is the linear velocity of the cold fluid. A plot of $1/U$ v/s $1/(u)^{0.8}$ results in a straight line with a slope equal to $1/a$ and an intercept equal to $\dfrac{x_w}{k} + \dfrac{1}{h_o}$. The value of h_o is obtained from the intercept and 'a' represents the value of film coefficient h_i for unit velocity of the cold fluid. Such a plot shown in Fig. 3.4 is known as the Wilson plot.

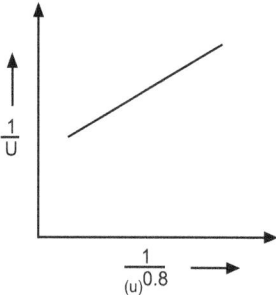

Fig. 3.4 : Wilson plot

Flow arrangements in heat exchangers :

There are three basic flow arrangements.

1. Parallel flow/Co-current flow 2. Counter current flow and 3. Cross flow

Consider a double pipe heat exchanger wherein a hot fluid is flowing through the inside pipe and a cold fluid is flowing through the annular space for the explanation of parallel and counter current flow.

When both fluids flow in the same direction from one end of a heat exchanger to other end through the heat exchanger, then the flow is called as **co-current or parallel flow.** Such a flow is shown in Fig. 3.5 (a). The temperature - length curve for parallel flow arrangement is shown in Fig. 3.5 (b).

When fluids are flowing through a heat exchanger in opposite directions with respect to each other (i.e., one fluid enters at one end of the heat exchanger and the other fluid enters at the opposite end of the heat exchanger), then the flow is termed as **counter current flow.** Such a flow arrangement is shown in Fig. 3.6 (a). The temperature - length curve for counter flow arrangement is shown in Fig. 3.6 (b).

When fluids are directed at right angles to each other through a heat exchanger, then the flow arrangement is called **cross-flow.**

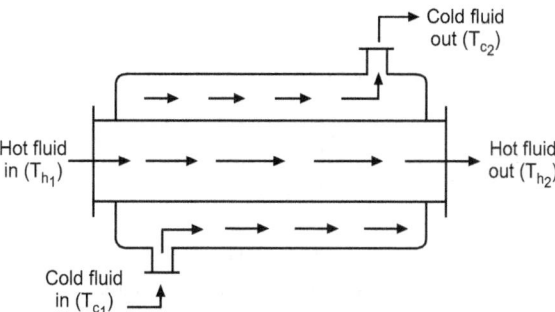

Fig. 3.5 (a) : Co-current/Parallel flow in heat exchanger

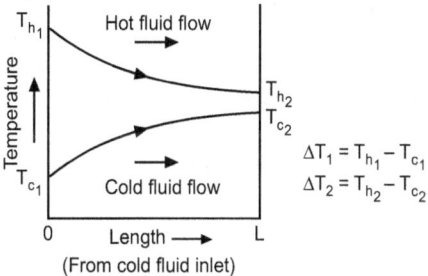

Fig. 3.5 (b) : Temperature - length curve for parallel flow

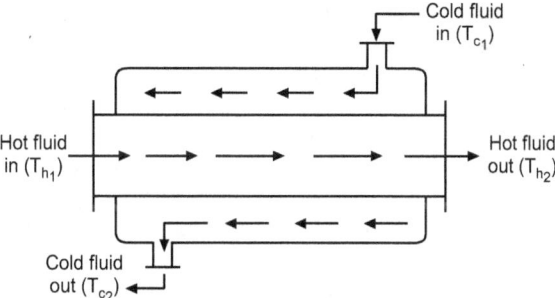

Fig. 3.6 (a) : Counter-current flow in heat exchanger

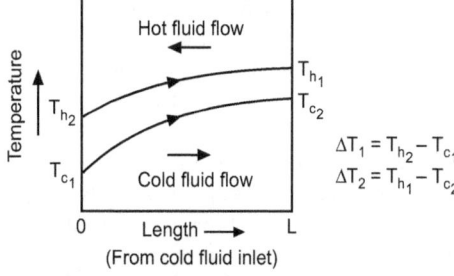

Fig. 3.6 (b) : Temperature - length curve for counter-current flow

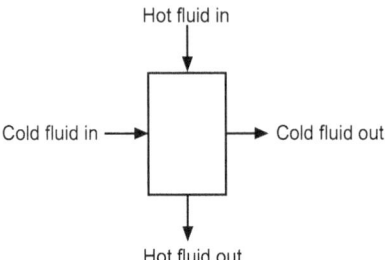

Fig. 3.7 : Cross flow heat exchanger

Heat exchangers according to flow pattern :

Parallel flow heat exchanger : It is the one in which two fluid streams enter at one end, flow through in the same direction and leaves at the other end. For example, double pipe heat exchanger, shell and tube heat exchanger can be operated in a parallel flow fashion.

Counter current flow heat exchanger : It is the one in which two fluid streams flow in opposite directions.

For example, double pipe heat exchanger, shell and tube heat exchanger can be operated in this way.

Cross flow heat exchanger : It is the one in which one fluid moves through the exchanger at right angles to the flow path of other fluid. For example, plate-fin heat exchanger.

Counter current flow v/s Co-current flow :

The temperature gradient in case of parallel flow is maximum at the entrance and continuously decreases towards the exit while the temperature gradient is fairly constant over the length of heat exchanger in case of counter current flow. Hence, with counter current flow arrangement, the heating surface has nearly constant capacity through the exchanger and with parallel flow, the capacity at exit is much less as compared to that at entrance. With parallel flow arrangement the lowest temperature theoretically attainable by a hot fluid is that of outlet temperature of a cold fluid. Under this condition, the log mean temperature difference would be zero and heat transfer surface requirement would be infinite. [$Q = U.A. \Delta Tlm$, U and A are finite]. With this method (parallel flow), it is not possible to bring the hot fluid temperature below the outlet temperature of the cold fluid and thus has marked effect on the ability of heat exchanger to recover heat. In parallel flow heat exchanger, heat transfer is restricted by the cold fluid outlet temperature rather than the cold fluid inlet temperature and hence the counter flow arrangement is very common in heat transfer apparatus. The parallel flow arrangement is used whenever it is necessary to limit the maximum temperature of the cooler fluid.

In counter current flow, it is possible for the cooling liquid to leave at a higher temperature than the heating fluid, and one of the greatest advantages of counter-flow is that it is possible to extract a higher proportion of the heat content of the heating fluid. For the same terminal temperatures, it is important to note that the value of the logarithmic mean temperature difference for counter flow is appreciable greater than the value for co-current flow. For the same terminal temperatures and same heat load, the heat transfer area required for counter flow heat exchanger is less than it for parallel flow heat exchanger. The rate of heat transfer in counter current flow heat exchanger is more than it in co-current flow exchanger.

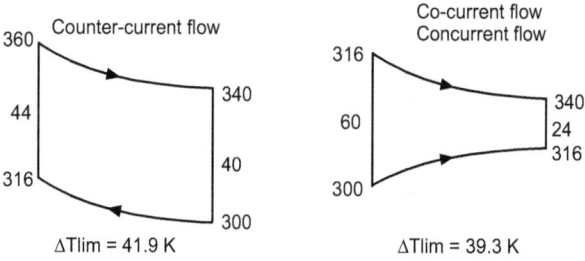

Fig. 3.8

In counter current flow arrangement, temperature difference will show less variation throughout the heat exchanger. In co-current flow, the temperatures of the two streams progressively approach one another. Temperature difference will show more variation throughout the heat exchanger.

Range :

It is the actual rise or fall of temperature of a fluid. If T_{h_1} is the inlet temperature and T_{h_2} is the outlet temperature of a hot fluid, then $T_{h_1} - T_{h_2}$ is the range for the hot fluid. Similarly if T_{c_1} and T_{c_2} are the inlet and outlet temperatures of a cold fluid, then $T_{c_2} - T_{c_1}$ is the range for the cold fluid.

Approach :

It is the terminal point temperature difference between hot and cold fluids. Thus T_{h_1} is the inlet temperature of a hot fluid and T_{c_2} is the outlet temperature of a cold fluid at one end of counter current heat transfer apparatus, then $T_{h_1} - T_{c_2}$ is called the approach.

In a condenser where the vapour entering it is not superheated and condensate is not subcooled below its boiling temperature, the temperature throughout the shell side of the condenser is constant as pressure in the shell space is constant. The temperature – length curve for the condenser is shown in Fig. 3.9. The temperature of the coolant used continuously increases as it passes through the tubes of the condenser.

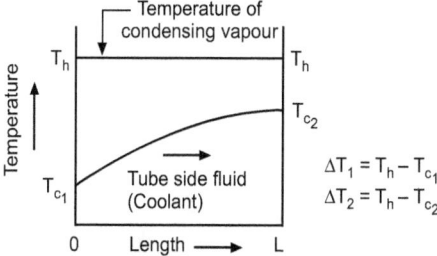

Fig. 3.9 : Temperature-length curve for condenser

Energy balances :

The energy balances are of a great importance in attacking the heat transfer problems.

Consider the heat exchanger shown in Fig. 3.10.

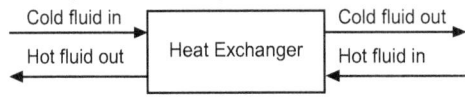

Fig. 3.10 : Energy balance

Let $\dot{m}_c$ and $\dot{m}_h$ be the mass flow rates of the cold and hot fluids respectively.

Let H_{c_1} and H_{c_2} be the enthalpies per unit mass of the cold fluid entering and leaving the heat exchanger respectively.

Similarly, let H_{h_1} and H_{h_2} be the enthalpies per unit mass of the hot fluid entering and leaving the heat exchanger respectively.

Q_c and Q_h be the rate of heat addition to the cold fluid and hot fluid respectively. The sign of Q_h is negative since the hot fluid losses/gives out, rather than gains, heat; while the sign of Q_c is positive. At steady state, the heat given out by the hot fluid is equal to the heat gained by the cold fluid.

$$\therefore \qquad Q_c = -Q_h \qquad \ldots (3.78)$$

$$\dot{m}_c (H_{c_2} - H_{c_1}) = -\dot{m}_h [H_{h_2} - H_{h_1}] = Q \qquad \ldots (3.79)$$

$$\dot{m}_c [H_{c_2} - H_{c_1}] = \dot{m}_h [H_{h_2} - H_{h_1}] = Q \qquad \ldots (3.80)$$

If only sensible heat transfer takes place between hot and cold fluids and if constant heat capacities are assumed, then Equation (3.80) can be written as :

$$\dot{m}_c C_{p_c} [T_{c_2} - T_{c_1}] = \dot{m}_h C_{p_h} (T_{h_1} - T_{h_2}) = Q \qquad \ldots (3.81)$$

where C_{p_c} and C_{p_h} are the heat capacities of the cold and hot fluids respectively.

T_{c_1}, T_{c_2} and T_{h_1} and T_{h_2} have their usual meaning. Equation (3.81) is the overall energy or enthalpy balance over a heat exchanger equipment for sensible heat changes in both the fluids.

For the latent heat transfer (i.e., condensation of vapours) from the condensing vapours to a coolant, the energy balance will be :

$$\dot{m}_h \cdot \lambda = \dot{m}_c C_{p_c} (T_{c_2} - T_{c_1}) = Q \qquad \ldots (3.82)$$

where
$\dot{m}_h$ – rate of condensation of vapour
λ – latent heat of condensation of vapour

Equation (3.82) is applicable to a condenser where the vapour entering is saturated and no subcooling of the condensed liquid takes place.

In the SI system, the mass flow rate is given usually in terms of kg/s, the specific heat in terms of J/(kg·K) or kJ/(kg·K) and the rate of heat transfer in terms of W ≡ J/s.

Sensible Heat :

It is the heat that must be transferred to raise or lower the temperature of a substance or a mixture of substances.

Latent Heat :

When matter undergoes a phase change (vapour to liquid, liquid to solid, etc.) the enthalpy change associated with a unit amount of matter at constant temperature and pressure is known as the latent heat of phase change. It is denoted by 'λ' and has the units of kJ/kg.

Heat Flux :

It is defined as the rate of heat transfer per unit area. It can be based on the outside or inside heat transfer area. It has the units of W/m².

Log mean temperature difference :

The heat transfer flux is directly proportional to a driving force. The driving force for heat flow is taken as $T_h - T_c$, where T_h and T_c are the temperatures of hot and cold fluids respectively. As the term $\Delta T = T_h - T_c$ varies along the length of a heat exchanger, the flux also varies over the entire length. Consider a differential element of area dA through which a differential amount of heat dQ flows under the driving force of ΔT. Then, dQ/dA is related to ΔT by the relation given below.

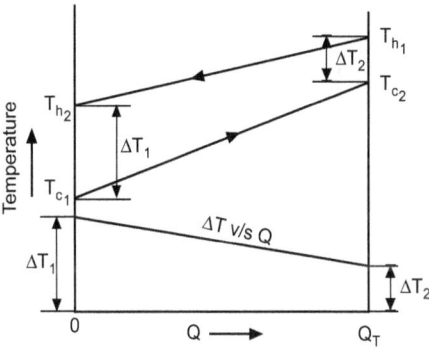

Fig. 3.11 : Temperature v/s heat flow rate (counter-current flow)

$$\frac{dQ}{dA} = U \cdot (\Delta T) = U \cdot (T_h - T_c) \qquad \ldots (3.83)$$

where U is the local overall heat transfer coefficient, dQ/dA is the local heat flux and ΔT is the local temperature difference.

Equation (3.83) needs to be integrated for its application to the entire area of a heat. Assumptions to be made for integration are :

1. Overall coefficient U is constant.
2. Specific heats of the hot and cold fluids are constant.
3. Heat flow to and from the ambient is negligible and
4. Flow is steady and may be parallel or counter current type.

Based on the assumptions (2) and (4), we get straight lines if T_c and T_h are plotted against Q and also a plot of ΔT v/s Q is a straight line. Such plots are shown in Fig. 3.11.

The slope of the plot of ΔT v/s Q is constant.

$$\text{Slope} = \frac{d(\Delta T)}{dQ} = \frac{\Delta T_2 - \Delta T_1}{Q_T} \quad \ldots (3.84)$$

where ΔT_1 and ΔT_2 are the terminal temperature differences (i.e., approaches) and Q_T is the rate of heat transfer in the entire heat exchanger.

Putting the value of dQ from Equation (3.83) into Equation (3.84) gives

$$\frac{d(\Delta T)}{U \cdot \Delta T \, dA} = \frac{\Delta T_2 - \Delta T_1}{Q_T} \quad \ldots (3.85)$$

Rearranging Equation (3.85),

$$\frac{d(\Delta T)}{\Delta T} = \frac{(\Delta T_2 - \Delta T_1) U}{Q_T} \cdot dA \quad \ldots (3.86)$$

Integrating the above equation over the limits :
$A = 0$, $\Delta T = \Delta T_1$ and $A = A$, $\Delta T = \Delta T_2$, gives

$$\int_{\Delta T_1}^{\Delta T_2} \frac{d(\Delta T)}{\Delta T} = \frac{(\Delta T_2 - \Delta T_1) U}{Q_T} \int_0^A dA \quad \ldots (3.87)$$

$$\ln\left(\frac{\Delta T_2}{\Delta T_1}\right) = \frac{(\Delta T_2 - \Delta T_1)}{Q_T} U \cdot A \quad \ldots (3.88)$$

$$Q_T = U.A. \frac{(\Delta T_2 - \Delta T_1)}{\ln\left(\frac{\Delta T_2}{\Delta T_1}\right)} \quad \ldots (3.89)$$

The heat transfer rate in the entire heat exchanger can be denoted by the symbol Q.

$$\therefore \quad Q = U.A \frac{(\Delta T_2 - \Delta T_1)}{\ln\left(\frac{\Delta T_2}{\Delta T_1}\right)} \quad \ldots (3.90)$$

$$Q = U.A. \, \Delta Tlm \quad \ldots (3.91)$$

where

$$\Delta Tlm = \frac{(\Delta T_2 - \Delta T_1)}{\ln\left(\frac{\Delta T_2}{\Delta T_1}\right)} \quad \ldots (3.92)$$

ΔTlm is referred to as the logarithmic mean or the log mean temperature difference (LMTD).

In counter current flow, the hot end approach ΔT_2 may be less than the cold end approach ΔT_1, so the subscripts may be interchanged for eliminating confusion due to negative (−) signs.

In a 1-2 heat exchanger, the tube side fluid flows twice through the exchanger and the shell side fluid flows once through it. Consequently, there is a combination of co-current and counter-current flow patterns in such multipass units. The rate of heat transfer in these units using the corrected LMTD is given by

$$Q = U.A. \, F_T (\Delta Tlm) \qquad \ldots (3.93)$$

where F_T = Correction factor for the LMTD and is usually taken as 0.85 – 0.90

and ΔTlm = Log mean temperature difference calculated for counter current flow from the terminal temperatures or counter current LMTD.

For **cross flow arrangement,** the true ΔTlm is calculated as :

ΔTlm for cross flow = $F_T \cdot \Delta Tlm$ for counter current flow, where F_T is a correction factor.

The heat transfer rate is given by Equation (3.93).

Heat transfer in condensation of single vapours :

The change from liquid to vapour state is known as vaporisation and that from vapour to liquid is known as condensation. In either case, the latent heats involved are identical. In the condensation of a pure vapour, it is necessary to remove the latent heat of vaporisation. Condensation is a convection process that involves a change of phase from vapour to liquid and it occurs whenever a saturated vapour comes into contact of a cold surface, for example, in surface condensers, heat transfer from the vapour to the surface takes place and the vapour gets condensed on the surface.

The process of condensation, which is the reverse of boiling, occurs by two distinct mechanisms and that too at very different rates of heat transfer. The two distinct mechanisms are :

(i) dropwise condensation and

(ii) filmwise condensation.

The condensing film coefficient depends upon the nature of surface and whether the surface, on which condensation occurs, is mounted vertically or horizontally.

For filmwise condensation on a vertical surface, the mean heat transfer coefficient is given by

$$h_m = 0.943 \left[\frac{\rho^2 g \lambda k^3}{\mu L \Delta T_f} \right]^{1/4} \qquad \ldots (3.94)$$

where
- h_m - mean heat transfer coefficient over the tube length
- L - tube length
- g - gravitational acceleration
- μ - liquid viscosity
- λ - latent heat of vaporisation
- k - thermal conductivity of liquid
- ΔT_f - temperature difference between vapour and metal

For filmwise condensation on a horizontal tube of outside diameter d_o, the mean heat transfer coefficient h_m is given as :

$$h_m = 0.725 \left[\frac{\rho^2 g \cdot \lambda k^3}{\mu \, d_o \, \Delta T_f} \right]^{1/4} \qquad \ldots (3.95)$$

Drop-wise Condensation :

When a saturated vapour comes into contact with a cold surface, it condenses and if condensate does not wet the surface, the droplets are formed on the surface. These droplets grow and ultimately fall from or fall down the surface under the influence of gravity leaving behind the bare metal surface on which further condensation takes place. The condensation occurring by this mechanism is known as drop-wise condensation.

Film-wise Condensation :

When a saturated vapour comes into contact with the cold surface, it condenses and if condensate wets the surface, it forms a continuous film of condensate through which heat must be transferred. The additional vapour is then required to condense into the liquid film rather than directly on the surface. The condensate ultimately flows down the surface under the influence of gravity. The condensation occurring by this mechanism is called as filmwise condensation.

In film-wise condensation, the film covering the surface acts as a resistance to heat transfer, while in drop-wise condensation, a large portion of the surface is directly exposed to the vapour. Because of this the heat transfer coefficients (hence the heat transfer rates) in drop-wise condensation are four to eight times larger than those for filmwise condensation.

Drop-wise condensation needs a physical preparation of surfaces which is very difficult and needs to be promoted by introducing an impurity into the vapour stream. This type of condensation is very unstable and also the design methods are not available. Because of these cited points, dropwise condensation is not common in industry. In general, smooth, clean surfaces seem to promote film-wise condensation and oily or greasy surfaces and presence of dirt on the surfaces, i.e., when impurities are present and surface is contaminated, seem to promote dropwise condensation.

Film-wise condensation is very common and reliable and therefore the condensing equipments in use are designed on the basis of film-wise condensation.

Condensers are widely used in chemical industry. For example, in the separation of the constituents of a liquid mixture by distillation, a condenser converts vapours from the top of the column into liquid distillate and reflux. In power plants the surface condensers are used for condensing steam from the exhaust of turbines into liquid. The home air conditioning unit makes a use of air cooled condenser for liquefication of refrigerant.

Effect of non-condensable gases :

If a non-condensable gas is also present, for example, air in the condensing vapours in a condenser because of say leakage it hinders the process of heat transfer. The non-condensable gas collects in the viscinity of condensate surface, and the condensing vapour must have to diffuse through the gas film. The presence of diffusion resistance into the process of condensation decreases the rate of condensation far below that for a pure material. Presence of air about 1% by volume can reduce the heat transfer coefficient by 60%

of its value for no air. Air vent is always provided on almost all the condensers to eliminate air in the system.

Difference between drop-wise and film-wise condensation :

Drop-wise condensation	Film-wise condensation
1. In drop-wise condensation the condensate (condensed liquid) does not wet the surface and collects in the form of droplets. These droplets grow for a while and then fall from the surface, leaving bare metal surface for further condensation.	1. In film-wise condensation the condensed liquid wets the surface and forms a continuous film of condensate through which heat transfer takes place. This condensate flows down under the action of gravity.
2. Heat transfer coefficients are very high as the heat does not have to flow through film by conduction.	2. Heat transfer coefficients are relatively very low since the heat does have to flow through a film by conduction.
3. Oily or greasy surfaces seem to tend towards drop-wise condensation.	3. Smooth, clean surfaces seem to tend towards film-wise condensation.
4. Drop-wise condensation is very difficult to achieve.	4. Film-wise condensation is easily obtainable.
5. Drop-wise condensation is unstable and difficult to maintain, uncommon and so not desired industrially.	5. Film-wise condensation is stable, easy, reliable, common and so desired industrially.
6. Methods for predicting the film coefficient are not available.	6. Methods for predicting the film coefficients are available.

Table 3.3 : Average values of film coefficients (h_m) for condensation of pure saturated vapour on horizontal tubes

Vapour	h_m in W/(m²·K)	Range of ΔT_f
Steam	10000 – 28000	1 – 11
Steam	18000 – 37000	4 – 37
Benzene	1400 – 2200	23 – 37
Methanol	2800 – 3400	8 – 16
Ethanol	1800 – 2600	6 – 22
Toluene	1100 – 1400	31 – 40

Heat transfer to boiling liquids :

The phenomena of boiling, opposite of condensation, is commonly encountered in the unit operations such as distillation and evaporation and steam generation. In almost all cases where the condensation is carried out, boiling apparatus associates it. In the chemical industry usually the boiling takes place either on a hot submerged surface, e.g., kettle reboiler or inside a vertical tube, e.g., vertical tube evaporator. In boiling practice, initially the vapour is formed in the form of bubbles and afterwards as a distinct vapour phase above the liquid interface.

Boiling is a convection process that involves a change in phase from liquid to vapour. Boiling may occur when a liquid is exposed to a solid surface maintained at a temperature higher than the saturation temperature of the liquid. In this case, the heat flux will depend upon the difference in temperature between the surface and the saturation temperature of the liquid. The rate of heat transfer from the solid surface to the liquid is given by

$$Q = h(T_w - T_s)$$

where T_w is the temperature of the surface and T_s is the saturation of the liquid and the difference $T_w - T_s$ is known as the excess temperature.

When heat is added to a liquid from a submerged solid surface then the boiling process is termed as pool boiling. (Pool boiling is the type of boiling in which the heating surface is surrounded by or submerged in a relatively large body of the liquid which is agitated by the motion of the bubbles and by natural convection currents.) If the bulk liquid temperature is less than the saturation temperature, the process is called as **subcooled** or **local boiling**. In this case, the bubbles formed at the surface eventually condense in the liquid. If the liquid temperature is equal to the saturation temperature, the boiling process is called as saturated or bulk boiling. *When heat is added to a liquid from a submerged surface and the liquid is maintained at saturation temperature, then the process is called as* **saturated pool boiling**. The process of boiling depends upon the nature of the surface, thermophysical properties of the liquid and vapour bubble dynamics. As the boiling process is complicated, general equations describing the process are not available.

In case of boiling accomplished by a hot submerged surface, the temperature of the liquid is the same as the boiling point of the liquid at pressure prevailing in the apparatus. Bubbles of vapour are formed at the heating surface, rise through the pool of liquid, and disengage from the surface of the liquid. Vapours accumulate in a vapour space above the liquid surface and finally the vapour from the vapour space is removed as fast as it is formed through a vapour outlet. This type of boiling is referred to as **pool boiling** of saturated liquid as the vapour leaving is in equilibrium with the liquid at its boiling temperature.

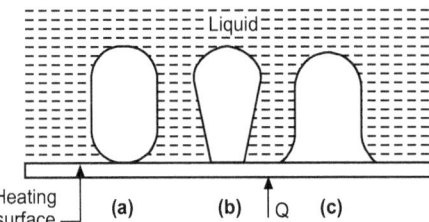

Fig. 3.12 : Effect of surface tension on bubble formation

Heat transfer by vaporisation in the absence of mechanical agitation is a combination of free convection and the additional convection generated by the rising stream of bubbles. The surface tension of liquid against the heating surface is the important factor in controlling the rate of bubble detachment is the another variable. If the surface tension of the liquid against the heating surface is large, the bubble tends to spread along the surface and blankets the surface rather than leaving from the surface to make a room for other bubbles. This is shown in Fig. 3.12 (c). If the surface tension is low, it tends to wet the surface and the bubble will pinch off easily and rises as shown in Fig. 3.12 (a). An example of a liquid having intermediate surface tension is shown in Fig. 3.12 (b).

Pool Boiling of Saturated Liquid :

Consider a heating element, e.g., a horizontal tube bundle submerged in a pool of boiling liquid and steam is condensing on the inside of tubes. Let $\frac{Q}{A}$ be the heat flux and $\Delta T = (T_w - T)$ be the difference in temperature between the tube wall and the boiling liquid. Start with a very small temperature drop and go on increasing ΔT (by increasing T_w and keeping T constant) in a stepwise manner. For each step, measure the value of $\frac{Q}{A}$ and ΔT till high values of ΔT are obtained.

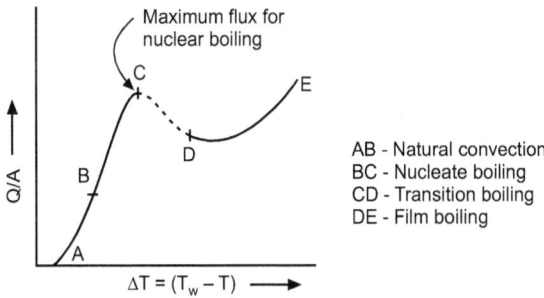

Fig. 3.13 : Heat flux v/s ΔT for water at 373 K (100 °C)

When we plot $\frac{Q}{A}$ v/s ΔT on logarithmic co-ordinates, we will get a curve as shown in Fig. 3.13.

The curve thus obtained can be divided into four segments : AB, BC, CD and DE. Under very small temperature drops, the rate of production of bubbles proceeds slowly and the mechanism is that of transfer of heat by free convection. Bubbles form on the surface, release from it, rise to the surface of the liquid and then disengaged into the vapour space and they are very few to disturb the natural convection currents set up in the liquid. This occurs over the segment AB wherein $\frac{Q}{A}$ is proportional to $\Delta T^{1.25}$. The segment BC of the curve is also a straight line with a slope greater than that for the segment AB. As the temperature of the surface is further increased (i.e., ΔT increased), the rate of bubble production is large and in turn it increases the velocity of the circulation currents in the mass of liquid and both the heat flux and heat transfer coefficient become greater than that in free convection. The temperature drop corresponding to point 'C' is called the critical temperature drop and the corresponding flux is called the peak flux (critical heat flux). The action occurring below the critical temperature drop over the segment BC is called **nucleate boiling** where vaporisation takes place directly from the surface. During **nucleate boiling** the most of the surface is in direct contact with the liquid, and only small portion is occupied by the bubbles. As the temperature drop is increased, more cite becomes active. Hence, more bubbles are generated, agitation of liquid is improved and both these lead to increase in the heat flux and the heat transfer coefficient.

Over the segment CD as the temperature drop increases, the flux decreases and reaches a minimum at point D. Point D is known as the **Leidenfrost point**. The boiling action over the segment CD is known as **transition boiling**. During this action the rate of bubble production is so large that they tend to coalesce on the heating surface forming a layer of insulating vapour. The layer is highly unstable and bubble issues from it in the form of jets. Further increase in ΔT increases the thickness of the insulating vapour layer which reduces the number of explosions in a given time and hence both heat flux and heat transfer coefficient decrease.

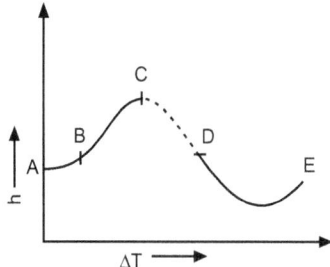

Fig. 3.14 : Heat transfer coefficient v/s ΔT

Beyond point D, the hot surface gets covered with a stable film of vapour through which heat transfer takes place by conduction and by radiation (at very high ΔT). As the ΔT increases, the heat flux rises slowly at first and then rapidly as the radiation heat transfer becomes important. Over the segment DE, vaporisation takes place through a blanketing film of gas/vapour and is known as **film boiling**. The relationship between ΔT and h (heat transfer coefficient) from A to E is shown in Fig. 3.14. In film boiling, the rate of heat transfer is low for a large temperature drop and the temperature drop is not utilised effectively. Hence, film boiling is not usually desired in commercial heat transfer equipment and the process equipments are generally designed for the temperature drop less than the critical temperature drop.

SOLVED EXAMPLES

Example 3.1 : *A hot fluid enters a double pipe heat exchanger at a temperature of 423 K (150 °C) and is to be cooled to 367 K (94°C) by a cold fluid entering at 311 K (38°C) and heated to 339 K (66°C). Shall they be directed in parallel or counter-current flow ?*

Solution : (I) For counter current flow :

$$T_{h_1}, 423 \text{ K} \xrightarrow{\text{Hot fluid}} 367 \text{ K}, T_{h_2}$$

$$T_{c_2}, 339 \text{ K} \xrightarrow{\text{Cold fluid}} 311 \text{ K}, T_{c_1}$$

Unit Operations – II   3.36   Convection

T_{h_1} – temperature of hot fluid at inlet = 423 K
T_{h_2} – temperature of hot fluid at outlet = 367 K
T_{c_1} – temperature of cold fluid at inlet = 311 K
T_{c_2} – temperature of cold fluid at outlet = 339 K

$\Delta T_2 = T_{h_2} - T_{c_1} = 367 - 311 = 56$ K
$\Delta T_1 = T_{h_1} - T_{c_2} = 423 - 339 = 84$ K

Log mean temperature difference = LMTD

$$\Delta Tlm = \frac{\Delta T_1 - \Delta T_2}{\ln(\Delta T_1/\Delta T_2)} = \frac{84 - 56}{\ln\left[\frac{84}{56}\right]} = 69 \text{ K}$$

LMTD (counter-current flow) = 69 K

(II) For parallel flow :

423 K $\xrightarrow{\text{hot fluid}}$ 367 K
311 K $\xrightarrow{\text{cold fluid}}$ 339 K

$\Delta T_2 = T_{h_2} - T_{c_2} = 367 - 339 = 28$ K
$\Delta T_1 = T_{h_1} - T_{c_1} = 423 - 311 = 112$ K

Log mean temperature difference for parallel flow :

$$\Delta Tlm = \frac{\Delta T_1 - \Delta T_2}{\ln\left(\frac{\Delta T_1}{\Delta T_2}\right)} = \frac{112 - 28}{\ln\left(\frac{112}{28}\right)}$$

LMTD (parallel flow) = 60.6 K

As LMTD for counter current flow is more than co-current / parallel flow, the fluids must be directed in counter current fashion.

Example 3.2 : *Thermic fluid flowing at a rate of 5000 kg/h is to be cooled from 423 K (150ºC) to 363 K (90ºC) by circulating water at a rate of 15000 kg/h. If the water is available at 303 K (30ºC), find the outlet temperature of water.*

Data : *Specific heat of thermic fluid = 2.72 kJ/(kg·K)*
Specific heat of water = 4.187 kJ/(kg·K)

Solution : Basis : 5000 kg/h of thermic fluid.

At steady state, the heat given out by thermic fluid is equal to the heat gained by circulating water.

$$Q = \dot{m}_t C_{p_t} (T_1 - T_2)$$
$$= \dot{m}_w C_{p_w} (t_2 - t_1)$$

where, $\dot{m}_t$ = 5000 kg/h (mass flow rate of thermic fluid)
C_{p_t} = 2.72 kJ/(kg·K)

$T_1 = T_{h_1}$ = Inlet temperature of thermic fluid
      = 423 K
$T_2 = T_{h_2}$ = Outlet temperature of thermic fluid
      = 363 K
$\dot{m}_w$ = 15000 kg/h (mass flow rate of circulating water)
C_{p_w} = 4.187 kJ/(kg·K)
$t_1 = T_{c_1}$ = Inlet temperature of water
      = 303 K
$t_2 = T_{c_2}$ = Outlet temperature of water = ?

$$\dot{m}_t C_{p_t} (T_1 - T_2) = \dot{m}_w C_{p_w} (t_2 - t_1)$$
$$5000 \times 2.72 \,(423 - 363) = 15000 \times 4.187 \,(t_2 - 303)$$
t_2 = Outlet temperature of water
    = **316 K (43°C)** ... **Ans.**

Example 3.3 : *Cold fluid is flowing through the heat exchanger at a rate of 15 m³/h. It enters the heat exchanger at 303 K [30°C] and leaves at 328 K [55°C]. The hot thermic fluid enters the heat exchanger at the rate of 21 m³/h at a temperature of 388 K [115°C]. Find out the area of heat transfer required assuming the flow is counter current and overall heat transfer coefficient be 3490 W/(m²·K).*

Data : *Density of cold fluid = 1000 kg/m³*
Density of thermic fluid = 950 kg/m³
Specific heat of cold fluid = 4.187 kJ/(kg·K)
Specific heat of thermic fluid = 2.93 kJ/(kg·K)

Solution : Basis : 21 m³/h of thermic fluid

$\dot{m}_t$ = mass flow rate of thermic fluid
   = 21 × ρ
   = 21 × 950
   = 19950 kg/h
(as mass flow rate = volumetric flow rate × density)
$\dot{m}_c$ = mass flow rate of the cold fluid
   = 15 × 1000
   = 15000 kg/h
T_1 = Inlet (initial) temperature of the thermic fluid = 388 K
T_2 = Outlet temperature of the thermic fluid, K
t_1 = Initial temperature of the cold fluid = 303 K
t_2 = Outlet temperature of the cold fluid = 328 K

At steady state, heat gained by the cold fluid is equal to heat given out by the thermic fluid.

$$Q = \dot{m}_t \cdot C_{p_t} (T_1 - T_2)$$
$$= \dot{m}_c \cdot C_{p_c} (t_2 - t_1)$$

∴ $19950 \times 2.93 \times (388 - T_2) = 15000 \times 4.187 (328 - 303)$

∴ $T_2 = 361.2 \text{ K } (88.2°C)$

For counter current flow :

$388 \text{ K} \xrightarrow{\text{Thermic fluid}} 361.2 \text{ K}$

$328 \text{ K} \xleftarrow{\text{Cold fluid}} 303 \text{ K}$

∴ $\Delta T_1 = 388 - 328 = 60 \text{ K}$

$\Delta T_2 = 361.2 - 303 = 58.2 \text{ K}$

∴ $\Delta T_{lm} = \text{LMTD}$

$$= \frac{(\Delta T_2 - \Delta T_1)}{\ln\left(\frac{\Delta T_2}{\Delta T_1}\right)} = \frac{60 - 58.2}{\ln\left(\frac{60}{58.2}\right)} = 59.1 \text{ K}$$

$Q = $ Rate of heat transfer

$= \dot{m}_t \cdot C_{p_t} (T_1 - T_2)$

$= 19950 \times 2.93 \times (388 - 361.2)$

$= 1566554 \text{ kJ/h}$

$= 435154 \text{ J/s} \equiv 435154 \text{ W}$

We know : $Q = \text{U.A. } \Delta T \text{ lm}$

where, $U = $ overall heat transfer coefficient

$= 3490 \text{ W/(m}^2 \cdot \text{K)}$

$A = $ area of heat transfer in m² = ?

∴ $\Delta T_{lm} = \text{LMTD} = 59.1 \text{ K}$

$Q = $ Rate of heat transfer

$= 435154 \text{ W}$

∴ $435154 = 3490 \times A \times 59.1$

$A = $ Area of heat transfer

$= \mathbf{2.11 \text{ m}^2}$ ... **Ans.**

Example 3.4 : *Calculate the heat transfer area of 1-2 heat exchanger from the following data : Inlet and outlet temperatures of hot fluid are 423 K (150°C) and 353 K (80°C) respectively. Inlet and outlet temperatures of cold fluid are 303 K (30°C) and 318 K (45°C) respectively.*

$\therefore$ Overall heat transfer coefficient = 4100 W/(m²·K)

Heat loss = 407 kW

L.M.T.D. correction factor = 0.84

Solution :   Q = U.A. F_T $\Delta T lm$

Q = rate of heat transfer

= 407 kW = 407 × 10³ W

U = Overall heat transfer coefficient

= 4100 W/(m²·K)

A = Area of heat transfer, m²

$\Delta T lm$ = log mean temperature difference for counter current flow

F_T = L.M.T.D. correction factor for 1-2 heat exchanger

= 0.84

423 K $\xrightarrow{\text{hot fluid}}$ 353 K

318 K $\xleftarrow{\text{cold fluid}}$ 303 K

ΔT_1 = 423 – 318 = 105 K

ΔT_2 = 353 – 303 = 50 K

$\Delta T lm$ = LMTD

$$= \frac{\Delta T_1 - \Delta T_2}{\ln\left(\frac{\Delta T_1}{\Delta T_2}\right)} = \frac{(105 - 50)}{\ln\left(\frac{105}{50}\right)}$$

= 74.13 K

Q = U.A. F_T · $\Delta T lm$

407 × 10³ = 4100 × A × 0.84 × 74.13

A = 1.594 m² ≃ 1.6 m²

Area of heat transfer = **1.6 m²**   ... **Ans.**

Example 3.5 : *Calculate the inside heat transfer coefficient for fluid flowing at a rate of 300 cm³/s through a 20 mm inside diameter tube of heat exchanger.*

Data : *Viscosity of flowing fluid = 0.8 (N.s)/m²*
Density of flowing fluid = 1.1 g/cm³
Specific heat of fluid = 1.26 kJ/(kg·K)
Thermal conductivity of fluid = 0.384 W/(m·K)
Viscosity at wall temperature = 1.0 (N.s)/m²
Length of heat exchanger = 5 m

Solution : Basis : 300 cm³/s of volumetric flow rate of fluid

$$\text{Volumetric flow rate} = 300 \text{ cm}^3/\text{s}$$
$$= 300 \times 10^{-6} \text{ m}^3/\text{s}$$
$$\text{Density of flowing fluid} = 1.1 \text{ g/cm}^3$$
$$\text{Density of flowing fluid} = 1100 \text{ kg/m}^3$$
$$\text{Mass flow rate of flowing fluid} = 300 \times 10^{-6} \times 1100 = 0.33 \text{ kg/s}$$
$$\text{Inside diameter of pipe} = D_i = 20 \text{ mm} = 0.02 \text{ m}$$
$$\text{Area of pipe (cross section)} = \pi/4 \, D_i^2$$
$$= \pi/4 \, (0.02)^2 = 3.14 \times 10^{-4} \text{ m}^2$$
$$\text{Velocity of flowing fluid} = \frac{\text{Volumetric flow rate}}{\text{Cross section area}}$$
$$= \frac{300 \times 10^{-6}}{3.14 \times 10^{-4}} = 0.955 \text{ m/s}$$
$$N_{Re} = \text{Reynold's number}$$
$$= \frac{D_i u \rho}{\mu}$$

where $D_i = 0.02$ m
$u = 0.955$ m/s
$\rho = 1100$ kg/m³
$\mu = 0.8$ (N.s)/m² = 0.8 kg/(m.s)

$$N_{Re} = \frac{0.02 \times 0.955 \times 1100}{0.8} = 26.26$$

As the Reynold's number is less than 2100, the flow is laminar.

$$N_{Pr} = \frac{C_p \mu}{k}$$

where, C_p = 1.26 kJ/(kg·K) = 1.26 × 10³ J/(kg·K)

μ = 0.8 kg/(m·s)

k = 0.384 W/(m·K)

$$N_{Pr} = \frac{1.26 \times 10^3 \times 0.8}{0.384} = 2625$$

$$N_{Re} \cdot N_{Pr} \cdot \frac{D}{L} = 26.26 \times 2625 \times \left(\frac{0.02}{5}\right) = 275.73$$

μ_w = 1.0 (N·s)/m² = 1.0 kg/(m·s)

∴ The empirical relation applicable is :

$$N_{Nu} = 1.86 \left[N_{Re} \cdot N_{Pr} \cdot \frac{D}{L}\right]^{1/3} \left[\frac{\mu}{\mu_w}\right]^{0.14}$$

$$N_{Nu} = 1.86 \left[(26.26)(2625) \times \frac{0.02}{5}\right]^{1/3} \times \left[\frac{0.8}{1.0}\right]^{0.14}$$

$$= 11.71$$

$$N_{Nu} = \frac{h_i D_i}{k}$$

where h_i – inside heat transfer coefficient

$$11.71 = \frac{h_i \times 0.02}{0.384}$$

h_i = **1225 W/(m²·K)**   ... **Ans.**

Example 3.6 : *Calculate the heat transfer coefficient for fluid flowing through a tube having inside diameter 40 mm at a rate of 5500 kg/h. Assume that fluid is being heated.*

Data : *Properties of fluid at mean bulk temperature :*

Viscosity of flowing fluid = 0.004 (N·s)/m²

Density of flowing fluid = 1.07 g/cm³

Specific heat of flowing fluid = 2.72 kJ/(kg·K)

Thermal conductivity of flowing fluid = 0.256 W/(m·K)

Make use of Dittus – Boelter equation.

Solution : Basis : 5500 kg/h of fluid flowing through tube

Mass flow rate = $\dot{m}$ = 5500 kg/h = $\frac{5500}{3600}$ = 1.53 kg/s

Density of fluid = ρ = 1.07 g/cm³ = 1070 kg/m³

Volumetric flow rate = $\dot{m}/\rho$ = $\frac{1.53}{1070}$ = 1.43 × 10⁻³ m³/s

Cross-sectional area of tube = $\frac{\pi}{4} D_i^2$

where $D_i = 40$ mm $= 0.04$ m

$$A = \frac{\pi}{4}(0.040)^2 = 1.256 \times 10^{-3} \, m^2$$

Velocity of flowing fluid $= \dfrac{1.43 \times 10^{-3}}{1.256 \times 10^{-3}} = 1.14$ m/s

Reynold's number $= N_{Re} = \dfrac{D_i u \rho}{\mu}$

where, D_i = inside diameter of pipe
$= 40$ mm $= 0.04$ m
$\rho = 1070$ kg/m³
$u = 1.14$ m/s
μ = Viscosity
$= 0.004$ (N·s)/m² $= 0.004$ kg/(m·s)

$$N_{Re} = \frac{0.04 \times 1.14 \times 1070}{0.004} = 12198$$

As N_{Re} is greater than 10000, the flow is turbulent.

The empirical relationship for turbulent flow, i.e., the Dittus–Boelter equation for heating is :

$$N_{Nu} = 0.023 \, (N_{Re})^{0.8} \, (N_{Pr})^{0.4}$$

$$N_{Pr} = \frac{C_p \cdot \mu}{k}$$

$C_p = 2.72$ kJ/(kg·K) $= 2.72 \times 10^3$ J/(kg·K)
$k = 0.256$ W/(m·K)
$\mu = 0.004$ kg/(m·s)

$$N_{Pr} = \frac{2.72 \times 10^3 \times 0.004}{0.256} = 42.5$$

$N_{Nu} = 0.023 \, (12198)^{0.8} \, (42.5)^{0.4} = 191.5$
N_{Nu} = Nusselt number

$$\frac{h_i \, D_i}{k} = 191.5$$

where, h_i = inside heat transfer coefficient
D_i = inside diameter of pipe
$= 0.04$ m
k = thermal conductivity of fluid
$= 0.256$ W/(m·K)

$$\frac{h_i \, (0.04)}{0.256} = 191.5$$

$h_i = \mathbf{1225.5 \; W/(m^2 \cdot K)}$ ... **Ans.**

Example 3.7 : *Calculate the overall heat transfer coefficient from the following data :*

Inside heat transfer coefficient = 5800 W/(m²·K)

Outside heat transfer coefficient = 1750 W/(m²·K)

Outside diameter of tube = 30 mm

Inside diameter of tube = 20 mm

Thermal conductivity of metal wall = 46.52 W/(m·K)

Solution : The equation to be used is :

$$\frac{1}{U} = \frac{1}{h_o} + \frac{1}{h_i} + \frac{1}{k/x}$$

where U = overall heat transfer coefficient

h_o = outside heat transfer coefficient

= 1750 W/(m²·K)

h_i = inside heat transfer coefficient

= 5800 W/(m²·K)

k = thermal conductivity of metal wall

= 46.52 W/(m·K)

x = thickness of metal wall of tube

= (O.D. − I.D.) / 2

= $\frac{(30-20)}{2}$ = 5 mm = 0.005 m

$$\frac{1}{U} = \frac{1}{1750} + \frac{1}{5800} + \frac{1}{\frac{46.52}{0.005}}$$

U = 1175 W/(m²·K)

Overall heat transfer coefficient = **1175 W/(m²·K)** ... **Ans.**

Example 3.8 : *A hot fluid enters a double pipe heat exchanger at a temperature of 423 K (150°C) and to be cooled to 363 K (90°C) by a cold fluid entering at 308 K (35°C) and heated to 338 K (65°C). Shall they be directed in parallel flow or counter current flow to have more rate of heat transfer ?*

Solution :

(I) Parallel flow arrangement :

423 K $\xrightarrow{\text{Hot fluid}}$ 363 K

308 K $\xleftarrow{\text{Cold fluid}}$ 338 K

$\Delta T_1 = T_{h_1} - T_{c_1}$ = 423 − 308 = 115 K

$\Delta T_2 = T_{h_2} - T_{c_2}$ = 363 − 338 = 25 K

LMTD for parallel flow $= \dfrac{\Delta T_1 - \Delta T_2}{\ln(\Delta T_1/\Delta T_2)}$

$= \dfrac{115 - 25}{\ln\left(\dfrac{115}{25}\right)} = 58.97 \text{ K}$

(II) Counter current flow arrangement :

423 K $\xrightarrow{\text{Hot fluid}}$ 363 K

338 K $\xleftarrow{\text{Cold fluid}}$ 308 K

$\Delta T_1 = T_{h_1} - T_{c_2} = 423 - 338 = 85 \text{ K}$

$\Delta T_2 = T_{h_2} - T_{c_1} = 363 - 308 = 55 \text{ K}$

LMTD for counter current flow $= \dfrac{\Delta T_1 - \Delta T_2}{\ln(\Delta T_1/\Delta T_2)}$

$= \dfrac{85 - 55}{\ln(85/55)} = 68.91 \text{ K}$

As LMTD for counter current flow is more than that for co-current / parallel flow, the fluids should be directed in counter current fashion. ... **Ans.**

Example 3.9 : *A cold fluid is flowing through a double pipe heat exchanger at a rate 15 m³/h. It enters at 303 K (30°C) and is to be heated to 328 K (55°C). Hot thermic fluid is available at the rate of 21 m³/h and at 383 K (110°C). Find out the mean temperature difference for co-current and counter-current type of flow.*

Data : *Sp. heat of thermic fluid = 2.72 kJ/(kg·K)*

Density of thermic fluid = 0.95 g/cm³.

Density of water = 1 g/cm³, Specific heat of water = 4.187 kJ/(kg·K)

Solution : 303 K $\xrightarrow{\text{Cold fluid}}$ 328 K   303 K $\xrightarrow{\text{Cold fluid}}$ 328 K

383 K $\xleftarrow{\text{Thermic fluid}}$ T₂ K   T₂ $\xleftarrow{\text{Thermic fluid}}$ 383 K

Co-current flow   Counter current flow

Mass flow rate of water (cold fluid) = Volumetric flow rate × density

$= 15 \times 1000$

$\dot{m}_c = 15000 \text{ kg/h}$

Mass flow rate of thermic fluid = Volumetric flow rate × density

$= 21 \times 950$

$\dot{m}_t = 19950 \text{ kg/h}$

Heat Balance :

$$\text{Heat lost by thermic fluid} = \text{Heat gained by cold fluid}$$

$$\dot{m}_t C_{p_t} (T_1 - T_2) = \dot{m}_c C_{p_c} (t_2 - t_1)$$

$T_1 = 383 \text{ K}, \quad t_2 = 328 \text{ K}, \quad t_1 = 303 \text{ K}$

$19950 \times 2.72 (383 - T_2) = 15000 \times 4.187 \times (328 - 303)$

∴ $T_2 = 354 \text{ K } (81°\text{ C})$

$$\text{LMTD for co-current flow} = \frac{\Delta T_1 - \Delta T_2}{\ln (\Delta T_1 / \Delta T_2)}$$

$\Delta T_1 = T_{h_1} - T_{c_1} = T_1 - t_1 = 383 - 303 = 80 \text{ K}$

$\Delta T_2 = T_2 - t_2 = 354 - 328 = 26 \text{ K}$

$$\text{LMTD for co-current flow} = \frac{\Delta T_1 - \Delta T_2}{\ln (\Delta T_1 / \Delta T_2)} = \frac{80 - 26}{\ln (80/26)} = 48 \text{ K}$$

LMTD for counter current flow :

$\Delta T_1 = T_1 - t_2 = 383 - 328 = 55 \text{ K}$

$\Delta T_2 = T_2 - t_1 = 354 - 303 = 51 \text{ K}$

$$\text{LMTD} = \frac{55 - 51}{\ln (55/51)} = 53 \text{ K}$$

LMTD for concurrent/co-current flow = **48 K**

LMTD for counter current flow = **53 K** ... **Ans.**

Example 3.10 : *Find out the overall heat transfer coefficient if :*

(i) *Inside and outside film heat transfer coefficients are 12 and 11600 W/(m²·K) respectively.*

(ii) *Inside and outside diameters are 25 mm and 29 mm respectively.*

(iii) *Thermal conductivity of metal = 34.9 W/(m·K).*

Solution : The relationship among U, h_o, h_i and k/x is

$$\frac{1}{U} = \frac{1}{h_i} + \frac{1}{h_o} + \frac{1}{k/x} \quad \ldots (1)$$

where h_i = Inside heat transfer coefficient = 12 W/(m²·K)

h_o = Outside heat transfer coefficient = 11600 W/(m²·K)

k = Thermal conductivity of pipe wall material = 34.9 W/(m·K)

D_i = Inside diameter of pipe = 25 mm = 0.025 m

D_o = Outside diameter of pipe = 29 mm = 0.029 m

x = Thickness of pipe wall

$x = \frac{D_o - D_i}{2} = \frac{29 - 25}{2} = 2 \text{ mm} = 0.002 \text{ m}$

Putting values in equation (1),

$$\frac{1}{U} = \frac{1}{12} + \frac{1}{11600} + \frac{1}{34.9/0.002}$$

$$\frac{1}{U} = 0.0835$$

$$U = 11.97 \text{ W/(m}^2\cdot\text{K)} \qquad \ldots \text{Ans.}$$

Example 3.11 : *Find the overall heat transfer coefficient from the following data :*

(i)   LMTD = 23 K for counter current flow

(ii)   Heat transfer area = 1.5 m²

(iii)   Rate of heat transfer = 116 kW

(iv)   Correction factor for LMTD = 0.85

Solution : The rate of heat transfer in this case is given by

$$Q = U.A. F_T \text{ (LMTD) for counter current flow}$$

where,   Q = rate of heat transfer = 116 kW = 116 × 10³ W

           A = Area of heat transfer = 1.5 m²

           F_T = correction factor for LMTD = 0.85

      LMTD = Log mean temperature difference for counter current flow = 23 K

           U = Heat transfer coefficient (overall) in W/(m²·K)

$$116 \times 10^3 = U \times 1.5 \times 0.85 \times 23$$

$$U = \frac{116 \times 10^3}{1.5 \times 0.85 \times 23}$$

$$= \textbf{3956 W/(m}^2\cdot\text{K)} \qquad \ldots \text{Ans.}$$

Example 3.12 : *Find the inside heat transfer coefficient using Sieder-Tate equation for turbulent flow.*

Data : *I.d. of tube = 20 mm, N_{Re} = 15745*

Viscosity of fluid at bulk mean temperature = 550 × 10⁻⁵ Pa·s

Viscosity of fluid at average wall temperature = 900 × 10⁻⁶ Pa·s

Prandtl number = 36, Thermal conductivity of fluid = k = 0.25 W/(m·K)

Solution : The Sieder-Tate equation is

$$\frac{h_i D_i}{k} = 0.023 \, (N_{Re})^{0.8} \, (N_{Pr})^{1/3} \left(\frac{\mu}{\mu_w}\right)^{0.14} \qquad \ldots (1)$$

where, $\left(\dfrac{\mu}{\mu_w}\right)^{0.14}$ = Sieder-Tate correction factor

N_{Re} = Reynolds number = 15745

N_{Pr} = Prandtl number = 36

h_i = inside heat transfer coefficient, W/(m²·K)

D_i = inside diameter of pipe = 20 mm = 0.002 m

k = Thermal conductivity of fluid = 0.25 W/(m·K)

μ = 550×10^{-6} Pa·s

μ_w = 900×10^{-6} Pa·s

Putting values in Equation (1),

$$\frac{h_i (0.02)}{0.25} = 0.023 \times (15745)^{0.8} (36)^{1/3} \times \left(\frac{550 \times 10^{-6}}{900 \times 10^{-6}}\right)^{0.14}$$

$$\frac{h_i (0.02)}{0.25} = 0.023 \times 2278.84 \times 3.3 \times 0.933$$

$$\frac{h_i (0.02)}{0.25} = 161.37$$

h_i = 2017

Inside heat transfer coefficient = **2017 W/(m²·K)** ... **Ans.**

Example 3.13 : *Water enters a two-fluid heat exchanger at 328 K and leaves at 358 K. Hot gases enter at 578 K and leave at 433 K. If the total heat transfer area is 500 m² and the overall heat transfer coefficient is 700 W/(m²·K), determine the total heat transferred for*

(i) *parallel flow and*

(ii) *counter current flow of the two fluids.*

Solution : **(I) Parallel flow**

578 K $\xrightarrow{\text{Hot gas}}$ 433 K

328 K $\xrightarrow{\text{Water}}$ 358 K

ΔT_1 = 578 − 328 = 250 K

ΔT_2 = 433 − 358 = 75 K

$$\Delta T_{lm} = \frac{250 - 75}{\ln\left(\frac{250}{75}\right)} = 145.35 \text{ K}$$

Q = Total heat transferred

= UA ΔT_{lm}

= 700 × 500 × 145.35

= **50.87 × 10³ kW** ... **Ans. (i)**

(II) Counter current flow

578 K $\xrightarrow{\text{Hot gas}}$ 433 K

358 K $\xleftarrow{\text{Water}}$ 328 K

$\Delta T_1 = 578 - 358 = 220$ K

$\Delta T_2 = 433 - 328 = 105$ K

$\Delta T_{lm} = \dfrac{220 - 105}{\ln\left(\dfrac{220}{105}\right)} = 155.5$ K

$Q = U.A. \Delta T_{lm}$
$= 700 \times 500 \times 155.5$
$= 54.42 \times 10^3$ kW ... Ans. (ii)

Example 3.14 : *Crude oil flows at the rate of 1000 kg/h through the inside pipe of a double pipe heat exchanger and is heated from 303 K (30ºC) to 363 K (90ºC). The heat is supplied by kerosene initially at 473 K (200ºC) flowing through the annular space. If the temperature of approach (minimum temperature difference) is 10 K, determine the heat transfer area for co-current flow and kerosene flow rate.*

C_p for crude oil $= 2.1$ kJ/(kg·K)
C_p for kerosene $= 2.51$ kJ/(kg·K)
$U_o = 465$ W/(m²·K)

Solution : Let T be the outlet temperature of kerosene.

Temperature of approach (minimum temperature difference) = 10 K

363 K $\xleftarrow{\text{Crude oil}}$ 303 K

T, K $\xleftarrow{\text{Kerosene}}$ 473 K

Hence, outlet temperature of kerosene is :

$363 + 10 = 373$ K

For co-current flow :

$\Delta T_1 = 473 - 303 = 170$ K

$\Delta T_2 = 373 - 363 = 10$ K

$\Delta T_{lm} = \dfrac{170 - 10}{\ln\left(\dfrac{170}{10}\right)} = 56.47$ K

$Q = U_o A_o \Delta T_{lm} = \dot{m}_c C_{pc} \Delta T_c$

where $U_o = 465$ W/(m²·K)

$\Delta T_{lm} = 56.47$ K

$$\begin{bmatrix}\text{Mass flow rate of} \\ \text{crude oil}\end{bmatrix} = \dot{m}_c = 1000 \text{ kg/h} = 0.278 \text{ kg/s}$$

$$C_{p_c} = 2.1 \text{ kJ/(kg·K)}$$
$$= 2.1 \times 10^3 \text{ J/(kg·K)}$$

$$A_o = \dot{m}_c C_{p_c} \Delta T_c / U_o \Delta T \text{lm} = \frac{0.278 \times 2.1 \times 10^3 \times (363 - 303)}{465 \times 56.47}$$
$$= 1.33 \text{ m}^2$$

$$\dot{m}_c C_{p_c} \Delta T_c = \dot{m}_k C_{p_k} \Delta T_k$$

where
$$C_{p_k} = 2.51 \text{ kJ/(kg·K)}$$
$$\dot{m}_c = 1000 \text{ kg/h}, \quad \Delta T_c = 60 \text{ K}$$
$$\dot{m}_k = \text{mass flow rate of kerosene}$$
$$\Delta T_k = 473 - 373 = 100 \text{ K}$$
$$\dot{m}_k = \frac{1000 \times 2.1 \times 60}{2.51 \times 100}$$
$$= \mathbf{502 \text{ kg/h}} \qquad \text{... Ans.}$$

Example 3.15 : *Methyl alcohol flowing in the inner pipe of a double pipe heat exchanger is cooled with water flowing in the outer pipe. The inside and outside diameters of the inner pipe are 26 mm and 35 mm respectively. The thermal conductivity of steel is 50 W/(m·K). The individual film coefficients and fouling factors are :*

Alcohol coefficients = 250 W/(m²·K)
Water coefficients = 500 W/(m²·K)
Inside fouling factor = 0.86 × 10⁻³ (m²·K)/W
Outside fouling factor = 1.7 × 10⁻³ (m²·K)/W

Calculate the overall coefficients based on the outside area of the inner pipe including dirt factors and excluding dirt factors.

Solution :

$$\text{Inside diameter} = D_i = 26 \text{ mm} = 0.026 \text{ m}$$
$$\text{Outside diameter} = D_o = 35 \text{ mm} = 0.035 \text{ m}$$
$$x_w = \frac{35 - 26}{2} = 4.5 \text{ mm} = 0.0045 \text{ m}$$
$$D_w = \text{log mean diameter}$$
$$= \frac{D_o - D_i}{\ln\left(\frac{D_o}{D_i}\right)}$$
$$= \frac{0.035 - 0.026}{\ln\left(\frac{0.035}{0.026}\right)} = 0.0303 \text{ m}$$

$$k \text{ for steel} = 50 \text{ W/(m·K)}$$

Overall heat transfer coefficient based on the outside area of inner pipe (U_o) is given by :

$$\frac{1}{U} = \frac{1}{h_o} + \frac{1}{h_i} \cdot \frac{D_o}{D_i} + \frac{x_w \cdot D_o}{k \cdot D_w} + Rd_o + Rd_i \left(\frac{D_o}{D_i}\right)$$

The above equation includes dirt factors.

$$\frac{1}{U_o} = \frac{1}{500} + \frac{0.035}{0.026} \times \frac{1}{250} + \frac{0.0045}{50} \times \frac{0.035}{0.0303} + 1.7 \times 10^{-3} + 0.86 \times 10^{-3} \left(\frac{0.035}{0.026}\right)$$

U_o (inclusive of dirt factors) = **96.65 W/(m²·K)** ... Ans.

U_o excluding dirt factors :

$$\frac{1}{U_o} = \frac{1}{h_o} + \frac{1}{h_i} \times \frac{D_o}{D_i} + \frac{x_w \cdot D_o}{k \cdot D_w}$$

$$\frac{1}{U_o} = \frac{1}{500} + \frac{1}{250} \cdot \left(\frac{0.035}{0.026}\right) + \frac{0.0045}{50} \left(\frac{0.035}{0.0303}\right)$$

$$U_o = 133.56 \text{ W/(m}^2\text{·K)}$$

U_o (excluding dirt factors) = **133.56 W/(m²·K)** ... Ans.

Example 3.16 : *Heat is transferred from one fluid to a second fluid across a heat transfer surface. If the heat transfer coefficients for the two fluids are 1.0 and 1.5 kW/(m²·K) respectively, the metal is 6 mm thick and the scale coefficient is equivalent to 850 W/(m²·K), calculate the overall heat transfer coefficient.*

Take thermal conductivity of metal as 20 W/(m·K).

Solution : $\dfrac{1}{U} = \dfrac{1}{h_o} + \dfrac{x_w}{k} + \dfrac{1}{h_i} + R_d$

where
- h_o = 1 kW/(m²·K) = 1000 W/(m²·K)
- h_i = 1.5 kW/(m²·K) = 1500 W/(m²·K)
- x_w = 6 mm = 0.006 m
- k = 20 W/(m·K)
- R_d = 1/850 (m²·K)/W

$$\frac{1}{U} = \frac{1}{1000} + \frac{0.006}{20} + \frac{1}{1500} + \frac{1}{850}$$

$$= 0.001 + 0.003 + 0.00118 + 0.00067 = 0.00315$$

∴ U = 317.5 W/(m²·K) = **0.318 kW/(m²·K)** ... Ans.

Example 3.17 : *27 t/h of pure isobutane is to be condensed at 332 K in a horizontal tubular heat exchanger using water as a cooling media. Water enters at 300 K and leaves the exchanger at 315 K. Calculate the log mean temperature difference, heat load, and mass flow rate of cooling water.*

Data : *Latent heat of vaporisation of isobutane is 286 kJ/kg and specific heat of water is 4.187 kJ/(kg·K).*

Solution :

Mass flow rate of isobutane $(\dot{m}_1)$ = 27 t/h
= 7.5 kg/s
λ for isobutane = 286 kJ/kg

$\therefore$ Heat load = Q = $\dot{m}_1 \lambda$
= 7.5 × 286
= 2145 kJ/s
= 2145 kW
= **2145 × 10³ W** ... Ans.

$Q = \dot{m}_2 C_{p_2} (t_2 - t_1)$

where $\dot{m}_2$ = ?, t_2 = 315 K, t_1 = 300 K
C_{p_2} = 4.187 kJ/(kg·K)

$2145 = \dot{m}_2 \times 4.187 \times (315 - 300)$

$\dot{m}_2$ = 34.15 kg/s

Mass flow rate of cooling water = **34.15 kg/s** ... Ans.

ΔTlm – log mean temperature difference

332 K $\xrightarrow{\text{Isobutane}}$ 332 K
300 K $\xrightarrow{\text{Water}}$ 315 K
ΔT_1 = 32 K, ΔT_2 = 17 K

$$\Delta Tlm = \frac{\Delta T_1 - \Delta T_2}{\ln\left(\frac{\Delta T_1}{\Delta T_2}\right)}$$

$$= \frac{(32 - 17)}{\ln\left(\frac{32}{17}\right)}$$

= **23.8 K (23.8°C)** ... Ans.

Ex. 3.18 : *Determine the heat transfer coefficient for water flowing in a tube of 16 mm diameter at a velocity of 3 m/s. The temperature of the tube is 297 K (24°C) and the water enters at 353 K (80°C) and leaves at 309 K (36°C). Use (i) the Dittus – Boelter equation and (ii) Sieder-Tate equation.*

Data : *Properties of water at 331 K (58°C) i.e. at arithmetic mean-bulk temperature are :*
ρ = 984.1 kg/m³, C_p = 4187 J/(kg·K), μ = 485 × 10⁻⁶ Pa·s, k = 0.657 W/(m·K)
Viscosity of water at 297 K (24°C), μ_w = 920 × 10⁻⁶ Pa·s

Solution : $N_{Re} = \dfrac{Du\rho}{\mu}$

where,
$D = 16$ mm $= 0.016$ m, $u = 3$ m/s
$\mu = 485 \times 10^{-6}$ Pa·s or (N·s)/m² $= 485 \times 10^{-6}$ kg/(m·s)
$\rho = 984.1$ kg/m³ at arithmetic mean bulk temperature

$$N_{Re} = \dfrac{0.016 \times 3 \times 984.1}{485 \times 10^{-6}} = 97395$$

$$N_{Pr} = \dfrac{C_p \mu}{k}$$

where
$k = 0.657$ W/(m·K)
$C_p = 4187$ J/(kg·K)

$$= \dfrac{4187 \times 485 \times 10^{-6}}{0.657} = 3.09$$

(i) The Dittus-Boelter equation for cooling is

$N_{Nu} = 0.023 \, (N_{Re})^{0.8} (N_{Pr})^{0.3}$

$\dfrac{hD}{k} = 0.023 \, (N_{Re})^{0.8} (N_{Pr})^{0.3}$

$h = 0.023 \times (N_{Re})^{0.8} (N_{Pr})^{0.3} \times \dfrac{k}{D}$

$h = 0.023 \, (97395)^{0.8} (3.09)^{0.3} \times \left(\dfrac{0.657}{0.016}\right)$

$h = \mathbf{12972.6\ W/(m^2 \cdot K)}$ ... **Ans.**

(ii) The Sieder-Tate equation is

$N_{Nu} = 0.023 \, (N_{Re})^{0.8} (N_{Pr})^{1/3} (\mu/\mu_w)^{0.14}$

$h = 0.023 \, (N_{Re})^{0.8} (N_{Pr})^{1/3} (\mu/\mu_w)^{0.14} (k/D)$

where $\mu = 485 \times 10^{-6}$ Pa·s, $\mu_w = 920 \times 10^{-6}$ Pa·s

$h = 0.023 \, (97395)^{0.8} (3.09)^{1/3} \left(\dfrac{485 \times 10^{-6}}{920 \times 10^{-6}}\right)^{0.14} \times \left(\dfrac{0.657}{0.016}\right)$

$= \mathbf{12267.7\ W/(m^2 \cdot K)}$ ... **Ans.**

Example 3.19 : *A heat exchanger is required to cool 20 kg/s of water from 360 K (87°C) to 340 K (67°C) by means of 25 kg/s of water entering at 300 K (27°C). If the overall coefficient of heat transfer is constant at 2000 W/(m²·K), calculate the surface area required in*

(a) *a counter current concentric tube exchanger, and*
(b) *a co-current flow concentric tube exchanger.*

Data : *Take C_p for water $= 4.187$ kJ/(kg·K)*

Solution : Mass flow rate of hot water ($\dot{m}_{hw}$) is 20 kg/s.

$$\text{Heat load} = Q = \dot{m}_{hw} \cdot C_p \cdot (T_1 - T_2)$$
$$= 20 \times 4.187 (360 - 340)$$
$$= 1674.8 \text{ kJ/s}$$
$$= 1674.8 \times 10^3 \text{ W}$$

Let t_2 be the cooling water outlet temperature.

$$Q = \dot{m}_{cw} C_p (t_2 - t_1)$$
$$1674.8 = 25 \times 4.187 (t_2 - 300)$$
$$t_2 = 316 \text{ K } (43^\circ \text{C})$$

(I) Counter current flow :

(360 K) $T_1 \longrightarrow T_2$ (340 K)

(316 K) $t_2 \longleftarrow t_1$ (300 K)

$$\Delta T_1 = T_1 - t_2 = 360 - 316 = 44 \text{ K}$$
$$\Delta T_2 = T_2 - t_1 = 340 - 300 = 40 \text{ K}$$
$$\Delta T_{lm} = (\Delta T_1 - \Delta T_2) / \ln(\Delta T_1 / \Delta T_2)$$
$$\Delta T_{lm} = \frac{(44 - 40)}{\ln(44/40)} = 41.9 \text{ K}$$

$$Q = U.A. \Delta T_{lm}$$
$$Q = 1674.8 \times 10^3 \text{ W}$$

Heat transfer area :

$$A = \frac{Q}{U \cdot \Delta T_{lm}}$$
$$= \frac{1674.8 \times 10^3}{2000 \times 41.9}$$
$$= \mathbf{19.98 \text{ m}^2} \qquad \ldots \text{Ans. (a)}$$

(II) Parallel / Co-current flow :

(360 K) $T_1 \longrightarrow T_2$ (340 K)

(300 K) $t_1 \longrightarrow t_2$ (316 K)

$$\Delta T_1 = 360 - 300 = 60 \text{ K}$$
$$\Delta T_2 = 340 - 316 = 24 \text{ K}$$

$$\Delta Tlm = \frac{\Delta T_1 - \Delta T_2}{\ln\left(\frac{\Delta T_1}{\Delta T_2}\right)}$$

$$= \frac{60 - 24}{\ln\left(\frac{60}{24}\right)}$$

$$= 39.3 \text{ K}$$

Heat transfer area :

$$A = \frac{Q}{U \, \Delta Tlm}$$

$$= \frac{1674.8 \times 10^3}{2000 \times 39.3}$$

$$= \mathbf{21.31 \text{ m}^2} \qquad \ldots \text{ Ans. (b)}$$

More heat transfer area is required for co-current heat exchanger.

Example 3.20 : *Fuel oil in a tank is to be heated from 288.5 K to 316 K by means of steam coil. The coil has a pour point below 288.5 K. This oil stands in the tank and circulates only by natural convection. Exhaust steam is used and it leaves the coil at atmospheric pressure but not cooled below 373 K. The film heat transfer coefficient for fuel oil is 18.26 and the heat transfer coefficient for condensing steam is 4070 W/(m²·K). The fouling factor for oily steam is 0.215 (m²·K)/W and for fuel oil is 0.123 (m²·K)/W. The coil is required to heat 2250 kg/h of fuel oil of specific heat 3.35 kJ/(kg·K). The inside diameter of pipe is 40 mm and the outside diameter is 48 mm. Calculate,*

(a) *the overall co-efficient of heat transfer,*

(b) *the heat transfer surface area.*

Solution :

Q = rate of heat transfer

$Q = \dot{m} \, C_p \, \Delta T$

where

$\dot{m}$ = 2250 kg/h
C_p = 3.35 kJ/(kg·K)
ΔT = (316 − 288.5) temperature drop for oil
Q = 2250 × 3.35 × (316 − 288.5)
   = 20.73 × 10⁴ kJ/h
   = 57578 J/s ≡ 57578 W
D_i = 40 mm = 0.04 m
D_o = 48 mm = 0.048 m

Metal wall resistance is neglected.

h_i (for steam) = 4070 W/(m²·K)

h_o (for oil) = 18.26 W/(m²·K)

R_{d_o} = 0.123 (m²·K)/W

R_{d_i} = 0.215 (m²·K)/W

U_o = overall coefficient based on outside diameter

$$\frac{1}{U_o} = \frac{1}{h_o} + \frac{1}{h_i}\frac{D_o}{D_i} + R_{d_o} + R_{d_i}\left[\frac{D_o}{D_i}\right]$$

$$\frac{1}{U_o} = \frac{1}{18.26} + \frac{1}{4070}\left(\frac{0.0480}{0.040}\right) + 0.123 + 0.215\left[\frac{0.0480}{0.040}\right]$$

U_o = 2.3 W/(m²·K)

Steam temperature is constant and is equal to 373 K

ΔT_1 = 373 − 288.5 = 84.5 K

ΔT_2 = 373 − 316 = 57 K

$$\Delta Tlm = \frac{\Delta T_1 - \Delta T_2}{\ln(\Delta T_1/\Delta T_2)}$$

$$= \frac{84.5 - 57}{\ln(84.5/57)}$$

= 69.85 K

$Q = U_o\, A_o\, \Delta Tlm$

A_o = heat transfer area in m²

$$A_o = \frac{Q}{U_o\, \Delta Tlm}$$

$$A_o = \frac{57578}{2.3 \times 69.85} = 358.4 \text{ m}^2$$

Heat transfer area = **358.4 m²** ... **Ans.**

Example 3.21 : *A heat exchanger is to be designed to heat 1720 kg/h of water from 293 K to 318 K with steam condensing on the outside surface of brass tubes of o.d. 25 mm and i.d. 22.5 mm and 4 m long. The water velocity is 1.02 m/s, find the number of tubes.*

$k_{tube\ material}$ = 111.65 W/(m·K)

Weight of steam condensed = 4500 kg/h

Latent heat of vaporization of water = 2230 kJ/kg

Temperature of steam = 383 K

Steam side film coefficient = 4650 W/(m²·K)

Physical properties of water at mean temperature are given as follows :

$$\rho = 995.7 \text{ kg/m}^3$$
$$C_p = 4.174 \text{ kJ/(kg·K)}$$
$$k = 0.617 \text{ W/(m·K)}$$

(kinematic viscosity) $\quad \nu = 0.659 \times 10^{-6} \text{ m}^2/\text{s}$

Solution :

Mass flow rate of water = $\dot{m}$ = 1720 kg/h

C_p of water = 4.174 kJ/(kg·K)

T_1 = Initial temperature of water = 293 K

T_2 = Final temperature of water = 318 K

Rate of heat transfer = Q

$$Q = \dot{m}\, C_p\, \Delta T$$
$$= 1720 \times 4.174\, (318 - 293)$$
$$Q = 179482 \text{ kJ/h} = 49856 \text{ J/s} \equiv 49856 \text{ W}$$

$$N_{Re} = \frac{D_i\, u\, \rho}{\mu} = \frac{D_i\, u}{\nu}$$

$\left(\text{as } \nu = \dfrac{\mu}{\rho}\right)\quad \nu$ – kinematic viscosity

$$N_{Re} = \frac{D_i\, u}{\nu}$$

where
D_i = 22.5 mm = 0.0225 m
u = 1.2 m/s
ν = 0.659 × 10⁻⁶ m²/s

$$N_{Re} = \frac{0.0225 \times 1.2}{0.659 \times 10^{-6}} = 40970$$

As N_{Re} > 10000, Dittus-Boelter equation is applicable.

C_p = 4.174 kJ/(kg·K)
= 4.174 × 10³ J/(kg·K)
ν = Kinematic viscosity of water

where
$$\mu = \text{Viscosity of water}$$
$$\nu = \mu/\rho$$
$$\mu = \nu \times \rho$$
$$= 0.659 \times 10^{-6} \times 995.7$$
$$= 0.656 \times 10^{-3} \text{ kg/(m·s)}$$
$$N_{Pr} = \text{Prandtl number}$$
$$= \frac{C_p \mu}{k}$$

where $k = 0.617$ W/(m·K)

$$\therefore \quad N_{Pr} = \frac{4.174 \times 10^3 \times 0.656 \times 10^{-3}}{0.617} = 4.44$$

The Dittus-Boelter equation for heating is :

$$N_{Nu} = 0.023 \, (N_{Re})^{0.8} (N_{Pr})^{0.4}$$
$$= 0.023 \, (40970)^{0.8} (4.44)^{0.4} = 204.5$$
$$N_{Nu} = \frac{h_i \, D_i}{k} = 204.5$$
$$h_i = 204.5 \times \frac{0.617}{0.0225} = 5607 \text{ W/(m}^2\text{·K)}$$
$$D_i = 22.5 \text{ mm} = 0.0225 \text{ m}$$
$$D_o = 25 \text{ mm} = 0.025 \text{ m}$$
$$D_w = \text{log mean diameter}$$
$$= \frac{D_o - D_i}{\ln D_o/D_i}$$
$$= \frac{0.025 - 0.0225}{\ln \frac{0.025}{0.0225}} = 0.0237 \text{ m}$$

U_o = overall heat transfer coefficient based on outside diameter

$$\frac{1}{U_o} = \frac{1}{h_o} + \frac{1}{h_i} \times \frac{D_o}{D_i} + \frac{x_w}{k} \frac{D_o}{D_w}$$

where
$$h_i = 5607 \text{ W/(m}^2\text{·K)}$$
$$h_o = 4650 \text{ W/(m}^2\text{·K)}$$
$$k = 111.65 \text{ W/(m·K)}$$

$$x_w = (D_o - D_i)/2$$

$$= \frac{0.025 - 0.0225}{2}$$

$$= 1.25 \times 10^{-3} \text{ m}$$

$$\frac{1}{U_o} = \frac{1}{4650} + \frac{1}{5607}\left[\frac{0.025}{0.0225}\right] + \frac{1.25 \times 10^{-3}}{111.65}\left[\frac{0.025}{0.0237}\right]$$

∴ $\quad U_o = 2353 \text{ W/(m}^2 \cdot \text{K)}$

Temperature of condensing steam = 373 K

$$\Delta T_1 = 373 - 293 = 90 \text{ K}$$

$$\Delta T_2 = 373 - 318 = 65 \text{ K}$$

$$\Delta T\text{lm} = \frac{90 - 65}{\ln 90/65} = 76.8 \text{ K}$$

$$Q = U_o A_o \Delta T\text{lm}$$

$$A_o = \frac{49856}{2353 \times 76.8} = 0.276 \text{ m}^2$$

$$A_o = n \pi D_o L$$

where $\quad$ n = no. of tubes

$$n = A_o/\pi D_o L$$

$$= \frac{0.276}{\pi \times 0.025 \times 4} = 0.88$$

$$\simeq 1$$

∴ No. of tubes required = **1** ... **Ans.**

Example 3.22 : *Estimate the average value of convective film coefficient on the inside surface of a tube of 50 mm i.d. meant for heating water. The mass flow rate of water is 25000 kg/h, which enters at temperature of 293 K (20ºC) and leaves at 333 K (60ºC). Calculate also the heat transferred per unit length of the tube if the wall temperature is 10 K above the bulk temperature of the fluid.*

Physical properties of water at the mean temperature of 313 K (40º C) are given below :

$$\rho = 992.2 \text{ kg/m}^3$$

$$k = 0.634 \text{ W/(m·K)}$$

$$\nu = 0.659 \times 10^{-6} \text{ m}^2/\text{s}$$

and $\quad N_{Pr} = 4.31$

Solution : Mass flow rate of water = 25000 kg/h

Density of water = 992.2 kg/m³

Volumetric flow rate of water = $\dfrac{25000}{992.2}$ = 25.2 m³/h

Inside diameter of tube = D_i = 50 mm = 0.050 m

Velocity of water = u = $\dfrac{25.2}{3600} \times \dfrac{1}{\dfrac{\pi}{4}(0.05)^2}$

= 3.56 m/s

$$N_{Re} = \dfrac{D_i u \rho}{\mu} = \dfrac{D_i u}{\nu} \quad (\text{as } \nu = \dfrac{\mu}{\rho})$$

ν = 0.659 × 10⁻⁶ m²/s

$N_{Re} = \dfrac{0.05 \times 3.56}{0.659 \times 10^{-6}}$ = 270106

N_{Re} > 10000, flow is in turbulent region for heat transfer

The Dittus-Boelter equation for heating is

$$\dfrac{h_i D_i}{k} = 0.023 \, (N_{Re})^{0.8} \, (N_{Pr})^{0.4}$$

$\dfrac{h_i \times 0.05}{0.634} = 0.023 \, (270106)^{0.8} (4.31)^{0.4}$

h_i = **11,584 W/(m²·K)** ... **Ans.**

$\begin{bmatrix}\text{Heat transfer per unit} \\ \text{length of tube}\end{bmatrix} = h_i \pi D_i \Delta T$

∴ Q/L = $h_i \pi D_i \Delta T$

ΔT = 10 K as the wall is at a temperature of 10 K above the bulk temperature of fluid.

Q/L = 11584 × π × 0.05 × 10

= 18,196 W/m = **18.2 kW/m** ... **Ans.**

Example 3.23 : *Water at 303 K (30°C) enters a 25 mm i.d. tube at the rate of 1200 litres per hour. Steam condenses on the outside surface of the tube, (28 mm o.d.) at a temperature of 393 K (120°C) and its film heat transfer coefficient may be taken as 5800 W/(m²·K). Find the length of tube required to heat the water to 343 K (70°C). Assume the thermal conductivity of metal wall as 950 W/(m·K) and of water as 0.63 W/(m·K). The average density and viscosity of water may be taken as 0.98 g/cm³ and 0.0006 (Pa·s) respectively.*

Solution : Water flow rate = 1200 l/h

density of water = 0.980 g/cm³ = 0.980 kg/l

$\dot{m}$ = Mass flow rate of water = 1200×0.98 = 1176 kg/h = 0.33 kg/s

$$N_{Re} = \frac{DG}{\mu}$$

$$= \frac{D_i}{\mu} (\dot{m}/A_i)$$

D_i = 25 mm = 0.025 m

μ = 0.0006 Pa·s = [(N·s)/m²]

= 0.0006 kg/(m·s)

$$N_{Re} = \frac{0.025}{0.0006} \times \frac{0.33}{\frac{\pi}{4}(0.025)^2} = 28011$$

$$N_{Pr} = \frac{C_p \mu}{k}$$

$$= \frac{4.187 \times 10^3 \times 0.0006}{0.63} = 4.0$$

N_{Re} > 10,000

The Dittus-Boelter equation for heating is :

$$\frac{h_i D_i}{k} = 0.023 (N_{Re})^{0.8} (N_{Pr})^{0.4}$$

$$h_i = 0.023 (28011)^{0.8} (4)^{0.4} \times \frac{0.63}{0.025}$$

h_i = 3646 W/(m²·K)

D_o = 28 mm = 0.028 m

D_i = 0.025 m

$$x_w = \frac{0.028 - 0.025}{2} = 0.0015 \text{ m}$$

$$D_w = \frac{0.028 - 0.025}{\ln\left(\frac{0.028}{0.025}\right)} = 0.0265 \text{ m}$$

$$x_w = \frac{0.028 - 0.025}{2} = 0.0015 \text{ m}$$

$$\frac{1}{U_o} = \frac{1}{h_o} + \frac{1}{h_i} \frac{D_o}{D_i} + \frac{x_w}{k} \cdot \frac{D_o}{D_w}$$

where k for metal wall = 50 W/(m·K)

$$\frac{1}{U_o} = \frac{1}{5800} + \frac{1}{3646} \times \frac{0.028}{0.025} + \frac{0.0015}{50} \times \frac{0.028}{0.0265}$$

U_o = 1956 W/(m²·K)

ΔT_1 = 393 − 303 = 90 K

ΔT_2 = 393 − 343 = 50 K

$$\Delta T lm = \frac{(90 - 50)}{\ln(90/50)}$$

= 68.05 K

Rate of heat transfer = Q

Q = $\dot{m}\, C_p\, \Delta T$

= 1176 × 4.187 (343 − 303)

= 196957 kJ/h

= 54710 J/s ≡ 54710 W

Heat transfer area = A_o in m²

Q = $U_o\, A_o\, \Delta T lm$

$$A_o = \frac{Q}{U_o\, \Delta T lm}$$

$$= \frac{54710}{1956 \times 68.05} = 0.411\ m^2$$

$A_o = \pi\, D_o\, L = 0.411\ m^2$

L = $0.411/\pi D_o$

$$= \frac{0.411}{\pi \times 0.028}$$

= 4.67 m

≃ **5 m**   ... **Ans.**

Example 3.24 : *An oil is cooled from 353 K (80°C) to 313 K (40°C) in an oil cooler. The inlet temperature of water is 303 K (30°C). Calculate the temperature of cooling water leaving the cooler and logarithmic mean temperature difference assuming flow to be counter current, if the mass flow rate of oil and water are 1.4 kg/s and 2.9 kg/s respectively.*

C_p for oil = 2.135 kJ/(kg·K)

C_p for water = 4.187 kJ/(kg·K)

Solution : At steady state, heat gained by water = heat given by oil

$$Q = \dot{m}_w C_{p_w} (t_2 - t_1) = \dot{m}_o C_{p_o} (T_1 - T_2)$$

$\dot{m}_w$ = mass flow rate of water = 2.9 kg/s

$\dot{m}_o$ = mass flow rate of oil = 1.4 kg/s

C_{p_w} = 4.187 kJ/(kg·K), C_{p_o} = 2.135 kJ/(kg·K)

t_2 = ?, t_1 = 303 K, T_1 = 353 K, T_2 = 313 K

$Q = 2.9 \times 4.187 (t_2 - 303) = 1.4 \times 2.135 (353 - 313)$

∴ $t_2 = 312.9$ K

Outlet temperature of water = **312.9 K (39.9°C)** ... **Ans.**

353 K $\xrightarrow{\text{oil}}$ 313 K

312.9 K $\xleftarrow{\text{water}}$ 303 K

ΔT_1 = 40.1 K, ΔT_2 = 10 K

ΔT_{lm} = $(\Delta T_2 - \Delta T_1)$ / ln $(\Delta T_2/\Delta T_1)$

= (40.1 – 10) / ln (40.1/10)

= **21.67 K (°C)**   ... **Ans.**

Example 3.25 : *Air is heated in an air heater from 303 K (30°C) to 383 K (110°C), and hot gases cool from 483 K (210° C) to 418 K (145°C). Calculate the log mean temperature difference between air and gas with the two fluids in (a) parallel flow, and (b) counter current flow.*

Solution : (a) Parallel flow :

303 K $\xrightarrow{\text{Air}}$ 383 K

483 K $\xrightarrow{\text{Hot gas}}$ 418 K

ΔT_1 = 483 – 303 = 180 K

ΔT_2 = 418 – 383 = 35 K

$\Delta T_{lm} = \dfrac{\Delta T_1 - \Delta T_2}{\ln(\Delta T_1/\Delta T_2)} = \dfrac{(180 - 35)}{\ln(180/35)}$

= **88.54 K**   ... **Ans. (a)**

(b) Counter current flow :

$$303 \text{ K} \xrightarrow{\text{Air}} 383 \text{ K}$$

$$418 \text{ K} \xleftarrow{\text{Hot gas}} 483 \text{ K}$$

$\Delta T_1 = 418 - 303 = 115 \text{ K}$

$\Delta T_2 = 483 - 383 = 100 \text{ K}$

$\Delta Tlm = \dfrac{(115 - 100)}{\ln(115/100)}$

$= 107.32 \text{ K } (107.32 °C)$ ... **Ans.**

Example 3.26 : *A cooling coil is incorporated in the reaction vessel of which contents are kept uniformly at temperature of 360 K by means of stirrer. The inlet and outlet temperatures of the cooling water are 280 K and 320 K respectively. Find out the outlet temperature of water if the length of cooling coil were increased 5 times the original assuming that overall heat transfer coefficient to be constant over the length of the tube and is independent of water temperature.*

Solution : $Q = U A \Delta Tlm$

I. For initial conditions :

$\Delta T_1 = 360 - 280 = 80 \text{ K}, \quad \Delta T_2 = 360 - 320 = 40 \text{ K}$

$Q_1 = \dot{m}_1 C_{p_1} (T_2 - T_1) = U_1 A_1 \Delta Tlm \text{ (I)}$

$\dot{m}_1 \times 4.187 \,(320 - 280) = U_1 A_1 \,[(80 - 40) \ln(80/20)]$

$\dot{m}_1 / U_1 A_1 = 0.345$

II. For final conditions :

$\dot{m}_2 = \dot{m}_1, \quad U_2 = U_1 \text{ and } A_2 = 5 A_1 \text{ (as } L_2 = 5 L_1)$

Let T be the outlet temperature in final conditions.

$Q_2 = \dot{m}_2 \times 4.187\,(T - 280) = U_2 A_2 \Delta Tlm \text{ (II)} = U_2 A_2 \left[\dfrac{(360 - 280) - (360 - T)}{\ln\left[\dfrac{360 - 280}{360 - T}\right]} \right]$

$\therefore \quad Q_2 = \dot{m}_1 \times 4.187\,(T - 280) = 5 U_1 A_1 \left[\dfrac{(360 - 280) - (360 - T)}{\ln\left(\dfrac{360 - 280}{360 - T}\right)} \right]$

Substituting $\dot{m}_1 / U_1 A_1 = 0.345$

$0.289\,(T - 280) = (T - 280) / [\ln 80/(360 - T)]$

$\ln [80/(360 - T)] = 3.467$

$\therefore \quad T = \mathbf{357.5 \text{ K}}$ ... **Ans.**

Example 3.27: *In an oil cooler, 60 g/s of hot oil enters a thin pipe of diameter of 25 mm. An equal mass of cooling water flows through the annular space between pipe and a large concentric pipe. The oil and water are flowing in a counter current fashion. Calculate the outlet temperature of water and area of heat transfer required from the following data:*

Inlet temperature of oil = 420 K

Outlet temperature of oil = 320 K

Inlet temperature of water = 290 K

Oil side heat transfer coefficient = 1.6 kW/(m²·K)

Water side heat transfer coefficient = 3.6 kW/(m²·K)

Specific heat of oil = 2.0 kJ/(kg·K)

Specific heat of water = 4.18 kJ/(kg·K)

Metal wall resistance and scale resistance may be neglected.

Solution:

$$\text{Mass flow rate of oil} = \dot{m}_o = 60 \text{ g/s}$$
$$= 6.0 \times 10^{-2} \text{ kg/s}$$

$$\text{Rate of heat flow} = Q = \dot{m}_o \, C_{p_o} (T_1 - T_2)$$
$$= 6.0 \times 10^{-2} \times 2.0 \times (420 - 320)$$
$$= 12 \text{ kJ/s}$$
$$= 12 \text{ kW}$$

The outlet temperature of water is given by

$$Q = \dot{m}_w \, C_{p_w} (t_2 - t_1)$$

where $\dot{m}_w = \dot{m}_o = 6.0 \times 10^{-2}$ kg/s

$t_1 = 290$ K, $C_{p_w} = 4.18$ kJ/(kg·K)

$$12 = 6.0 \times 10^{-2} \times 4.18 \times (t_2 - 290)$$
$$t_2 = 338 \text{ K}$$

Outlet temperature of water = **338 K**   … **Ans.**

Logarithmic mean temperature difference:

$$\Delta T_1 = 420 - 338 = 82 \text{ K}$$
$$\Delta T_2 = 320 - 290 = 30 \text{ K}$$
$$\Delta T_{lm} = \frac{82 - 30}{\ln(82/30)} = 51.7 \text{ K}$$

Overall heat transfer coefficient :

$$\frac{1}{U} = \frac{1}{h_o} + \frac{1}{h_i}$$

$$= \frac{1}{1.6} + \frac{1}{3.6} = 1.108 \text{ kW/(m}^2\cdot\text{K)} = 1108 \text{ W/(m}^2\cdot\text{K)}$$

Q = rate of heat flow = 12 kW = 12000 W

$= U A \Delta T lm$

$$A = \frac{Q}{U \cdot \Delta T lm}$$

$$= \frac{12000}{1108 \times 51.7}$$

$= \mathbf{0.210 \text{ m}^2}$ ... Ans.

To find the length of tube required, the following procedure may be adopted.

D_o = 25 mm = 0.025 m

$A = \pi D_o L$

$L = A/\pi D_o = 0.210 / (\pi \times 0.025)$

$= \mathbf{2.67 \text{ m}}$ ... Ans.

Example 3.28 : *Determine the heating surface of an economiser in which a primary (hot gases) and a secondary fluid (water) are in counter current flow using the following data :*

Mass flow rate of gas = 1.22 kg/s

Specific heat of gas = 1.045 kJ/(kg·K)

Inlet temperature of gas = 693 K (420 ºC)

Mass flow rate of water = 0.67 kg/s

Inlet temperature of water = 378 K (105 ºC)

Rate of heat transfer from hot gas to water = 270 kW

Heat transfer coefficient from gases to water (i.e. U) = 80 W/(m²·K)

Solution : For water : Rate of heat transfer = $Q = \dot{m}_w C_{p_w} (t_2 - t_1)$

Q = 270 kW = 270 × 10³ W = 270 kJ/s

∴ 270 = 0.67 × 4.187 (t_2 – 378)

t_2 = 474 K

For hot gas :

$Q = \dot{m}_h C_{p_h} (T_1 - T_2)$

270 = 1.22 × 1.045 (693 – T_2)

T_2 = 481.2 K

693 K $\xrightarrow{\text{Hot gas}}$ 481.2 K

474 K $\xleftarrow{\text{Water}}$ 378 K

$\Delta T_1 = 693 - 474 = 219$ K, $\Delta T_2 = 481.2 - 378 = 103.2$ K

$\Delta T lm = (219 - 103.2)/\ln(219/103.2) = 153.9$ K

$Q = U A \Delta T lm$

$A = Q/(U \cdot \Delta T lm) = \dfrac{270 \times 10^3}{80 \times 153.9} = 21.93$ m²

Heating surface of economiser = **21.93 m².** ... **Ans.**

Example 3.29 : *Water is to be heated from 298 K (25ºC) to 313 K (40ºC) at a rate of 30 kg/s. Hot water is available at 353 K (80ºC) at a rate of 24 kg/s for heating in a counter current exchanger. Calculate the required heat transfer area, if the overall heat transfer coefficient is 1220 W/(m²·K).*

Solution : At steady state : Heat gained by cold water = Heat removed from hot water

$$Q = \dot{m}_c C_{p_c} (t_2 - t_1) = \dot{m}_h C_{p_h} (T_1 - T_2)$$

$\dot{m}_c$ = mass flow rate of cold water = 30 kg/s

$\dot{m}_h$ = mass flow rate of hot water = 24 kg/s

$C_{p_c} = C_{p_h} = 4.187$ kJ/(kg·K)

$t_2 = 313$ K, $t_1 = 298$ K, $T_1 = 353$ K, $T_2 = ?$

$Q = 30 \times 4.187 \times (313 - 298) = 1884.15$ kJ/s

$= 1884.15 \times 10^3$ J/s $\equiv 1884.15 \times 10^3$ W

Q = Heat gained by cold water = Heat lost by hot water

$1884.15 = 24 \times 4.187 (353 - T_1)$

$T_1 = 334.2$ K

298 K $\xrightarrow{\text{Cold water}}$ 313 K

334.2 K $\xleftarrow{\text{Hot water}}$ 353 K

$\Delta T_1 = 353 - 313 = 40$ K, $\Delta T_2 = 334.2 - 298 = 36.2$ K

$\Delta T lm$ for counter current flow $= (40 - 36.2)/\ln(40/36.2)$

$= 38.1$ K

$Q = U A \Delta T lm$

$A = Q/U \cdot \Delta T lm = \dfrac{1884.15 \times 10^3}{1220 \times 38.1}$

$= 40.53$ m²

Heat transfer area required = **40.53 m²** ... **Ans.**

Example 3.30 : *Evaluate the inside heat transfer coefficient. Heavy oil flows at a rate of 0.5 kg/s through a tube of 19 mm inside diameter and is heated from 311 to 327 K by condensing steam at 373 K.*

Data : *Properties of oil at 319 K (mean/average oil temperature)*

k for oil $= 0.14$ W/(m·K)

C_p for oil $= 2.1$ kJ/(kg·K)

μ for oil $= 154$ (mN·s)/m²

μ at mean wall temperature (346 K) $= 87.0$ (mN·s)/m²

Length of tube $= 1.5$ m

Solution : Mass flow rate of oil $= \dot{m} = 0.5$ kg/s

Diameter of tube $= 19$ mm $= 0.019$ m

Mean temperature of oil $= (311 + 327)/2 = 319$ K

μ of oil at 319 K $= 154$ (mN·s)/m²

$= 154 \times 10^{-3}$ (N·s)/m² [i.e. kg/(m·s)]

Cross sectional area of tube $= \pi/4 \times (0.019)^2 = 2.835 \times 10^{-4}$ m²

$G =$ mass velocity $= \dot{m}/A = 0.5 / 2.835 \times 10^{-4} = 1763.67$ kg/(m²·s)

$$N_{Re} = \frac{D u \rho}{\mu} = \frac{DG}{\mu} = \frac{0.019 \times 1763.67}{154 \times 10^{-3}} = 217.6$$

As N_{Re} is less than 2100, the flow is laminar.

The Sieder-Tate equation for laminar flow is :

$$\frac{h_i D_i}{k} = 2.0 \left[\frac{\dot{m} C_p}{k L}\right]^{1/3} \left[\frac{\mu}{\mu_w}\right]^{0.14}$$

where $\dot{m} = 0.5$ kg/s, $L = 1.5$ m, $k = 0.14$ W/(m·K)

$\mu = 154 \times 10^{-3}$ kg/(m·s)

$\mu_w =$ viscosity at the mean wall temperature [(373 + 319)/2] i.e. at 346 K

$\mu_w = 87$ (mN·s)/m² $= 87 \times 10^{-3}$ (N·s)/m² $= 87 \times 10^{-3}$ kg/(m·s)

$C_p = 2.1$ kJ/(kg·K) $= 2.1 \times 10^3$ J/(kg·K)

$$\frac{h_i \times 0.019}{0.14} = 2 \left[\frac{0.5 \times 2.1 \times 10^3}{0.14 \times 1.5}\right]^{1/3} \left[\frac{154 \times 10^{-3}}{87 \times 10^{-3}}\right]^{0.14}$$

∴ $h_i = 265.33$ W/(m²·K)

Inside heat transfer coefficient $= \mathbf{265.33 \ W/(m^2 \cdot K)}$ ... **Ans.**

Example 3.31 : *Pure iso-butane vapours are to be condensed at 331.7 K in a horizontal tubular heat exchanger using water as a cooling media. Determine the inside film heat transfer coefficient based on the outside diameter of tube.*

Outside diameter of tube = 19 mm

Wall thickness of tube = 1.6 mm

Inlet temperature of water = 301 K

Outlet temperature of water = 315 K

Water flow rate through each tube = 0.217 kg/s

Solution :

$$\text{Water flow rate} = 0.217 \text{ kg/s}$$
$$\text{i.d. of tube} = (19.0 - 2 \times 1.6) = 15.7 \text{ mm} = 0.0157 \text{ m}$$
$$\text{Cross sectional area for flow} = \pi/4 \times (0.0157)^2 = 0.000194 \text{ m}^2$$
$$\text{Water velocity through tube} = u = \dot{m}/\rho \cdot A_i$$
$$= \frac{0.217}{1000 \times 0.000194} = 1.12 \text{ m/s}$$
$$T = (T_1 + T_2)/2 = (301 + 315)/2 = 308 \text{ K}$$

The inside heat transfer coefficient (for water) may be calculated by :

$$h_i = 1063 (1 + 0.00293 \times T) u^{0.8} / (d_i)^{0.20}$$
$$= 1063 (1 + 0.00293 \times 308) (1.12)^{0.8} / (0.0157)^{0.20}$$
$$= 5084 \text{ W/(m}^2 \cdot \text{K)}$$

Inside heat transfer coefficient based on outside diameter : h_{io}

$$h_{io} = h_i \left(\frac{D_i}{D_o}\right) = 5084 \times \left(\frac{0.0157}{0.019}\right)$$
$$= 4201 \text{ W/(m}^2 \cdot \text{K)}$$
$$= 4.20 \text{ kW/(m}^2 \cdot \text{K)} \quad \text{... Ans.}$$

Example 3.32 : *A heat exchanger is required to cool 20 kg/s of hot water from 360 K to 335 K by means of cold water flowing at 25 kg/s. Inlet temperature of cold water is 300 K. Overall heat transfer coefficient is 2 kW/(m²·K). Calculate the area of heat transfer required in (a) counter current flow heat exchanger and (b) in 1–2 pass heat exchanger (cold water flowing twice through heat exchanger).*

Data : *Specific heat of cold and hot water may be taken as 4.187 kJ/(kg·K) and LMTD correction factor = 0.94*

Solution :

$$\text{Heat load} = Q = \dot{m}_1 C_{p_1} (T_1 - T_2)$$

where $\dot{m}_1$ = 20 kg/s, C_{p_1} = 4.187 kJ/(kg·K)

T_1 = 360 K, T_2 = 335 K

Q = 20 × 4.187 × (360 – 335)

Q = 2093.5 kJ/s = 2093.5 kW

t_1 = inlet temperature of cold water = 300 K

t_2 = outlet temperature of cold water

$\dot{m}_2$ = mass flow rate of cold water = 25 kg/s

At steady state, heat given out by the hot water is equal to heat gained by the cold water.

∴ $Q = \dot{m}_2 C_{p_2} (t_2 - t_1)$

2093.5 = 25 × 4.187 (t_2 – 300)

t_2 = 320 K

I. Case (a):

360 K $\xrightarrow{\text{Hot water}}$ 335 K

320 K $\xleftarrow{\text{Cold water}}$ 300 K

ΔT_1 = 360 – 320 = 40 K

ΔT_2 = 335 – 300 = 35 K

ΔTlm for counter current flow = $\dfrac{(\Delta T_1 - \Delta T_2)}{\ln(\Delta T_1/\Delta T_2)}$

ΔTlm = (40 – 35) / ln (40/35) = 37.4 K

Q = U A ΔTlm

A = Q/U ΔTlm

where Q = 2090 kW = 2090 × 10³ W

U = 2.0 kW/(m²·K) = 2 × 10³ W/(m²·K)

∴ $A = \dfrac{2090 \times 10^3}{2.0 \times 10^3 \times 37.4}$

= **27.94 m²** ... **Ans. (a)**

II. Case (b):

ΔTlm = 37.4 K

LMTD correction factor = F_T = 0.94

Q = U A F_T ΔTlm

$A = \dfrac{Q}{U \cdot F_T \cdot \Delta Tlm}$

$A = \dfrac{2090 \times 10^3}{2.0 \times 10^3 \times 0.94 \times 37.4}$

= **29.73 m²** ... **Ans. (b)**

Example 3.33 : *It is desired to warm 0.90 kg/s of air flowing through tubes from 283 to 366 K with the help of flue gas entering at 700 K and leaving at 366 K in counter current fashion. Calculate heat transfer area of heat exchange equipment.*

Data : *Pipe diameter = 12 mm*

$\quad$ *Mass flow velocity = G = 19.9 kg/(m²·s)*

$\quad$ *k for air 324.5 K = 0.029 W/(m·K)*

$\quad$ *μ for air 324.5 K = 0.0198 (mN·s)/m²*

$\quad$ *C_p for air = 1.0 kJ/(kg·K)*

$\quad$ *h_o = 232 W/(m²·K)*

Solution : $\dot{m}_{air} = 0.90$ kg/s, $\quad D_i = 12$ mm $= 0.012$ m

Mean temperature of air $= (283 + 366)/2 = 324.5$ K

$G = 19.9$ kg/(m²·s)

$\mu = 0.0198$ (mN·s)/m² $= 1.98 \times 10^{-5}$ (N·s)/m² $= 1.98 \times 10^{-5}$ kg/(m·s)

$$N_{Re} = \frac{D_i \, G}{\mu}$$

$$= \frac{0.012 \times 19.9}{1.98 \times 10^{-5}} = 1.206 \times 10^4$$

$C_p = 1.0$ kJ/(kg·K) $= 1.0 \times 10^3$ J/(kg·K)

$k = 0.029$ W/(m·K)

$N_{Pr} = C_p \mu / k$

$$= \frac{1.0 \times 10^3 \times 1.98 \times 10^{-5}}{0.029} = 0.683$$

The Dittus-Boelter equation for heating is

$$\frac{h_i \, D_i}{k} = 0.023 \, (N_{Re})^{0.8} \, (N_{Pr})^{0.4}$$

$$\frac{h_i \times 0.012}{0.029} = 0.023 \, (1.206 \times 10^4)^{0.8} \, (0.683)^{0.4}$$

$h_i = 87.85$ W/(m²·K)

$h_o = 232$ W/(m²·K)

The overall heat transfer coefficient is given by

$$\frac{1}{U} = \frac{1}{h_i} + \frac{1}{h_o}$$

$$= \frac{1}{87.85} + \frac{1}{232} = 0.0114 + 0.0043 = 0.0157$$

$U = 63.7 \text{ W/(m}^2\cdot\text{K)}$

$Q = (\dot{m} \times C_p)_{air} (T_2 - T_1)$

$Q = 0.9 \times 1.0 \times (366 - 283) = 74.7 \text{ kJ/s}$

$= 74.7 \times 10^3 \text{ J/s} \equiv 74.7 \times 10^3 \text{ W}$

283 K $\xrightarrow{\text{Air}}$ 366 K

366 K $\xleftarrow{\text{Flue gas}}$ 700 K

$\Delta T_1 = 700 - 366 = 334 \text{ K}$

$\Delta T_2 = 366 - 283 = 83 \text{ K}$

$\Delta Tlm = \dfrac{(\Delta T_1 - \Delta T_2)}{\ln(\Delta T_1/\Delta T_2)}$

$= \dfrac{(334 - 83)}{\ln(334/83)} = 180 \text{ K}$

$Q = U A \Delta Tlm$

$A = Q/U \cdot \Delta Tlm$

$= 74.7 \times 10^3 / (63.7 \times 180)$

$= \mathbf{6.52 \text{ m}^2}$ ... **Ans.**

Ex. 3.34 : *A light motor oil is to be heated from 338.5 K (65.5°C) to 394.1 K (121.1°C). The pipe wall is at 449.7 K (176.7°C). A light motor oil flows through a 10 mm pipe, 5 m long at a rate of 41 kg/h. Calculate the heat transfer coefficient using the following data :*

Data : *Properties of oil at the average bulk temperature are :*

$C_p = 2.01 \text{ kJ/(kg·K)}, \quad k = 0.142 \text{ W/(m·K)}$

$\mu = 4.65 \times 10^{-3} \text{ kg/(m·s)}$

Viscosity of oil at the wall temperature $= \mu_w = 1.37 \times 10^{-3} \text{ kg/(m·s)}$

Solution : Mass flow rate of oil = 41 kg/h = 0.0114 kg/s

$D_i = 10 \text{ mm} = 0.01 \text{ m}$

Area of pipe $= \pi/4 \; D_i^2 = \pi/4 \; (0.01)^2 = 7.85 \times 10^{-5} \text{ m}^2$

G = mass velocity of oil $= \dfrac{0.0114}{7.85 \times 10^{-6}} = 145.15 \text{ kg/(m}^2\cdot\text{s)}$

$N_{Re} = \dfrac{D_i G}{\mu} = \dfrac{0.01 \times 145.15}{4.65 \times 10^{-3}}$

$= 312.15$

As N_{Re} is less than 2100, flow is laminar.

The Sieder-Tate equation for laminar flow is

$$\frac{hD}{k} = 2\left[\frac{\dot{m} C_p}{kL}\right]^{1/3} \left[\frac{\mu}{\mu_w}\right]^{0.14}$$

where $k = 0.142$ W/(m·K), $\dot{m} = 0.0114$ kg/s
 $L = 5$ m, $C_p = 2.01 \times 10^3$ J/(kg·K)
 $\mu = 4.65 \times 10^{-3}$ kg/(m·s), $\mu_w = 1.37 \times 10^{-3}$ kg/(m·s)
 $D = 0.01$ m

$$\frac{h \times 0.01}{0.142} = 2\left[\frac{0.0114 \times 2.01 \times 10^3}{0.142 \times 5}\right]^{1/3} \left[\frac{4.65 \times 10^{-3}}{1.37 \times 10^{-3}}\right]^{0.14}$$

$h \times 0.0704 = 7.56$
$h = 107.4$ W/(m²·K)

Film heat transfer coefficient $= \mathbf{107.4}$ **W/(m²·K)** ... **Ans.**

Example 3.35 : *Ethylene glycol at 273 K enters 40 mm diameter pipe with a velocity of 5 m/s. The tube wall is maintained at a temperature of 353 K. Calculate the heat transfer coefficient using Sieder-Tate equation.*

Data : *Exit temperature is 313 K.*

Properties of ethylene glycol at 293 K are as follows :

$\rho = 1117$ kg/m³, $C_p = 2.39$ kJ/(kg·K), $\nu = 19.18 \times 10^{-6}$ m²/s
$k = 0.249$ W/(m·K)
μ_w = viscosity at 353 K = 3.21×10^{-3} kg/(m·s)

Solution : u = velocity of glycol through pipe = 5 m/s
D_i = 40 mm = 0.04 m
ρ = 1117 kg/m³
$\nu = 19.18 \times 10^{-6}$ m²/s = μ/ρ

$$N_{Re} = \frac{Du\rho}{\mu} = \frac{Du}{\mu/\rho} = \frac{0.04 \times 5}{19.18 \times 10^{-6}} = 10427.5$$

$N_{Pr} = 204$

μ = Viscosity at average temperature of 293 K
 $= \nu \times \rho = 19.18 \times 10^{-6} \times 1117 = 0.0214$ kg/(m·s)

Average temperature of glycol $= \dfrac{273 + 313}{2} = 293$ K

At 293 K, we have :

$$\mu = 0.0214 \text{ kg/(m·s)}$$
$$k = 0.249 \text{ W/(m·K)}$$
$$C_p = 2.39 \text{ kJ/(kg·K)} = 2.39 \times 10^{-3} \text{ J/(kg·K)}$$
$$N_{Pr} = \frac{C_p \mu}{k} = \frac{2.39 \times 10^{-3} \times 0.0214}{0.249} = 205.4$$
$$N_{Nu} = 0.023 \, (N_{Re})^{0.8} (N_{Pr})^{1/3} (\mu/\mu_w)^{0.14}$$
$$N_{Nu} = 0.023 \, (10427.5)^{0.8} (205.4)^{1/3} \left(\frac{0.0214}{3.21 \times 10^{-3}}\right)^{0.14}$$
$$= 290.06$$
$$\frac{h_i D_i}{k} = 290.06$$
$$h_i = 290.06 \times \frac{k}{D_i} = 290.06 \times \frac{0.249}{0.04}$$
$$= \mathbf{1805.6 \ W/(m^2 \cdot K)} \quad \ldots \text{Ans.}$$

Example 3.36 : *A vertical plate, 30 by 30 cm, is exposed to steam at atmospheric pressure. The plate is at 371 K (98ºC). Calculate the mean heat transfer coefficient and the heat transfer rate and mass of steam condensed per hour.*

Data : *Properties of condensate at the film temperature are :*
$\rho = 960 \text{ kg/m}^3$, $\mu = 2.82 \times 10^{-4} \text{ kg/(m·s)}$, $k = 0.68 \text{ W/(m·K)}$
$\lambda = 2225 \text{ kJ/kg}$, *Saturation temperature of steam* $= 373 \text{ K } (100º \text{ C})$.
Assume that condensate film is laminar.

Solution :
$$\rho = 960 \text{ kg/m}^3, \ \lambda = 2225 \times 10^3 \text{ J/kg}, \ L = 0.3 \text{ m}$$
$$\Delta T = 373 - 371 = 2 \text{ K}$$
$$\mu = 2.82 \times 10^{-4} \text{ kg/(m·s)}, \ k = 0.68 \text{ W/(m·K)}$$
$$g = 9.81 \text{ m/s}^2$$
$$h_m = 0.943 \left[\frac{\rho^2 g \lambda k^3}{L \mu (\Delta T)}\right]^{1/4}$$
$$\therefore \quad h_m = 0.943 \left[\frac{(960)^2 \times 9.81 \times 2225 \times 10^3 \times (0.68)^3}{(0.3)(2.82 \times 10^{-4})(2)}\right]^{1/4}$$
$$= 13150 \text{ W/(m}^2\text{·K)}$$

The heat transfer rate is :
$$Q = h_m A (T_{sat} - T_w)$$
$$= 13150 \times 0.3 \times 0.3 \, (373 - 371) = 2367 \text{ W}$$

Mass flow of condensate $= \dfrac{Q}{\lambda} = \dfrac{2367}{2225 \times 10^3}$

$= 1.05 \times 10^{-3}$ kg/s

$= \mathbf{3.78\ kg/h}$ ... **Ans.**

Example 3.37 : *Dry steam at 373 K (100°C) condenses on the outside surface of a horizontal pipe of 25 mm O.D. The pipe surface is maintained at 357 K (84°C) by circulating water through it. Determine mean heat transfer coefficient, heat transfer per unit length of pipe and condensate rate per unit length of pipe.*

Data : *The properties of condensate at the film temperature of 350 K are :*

$\mu = 306 \times 10^{-6}$ N·s/m², $k = 0.668$ W/(m·K), $\rho = 974$ kg/m³, $\lambda = 2225$ kJ/kg

Solution : h_m = mean heat transfer coefficient

$\rho = 974$ kg/m³, $\lambda = 2225 \times 10^3$ J/kg, $k = 0.668$ W/(m·K)

$\mu = 306 \times 10^{-6}$ N·s/m², $g = 9.81$ m/s²

$h_m = 0.725 \left[\dfrac{\rho^2 g \lambda k^3}{\mu\, d_o\, \Delta T_f} \right]^{1/4}$

$h_m = 0.725 \left[\dfrac{(974)^2 \times 9.81 \times 2225 \times 10^3 \times (0.668)^3}{306 \times 10^{-6} \times 0.025 \times 16} \right]^{1/4}$

$= \mathbf{10864\ W/(m^2 \cdot K)}$ ... **Ans.**

The heat transfer per unit length is

$Q/L = h_m \pi d_o (T_{sat} - T_s)$

$= 10864 \times \pi \times 0.025\, (373 - 357) = \mathbf{13652\ W/m}$ ... **Ans.**

The mass flow rate of the condensate per unit length is

$= 13652/2225 \times 10^3$

$= 6.13 \times 10^{-3}$ kg/s $= \mathbf{22.1\ kg/h}$ ... **Ans.**

EXERCISES

1. Fill in the blanks :

(a) Heat transfer in fluids occurs by mechanism known as ....
    Ans. convection

(b) Heat transfer from hot fluid to cold fluid in heat exchange equipment takes place by conduction and .... mode. **Ans.** convection

(c) Overall heat transfer coefficient has .... units in SI system. **Ans.** W/(m²·K)

(d) When hot and cold fluid flow in same direction in heat exchanger then flow is called .... flow. **Ans.** parallel / co-current

(e) When hot and cold fluid flow in opposite direction in heat exchanger then flow is called as .... flow. **Ans.** counter current

(f) Film heat transfer coefficients are higher for .... condensation than for filmwise condensation. **Ans.** dropwise

(g) In case of .... boiling, vaporisation takes place directly from the surface.
Ans. nucleate

(h) SI unit of film heat transfer coefficient is .... **Ans.** W/(m²·K)

(i) The dirt factor / fouling factor has .... unit in SI units. **Ans.** (m²·K)/W

(j) The ratio of $C_p \cdot \mu$ to k is known as .... number. **Ans.** Nusselt

(k) Thermal resistance in case of convection heat transfer has SI units of ....
Ans. (m²·K)/W

(l) In forced convection, liquid viscosity effect (for viscous liquids) is taken into account in case of .... equation. **Ans.** Sieder-Tate

2. Give Dittus-Boelter equation for turbulent flow for heating.

3. Write down Dittus-Boelter equation for turbulent flow in case of cooling.

4. Give the Sieder-Tate equation for calculation of film coefficient in case of laminar flow.

5. Give Sieder-Tate equation for calculation of film coefficient in case of turbulent flow.

6. What do you mean by film heat transfer coefficient ?

7. For double pipe heat exchanger, give equivalent diameter in terms of D_1 and D_2, where D_1 is the outside diameter of inside pipe and D_2 is inside diameter of outside pipe.

8. What do you mean by natural convection ? Give example of heat transfer by natural convection.

9. Define forced convection and give suitable example of it.

10. Compare natural convection with forced convection (Three points).

11. Compare parallel flow with counter current flow in heat exchangers (Three points).

12. Define drop-wise condensation.

13. Compare drop-wise condensation with film-wise condensation (Three points).

14. Define co-current and counter current flow with neat sketches.

15. State the relationship between overall heat transfer coefficient and individual heat transfer coefficients.

16. Write the relationship between U and h_i, h_o, x_w/k and R_d.

17. Explain in brief heat transfer to boiling liquid.
18. Derive the relationship Q = UA ΔTlm.
19. Write in brief on dirt factor / fouling factor with respect to heat transfer.
20. State various resistances in series when heat flows from one fluid to another through a solid wall in heat exchange equipment.

    (**Ans.** Resistances are : hot fluid film resistance, solid wall resistance, cold fluid film resistance and dirt or fouling resistances.)
21. State different types of flow arrangement in heat exchanger.
22. What do you mean by counter current heat exchanger and cross flow heat exchanger ?
23. Define the terms nucleate boiling and film boiling.
24. Give physical significance of

    (1) Reynolds number (2) Nusselt number and (3) Prandtl number.

□□□

CHAPTER FOUR

RADIATION

Heat transfer by radiation usually takes place simultaneously with heat transfer by convection and conduction. The heat transfer by radiation is of much more importance at high temperature levels as compared to the other two mechanisms. Direct fired kettles, electric heaters, steam boilers, rotary kiln, etc. are the examples of chemical process equipments where radiation is a major energy transfer mechanism.

Radiation : It refers to the transport of energy through space by electromagnetic waves.

It depends upon the electromagnetic waves as a means for transfer of energy from a source to a receiver.

Radiant energy is of the same nature as the ordinary visible light. It travels in the straight lines and it may be reflected from a surface. The electromagnetic waves with wavelength ranging from 0.50 to 50 μm (microns, 1 μm = 10^{-6} m) are of importance to radiant-heat transfer. Radiation of a single wavelength is called as monochromatic. Thermal radiation is the energy emitted by a body due to its temperature and we restrict our discussion to this type of radiation.

Typical examples of heat transfer by radiation :
(i) Transfer of heat from the sun to the earth.
(ii) Heat loss from an unlagged steam pipe.
(iii) Use of energy from the sun in solar heaters.
(iv) Heating of a cold room by a radiant electric heater.

Unlike conduction and convection, radiation heat transfer does not require an intervening medium (solid or liquid) and heat can be transmitted by radiation mode across an absolute vacuum.

Radiation is the only significant mode of energy/heat transfer when no medium is present (e.g., the heat leakage through the evacuated walls of a thermos flask).

Absorptivity, Reflectivity and Transmissivity :

Any substance receives and gives off/emits energy in the form of electromagnetic waves. When energy emitted by a heated body falls on a second body (i.e., thermal radiation falling on a body), it will be partly absorbed, partly reflected and partly transmitted. It is only the absorbed energy that appears as a heat in the body and this transformation is quantitative.

The proportions of the incident energy that are absorbed, reflected and transmitted depend mainly on the characteristics of a receiver and the temperature of the receiver.

The fraction of the incident radiation on a body that is absorbed by the body is known as the **absorptivity** and may be denoted by the letter **'a'**.

The fraction of the incident radiation on a body that is reflected by the body is known as the **reflectivity** and may be denoted by the letter **'r'**.

Fig. 4.1 : Reflection, absorption and transmission of radiation

The fraction of the incident radiation on a body that is transmitted through the body is known as the **transmissivity** and may be denoted by the letter 'τ'. The energy balance about a body (a receiver) on which the total incident energy falling is unity (i.e., the sum of these fractions is unity) is given as :

$$a + r + \tau = 1.0 \qquad \ldots (4.1)$$

A majority of engineering materials are opaque (i.e., for which the amount transmitted is very negligible) and in such cases Equation (4.1) simplifies to :

$$a + r = 1.0 \quad \ldots \text{ for an opaque material/surface} \qquad \ldots (4.2)$$

If $\tau = 1$, $a = r = 0$ all incident energy passes through the body and it is called perfectly transparent, e.g., rock salt (NaCl), quartz and fluorite.

If $r = 1$, $a = \tau = 0$, all the incident energy is supposed to be entirely reflected by the body and is specular. If the surface gives diffused reflection, the body is called as a white body, e.g., a piece of white chalk (white body).

(i) $r = 0$ represents a nonreflecting surface.

(ii) $a = 1$ represents a perfectly absorbing surface or a black surface.

(iii) $\tau = 1$ represents a perfectly transparent surface.

(iv) $r = 1$ represents a perfect reflector.

Black Body :

A body for which $a = 1$, $r = \tau = 0$, i.e., which absorbs all the incident radiant energy, is called **a black body**. It neither reflects nor transmits but absorbs all the radiation incident on it, so it is treated as an ideal radiation receiver. It is not necessary that the surface of the body be black in colour. The black body radiates maximum possible amount of energy at a given temperature and though perfectly black bodies do not exist in nature, some materials may approach it. Lampblack is the nearest to a black body. It absorbs 96 % of the visible light.

Both the absorptivity and emissivity of perfect block body are unity.Laws of Black Body Radiation

Kirchhoff's Law :

Consider that the two bodies are kept into a furnace held at constant temperature of T K. Assume that, of the two bodies one is a black body and the other is a non-black body, i.e., the body having **'a'** value less than one. Both the bodies will eventually attain the temperature of T K and the bodies neither become hotter nor cooler than the furnace. At this condition of thermal equilibrium, each body absorbs and emits thermal radiation at the same rate. The rate of absorption and emission for the black body will be different from that of the non-black body.

Let the area of non-black body and black body be A_1 and A_2 respectively. Let 'I' be the rate at which radiation falling on bodies per unit area and E_1 and E_b be the emissive powers **(emissive power is the total quantity of radiant energy emitted by a body per unit area per unit time)** of non-black and black body respectively.

At thermal equilibrium, absorption and emission rates are equal, thus,

$$I a_1 A_1 = A_1 E_1 \quad \ldots (4.3)$$

$\therefore \quad I a_1 = E_1 \quad \ldots (4.4)$

and $\quad I a_b A_2 = A_2 E_b \quad \ldots (4.5)$

$$I a_b = E_b \quad \ldots (4.6)$$

From Equations (4.4) and (4.6), we get

$$\frac{E_1}{a_1} = \frac{E_b}{a_b} \quad \ldots (4.7)$$

where a_1, a_b = absorptivities of non-black and black bodies respectively.

If we introduce a second body (non-black) then for the second non-black body, we have :

$$I A_3 a_2 = E_2 A_3 \quad \ldots (4.8)$$

$$I a_2 = E_2 \quad \ldots (4.9)$$

where a_2 and E_2 are the absorptivity and emissive power of the second non-black body.

Combining Equations (4.4), (4.6) and (4.9), we get

$$\frac{E_1}{a_1} = \frac{E_2}{a_2} = \frac{E_b}{a_b} = E_b \quad \ldots (4.10)$$

(As the absorptivity of the black body is 1.0)

Statement of Kirchhoff's law

It states that, *at thermal equilibrium the ratio of the total emissive power to its absorptivity is the same for all bodies.* Equation (4.10) is a mathematical statement of Kirchhoff's law.

The **emissivity** 'e' of any body is defined as the **ratio of the total emissive power E of the body to that of a black body E_b at the same temperature.** The emissivity depends on the temperature of the body only.

$$e = \frac{E}{E_b} \quad \ldots (4.11)$$

Since $\quad \frac{E}{a}$ is constant for all bodies

$$\frac{E}{a} = \frac{E_b}{a_b} \qquad \ldots (4.12)$$

$$e = \frac{E}{E_b} = \frac{a}{a_b} \qquad \ldots (4.13)$$

but $\quad a_b = 1$ (for black body)

$\therefore \quad e = a \qquad \ldots (4.14)$

Thus, *when any body is in thermal equilibrium with its surroundings, its emissivity and absorptivity are equal.* Equation (4.14) may be taken as the another statement of **Kirchhoff's law**.

Monochromatic emissive power : It is the radiant energy emitted from a body per unit area per unit time per unit wavelength about the wavelength λ. It is denoted by E_λ. It has the units of $W/(m^2 \cdot \mu m)$.

Total emissive power : It is the total quantity of radiant energy of all wavelength emitted by a body per unit area per unit time. It is denoted by symbol E. It has units of W/m^2.

For the entire spectrum of radiation from a surface, it is the sum of all the monochromatic radiations from the surface.

$$E = \int_0^\infty E_\lambda \, d\lambda \qquad \ldots (4.15)$$

Monochromatic emissivity : *It is the ratio of the monochromatic emissive power of a body to that of a black body at the same wavelength and temperature.*

$$e_\lambda = \frac{E_\lambda}{E_{b,\lambda}} \qquad \ldots (4.16)$$

Gray body :

A body having the same value of the monochromatic emissivity at all wavelengths is called a gray body.

A gray body is the one of which emissivity is independent of wavelength.

[The adjective monochromatic indicates that the quantity being defined for a particular wavelength / single wavelength. Monochromatic property refers to a single wavelength and total property is the sum of monchromatic values of property. Monochromatic values are not important to the direct solution of engineering problems.]

Laws of black body radiation :

Steafan-Boltzmann law : It states that *the total energy emitted per unit area per unit time by a black body is directly proportional to the fourth power of its absolute temperature.*

$$E_b \propto T^4 \qquad \ldots (4.17)$$

$$E_b = \sigma \cdot T^4$$

where $\quad T = $ Temperature in K

σ = Steafan-Boltzmann constant
= 5.67×10^{-8} W/(m²·K⁴)

For a non-black body,

$$\frac{E}{E_b} = e \qquad \ldots (4.18)$$

$$E = e \cdot E_b \qquad \ldots (4.19)$$

Combining Equations (4.17) and (4.19), we get

$$E = e \cdot \sigma \cdot T^4 \qquad \ldots (4.20)$$

where 'e' is the emissivity of the non-black body.

The Steafan-Boltzmann equation is a fundamental relation for all the radiant energy transfer calculations.

Planck's law :

This law gives a relationship between the monochromatic emissive power of a black body, absolute temperature and the corresponding wavelength.

$$E_{b,\lambda} = \frac{2\pi hc^2 \lambda^{-5}}{e^{hc/k\lambda T} - 1} \qquad \ldots (4.21)$$

where $E_{b,\lambda}$ is the monochromatic emissive power of the black body / black surface, W/(m²·μm), **h** is the Planck's constant, **k** is the Boltzmann constant, c is speed of light, T is the absolute temperature and λ is the wavelength of radiation.

Equation (4.21) can be written as

$$E_{b,\lambda} = \frac{C_1 \lambda^{-5}}{\left(e^{C_2/\lambda T} - 1\right)} \qquad \ldots (4.22)$$

where C_1 and C_2 are constants.

$C_1 = 3.472 \times 10^{-16}$ W·m² and $C_2 = 0.01439$ m·K

Wiens displacement law :

It states that the wavelength at which the maximum monochromatic emissive power is obtained (i.e., λ_{max}) is inversely proportional to the absolute temperature, or

$$T \lambda_{max} = C \qquad \ldots (4.23)$$

when λ_{max} is in micrometers and T is in Kelvins, the value of constant C is equal to 2890.

Heat transfer by radiation :

A body having emissivity 'e' at temperature T_1 emits the radiant energy equal to $e \sigma T_1^4$ per unit area. If the surroundings are black, none of this radiation will be reflected by them and if surroundings are at temperature T_2, they will emit the radiation equal to σT_2^4. If a body is grey, it will absorb fraction 'e' of this energy, so that the net rate of radiant energy flow from the grey body to the black surrounding is given by the expression

$$\frac{Q}{A} = e \cdot \sigma \left(T_1^4 - T_2^4\right) \qquad \ldots (4.24)$$

where 'e' = the emissivity of grey body.

T_1 = absolute temperature of grey body

T_2 = absolute temperature of surroundings.

Equation (4.24) is also applicable when a heat source is small as compared to the surroundings (so that none of heat radiated from source is reflected to it, i.e., a body radiating to the atmosphere (in the calculation of heat loss from a steam pipe).

Concept of a Black body :

A black body is the one which absorbs all radiation incident upon it, whatever be the wave length, λ. It is an ideal body that absorbs all incident radiation energy and reflects or transmits none. This means that the black body is perfectly non-reflecting and non-transmitting. Actually no matter with **a = 1** and **τ = r = 0** exists. Even the blackest surfaces occurring in nature still have reflectivity of about 1 per cent (r = 0.01).

Hence, although a black body must be black in colour, this is not a sufficient condition. Kirchhoff, however, conceived the following possibility of making a practically perfect black body. If a hollow body is provided with only one very small opening and is held at uniform temperature, then any beam of radiation entering through the hole is partly absorbed, and partly reflected inside. The reflected radiation will not find the outlet, but will fall again on the inside the wall. There it will be only partly reflected and so on. By such a sequence of reflections, the entering radiation will be almost absorbed by the body, and an arrangement of this kind will act just as a perfectly black body as shown in Fig. 4.2.

All substances emit radiation, the quality and quantity depending upon the absolute temperature and the properties of the material composing a radiating body. It may be shown that, at a given temperature, good absorbers of any particular wavelength are also good emitter of that wavelength. Thus, since by definition a black body is a complete radiator of all wave lengths it is also the best possible emitter of thermal radiation, i.e., it is a full radiator.

Fig. 4.2 : Black body

Transfer coefficient for radiation :

The net heat transfer by radiation from a unit surface area of a grey body at temperature T_1 to the black surroundings at temperature T_2 may be expressed as

$$Q_r = h_r (T_1 - T_2)$$

Therefore,
$$h_r = \frac{Q_r}{(T_1 - T_2)} = \frac{e \cdot \sigma}{(T_1 - T_2)} (T_1^4 - T_2^4) \quad \ldots (4.25)$$

where h_r is a radiation heat transfer coefficient. Equation (4.21) is also applicable if the surroundings are not black, the body is small and none of its radiation is reflected back to it.

SOLVED EXAMPLES

Ex. 4.1 : Calculate the heat loss by radiation from an unlagged horizontal steam pipe, 50 mm o.d. at 377 K (104° C) to air at 283 K (10° C).

Data : Emissivity, e = 0.90.

Solution : The heat loss by radiation is given by

$$\frac{Q_r}{A} = e \cdot \sigma \cdot (T_1^4 - T_2^4)$$

where
$$e = 0.90$$
$$\sigma = 5.67 \times 10^{-8} \text{ W/(m}^2 \cdot \text{K}^4)$$
$$T_1 = 377 \text{ K and } T_2 = 283 \text{ K}$$

$$\frac{Q_r}{A} = 0.90 \times 5.67 \times 10^{-8} \left(\overline{377}^4 - \overline{283}^4\right)$$

$$= 704 \text{ W/m}^2 \quad \ldots \text{Ans.}$$

Ex. 4.2 : Calculate the rate of heat transfer by radiation from an unlagged steam pipe, 50 mm, o.d. at 393 K (120° C) to air at 293 K (20° C).

Assume emissivity 'e' of 0.9

Solution : Given :
$$e = 0.90$$
$$T_1 = 393 \text{ K}, \quad T_2 = 293 \text{ K}$$
$$\sigma = 5.67 \times 10^{-8} \text{ W/(m}^2 \cdot \text{K}^4)$$

The rate of heat transfer by radiation per unit area is

$$\frac{Q_r}{A} = e \cdot \sigma (T_1^4 - T_2^4)$$

$$= 0.90 \times 5.67 \times 10^{-8} \left(\overline{393}^4 - \overline{293}^4\right)$$

$$= 841.2 \text{ W/m}^2 \quad \ldots \text{Ans.}$$

Ex. 4.3 : A 50 mm i.d. iron pipe at 423 K (150° C) passes through a room in which the surroundings are at temperature of 300 K (27° C). If the emissivity of the pipe metal is 0.8, what is the net interchange of radiation energy per meter length of pipe ? The outside diameter of pipe is 60 mm.

Solution :

Length of pipe = 1 m

e = 0.8, $\quad\quad\quad\sigma = 5.67 \times 10^{-8}$ W/(m²·K⁴)

$T_1 = 423$ K, $\quad T_2 = 300$ K, $\quad\quad D_o = 60$ mm $= 0.06$ m

Outside surface area per 1 meter length of pipe

$$A = \pi D_o L = \pi \times 0.06 \times 1 = 0.189 \text{ m}^2$$

The net radiation rate per 1 m length of pipe is

$$Q_r = e \, \sigma \, A \, (T_1^4 - T_2^4) = 0.8 \times 5.67 \times 10^{-8} \times 0.189 \, (\overline{423}^{\,4} - \overline{300}^{\,4})$$

$$= 205 \text{ W/m length of pipe} \quad\quad\quad \text{... Ans.}$$

Ex. 4.4 : Estimate the total heat loss by convection and radiation from an unlagged steam pipe, 50 mm o.d. at 415 K (142° C) to air at 290 K (17° C).

Data : Take emissivity, e = 0.90

Film coefficient (h_c) for calculation of heat loss by natural convection is given by

$$h_c = 1.18 \, (\Delta T/D_o)^{0.25}, \text{ W/(m}^2\cdot\text{K)}$$

Solution : Outside area of pipe $= \pi D \cdot L$

Assume $\quad\quad L = 1$ m

$\quad\quad\quad\quad\quad D_o = 50$ mm $= 0.05$ m

Outside area per unit length of pipe $= \pi \times 0.05 \times 1.0 = 0.157$ m²/m

$\Delta T = 415 - 290 = 125$ K

$h_c = 1.18 \, (\Delta T/D_o)^{0.25} = 1.18 \, (125/0.05)^{0.25} = 8.34$ W/(m²·K)

The heat loss by convection per unit length of pipe is

$$Q_c = h_c \cdot A \, (T_1 - T_2)$$

$$= 8.34 \times 0.157 \, (415 - 290) = 163.7 \text{ W/m}$$

The heat loss by radiation per unit length of pipe is

$$Q_r = e \sigma A \, (T_1^4 - T_2^4)$$

$$= 0.9 \times 5.67 \times 10^{-8} \times 0.157 \, (\overline{415}^{\,4} - \overline{290}^{\,4}) = 181 \text{ W/m}$$

∴ The total heat loss by convection and radiation per unit length of pipe is

$$Q_t = Q_c + Q_r$$

$$= 163.7 + 181$$

$$= 344.7 \text{ W/m length of pipe} \quad\quad\quad \text{... Ans.}$$

Ex. 4.5 : Calculate the rate of heat loss from a 6 m long horizontal steam pipe, 60 mm o.d. when carrying steam at 800 kN/m². The temperature of atmosphere and surroundings is 290 K.

Data: Take emissivity, $e = 0.85$ and Stefan-Boltzmann constant,
$\sigma = 5.67 \times 10^{-8}$ W/(m²·K⁴).

Film coefficient (h_c) for heat loss by natural convection can be calculated by:
$$h_c = 1.64 \, (\Delta T)^{0.25}, \text{ W/(m}^2\cdot\text{K)}$$

Steam is saturated at 800 kN/m² and 443 K (170° C).

Solution: Neglecting the inside resistance and resistance of the metal wall, it may be assumed that the surface temperature of pipe is 443 K.

$T_1 = 443$ K, $T_2 = 290$ K, $D_o = 60$ mm $= 0.06$ m

$\Delta T = 443 - 290 = 153$ K, $L = 6$ m

For radiation from pipe:

Surface area of pipe $= \pi D \cdot L$
$= \pi \times 0.06 \times 6.0 = 1.131$ m²

The rate of heat loss by radiation from the pipe is

$$Q_r = e \, \sigma \, A \, (T_1^4 - T_2^4)$$
$$= 0.85 \times 5.67 \times 10^{-8} \times 1.131 \, (\overline{443}^4 - \overline{290}^4)$$
$$= 1714 \text{ W}$$

The rate of heat loss by convection from the pipe is
$$Q_c = h_c \, A \, (T_1 - T_2)$$
$$= 1.64 \, (\Delta T)^{0.25} \times A \, (T_1 - T_2)$$
$$= 1.64 \, (153)^{0.25} \times 1.131 \, (443 - 290)$$
$$= 998 \text{ W}$$

$\therefore$ Total heat loss $= Q_r + Q_c = 1714 + 998$
$= 2712$ W ... **Ans.**

Exchange of energy between two parallel plates / planes of different emissivities:

(Multiple Reflection Method)

When two non-black bodies are situated in fairly close proximity, part of the energy emitted by one body will be reflected back to it by the second body and will then be partly reabsorbed and partly reflected again. Thus, the heat undergoes a series of internal reflections and absorptions.

Consider two large gray planes/surfaces that are maintained at absolute temperatures T_1 and T_2 respectively. Let e_1 and e_2 be the emissivities of the surfaces.

Fig. 4.3 : Radiant heat exchanger between infinite parallel surfaces (energy originating at surface-1 absorbed by surface-2)

Consider the energy radiated from the surface-1. Then, per unit area per unit time :

- energy radiated from surface 1 $= \sigma \cdot e_1 T_1^4$ ... (a)
- of this, amount absorbed by surface 2 $= \sigma e_1 T_1^4 e_2$ ... (b)
- and amount reflected by surface 2 $= e_1 T_1^4 (1 - e_2)$ ... (c)
- of this, amount re-absorbed by surface 1 $= \sigma e_1 T_1^4 (1 - e_2) e_1$ ... (d)
- and amount re-reflected by surface 1 $= \sigma e_1 T_1^4 (1 - e_2)(1 - e_1)$ ... (e)
- and, of this, amount absorbed by surface $-2 = \sigma e_1 T_1^4 (1 - e_2)(1 - e_1) e_2$ ... (f)

Hence, as a result of each complete cycle of internal reflection, it is seen by comparing (b) and (f) that the absorption is reduced by factor $(1 - e_1)(1 - e_2)$. As the energy suffers an infinite number of reflections :

Total transfer of energy from surface 1 to surface 2 per unit area and unit time =

$$= \sigma \cdot e_1 e_2 T_1^4 \,[1 + (1 - e_1)(1 - e_2) + (1 - e_1)^2 (1 - e_2)^2 \ldots \text{to } \infty\,]$$

$$= \sigma \cdot e_1 e_2 T_1^4 \, \frac{1}{1 - (1 - e_1)(1 - e_2)}$$

$$= \frac{\sigma \cdot e_1 e_2}{e_1 + e_2 - e_1 e_2} \, T_1^4$$

In a similar manner, considering the radiation emitted by the surface 2, it can be shown that the total transfer of energy from surface 2 to surface 1 per unit area per unit time (i.e., emitted by the surface 2 and absorbed by the surface 1)

$$= \frac{e_1 e_2 \sigma}{e_1 + e_2 - e_1 e_2} \, T_2^4$$

Thus, the net energy transferred per unit area per unit time is

$$\left(\frac{Q}{A}\right)_{12} = \frac{e_1 e_2 \sigma}{e_1 + e_2 - e_1 e_2} \, (T_1^4 - T_2^4)$$

$$\left(\frac{Q}{A}\right)_{12} = \frac{\sigma (T_1^4 - T_2^4)}{\dfrac{1}{e_1} + \dfrac{1}{e_2} - 1} \qquad \ldots (4.26)$$

$$\left(\frac{Q}{A}\right)_{12} = \sigma \cdot F_{12} \, (T_1^4 - T_2^4) \qquad \ldots (4.27)$$

Unit Operations – II 4.11 Radiation

where,
$$F_{12} = \frac{1}{\frac{1}{e_1} + \frac{1}{e_2} - 1} \qquad \ldots (4.28)$$

(F_{12} is called overall interchange factor and is function of e_1 and e_2)

Spheres or cylinders with spherical or cylindrical enclosures :

The net exchange between the inner and outer sphere is given by

$$Q = \frac{\sigma A_1}{\frac{1}{e_1} + \left(\frac{r_1}{r_2}\right)^2 \left(\frac{1}{e_2} - 1\right)} (T_1^4 - T_2^4) \qquad \ldots (4.29)$$

$$= \frac{\sigma A_1}{\frac{1}{e_1} + \frac{A_1}{A_2}\left(\frac{1}{e_2} - 1\right)} (T_1^4 - T_2^4) \qquad \ldots (4.30)$$

The net exchange between infinitely large concentric cylinders is given by

$$Q = \frac{\sigma \cdot A_1 (T_1^4 - T_2^4)}{\frac{1}{e_1} + \frac{A_1}{A_2}\left(\frac{1}{e_2} - 1\right)} = \frac{\sigma \cdot A_1 (T_1^4 - T_2^4)}{\frac{1}{e_1} + \frac{r_1}{r_2}\left(\frac{1}{e_2} - 1\right)} \qquad \ldots (4.31)$$

where A_1 and A_2 are the areas of the inner and outer cylinders/spheres respectively, e_1 and e_2 are the emissivities of the inner and outer cylindrical/spherical surfaces. T_1 and T_2 are the respective temperatures.

$$Q = \sigma A_1 F_{1-2} (T_1^4 - T_2^4) \qquad \ldots (4.32)$$

where
$$F_{12} = \frac{1}{\frac{1}{e_1} + \frac{A_1}{A_2}\left(\frac{1}{e_2} - 1\right)} \qquad \ldots (4.33)$$

Ex. 4.6 : Calculate the loss of heat by radiation from a steel tube of diameter 70 mm and 3 m long at a temperature of 500 K (227º C), if the tube is located in a square brick conduit 0.3 m side at 300 K (27º C). Assume e for steel as 0.79 and for brick conduit as 0.93.

Solution :
$$Q = \frac{\sigma \cdot A_1 (T_1^4 - T_2^4)}{\frac{1}{e_1} + \frac{A_1}{A_2}\left(\frac{1}{e_2} - 1\right)}$$

where, $\sigma = 5.67 \times 10^{-8}$ W/(m²·K⁴)

$e_1 = 0.79$, $e_2 = 0.93$

$T_1 = 500$ K

$T_2 = 300$ K

$A_1 = \pi \times \frac{70}{1000} \times 3 = 0.659$ m²

$A_2 = 4(0.3 \times 3) = 3.6$ m²

$$Q = \frac{5.67 \times 10^{-8} \times 0.659 \times [\overline{500}^4 - \overline{300}^4]}{\frac{1}{0.79} + \frac{0.659}{3.6}\left(\frac{1}{0.93} - 1\right)}$$

$$Q = 1588.5 \text{ W} \quad \text{... Ans.}$$

Ex. 4.7 : Calculate the net radiant interchange per square meter for very large planes at temperatures of 703 K (430° C) and 513 K (260° C) respectively. Assume that the emissivity of the hot and cold planes are 0.85 and 0.75 respectively.

Solution :
$$\left(\frac{Q}{A}\right)_r = \frac{\sigma(T_1^4 - T_2^4)}{\frac{1}{e_1} + \frac{1}{e_2} - 1}$$

where
$$\sigma = 5.67 \times 10^{-8} \text{ W/(m}^2\cdot\text{K}^4)$$
$$T_1 = 703 \text{ K}$$
$$T_2 = 513 \text{ K}$$
$$e_1 = 0.85 \quad \text{and} \quad e_2 = 0.75$$

$$\left(\frac{Q}{A}\right)_r = \frac{5.67 \times 10^{-8} [(703)^4 - (513)^4]}{\frac{1}{0.85} + \frac{1}{0.75} - 1}$$

$$= 6571 \text{ W/m}^2 \quad \text{... Ans.}$$

Ex. 4.8 : Determine the net radiant interchange between two parallel oxidised iron plates, placed at a distance of 25 mm having sides 3 × 3 m. The surface temperatures of two plates are 373 K (100° C) and 313 K (40° C) respectively. Emissivities of the plates are equal. Given – $e_1 = e_2 = 0.736$.

Solution : The interchange factor is given by –

$$F_{12} = \frac{1}{\frac{1}{e_1} + \frac{1}{e_2} - 1}$$

$$= \frac{1}{\frac{1}{0.736} + \frac{1}{0.736} - 1} = 0.5823$$

$$Q = \sigma A \, F_{12} \, (T_1^4 - T_2^4)$$

where
$$F_{12} = 0.5823$$
$$A = 3 \times 3 = 9 \text{ m}^2$$
$$\sigma = 5.67 \times 10^{-8} \text{ W/(m}^2\cdot\text{K}^4)$$
$$T_1 = 373 \text{ K}$$
$$T_2 = 313 \text{ K}$$
$$Q = 5.67 \times 10^{-8} \times 9 \times 0.5823 \times [(373)^4 - (313)^4]$$
$$= 2900 \text{ W} \quad \text{... Ans.}$$

The net radiant interchange between two parallel oxidised iron plates is 2900 W.

Ex. 4.9 : Calculate the rate of heat loss from a thermoflask if the polished silvered surfaces have emissivities of 0.05, the liquid in the flask is at 368 K (95° C) and the casing is at 293 K (20° C). Calculate the loss if both surfaces were black.

Stefan Boltzmann constant = 5.67×10^{-8} W/(m²·K⁴)

Solution :
$$F_{12} = \frac{1}{\frac{1}{e_1} + \frac{A_1}{A_2}\left(\frac{1}{e_2} - 1\right)}$$

As the areas are equal $A_1 = A_2$. Further, $e_1 = e_2 = 0.05$

$$F_{12} = \frac{1}{\frac{1}{0.05} + \left(\frac{1}{0.05} - 1\right)} = 0.0256$$

T_1 = 368 K

T_2 = 293 K

The heat loss per unit area of the silvered surface is

$$\frac{Q}{A} = \sigma F_{12} (T_1^4 - T_2^4)$$

$\phantom{\frac{Q}{A}}$ = $5.67 \times 10^{-8} \times 0.0256 [(368)^4 - (293)^4]$

$\phantom{\frac{Q}{A}}$ = **15.92 W/m²** ... **Ans.**

where the two surfaces are black.

$e_1 = e_2 = 1$

$$F_{12} = \frac{1}{\frac{1}{1} + \left(\frac{1}{1} - 1\right)} = 1$$

$$\frac{Q}{A} = 5.67 \times 10^{-8} \times 1 \times [(368)^4 - (293)^4]$$

$\phantom{\frac{Q}{A}}$ = **622 W/m²** ... **Ans.**

Ex. 4.10 : The inner sphere of a Diwar flask is 30 cm diameter and outer sphere is 36 cm diameter. Both spheres are coated for which emissivity is 0.05. Determine the rate at which liquid oxygen (latent heat = 21.44 kJ/kg) would evaporate at 90 K (– 183° C) when outer sphere temperature is 293 K (20° C). Assume that the other modes of heat transfer are absent.

Solution :
$$\frac{A_1}{A_2} = \frac{d_1^2}{d_2^2} = \frac{(30)^2}{(36)^2} = 0.6944$$

$e_1 = e_2 = 0.05$

$$F_{12} = \cfrac{1}{\cfrac{1}{e_1} + \cfrac{A_1}{A_2}\left(\cfrac{1}{e_2} - 1\right)}$$

$$= \cfrac{1}{\cfrac{1}{0.05} + 0.6944\left(\cfrac{1}{0.05} - 1\right)} = 0.03$$

$$\frac{Q}{A} = \sigma \cdot F_{12}\left(T_1^4 - T_2^4\right)$$

$$= 5.67 \times 10^{-8} \times 0.03 \,[\overline{293}^{\,4} - \overline{90}^{\,4}] = 12.42 \text{ W/m}^2$$

∴ $\quad Q = 12.42 \times A$

$\quad\quad = 12.42 \times \pi\,(0.3)^2 = 3.51 \text{ W} + 12.64 \text{ kJ/h}$

Latent heat of liquid oxygen = 21.44 kJ/kg

Amount of oxygen evaporated = $\dfrac{12.64}{21.44}$ = 0.59 kg/h ... **Ans.**

Ex. 4.11 : Liquid oxygen at atmospheric pressure (boiling point = 90 K (– 183° C) is stored in a spherical vessel of 300 mm outside diameter. The system is insulated by enclosing the container inside another concentric sphere of 500 mm inside diameter with space between them evacuated. Both the sphere surfaces are made of aluminium for which emissivity may be taken as 0.3. The temperature of the outer sphere is 313 K (40° C).

Calculate the rate of heat flow due to radiation.

What will be the reduction in heat flow if polished aluminium with an emissivity of 0.5 is used for the container walls ?

Solution :

$$Q = \cfrac{\sigma \cdot A_1\left(T_1^4 - T_2^4\right)}{\cfrac{1}{e_1} + \cfrac{A_1}{A_2}\left(\cfrac{1}{e_2} - 1\right)}$$

where, $\quad \sigma = 5.67 \times 10^{-8}$ W/(m²·K⁴)

$\quad\quad e_1 = e_2 = 0.3$

$\quad\quad T_1 = 90$ K

$\quad\quad T_2 = 313$ K

$\quad\quad A_1 = \pi D_1^2 = \pi \times (0.3)^2 = 0.283$ m²

$\quad\quad A_2 = \pi D_2^2 = \pi \times (0.5)^2 = 0.785$ m²

$$Q = \cfrac{5.67 \times 10^{-8} \times 0.283\,[\overline{90}^{\,4} - \overline{313}^{\,4}]}{\cfrac{1}{0.3} + \cfrac{0.283}{0.785}\left[\cfrac{1}{0.3} - 1\right]} = -36.64 \text{ W}$$

Rate of heat flow = 36.64 W

Emissivity of polished aluminium = e_1 = 0.05

Emissivity of aluminium = e_2 = 0.5

$$Q = \frac{\sigma A_1 (T_1^4 - T_2^4)}{\frac{1}{e_1} + \frac{A_1}{A_2}\left(\frac{1}{e_2} - 1\right)}$$

$$Q = \frac{5.67 \times 10^{-8} \times 0.283 \,[(90)^4 - (313)^4]}{\frac{1}{0.05} + \frac{0.283}{0.785}\left(\frac{1}{0.30} - 1\right)} = -7.34 \text{ W}$$

Rate of heat flow = − 7.34 W

∴ Reduction in heat flow = $\frac{36.64 - 7.34}{36.64} \times 100$

= **79.97 %** ... Ans.

Ex. 4.12 : Liquid nitrogen boiling at 77 K (− 196º C) is stored in a 15 litre spherical container of diameter 32 cm. The container is surrounded by a concentric spherical shell of diameter 36 cm at a temperature of 303 K (30º C) and the space between the two spheres is evacuated. The surfaces of the spheres facing each other are silvered and have an emissivity of 0.03. Taking the latent heat of vaporisation for liquid nitrogen to be 201 kJ/kg, find the rate at which the nitrogen evaporates.

Solution : The radiant heat exchange rate between the inner and outer shell is given by −

$$Q = \frac{\sigma A_1 (T_1^4 - T_2^4)}{\frac{1}{e_1} + \frac{A_1}{A_2}\left(\frac{1}{e_2} - 1\right)}$$

where, T_1 and T_2 are temperatures of the inner and outer surfaces respectively.

σ = 5.67 × 10^{-8} W/(m²·K⁴)

T_1 = 77 K

T_2 = 303 K

D_1 = 32 cm = 0.32 m, D_2 = 36 cm = 0.36 m

A_1 = πD_1^2 = $\pi (0.32)^2$ = 0.3217 m²

A_2 = πD_2^2 = $\pi (0.36)^2$ = 0.407 m²

e_1 = e_2 = 0.3

$$Q = \frac{5.67 \times 10^{-8} \times 0.3217 \,[\overline{77}^4 - \overline{303}^4]}{\frac{1}{0.03} + \frac{0.3217}{0.407}\left(\frac{1}{0.03} - 1\right)}$$

$Q = -2.63\ W + -9.5\ kJ/h$

Radiant heat exchange = $2.63\ W + 9.5\ kJ/h$

Latent heat of vaporisation of liquid nitrogen = $201\ kJ/kg$

Evaporation rate = $\frac{Q}{\lambda} = \frac{9.5}{201} = 0.047\ kg/h$ ... **Ans.**

Ex. 4.13 : The space between the two concentric spherical vessels is completely evacuated. The inner sphere contains air at 76 K (– 197° C). The ambient temperature is 300 K (27° C). The surface of the spheres are highly polished (e = 0.04). Find the rate of evaporation of liquid air per hour.

Diameter of inner sphere = 250 mm

Diameter of outer sphere = 350 mm

Latent heat of vaporisation of air = 200 kJ/kg

Solution :
$$Q = \frac{\sigma A_1 (T_1^4 - T_2^4)}{\frac{1}{e_1} + \frac{A_1}{A_2}\left(\frac{1}{e_2} - 1\right)}$$

$$= \frac{\sigma \pi D_1^2 (T_1^4 - T_2^4)}{\frac{1}{e_1} + \left(\frac{D_1^2}{D_2^2}\right)\left(\frac{1}{e_2} - 1\right)}$$

where, $\sigma = 5.67 \times 10^{-8}\ W/(m^2 \cdot K^4)$

$A_1 = \pi D_1^2 \qquad A_2 = \pi D_2^2$

$D_1 = 250\ mm = 0.25\ m, \quad D_2 = 350\ mm = 0.35\ m$

$T_1 = 76\ K$

$T_2 = 300\ K$

$$Q = \frac{5.67 \times 10^{-8} \times \pi\,(0.25)^2\,[\overline{76}^4 - \overline{300}^4]}{\frac{1}{0.04} + \left(\frac{0.25}{0.35}\right)^2 \left[\frac{1}{0.04} - 1\right]} = -2.45\ W$$

Net heat exchange = $2.45\ W$

$+ 2.45\ J/s + 8.82\ kJ/h$

Rate of evaporation = $\frac{8.82}{200} = 0.0441\ kg/h$ ... **Ans.**

EXERCISE

1. Fill in the blanks :
   (a) Radiation refers to the transport of energy through space by .... waves.
   Ans. electromagnetic
   (b) Heat can be transmitted by .... mode across absolute vacuum. **Ans.** radiation
   (c) The fraction of the incident radiation absorbed is known as .... **Ans.** absorptivity
   (d) For perfectly black body absorptivity is equal to .... **Ans.** one
   (e) For specular body the reflectivity is equal to .... **Ans.** one
   (f) As per Kirchhoff's law, at thermal equilibrium for all bodies the ratio of ..... to the absorptivity will be same. **Ans.** emissive power
   (g) The emissivity 'e' of a body is equal to its .... 'a'. **Ans.** absorptivity
   (h) As per Stefan-Boltzmann law the total energy emitted by a black body is directly proportional to the fourth power of its absolute .... **Ans.** temperature
   (i) .... Boltzmann equation is a fundamental relation for all radiant energy transfer calculations. **Ans.** Stefan
   (j) Emissivity of any body is the ratio of its ..... to that of black body at the same temperature. **Ans.** emissive power

2. Define the following terms :
   (a) Radiation (b) Absorptivity (c) Emissivity (d) Opaque material (e) Gray body.

3. What do you mean by black body ?

4. Give the example of radiation heat transfer.

5. State Kirchhoff's law of radiation.

6. State Stefan-Boltzmann law of radiation.

7. Write in brief on concept of black body.

8. Calculate the loss of heat per unit area from steam pipe to the surrounding air by radiation mode. Take emissivity of 0.90.

   Data : Temperature of steam pipe = 398 K (125° C)

   Temperature of air = 303 K (30° C) **Ans.** 851 W/m²

CHAPTER FIVE

HEAT EXCHANGE EQUIPMENTS

Various types of heat transfer equipment are used in the chemical industry depending upon the applications involved (i.e. based on service), but their common task is to transfer heat from a hot fluid to a cold one. The heat exchange equipments involve heat energy transfer either by conduction-convection or by radiation mode. In the chemical industry, shell and tube type heat exchangers constitute the bulk of unfired heat transfer equipment.

Based upon the function, heat transfer equipments can be referred as cooler, heater, condenser, etc.

Cooler :

It is a heat exchange equipment employed to cool a process fluid (gas or liquid) by means of water or atmospheric air. It involves the removal of sensible heat from the process fluid (stream).

Condenser :

It is a heat exchange equipment employed to condense a vapour or a mixture of vapours (in the presence or absence of noncondensable gas). It involves the removal of latent heat with the help of a suitable cooling medium, e.g., cooling tower water or chilled water.

Chiller :

It is a heat exchange equipment employed to cool a process fluid (stream) to a temperature below that can be obtained by using water as a cooling medium. It employs a refrigerant such as ammonia or freon (cooling medium).

Exchanger :

It is a heat exchange equipment that allows exchange of heat between hot and cold process streams/fluids.

Heater :

It is a heat exchange equipment which imparts sensible heat to a process fluid (stream). Condensing steam or dowtherm may be employed as a heating medium.

It heats a process stream by condensing steam.

Reboiler :

It is a heat exchange equipment, employed to meet the latent heat requirement at the bottom of a distillation column. The heating medium may be either steam or a hot process fluid.

Vaporiser :

It is a heat exchange equipment (unfired) which vaporises part of the liquid.

Waste - heat boiler :

It is a heat exchange equipment employed for the production of steam using a hot gas or a hot liquid stream produced in a chemical reaction as a heating medium.

Evaporator :

It is a heat exchange equipment employed for the concentration of a solution by evaporation of water. Condensing steam is used as a heating medium.

Double pipe heat exchanger :

It is the simplest type of heat exchanger used in industry. It is used when the required heat transfer area is relatively small.

It consists of concentric pipes, connecting tees, return heads and return bends. The packing glands support the inner pipe within the outer pipe. A double pipe heat exchanger arranged in two legs [i.e. when two lengths of inner pipe are connected by return bend] as shown in Fig. 5.1 is known as a single hair-pin. Tees are provided with nozzles or screwed connections for permitting the entry and exit of the annulus fluid which crosses from one leg to the other through the return head. The return bend connects two legs of inner pipes to each other. This exchanger can be very easily assembled in any pipe-fitting shop as it consists of standard parts and it provides inexpensive heat transfer surface. In this exchanger, one of the fluids flows through the inside pipe and the other fluid flows through the annular space created between two concentric pipes either in co-current or counter-current fashion. It is usually employed for decreasing the temperature of a hot fluid with the help of a cold fluid when flow rates are low. These are commonly used in refrigeration services.

These exchangers are usually assembled in effective lengths of 3.65, 4.57, 6 m. The distance in each leg over which the heat transfer occurs is termed as the effective length.

Fig. 5.1 (a) : Double pipe heat exchanger

Fig. 5.1 (b) : Schematic diagram of double pipe heat exchanger (counter current)

The major disadvantages of double pipe heat exchanger are :

1. Small heat transfer surface in large floor space as compared to other type (e.g. shell and tube heat exchanger).
2. Dismantling requires large time and
3. Maximum leakage points.

Apart from this, double pipe heat exchanger is very attractive where the total heat transfer surface required is small, 9.29 m² to 14 m² or less. It is simple in construction, cheap and easy to clean.

Shell and Tube Heat Exchanger :

For a variety of industrial services where large heat transfer surfaces are required, shell and tube heat exchangers are commonly used. These heat exchange equipments can be fabricated from a wide range of materials of construction.

A shell and tube heat exchanger consists of a number of parallel tubes, ends of which are mounted in the tube sheets and the entire tube bundle is enclosed in a close fitting cylindrical shell. In this exchanger, heat transfer surface is the one that is offered by tubes. One of the fluid flows through the tubes and is called as the tube side fluid while the outer fluid flows through the space created between tubes and shell, i.e., outside the tubes and is called as the shell side fluid. Two fluids are in thermal contact but are physically separated by a metal wall of the tubes. Heat flows through the metal wall of the tubes from a hot fluid to a cold fluid.

If none of the fluids condenses or evaporates the unit is known as **heat exchanger**. When one of the fluids condenses it is known as **condenser** or as **heater** depending on whether the primary purpose of the unit is to condense one fluid or to heat the other. Similarly such units may be called as cooler, evaporator, etc. based on a primary purpose for which they are employed.

Shell :

It is usually a cylindrical casing through which one of the fluid flows in one or more passes. Shell is commonly made of carbon steel. It may be cut to the required length from a standard pipe upto 60 cm diameter or fabricated from plate. The minimum thickness of shell made of carbon steel varies from 5 mm to 11 mm depending upon the diameter.

Tubes :

Standard heat exchanger tubes used in many industrial processes may be of various sizes and lengths. The outside diameter of tubes vary from 6 mm to 40 mm. The tubes with outside diameters of 19 mm and 25 mm are very common. The tube lengths used are 0.5, 2.5, 3, 4, 5 and 6 meters. The wall thickness of tubes is usually expressed in terms of Birmingham Wire Gauge (BWG). It depends upon the material of construction and diameter. For 19 or 25 mm outside diameter tube of mild steel 10 or 12 BWG is common. The tubes that are placed in a tube bundle inside the shell are either rolled or welded to the tube sheet. The tube side fluid first enters a header (bonnet) or channel through nozzles, then flows through tubes in parallel flow. It may flow in one pass or in more than one pass. In general, an even number of the tube side passes are used.

Tube pitch : The shortest centre-to-centre distance between the adjacent tubes is called as the tube pitch.

Clearance : The shortest distance between two tubes is called as the clearance.

The minimum pitch is 1.25 times the outside diameter of tube. The clearance should not be less than 0.25 times the outside diameter of tube, the minimum clearance being 4.76 mm.

The tubes are commonly laid out either on a square pitch or on an equilateral triangular pitch as shown in Fig. 5.2 (a). The advantages of the square pitch is that it permits external cleaning of the tubes and causes a low pressure drop on the shell side fluid. If the fluids are very clean, a triangular pitch is used. The triangular pitch arrangement incorporates a larger number of tubes in a given shell diameter than with a square pitch and usually creates a large turbulence in the shell side fluid.

Fig. 5.2 (a) : Square and Triangular pitch

Baffles :

Baffles are commonly employed within the shell of a heat exchanger to increase the rate of heat transfer by increasing the velocity and turbulence of the shell side fluid and also as structural supports for the tubes and dampers against vibration. The baffles cause the fluid to flow through the shell at right angles to the axes of the tubes. To avoid bypassing of the shell side fluid the clearance between the baffles and shell, and the baffles and tubes must be minimum.

The centre-to-centre distance between adjacent baffles is known as baffle spacing or baffle pitch. The baffle spacing should not be greater than the inside diameter of the shell and should not be less than one-fifth of the inside diameter of the shell. The optimum baffle spacing is 0.3 to 0.50 times the shell diameter.

Various transverse baffles used are : segmental, disc and ring, orifice, etc. The segmental baffles are most commonly used. **Segmental baffle** is a drilled circular disk of sheet metal with one side cut away. **When the height of the baffle is 75 % of the inside diameter of the shell, it is called as 25 % cut segmental baffle.** 25 % cut segmental baffle is the optimum one giving good heat transfer rates without excessive pressure drop. The baffle thickness usually ranges from 3 mm to 6 mm. Fig. 5.2 (b) shows a segmental baffle.

Fig. 5.2 (b) : Segmental baffle detail

Tie rods are used to hold the baffles in place, with spacers to position / locate the baffles. Tie rods are fixed at one end in the tube sheet by making blind holes. Usually 4 to 6 tie rods with atleast 10 mm diameter are necessary.

Tube sheet :

It is essentially a flat circular plate with a provision for making gasketed joint, around a pheriphery. A large number of holes are drilled in the tube sheet according to the pitch requirements.

(i) Tube sheet triangular pitch of tubes   (ii) Tube sheet square pitch of tubes

Fig. 5.2 (c)

Tube sheet thickness ranges from 6 mm to 25.4 mm for tube outside diameter of 6 mm to 40 mm.

Shell Side and Tube Side Passes :

With the help of passes (i.e. flow paths) we can change the direction of flow in the shell and tubes. Passes are generally used to obtain higher velocities and longer paths for a fluid to travel, without increasing the length of the exchanger, that leads to high heat transfer rates.

The passes on shell side are single pass, two pass, single split pass. The passes on the tube side are one, two, four, six upto twelve. Passes on tube side are formed by partitions placed in the shell cover and channels.

When we use single pass partition on tube side, the tube side fluid flows twice through the heat exchanger. In this case the pass partition divides the tubes equally in two sections. It is provided in the channel so that inlet and outlet for tube side fluid are provided on the same channel. Fig. 5.3 shows the incorporated pass partition in shell and tube heat exchanger.

Multipass construction decreases the cross section of the fluid path that increases the fluid velocity which in turn increases the heat transfer coefficients. But these have certain disadvantages such as more complicated constructions and high friction losses.

Fig. 5.3 : Heat exchanger with pass partition

Difference between single pass and multipass shell and tube heat exchanger :
1. Single pass heat exchanger is simple in construction.
   Multipass heat exchanger is complex in construction.
2. In single pass heat exchanger, the flow may be parallel or counter-current.
   In multipass heat exchanger, the flow is parallel as well as counter current.
3. It is relatively inexpensive.
   It is relatively expensive.
4. Heat transfer coefficients are relatively low.
   Heat transfer coefficients are high.
5. For a given duty, floor space requirement is large.
   For a given duty, floor space requirement is low.
6. Friction losses are low.
   Frictional losses are high.

7. Heat transfer rates are low.
   Heat transfer rates are high.
8. Fluids flow once through the exchanger.
   Fluids flow number of times through the exchanger depending upon the number of passes.
9. Small to modest U valves and larger areas. Larger U valves and smaller areas.
10. Easier to assemble, dismantle and clean. Relatively difficult to assemble, dismantle and clean.

Based upon the number of passes provided on the tube side as well as on the shell side, the shell and tube heat exchangers are referred as 1 - 2 shell and tube heat exchanger, 1 - 4 shell and tube heat exchanger, 2 - 4 shell and tube heat exchanger, etc.

In 1 - 2 shell and tube heat exchanger, the shell side fluid flows once through the exchanger and the tube side fluid flows twice through the exchanger (Number - 1 stands for shell side pass and number - 2 stands for tube side passes).

In 2 - 4 shell and tube heat exchanger, the shell side fluid flows twice through the exchanger and the tube side fluid flows four times through the exchanger. Figs. 5.4 and 5.5 show the passes on tube side as well as on shell side. Basically, passes are provided to increase the heat recovery.

(a) **Single pass**   (b) **Two passes**   (c) **Four passes**   (d) **Six passes**
Fig. 5.4 : Tube side passes

Fig. 5.5 : Shell side pass (two pass)

Guideline for directing fluids :

As the shell side of the exchanger is difficult to clean, the least corrosive and cleanest fluid should be admitted in the shell. The scale forming fluids should always be directly through tubes. The corrosive fluids should be admitted through the tubes to save the cost of an expensive alloy shell. When both the fluids are corrosive, the fluid which is more corrosive should be directed through the tubes. To improve the heat transfer characteristics dealing with a viscous liquid, the viscous liquid should be introduced on the shell side as baffles induce the turbulence. To avoid expensive high-pressure shells, the high pressure fluids should flow through the tubes. The vapours or gases should always be directed through the shell.

Classification of Shell and Tube Heat Exchangers :

Shell and tube heat exchangers are built of a shell in which a number of round tubes are mounted by means of tube sheets. Many variations of this basic type are available with difference lying mainly in constructional features and provisions for differential thermal expansion between shell and tubes.

These exchangers are classified as :
1. Fixed tube sheet heat exchanger.
2. Floating head heat exchanger.
    (a) Internal floating head and (b) Outside packed floating head
3. U-tube type heat exchanger and
4. Reboiler / Kettel type heat exchanger
    (i) with internal floating head or (ii) with U-tube (hair pin).

The main components of all these exchangers are **shell, shell cover, tubes, tube sheets, channel, channel cover, nozzles (inlet/outlet), pass partitions, baffles, tie rods and spacers.**

Fixed tube-sheet exchanger :

This is the simplest form of heat exchanger wherein the tube sheets are welded to a shell at both ends. The shell is equipped with two nozzles. The tube sheets usually extend beyond the shell and serve as flanges for the attachments of the channels on either side as shown in Fig. 5.6. In a fixed tube type construction, the shell and tube sheet materials must be weldable to each other. The channels on either sides are covered by means of channel covers and are provided with nozzle connections for the entry and exist of the tube side fluid. The shell side passes more than two are rarely used but as such there is no limitation on the tube side passes.

In the another variation of fixed tube sheet heat exchanger shown in Fig. 5.7 in which a tube side header (i.e., a channel) may be welded to the tube sheet and channels on the either sides are closed with removable covers. In order to account for the differential expansion between shell and tubes occurring because of differences in the thermal properties of materials of shell and tubes, expansion joints such as expansion bellows are used on the shell (to eliminate excessive stresses caused by the thermal expansion).

Fig. 5.6 : Fixed tube sheet heat exchanger

Fig. 5.7 : Fixed tube sheet exchanger with integral channels

This type of heat exchanger is used only when the shell side fluid is clean and non fouling.

The problem with this type of heat exchanger is that tube bunddle cannot be removed from shell for mechanical cleaning and usual inspection of outside of the tubes.

Fixed tube sheet 1 – 2 heat exchanger :

In the 1 - 1 shell and tube heat exchanger operated in counter current flow, it is very difficult to obtain high velocity of the tube side fluid. Thus, multipass construction is used to increase the fluid velocity which in turn increases the heat transfer coefficient. But with multipass construction the exchanger becomes more complicated and the friction loss through the exchanger is more, which calls for a high pumping cost. For economic design, the balance should be done between fluid velocity and pumping cost.

In a 1 – 2 shell and tube heat exchanger (Fig. 5.8), the tubes are fixed into two tube sheets and the tube sheets are welded to a shell which also serve as flanges for attachment of a channel and a cover. On one side of the shell, the channel is employed with a pass partition to permit the entry and exists of the tube side fluid through it.

On the other side of the shell, the cover is clamped to the tube sheet with the help of nuts and bolts to permit the tube side fluid to cross from the first to second pass. The outsides of the tubes are not accessible for inspection and mechanical cleaning, (while inside of the tubes can be cleaned by removing the channel cover). The shell is provided with nozzles for entry and exit of the shell side fluid.

Fig. 5.8 : Fixed tube sheet 1–2 heat exchanger

In the 1 - 2 shell and tube heat exchanger shown in Fig. 5.8, the shell side fluid flows once through the exchanger and the tube side fluid flows twice through the exchanger. In this exchanger, the tube side fluid flows in co-current as well as in counter current fashion with respect to the shell side fluid (i.e. in this exchanger, the shell side fluid flows in one pass and the tube side fluid flows in two passes).

Removable – bundle heat exchanger :

A fixed-tube sheet heat exchanger is the cheapest because of the ease of fabrication. The heat exchangers require periodic cleaning, replacement of tubes, etc. The inside of the tubes can be easily cleaned by mechanical means (by forcing wire brush or worm) and cleaning of the tubes from the outside require removal of a tube bundle from a heat exchanger, this is not possible with the fixed tube sheet-type. With the fixed tube heat exchanger, in addition to the above cited difficulty, the high stresses developed between shell and tube may lead to the loosening of tubes. Consequently, many heat exchangers are provided with removable tube bundles.

Internal floating head heat exchanger :

So as to make removal of a tube bundle possible and to allow for a considerable expansion of the tubes, a floating head exchanger is used.

In this exchanger (Fig. 5.9), tubes are fixed in a floating tube sheet at one end and in a stationary tube sheet at the other end. The stationary tube sheet is clamped between a shell and a channel (by a flange joint).

Fig. 5.9 : Internal floating head exchanger

The floating tube sheet is clamped between a floating head and a clamp ring. The clamp ring (split backing ring) which is split in half to permit dismantling is placed at the back of the tube sheet. Fig. 5.10 shows the details of a split ring assembly. The floating tube sheet is kept slightly smaller in diameter than the inside diameter of shell so as to withdraw the entire tube bundle from the channel end. The channel is provided with inlet and outlet connections for the tube side fluid. The shell is closed by shell cover or bonnet on a floating head side. Shell cover at the floating head end is larger than the other end so as to enable the tubes to be placed as near as possible to the edge of the fixed tube sheet. The tube sheet along with the floating head is free to move and thus, this exchanger takes into account differential thermal expansion between shell and tubes (tube bundle).

Fig. 5.10 : Split-ring assembly

It is widely used in chemical industry and petroleum refinery. It is suitable for rigorous duties associated with high pressures and temperatures and also with dirty fluids.

Advantages :
(i) The tube bundle of the exchanger is removable for inspection and mechanical cleaning of the tubes (from outside).
(ii) It eliminates differential expansion problems.

U-tube heat exchanger :

A U-tube 1-2 heat exchanger (shown in Fig. 5.11) consists of U-shaped tubes, both the ends of which are fixed to a single stationary tube sheet. At one end of a shell, a channel is provided with pass partition and is used for entry and exit of the tube side fluid. At the opposite end of the shell, there is a cover which is integral with it. The shell is provided with two nozzles for entry and exit of the shell side fluid. The tube sheet is clamped between shell flange and channel flange. The entire tube bundle can be removed from the shell from the channel end. The differential thermal expansion between shell and tubes is absorbed by U-bends. Each tube can expand or contract freely without affecting the other tubes. As there is a limitation of bending tubes of a very short radius, the number of tube holes in the tube sheet of a given diameter with this exchanger are less than that with a fixed tube sheet exchanger.

In this exchanger, the tube side fluid enters through channel, it flows first through one arm of U - shaped tubes, it comes at other end, travels down through the bend, flows through the other arm of U-shaped tubes and ultimately leaves the exchanger through the outlet provided on the channel. During its passage through the exchanger, it exchanges heat with the shell side fluid.

Fig. 5.11 : U-tube exchanger

The tube bundle can be removed for cleaning of the tubes from outside. The inside of the tube can be cleaned only by chemical means.

Commonly used for the reboiler on large fractionating columns (with enlarged shell) where steam is condensed in the tubes. Also used for high pressure and temperature applications.

Kettle Reboilers / Reboiler exchanger :

It is either provided with an internal floating head arrangement or a U-tube arrangement. To provide a vapour space above a tube bundle, a shell is made larger in diameter.

In distillation operation, a reboiler is used to meet the latent heat requirements at the bottom of a column (i.e., for converting liquid into vapour). Fig. 5.12 shows a kettle type reboiler. It consists of a enlarged shell containing a relatively small tube bundle. At one end of the bundle, the tubes are expanded into a stationary tube sheet clamped between shell and channel flange. In a channel, pass partition is incorporated so that inlet and outlet for the tube side fluid is provided on the same channel. At opposite end of the bundle, tubes are expanded into a freely riding floating tube sheet. The tubes are free to expand. The shell is provided with liquid inlet and outlet at the bottom as shown in Fig. 5.12. A vapour outlet is provided at the top. A weir is incorporated in the shell to maintain a pool of liquid in it.

Fig. 5.12 : Kettle type reboiler with floating head arrangement

Fig. 5.13 : Kettle-type reboiler with U-tube arrangement

The heating media, usually steam, flows through the tubes and condensate is removed through a steam trap. The liquid to be vaporised is introduced in the enlarged shell through the liquid inlet. The tube bundle is always submerged in a pool of boiling liquid and for this purpose an over-flow weir is incorporated in the shell, which is set aside of the floating head. Heat transfer to boiling liquid takes place from a submerged surface. The shell is of a large diameter mainly for vapour-liquid separation. The vapours are generated, disengaged and removed from the top, and unvaporised liquid spills over the weir, and is withdrawn as the bottom product, through the liquid outlet provided at the bottom of shell.

Finned tube heat exchanger / Extended surface exchanger :

When the heat transfer coefficient of one of the process fluids is very low as compared to the other, the overall heat transfer coefficient becomes approximately equal to the lower coefficient. This reduces the capacity per unit area of heat transfer surface, making it necessary to provide very large heat transfer area.

Such situations often arise in (i) heating of viscous liquids by condensing steam or a hot liquid of low viscosity and (ii) heating of a air or a gas stream by condensing steam.

Air or gas side heat transfer coefficient is very low in comparison with the film coefficient on the condensing steam side (condensing steam side coefficient may be 100 to 200 times the film the coefficient on air/gas side). In such cases, it is possible to increase heat transfer by increasing / extending the surface area on the side with the limiting coefficient (air, gas or viscous liquid side) with the help of fins.

The heat transfer area of the tube and pipe is increased substantially by attaching the metal pieces. *The metal pieces employed to extend or increase the heat transfer surface are known as fins.* The fins are most commonly employed on the outside of the tubes. The good example of the extended surface heat exchangers is some automobile radiators.

Common types of fins / extended surfaces are :

(i) Longitudinal fins and (ii) Transverse fins.

Longitudinal fins are used when the direction of flow is parallel to the axis of the tube whereas transverse fins are used when the direction of flow is across the tubes.

(a) **Longitudinal fins**   (b) **Transverse fins**

Fig. 5.14 : Extended surface heat exchangers

In case of longitudinal fins, long metal strips or channels are attached to the outside of a pipe. The strips are attached either by grooving and peening the tube or by welding the strips continuously along the base. Longitudinal fins are commonly employed in double pipe heat exchangers in situations involving gases and viscous liquid, where flow is parallel to the axis of tubes, these fins are used. Longitudinal fin heat exchangers are relatively expensive and are not cleanable so they are especially used for fluids having low heat transfer coefficients and which are clean or form dirt that can be boiled out easily. Fig. 5.14 (a) shows longitudinal fins.

In case of transverse fins, the metal pieces are attached to an ordinary pipe or a tube by grooving and pinning, etc. at right angle to the axis of the pipe or tube. Disc type fins shown in Fig. 5.14 (b) are transverse fins and are usually welded to the tube. Helical fins are the transverse fins and are usually attached in a variety of ways such as welding a ribbon to a tube continuously, etc. as shown in Fig. 5.14 (b).

Transverse fins are commonly employed for cooling and heating of large quantities of gases in cross-flow e.g. economiser, air cooled steam condensers for turbine and engine works, etc.

Plate-type heat exchanger :

It consists of a series of rectangular, parallel plates held firmly together between substantial head frames. The plates have corner ports and are sealed and spaced by rubber gaskets around the ports and along the plate edges. The plates are having corrugated faces. These plates serve as the heat transfer surfaces and are frequently of stainless steel. Corrugated plates provide a high degree of turbulence even at low flow rates. In general, a gap between plates is 1.3 to 1.5 mm. It is provided with inlet and outlet nozzles for fluids at ends.

In this exchanger, a hot fluid passes between alternate pairs of plates, transferring heat to a cold fluid in the adjacent spaces.

The plates can be readily separated for cleaning and the heat transfer area can be increased by simply adding more plates.

Advantages include – it being very compact requires very small floor space, low pressure drop, absence of inter leakage of fluids, ease in dismantling for inspection and cleaning, high heat transfer coefficients, and provide large heat transfer areas in a small volume.

Plate heat exchangers are competitive with shell-and-tube exchangers where corrosion resistant materials are required. As large surface is available for a given duty, the operation with a small temperature difference is possible. Thus for heat sensitive materials and where a close temperature control is required, these units are used. These are successfully used in dairy and brewery industries, where close control of temperature is a valuable feature.

Plate exchangers are relatively effective with viscous fluids with viscosities upto about 30 kg/(m·s) (300 Poise). These can be employed upto temperature of 423 K (150°C) and pressure of 900 kN/m². These units are easily dismantled for the inspection of plates. The weakness of these units is the necessity of long gaskets.

Fig. 5.15 shows a typical plate type unit.

(a) (b)

(c) (d)

(e) **Plates with rubber sealing gaskets**

Fig. 5.15 : Plate heat exchanger

Scrapped surface heat exchanger :

Scrapped surface heat exchanger is basically a double pipe heat exchanger with a fairly large central tube, 100 to 300 mm in diameter, jacketed with steam or a cooling liquid. A scrapping mechanism-rotating shaft provided with one or more longitudinal scrapping blades is incorporated in the inner pipe to scrape the inside surface. The process fluid (viscous liquid) flows at a low velocity through inside pipe and a cooling or heating medium flows through the annular space created between two concentric pipes. The rotating scrapper continuously scraps the surface thus preventing localised heating and facilitating rapid heat transfer.

This heat exchanger is used for heating or cooling of liquid-solid suspensions, viscous, aqueous and organic solutions and food products, such as margarine and orange juice concentrates. It is also widely used in paraffin wax plants.

Fig. 5.16 : Scrapped surface heat exchanger

Graphite block heat exchanger :

Graphite heat exchangers are well suited for handling corrosive fluids. Graphite is inert towards most corrosive fluids and has very high thermal conductivity. Graphite being soft, these exchangers are made in cubic or cylindrical blocks. In cubic exchangers, parallel holes are drilled in a solid cube such that parallel holes of a particular row are at right angles to the holes of the row above and below. Headers bolted to the opposite sides of the vertical faces of the cube provide the flow of process fluid through the block. The headers located on the remaining vertical faces direct the service fluid through the exchanger in a cross flow.

Fig. 5.17 : Graphite heat exchanger

Heat Transfer in Agitated Vessel :

An agitated vessel is a vertical cylindrical vessel incorporating a suitable type of agitator that brings out even distribution in the vessel. The agitator may be a paddle, anchor or turbine depending upon a situation. Anchors are used for contents of high viscosity and turbines for moderate viscosities.

Agitated vessels are commonly employed in chemical industries for a variety of purposes such as mixing, dissolution (e.g. dissolution of caustic soda in water), dilution (i.g. dilution of sulphuric acid), neutralisation (e.g. acidic stream by alkali and vice-versa), absorption (e.g. absorption of ammonia in water), crystallisation (e.g. crystallisation by cooling) and to carry out a number of chemical reactions. In such cases, addition or removal of heat is conveniently done by a heat transfer surface, the surface that may be in the form of a jacket fitted on the outside the vessel or a helical coil fitted to the inside.

Jacket as well as helical coils are used for heating or cooling purpose depending upon a situation.

For carrying out exothermic or endothermic reaction in agitated vessel one can use either a jacket or a coil, although generally the jacket is installed when it is necessary to supply the heat and the coil to remove the heat. In a majority of cases, the heat is supplied by condensation of vapours and for given heat transfer area there is greater space for condensation in jacket than in a coil. The condensate removal is also easy with jackets. A cooling coil is more suitable than a cooling jacket as the heat transfer coefficient is high in the coil than in the jacket due to higher velocities of the coolant in the coils. Jackets can be constructed out of cheaper material like mild steel, whereas coils as they are immersed in the contents of vessel are constructed out of expensive materials from a corrosion point of view. Generally, use of coil or jacket depends upon a number of factors.

The rate of heat transfer depends upon the physical properties of the agitated liquid, heating and cooling media, vessel geometry, degree of agitation, etc.

Fig. 5.18 : Agitated vessel with jacket and helical coil

Film coefficients for jacket and coil :

(i) Coil :

h_i-inside film coefficient is given by

$$\frac{hD}{k} = 0.023 \left(\frac{Du\rho}{\mu}\right)^{0.8} \left(\frac{C_p \mu}{k}\right)^a \qquad \ldots (5.1)$$

where $\quad a$ = 0.4 for heating and 0.3 for cooling.

This equation is applicable for a straight tube.

For a coil, h_i is given by

$$h_{i\,(coil)} = h_{i\,(straight\,tube)} \left[1 + 3.5\,\frac{D}{D_c}\right] \qquad \ldots (5.2)$$

where D is the inside diameter of coil and D_c is the diameter of helix (coil diameter).

The agitator Reynolds number is given by

$$N_{Re,\,a} = \frac{D_a^2 N \rho}{\mu}$$

This number is very useful as a correlating variable for heat transfer to jackets or coils in an agitated vessel.

For heating or cooling liquids in a baffled agitated vessel equipped with a helical coil and a turbine agitator, h_c is given by the following equation :

$$\frac{h_c D_c}{k} = 0.17 \left(\frac{D_a^2 N \rho}{\mu}\right)^{0.67} \left(\frac{C_p \mu}{k}\right)^{0.37} \left(\frac{D_a}{D_t}\right) \left(\frac{D_c}{D_t}\right)^{0.5} \left(\frac{\mu}{\mu_w}\right)^{0.24} \qquad \ldots (5.3)$$

where $\quad D_a$ – impeller diameter

$\quad\quad\quad\; D_t$ – vessel diameter

$\quad\quad\quad\; N$ – r.p.m.

and h_c is the film coefficient between coil surface and liquid (content of vessel).

(ii) Jacket :

For heat transfer to or from the jacket of a baffled agitated vessel, when pitched blade turbine is used, h_j is given by

$$\frac{h_j D_t}{k} = 0.44 \left(\frac{D_a^2 N \rho}{\mu}\right)^{2/3} \left(\frac{C_p \mu}{k}\right)^{1/3} \left(\frac{\mu}{\mu_w}\right)^{0.24} \qquad \ldots (5.4)$$

where h_j is the film coefficient between the liquid (the content of the vessel) and the jacketed inner surface of the vessel.

Maintenance of Heat Exchanger :

The main maintenance of a heat exchanger is cleaning of the tubes as the surface of the tubes is the heat transfer surface. The cleaning of the tubes is required from both inside and outside as deposits/scales can form on both the sides. Cleaning of the tubes is done by mechanical or chemical means. Usually, cleaning of the tubes from the inside is done by brushing (round wire brush is used) or by acid cleaning. For mechanical cleaning, the heat exchanger should be opened. Replacement of gaskets is essential to avoid the leakage when opened for cleaning. In case of acid cleaning, the dilute acid (hydrochloric) is circulated through the heat exchanger for predetermined period then alkali for neutralisation of the residual acid is circulated and finally the heat exchanger is flushed with fresh soft water. Acid cleaning may be adopted for external cleaning of the tubes. Cleaning may be done periodically or during shutdown of the plant.

There are chances of leakage occurring through the tube sheet which may be rectified by welding. After a long period of operation depending upon the service conditions the tubes may get corroded which results in decrease in the thickness of the tubes which can be judged by sound test. The corroded tube may require replacement or filling by welding. A tube which leaks at a certain point should be isolated from the service by plugging both ends of the tube.

Ex. 5.1 : In a double pipe counter current flow heat exchanger, 10000 kg/h of an oil having a specific heat of 2095 J/(kg·K) is cooled from 353 K (80° C) to 323 K (50° C) by 8000 kg/h of water entering at 298 K (25° C). Calculate the heat exchanger area for an overall heat transfer coefficient of 300 W/(m²·K). Take C_p for water as 4180 J/(kg·K).

Solution : Heat gained by water = Heat removed from oil

$$Q = \dot{m}_w C_{pw} (t_2 - t_1) = \dot{m}_o C_{po} (T_1 - T_2)$$

$$8000 \times 4180 (t_2 - 298) = 10000 \times 2095 (353 - 323)$$

∴ $t_2 = 316.8$ K (43.8° C)

$$353 \xrightarrow{\text{oil}} 323 \text{ K}$$
$$316.8 \text{ K} \xleftarrow{\text{water}} 298 \text{ K}$$

$\Delta T_1 = 353 - 316.8 = 36.2$ K, $\Delta T_2 = 323 - 298 = 25$ K

$\Delta Tlm = (36.2 - 25) / \ln (36.2/25) = 30.25$ K

$Q = UA \Delta Tlm$

$Q = \dot{m}_o C_{po} (T_1 - T_2) = \dfrac{10000}{3600} \times 2095 (353 - 323) = 174583$ W

$U = 300$ W/(m²·K)

$A = Q/(U \Delta Tlm) = \dfrac{174583}{300 \times 30.25} = 19.24$ m² ... **Ans.**

Ex. 5.2 : Hot oil at a rate of 1.2 kg/s [C_p = 2083 J/(kg·K)] flows through double pipe heat exchanger. It enters at 633 K (360° C) and leaves at 573 K (300° C). The cold fluid enters at 303 K (30° C) and leaves at 400 K (127° C). If the overall heat transfer coefficient is 500 W/(m²·K), calculate the heat transfer area for (i) parallel flow and (ii) countercurrent flow.

Solution : (i) Parallel flow :

$$633 \text{ K} \xrightarrow{\text{oil}} 573 \text{ K}$$

$$303 \text{ K} \xrightarrow{\text{coolant}} 400 \text{ K}$$

ΔT_1 = 633 – 303 = 330 K, ΔT_2 = 573 – 400 = 173 K

ΔTlm = (330 – 173)/ln (330/173) = 243 K

Q = 1.2 × 2083 (633 – 573) = 149976 W

Q = UA ΔTlm

A = Q/U ΔTlm = $\dfrac{149976}{243 \times 500}$ = 1.234 m² ... **Ans.**

(ii) Countercurrent flow :

$$633 \text{ K} \xrightarrow{\text{oil}} 573 \text{ K}$$

$$400 \text{ K} \xleftarrow{\text{water}} 303 \text{ K}$$

ΔT_2 = 633 – 400 = 233 K, ΔT_2 = 573 – 303 = 270 K

ΔTlm = (270 – 233)/ln (273/233) = 251 K

Q = 149976 m

A = Q/U ΔTlm

= 149976/500 × 251 = 1.195 m² ... **Ans.**

For the same thermal temperature of the fluids, the surface area for counterflow arrangement is less than that required for parallel flow.

Ex. 5.3 : Calculate the total length of double pipe heat exchanger required to cool 5500 kg/h of ethylene glycol from 358 K (85° C) to 341 K (68° C) using toluene as a cooling media which flows in counter current fashion. Toluene enters at 303 K (30° C) and leaves at 335 K (62° C).

Data :

Outside diameter of outside pipe = 70 mm

Outside diameter of inside pipe = 43 mm

Wall thickness of both pipes = 3 mm

Mean properties of two fluids are given as below :

Property	Ethylene glycol	Toluene

Density	1080 kg/m³	840 kg/m³
Specific heat	2.680 kJ/(kg·K)	1.80 kJ/(kg·K)
Thermal conductivity	0.248 W/(m·K)	0.146 W/(m·K)
Viscosity	3.4×10^{-3} Pa·s	4.4×10^{-4} Pa·s

Thermal conductivity of metal pipe is 46.52 W/(m·K) and ethylene glycol is flowing through the inner pipe.

Solution :

For ethylene glycol flowing through the inner pipe :

$\dot{m}_e$ = mass flow rate of ethylene glycol
= 5500 kg/h = 1.528 kg/s

O.D. of inner pipe = 42 mm

I.D. of inner pipe = 43 – 2 × 3 = 37 mm = 0.037 m

Area of inner pipe = $A_i = \frac{\pi}{4} D_i^2 = \frac{\pi}{4} \times (0.037)^2$

A_i = 0.001075 m²

G = mass velocity = $\dot{m}_e / A_i = \frac{1.528}{0.001075}$

= 1421.4 kg/(m²·s)

$$N_{Re} = \frac{D_i u \rho}{\mu} = \frac{D_i G}{\mu}$$

where $\mu = 3.4 \times 10^{-3}$ Pa·s + 3.4×10^{-3} kg/(m·s)

$$N_{Re} = \frac{0.037 \times 1421.4}{3.4 \times 10^{-3}} = 15468$$

C_p = 2.68 kJ/(kg·K) = 2.68×10^3 J/(kg·K)

$\mu = 3.4 \times 10^{-3}$ kg/(m·s), k = 0.248 W/(m·K)

$$N_{Pr} = \frac{C_p \mu}{k} = \frac{2.68 \times 10^3 \times 3.4 \times 10^{-3}}{0.248} = 36.74$$

As N_{Re} > 10,000 we can use the Dittus-Boelter equation [for cooling]

N_{Nu} = 0.023 $(N_{Re})^{0.8} (N_{Pr})^{0.3}$

= 0.023 $(15468)^{0.8} (36.74)^{0.3}$ = 152.32

$$\frac{h_i D_i}{k} = 152.34$$

$$h_i = \frac{152.34 \times 0.248}{0.037} = 1021 \text{ W/(m}^2\cdot\text{K)}$$

For toluene flowing through the annulus :

$\dot{m}_t$ = mass flow rate of toluene

Heat balance :

Heat lost by ethylene glycol = Heat gained by toluene

$$5500 \times 2.68 \, (358 - 341) = \dot{m}_t \times 1.80 \, (335 - 303)$$

$$\dot{m}_t = 4350.35 \text{ kg/h} = 1.21 \text{ kg/s}$$

Inside diameter of outside pipe = $70 - 2 \times 3 = 64$ mm = 0.064 m

$$D_e = \text{equivalent diameter for annulus} = \frac{D_2^2 - D_1^2}{D_1}$$

$$= \frac{(0.064)^2 - (0.043)^2}{(0.043)} = 0.052 \text{ m}$$

Area of cross section for flow $= \frac{\pi}{4} \left[D_2^2 - D_1^2 \right]$

$$= \frac{\pi}{4} \left[(0.064)^2 - (0.043)^2 \right]$$

$$A_a = 0.00176 \text{ m}^2$$

G_a = mass velocity through annulus $= \dfrac{1.21}{0.00176} = 687.5$ kg/(m²·s)

$$N_{Re} = \frac{D_e \, G_a}{\mu} = \frac{0.052 \times 687.5}{4.4 \times 10^{-4}} = 81250$$

$$N_{Pr} = \frac{C_p \mu}{k} = \frac{1.80 \times 10^3 \times 4.4 \times 10^{-4}}{0.146} = 5.42$$

Dittus-Boelter equation for heating :

$$N_{Nu} = 0.023 \, (N_{Re})^{0.8} \, (N_{Pr})^{0.4}$$

$$= 0.023 \, (81250)^{0.8} \, (5.42)^{0.4}$$

$$= 383$$

$$\frac{h_o \, D_e}{k} = 383$$

$$h_o = \frac{383 \times 0.146}{0.052} = 1075.3 \text{ W/(m}^2\cdot\text{K)}$$

D_w = log mean diameter of inside pipe

$$= \frac{0.043 - 0.037}{\ln (0.043/0.037)} = 0.0399 \text{ m}$$

$$\frac{1}{U_o} = \frac{1}{h_o} + \frac{1}{h_i} \times \frac{D_o}{D_i} + \frac{x}{k} \frac{D_o}{D_w}$$

$$\frac{1}{U_o} = \frac{1}{1075.3} + \frac{1}{1021} \times \frac{0.043}{0.037} + \frac{0.003}{46.52} \times \frac{0.043}{0.0399}$$

$$U_o = 468 \text{ W/(m}^2\cdot\text{K)}$$

ΔTlm = log mean temperature difference for counter current flow

$$358 \text{ K} \xrightarrow{E.G.} 341 \text{ K}$$
$$335 \text{ K} \xleftarrow{Toluene} 303 \text{ K}$$

$\Delta T_1 = 38$ K   and $\Delta T_2 = 23$ K

$\Delta Tlm = (38 - 23) / \ln(38/23) = 29.87$ K

$$Q = \dot{m}C_{p_e}(T_1 - T_2) = 1.528 \times 2.680 \,(358 - 341)$$
$$= 69.61 \text{ kJ/s} = 69.61 \times 10^3 \text{ J/s} + 69.61 \times 10^3 \text{ W}$$

We have,

$$Q = U_o \cdot A_o \cdot \Delta Tlm$$
$$69.61 \times 10^3 = 468 \times A_o \times 29.87$$
$$A_o = 4.98 \text{ m}^2$$
$$A = 4.98 = \pi D \cdot L$$
$$4.98 = \pi(0.043) L$$

∴ $L = 36.86$ m   … **Ans.**

EXERCISE

1. Fill in the blanks :
1.1 The centre-to-centre distance between baffles is known as baffle ....
 Ans. spacing or pitch
1.2 The shortest centre-to-centre distance between the adjacent tubes is known as the .... **Ans.** tube pitch
1.3 The heat transfer equipment which consists of two concentric pipes is called as .... heat exchanger. **Ans.** double pipe
1.4 External cleaning of the tubes is easy in case of ..... pitch arrangement than triangular pitch arrangement of tube lay-out. **Ans.** square
1.5 In 1-2 shell and tube heat exchanger the ..... side fluid flows once through exchanger while ...... side fluid flows twice through exchanger. **Ans.** shell, tube
1.6 For external cleaning of the tubes, tube bundle can be taken out of shell in .... heat exchanger. **Ans.** floating
1.7 The .... baffles are the drilled plate with heights equal to 75% of the inside diameter of the shell. **Ans.** segmental

1.8 Kettle reboilers generally incorporates .... head arrangement or .... arrangement. **Ans.** floating, U-tube

1.9 The metal pieces examployed to extend or increase the heat transfer surface are called as .... **Ans.** fins

1.10 In case of .... fins, long metal strips are attached to the outside of the pipe. **Ans.** longitudinal

2. Define the following terms :
   (a) condenser (b) cooler (c) vaporiser (d) heater (e) reboiler (f) chiller
3. Give the classification of shell and tube heat exchanger.
4. Write in brief on double pipe heat exchanger.
5. Draw neat sketch of fixed tube sheet heat exchanger and label its parts.
6. Write in brief on plate heat exchanger.
7. Write in brief on scrapped surface heat exchanger.
8. Draw neat sketch of kettle reboiler and explain its construction.
9. Draw neat sketch of floating heat exchanger and explain its construction.
10. What do you mean by term fins. Draw neat sketches of longitudinal and transverse fins.
11. Write in brief in finned tube heat exchanger.
12. Draw neat sketch of U-tube heat-exchanger and explain briefly its construction.
13. Draw the neat sketch of kettle reboiler and explain in brief its working.
14. Draw the neat sketch of 1-2 shell and tube heat exchanger and label its parts.
15. State the advantages of floating head heat exchanger.
16. State the advantages of double pipe heat-exchanger and its drawbacks.

CHAPTER SIX

EVAPORATION

Evaporation is an operation that is carried out in the industry as a means of concentrating a weak liquor/solution by vaporising a portion of the solvent.

The weak liquor/solution is composed of a non-volatile solute and a volatile solvent.

Objective : The objective of evaporation is to concentrate a solution consisting of a non-volatile solute and a volatile solvent.

In this operation, the solvent to be evaporated is generally water and the concentrated solution/thick liquor is the desired product. The vapour generated usually has no value, it is condensed and discarded.

It differs from drying in that the residue obtained is a liquid rather than a solid.

It differs from distillation in that the vapour is usually a single component and even if it is a mixture, it is not separated into fractions.

It differs from crystallisation in that the purpose is to concentrate a solution rather than to form and build crystals.

Evaporation is generally followed by crystallisation and drying.

Evaporation is carried by supplying heat to a solution to vaporise the solvent. The common heating medium (heat source) is generally low pressure steam but in some situations other sources that might be used : solar energy, fuel, electricity, hot oil and flue-gas. The heat is utilised to –

(i) increase the temperature of the solution to its boiling point and

(ii) supply the latent heat of vaporisation of the solvent.

Though the several rate processes occur (heat transfer from a heating medium to a solution through the solid surface, simultaneous heat and mass transfer from a liquid to a vapour phase), the operation can usually be considered in terms of heat transfer from a heater to the solution (heat transfer to boiling liquids) for the design of evaporators.

There is a wide variation in characteristics of the liquor to be concentrated that requires judgement and experience in designing and operating evaporators. Some of the properties of evaporating liquids that influence the process of evaporation are :

(i) Concentration : As the concentration increases, the solution become more and more individualistic. The viscosity and density increase with solid content. The boiling point of the solution also increases considerably with the solid content so that it may be much higher than B.P. of water at the same pressure.

(ii) Foaming : Some materials have tendency to foam that causes heavy entrainment (carry over of a portion of the liquid by the rising vapour is called as an entrainment).

(iii) Scale : Some solutions deposit scale on the heat transfer surfaces that results in reduction of the heat transfer coefficient and hence the heat transfer rate. It is therefore necessary to clean the tubes at definite intervals.

(iv) Temperature sensitivity : Some materials especially pharmaceuticals and food products are damaged when heated to moderate temperatures even for short times. For concentrating such materials special techniques are to be used that reduce the temperature and also the time of heating.

(v) Materials of construction : Generally evaporators are made of mild steel. Whenever contamination and corrosion is not a problem special materials such as copper, nickel, stainless steels may be used. Other liquid characteristics that must be considered in the design are specific heat, freezing point, toxicity, explosion hazards and radioactivity.

The selection of an evaporator for a particular application is based on the analysis of the factors such as the properties of liquid to be concentrated, operating cost, capacity, hold ups and residence time. High product viscosity, heat sensitivity, scale formation and deposition are the major problems encountered during the operation of evaporators and should be taken into account while designing evaporator for a new installation.

Usually, the desired product of an evaporation operation is the concentrated solution (called as thick liquor), but occasionally the evaporated solvent is the primary product as in the evaporation of sea water to obtain potable water.

Common examples of evaporation are :

Concentration of aqueous solutions of sugars, sodium chloride, sodium hydroxide, glycerol, milk and fruit juices.

Performance of tubular evaporators :

The performance of a steam heated tubular evaporator is evaluated in terms of

(i) capacity and (ii) economy

Capacity : Capacity of an evaporator is defined as the *number of kilogram of water vaporised / evaporated per hour.*

The rate of heat transfer Q, through the heating surface of an evaporator, is the product of the area of heat transfer surface A, the overall heat transfer coefficient U, and the overall temperature drop ΔT.

$$Q = U \cdot A \, \Delta T \qquad \ldots (6.1)$$

ΔT is the temperature difference between the heating medium and the boiling liquor. (saturation temperature of steam minus the boiling point of solution).

If the feed solution is at the boiling temperature corresponding to the pressure in the vapour space of an evaporator, then all the heat transferred through the heating surface is available for evaporation and the capacity is proportional to the heat transfer rate. If the cold feed solution is fed to the evaporator, the heat is required to increase its temperature to the boiling point and it may be a quite large and thus, the capacity for a given rate of heat transfer will be reduced accordingly as heat used to increase the temperature to the boiling point is not available for evaporation. When the feed solution to the evaporator is at a temperature higher than the boiling point corresponding to the pressure in the vapour space, a portion of the feed evaporates adiabatically and the capacity is greater than that corresponding to the heat transfer rate. The process is called as flash evaporation.

Evaporator economy : Economy of an evaporator is defined as the *number of kilogram of water evaporated per kilogram of steam fed to the evaporator*. It is also called as steam economy.

In a single-effect evaporator the amount of water evaporated per kg of steam fed is always less than one and hence economy is less than one. The fact that the latent heat of evaporation of water decreases as the pressure increases tends to make the ratio of water vapour produced per kg of steam condensed less than unity.

Increase in the economy of an evaporator is achieved by reusing the vapour produced.

The methods of increasing the economy are :

(i) use of multiple effect evaporation system

(ii) vapour recompression.

In a multiple effect evaporation system, the vapour produced in first effect is fed to the steam chest of second-effect as a heating medium in which boiling takes place at low pressure and temperature and so on. Thus in a triple-effect evaporator, 1 kg of steam fed to first-effect evaporates approximately 2.5 kg of steam.

The another method to increase the economy of an evaporator is to use principle of thermo compression. Here, the vapour from the evaporator is compressed to increase its temperature so that it will condense at a temperature higher enough to permit its use as a heating media in the same evaporator.

Boiling point elevation :

In actual practice, the boiling point of a solution is affected by a boiling point elevation and a liquid head.

As the vapour pressure of most aqueous solutions is less than that of water at any given temperature, the boiling point of the solution is higher than that of pure water at a given pressure. **The difference between the boiling point of a solution and that of pure water at any given pressure is known as the boiling point rise/elevation of the solution.** The boiling point elevation is small for dilute solutions and large for concentrated solutions of inorganic salts.

The boiling point elevation of strong solutions can be obtained from an empirical rule known as *Duhring's rule*. It states that *the boiling point of a given solution is a linear function of the boiling point of pure water at the same pressure.* So, when the boiling point of a solution is plotted against the boiling point of water, we get a straight line. Fig. 6.1 shows such a plot for an aqueous solution of caustic soda of various concentrations.

Fig. 6.1 : Duhring's plot for NaOH

Material and enthalpy balances for single-effect evaporator :

Consider an evaporator which is fed with $\dot{m}_f$ kg/h of the weak solution containing w_1 % solute and the thick liquor is withdrawn at $\dot{m}'$ kg/h containing w_2 % solute by weight. Let $\dot{m}_v$ be the kg/h of water evaporated. Then :

Fig. 6.2 : Block diagram of evaporator

Overall material balance :

$$\dot{m}_f = \dot{m}_v + \dot{m}' \qquad \ldots (6.2)$$

Material balance of the solute :

Solute in feed = Solute in thick liquor

$$\frac{w_1 \times \dot{m}_f}{100} = \frac{w_2 \dot{m}'}{100}$$

$$w_1 \times \dot{m}_f = w_2 \dot{m}' \qquad \ldots (6.3)$$

Knowing three out of the above mentioned five quantities we can find the values of other two with the help of the above two equations.

Let T_f, T and T_s be the temperatures, of feed entering the evaporator, solution in the evaporators and condensing steam respectively.

Let 'λ_s' be the latent heat of condensation of the steam at saturation temperature and assume that only the latent heat of condensation is used. Then, the rate of heat transfer through the heating surface from the steam side is :

$$Q_s = \dot{m}_s \lambda_s \qquad \ldots (6.4)$$

where $\dot{m}_s$ is mass flow rate of the steam to the evaporator in kg/h.

Assuming heat losses to be negligible, the enthalpy balance over the evaporator is :

Heat associated with feed + Heat (latent) associated with steam =

Heat associated with vapour leaving + Heat associated with thick liquor

$$\dot{m}_f \cdot H_f + \dot{m}_s \lambda_s = \dot{m}\dot{m}_v H_v + \dot{m}' H' \qquad \ldots (6.5)$$

$$\dot{m}_f \cdot H_f + \dot{m}_s \lambda_s = (\dot{m}_f - \dot{m}') H_v + \dot{m}' H' \qquad \ldots (6.6)$$

where H_v, H_f and H' are enthalpies of the vapour, feed solution and thick liquor, respectively.

Rearranging we get :

$$\dot{m}_s \lambda_s = (\dot{m}_f - \dot{m}') H_v + \dot{m}' H' - \dot{m}_f H_f \qquad \ldots (6.7)$$

Heat transfer rate on the steam side = Heat transfer rate on the liquor side.

In case of solutions having negligible heats of dilution, the enthalpy balance can be written in terms of the specific heats and temperatures of the solutions.

Heat transferred to solution in the evaporator by the condensing steam (in absence of heat losses) is utilised to heat the feed solution from T_f to T and for the vaporisation of water from the solution.

$$Q_s = Q$$
$$= \dot{m}_f C_{p_f} (T - T_f) + (\dot{m}_f - \dot{m}') \lambda_v \qquad \ldots (6.8)$$

$$\dot{m}_s \lambda_s = \dot{m}_f \cdot C_{p_f} (T - T_f) + (\dot{m}_f - \dot{m}') \lambda_v \qquad \ldots (6.9)$$

where $\quad C_{p_f}$ = specific heat of feed solution

λ_v = latent heat of evaporation from thick liquor

For a negligible boiling point rise $\lambda_v = \lambda$

where $\quad \lambda$ = latent heat of vaporisation of water at pressure in the vapour space and can be read from steam tables

Equation (6.9) becomes :

$$\dot{m}_s \lambda_s = \dot{m}_f C_{p_f} (T - T_f) + (\dot{m}_f - \dot{m}') \lambda \qquad \ldots (6.10)$$

$$\dot{m}_s \lambda_s = \dot{m}_f \cdot C_{p_f} (T - T_f) + \dot{m} \lambda \qquad \ldots (6.11)$$

The boiling point of solution (T) at the pressure in the vapour space can be obtained by knowing the boiling point elevation and boiling point of pure water at that pressure, e.g. if T' is the boiling point of water at a certain pressure of operation and 'P' is the boiling point elevation, then

$$T = T' + P$$

Area of heat transfer of an evaporator is calculated with the help of the following equation :

$$Q = U \cdot A \cdot \Delta T \qquad \ldots (6.12)$$

$$Q = \dot{m}_s \lambda_s = U \cdot A \cdot \Delta T \qquad \ldots (6.13)$$

where U = overall heat transfer coefficient

A = area of heat transfer

and ΔT = the temperature difference

$\Delta T = T_s - T$

ΔT = Condensing steam temperature – Boiling point of a solution

When 'Q' is in W, 'U' is in W/(m²·K) and 'ΔT' is in K then 'A' will be in m².

λ_s = Specific enthalpy of saturated steam
– Specific enthalpy of saturated water (i.e. of condensate)

Evaporator Types :

Evaporators used in process industries can be classified as :

(i) Natural circulation evaporators, and

(ii) Forced circulation evaporators.

Natural circulation evaporators are commonly employed for simpler evaporation operations singly or in multiple effect e.g. horizontal tube evaporator, vertical tube evaporator etc., while forced circulation evaporators are commonly employed for salting, viscous and scale forming solutions. These units may be provided with external horizontal or vertical heating element.

Open pan evaporator / Jacketed pan evaporator :

The simplest method of concentrating a solution is by use of jacketed pans, in which the condensing steam is used in the jacket for evaporating a part of the solvent. Such type of evaporator is particularly suitable when small quantities are to be handled. These are available in a great variety of materials. Pans of stainless steel, copper, aluminium etc. are widely used in the food process industries. Mild steel jacket may be welded to the pan.

Fig. 6.3 : Jacketed pan evaporator

Pan is made of a single sheet of metal for small size, or several sheets joined by welding / brazing. A jacket is welded to the pan. The jacket is provided with steam inlet at the top while a condensate drain is provided at its bottom. The pan is provided with the outlet at the bottom for draining its contents.

The solution to be concentrated is taken into the pan and steam is admitted in the jacket. Evaporation is carried out for a predetermined time to achieve a desired concentration level. The thick liquor is then drained from the outlet.

Horizontal tube evaporator :

It is the oldest type of evaporator. It consists of a vertical cylindrical shell incorporating a horizontal square tube bundle at the lower portion of the shell. Channels are provided on either ends of the tube bundle for introduction of steam and withdrawal of condensate. The shell is closed by dished heads at both the ends. A vapour outlet is provided on the top cover and a thick liquor outlet is provided at the bottom. Feed point is located at a convenient point. In this evaporator, steam is inside the tube and a liquor to be concentrated surrounds the tubes. Steam which is admitted through one of the steam chest/channel flows through tubes. Steam gets condensed by transferring its latent heat and the condensate is removed from the outlet provided at the bottom of opposite steam chest. This type of evaporator is shown in Fig. 6.4.

Heat given out by the condensing steam will be gained by a solution in the evaporator and the solution boils. Vapours formed are removed from the top while the thick liquor is removed from the bottom. In this evaporator as evaporation occurs outside the tube, it eliminates scale formation problem inside the tubes. Small diameter tubes than any other types are used.

Fig. 6.4 : Horizontal tube evaporator

Main advantages : Very low head room requirements and large vapour-liquid disengaging area.

It is not suited for salting and scaling liquids as deposits form on the outside of the tubes.

It is commonly employed for small capacity services and for simpler problems of concentrations, i.e., for processes wherein the final product is liquor, such as industrial sirups.

Calendria - type / Standard vertical tube evaporator / Short tube evaporator :

Construction :

It consists of a vertical cylindrical shell incorporating (at the lower portion) a short vertical tube bundle with horizontal tube sheets bolted to shell flanges. Vapour outlet is provided at the top cover while thick liquor discharge is provided at the bottom. Usually the tube bundle is not more than 150 cms high and tube diameter (outside) not more than 75 mm (25 mm to 75 mm). A downtake is provided at the centre of the tube bundle with flow area about 40 to 100 per cent of the total cross sectional area of the tubes for circulating cooler liquid back to the bottom of the tubes. In this evaporator, the solution to be evaporated is inside the tubes and steam flows outside the tubes in the steam chest. Baffles are incorporated in the steam chest to promote uniform distribution of steam. The condensate is withdrawn at any convenient point near the lower tube sheet, while the non-condensable gas such as air is vented to the atmosphere from a point near the top tube sheet.

Fig. 6.5 : Calendria type evaporator

Working : Thin liquor is introduced to the tube side and steam into the steam chest. The liquor covers the top of tubes. Heat transfer to the boiling liquid inside the tubes takes place from condensing steam on the outside of the tubes. Vapours formed will rise through the tubes, come to a liquid surface from which they are disengaged into a vapour space and removed from a vapour outlet. Circulation of the cold liquor is promoted by a central downtake and the concentrated / thick liquor is removed from the bottom of the evaporator.

Advantages :
(i) Relatively inexpensive.
(ii) As scaling occurs inside the tubes, it can be easily removed by mechanical or chemical means.
(iii) Provide moderately good heat transfer at reasonable cost.
(iv) Can be put into more rigorous services than horizontal tube evaporators.
(v) High heat transfer coefficients.
(vi) Requires low head room.

Disadvantages :
(i) Floor space required is large.
(ii) Amount of liquid help up in the evaporator is large.
(iii) Since there is no circulation these are not suitable for viscous liquid.

Long tube vertical evaporator :

Construction : A long tube evaporator consists of a long tubular heating element incorporating tubes 25 mm to 50 mm in diameter and 4 to 8 metres in length. The tubular heating element projects into a vapour space/separator for removing entrained liquid from the vapour. The upper tube sheet of tubular exchanger is free and a vapour deflector is incorporated in the vapour space just above it. A return pipe connecting the vapour space to the bottom of the exchanger is provided for natural circulation of a unvaporised liquid. It is provided with inlet connections for feed, steam and outlet connections for vapour, thick liquor, condensate, etc. In this evaporator, the liquor to be concentrated is in tubes and condensing steam surrounds the tubes. Fig. 6.6 shows a long-tube vertical evaporator.

Fig. 6.6 : Long-tube vertical evaporator

Working :

In this evaporator, feed enters the bottom of the tubes, gets heated by the condensing steam, starts to boil part way up the tubes and the mixture of vapour and liquid issues from the top of tubes and finally impinges at high velocity on a deflector. The deflector acts both as a primary separator and a foam breaker. The separated liquid enters the bottom of the exchanger and part of this liquid is taken out as a product.

The long tube vertical evaporator competes most favourably with forced circulation evaporators as compared to other natural circulation evaporators.

This type of evaporator is widely used for handling of foamy, frothy liquors.

Used for the production of condensed milk and concentrating black liquor in the pulp and paper industry.

Forced Circulation Evaporators :

Whenever we are dealing with concentration problems involving solutions of high viscosities, of scale forming tendencies there is no other alternative than to use a forced circulation evaporator as increasing the velocity of flow of liquor through tubes increases remarkably the liquid film heat transfer coefficients and the high velocity resulting by use of a centrifugal pump prevents the formation of excessive deposits on the heat transfer surfaces. In a natural circulation evaporator, the liquid enters the tube at a velocity of 0.3 to 1 metre per second; while in a forced circulation evaporator, the velocity is of the order of 2 to 6 metres per second. In the forced circulation evaporator, smaller diameter tubes are used than in the natural circulation evaporator, generally not larger than 50 mm.

Forced circulation evaporators with horizontal external heating element :

Construction :

Fig. 6.7 shows a forced circulation evaporator with horizontal external heating element. It consists of a circulating pump, a separating space (separator), an evaporator body with a vapour outlet at the top, a deflector plate, an outlet for discharge of thick liquor and an external heating surface - a horizontal shell and tube heat exchanger having two passes on both shell and tube sides.

Working :

A centrifugal pump forces liquid through the tubes at high velocity and is heated as it passes through tubes due to heat transfer from condensing steam on the shell side. Boiling does not take place in the tubes as they are under sufficient static head which raises the boiling point above that in the separating space.

Fig. 6.7 (a) : Forced circulation evaporator with horizontal external heating element

Fig. 6.7 (b) : Forced circulation evaporator with vertical heating element

The solution becomes superheated and flashes into a mixture of vapour and liquid just before entering the separator due to reduction in the static head when it flows from the exchanger to the separator. The two-phase mixture impinges on a deflector plate in the separating space, and the vapours are removed from the top, and the liquid is returned to the centrifugal pump. Part of liquid/solution leaving the separating space is withdrawn as concentrated liquor and makeup feed is continuously introduced at the pump inlet.

In case of vertical heating element, single pass shell and tube heat exchanger is used.

Advantages of forced circulation evaporators :

1. High heat transfer coefficients are obtained even with viscous material.
2. Positive circulation and close control of flow.
3. Whenever there is a tendency to form scale or deposit salts, use of forced circulation units prevents the formation of excessive deposits due to high velocities.
4. Residence time of liquid in tube is very small (1– 3 s) because of high velocities in these units so that moderately heat sensitive liquids can be handled.

Main disadvantage lies in high pumping cost.

The forced circulation evaporators are commonly employed for crystalline product, viscous, salting, scaling and corrosive and foaming solutions / liquors.

Multiple-effect evaporation :

Most of the evaporators use low pressure steam for heating purpose. Due to addition of heat to a solution in the evaporator by condensation of steam, the solution in the evaporator will boil. If the vapours leaving the evaporator are fed to some form of a condenser then the heat associated with the vapour will be lost and the system is said to make poor use of steam.

The vapour coming out of an evaporator can be used as the heating media for the another evaporator which will be operating at the pressure lower than the pressure in the evaporator from which the vapours are issuing so as to provide a sufficient temperature gradient for the heat transfer in that evaporator.

When a single evaporator is put into service and vapours leaving the evaporator are condensed and discarded the method is known as *single-effect evaporation*. The economy of a single effect evaporator is always less than one. Generally for evaporation of one kg of water from a solution, 1 to 1.3 kg of steam is required.

Method of increasing the evaporation per kilogram of steam by employing a series of evaporators between steam supply and condenser is known as *multiple-effect evaporation*. It is the one way to increase the economy of evaporator system.

Multiple effect evaporation system is commonly used in large scale operations. In such system, evaporators are arranged in a series so that the vapour from one evaporator is used as the heat source for the next one that is operating under lower pressure and temperature. Each unit in a series is called as an **effect**. In case of a tripple-effect evaporator, if the first effect is operating at atmospheric pressure, then the second and third effect operate under vacuum. Steam is fed to the first effect and the vapour from the third-effect is condensed in the condenser connected to a vacuum pump.

With multiple-effect evaporation system, it is possible theoretically to evaporate N kg of water from 1 kg of initial steam fed, where N is the number of effects.

If the vapour (as heat source / as steam supply) from one evaporator is fed to the steam chest of the second evaporator, the system is called as *double-effect evaporator system* and so on.

Increasing the number of effects between steam supply and condenser increases the amount of evaporation per kg of steam fed to the first effect and also the operating cost will be less but capital cost and repair and maintenance charges increase with increase in number of effects. Supervisory labour will be the same for operating any number of effects. The optimum number of effects for a given duty must be found out by analysis of the above cited factors. At the optimum number of effects, a minimum of total cost occurs on a plot of total cost against number of effects.

Most common methods used in chemical industry for feeding a multiple evaporation system are :

1. Forward feed, 2. Backward feed, and 3. Mixed feed.

1. Forward feed :

In this arrangement, the liquid feed flows in the same direction as the vapour flow. Fresh feed enters the first effect and steam is also fed to the steam chest of the first effect. The vapours produced in the first effect are fed to the steam chest of the second effect as a heating medium and the concentrated liquor from the first effect is fed to the next effect in series. The pressure in the second effect is less than in the first effect and so on. For effectively utilising temperature potentials, this arrangement is preferable. Fig. 6.8 shows such a arrangement.

2. Backward feed :

In this arrangement the feed solution and the vapour flow in opposite direction to each other. Fresh feed (thin liquid) is admitted to the last effect and then pumped through other

Fig. 6.8 : Forward feed arrangement for feeding multiple effect evaporator system

effects. The steam is admitted to the steam chest of the first effect and vapours produced in the first effect are fed to the steam chest of the second effect (evaporator) and so on. The pressure in the first evaporator is highest and that in the last effect is lowest. If the liquid is very viscous then we have to adopt backfeed arrangement as the temperature of the first effect is highest and the corresponding viscosity will be less. Fig. 6.9 shows such a arrangement.

Fig. 6.9 : Backward feed arrangement for feeding multiple-effect evaporation system

Fig. 6.10 : Mixed feed arrangement for feeding multiple-effect evaporation system

3. Mixed feed :

In this feed arrangement, steam is admitted to the steam chest of the first effect and the vapours leaving the first effect are fed to the steam chest of the second effect and so on. Feed solution is admitted to an intermediate effect and flows to the first effect from where it is fed to the last effect for final concentration. This arrangement is a combination of the forward and backward feed adopted for the best overall performance. Fig. 6.10 shows this type of feeding arrangement.

Comparison of forward feed and backward feed arrangements :

1. In forward feed, the flow of the solution to be concentrated is parallel to the steam/vapour flow.

In backward feed, the flow of the solution to be concentrated is in opposite direction to that of steam/vapour (counter current).

2. Forward feed arrangement does not need a pump for moving the solution from effect to effect as vacuum is maintained in the last effect.

Backward feed arrangement needs pumps for moving the solution from effect to effect as transfer of the solution is to be done from the evaporator operating at a low pressure to that operating at a high pressure.

3. In forward feed as all heating of the cold feed solution is done in the first effect, less vapour is produced per kilograms of steam fed, resulting into a lower economy.

In backward feed, the solution is heated in each effect which usually results in better economy than that with forward feed.

4. With forward feed, the most concentrated liquor is in the last effect wherein the temperature is lowest and the viscosity is highest. These conditions lead to reduction in the capacity of the system as a whole due to low overall coefficient in the last effect in case of thick liquors which are very viscous.

In case of backward feed, the concentrated liquor is in the first effect wherein the temperature is highest as steam is admitted to that effect and the viscosity is lowest, thus the overall coefficient can be moderately high inspite of high viscosity.

5. In case of forward feed, the maintenance charges and power cost is less.

In case of backward feed, the maintenance charges and power cost is more for the same duty.

6. Forward feed arrangement is less effective thermally.

Backward feed arrangement is more effective thermally. (At high values of feed temperature).

7. Forward feed is more economical in steam.

At low values of feed temperature, backward feed gives higher economy.

8. Forward feed is the commonest one, largely used as it is simple to operate.

Backward feed is not common as it necessitates the use of pump between effects.

The choice of optimum number of effects will be dictated by an economic balance between the savings in steam obtained by multiple-effect evaporation and the added investment costs that results from the added area.

Fig. 6.11 : Optimum number of effects in a multiple-effect evaporation system

Vapour Recompression

Thermal energy in the vapour generated/produced from a boiling solution can be utilised to vaporise more water if at all there is a temperature drop for heat transfer in the desired direction. In a multiple-effect evaporation systems, this temperature drop is created by progressively lowering the boiling point of the solution in a series of evaporators by operating them successively under lower absolute pressures.

The desired driving force (temperature drop) can also be created by increasing the pressure (and, therefore, the condensing temperature) of the vapour evolved by (a) mechanical recompression or (b) thermal recompression.

The compressed vapours having a higher condensing temperature is then fed to the steam chest of the evaporator from which it evolved. So economy of the evaporator is also increased by recompressing the vapour from evaporator and condensing it in the steam chest of the same evaporator.

In this method, the vapours from the evaporator are compressed to a saturation pressure of steam to upgrade the vapours to the condition of the original steam to permit their use as the heating media. The cost of supplying the required amount of compression is usually smaller than the value of latent heat in the vapour. By this we can obtain the multiple effect economy in a single effect.

Mechanical recompression :

In this method, the vapour evolved from an evaporator is compressed to a somewhat higher pressure by a positive displacement or centrifugal compressor and fed to a heater (as steam). As the saturation temperature of the compressed vapour is higher than the boiling point of the solution, heat flows from the vapour to the solution and more vapours are generated. The principle of mechanical vapour recompression is depicted in Fig. 6.12.

It is used for the concentrations of very dilute radioative solutions and production of distilled water.

Fig. 6.12 : Mechanical recompression applied to forced circulation evaporator

Thermal recompression :

In this method, the vapour is compressed by means of a steam jet ejector. Here the high pressure steam is used to draw and compress the major part of vapours from the evaporator while the remaining part of vapours is separately condensed for compensating motive steam added.

Fig. 6.13 : Thermal recompression

Thermal recompression is better suited than mechanical recompression to vacuum operation as steam jets can handle large volumes of vapour. Jets are cheap and easy to maintain compared to compressors/blowers. Disadvantages of thermal recompression include : (i) low mechanical efficiency of the jets and (ii) lack of flexibility in the system to meet changed operating conditions.

By this vapour recompression, we can obtain the multiple-effect economy in a single-effect. The question that arises is that why not compress the vapour from the evaporator and expend a small amount of heat to get a kg of steam instead of spending large amount of heat energy in a boiler to obtain the same kg of steam ? The major reasons are : (i) The vapour compression evaporator operates on a small temperature drop to make the compression economical. Optimum temperature drop is 10 °F whereas a multiple effect evaporator may work on a temperature drop of 100 °F. Thus, the single effect must have as much surface in one-effect as the sum of all the heating surfaces in the multiple-effect. (ii) The compression equipment is expensive. (iii) There must be stand-by steam capacity for supplying heat for starting and (iv) If the boiling point elevation of the solution is appreciable then the energy needed for the compression increases very rapidly.

Choice of steam pressure :

In case of an evaporation operation, generally, a low pressure steam is used. Why one cannot use a high pressure steam that gives a larger temperature drop that consequently decrease the size and therefore the cost of the evaporator. The reason for not making use of high pressure steam for the evaporation is that it is much more valuable as a source of power than as a source of heat. High pressure steam has a lower latent heat than a low pressure steam and hence the low pressure steam delivers more latent heat than the high pressure steam for evaporating a solvent. The construction of the evaporator to hold the high pressure steam would be much more expensive than the construction to hold the low pressure steam.

Pressure in the vapour space :

It is often desirable to have a larger temperature drop between condensing steam and boiling point of solution because as the temperature drop increases, the heating surface and in turn the cost of evaporator decreases. By making use of a condenser and a vacuum pump, the pressure in the vapour space of the evaporator is made less than atmospheric. So by operating the evaporator at pressure less than atmospheric, i.e., operating under a vacuum results in decrease in the boiling point of solution which in turn leads to a larger value of temperature drop that decreases a heating surface required.

It is not necessarily required to operate the evaporators under vacuum, but because it is most economical to feed them with steam at modest pressure, a vacuum is necessary in order to get an economical temperature drop (ΔT). There are certain cases where the operation under vacuum is necessary, for example while dealing with heat sensitive materials (they may be decomposed or altered if boiled at higher temperatures). Evaporators operating at high pressure requires much more expensive construction than when operating at lower pressures. Basically evaporators are operated under vacuum for obtaining a larger temperature drop (ΔT).

Evaporator accessories :

These are devices that must be supplied with every evaporator in addition to it.

(i) condensers (ii) vacuum pump / steam jet ejector.

There are two types of condensers :

Surface condensers and

Contact condensers $\begin{Bmatrix} \text{parallel current} \\ \text{counter current} \end{Bmatrix} \begin{Bmatrix} \text{wet} \\ \text{dry} \end{Bmatrix} \begin{Bmatrix} \text{barometric} \\ \text{low level} \end{Bmatrix}$

In a surface condenser, the vapour to be condensed and cooling medium are separated by a metal wall while in a contact condenser the vapour and the cooling medium/liquid are mixed directly.

Parallel-current condenser : It is the one in which the non-condensed gases leave at a temperature of the exit cooling water.

Counter-current condenser : It is the one in which the non-condensed gases leave at a temperature of the entering cooling water.

Wet condenser : It is the one in which the non-condensed gases and cooling water are removed by the same pump.

Dry condenser : It is the one in which the non-condensed gases and cooling water are removed by separate pumps.

Barometric condenser : It is the one that is placed high enough so that water escape from it by a barometric leg.

Low level condenser : It is the one in which water is removed by a pump.

In practice parallel current condenser are almost always wet condensers while counter-current condensers are always dry.

Materials of construction for evaporators : Evaporator bodies are generally fabricated from mild steel as it is least expensive and easy to fabricate. When corrosive action is to be prevented, materials like monel, inconel and stainless steel are used. The tubes are made of copper, stainless steel and the tube sheet may be of cast bronze, nickel clad steel or stainless steel.

SOLVED EXAMPLES

Ex. 6.1 : What is the boiling point elevation of the solution and driving force for heat transfer ?

Data : Solution boils at a temperature of 380 K (107 °C) and boiling point of water at a pressure in the vapour space is 373 K (100 °C)

Temperature of condensing steam is 399 K (126° C).

Solution : Boiling point of solution = T = 380 K

Boiling point of water = T' = 373 K

Boiling point elevation = T – T' = 380 – 373 K

= 7 K (or °C) ... **Ans.**

Saturation temperature of condensing steam = T_s

= 399 K

Driving force for heat transfer = $T_s - T$ = 399 – 380

= 19 K   ... Ans.

Note : Whenever pressure at which the steam is available and pressure prevailing in the vapour space of the evaporator are given, then steam table should be referred to find out temperature of steam, latent heat of condensation of steam based on steam pressure and latent heat of evaporation of water i.e. latent heat of vapour based on pressure prevailing in the vapour space of the evaporator.

Ex. 6.2 : An evaporator operating at atmospheric pressure (101.325 kPa) is fed at the rate of 10000 kg/h of weak liquor containing 4 % caustic soda. Thick liquor leaving the evaporator contains 25% caustic soda. Find the capacity of the evaporator.

Solution :

Basis : 10,000 kg/h of weak liquor entering the evaporator.

Let $\dot{m}'$ be the kg/h of thick liquor leaving the evaporator.

Material balance of caustic soda :

Caustic soda in feed = Caustic soda in thick liquor

$$0.04 \times 10000 = 0.25 \times \dot{m}'$$

$$\dot{m}' = 1600 \text{ kg/h}$$

Overall material balance :

kg/h of feed = kg/h water evaporated + kg/h of thick liquor

10000 = kg/h water evaporated + 1600

water evaporated = 10000 − 1600

= 8400 kg/h

∴ Capacity of evaporator = 8400 kg/h   ... **Ans.**

Ex. 6.3 : An evaporator is operating at atmospheric pressure. It is desired to concentrate the feed from 5 % solute to 20 % solute (by weight) at a rate of 5000 kg/h. Dry saturated steam at a pressure corresponding to saturation temperature of 399 K (126° C) is used. The feed is at 298 K (25° C) and boiling point rise (elevation) i.e. B.P.E. (B.P.R.) is 5 K. Overall heat transfer coefficient is 2350 W/(m²·K). Calculate economy of evaporator and area of heat transfer to be provided.

Data : Treating solution as pure water and neglecting B.P.R. Latent heat of condensation of steam at 399 K = 2185 kJ/kg.

Latent heat of vaporisation of / evaporation of water at 101.325 kPa and 373 K = 2257 kJ/kg

Specific heat of feed = 4.187 kJ/(kg·K)

Solution : Basis : 5000 kg/h of feed to evaporator.

Let $\dot{m}_f$, $\dot{m}'$ and $\dot{m}_v$ be the kg/h of feed, thick liquor and water vapour / water evaporated.

Material balance of solute :

Solute in feed = Solute in thick liquor

$$0.05 \times 5000 = 0.20 \times \dot{m}'$$

$$\dot{m}' = 1250 \text{ kg/h}$$

Overall material balance :

kg/h feed = kg/h water evaporated + kg/h thick liquor

Water evaporated = $\dot{m}_v$ = 5000 – 1250 = 3750 kg/h

Let $\dot{m}_s$ be kg/h of steam required (steam consumption)

λ_s = latent heat of condensation of steam at 399 K = 2185 kJ/kg

$\lambda_v = \lambda$ = latent heat of vaporisation of water at 373 K = 2257 kJ/kg

T = temperature of thick liquor
  = T' + B.P.E. = 373 + 5 = 378 K

(λ_v is taken as equal to λ for calculation purpose, effect of B.P.E. is eliminated)

T_f = temperature of feed = 298 K

$\dot{m}_f$ = 5000 kg/h

C_{p_f} = 4.187 kJ/(kg·K)

Heat balance over evaporator :

Heat lost by condensing steam (latent heat) =

= Heat gained by solution to increase its temperature to boiling point
+ Heat required to vaporise / evaporate water

$$\dot{m}_s \lambda_s = \dot{m}_f C_{p_f} (T - T_f) + \dot{m}_v \lambda$$

$$\dot{m}_s \times 2185 = 5000 \times 4.187 (378 - 298) + 3750 \times 2257$$

$$\dot{m}_s = 4640.1 \text{ kg/h}$$

Steam consumption = 4640.1 kg/h

Economy of evaporator = $\dfrac{\text{kg/h water evaporated}}{\text{kg/h steam consumed}}$

$$= \dfrac{3750}{4640.1} = 0.808 \qquad \text{... Ans.}$$

T_s = saturation temperature of steam = 399 K

Temperature driving force = ΔT = $T_s - T$
= 399 – 378
= 21 K (21° C)

U = 2350 W/(m²·K)

$$\text{Rate of heat transfer} = \dot{Q} = \dot{m}_s \lambda_s$$
$$= 4640.1 \times 2185$$
$$= 10138619 \text{ kJ/kg}$$
$$= \frac{10138619 \times 1000}{3600}$$
$$= 2816283 \text{ J/s} + 2816283 \text{ W}$$
$$Q = UA \Delta T$$
$$A = Q/U \Delta T = 2816283 / (2350 \times 21)$$
$$= 57.07 \text{ m}^2$$

Heat transfer area to be provided = 57.07 m² ... **Ans.**

Ex. 6.4 : A solution containing 10 % solids is to be concentrated to a level of 50 % solids. Steam is available at a pressure of 0.20 MPa [saturation temperature of 393 K (120° C)]. Feed rate to the evaporator is 30000 kg/h. The evaporator is working at reduced pressure such that boiling point is 323 K (50° C). The overall heat transfer coefficient is 2.9 kW/(m²·K). Estimate steam economy and heat transfer surface for :

(i) Feed introduced at 293 K (20° C)

(ii) Feed introduced at 308 K (35° C).

Data : Specific heat of feed = 3.98 kJ/(kg·K)

Latent heat of condensation of steam at 0.20 MPa = 2202 kJ/kg

Latent heat of vaporisation of water at 323 K (i.e. at pressure in the vapour space = 2383 kJ/kg.

Solution : Basis : 30000 kg/h of feed to the evaporator.

Let $\dot{m}_f$, $\dot{m}'$ and $\dot{m}_v$ be the mass flow rate of feed, thick liquor and water vapour respectively.

Material balance of solids :

$$\text{Solids in feed} = \text{Solids in thick liquor}$$
$$0.10 \times 30000 = 0.05 \, \dot{m}'$$
$$\dot{m}' = 6000 \text{ kg/h}$$

Overall material balance :

Feed = water evaporator + thick liquor

$$\text{Water evaporated} = \dot{m}_v = 30000 - 6000 = 24000 \text{ kg/h}$$

(I) Feed at 293 K (T_f) :

$\dot{m}_s$ = mass flow rate of steam in kg/h

$\dot{m}_f$ = 30000 kg/h, $\dot{m}_v$ = 24000 kg/h

C_{p_f} = 3.98 kJ/(kg·K)

T_s = saturation temperature of steam = 393 K

T = boiling point of solution = 323 K

λ_s = latent heat of condensation of steam at 0.20 MPa

= 2202 kJ/kg

λ = latent heat of vaporisation of water at 323 K = 2383 kJ/kg

Enthalpy balance over evaporator assuming no heat loss :

$$Q = \dot{m}_s \lambda_s = \dot{m}_f \cdot C_{p_f}(T - T_f) + \dot{m}\dot{m}_v \lambda$$

$\dot{m}_s \times 2202$ = 30000 × 3.98 × (323 − 293) + 24000 × 2383

$\dot{m}_s$ = 27599.5 kg/h

Steam consumption = 27599.5 kg/h

Steam economy = water evaporated / steam consumed

$= \dfrac{24000}{27599.5} = 0.87$ ... **Ans.** (i)

∴ ΔT = T_s − T = 393 − 323 = 70 K

U = 2.9 kW/(m²·K) = 2900 W/(m²·K)

Heat load = Rate of heat transfer = Q = $\dot{m}_s \lambda_s$

Q = 27599.5 × 2202

= 60774099 kJ/h

$= \dfrac{60774099 \times 1000}{3600}$

= 16881694 J/s + 16881694 W

Q = U A ΔT

A = Q / U ΔT

$= \dfrac{16881694}{2900 \times 70} = 83.16$ m²

Heat transfer area required = 83.16 m² ... **Ans.** (i)

(II) Feed at 308 K :

Heat balance gives

$\dot{m}_s \times 2202$ = 30000 × 3.98 × (323 − 308) + 24000 × 2383

Unit Operations – II   6.24   Evaporation

$$\dot{m}_s = 26786 \text{ kg/h}$$

Steam consumption = 26786 kg/h

$$\text{Economy of evaporator} = \frac{24000}{26786}$$

$$= 0.896 \quad \quad \text{... Ans. (ii)}$$

Heat load = Rate of heat transfer = $Q = \dot{m}_s \lambda_s$

$$= 267866 \times 2202$$
$$= 58982772 \text{ kJ/h}$$
$$= \frac{58982772 \times 1000}{3600}$$
$$= 16384103 \text{ J/s} + 16384103 \text{ W}$$

$$Q = U A \Delta T$$
$$A = Q/(U \cdot \Delta T)$$
$$= \frac{16384103}{2900 \times 70} = 80.71 \text{ m}^2$$

Heat transfer area required = 80.71 m²   ... **Ans. (ii)**

As the feed temperature goes down, economy decreases and as ΔT and U do not change area increases due to increase in heat load.

$T_f = 308$ K   Economy = 0.896, Area = 80.71 m²
$T_f = 293$ K   Economy = 0.87,   Area = 83.16 m²

Ex. 6.5 : An evaporator is to be fed with 5000 kg/h solution containing 10 % solute by weight. The feed at 313 K (40° C) is to be concentrated to a solution containing 40 % by weight of the solute under an absolute pressure of 101.325 kPa. Steam is available at an absolute pressure of 303.975 kPa (saturation temperature of 407 K (134° C). The overall heat transfer coefficient is 1750 W/(m²·K).

Calculate :

(i) heat transfer area that should be provided

(ii) economy of an evaporator.

Data : C_p of feed = 4.187 kJ/(kg·K)

Treat solution as pure water for purpose of calculation of enthalpies.

Temperature, K	Enthalpy, kJ/kg	
	Vapour	Liquid

313 K		170
373 K	2676	419
407 K	2725	563

Solution : Basis : 5000 kg/h of feed to the evaporator.

Let $\dot{m}_f$, $\dot{m}'$ be the kg/h of feed and thick liquor respectively.

Material balance of solute :

$$\text{Solute in feed} = \text{Solute in thick liquor}$$

$$0.10 \times 5000 = 0.40 \times \dot{m}'$$

$$\dot{m}' = 1250 \text{ kg/h}$$

Overall material balance :

$$\text{Feed} = \text{Water evaporated} + \text{Thick liquor}$$

$$\text{Water evaporated} = 5000 - 1500$$

$$\dot{m}_v = 3750 \text{ kg/h}$$

Let H_f, H', H_v be the enthalpies of feed, thick liquor and water vapour respectively.

λ_s = latent heat of condensing steam

= specific enthalpy of saturated steam − specific enthalpy of saturated water

= Enthalpy of water vapour − Enthalpy of liquid water at 407 K

= 2725 − 563 = 2162 kJ/kg

Pressure in the evaporator = 101.325 kPa

Boiling point of solution = Boiling point of water at 101.325 kPa

= 373 K

H_v = Enthalpy of water vapour at 373 K

= 2676 kJ/kg

H' = enthalpy of product (thick liquor) at 373 K

= 419 kJ/kg

H_f = enthalpy of feed at 313 K

= 170 kJ/kg

Heat balance over evaporator :

$$\dot{m}_f H_f + \dot{m}_s \lambda_s = \dot{m}_v \cdot H_v + \dot{m}' H'$$

(feed) (steam) (water vapour) (thick liquor)

$$5000 \times 170 + \dot{m}_s \times 2162 = 3750 \times 2676 + 1250 \times 419$$

$$\dot{m}_s = 4490.6 \text{ kg/h}$$

Steam consumption = 4490.6 kg/h

Steam economy of an evaporator = $\dfrac{\text{kg/h water evaporated}}{\text{kg/h steam consumed}}$

$$= \dfrac{3750}{4490.6} = 0.835$$

Alternatively :

$$Q = \dot{m}\dot{m}_s \lambda_s = \dot{m}_f C_{p_f} (T - T_f) + (\dot{m}_f - \dot{m}') \lambda_v$$

$\dot{m}_f - \dot{m}' = 5000 - 1250 = 3750$ kg/h

λ_v = latent heat of evaporation of water at pressure in the evaporator (i.e. at 373 K)

$= 2676 - 419 = 2257$ kJ/kg

$C_{p_f} = 4.187$ kJ/(kg·K)

$\dot{m}_s \times 2162 = 5000 \times 4.187 \times (373 - 313) + 3750 \times 2257$

$\dot{m}_s = 4495$ kg/h

T_s = Saturation temperature of condensing steam = 407 K

T = B.P. of solution = 373 K

$\Delta T = T_s - T = 407 - 373 = 34$ K

$U = 1750$ W/(m²·K)

$Q = \dot{m}_s \lambda_s = U \cdot A \Delta T$

$Q = 4490.6 \times 2162 = 9708677.2$ kJ/h = 2696855 J/h + 2696855 W

$Q = \dfrac{Q}{U \Delta T} = \dfrac{2696855}{1750 \times 34} = 45.32$ m²

Heat transfer area to be provided = 45.32 m² ... **Ans.**

Ex. 6.6 : A single effect evaporator is fed with 5000 kg/h of solution containing 1 % solute by weight. Feed temperature is 303 K (30° C) and is to be concentrated to a solution of 2 % solute by weight. The evaporation is at atmospheric pressure (101.325 kPa) and area of evaporator is 69 m². Saturated steam is supplied at 143.3 kPa as a heating medium. Calculate steam economy and overall heat transfer coefficient.

Data :

Enthalpy of feed at 303 K = 125.79 kJ/kg
Enthalpy of vapour at 101.325 kPa = 2676.1 kJ/kg
Enthalpy of saturated steam at 143.3 kPa = 2691.5 kJ/kg
Saturation temperature of steam = 383 K (110° C)
Boiling point of saturation = 373 K
Enthalpy of product = 419.04 kJ/kg
Enthalpy of saturated water at 383 K = 461.30 kJ/kg
Solution : Basis : 5000 kg/h of feed to evaporator.

Let $\dot{m}'$, $\dot{m}_v$ be the flow rate of product and water vapour.

Material balance of solute :

$$0.01 \times 5000 = 0.02 \times \dot{m}'$$
$$\dot{m}' = 2500 \text{ kg/h}$$

Overall material balance :

Feed = water evaporated + thick liquor

Water evaporated = 5000 – 2500 = 2500 kg/h

Assuming no heat loss, the heat balance is :

$$\dot{m}_f H_f + \dot{m}_s \lambda_s = \dot{m}' H' + \dot{m}_v H_v$$

where
$\dot{m}_f$ = 5000 kg/h,

$\dot{m}'$ = 2500 kg/h,

$\dot{m}_v$ = 2500 kg/h

H_f, H', H_v are enthalpies of feed, thick liquor and water vapour respectively.

H_f = 125.79 kJ/kg

H' = 419.04 kJ/kg, H_v = 2676.1 kJ/kg

λ_s = latent heat of condensing steam

   = enthalpy of saturated steam – enthalpy of saturated water

   = 2691.5 – 461.30 = 2230.2 kJ/kg

$5000 \times 125.79 + \dot{m}_s (2230.2) = 2500 \times 419.04 + 2500 \times 2676.1$

$\dot{m}_s$ = 3187.56 kg/h

Steam consumption = steam flow rate = 3187.56 kg/h

Steam economy = 2500 / 3187.56

   = 0.784   ... **Ans.**

Rate of heat transfer = $\dot{m}_s \lambda_s$

$$= 3187.56 \times 2230.2$$
$$= 71088963 \text{ kJ/h}$$
$$= \frac{71088963 \times 1000}{3600} = 1974693.4 \text{ J/s (i.e. W)}$$
$$\Delta T = T_s - T = 383 - 373 = 10 \text{ K}$$
$$Q = U A \Delta T$$
$$U = Q/(A \Delta T)$$
$$U = \frac{1974693.4}{69 \times 10} = 2862 \text{ W/(m}^2\cdot\text{K)}$$

Overall heat transfer coefficient = 2862 W/(m²·K) ... **Ans.**

Ex. 6.7 : If the evaporator pressure is reduced to 38.58 kPa, what would be the change in heat transfer area ? Use the same steam pressure and overall heat transfer coefficient as in Ex. 6.6.

Data :

Boiling point of water / solution at 38.58 kPa = 348 K
Enthalpy of water vapour = 2635.3 kJ/kg
Enthalpy of product = 313.93 kJ/kg

Solution : Heat balance is :

$$\dot{m}_f H_f + \dot{m}_s \lambda_s = \dot{m}' H' + \dot{m}_v H_v$$
$$5000 \times 125.79 + \dot{m}_s \times 2230.2 = 2500 \times 313.93 + 2500 \times 2635.3$$
$$\dot{m}_s = 2320.18 \text{ kg/h}$$
$$Q = \dot{m}_s \lambda_s = 2320.8 \times 2230.2$$
$$= 5174465.4 \text{ kJ/h}$$
$$= \frac{5174465.4 \times 1000}{3600} = 1437351.5 \text{ J/s} + 1437351.5 \text{ W}$$

where
$$Q = U A \Delta T$$
$$U = 2862 \text{ W/(m}^2\cdot\text{K)}$$
$$\Delta T = 383 - 348 = 35 \text{ K}$$
$$A = Q / (U \cdot \Delta T)$$
$$= \frac{1437351.5}{2862 \times 35} = 14.35 \text{ m}^2 \quad \text{... \textbf{Ans.}}$$

Heat transfer area in this case is 14.35 m².

Heat transfer area decreases from 69 m² to 14.35 m². In this case a condenser and vacuum pump should be used.

Ex. 6.8 : If the feed rate is increased to 6000 kg/h what would be mass flow rate of product, water evaporated and product concentration ? Use the same area, value of U, steam pressure, evaporator pressure and feed temperature as in Ex. 6.6.

Solution : Basis : 6000 kg/h of feed to evaporator.

Heat balance over evaporator :

$$\dot{m}_f H_f + \dot{m}_s \lambda_s = \dot{m}' H' + \dot{m}_v H_v$$

$$6000 \times 125.79 + 3187.56 \times 2230.2 = \dot{m}' \times 419.04 + \dot{m}_v \times 2676.1$$

We know that

$$\dot{m}_f = \dot{m}' + \dot{m}_v$$

∴
$$6000 = \dot{m}' + \dot{m}_v$$

$$\dot{m}' = 6000 - \dot{m}_v$$

$$6000 \times 125.79 + 3187.56 \times 2230.2 = (6000 - \dot{m}_v) \times 419.04 + \dot{m}_v \times 2676.1$$

$$\dot{m}_v = 2370.1 \text{ kg/h}$$

$$\dot{m}' = 6000 - 2370.1 = 3629.9 \text{ kg/h}$$

Water evaporated = 2370.1 kg/h

Mass flow rate of product = 3629.9 kg/h … **Ans.**

Let x be the wt. % solute in product.

Material balance of solids :

$$0.01 \times 6000 = \frac{x}{100} \times 3629.9$$

$$x = 1.653$$

Concentration of product = 1.653% by weight … **Ans.**

Ex. 6.9 : A single effect evaporator is to concentrate 20000 kg/h of a solution having a concentration of 5 % salt to a concentration of 20 % salt by weight. Steam is fed to the evaporator at a pressure corresponding to the saturation temperature of 399 K (126° C). The evaporator is operating at atmospheric pressure and boiling point rise is 7 K. Calculate the heat load and steam economy.

Data : Feed temperature = 298 K (25° C)

Specific heat of feed = 4.0 kJ/(kg·K)

Latent heat of condensation of steam at 399 K = 2185 kJ/kg

Latent heat of vaporisation of water at 373 K = 2257 kJ/kg

Solution : Basis : 20000 kg/h of solution to the evaporator.

Evaporator is operating at atmospheric pressure i.e. at 101.325 kPa. Boiling point of pure water at 101.325 kPa is 373K (100° C).

Let $\dot{m}_f$, $\dot{m}'$ and $\dot{m}_v$ be the flow rate of feed, thick liquor and water vapour.

Material balance of salt :

$$0.05 \times 20000 = 0.20 \times \dot{m}'$$

$$\dot{m}' = 5000 \text{ kg/h}$$

Overall material balance over evaporator :

Feed = Water evaporated + Thick liquor

Water evaporated = 20000 – 5000

$$\dot{m}_v = 15000 \text{ kg/h}$$

$$\lambda_s = 2185 \text{ kJ/kg}$$

$$\lambda_v = \lambda = 2257 \text{ kJ/kg}$$

$$C_{p_f} = 4.0 \text{ kJ/(kg·K)}$$

$$T_f = 298 \text{ K}$$

Boiling point of solution = T = T' + B.P.R.

$$= 373 + 7 = 380 \text{ K}$$

Temperature of condensing steam = Saturation temperature of steam

$$= 399 \text{ K}$$

Heat balance over evaporator :

Heat load = Q

$$Q = \dot{m}_s \lambda_s = \dot{m}_f C_{p_f} (T - T_f) + \dot{m}_v \cdot \lambda$$

$$\dot{m}_s \times 2185 = 20000 \times 4.0 \, (380 - 298) + 15000 \times 2257$$

$$\dot{m}_s = 18496.6 \text{ kg/h}$$

Steam consumption = 18496.6 kg/h

Economy of evaporator = $\dfrac{15000}{18496.6}$

$$= 0.811 \qquad \text{... \textbf{Ans.}}$$

Heat load = Q = $\dot{m}_s \lambda_s$

$$= 18496.6 \times 2185$$

$$= 4041507.1 \text{ kJ/h}$$

$$= \frac{4041507.1 \times 1000}{3600}$$

$$= 1122641 \text{ J/s}$$

$$= 1122641 \text{ W} \qquad \text{... Ans.}$$

Calculation of Multiple-Effect Evaporators

Assumptions generally made in calculation procedure are :

(i) equal heat transfer rate in each of the effects,

(ii) equal heat transfer surface in each of the effects, and

(iii) equal evaporation in each of the effects.

In actual practice, however, the above cited assumptions cannot hold good simultaneously. With equal heat load, a trial and error procedure is adopted to get equal heat transfer area in every effect. The actual evaporation in each effect is obtained by subsequent calculations.

Consider a tripple-effect evaporator.

Let Q_1, Q_2 and Q_3 be the heat transmitted in the first, second and third-effect respectively.

ΔT_1, ΔT_2 and ΔT_3 are the corresponding temperature drops.

U_1, U_2 and U_3 be the overall heat transfer coefficient in the first, second and third-effect respectively.

A_1, A_2 and A_3 be the heat transfer surface of the first, second and third-effect respectively.

For a tripple effect evaporator, we have

$$Q_1 = Q_2 = Q_3$$

$$U_1 A_1 \Delta T_1 = U_2 A_2 \Delta T_2 = U_3 A_3 \Delta T_3 \qquad \text{... (1)}$$

To obtain the economy of construction, in practice, heat transfer areas in all effects are equal.

So, with $A_1 = A_2 = A_3$, we get

$$U_1 \Delta T_1 = U_2 \Delta T_2 = U_3 \Delta T_3 \qquad \text{... (2)}$$

It follows from the equation (2) that the temperature drops in the multiple effect evaporator are approximately inversely proportional to the heat transfer coefficients.

$$\Delta T_2 = \frac{U_1}{U_2} \Delta T_1 \qquad \text{... (3)}$$

$$\Delta T_3 = \frac{U_1}{U_3} \Delta T_1 \qquad \text{... (4)}$$

where, ΔT = overall temperature drop over the system

$$\Delta T = \Delta T_1 + \Delta T_2 + \Delta T_3$$

$$\Delta T = \Delta T_1 [1 + U_1/U_2 + U_1/U_3] \qquad \ldots (5)$$

Also $\quad \Delta T = T_s - T_{v_3} \qquad \ldots (6)$

where T_s = saturation temperature of condensing (first effect) steam corresponding to steam pressure. T_{v_3} = temperature of the vapour corresponding to the pressure in the vapour space of third-effect. With equation (6) overall temperature drop is calculated. With the help of equations (3), (4) and (5) and values of U_1, U_2 and U_3, the temperature drops in each of the effects are calculated and hence the temperature distribution in each of the effects.

	First effect	**Second effect**	**Third effect**
Steam	T_s	T_{v_1}	T_{v_2}
Liquor	T_{L_1}	T_{L_2}	T_{L_3}
Vapour	T_{v_1}	T_{v_2}	T_{v_3}
ΔT	$T_s - T_{L_1}$	$T_s - T_{L_2}$	$T_s - T_{L_3}$
BPR/BPE	$T_{L_1} - T_{v_1}$	$T_{L_2} - T_{v_2}$	$T_{L_3} - T_{v_3}$

Knowing the temperature distribution, enthalpies of various streams are obtained.

Evaporation in each effect and steam consumption are computed with the help of material balance and energy balance equations.

The areas of the individual effects are calculated as follows :

$$A_1 = \frac{\dot{m}_s \lambda_s}{U_1 \Delta T_1} \qquad \ldots (7)$$

$$A_2 = \frac{\dot{m}_{v_1} \lambda_{v_1}}{U_2 \Delta T_2} \qquad \ldots (8)$$

and $\quad A_3 = \dfrac{\dot{m}_{v_2} \lambda_{v_2}}{U_3 \Delta T_3} \qquad \ldots (9)$

If $A_1 \ne A_2 \ne A_3$, and the deviation is more than $\pm 10\%$, a fresh trial with new temperature distribution is performed. The new temperature drops are calculated as :

$$\Delta T_1' = \Delta T_1 \times \frac{A_1}{A_{avg.}} , \quad A_{avg.} = \frac{A_1 + A_2 + A_3}{3}$$

$$\Delta T_2' = \Delta T_2 \times \frac{A_2}{A_{avg.}}$$

$$\Delta T_3' = \Delta T_3 \times \frac{A_3}{A_{avg.}}$$

The above mentioned procedure is repeated till the deviation is within $\pm 10\%$.

Ex. 6.10 : A tripple-effect evaporator is concentrating a solution that has no appreciable boiling point elevation. The temperature of steam to the first effect is 381.3 K (108.3° C) and boiling point of the solution in the last effect is 324.7 K (51.7° C). The overall heat transfer coefficients in the first, second and third-effect are 2800, 2200 and 1100 W/(m²·K) respectively. At what temperatures will the solution boil in the first and second effects ?

Solution : Total temperature drop $= \Delta T = 381.3 - 324.7$
$$= 56.6 \text{ K}$$

$\Delta T = \Delta T_1 [1 + U_1/U_2 + U_1/U_3]$

$56.6 = \Delta T_1 [1 + 2800/2200 + 2800/1100]$

$\therefore \quad \Delta T_1 = 11.75 \text{ K}$

$\Delta T = \Delta T_2 [1 + U_2/U_1 + U_2/U_3]$

$56.6 = \Delta T_2 [1 + 2200/2800 + 2200/1100]$

$\Delta T_2 = 14.95 \text{ K}$

and $\therefore \Delta T_3 = 56.6 - [11.75 + 14.95]$
$$= 29.9 \text{ K}$$

$\Delta T_1 = T_s - T_1'$

$\therefore \quad T_1' = 381.3 - 11.75 = 369.55 \text{ K } (96.55° \text{ C})$

$\Delta T_2 = T_1' - T_2'$

$T_2' = 369.55 - 14.95$
$$= 354.6 \text{ K } (81.6 \text{ °C})$$

Boiling point in first effect $= 369.55 \text{ K } (96.55° \text{ C})$

Boiling point in second effect $= 354.6 \text{ K } (81.6° \text{ C})$

Ex. 6.11 : A double-effect evaporator is employed to concentrate 10,000 kg/h of caustic soda solution from 9% to 47% by wt. NaOH. For this purpose backward feed arrangement is used. The feed enters the evaporator at 309 K (36° C). Process steam at 686.616 kPa.g is available and in the second effect a vacuum of 86.66 kPa is maintained. Design a suitable forced circulation system with equal heating surface in both the effects. Calculate the steam consumption and evaporation in each effect. Neglect boiling point rise. The overall heat transfer coefficients in the first and second effects are 2326 and 1744.5 W/(m²·K) respectively. Take a specific heat value of 3.77 kJ/(kg·K) for all caustic streams.

Solution : 10,000 kg/h of feed.

Fig. 6.14

Overall material balance :

$$\dot{m}_f = \dot{m}_1' + \dot{m}_{v_1} + \dot{m}_{v_2}$$

Material balance of solute :

$$0.09 \times 10000 = 0.47 \times \dot{m}_1'$$

$$\dot{m}_1' = 1915 \text{ kg/h}$$

$$\text{Steam pressure} = 686.616 \text{ kPa.g.}$$
$$= 686.616 + 101.325 = 787.941 \text{ kPa}$$

Hence, saturation temperature, $T_s = 442.7$ K (169.7 °C)

$$\text{Vacuum in second effect} = 86.660 \text{ kPa}$$
$$\text{Absolute pressure in second effect} = 101.325 - 86.660$$
$$= 14.665 \text{ kPa}$$
$$\text{Corresponding temperature} = 326.3 \text{ K (53.3 °C)}$$

∴ Overall temperature drop $= \Delta T = 442.7 - 326.3$
$$= 116.4 \text{ K (°C)}$$

Assuming heat loads equal in both the effects

$$Q_1 \simeq Q_2$$
$$U_1 A_1 \Delta T_1 = U_2 A_2 \Delta T_2$$

For equal heat transfer surface,

$$U_1 \Delta T_1 = U_2 \Delta T_2$$

$$\Delta T_1 = \frac{U_2}{U_1} \Delta T_2 = \frac{2326}{1744.5} \Delta T_2 = 0.75 \Delta T_2$$

$$\Delta T = \Delta T_1 + \Delta T_2 = 0.75 \Delta T_2 + \Delta T_2$$

$$116.4 = 1.75 \Delta T_2$$

∴ $\Delta T_2 = 66.5$ K, and $\Delta T_1 = 49.9$ K

Since there is no B.P.R.

$$\Delta T_1 = T_s - T_{v_1}$$

where T_{v_1} – temperature in the vapour space of first effect

$$T_{v_1} = T_s - \Delta T_1 = 442.7 - 49.9$$
$$T_{v_1} = 392.8 \text{ K } (119.8 \text{ °C})$$
$$T_{v_2} = T_{v_1} - \Delta T_2$$
$$= 392.8 - 66.5 = 326.3 \text{ K } (53.3 \text{ °C})$$

Enthalpy of various streams :

$$H_f = \text{feed enthalpy}$$
$$H_f = 3.768 \times (309 - 273)$$
$$= 135.66 \text{ kJ/kg}$$
$$H_1' = \text{enthalpy of the final product}$$
$$= 3.768 \, (392.8 - 273)$$
$$= 451.4 \text{ kJ/kg}$$
$$H_2' = \text{enthalpy of the intermediate product}$$
$$= 3.768 \, (326.3 - 273) = 200.83 \text{ kJ/kg}$$

For steam at 442.7 K (169.7 °C), $\lambda_s = 2048.7$ kJ/kg

For vapour at 392.8 K (119.8 °C)

$$H_{v_1} = 2705.22 \text{ kJ/kg}, \quad \lambda_{v_1} = 2202.8 \text{ kJ/kg}$$

For vapour at 326.3 K (53.3 °C)

$$H_{v_2} = 2597.61 \text{ kJ/kg}$$
$$\lambda_{v_2} = 2377.8 \text{ kJ/kg}$$

Material balances and energy balance around the effects :

First effect

Material balance :

$$\dot{m}_2' = \dot{m}_1' + \dot{m}_{v_1} \qquad \ldots (1)$$

Energy balance :

$$\dot{m}_s \lambda_s + \dot{m}_2' H_2' = \dot{m}_{v_1} H_{v_1} + \dot{m}_1' H_1' \qquad \ldots (2)$$

Second effect

Material balance :

$$\dot{m}_f = \dot{m}_2' + \dot{m}_{v_2} \qquad \ldots (3)$$

Energy balance :

$$\dot{m}_{v_1} \lambda_{v_1} + \dot{m}_f H_f = \dot{m}_{v_2} H_{v_2} + \dot{m}_2' H_2' \qquad \ldots (4)$$

Overall material balance :

$$\dot{m}_f = \dot{m}_v + \dot{m}_1'$$

$$\dot{m}_v = \dot{m}_{v_1} + \dot{m}_{v_2}$$

$$\dot{m}_v = \dot{m}_f - \dot{m}_1' = 10000 - 1915 = 8085 \text{ kg/h}$$

$$\dot{m}_{v_2} = \dot{m}_v - \dot{m}_{v_1} \qquad \ldots (5)$$

Putting the value of $\dot{m}_{v_2}$ from equation (5) in equation (4), we have

$$\dot{m}_2' = \dot{m}_f - \dot{m}_{v_2} \text{ from equation (3)}$$

∴ Equation (4) becomes

$$\dot{m}_{v_1} \lambda_{v_1} + \dot{m}_f H_f = (\dot{m}_v - \dot{m}_{v_1}) H_{v_2} + (\dot{m}_f - \dot{m}_{v_2}) H_2'$$

$$\dot{m}_{v_1} \lambda_{v_1} + \dot{m}_f H_f = (\dot{m}_v - \dot{m}_{v_1}) H_{v_2} + [\dot{m}_f - (\dot{m}_v - \dot{m}_{v_1})] H_2' \qquad \ldots (6)$$

Only unknown in above equation is $\dot{m}_{v_1}$

$$2202.8\,\dot{m}_{v_1} + 10000 \times 135.66 = (8085 - \dot{m}_{v_1}) \times 2597.61 + [10000 - (8085 - \dot{m}_{v_1})] \times 200.83$$

$$2202.8\,\dot{m}_{v_1} + 1356600 = 21001677 - 2597.66\,\dot{m}_{v_1} + 2008300$$

$$- 1623710.6 + 200.83\,\dot{m}_{v_1}$$

$$4599.58\,\dot{m}_{v_1} = 20029666$$

$$\dot{m}_{v_1} = 4354.7 \text{ kg/h}$$

$$\dot{m}_{v_2} = \dot{m}_v - \dot{m}_{v_1} = 8085 - 4354.7$$

$$= 3729.3 \text{ kg/h}$$

Putting values of $\dot{m}_{v_1}$, $\dot{m}_{v_2}$, $\dot{m}_1'$ and $\dot{m}_f$ and thermal quantities in equation (2), we get

$$\dot{m}_s = 5557 \text{ kg/h}$$

Heat transfer area :

First effect :

$$A_1 = \frac{Q_1}{U_1 \Delta T_1} = \frac{\dot{m}_s \lambda_s}{U_1 \Delta T_1}$$

$$A_1 = \frac{5557 \times 2048.7 \times 10^3}{2326 \times 49.9 \times 3600} = 27.25 \text{ m}^2$$

Second effect :

$$A_2 = \frac{Q_2}{U_2 \Delta T_2} = \frac{\dot{m}_{v_1} \lambda_{v_1}}{U_2 \Delta T_2}$$

$$= \frac{4354.7 \times 2202.8 \times 10^3}{1744.5 \times 66.5 \times 3600}$$

$$= 22.97 \text{ m}^2$$

Since $A_1 \neq A_2$ and difference is more than 10% a second trial is required.

Second trial :

$$A_{avg} = \frac{A_1 + A_2}{2} = \frac{27.25 + 22.97}{2} = 25.11 \text{ m}^2$$

$$\Delta T_1' = \Delta T_1 \times \frac{A_1}{A_{avg}} = \frac{49.9 \times 27.25}{25.11} = 54.2 \text{ K}$$

$$\Delta T_2' = \Delta T - \Delta T_1 = 116.4 - 54.2 = 62.2 \text{ K}$$

Temperature distribution :

$$T_{v_1} = T_s - \Delta T_1' = 442.7 - 54.2 = 388.5 \text{ K } (115.5 \text{ °C})$$

$$T_{v_2} = T_{v_1} - \Delta T_2' = 388.5 - 62.2 = 326.3 \text{ K } (53.3 \text{ °C})$$

Enthalpy of streams :

$$H_f = 135.66 \text{ kJ/kg}$$

$$H_1' = 3.768 (388.5 - 273) = 424.81 \text{ kJ/kg}$$

$$H_2' = 200.83 \text{ kJ/kg}$$

Vapour at 388.5 K (115.5 °C)

$$H_{v_1} = 2699.8 \text{ kJ/kg}$$

$$\lambda_{v_1} = 2214.92 \text{ kJ/kg}$$

Putting new values, energy balance for second effect equation (5) becomes :

$$\dot{m}_{v_1} \times 2214.92 + 10000 \times 135.66 = (8085 - \dot{m}_{v_1}) \, 2597.01 + [10000 - (8085 - \dot{m}_{v_1})] \times 200.83$$

Solving, we get : $\dot{m}_{v_1} = 4343 \text{ kg/h}$

$$\dot{m}_{v_2} = \dot{m}_v - \dot{m}_{v_1} = 8085 - 4343$$
$$= 3742 \text{ kg/h}$$

First-effect energy balance :

$$\dot{m}_s \lambda_s + \dot{m}_2 H_2' = \dot{m}_{v_1} H_{v_1} + \dot{m}_1' H_1'$$

$$\dot{m}_2 = \dot{m}_1' + \dot{m}_{v_1}$$

$$= \dot{m}_f - \dot{m}_v + \dot{m}_{v_1}$$

$$= \dot{m}_f - (\dot{m}_{v_1} + \dot{m}_{v_2}) + \dot{m}_{v_1} = \dot{m}_f - \dot{m}_{v_2}$$

$$\therefore \dot{m}_s \lambda_s + (\dot{m}_f - \dot{m}_{v_2}) H_2' = \dot{m}_{v_1} H_{v_1} + \dot{m}_1' H_1'$$

$$\dot{m}_s \times 2048.7 + (10000 - 3742) \times 200.83$$
$$= 4343 \times 2699.8 + 1915 \times 424.81$$

Solving, we get

$$\dot{m}_s = 5516 \text{ kg/h}$$

Area of heat transfer :

First effect :

$$A_1 = \frac{5516 \times 2048.7 \times 10^3}{2326 \times 54.2 \times 3600}$$
$$= 24.9 \text{ m}^2$$

Second effect : $\quad A_2 = \dfrac{4343 \times 2214.92 \times 10^3}{1744.5 \times 62.2 \times 3600} = 24.62 \text{ m}^2$

$$A_1 \simeq A_2$$

So area in each effect can be 24.90 m² (recommending higher value).

∴ Steam consumption = 5516 kg/h ... **Ans.**
Evaporation in first effect = 4343 kg/h
Evaporation in second effect = 3742 kg/h ... **Ans.**

EXERCISES

1. 1.1 The weak liquor to be fed to the evaporator is composed of non-volatile .... and .... solvent. **Ans.** solute, volatile
   1.2 In most of the evaporation operation .... are condensed and discarded. **Ans.** water vapour
   1.3 .... is carried out by supplying heat to a solution to vaporise solvent. **Ans.** Evaporation
   1.4 In case of evaporation generally .... is the valuable product.

Unit Operations – II 6.39 Evaporation

Ans. concentrated solution / thick liquor

1.5   In .... feed system, vapour and liquor flow in counter current fashion.
Ans. backward

1.6   Economy of single-effect evaporator is always less than ....   **Ans.** one

1.7   Economy of multiple effect evaporator system is always .... than one.
Ans. more greater

1.8   In .... evaporator the velocity of liquid entering the tube is of the order of 2 to 6 m/s.   **Ans.** forced circulation

1.9   .... tube vertical evaporator is commonly used for handling solutions that tend to foam.   **Ans.** Long

1.10   In case of Calendria type evaporator the solution to be evaporated is .... the tubes and steam flows .... the tubes in the steam chest. **Ans.** inside, outside

2. Define the following terms :
    (i) evaporation (ii) boiling point elevation (iii) capacity of evaporator and
    (iv) economy of an evaporator.

3. State why the economy of single effect evaporator is less than one ?
4. State the method of increasing the economy of an evaporator.
5. What do you mean by multiple effect evaporation system ?
6. What do you mean by double effect evaporator.
7. State the method of feeding multiple effect evaporation system.
8. Compare forward feed arrangement with backward feed arrangement in case of multiple effect evaporation system.
9. State the advantages of forced circulation evaporators and its application.
10. Write construction with neat sketch of standard vertical tube evaporator.
11. Draw the neat diagrams of forward feed arrangement and backward feed arrangement for feeding multiple effect evaporation system.
12. Mention the common examples of evaporation operation.
13. Draw neat sketch of long tube evaporator and explain briefly its construction and working.
14. Explain in brief forced circulation evaporator with external horizontal heating surface with reference to its construction and working.
15. Explain in brief vapour recompression with neat sketch.

CHAPTER SEVEN

DIFFUSION

In a mixture consisting of two or more components, if the concentrations of the components vary from point to point then there is a natural tendency for each component to migrate/ transport from regions of high concentration to those of low concentration. This process of transfer of mass as a result of the concentration difference of the component in a mixture is called as **mass transfer**. (The transport of a component present in a mixture from a rigion of higher concentration to a region of lower concentration within the mixture is called as mass transfer.)

The operations carried out for separating the components of mixtures, involving the transfer of material from one homogeneous phase to another, utilising differences in vapour pressure, solubility or diffusivity, – in which the driving force for transfer is a concentration difference are called as **mass transfer operations**.

In case of evaporation of water from a pool of water into a stream of air flowing over the water surface, molecules of water vapour diffuse through those of the air at the surface into the main portion of air stream, as a consequence of which they are carried away with air. In this case, mass transfer is a result of a concentration difference, or gradient, the diffusing substance (water) moving from a region of high concentration to one of low concentration. Hence, the driving force for mass transfer is a concentration difference just as a temperature difference in heat transfer.

Fractional distillation (one of the methods of separation) depends on the difference in vapour pressures of different components at the same temperature (volatility), while gas absorption depends on the difference in solubility of gases in a selective solvent. Liquid-liquid extraction and leaching depend on the difference in solubility in a liquid solvent.

Mass transfer operations include separation techniques such as distillation, gas absorption, liquid extraction, drying, crystallisation, etc.

In mass transfer operations, mass transfer may occur :
(a) In one direction, e.g., gas absorption.
(b) In opposite directions, e.g., distillation.
(c) With simultaneous heat transfer, e.g., drying and crystallisation.
(d) With a simultaneous chemical reaction, e.g., gas absorption accompanied by a chemical reaction (absorption of CO_2 in an aqueous solution of KOH)
(e) With the exchange of one or more components.
(f) Isothermally (at constant T) and non-isothermally.

In mass transfer operations, the following phenomena must exist :
(a) At least two phases must come in contact with each other.

(b) Materials should flow from one phase to the other.

(c) A part of the total flow of material must occur by molecular diffusion.

Three states of aggregation of a substance are gas, liquid and solid and this permit six possibilities of the phase contact. Gas-gas (not practically realised), gas-liquid, gas-solid, liquid-liquid, liquid-solid and solid-solid (no industrial separation operation in this category).

Mass transfer operations have been classified according to the **phases in contact** as given in Table 7.1.

Table 7.1

Phases in contact	Mass transfer operation
Liquid-vapour (gas)	Distillation (Fractionation)
Liquid-gas	Gas absorption
	Stripping
	Humidification
	Dehumidification
Liquid-solid	Crystallisation
	Leaching
	Adsorption
Liquid-liquid	Extraction
Solid-vapour	Sublimation
Solid-gas	Adsorption
Wet solid-gas (usually air)	Drying

Hence, distillation, gas absorption, stripping are gas-liquid operations, liquid extraction is a liquid-liquid operation, crystallisation is a liquid-solid operation and drying is a gas-solid operation.

As the basic mechanism is the same whether the phase is a gas, liquid or solid, there are some similarities between the various mass transfer operations and these are :

(a) Equilibrium between the phases is attained after a sufficiently long time/period of phase contact.

(b) Material transfer is caused by the combined effect of molecular diffusion and turbulence.

(c) There is no resistance to mass transfer at the phase interface (because of the existence of equilibrium at the interface).

(d) Rate of mass transfer is evaluated by deviation/departure from equilibrium concentration.

1. Distillation : Distillation is a gas-liquid operation. It is a method of separating the components of a liquid mixture by use of thermal energy. The difference in vapour pressures of different components is responsible for such a separation. It is also called as fractionation or fractional distillation. (The term fractionation is commonly used in petroleum refineries).

The separation of a crude petroleum into gasoline, kerosene, etc. is a typical example of distillation.

Consider a binary liquid mixture. For this, we have : C = 2, P = 2.

∴ F = 2 (as F = C − P + 2). These are four variables; temperature, pressure, composition of A in the liquid and vapour phases. If the pressure is fixed, only one variable, e.g., the liquid phase concentration can be varied and the temperature and vapour phase concentration follow. Here the equilibrium data are presented in temperature-composition diagram at constant pressure or by plotting vapour phase composition against liquid phase composition. Such a plot is called the equilibrium curve.

2. Gas absorption : Gas absorption is a gas-liquid operation. It is a method of separating one or more constituents of a gas mixture by contacting it with a suitable solvent. The necessary condition is the solubility of the constituents in a given solvent. The washing of ammonia from a ammonia-air mixture by means of water is a typical example of gas absorption.

Consider that a gas mixture contains two components and one component is transferred. We have C = 3, P = 2 and ∴ F = 3. There are four variables; temperature pressure, and the concentration of A in liquid and gas. If the temperature and pressure are fixed, one concentration may be chosen as the remaining independent variable that may be varied and the value of other concentration follows. A plot of equilibrium concentration in gas v/s concentration in liquid phase gives an equilibrium relationship.

3. Liquid extraction : Liquid extraction is a liquid-liquid operation. It is a method of separating the constituents of a liquid mixture by treating it with a suitable solvent that preferentially dissolves one or more of the constituents of a mixture. It is also called as solvent extraction. It is used as a separation technique only when distillation is ineffective and difficult. The separation of penicillin from fermentation mixtures is a typical example of application of liquid extraction.

4. Crystallisation : It is liquid-solid operation and used to obtain materials in attractive and uniform crystals of good purity. Crystallisation is the formation of solid particles within a homogeneous liquid phase.

5. Drying : Drying is gas-solid operation. In general, it means the removal of a relatively small amounts of water from a solid material.

In case of drying, there are two phases and three components. C = 3, P = 2, ∴ F = 3.

The variables are : temperature, pressure, the concentration of water in solid and gas. If the temperature and pressure are fixed, one concentration may be taken as the remaining independent variable and the other concentration follows. These two concentrations can be plotted as the equilibrium curve.

DIFFUSION

It is the movement of an individual component through a mixture from a region of higher concentration to one of lower concentration at fixed temperature and pressure with or without the help of an external force.

A mixture non-uniform initially will be ultimately brought to uniformity (a mixture is everywhere uniform in the concentration of its constituents) by diffusion as a concentration gradient which is the common cause of diffusion tends to move the component in such a direction as to equalise concentrations and destroy the gradient. If we maintain the concentration gradient by constantly supplying the diffusing component to the high concentration end and removing it at low concentration end then the flow of diffusing component is continuous. This movement is utilised in mass transfer operations.

When diffusion results from the random movement/motion of the molecules, it is called as **molecular diffusion**. As the molecular diffusion requires actual migration of molecules, the rate of mass transfer is higher in gases than liquids and very slow in solids. When the movement of the molecules occurs with the help of an external force (e.g., mechanical stirring and convective movement of the fluid) then it is called as **eddy or turbulent diffusion**. The molecular diffusion is a slow process whereas eddy diffusion is a fast process. The molecular diffusion is the mechanism of mass transfer in a stationary fluid, i.e., a fluid at rest and fluids in laminar flow. In case of mass transfer in fluids in turbulent flow, the mechanism of mass transfer is by eddy diffusion. The transfer of material in the presence of a concentration gradient is classified as molecular transfer and eddy transfer. Molecular transfer of mass is encountered in stationary fluids or fluids in laminar flow whereas eddy transfer is encountered in the case of fluids under turbulent conditions.

Role of diffusion in mass transfer :

Diffusion may occur in one phase or in both phases in all the mass transfer operations. In case of distillation, the more volatile component diffuses through the liquid phase to the interface between the phases (liquid and vapour phases) and away from the interface into the vapour phase. The less volatile component diffuses in the opposite direction and passes from the vapour phase to the liquid phase. In case of gas absorption, the solute gas diffuses through the gas phase to the interface and then through the liquid phase (liquid solvent phase) from the interface between the phases. In case of crystallisation, the solid solute diffuses through the mother liquor to the crystals and deposit on the solid surfaces. In case of drying operation, liquid water (moisture) diffuses through the solid towards the surface of the solid, evaporates and diffuses as a vapour into the gas phase (drying medium). In case of liquid-liquid extraction, the liquid solute diffuses through the raffinate phase and then into the extract phase (solvent phase) from the interface between the phases.

Molecular Diffusion :

Concentrations, velocities and fluxes :

Let us consider two chemical species A and B are placed in two compartments that are separated by a impermeable partition. Now, assume that the partition is suddenly removed so that the species A will diffuse into B and the species B will diffuse in A and this will continue at a constantly decreasing rate until the mixture becomes everywhere uniform in the concentration of its constituents. The process is one of molecular diffusion in which the species are diffused in one another solely as a result of the random motion of molecules. The rate of diffusion is governed by Fick's law and before dealing with this law, we will define the above mentioned terms based on the combination of such species. We make it clear that by word *solution* we mean a mixture of species of the same phase – gas in gas, liquid in liquid, etc., i.e., one phase - a gaseous, a liquid or a solid mixture.

Concentration :

There are various ways to express the concentration of the various species in a multicomponent system/mixture. We limit our discussion to mass concentration, molar concentration, mass fraction and mole fraction.

Mass concentration : It is the mass of species A per unit volume of the solution (mixture). It is equivalent to the density of A and designated as ρ_A.

For the above binary system composed of A and B,

$$\rho_A + \rho_B = \rho \qquad \ldots (7.1)$$

where ρ is the mass density of the solution.

Molar concentration : It is the number of moles of species A per unit volume of the solution.

$$C_A = \frac{\rho_A}{M_A} \qquad \ldots (7.2)$$

where M_A is the molecular weight of component A. The units of molar concentration in SI system are $kmol/m^3$.

Hence, for a binary system of A and B, the total molar concentration of the mixture is given by

$$C = C_A + C_B \qquad \ldots (7.3)$$

Mass fraction : The mass fraction x_A' of a species A may be defined as the ratio of the mass concentration of species A to the mass density of the solution.

$$x_A' = \frac{\rho_A}{\rho} \qquad \ldots (7.4)$$

Mole fraction : The mole fraction (x_A) of a species A can be defined as the ratio of the molar concentration of A to the molar concentration of the solution.

$$x_A = \frac{C_A}{C} \qquad \ldots (7.5)$$

For a binary system, we have :

$$x_A' + x_B' = 1$$

and $\qquad x_A + x_B = 1$

In the gas phase, concentrations are usually expressed in terms of partial pressures.

For the ideal gas A, $\quad p_A V = n_A RT$

$$C_A = \frac{n_A}{V} = \frac{p_A}{RT} \qquad \ldots (7.6)$$

where p_A is the partial pressure of species A in the mixture, n_A is the number of moles of A in the mixture, V is the molar volume of the mixture, T is the temperature (absolute), and R is the univeral gas constant.

x_A in terms of p_A is given as :

$$x_A = \frac{C_A}{C} = \frac{p_A/RT}{P/RT} = \frac{p_A}{P} \qquad \ldots (7.7)$$

where P is the total pressure exerted by the gas mixture.

Also, we have $\qquad C = C_A + C_B = \frac{p_A}{RT} + \frac{p_B}{RT} = \frac{P}{RT} \qquad \ldots (7.8)$

Velocities :

In a diffusing mixture, various chemical species are moving at different velocities as they may have different mobilities. The bulk velocity of the mixture would be some sort of an average velocity. Let u_i be the velocity of the ith species with respect to the stationary coordinate system. Then, for a mixture of n species, the local mass average velocity u is defined by,

$$u = \frac{\sum_{i=1}^{n} \rho_i u_i}{\sum_{i=1}^{n} \rho_i} \qquad \ldots (7.9)$$

ρu is the local rate at which mass passes through a unit cross-section when it is placed perpendicular to u.

In a binary system of A and B components

$$u = \frac{\rho_A u_A + \rho_B u_B}{\rho} \qquad \ldots (7.10)$$

The local molar average velocity of the mixture U, is defined by

$$U = \frac{\sum_{i=1}^{n} C_i u_i}{\sum_{i=1}^{n} C_i} \qquad \ldots (7.11)$$

Cu is the local rate at which moles pass through a unit cross-section which is placed perpendicular to U.

In a binary system,

$$U = \frac{C_A u_A + C_B u_B}{C} \qquad \ldots (7.12)$$

Let us define two diffusion velocities relative to/with respect to the two bulk velocities (mass and molar average velocities of the mixture).

The mass diffusion velocity of a species is the velocity of that species relative to the local mass average velocity of the mixture.

Mass diffusion velocity of species i w.r.t. $u = u_i - u$

Mass diffusion velocity of species A w.r.t. $u = u_A - u$.

The molar diffusion velocity of a species is the velocity of species with respect to/relative to the local molar average velocity of the mixture.

Molar diffusion velocity of species i w.r.t. $U = u_i - U$ $\qquad \ldots (7.13)$

Molar diffusion velocity of species A w.r.t. $U = u_A - U$ $\qquad \ldots (7.14)$

Mass flow rate : It is the quantity of material flow in mass units per unit time.

Molar flow rate : It is the quantity of material flow in molar units per unit time.

Flux : The mass transfer flux of a given species (vector quantity) is defined as the amount of that species, in either mass or, molar units, that crosses a unit area per unit time. We will define four types of fluxes, two with reference to fixed coordinates in space and two with respect to local mass average velocity and local molar average velocity (w.r.t. coordinates moving with mass average velocity and molar average velocity).

Mass flux : The mass flux of a species i is defined as the mass of the species i that passes through a unit area per unit time.

The mass flux relative to the stationary/fixed coordinates is given by,

$$n_i = \rho_i u_i \quad \ldots (7.15)$$

The mass flux relative to the mass average velocity u is given by,

$$j_i = \rho_i (u_i - u) \quad \ldots (7.16)$$

Molar flux : It is defined as the moles of species i that passes through a unit area per unit time.

The molar flux relative to the stationary coordinates is given by,

$$N_i = C_i u_i \quad \ldots (7.17)$$

The molar flux relative to the molar average velocity U is given by,

$$J_i = C_i (u_i - U) \quad \ldots (7.18)$$

It is true that any one of the above mentioned notation used for the flux is adequate for all diffusion problems, but each has certain advantages. In process calculations, it is usually desirable to refer to a coordinate system fixed in an equipment so the flux N_i is used in engineering. The fluxes j_i and J_i are the usual measures of rates of diffusion and are useful in formulating the equations of change for multicomponent systems.

For a binary system of A and B :

The mass fluxes of A and B relative to stationary coordinates are :

$$n_A = \rho_A u_A \quad \ldots (7.19)$$

$$n_B = \rho_B u_B \quad \ldots (7.20)$$

The mass fluxes of A and B relative to mass average velocity are :

$$j_A = \rho_A (u_A - u) \quad \ldots (7.21)$$

$$j_B = \rho_B (u_B - u) \quad \ldots (7.22)$$

The molar fluxes of A and B with respect to stationary coordinates are :

$$N_A = C_A u_A \quad \ldots (7.23)$$

$$N_B = C_B u_B \quad \ldots (7.24)$$

The molar fluxes of A and B relative to molar average velocity U are :

$$J_A = C_A (u_A - U) \quad \ldots (7.25)$$

$$J_B = C_B (u_B - U) \quad \ldots (7.26)$$

J_A and J_B are diffusion flux of components A and B. The various fluxes can be interrelated as,

$$n_A = \rho_A u_A$$
$$= \rho_A(u + u_A - u)$$
$$= \rho_A u + \rho_A(u_A - u)$$
$$= \rho_A u + j_i \qquad \ldots (7.27)$$

We have, $x'_A = \dfrac{\rho_A}{\rho} \quad \therefore \quad \rho_A = x'_A \rho$

$$n_A = x'_A (\rho u) + j_i$$

Since, $\sum n_i = \sum \rho_i u_i = \rho v$

$\therefore \quad n_A = x'_A \sum n_i + j_i \qquad \ldots (7.28)$

Similarly,
$$N_A = C_A u_A$$
$$= C_A(U + u_A - U)$$
$$= C_A U + C_A(u_A - U)$$
$$N_A = C_A U + J_A \qquad \ldots (7.29)$$
$$N_A = x_A(CU) + J_A$$
$$\sum N_i = \sum C_i u_i = CU$$
$$N_A = x_A \left(\sum N_i\right) + J_A \qquad \ldots (7.30)$$

Fick's law of diffusion :

A relation between the flux of the diffusing substance and the concentration gradient responsible for molecular diffusion-mass transfer was first proposed by FICK in 1855 and is therefore referred to as Fick's first law of diffusion.

The flux of diffusing component A (diffusion flux of A) in z direction in a binary mixture of A and B is proportional to the molar concentration gradient.

So Fick's law of diffusion for a binary mixture for steady state diffusion can be expressed as

$$J_A = -D_{AB} \cdot \dfrac{dC_A}{dz} \qquad \ldots (7.31)$$

where J_A is the molar flux of A in the z direction relative to the molar average velocity [moles per unit area per unit time, $kmol/(m^2 \cdot s)$].

C_A is the concentration of A [moles of A per unit volume, $kmol/m^3$]

$\dfrac{dC_A}{dz}$ is the concentration gradient in the z-direction.

D_{AB} is the proportionality constant, known as the molecular diffusivity or diffusion coefficient for component A diffusing through B, m^2/s and z is the distance in the direction of diffusion, m.

The negative sign indicates/implies that diffusion occurs in the direction of a drop in concentration.

Diffusivity is defined as the ratio of the flux to the corresponding concentration gradient. The dimensions of the diffusivity are L^2/θ and its SI units are m^2/s. The diffusivity of any component is a measure of its diffusive mobility and is a function of the temperature, pressure, nature, and concentration of the other components.

Diffusive mobility is a function of the number of collisions. Therefore, diffusivity increases with decrease in pressure because number of collisions are less at lower pressure. However, the effect of pressure is negligible in case of liquids. Also, as the random motion of the molecules increases with increase in temperature, diffusivity increases with increase in temperature.

For a binary system in the z direction, dropping the subscript z :

$$J_A = C_A(u_A - U) \quad \ldots (7.32)$$

Equating equations (7.31) and (7.32), we get

$$J_A = C_A(u_A - U) = -D_{AB}\frac{dC_A}{dz}$$

$$C_A u_A = -D_{AB}\frac{dC_A}{dz} + C_A U \quad \ldots (7.33)$$

Now, U according to equation (7.12) is given by

$$U = \frac{1}{C}(C_A u_A + C_B u_B)$$

$$C_A U = \frac{C_A}{C}(C_A u_A + C_B u_B)$$

$$C_A U = x_A(C_A u_A + C_B u_B)$$

Substituting $C_A U$ in equation (7.33), we get

$$C_A u_A = -D_{AB}\frac{dC_A}{dz} + x_A(C_A u_A + C_B u_B)$$

Using equation (7.23), the above expression becomes

$$N_A = -D_{AB}\frac{dC_A}{dz} + x_A(N_A + N_B)$$

$$N_A = J_A + x_A(N_A + N_B) \quad \ldots (7.34)$$

Here, J_A is the contribution due to concentration gradient, diffusion flux and $x_A(N_A + N_B)$ is the bulk motion contribution, flux due to bulk flow.

Molecular Diffusion in Gases :

For the diffusion in the z direction and for N_A and N_B both constant (steady state), we will derive equations for the flux.

For an ideal gas, we have

$$\frac{C_A}{C} = \frac{p_A}{P} = y_A \quad \ldots (7.35)$$

where p_A is the partial pressure of component A.

and P is the total pressure.

1. Steady state equimolar counter diffusion : For the steady state diffusion of two ideal gases, where an equal number of moles the gases are diffusing counter current to each other (in opposite directions to each other), the flux is given by

$$N_A = \frac{D_{AB}}{RTz} (p_{A1} - p_{A2}) \quad \ldots (7.36)$$

where N_A is the molar flux of A in kmol/(m².s), D_{AB} is the diffusivity of A in B in m²/s, $z\ (z_2 - z_1)$ is the distance through which diffusion occurs in m and p_{A1} and p_{A2} are the partial pressures of the component A (in Pa) at the beginning and end of the diffusion path respectively.

We have :
$$N_A = J_A + x_A (N_A + N_B)$$
$$N_A = -D_{AB} \frac{dC_A}{dz} + \frac{C_A}{C} (N_A + N_B)$$

For an ideal gas :
$$p_A = C_A RT$$
$$\therefore \quad C_A = \frac{p_A}{RT}$$
$$dC_A = \frac{dp_A}{RT}$$
$$C = \frac{P}{RT}$$

Putting values of C_A, C, and dC_A, we get

$$N_A = -\frac{D_{AB}}{RT} \frac{dp_A}{dz} + \frac{p_A}{P} (N_A + N_B) \quad \ldots (7.37)$$

For equimolar counter diffusion,
$$N_A = -N_B = \text{constant and the above equation reduces to}$$

$$\therefore \quad N_A = -\frac{D_{AB}}{RT} \frac{dp_A}{dz} \quad \ldots (7.38)$$

If D_{AB} is constant, then the above equation can be integrated.

$$N_A \int_{z_1}^{z_2} dz = -\frac{D_{AB}}{RT} \int_{p_{A1}}^{p_{A2}} dp_A$$

$$N_A (z_2 - z_1) = \frac{-D_{AB}}{RT} (p_{A2} - p_{A1})$$

Let $z_2 - z_1 = z$. Rearranging the above equation, we get

$$N_A = \frac{D_{AB}}{RTz} (p_{A1} - p_{A2}) \quad \ldots (7.39)$$

Here, the concentration difference is expressed in terms of partial pressure. It can also be expressed in terms of mole fraction or molar concentration.

2. Steady state diffusion of A through nondiffusing/stagnant B :

For the steady state diffusion of an ideal gas A through a stagnant gas B, the flux is given by

$$N_A = \frac{D_{AB} P}{RTz \cdot p_{B,M}} (p_{A1} - p_{A2}) \qquad \ldots (7.40)$$

where $p_{B,M}$ is the log mean partial pressure of gas B.

We have:
$$N_A = -D_{AB} \frac{dC_A}{dz} + \frac{C_A}{C} (N_A + N_B)$$

$$N_A = \frac{-D_{AB}}{RT} \frac{dp_A}{dz} + \frac{p_A}{P} (N_A + N_B)$$

For the steady state diffusion of A through nondiffusing B, we have:
$$N_A = \text{constant and } N_B = 0$$

With this, the above equation reduces to
$$N_A = \frac{-D_{AB}}{RT} \frac{dp_A}{dz} + \frac{p_A}{P} \cdot N_A$$

Rearranging, we get
$$N_A \left(\frac{P - p_A}{P}\right) = \frac{-D_{AB}}{RT} \frac{dp_A}{dz}$$

If D_{AB} is constant, then the above equation can be integrated.

$$N_A \int_{z_1}^{z_2} dz = \frac{-D_{AB} \cdot P}{RT} \int_{p_{A1}}^{p_{A2}} \frac{dp_A}{P - p_A}$$

$$N_A = \frac{D_{AB} P}{RTz} \ln \left[\frac{P - p_{A2}}{P - p_{A1}}\right] \qquad \ldots (7.41)$$

We have,
$$p_{A1} + p_{B1} = P \qquad p_{B1} = P - p_{A1}$$
and $\quad p_{A2} + p_{B2} = P \qquad p_{B2} = P - p_{A2}$
$$\therefore \qquad p_{B2} - p_{B1} = p_{A1} - p_{A2}$$

$$\therefore \qquad N_A = \frac{D_{AB} P}{RTz} \ln \left(\frac{p_{B2}}{p_{B1}}\right)$$

$$N_A = \frac{D_{AB} P}{RTz} \frac{(p_{B2} - p_{B1})}{(p_{B2} - p_{B1})} \ln (p_{B2}/p_{B1})$$

$p_{B,M}$ is the log mean partial pressure of B.

$$p_{B,M} = \frac{p_{B2} - p_{B1}}{\ln (p_{B2}/p_{B1})}$$

Replacing $p_{B2} - p_{B1}$ by $p_{A1} - p_{A2}$ in the numerator and putting $p_{B,M}$ for $(p_{B2} - p_{B1})/\ln (p_{B2}/p_{B1})$, we get

$$N_A = \frac{D_{AB} P}{RTz \cdot p_{B,M}} (p_{A1} - p_{A2}) \qquad \ldots (7.42)$$

Here, the flux is proportional to the concentration difference expressed in terms of partial pressure of A and inversely proportional to the distance z and the concentration of the stagnant gas ($p_{B,M}$). With increase in z and $p_{B,M}$, resistance to diffusion increases and therefore, flux decreases.

Molecular Diffusion in Liquids :

1. **Steady-state equimolar counter diffusion :**

   We have : $N_A = -N_B$ = constant

   The flux equation for steady state equimolar counter diffusion is given by

   $$N_A = \frac{D_{AB}}{z}(C_{A1} - C_{A2}) = \frac{D_{AB}}{z}\left(\frac{\rho}{M}\right)_{avg.}(x_{A1} - x_{A2}) \quad \ldots (7.43)$$

   where $x_{A1} - x_{A2}$ is the concentration difference in terms of mole fraction.

   $$(\rho/M)_{avg.} = C_{avg.} = [\rho_1/M_1 + \rho_2/M_2]/2 \quad \ldots (7.44)$$

   $C_{avg.}$ is the total average concentration of A and B in kmol/m³, ρ_1 and ρ_2 are the average densities of the solution in kg/m³ at locations 1 and 2 respectively, and M_1 and M_2 are the average molecular weights of the solution at locations 1 and 2 respectively in kg/kmol.

2. **Steady state diffusion of A through nondiffusing B :**

   N_A = constant, $N_B = 0$

   The flux is given by

   $$N_A = \frac{D_{AB}}{z \cdot x_{A,M}}(\rho/M)_{avg.}(x_{A1} - x_{A2}) \quad \ldots (7.45)$$

   where $x_{B,M} = (x_{B2} - x_{B1})/\ln(x_{B2}/x_{B1})$

Diffusion in Solids :

The operations like leaching, drying, etc. involve contact of fluids with solids and involve diffusion in the solid phase.

Fick's law for the steady state diffusion can be written as

$$N_A = -D_A \frac{dC_A}{dz} \quad \ldots (7.46)$$

where N_A is the rate of diffusion of A per unit cross-section of solid. D_A is the diffusivity of A through the solid, $-dC_A/dz$ is the concentration gradient in the direction of diffusion.

1. **Diffusion through a flat slab of thickness z :**

   Taking D_A constant, integration of the above equation (7.46) yields

   $$N_A = \frac{D_A[C_{A1} - C_{A2}]}{z} \quad \ldots (7.47)$$

   $z = z_2 - z_1$ = thickness of the slab

   C_{A1} and C_{A2} are concentrations of A at the opposite sides of the slab.

For other solid shapes, the rate of diffusion is given by

$$W = N_A A_{avg.} = \frac{D\, A_{avg.}\, (C_{A1} - C_{A2})}{z} \qquad \ldots (7.48)$$

$A_{avg.}$ is the average cross-section available for diffusion.

For the radial diffusion through a solid cylinder of inner and outer radii r_1 and r_2 and length L :

$$A_{avg.} = \frac{2\pi\, (r_2 - r_1)\, L}{\ln\, (r_2/r_1)}, \quad \text{and } z = r_2 - r_1$$

For the radial diffusion through a spherical shell of inner and outer radii r_1 and r_2,

$$A_{avg.} = 4\pi\, r_1 r_2 \quad \text{and} \quad z = r_2 - r_1$$

Steady State Equimolar Counter Diffusion :

The diffusion of two components in opposite directions in each other in a stationary mixture is of importance in distillation of a binary system. If the two components are at the same temperature and the same total pressure, then no net movement of the mixture will take place and it will be simply the replacement of the molecules of one component by the molecules of other component. In a language of diffusion, two components diffuse at the same molar flow rate in the opposite directions in each other. This overall transfer process is called as *equimolar counter diffusion*.

Consider a case of two gases A and B at constant total pressure P in two chambers.

Let us consider that the two large chambers containing gases A and B are connected by a tube in such a way that molecular diffusion at steady state is occurring. The total pressure P is uniform/constant throughout.

(a)

(b)

Fig. 7.1 : Equimolar counter diffusion of gases A and B;
(a) system, (b) concentration profile

Stirring provided in each chamber keeps the concentration in each chamber uniform. The partial pressure $p_{A1} > p_{A2}$ and $p_{B2} > p_{B1}$. The molecules of A diffuse to the right, while the molecules of B diffuse to the left.

As the temperature and total pressure P is constant throughout, the net moles of A diffusing to the right must be equal to the net moles of B diffusing to the left. If this is not so, the total pressure would not remain constant throughout the system. This implies/indicates that

$$J_A = -J_B \quad \ldots (7.49)$$

J_A is the molar flux of component A in the x-direction due to molecular diffusion in kmol A/(m².s).

Writing Fick's law for component B for constant molar concentration, C,

$$J_B = -D_{BA} \frac{dC_B}{dx} \quad \ldots (7.50)$$

Here the flux is in the x-direction.

Now as the total pressure is the sum of the partial pressures of A and B,

$$P = p_A + p_B \quad \ldots (7.51)$$

and

$$p \propto C \text{ [for gases]} \quad \ldots (7.52)$$

The total molar concentration for the gaseous mixture is given by

$$C = C_A + C_B \quad \ldots (7.53)$$

Differentiating both the sides of equation (7.53) with respect to x,

$$0 = \frac{dC_A}{dx} + \frac{dC_B}{dx} \quad \ldots (7.54)$$

or

$$\frac{dC_A}{dx} = \frac{-dC_B}{dx} \quad \ldots (7.55)$$

Therefore, if a gradient exists in the gas A, a gradient exists in the gas B. The gradient of B is equal but opposite in sign to that of A.

Fick's law for component A for constant total concentration is

$$J_A = -D_{AB} \frac{dC_A}{dx} \quad \ldots (7.56)$$

Combining equations (7.49), (7.50) and (7.51),

$$J_A = -D_{AB} \frac{dC_A}{dx}$$

$$= -J_B = -\left[-D_{BA} \frac{dC_B}{dx}\right] \quad \ldots (7.57)$$

$$-D_{AB} \frac{dC_A}{dx} = D_{BA} \frac{dC_B}{dx} \quad \ldots (7.58)$$

but

$$\frac{dC_A}{dx} = -\frac{dC_B}{dt} \quad \ldots (7.59)$$

$$\therefore \quad D_{AB} = D_{BA} \quad \ldots (7.60)$$

This shows that for a binary mixture of A and B, the diffusivity coefficient D_{AB} for A diffusing in B is the same as D_{BA}, for B diffusing in A.

We have :
$$J_A = -D_{AB} \frac{dC_A}{dx} \quad \ldots (7.61)$$

For ideal gases, molar concentration of A is related to the partial pressure of A by

$$C_A = \frac{N_A}{V} = \frac{p_A}{RT} \quad \ldots (7.62)$$

$$\therefore \quad \frac{dC_A}{dx} = \frac{1}{RT} \frac{dp_A}{dx} \quad \ldots (7.63)$$

$$\therefore \quad J_A = -\frac{D_{AB}}{RT} \frac{dp_A}{dx} \quad \ldots (7.64)$$

Integrating, we get

$$J_A = \frac{D_{AB}}{RT} \frac{(p_{A1} - p_{A2})}{(x_2 - x_1)} \quad \ldots (7.65)$$

$$= \frac{D_{AB}}{RT} \frac{(p_{A1} - p_{A2})}{x} \, , \, x = x_2 - x_1 \quad \ldots (7.66)$$

For species B,

$$J_B = \frac{D_{BA}}{RT} \frac{(p_{B1} - p_{B2})}{x} \quad \ldots (7.67)$$

Equations (7.66) and (7.67) are the equations for steady state equimolar counter diffusion.

We know that

$$\frac{dC_A}{dx} = -\frac{dC_B}{dx} \quad \ldots (7.68)$$

The gradient of B is equal but opposite in sign to that of A. Since the gradient for B exists, there must be molar flux of B, as stated by equation (7.50). Combination of equations (7.50), (7.56) and (7.68) gives

$$J_A = -J_B \quad \ldots (7.69)$$

This shows that the rates of diffusion are equal but in opposite directions. Equation (7.69) is always true in the binary mixtures, irrespective of what other mechanisms for mass transfer may be operating. The rates of transfer of the two species by molecular transport (diffusion) are always equal but in opposite directions. When molecular transport is the only mechanism, the overall transfer process is called as an *equimolar counter diffusion*.

Mass Transfer Coefficients :

In most mass transfer operations, the turbulent flow is desired to increase the rate of transfer per unit area. In such cases, the mass transfer rate is expressed in terms of mass transfer coefficients. In turbulent flow there are three regions of mass transfer but as it is very difficult to know the value of distance in turbulent region through which diffusion occurs, it is considered that the entire resistance to mass transfer lies in a laminar sublayer of thickness z (effective laminar film thickness). The resistance offered by the effective laminar film thickness is approximately the same as the combined resistance offered by three regions in turbulent motion. The flux equations for such situations are of the type :

$$\text{Flux} = (\text{Mass transfer coefficient}) \times (\text{Concentration difference})$$

As the concentration can be expressed in number of ways, we have a variety of types of mass transfer coefficients.

Mass transfer coefficient is thus defined as *the rate of mass transfer per unit area per unit concentration difference.*

The flux equation obtained for the steady state equimolar counter diffusion (components A and B diffusing at the same molar rates in opposite directions) for turbulent motion becomes

$$N_A = \frac{D_{AB}}{RTz_G} (p_{A1} - p_{A2}) \qquad \ldots (7.70)$$

For a given situation, the term $\dfrac{D_{AB}}{RTz_G}$ is constant and it can be termed as the mass transfer film coefficient for the gas, k_G'

$$\therefore \qquad N_A = k_G' (p_{A1} - p_{A2}) \qquad \ldots (7.71)$$

The flux equation obtained for the steady state diffusion of A through non-diffusing (stationary) B for turbulent motion may be written as :

$$N_A = \frac{D_{AB} P}{RTz \, p_{B,M}} (p_{A1} - p_{A2}) \qquad \ldots (7.72)$$

$$N_A = k_G (p_{A1} - p_{A2}) \qquad \ldots (7.73)$$

where, $\qquad k_G = \dfrac{D_{AB} P}{RTz \, p_{B,M}}$

Similar equations can be written for the liquid phase.

The flux equation for the equimolar counter diffusion for the liquid phase is

$$N_A = \frac{D_{AB}}{z_L} (C_{A1} - C_{A2}) = k_L' (C_{A1} - C_{A2}) \qquad \ldots (7.74)$$

where z_L is the effective laminar film thickness and k_L' is the mass transfer film coefficient for the liquid or the liquid film mass transfer coefficient/individual mass transfer coefficient for the liquid phase.

Mass transfer film coefficient may be defined as *the rate of mass transfer from the bulk of one phase to an interface of unit area for unit driving force.*

The flux equations for transfer of A through non-transferring B (i.e., diffusion of A through non-diffusing B) in terms of the driving force expressed in terms of concentration and molefraction are :

$$N_A = k_y (y_{A1} - y_{A2}), \quad N_A = k_C (C_{A1} - C_{A2}) \qquad \text{for gases} \ldots (7.75)$$

$$N_A = k_x (x_{A1} - x_{A2}), \quad N_A = k_L (C_{A1} - C_{A2}) \qquad \text{for liquids} \ldots (7.76)$$

Similar equations for equimolecular counter diffusion are :

$$N_A = k'_y (y_{A1} - y_{A2}), \quad N_A = k'_c (C_{A1} - C_{A2}) \quad \text{for gases} \ldots (7.77)$$

$$N_A = k'_x (x_{A1} - x_{A2}), \quad N_A = k'_c (C_{A1} - C_{A2}) \quad \text{for liquids} \ldots (7.78)$$

In two film concepts, z is the effective thickness of the film.

Relation between film coefficients :

Gases : $\quad k'_c \dfrac{P}{RT} = k'_c C = k'_c \dfrac{p_{B,M}}{RT} = k'_G P = k'_y = \dfrac{k_y}{M_B} = k_G \, p_{B,M} = k_G \, y_{B,M} \cdot P$

$p_{B,M} = (p_{B1} - p_{B2})/\ln(p_{B1}/p_{B2})$, $\quad y_{B,M} = (y_{B1} - y_{B2})/\ln(y_{B1}/y_{B2})$,

Liquids : $\quad k'_L C = k'_L \rho/M = k'_c C = k'_x = k_x \, x_{B,M} = k_L \, x_{B,M} C$

Overall Mass Transfer Coefficient :

The mass transfer film coefficients are difficult to measure except for cases where the concentration difference across one of the phases is small and can thus be neglected.

In such cases, the overall mass transfer coefficients are measured on the basis of the gas phase or the liquid phase driving force.

The flux equation in terms of the overall mass transfer coefficient and the overall driving force for diffusion of A through non-diffusion B is given as :

$$N_A = K_G (p_A - p_A^*) \quad \ldots (7.79)$$

K_G is the overall gas phase mass transfer coefficient and $(p_A - p_A^*)$ is the overall driving force for the gas phase in terms of partial pressure.

p_A^* is the partial pressure of solute A over a solution having the composition of bulk liquid of C_A. (Partial pressure of A in the gas phase that would be in equilibrium with C_A, the concentration of A in the bulk liquid phase.)

The flux can also be written as :

$$N_A = K_y (y_A - y_A^*) \quad \ldots (7.80)$$

Similarly,

$$N_A = K_L (C_A^* - C_A) \quad \ldots (7.81)$$

where K_L is based on the concentration difference overall driving force for the liquid phase. C_A^* is the concentration of solute A in liquid phase that would be in equilibrium with p_A, partial pressure of A in the bulk gas phase.

Mass transfer (film) coefficients may also be expressed in terms of driving forces in each of the phases as

$$N_A = k_G (p_A - p_{Ai}) = k_L (C_{Ai} - C_A) \quad \ldots (7.82)$$

$$p_A - p_A^* = (p_A - p_{Ai}) + (p_{Ai} - p_A^*) \quad \ldots (7.83)$$

A state of equilibrium can be given by Henry's law

$$p_A^* = H C_A, \quad p_{Ai} = H C_{Ai} \quad \text{and} \quad p_A = H C_A^*$$

$$\therefore \quad p_A - p_A^* = (p_A - p_{Ai}) + H(C_{Ai} - C_A)$$

$$\therefore \quad p_A - p_A^* = \frac{N_A}{K_G}, \quad p_A - p_{Ai} = \frac{N_A}{k_G}, \quad C_{Ai} - C_A = \frac{N_A}{k_L}$$

$$\therefore \quad \frac{1}{K_G} = \frac{1}{k_G} + \frac{H}{k_L} \qquad \ldots (7.84)$$

Here $\frac{1}{K_G}$ is the total resistance, in both the phases, based on the overall gas phase driving force and is equal to the sum of the gas film resistance $1/k_G$ and the liquid film resistance $\frac{H}{k_L}$.

The overall driving force for the liquid phase :

$$C_A^* - C_A = (C_A^* - C_{Ai}) + (C_{Ai} - C_A)$$

$$C_A^* - C_A = \frac{p_A - p_{Ai}}{H} + (C_{Ai} - C_A)$$

$$\therefore \quad \frac{1}{K_L} = \frac{1}{H k_G} + \frac{1}{k_L} \qquad \ldots (7.85)$$

C_{Ai} is the concentration of A at an interface between the phases.

Controlling Film Concept :

We have :
$$\frac{1}{K_G} = \frac{1}{k_G} + \frac{H}{k_L} \qquad \ldots (7.86)$$

If H is very small, $H \simeq 0$ (a case with a highly soluble gas), the liquid film resistance $\frac{H}{k_L}$ is negligible compared to $\frac{1}{k_G}$ and the total resistance equals the gas film resistance (i.e. gas film offers entire resistance to transfer). Such transfer process is called gas film (gas phase) controlling as the resistance to transfer lies entirely in the gas film.

$$\therefore \quad \frac{1}{K_G} = \frac{1}{k_G}$$

or $\quad K_G \simeq k_G$

The overall mass transfer coefficients in such cases are based on the gas film coefficients only. The absorption of ammonia in water is an example of this kind.

We have :
$$\frac{1}{K_L} = \frac{1}{H k_G} + \frac{1}{k_L} \qquad \ldots (7.87)$$

When H is very large, $H \gg 1$ (a case with a insoluble gas), the gas film resistance $\frac{1}{H k_G}$ is negligible and the total resistance equals the liquid film resistance $\frac{1}{k_L}$ and the transfer process in such cases is considered to be liquid film controlling. The absorption of a gas of low solubility such as CO_2 or O_2 in water is an example of this kind.

$$\frac{1}{K_L} \approx \frac{1}{k_L}$$

∴ $K_L \approx k_L$

The overall mass transfer coefficients in such cases are based on liquid film coefficients only.

For absorption of a moderately soluble gas obeying Henry's law either K_G or K_L can be used for mass transfer calculations. The absorption of sulphur dioxide in water is an example of this kind.

Interphase Mass Transfer :

In most important industrial applications of mass transfer, the material is transferred across a phase boundary (called the interface). For example, in distillation the vapour and liquid are brought into contact in a fractionating column and the more volatile component is transferred from the liquid to vapour while the less volatile component is transferred from the vapour to liquid. In gas absorption, the solute gas is transferred from the gas to the liquid. In both of these examples, one phase is liquid and the other is gas.

Phase : It is a homogeneous and physically distinct part of a system which is bounded by a surface and, therefore, can be separated from the other parts of the system, e.g., water is one phase, but ice is another phase. Phases may be liquid, solid or gaseous.

Interphase mass transfer : *It is the process of mass transfer from the bulk of one phase to the interphase surface, and then from the interphase to the bulk of another phase.*

In absorption of ammonia by water from an ammonia-air mixture, the solute ammonia may diffuse through the gas phase and then pass through the interface between the phases, and finally diffuse through the adjacent immiscible water phase (liquid phase).

Mass transfer occurs in each phase due to the concentration gradient existing in that phase and a state of equilibrium is assumed to exist at the interface between the two fluid phases.

Fig. 7.2

In absorption of a solute gas A in a liquid solvent from a gas mixture, as shown in Fig. 7.2, mass transfer occurs in the gas phase from p_A to p_{Ai} (at the interface) and in the liquid phase from C_{Ai} (at the interface) to C_A. As equilibrium exists at the interface (between the phases), there is no resistance to mass transfer at the interface and p_{Ai} and C_{Ai} are related through the equilibrium relationship :

$$p_{Ai} = H\,C_{Ai} \qquad \ldots (7.88)$$

where H is the Henry's constant for the system under consideration.

Equilibrium :

In mass transfer operations usually there are two phases which are brought in contact for the transfer of constituent material(s) from one phase to another or in both the phases. If two phases come to a state of equilibrium, the net transfer of material ceases. The equilibrium relationship between the phases involved is of basic importance in all the mass transfer calculations. The equilibrium relationships can be expressed by an equation or can be shown graphically.

For gas absorption operation, the relationship between the equilibrium concentrations of solute in a gas phase and a liquid phase at constant temperature and pressure is the desired equilibrium relationship between the two phases. Now we will obtain the equilibrium relationship for absorption of ammonia by liquid water from an ammonia-air mixture. Consider that a definite amount of liquid water along with a gaseous mixture of ammonia and air is placed in a closed container which is maintained at constant temperature and pressure. As the ammonia is very soluble in water, some of the ammonia molecules will transfer from the gas phase to the liquid phase, crossing the interface separating the two phases. Some of the ammonia molecules return back into the gas, at a rate proportional to the ammonia concentration in the liquid. As more and more ammonia enters the liquid, its concentration in that phase increases and due to this the rate at which ammonia returns back to the gas phase increases. This will continues and ultimately a stage will reach at which the rate with which ammonia enters the liquid phase becomes exactly equal to the rate with which it leaves the liquid phase and also at the same time ammonia concentration throughout each phase becomes uniform through the mechanism of diffusion. A dynamic equilibrium is now said to exist between the phases. In a state of equilibrium, the net transfer of ammonia ceases even though ammonia molecules continue to transfer back and forth from one phase to another. The concentrations of ammonia within each phase do not change with time. Then these concentrations of ammonia in these two phases are its equilibrium concentrations.

If we further inject additional ammonia into the container, equilibrium will be disturbed, the system will try to attain the state of equilibrium and finally we get a new set of equilibrium concentrations. These equilibrium values of concentrations are higher than the previous obtained values. In this way we can obtain the complete relationship between the equilibrium concentrations in both phases at constant temperature and pressure. If we express the equilibrium concentrations of ammonia (A) in both phases in terms of its mole fractions x_A and y_A in the liquid and the gas phase respectively and plot the values of y_A (as ordinate) against the corresponding values of x_A (as abscissa), we obtain a curve as shown in Fig. 7.3. Such a curve is called an equilibrium distribution curve. This curve changes only by conditions imposed on the system such as temperature and pressure. One should note here that at equilibrium, the concentrations of ammonia in the two phases are not equal but it is the chemical potential of ammonia that is the same in both phases and it is this equality of chemical potentials and not of concentrations, which causes the net transfer of solute (ammonia) to cease.

Fig. 7.3 : Equilibrium-distribution curve at constant temperature

Mechanism of Mass Transfer :

The mechanism of mass transfer across a phase boundary (an interface) can be explained by the various theories such as :
- (i) Whitman's two-film theory
- (ii) Higbie's penetration theory
- (iii) Danckwert's surface renewal theory
- (iv) Toor and Marchello's film penetration theory.

The Two-film Theory :

Salient features of Whitman's two film theory are :
- (i) Resistance to transfer in each phase is regarded as lying in a thin film close to the interface (i.e., in two fictitious films one on each side close to the interface).
- (ii) The transfer in these films is by a steady state process of molecular diffusion.
- (iii) The concentration gradient is assumed to be linear in these films and it is zero outside the films, i.e., zero in the bulk fluid.

Fig. 7.4

(iv) The theory assumes that the turbulence in the bulk fluid die out at the interface of the films.

(v) The film capacity is negligible i.e. time taken for concentration gradient to establish is small compared to time of transfer.

Consider a case of a solute gas (A) diffusing from a gas phase into a liquid phase. There must be a concentration gradient in the direction of mass transfer within each phase. This is shown in Fig. 7.4 graphically in terms of distance through the phases.

The concentration of solute A in the bulk of gas phase is y_A molefraction, and it falls to y_{Ai} at the interface. The concentration of solute A in the liquid phase falls from x_{Ai} at the interface between the phases to x_A in the bulk liquid. The bulk concentrations y_A and x_A are not in equilibrium because otherwise the solute will not be diffused from the gas to the liquid phase.

Whitman assumed that the resistance to transfer of solute A lies in two hypothetical films, one on each side of the interface, in which the transfer is entirely by molecular diffusion. There is no resistance to transfer across the interface and as a result the concentrations

y_{Ai} and x_{Ai} are the equilibrium values.

For steady state mass transfer, the rate of transfer of A to the interface must be equal to the rate at which A is transferred from the interface to the bulk of liquid phase so that there is no accumulation or depletion of A at the interface.

Therefore, we can write the mass transfer flux of A or rate of transfer of A in terms of mass transfer coefficients and concentration changes occurring in the phases involved.

$$N_A = k_y (y_A - y_{Ai})$$
$$= k_x (x_{Ai} - x_A) \quad \ldots (7.89)$$

The differences in y's and x's are the driving forces for mass transfer.

Rearranging equation (7.89), we get

$$\frac{k_x}{k_y} = \frac{y_A - y_{Ai}}{x_{Ai} - x_A} \quad \ldots (7.90)$$

$$\frac{y_A - y_{Ai}}{x_A - x_{Ai}} = -\frac{k_x}{k_y} \quad \ldots (7.91)$$

Fig. 7.5 shows typical values of the concentrations of the bulk phases (P) and at the interface (Q).

Fig. 7.5

In experimental determinations of the rate of transfer of solute A, it is possible to measure only the bulk concentrations of the solute A and to measure the interface concentrations is ordinarily impossible. The equilibrium-distribution curve shown in Fig. 7.5 is unique at fixed T and P, so y_A^* in equilibrium with x_A is a good measure of x_A. Therefore, the entire two phase mass transfer effects can be measured in terms of an overall mass transfer coefficient K_y, i.e., the rate of mass transfer can also be set equal to the overall coefficient K_y times the driving force $(y_A - y_A^*)$, where y_A^* is the composition of solute in the gas phase which is in equilibrium with x_A.

$$N_A = K_y (y_A - y_A^*) \qquad \ldots (7.92)$$

$$\frac{1}{K_y} = \frac{y_A - y_A^*}{N_A} = \frac{(y_A - y_{Ai}) + (y_{Ai} - y_A^*)}{N_A}$$

$$\frac{1}{K_y} = \frac{y_A - y_{Ai}}{N_A} + \frac{y_{Ai} - y_A^*}{N_A}$$

$$\frac{1}{K_y} = \frac{1}{k_y} + \frac{y_{Ai} - y_A^*}{k_x (x_{Ai} - x_A)}$$

$$\frac{1}{K_y} = \frac{1}{k_y} + \frac{m}{k_x} \qquad \ldots (7.93)$$

where, $m = \text{slope} = (y_{Ai} - y_A^*) / (x_{Ai} - x_A)$

$1/K_y$ is the overall resistance to mass transfer and $1/k_y$ and m/k_x are the resistances in the liquid and gas films. The resistances in two phases are added to get an overall resistance and hence it is also called as two resistance theory.

On a similar line, x_A^* is a measure of y_A and it can be readily shown that

$$\frac{1}{K_x} = \frac{1}{m\,k_y} + \frac{1}{k_x} \qquad \ldots (7.94)$$

The Penetration Theory :

The penetration theory was proposed by Higbie. The main features of this theory are :
1. As the time of exposure of fluid for mass transfer generally being short, development/establishment of the concentration gradient of film theory (characteristic of steady state) is not possible.
2. The transfer is largely because of fresh material brought to the interface by the eddies.
3. A process of unsteady state transfer occurs for a fixed period at the freshly exposed surface.
4. Each fluid element (eddy) resides for the same length of time period at the surface. According to this theory, the mass transfer coefficient is proportional to the square root of the diffusivity.

Surface Renewal Theory :

According to this theory proposed by Danckwerts

1. The eddies of the fluid at the surface are exposed to varying lengths of time.
2. On the basis of exposure-time histories, an age distribution for the surface elements is calculated.
3. The mass transfer coefficient is proportional to the square root of the diffusivity regardless of the nature of the surface renewal rate.

Counter current and Cocurrent Mass Transfer :

Mass transfer processes that involve two fluid streams are frequently carried out continuously by passing the fluid streams either in a counter current or a cocurrent fashion in a column device. The average driving force for a given situation will be larger in the countercurrent operation than in the cocurrent operation and because of which smaller size equipment is needed for a given set of flow conditions for countercurrent operation. The counter current flow is more common.

The examples of counter current mass transfer processes are :

(i) **Distillation in packed column :** In this case, a vapour stream (thermally created) is moving up against the downward flow of a liquid reflux. At steady state, a state of dynamic equilibrium is set up. The more volatile component under the action of a concentration gradient is transferred from the liquid phase to the interface and then from the interface into the vapour phase. The less volatile component is transferred in the opposite direction and passes through the vapour into the liquid. Here equimolar counter diffusion takes place if the molar latent heats of the components are of the same magnitude.

(ii) **Absorption in packed column :** In this case, a solute gas together with a carrier gas moves up against the downward flow of a liquid (solvent). The solute gas diffuses through the gas phase to the interface where it dissolves and is then transferred into the bulk of the liquid.

(iii) **Liquid-liquid extraction in packed/spray column :** In this case, both the streams are liquid. The lighter liquid rises through the denser one. The solute diffuses from the raffinate phase to the interface and away from the interface into the extract phase.

Examples of Cocurrent Flow :

The cocurrent flow of gas and liquid streams usually in the downward direction through a packed column is used for – catalytic chemical reaction between components of fluids, diffusional operation when a gas to be dissolved in a liquid is a pure substance and for diffusional operation accompanying a chemical reaction, e.g., in absorption of hydrogen sulfide in sodium hydroxide solution. The cocurrent flow produces a separation effect equivalent to that obtained with only one theoretical stage so used for such cases only. With cocurrent flow there is no flooding and there is no upper limit for permissible phase flow rates. The cocurrent flow is rarely used in the absence of a chemical reaction.

Analogies among Heat, Mass and Momentum Transfer :

Depending upon the fluid flow conditions, the mechanism of the transfer process can be classified as molecular transport (characteristic of stream line flow) and combined molecular and eddy transfer (characteristic of total flow regime). There are similarities in governing equations for molecular transport as well as for turbulent transport and we can say that we have analogies among these transport processes. A great deal of effort has been devoted in the literature in developing analogies among these three transport processes for turbulent transfer.

General Molecular Transport Equation :

The molecular transport of momentum, heat and mass is characterised by the same general equation of the type :

$$\text{Rate of a transfer process} = \frac{\text{Driving force}}{\text{Resistance}} \qquad \ldots (7.95)$$

Molecular transport or molecular diffusion equations for momentum, heat and mass transfer :

These equations are applicable to laminar flow as molecular transport is a characteristic of laminar/stream line flow.

Newton's law for momentum transport, i.e., Newton's equation for molecular diffusion of momentum for constant density is

$$\tau_{zx} = \frac{-\mu}{\rho} \frac{d(u_x \rho)}{dz} \qquad \ldots (7.96)$$

$$\tau_{zx} = -\nu \frac{d(u_x \rho)}{dz} \qquad \ldots (7.97)$$

where τ_{zx} is the momentum transferred per unit time per unit area, where momentum has units of (kg.m)/s. [It is also called as the momentum flux], μ is viscosity and ρ is the density of fluid. ν is the kinematic viscosity and also called as the diffusivity of momentum having units of m²/s.

Fourier's law for heat transport, i.e., Fourier's equation for molecular diffusion of heat for constant ρ and C_p is

$$\frac{q_z}{A} = -\alpha \frac{d(\rho C_p T)}{dz} \qquad \ldots (7.98)$$

where $\frac{q_z}{A}$ is the heat transferred per unit time per unit area and is called as heat flux having units of W/m² [J/(m².s)]. α is the thermal diffusivity or diffusivity of heat in m²/s.

Fick's law of molecular mass transport or Fick's equation for molecular diffusion of mass for constant total concentration in a fluid is

$$J_{Az} = -D_{AB} \frac{dC_A}{dz}$$

$$= -D_{AB} \frac{d(\rho_A/M_A)}{dz} \qquad \ldots (7.99)$$

where J_{Az} is the molar flux of component A in the z direction due to molecular diffusion in kmol A/(m².s), D_{AB} is the molecular diffusivity of molecule A in B or mass diffusivity in m²/s. C_A is the molar concentration of A in kmol/m³.

These equations state, respectively, that (a) momentum transport occurs because of a gradient in momentum concentration, (b) energy transport occurs because of a gradient in energy concentration, and (c) the mass transport occurs because of a gradient in mass concentration.

Turbulent diffusion equations for momentum, heat and mass transfer :

For combined molecular and eddy transfer, the relations for momentum, heat and mass are :

For turbulent momentum transfer for constant density,

$$\tau_{zx} = -(\mu/\rho + \varepsilon_M) \frac{d(u_x \rho)}{dz} \quad \ldots (7.100)$$

$$\tau_{zx} = -(\nu + \varepsilon_M) \frac{d(\rho u_x)}{dz} \quad \ldots (7.101)$$

For turbulent heat transfer for constant ρ and C_p,

$$\frac{q_z}{A} = -(\alpha + \varepsilon_H) \frac{d(\rho C_p T)}{dz} \quad \ldots (7.102)$$

For turbulent mass transfer for constant total molar concentration,

$$J_{Az} = -(D_{AB} + \varepsilon_D) \frac{dC_A}{dz} \quad \ldots (7.103)$$

In the above equations, ε_m is the turbulent or eddy diffusivity of momentum in m²/s, ε_H is the turbulent or eddy diffusivity of heat or eddy thermal diffusivity in m²/s and ε_M is the turbulent or eddy diffusivity of mass in m²/s. Again, these equations are quite similar or analogous to each other.

Equations (7.97), (7.98) and (7.99) for momentum, heat and mass transfer are similar to each other and to the general molecular transport equation (7.95). All these equations have a flux on the left hand side having the units of a quantity of momentum, heat or mass transferred per unit time per unit area; a diffusivity of momentum, heat and mass (i.e., transport properties, ν, α and D_{AB}) all in m²/s, and a derivative of the concentration of a property with respect to the distance on the right hand side. In all the above cases, the flux is proportional to the driving force. All three of the molecular transport equations are mathematically identical. Thus, we state we have an analogy or similarity among them. Even though there is a mathematical analogy among them, the actual physical mechanisms occurring can be totally different.

The mass diffusivity D_{AB}, the kinematic viscosity, ν and thermal diffusivity, α are analogous as seen from the above equations.

The similarity in nature of transfer of these three processes are referred to as analogy. Looking at similarities between governing equations of heat, mass and momentum transfer, it is to be expected that the correlations for heat transfer coefficients and mass transfer coefficients would also be similar. Various quantitative relations are available to describe the analogical behaviour. The simplest and oldest is due to Reynolds.

The Reynolds Analogy :

Reynolds was first to note similarities in transport processes and relates turbulent momentum and heat transfer.

The basic assumption of the Reynolds analogy is that the ratio of two molecular diffusivities equals to that of two eddy diffusivities.

$$\frac{\nu}{\alpha} = N_{Pr} = \frac{\varepsilon_M}{\varepsilon_H} \qquad \ldots (7.104)$$

For turbulent flow conditions, the Reynolds analogy equations are :

The statement of Reynolds analogy between heat and momentum transfer is :

$$\frac{h}{C_p\, u\, \rho} = \frac{h}{C_p\, G} = N_{St} = \frac{f}{2} \qquad \ldots (7.105)$$

The statement of Reynolds analogy between mass and momentum transfer is :

$$\frac{k'_c}{u} = \frac{f}{2} \qquad \ldots (7.106)$$

Therefore, the complete Reynolds analogy is

$$\frac{h}{C_p\, u\, \rho} = \frac{k'_c}{u} = \frac{f}{2} \qquad \ldots (7.107)$$

$$N_{St} = N_{St_m} = \frac{f}{2} \qquad \ldots (7.108)$$

where f is the Fanning friction factor (measure of skin friction), u is the average velocity of fluid, k'_c is the convective mass transfer coefficient, h is the convective heat transfer coefficient.

Equation (7.107) agrees well with experimental data (correlates data) for gases in turbulent flow if the Schmidt and Prandtl numbers are about unity and only the skin friction is present in a flow past a flat plate or inside pipe. The equations do not correlate the data for liquids in turbulent flow nor for any fluids in laminar flow, i.e., in such cases the analogy is not valid.

Although the Reynolds analogy is of limited utility, significant conclusion may be drawn that, at $N_{Pr} = N_{Sc} = 1.0$, the mechanisms for momentum, heat and mass are identical.

If the measure of the skin friction-fanning friction factor is known, the analogy may be used to find the heat transfer coefficient from the mass transfer coefficient and vice-versa.

SOLVED EXAMPLES

Ex. 7.1 : A large tank filled with a mixture of gases A and B at 101 kPa and 298 K (25 °C) is connected to another large tank filled with a mixture of A and B of different compositions of A and B at 101 kPa and 298 K (25 °C). The tanks are connected by a tube of inner diameter of 50 mm and is 150 mm long. Calculate the steady state rate of transport of A through the tube when concentration of A in one tank is 90 mole % and other, 5 mole %

assuming, uniformity in composition in each tank and transfer takes by molecular diffusion. The diffusivity of A in B is 4.3×10^{-3} m²/s.

Solution : Mole fraction of A in tank–1 = $x_{A1} = \dfrac{90}{100} = 0.90$

Mole fraction of A in tank–2 = $x_{A2} = \dfrac{5}{100} = 0.05$

$D_{AB} = 4.3 \times 10^{-3}$ m²/s

$z = 150$ mm $= 0.15$ m = length of diffusion path

Area $= \dfrac{\pi}{4} D^2 = \dfrac{\pi}{4} \times (0.05)^2 = 1.963 \times 10^{-3}$ m²

$p_{A1} = x_{A1} \cdot P = 0.9 \times 101 = 90.9$ kPa

$p_{A2} = x_{A2} \cdot P = 0.05 \times 101 = 5.05$ kPa

$R = 8.31451$ m³·kPa/(kmol·K)

Rate of transport of A $= N_A \cdot A = \dfrac{D_{AB} (p_{A1} - p_{A2})}{RTz} \times A$

$= \dfrac{4.3 \times 10^{-3} \times (90.9 - 5.05) \times 1.963 \times 10^{-3}}{8.31451 \times 298 \times 0.15}$

$= 1.95 \times 10^{-6}$ kmol/s ... **Ans.**

Ex. 7.2 : In an oxygen – nitrogen gas mixture at 101.3 kPa and 298 K, the concentrations of oxygen at two phases 2 mm apart are 10 and 20% by volume respectively. Calculate the flux of diffusion of oxygen for the cases where :

(i) the nitrogen is non-diffusing

(ii) there is equimolar counter diffusion of the two gases. Diffusivity of O_2 in N_2 is 1.81×10^{-5} m²/s.

Solution : 1. For diffusion of A through non-diffusing B, the flux is given by

$$N_A = \dfrac{D_{AB} P}{RTz\, p_{B,M}} (p_{A1} - p_{A2})$$

Total pressure, $P = 101.3$ kPa

For ideal gas, volume % = mole % A

$x_{A1} = \dfrac{20}{100} = 0.20$

$x_{A2} = \dfrac{10}{100} = 0.10$

Partial pressure of A = Molefraction of A × Total pressure

$p_{A1} = x_{A1} P = 0.20 \times 101.3 = 20.26$ kPa

$p_{A2} = x_{A2} P = 0.10 \times 101.3 = 10.13$ kPa

We have, $P = p_{A1} + p_{B1}$

∴ p_{B1} = 101.3 − 20.26 = 81.04 kPa
  p_{B2} = 101.3 − 10.13 = 91.17 kPa
  $p_{B,M}$ = $(p_{B2} − p_{B1}) / \ln(p_{B2} / p_{B1})$
   = (91.17 − 81.04) / ln (91.17 / 81.04) = 86 kPa
  z = 2 mm = 2×10^{-3} m, D_{AB} = 1.81×10^{-5} m²/s
  R = 8.31451 m³.kPa / (kmol.K), T = 298 K

∴ $N_A = \dfrac{1.81 \times 10^{-5} [20.26 − 10.13] \times 101.3}{8.31451 \times 298 \times 2 \times 10^{-3} \times 86}$

   = 4.356×10^{-5} kmol/(m².s)   ... Ans.

2. The flux for equimolar counter diffusion is given by :

$$N_A = \frac{D_{AB}}{RTz} (p_{A1} − p_{A2})$$

$$= \frac{1.81 \times 10^{-5} \times (20.26 − 10.13)}{8.31451 \times 298 \times 2 \times 10^{-3}}$$

= 3.7×10^{-5} kmol/(m².s)   ... Ans.

Ex. 7.3 : Methane diffuses at steady state through the tube containing helium. At point 1, the partial pressure of methane is 55 kPa and at point 2 it is 15 kPa. The points 1 and 2 are 30 mm apart. The total pressure is 101.3 kPa and temperature is 298 K (25 °C). Calculate the flux of CH_4 at steady state for equimolar counter diffusion. Take the value of diffusivity as 6.75×10^{-5} m²/s.

Solution : The flux for equimolar counter diffusion is given by

$$N_A = \frac{D_{AB}}{RTz} (p_{A1} − p_{A2})$$

where, D_{AB} = 6.75×10^{-5} m²/s, R = 8.31451 m³.kPa/(kmol.K)
    T = 298 K, z = 30 mm = 0.03 m
    p_{A1} = 55 kPa, p_{A2} = 15 kPa

$$N_A = \frac{6.75 \times 10^{-5} (55 − 15)}{8.31451 \times 298 \times 0.03}$$

   = 3.63×10^{-5} kmol / (m².s)   ... Ans.

Ex. 7.4 : Ammonia gas (A) diffuses through nitrogen gas (B) under steady state conditions with nitrogen non-diffusing. The partial pressure of A at location 1 is 1.5×10^4 Pa and that at location 2 is 5×10^3 Pa (Pascal). The locations 1 and 2 are 0.15 m apart. The total pressure is 1.103×10^5 Pa and temperature is 298 K. Calculate the flux of diffusion of ammonia. Also calculate the flux of diffusion for equimolar counter diffusion assuming that nitrogen is also diffusing. Take the value of diffusivity at prevailing conditions as 2.30×10^{-5} m²/s.

Solution : 1. The flux equation for diffusion of A through non-diffusing B is

$$N_A = \frac{D_{AB} P}{RTz\, p_{B,M}} (p_{A1} - p_{A2})$$

where,
$D_{AB} = 2.30 \times 10^{-5}$ m²/s
$P = 1.103 \times 10^5$ Pa
$p_{A1} = 1.5 \times 10^4$ Pa
$p_{A2} = 5 \times 10^3$ Pa
$p_{B1} = P - p_{A1} = 1.103 \times 10^5 - 1.5 \times 10^4 = 8.63 \times 10^4$ Pa
$p_{B2} = P - p_{A2} = 1.103 \times 10^5 - 5 \times 10^3 = 9.63 \times 10^4$ Pa

$$p_{B,M} = \frac{p_{B2} - p_{B1}}{\ln(p_{B2}/p_{B1})}$$

$$= \frac{(9.63 \times 10^4 - 8.63 \times 10^4)}{\ln(9.63 \times 10^4 / 8.63 \times 10^4)}$$

$$= 9.121 \times 10^4 \text{ Pa}$$

$T = 298$ K, $z = 0.15$ m
$R = 8.31451$ m³·kPa/(kmol·K) $= 8314.51$ m³·Pa/(kmol·K)

$$N_A = \frac{2.30 \times 10^{-5} \times 1.103 \times 10^5 (1.5 \times 10^4 - 5 \times 10^3)}{8314.51 \times 298 \times 0.15 \times 9.121 \times 10^4}$$

$$= 7.484 \times 10^{-7} \text{ kmol/(m}^2\text{.s)} \qquad \text{... Ans.}$$

2. The flux equation for equimolar counter–diffusion is

$$N_A = \frac{D_{AB}}{RTz} (p_{A1} - p_{A2})$$

$$= \frac{2.30 \times 10^{-5} (1.5 \times 10^4 - 5 \times 10^3)}{8314.51 \times 298 \times 0.15}$$

$$= 6.19 \times 10^{-7} \text{ kmol/(m}^2\text{.s)} \qquad \text{... Ans.}$$

Ex. 7.5 : Hydrochloric acid (A) at 283 K diffuses through a thin film of water (B) 4 mm thick. The concentration of A at location 1 on one boundary of the film is 12 weight % (density $\rho_1 = 1060.7$ kg/m³) and on other boundary, at location 2, is 4 weight % (density $\rho_2 = 1020.15$ kg/m³). The diffusivity of HCl in water is 2.5×10^{-9} m²/s. Calculate the flux of diffusion of A assuming water to be stagnant (i.e. non-diffusing).

Solution : Molecular weight of HCl = 36.5, Molecular weight of H$_2$O = 18

At location 1 : Mole fraction of HCl (A)

$$x_{A1} = \frac{12/36.5}{12/36.5 + (100 - 12)/18}$$

$$= 0.063$$
$$x_{B1} = 1 - 0.063$$
$$= 0.937$$

Average molecular weight at location–1 is

$$M_1 = \frac{100}{12/36.5 + (100-12)/18}$$
$$= 19.166 \text{ kg/kmol}$$

In 100 kg of HCl – water mixture, there are 12 kg of HCl and 100 – 12 = 88 kg of H_2O at location–1 (as at location–1, HCl concentration is 12 weight %).

moles of HCl $= \frac{12}{36.5} = 0.3287$ kmol, moles of $H_2O = \frac{88}{18} = 4.8888$ kmol

Total moles of mixture of HCl $= 0.3287 + 4.8888 = 5.2175$ kmol

$$\therefore \quad x_{A1} = \frac{\text{Moles of HCl}}{\text{Total moles}} = \frac{0.3287}{5.2175} = 0.063$$

$$M_1 = \text{kg of mixture / kmol of mixture}$$
$$= \frac{100}{5.2175} = 19.166 \text{ kg/kmol}$$

At location–2, the molefraction of HCl is

$$x_{A2} = \frac{4/36.5}{(4/36.5) + (100-4)/18}$$
$$= \frac{0.1096}{0.1096 + 5.3333} = 0.0201$$
$$x_{B2} = 1 - 0.0201$$
$$= 0.9799$$

Average molecular weight at location-2 is

$$M_2 = \frac{100}{4/36.5 + 96/18}$$
$$= 18.3728 \text{ kg/kmol}$$

$$C_{avg} = \frac{\rho_1/M_1 + \rho_2/M_2}{2}$$
$$= \frac{(1060.7/19.166) + (1020.15/18.3728)}{2}$$
$$= 55.4336 \text{ kmol/m}^3$$

$$x_{B,M} = (x_{B2} - x_{B1}) / \ln(x_{B2}/x_{B1})$$
$$= (0.9799 - 0.937) / \ln(0.9799/0.937)$$
$$= 0.958$$
$$z = 4 \text{ mm} = 0.004 \text{ m}$$

The diffusional flux for HCl with non-diffusing water is given by

$$N_A = \frac{D_{AB}\, C_{avg}}{x_{B,M} \cdot z}\,(x_{A1} - x_{A2})$$

$$= \frac{2.5 \times 10^{-9} \times 55.4336\,(0.063 - 0.0201)}{0.958 \times 0.004}$$

$$= 1.55 \times 10^{-6} \text{ kmol/(m}^2\text{.s)} \qquad \text{... Ans.}$$

Ex. 7.6 : Calculate the rate of diffusion of acetic acid (A) across a film of non-diffusing water (B) 1 mm thick at 290 K if the concentrations of acetic acid on the opposite sides of the film are 9% and 3% respectively. The densities of 9% and 3% solutions are 1012 kg/m³ and 1003.2 kg/m³ respectively. The diffusivity of acetic acid in water is 0.95×10^{-9} m²/s.

Solution : $D_{AB} = 0.95 \times 10^{-9}$ m²/s, $z = 1$ mm $= 1 \times 10^{-3}$ m

At location 1, on one side of film :

$\rho_1 = 1012$ kg/m², Acetic acid = 9% by weight

Mol. Wt. of acetic acid (CH_3COOH) = 60, Mol. Wt. of water (H_2O) = 18

$$\therefore \quad x_{A1} = \frac{9/60}{9/60 + (100-9)/18}$$

$$= \frac{0.15}{0.15 + 5.05}$$

$$= \frac{0.15}{5.2} = 0.0288$$

M_1 = Average molecular weight of solution = $\frac{100}{5.2}$ = 19.21 kg/kmol

$$x_{B1} = 1 - 0.0288 = 0.9712$$

At location-2, on other / opposite side of film :

Weight % of acetic acid = 3%, $\rho_2 = 100.3$ kg/m³

$$x_{A2} = \frac{3/60}{3/60 + (100-3)/18} = 0.0092$$

$$x_{B2} = 1 - 0.0092 = 0.9908$$

$$M_2 = \frac{100}{3/60 + (100-3)/18} = 18.40$$

$$C_{avg.} = \frac{\rho_1/M_1 + \rho_2/M_2}{2}$$

$$= \frac{(1012/19.21) + (1003.2/18.40)}{2}$$

$$= 53.6 \text{ kmol/m}^3$$

$$x_{B,M} = (x_{B2} - x_{B1})/\ln(x_{B2}/x_{B1})$$

$$= (0.9908 - 0.9712)/\ln(0.9908/0.9712)$$

$$= 0.980$$

The flux of acetic acid is given by :

$$N_A = \frac{D_{AB} \cdot C_{avg}}{z \cdot x_{B,M}} (x_{A1} - x_{A2})$$

$$= \frac{0.95 \times 10^{-9}}{1 \times 10^{-3} \times 0.98} (0.0288 - 0.0092)$$

$$= 1.018 \times 10^{-6} \text{ kmol/(m}^2\text{.s)} \qquad \text{... Ans.}$$

Ex. 7.7 : Hydrogen gas at 202.6 kPa (2 atm) and 298 K (25°C) flows through a pipe made of unvulcanised neoprene rubber with i.d. and o.d. 25 and 50 mm respectively. The diffusivity of hydrogen through rubber is 1.8×10^{-6} cm²/s. Calculate the rate of loss of hydrogen by diffusion per meter length of pipe.

The solubility of hydrogen is 0.053 cm³ (NTP)/cm³·atm.

Solution : 1 m length of pipe,

$$z = r_2 - r_1 = \frac{\text{o.d.} - \text{i.d.}}{2} = \frac{50 - 25}{2} = 12.5 \text{ mm} = 0.0125 \text{ m}$$

$$D_A = 1.8 \times 10^{-6} \text{ cm}^2/\text{s} = 1.8 \times 10^{-10} \text{ m}^2/\text{s}$$

$$L = 1 \text{ m}$$

$$A_{avg.} = \frac{2\pi L (r_2 - r_1)}{\ln (r_2/r_1)} = \frac{2\pi (1)(0.0125)}{\ln (0.025/0.0125)}$$

$$= 0.1133 \text{ m}^2$$

At 202.6 kPa (2 atm) hydrogen pressure, the solubility is

$$= 0.053 \times \frac{2}{1} = 0.106 \text{ cm}^3 \text{(NTP)/cm}^3$$

$$= 0.106 \text{ m}^3 \text{(NTP)/m}^3$$

$\therefore$ C_{A1} at the inner surface of pipe $= \frac{0.106}{22.4} \times 1 = 4.73 \times 10^{-3}$ kmol H_2/m^3

At the outer surface, $C_{A2} = 0$

$\therefore$ Rate of loss of hydrogen =

$$w = N_A \cdot A_{avg.} = D_A \cdot A_{avg.} [C_{A1} - C_{A2}]/z$$

$$= 1.8 \times 10^{-10} \times 0.1133 \ (4.73 \times 10^{-3} - 0)/0.0125$$

$$= 7.72 \times 10^{-2} \text{ kmol } H_2/\text{s, per 1 m length of pipe} \qquad \text{... Ans.}$$

Some Important Definitions :

1. Gram mole : It is defined as the *mass in grams of a substance that is numerically equal to its molecular weight.*

In this book, gram mole and kilogram mole are specified as mol and kmol respectively.

2. Weight fraction : It is the *ratio of the weight of the individual component to the total weight of the system*. It is denoted by x'. For two component system : $x'_A + x'_B = 1.0$

Weight % of A = Weight fraction of A × 100

3. Mole fraction : It is the *ratio of the moles of individual component to the total moles of the system.* It is denoted by x.

For a binary system of A and B : $x_A + x_B = 1.0$.

Mole % of A = mole fraction of A × 100.

4. More volatile component : It is the *component with lower boiling point or with higher vapour pressure at a given temperature (in a binary system).* It is also called as the lighter component.

In case of distillation, compositions of vapour and liquid phases are expressed in terms of mole fraction of the more volatile component.

5. Less volatile component : In a binary system, it is the component with higher boiling point or with lower vapour pressure at a given temperature. It is also called as the heavier component.

6. Vapour pressure : The vapour pressure of a liquid is defined as the *absolute pressure at which the liquid and its vapour are in equilibrium at a given temperature.*

Pure water exerts a vapour pressure of 101.325 kPa at 373.15 K (100°C).

7. Partial pressure : The partial pressure of a component gas that is present in a mixture of gases in the pressure that would be exerted by that component if it alone were present in the same volume and at the same pressure.

8. Ideal gas law : Mathematically, an ideal gas law is given as :

$$PV = nRT$$

if P is in kPa, V in m^3, n in kmol and T in K then units of R will be $m^3 \cdot kPa/(kmol \cdot K)$.

(R (gas constant) = $8.31451 \ m^3 \cdot kPa/(kmol \cdot K)$)

9. Dalton's law : Mathematically, Dalton's law is given as

$$P = p_A + p_B + p_C + \ldots$$

where P is the total pressure exerted by a gaseous mixture and $p_A, p_B, p_C \ldots$ are the partial pressures of component gases A, B, C, ….

10. Raoult's law : It states that the equilibrium pressure of component A is equal to the product of the vapour pressure and the mole fraction of A in the liquid phase.

$$\therefore \quad p_A = p_A^0 \cdot x_A$$

p_A is also related to y_A by equation

$$p_A = y_A \cdot P$$

y_A is the mole fraction of A in gas phase.

11. Henry's law : Mathematically Henry's law is given as,

$$p_A = H \, x_A$$

where H is the Henry's law constant.

Henry's law expresses the relationship between the concentration of a gas dissolved in a liquid and the equilibrium partial pressure of the gas above the liquid surface.

12. Gibb's phase rule : It is the relationship that governs all heterogeneous equilibria. It is given as

where
$$F = C - P + 2$$
$$C = \text{number of components}$$
$$P = \text{number of phases}$$

and F is the number of degrees of freedom or number of intensive variables (temperature, pressure, composition) that must be specified so that remaining variables will be fixed automatically and the system will be defined completely.

EXERCISES

1. Give mathematical statement of Fick's law of diffusion and give the meaning of each terms involved in equation.
2. Define with formula of each :
   (i) Mass fraction,
   (ii) Mole fraction,
   (iii) Molar concentration,
   (iv) Mass average velocity, and
   (v) Molar average velocity.
3. Define : Mass flux and Molar flux and give the expressions for Mass and Molar fluxes relative to the mass average velocity and molar average velocity.
4. Define Diffusion, Molecular diffusion, Eddy/turbulent diffusion and explain briefly the role of diffusion in mass transfer.
5. Explain briefly analogy between heat, mass and momentum.
6. Explain briefly Reynolds analogy.
7. Show that for equimolar counter diffusion, $D_{AB} = D_{BA}$.
8. State the Fick's law of diffusion.
9. Give the mathematical expression for analogy between heat, mass and momentum transport for laminar and turbulent flow. Give the meaning of each terms.
10. Define mass transfer coefficient. Give its unit.
11. What do you mean by interphase mass transfer ?
12. State salient features of two-film theory.
13. Explain the controlling film concept.

CHAPTER EIGHT

DISTILLATION

Distillation is *a unit operation in which the constituents of a liquid mixture (solution) are separated using thermal energy.* Basically, the difference in **vapour pressures** (volatilities) of different constituents at the same temperature is responsible for such a separation. This unit operation is also termed as **fractional distillation** or **fractionation**. With this technique it is possible to separate the liquid mixture into its components in almost pure form and this fact has made distillation perhaps the most important of all the mass transfer operations.

In distillation, the phases involved are : liquid and vapour or gas (the vapour phase is created by supplying heat to the liquid) and mass is transferred from both the phases to one another, by vaporisation from the liquid phase and by condensation from the vapour phase. The net effect is an increase in composition of the more volatile component in the vapour (phase) and that of the less volatile component in the liquid. The basic requirement for a separation of components by distillation is that the composition of the vapour be different from the composition of the liquid with which it is in equilibrium - the vapour is always richer in the more volatile component than the liquid from which it is formed. If the vapour composition is the same as the liquid composition, distillation technique will not effect a separation.

Distillation is commonly encountered in chemical and petroleum industries as a means of separating the liquid mixture into its component parts. Separation of ethanol and water mixture, production of absolute alcohol from 95% ethanol using benzene, separation of petroleum crude into gasoline, kerosene, fuel oils etc. are **the typical examples of distillation**.

Evaporation is concerned with the separation of a solution containing a non-volatile solute and a volatile solvent, whereas distillation is concerned with the separation of solution where all the components are appreciably volatile. Thus, the separation of a brine into salt and water is a evaporation whereas the separation of a mixture of alcohol and water into its components is a distillation.

Boiling Point :

For any given pressure, a pure liquid when heated will boil or vaporise at a certain single temperature known as the boiling point of the liquid. It is the temperature of a liquid at which the vapour pressure of a liquid equals the prevailing pressure. The boiling point of a liquid increases with increase in pressure and vice versa. The normal boiling of a liquid is the temperature at which its boiling takes place under a pressure of 1 atm. Boiling points at a given pressure vary greatly for different liquids. For example, the boiling point of water is

373 K (100° C), that of toluene is 383.6 K (110.6° C) and that of methanol is 337.7 K (64.7° C) at one atmosphere (101.325 kPa).

In a binary mixture (a two component system), the component with lower boiling point, i.e., the component with higher vapour pressure at a given temperature is termed as the **more volatile or lighter**, while the component with higher boiling point or with lower vapour pressure at a given temperature is termed as the **less volatile or heavier**.

Thus, in case of a binary mixture of methanol and water, methanol (B.P. = 64.7°C) is a more volatile component and water (B.P. = 100°C) is a less volatile component, since the vapour pressure of methanol is higher than that of water at any given temperature. The whole mixture of methanol and water will boil somewhere between 337.7 K (64.7° C) and 373 K (100° C) at atmospheric pressure (101.325 kPa).

Equilibrium :
- It is a static condition in which the net transfer of material between the phases ceases for a given set of operating conditions that exists for all combinations of phases.
- Equilibrium refers to the absence of any tendency for a change to take place.

Driving force :

When the two phases, which are not at equilibrium are brought into intimate contact, the phases will tend to approach equilibrium due to a tendency for change to take place. The difference between the existing condition and equilibrium condition is the driving force which causes a change. A concentration difference is the driving force for mass transfer analogous to a temperature difference for heat transfer.

Equilibrium stage :

It is the one in which the two phases not at equilibrium are brought into contact, time is provided to attain equilibrium, the phases are separated and streams leave the stage in equilibrium. For a given set of operating conditions, an equilibrium stage gives the maximum possible composition change, so it is also known as the ideal or theoretical stage. In actual practice, equilibrium is not achieved and hence stage efficiencies are always less than 100 percent.

Vapour - Liquid Equilibrium :

The basic data for distillation are the equilibria existing between the vapour and liquid phases of a system under consideration. The equilibrium in vapour-liquid systems is governed by phase rule. In a binary mixture subjected to distillation, we have : C (components) = 2, P (phases) = 2. So, according to the phase rule [F = C – P + 2], the degrees of freedom (F) or the number of intensive variables that must be fixed to define the equilibrium state of the system are two. In distillation, there are four variables : temperature, pressure, vapour phase composition and liquid phase composition. Thus, if the pressure is fixed then only one variable say, for example, liquid phase composition, can be changed independently and temperature and vapour phase composition follow :

Constant-Pressure Vapour-Liquid Equilibria :

The compositions of the vapour and liquid phases, that are in equilibrium, are usually expressed in terms of mole fractions of the more volatile component in the respective phases (y and x) - we use molefractions as a measure of concentrations.

Equilibrium data for a binary mixture at constant total pressure are represented in graphical forms by means of (i) the temperature-composition diagram or (ii) the x-y diagram where the vapour phase composition (y) is plotted against the liquid phase composition (x).

Boiling Point Diagram :

It is used to show how the equilibrium vapour and liquid phase compositions (i.e., y and x) change with temperature.

With the help of an equilibrium still one can determine experimentally the composition of the vapour in equilibrium with the liquid of a given composition and the results thus obtained can be shown on an temperature - composition diagram. Let us follow the whole process of boiling a binary mixture in an equilibrium still. For the situation under consideration refer to Fig. 8.1. Suppose that an mixture treated consists of benzene (the more volatile component) and toluene (the less volatile / heavier component). The composition of the mixture is plotted as abscissa in terms of the mole fraction of the more volatile component and temperature of the mixture is plotted as ordinate. The mixture presented by point A is at a temperature of T_1°C and contains 50 mole % of benzene. When we apply heating to the mixture it will start boiling at temperature T_2°C. The vapour given off by mixture on boiling will contain more of the more volatile component so the first quantity of the vapour issuing from the binary mixture 'B' will have the composition indicated by point 'C', i.e., this vapour will contain 91 mole % benzene at temperature T_2 °C. The vapour at 'C' is in equilibrium with the liquid at point 'B' and thus BC is known as the tie line. Hence, considerable enrichment in benzene has taken place from 50 mole % to 91 mole %. If we remove this portion of vapours and condense it completely in a condenser then we would obtain the liquid represented by point 'D' still containing 91 mole % benzene. If we reheat this portion of the liquid, it will boil at T_3 °C at point E ($T_3 < T_2$). The first portion of the vapours issuing from boiling liquid at point 'E' will contain more of the more volatile component, composition of it is represented by point 'F'. If we condense this part of the vapour completely, we get liquid containing almost 100 mole % of benzene indicating further enrichment in the vapour.

If we further heat the liquid at the point 'B' the boiling point of liquid rises to T' because of the removal of the majority of the more volatile component by vaporisation. At this temperature, the liquid phase composition is represented by 'L' and the vapour phase composition by 'N' and further heating to T" all the liquid get vaporised to give the vapour represented by point 'H'.

Alternatively, consider a mixture of vapours represented by point 'Q', when we cool it down to temperature T", condensation will start at point H. The first drop of the liquid formed will have the composition represented by point K (i.e., the less volatile component will tend to condense first). If we further cool the vapours to T' we will get liquid represented by point 'L' and the vapour represented by point N. This means that the vapour is richer in the more volatile component than the liquid. Hence we can say that partial vaporisation as well as partial condensation will both tend to enrich the vapour in the more volatile component.

In the process of boiling, the mixture boils over a temperature range from 'B' to 'K' (from the bubble point to the dew point), so the term boiling point has no meaning for the mixture and the correct term is the bubble point. **Bubble point** is the temperature at which a liquid mixture of a given composition starts to vaporise as the temperature is increased. The liquid represented by any point on the lower curve is at its bubble point and hence the lower curve is called as the saturated liquid curve or the **bubble point temperature curve** (T v/s x). The temperature at which a vapour mixture on cooling first begins to condense is called dew point. The condensation starts at any point on the upper curve and hence the upper curve is called as the saturated vapour curve or the **dew point temperature curve** (T v/s y).

For any pure liquid, the bubble point and dew point are identical and equal to the boiling point of liquid. Whereas the dew point and bubble point for a binary system are functions of its composition. The dew point and bubble point are identical at x, y = 0 and x, y = 1 as these compositions indicate pure toluene and pure benzene.

For systems that follow Raoult's law, the boiling point diagram can be constructed from the pure components vapour pressure data.

Fig. 8.1 : Boiling point diagram

(Constant pressure vapour-liquid equilibrium)

As the total pressure of the system is increased say, for example, from P_{t_1} to P_{t_2}, the spread between the bubble point curve and the dew point curve decreases and the separability by distillation becomes less, at high pressure owing to the decrease in the value of the relative volatility at higher pressure. The effect of increase in pressure is shown in Fig. 8.3.

Fig. 8.2 : Equilibrium diagram (Normal)/equilibrium curve/x-y diagram
(Constant pressure vapour-liquid equilibrium)

A large majority of distillation operations are carried out at a constant total pressure. For distillation calculations, the equilibrium vapour-liquid composition data can also be plotted as shown in Fig. 8.2 wherein the vapour phase composition (y) is plotted as ordinate and the liquid phase composition (x) is plotted as an abscissa. Such a diagram is called as an **equilibrium diagram** or **distribution diagram**. As the vapour is richer in the more volatile component than the liquid, the equilibrium curve lies above the 45° diagonal line which is drawn for comparison.

Fig. 8.3 : Effect of increased pressure - vapour-liquid equilibrium

Raoult's law :

It is commonly used for predicting the vapour-liquid equilibrium for an ideal solution in equilibrium with an ideal gas mixture from the pure component vapour pressure data. It states that the *equilibrium partial pressure of a constituent/component in a solution at a given temperature is equal to the product of its vapour pressure in the pure state and its mole fraction in the liquid phase.*

Thus, for a binary (two component) system, if p_A is the equilibrium partial pressure of A, p_A^o is the vapour pressure of 'A' in the pure state and x_A is the more fraction of 'A' in liquid phase, then,

$$p_A = p_A^o \, x_A \quad \ldots (8.1)$$

and

$$p_B = p_B^o \, x_B \quad \ldots (8.2)$$

$$= p_B^o \, (1 - x_A) \text{ as } x_A + x_B = 1$$

p_B = equilibrium partial pressure of B

x_B = mole fraction of B in liquid phase

p_B^o = vapour pressure of pure B.

Dalton's Law :

It states that *the total pressure exerted by gas/vapour mixture is equal to the sum of the partial pressures of components present in it.* Thus, it expresses the additive nature of the partial pressures.

Mathematically, for a binary system :

$$P = p_A + p_B \qquad \ldots (8.3)$$

where P is the total pressure.

For an ideal gas or vapour, the partial pressure is related to mole fraction of the component in gas or vapour phase by the relation :

$$\text{Partial pressure} = \text{Mole fraction} \times \text{Total pressure}$$

Thus, for component 'A'

$$p_A = y_A \cdot P \qquad \ldots (8.4)$$

where y_A is the mole fraction of 'A' in vapour phase.

Knowing the vapour pressures of components 'A' (more volatile) and 'B' at various values of temperatures, x - y data can be generated for an ideal solution as follows :

$$p_A = p_A^o \cdot x_A \qquad \ldots (8.5)$$

$$p_B = p_B^o \cdot (1 - x_A) \qquad \ldots (8.6)$$

$$p_A = y_A \cdot P \qquad \ldots (8.7)$$

$$p_B = y_B \cdot P \qquad \ldots (8.8)$$

From equations (8.5) and (8.7), we get

$$p_A^o \cdot x_A = y_A \cdot P \qquad \ldots (8.9)$$

$$y_A = \frac{p_A^o}{P} \cdot x_A \qquad \ldots (8.10)$$

Similarly, $\qquad y_B = \dfrac{p_B^o}{P} \cdot x_B \qquad \ldots (8.11)$

We have, $\qquad y_B + y_B = 1$ and $x_B = 1 - x_A$

$$y_A + y_B = 1$$

Putting values of y_A and y_B from equations (8.10) and (8.11), and of x_B in terms of x_A, we get

$$\frac{p_A^o}{P} \cdot x_A + \frac{p_B^o}{P} (1 - x_A) = 1 \qquad \ldots (8.12)$$

$$p_A^o \cdot x_A + p_B^o - p_B^o \cdot x_A = P \qquad \ldots (8.13)$$

$$\therefore \qquad x_A \left(p_A^o - p_B^o \right) = P - p_B^o \qquad \ldots (8.14)$$

$$\therefore \quad x_A = \frac{P - p_B^o}{p_A^o - p_B^o} \quad \ldots (8.15)$$

Knowing x_A, corresponding equilibrium value of vapour phase concentration (y_A) is obtained with the help of equation (8.10).

Relative volatility :

Volatility of A : It is defined as the *ratio of the partial pressure of 'A' to the mole fraction of 'A' in liquid phase*.

$$\text{Volatility of A} = \frac{p_A}{x_A} \quad \ldots (8.16)$$

Similarly,
$$\text{Volatility of B} = \frac{p_B}{x_B} \quad \ldots (8.17)$$

Relative volatility of a component A with respect to a component B is *the ratio of volatility of 'A' (the more volatile component) to the volatility of 'B'*. It is also known as volatility of 'A' with respect to 'B' and is denoted by a symbol α_{AB}.

$$\therefore \quad \alpha_{AB} = \frac{p_A \, x_B}{x_A \cdot p_B} \quad \ldots (8.18)$$

but
$$P y_A = p_A \text{ and } P y_B = p_B$$

$$\therefore \quad \alpha_{AB} = \frac{y_A \cdot x_B}{y_B \cdot x_A} \quad \ldots (8.19)$$

$$\alpha_{AB} = \frac{y_A / y_B}{x_A / x_B} \quad \ldots (8.20)$$

Thus, the relative volatility is the *ratio of the concentration ratio of A to B in vapour phase to that in liquid phase*.

$$\alpha_{AB} = \frac{y_A \, x_B}{y_B \cdot x_A}$$

We have,
$$y_B = 1 - y_A \quad \ldots (8.21)$$
$$x_B = 1 - x_A \quad \ldots (8.22)$$

$$\therefore \quad \alpha_{AB} = \frac{y_A (1 - x_A)}{(1 - y_A) \cdot x_A} \quad \ldots (8.23)$$

$$\alpha_{AB} (1 - y_A) \, x_A = y_A (1 - x_A)$$
$$\alpha_{AB} \, x_A - \alpha_{AB} \, y_A \, x_A = y_A - y_A \, x_A$$
$$\alpha_{AB} \cdot x_A = y_A + y_A \, x_A (\alpha_{AB} - 1)$$
$$\alpha_{AB} \, x_A = y_A [1 + (\alpha_{AB} - 1) \, x_A] \quad \ldots (8.24)$$

$$\therefore \quad y_A = \frac{\alpha_{AB} \cdot x_A}{1 + (\alpha_{AB} - 1) \, x_A} \quad \ldots (8.25)$$

Dropping subscripts, we get

$$y = \frac{\alpha x}{1 + (\alpha - 1) x} \qquad \ldots (8.26)$$

From the above equation knowing 'α' for a given binary system x – y data (equilibrium data) can be generated by taking x = 0, 0.1 …… to 1 and evaluating the corresponding values of 'y' (equilibrium vapour phase composition).

For an ideal system, volatility is equal to the vapour pressure of the pure component.

The relative volatility of a component A with respect to B is the ratio of the pure component vapour pressure of A to that of B at the same temperature.

Thus :

$$\text{Relative volatility} = \frac{p_A^o}{p_B^o} \qquad \ldots (8.27)$$

Relative volatility is a measure of the separability by distillation. When **$\alpha = 1$**, a separation by distillation is not possible. The separation by distillation is possible for relative volatility values greater than one. Larger the value of the relative volatility, the easier is the separation by distillation.

THE METHODS OF DISTILLATION - BINARY SYSTEMS :

Basically, distillation is carried out in two ways :

1. The liquid mixture to be separated is heated to create a vapour. The vapour formed is condensed in a condenser and withdrawn as product. As there is no reflux, products of relatively low purities are obtained.

2. The liquid mixture to be separated is heated to create a vapour, the vapour formed is condensed in a condenser. A part of the condensed liquid is returned to the distillation still (as reflux) and the remaining part is withdrawn as product. In this method, the liquid and vapour are brought into intimate contact for a number of times and almost pure product can be achieved. The part of the vapour returned as liquid to the distillation unit is called as reflux and the operation is called rectification or fractionation. The term rectification originated in the alcohol industry whereas the term fractionation is popular in the petroleum industry.

Common methods used in distillation practice are :

1. Differential or simple distillation,
2. Flash or equilibrium distillation,
3. Rectification or fractionation.

Out of these three methods, distillation with rectification or simply called rectification is the most important. The first two methods are carried out without reflux and the third one is carried out with reflux (which is nothing but returning a part of the condensed liquid back to the distillation system).

Differential or Simple Distillation :

In this distillation technique, a known quantity of a liquid mixture is charged into a jacketed kettle or still. The jacket is provided for heating the liquid mass in the still with the help of a heating media such as steam. The charge is boiled slowly, vapours formed are withdrawn and fed to a condenser where they are liquified and collected in a receiver as a distillate. In the early stage of distillation, vapours leaving the still are richest in the more volatile component and as the distillation proceeds the liquid in the still becomes lean with respect to the more volatile component. The composition of the less volatile component thereby increases and hence the boiling point increases. The product (distillate) from such units can be collected in several receivers, called cuts, to give products of various purities over the length of distillation period. The distillation is continued till the boiling point of liquid reaches a predetermined value and the content of the still is finally removed as residual liquid containing majority of the less volatile component.

Fig. 8.4 : Simple distillation unit

Material balance - binary mixtures :

As the composition of the vapour issuing from the distillation still and that of the liquid remaining in it changes during the course of operation, the mathematical approach should be differential.

Let 'F' be the kmol of a liquid mixture (A + B) containing x_F mole fraction of A which is charged to a distillation still. Let 'D' be kmol of distillate and 'W' be kmol of residual liquid in the still which are obtained at the end of operation. Let y_{Davg} and x_W be the mole fraction of 'A' in distillate and bottom residual liquid.

Let 'L' be kmol of liquid in the still at any time during the course of distillation and let 'x' be the mole fraction of 'A' in the liquid. Let a very small amount 'dD' kmol of the distillate of composition 'y' in equilibrium with the liquid is vaporised. Then, the composition and the quantity of liquid decreases from x to x − dx and L to L−dL respectively.

Then,

The overall material balance at any time is :

$$L = L - dL + dD \qquad \ldots (8.28)$$

$$\therefore \quad dL = dD \qquad \ldots (8.29)$$

A material balance of component 'A' gives

$$Lx = (L - dL)(x - dx) + y\, dD \qquad \ldots (8.30)$$

$$Lx = Lx - Ldx - xdL + dLdx + ydD$$

dLdx being very small can be neglected

$$0 = - Ldx - xdL + ydD \qquad \ldots (8.31)$$

Put the value of dD as dL from equation (8.29)

$$0 = - Ldx - xdL + ydL \qquad \ldots (8.32)$$

$$Ldx = (y - x)\, dL \qquad \ldots (8.33)$$

$$\therefore \quad \frac{dL}{L} = \frac{dx}{y - x} \qquad \ldots (8.34)$$

Integrating the above equation between two extreme conditions :

$$L = F, \quad x = x_F$$

and

$$L = W, \quad x = x_W$$

$$\int_W^F \frac{dL}{L} = \int_{x_W}^{x_F} \frac{dx}{y - x} \qquad \ldots (8.35)$$

$$\ln \frac{F}{W} = \int_{x_W}^{x_F} \frac{dx}{y - x} \qquad \ldots (8.36)$$

Equation (8.36) is known as the Rayleigh equation. It is used to determine F, W, x_F or x_W when three of these are known. The R.H.S. of equation (8.36) is evaluated graphically by plotting $1/(y - x)$ against x and determining the area under the curve between $x = x_F$ and $x = x_W$. The required data for the above procedure are taken from the vapour-liquid equilibrium relationship.

If $y_{D,\ avg.}$ is the composited distillate composition then

Material balance of the component 'A' is :

$$x_F \cdot F = y_{D,\ avg.}\, D + x_W \cdot W \qquad \ldots (8.37)$$

Though the simple or differential distillation as a method of separation is not effective, many such units are used, especially where (i) the components to be separated have widely different boiling points and (ii) methods giving sharp separations are not necessary.

Flash or Equilibrium distillation :

Flash distillation is normally carried out in a continuous manner. In this method, a liquid mixture is partially vaporised, the vapour and liquid are allowed to attain equilibrium and finally withdrawn separately.

Feed is heated in a tubular heat exchanger. The hot liquid mixture is then fed to a separator via pressure reducing valve whereby pressure is reduced and the vapour is formed at the expense of liquid adiabatically. The liquid is withdrawn from the bottom of the separator and the equilibrium vapour leaves the separator from the top which is then liquified in a condenser. Flash distillation is commonly used in petroleum industry, handling multi component systems in the pipe stills.

Fig. 8.5 : Flash/Equilibrium distillation

Consider one mole of a liquid mixture having x_F mole fraction of more volatile component, is fed to a flash distillation unit. Let 'f' be the fraction of feed that is vaporised and is of composition 'y'. Then $(1 - f)$ will be the moles of residual liquid obtained. Let 'x' be the mole fraction of more volatile component in liquid.

Then, a material balance of the more volatile component gives

$$x_F = f \cdot y + (1 - f) \cdot x \qquad \ldots (8.38)$$

$$f \cdot y = -(1 - f) x + x_F \qquad \ldots (8.39)$$

$$y = -\frac{(1-f)}{f} x + \frac{x_F}{f} \qquad \ldots (8.40)$$

Equation (8.40) is the material balance/operating line for flash distillation with a slope equal to $-(1 - f)/f$ and an intercept equal to x_F/f.

The point of intersection of the operating line and the diagonal $(x = y)$ is,

$$y = -\frac{(1-f)x}{f} + \frac{x_F}{f}$$

$$x = y$$

$$\therefore \quad x = -\frac{(1-f)x}{f} + \frac{x_F}{f}$$

$$x \cdot f = -x + x \cdot f + x_F$$

$$\therefore \quad x = x_F$$

and $\quad y = x_F$

For **f = 1**, feed totally vaporised (feed 100 mole per cent vaporised)

$$\text{Slope} = -\frac{(1-f)}{f} = 0$$

and hence operating line is parallel to x-axis through a point (x_F, x_F) on the diagonal.

For **f = 0**, – no feed is vaporised.

Slope = ∞ and the operating line will be parallel to y-axis through a point (x_F, x_F) on the diagonal.

The operating line for various values of 'f' on the xy equilibrium diagram is as shown in Fig. 8.6.

Fig. 8.6 : Plotting material balance line on equilibrium diagram

Fig. 8.7

Fig. 8.7 shows a method of obtaining the equilibrium compositions of vapour (y_1) and liquid (x_1) for a given f.

Continuous Rectification – Binary Systems :

Rectification is commonly encountered in industrial practice as it is possible to get almost pure product by this method.

The enrichment of the vapour stream as it passes through the column in contact with reflux is termed as *rectification*.

In this separation method, a part of the condensed liquid is returned back as reflux and a maximum enrichment of the more volatile component in the vapour is obtained by successive partial vaporisation and condensation by a multistage contact of the vapour and the liquid. This is achieved in a single unit called a fractionating column.

Fractionating Column :

A fractionating column or fractionator consists of (i) a cylindrical shell divided into sections by a series of perforated trays, (ii) a reboiler and (iii) a condenser. A liquid mixture to be separated is introduced in the cylindrical column more or less centrally. The column itself is divided into two sections - rectifying and stripping section. The section above the feed plate or tray is called the **rectifying section**, wherein vapour is washed to remove the less volatile component with the liquid returned to the column from top (known as reflux). The portion below the feed plate including feed plate is called the **stripping section** wherein liquid is stripped off more volatile component by rising vapour. Perforated trays are nothing but gas-liquid contacting devices on which gas/vapour and liquid are brought into intimate contact for mass transfer to occur.

Fig. 8.8 : Fractionating column

Vapours are generated in a reboiler (generally steam heated) and are fed to the bottom of the column. The liquid removed from the fractionator rich in less volatile component is called the bottoms or bottom product. The vapour issuing from the top of the column is fed to a condenser where the latent heat is removed with the help of a circulated coolant through the condenser. A part of condensed liquid is returned to the column (reflux) and the remaining part is withdrawn as the top product or distillate which is rich in more volatile component. As we move up the column, the vapour becomes richer and richer in the more volatile component and as we move down the column, the liquid becomes richer and richer in the less volatile component. As the liquid is at its bubble point and the vapour is at its dew point, temperature is maximum at the bottom and minimum at the top. The part of the condensed liquid returning to the top of the column is called as reflux.

Rectification on an ideal plate :

Refer to Fig. 8.9 wherein the plates are numbered serially from the top down. Consider the nth plate from the top in the cascade. The plate n–1 is immediately above the plate 'n' and plate n + 1 is immediately below the plate n. On every plate, two different fluid streams not at equilibrium are brought into intimate contact, mass transfer takes place, phases are separated, and finally the two fluid streams leave the plate in equilibrium with each other. Thus, the plate under consideration will receive a liquid stream of L_{n-1} moles/h of composition x_{n-1} and a vapour stream of V_{n+1} moles/h of composition y_{n+1} from plate n–1 and n+1 respectively. A liquid stream L_n moles/h of composition x_n and a vapour stream V_n moles/h of composition y_n leave this plate for plate n+1 and n – 1 respectively in equilibrium with each other.

When the vapour from plate n+1 is brought into intimate contact on the plate under consideration with the liquid from plate n–1 their compositions tend to change to attain equilibrium values. During the interchange process, some of the more volatile component is vaporised from the liquid L_{n+1}, decreasing the liquid concentration from x_{n-1} to x_n; and some of the less volatile component is condensed from the vapour V_{n+1}, increasing the vapour concentration from y_{n+1} to y_n. In the column, as the liquid is at its bubble point and the vapour is at its dew point, the heat to vaporise the more volatile component from the liquid is supplied by the heat released in the condensation of the less volatile component from the vapour. Thus, the net effect is that the more volatile component is transferred to the vapour rising up from the liquid running down the column, while the less volatile component is transferred to the liquid running down from the vapour rising up the column. Liquid and vapour phase composition increases along column height with respect to more volatile component and therefore the temperature decreases. The temperature of plate n is less than that of plate n + 1 and greater than that of plate n – 1.

Fig. 8.9 : Material balance over ideal plate   **Fig. 8.10 : Boiling point diagram showing rectification on an ideal plate**

Material balance :

Consider a column fed with 'F' moles/time of a liquid mixture (feed) with x_F mole fraction of the more volatile component. Let D moles/time of composition x_D are withdrawn as a distillate and W moles/time of composition x_W are withdrawn as a bottom product from the column.

Overall material balance :

$$\text{Feed} = \text{distillate} + \text{bottom product}$$

$$F = D + W \qquad \ldots (8.41)$$

Material balance of the more volatile component, (A) over the column/fractionator :

'A' in feed = 'A' in distillate + 'A' in bottom product.

$$x_F \cdot F = x_D \cdot D + x_W \cdot W \qquad \ldots (8.42)$$

With the help of equations (8.41), and (8.42), it is possible to calculate D and W knowing F, x_F, x_D and x_W.

Let L be the moles/time of liquid returned to the top of column then,

$$\text{Reflux ratio} = R = \frac{L}{D} \qquad \ldots (8.43)$$

This reflux ratio is also known as external reflux ratio.

If V is the (moles/time) molal flow rate of vapour leaving the top of column then, the ratio L/V is known as the internal reflux ratio.

Fig. 8.11 : Rectifying section including condenser

Material balance around the condenser :

$$V = L + D$$
$$\therefore \quad L = V - D \qquad \ldots (8.44)$$
and $$D = V - L$$

Overall material balance over Fig. 8.11 :

Vapour flow to plate 'n' = liquid flow from plate 'n' + distillate withdrawn

$$V_{n+1} = L_n + D \qquad \ldots (8.45)$$

Similarly, **material balance of the more volatile component (A) over Fig. 8.11 :**

$$V_{n+1}\, y_{n+1} = L_n\, x_n + D \cdot x_D \qquad \ldots (8.46)$$

$$\therefore \quad y_{n+1} = \frac{L_n}{V_{n+1}}\, x_n + \frac{D \cdot x_D}{V_{n+1}}$$

$$\therefore \quad y_{n+1} = \frac{L_n}{V_{n+1}}\, x_n + \frac{D \cdot x_D}{V_{n+1}} \qquad \ldots (8.47)$$

From equation (8.45)

$$V_{n+1} = L_n + D$$

Therefore equation (8.47) becomes :

$$y_{n+1} = \frac{L_n}{L_n + D}\, x_n + \frac{D\, x_D}{L_n + D} \qquad \ldots (8.48)$$

Equation (8.48) is known as the material balance line or the **operating line** of the **rectifying section**.

Fig. 8.12 : Stripping section including reboiler

Overall material balance over Fig. 8.12 :

Liquid flow to plate – m + 1 = Vapour flow from plate – m + 1
+ Bottom product withdrawn

$$L_m = V_{m+1} + W \qquad \ldots (8.49)$$

Similarly,

Material balance of more volatile component (A) :

$$L_m \cdot x_m = V_{m+1}\, y_{m+1} + W\, x_W \qquad \ldots (8.50)$$

Rearranging the equation (8.50)

$$y_{m+1} = \frac{L_m}{V_{m+1}} x_m - \frac{W x_W}{V_{m+1}} \qquad \ldots (8.51)$$

We know from equation (8.49), that $V_{m+1} = L_m - W$.

$$\therefore \quad y_{m+1} = \frac{L_m}{L_m - W} x_m - \frac{W x_W}{L_m - W} \qquad \ldots (8.52)$$

Equation (8.52) is known as the material balance line or the **operating line** for the **stripping section**.

Analysis of fractionating columns :

The theoretical/ideal stages/plates required for given degree of separation can be obtained by :

1. McCabe – Thiele method.
2. Lewis – Sorel method.

McCabe – Thiele Method :

It is a graphical procedure of obtaining theoretical plates.

Assumptions underlying this method are :

1. Constant molal heat of vaporisation.
2. No heat losses.
3. No heat of mixing.

The above cited assumptions leads to a concept of constant molal vapour flow and constant molal liquid flow in any section of the column. In other words, for one mole of liquid vaporised one mole of vapour is condensed. Thus $V_n = V_{n+1}$, $L_n = L_{n+1}$ ... etc.

The subscripts n, n + 1, m, m + 1 ... etc. may be dropped and the operating lines then plotted on the equilibrium diagram are straight.

Therefore, operating line for the rectifying section becomes :

$$y = \frac{L}{L+D} x + \frac{D x_D}{L+D} \qquad \ldots (8.53)$$

As $R = \frac{L}{D}$, above equation becomes :

$$y = \frac{R}{R+1} x + \frac{x_D}{R+1} \qquad \ldots (8.54)$$

On the xy diagram, it is a straight line with a slope equal to $R/(R+1)$ and an intercept equal to $x_D/(R+1)$.

The point of intersection of the operating line for rectifying section and the diagonal $y = x$ is obtained as –

$$y = \frac{R}{R+1} x + \frac{x_D}{R+1}$$

Putting $\qquad y = x$

$\therefore \qquad x = \frac{R}{R+1} x + \frac{x_D}{R+1}$

$(R+1) x = R \cdot x + x_D$

$\therefore \qquad x = x_D$

and $\qquad y = x_D$

Thus, the operating line of the rectifying section is to be drawn on the equilibrium diagram through the point (x_D, x_D) on the diagonal and with a slope equal to $R/(R+1)$ or an intercept on y-axis equal to $x_D/(R+1)$.

The equation of operating line of the stripping section becomes :

$$y = \frac{L'}{L'-W} x - \frac{W x_W}{L'-W} \qquad \ldots (8.55)$$

On the xy diagram, i.e., on the equilibrium diagram, it is a straight line with a slope of $L'/(L'-W)$ and an intercept of $W x_W/(L'-W)$.

The point of intersection of the operating line of stripping section and the diagonal is obtained as follows :

$$y = \frac{L'}{L'-W} x - \frac{W x_W}{L-W}$$

Diagonal : $\qquad y = x$

$\therefore \qquad x = \frac{L'}{L'-W} x - \frac{W x_W}{L'-W}$

$\therefore \qquad L' \cdot x - W \cdot x = L' \cdot x - W x_W$

$\therefore \qquad x = x_W$

and $\qquad y = x_W$

Thus, the operating line of stripping section is to be drawn through point (x_W, x_W) on the diagonal with slope equal to $\dfrac{L'}{L' - W}$.

Step wise procedure for obtaining theoretical plates :
1. By material balances, evaluate the terms D, W, L, etc.
2. Draw the equilibrium curve and diagonal with the help of x – y data given.
   If the relative volatility is given, generate x – y data using the relativity value provided.
3. Draw the operating line of rectifying section through point (x_D, x_D) on the diagonal and with an intercept equal to $x_D/(R + 1)$ or $Dx_D/(L + D)$ or a slope equal to $R/(R + 1)$.
4. Draw the operating line of stripping section through point (x_W, x_W) on the diagonal and with a slope of $\dfrac{L'}{L' - W}$.
5. Starting from the (x_D, x_D) on diagonal, draw a horizontal line to meet the equilibrium curve at point 'a'. Drop a vertical from point 'a' to meet the operating line at point 1.

Fig. 8.13 : Determination of theoretical plates by McCabe – Thiele Method

6. Proceed in this way, that is constructing the triangles between equilibrium curve and operating line of rectifying section, till we are above the point of intersection of the two operating lines. Once we cross this point of intersection, construct the triangles between equilibrium curve and operating line of stripping section, i.e., dropping verticals on operating line of stripping section.
7. Proceed in the same manner till we reach/across the point (x_W, x_W).
8. Count the number of triangles constructed between – x_D and x_W. Each triangle on the x – y diagram represents a theoretical plate.
9. If the number of triangles are 'n', then 'n' represents the theoretical number of plates including reboiler and n –1 represents the number of theoretical plates in a column.

Since the vapour and liquid leaving reboiler are in equilibrium, the reboilers is equivalent to one theoretical plate.

Limitations of McCabe – Thiele Method :
1. It is not used when the relative volatility is less than 1.3 or greater than 5.
2. It is not used when more than 25 theoretical stages/plates are required, and
3. It is not used when the operating reflux ratio is less than 1.1 times the minimum reflux ratio.

Lewis – Sorel method of determination of number of theoretical stages/plates :

Equation of the operating line for the rectifying section is :

$$y_{n+1} = \frac{L_m}{L_n + D} x_n + \frac{D \cdot x_D}{L_n + D} \quad \ldots (8.56)$$

Equation of the operating line for the stripping section is :

$$y_{n+1} = \frac{L_n}{L_m - W} x_m - \frac{W\, x_W}{L_m - W} \quad \ldots (8.57)$$

1. From the data cited in a given problem, evaluate the terms - D, W, L, etc.
2. From the x – y data provided (or can be generated knowing the relative volatility) draw an equilibrium diagram.
3. Put the values of L_n (L), x_D, D in equation (8.56), so that it will be a relationship between y_{n+1} and x_n.
4. Similarly, put the values L_m, W, x_W in equation (8.57), so that it will be a relationship between y_{m+1} and x_m. L_m is to be evaluated by taking into consideration the condition of feed. For example, if it is a liquid at its bubble point $L_m = L_n + F$ (i.e. L + F).
5. Given distillate composition (x_D) in the problem statement represents the composition of vapour (y_n) as it is obtained by condensing the vapour leaving the top of column.
6. From the vapour phase composition – $y_n = x_D$, find from the equilibrium diagram the liquid phase composition x_{n+1} and put this value of x_{n+1} in the equation of the operating line of rectifying section to get y_2.
7. Find x_{n+2} value from the equilibrium diagram corresponding to y_{n+2}.
8. Find y_{n+3} and proceed with same equation till we reach the point when liquid phase composition equal to or less than x_F.
9. Then make use of material balance equation or operating line of the stripping section and proceed in the same way as described above till we get liquid phase composition equal to or below x_W. Suppose we end with y_{n+10} it means that there will be 10 plates in column.

Feed Plate and Feed Line :

The plate on which feed is introduced is called the **feed plate**. The feed to the column may be introduced as : (a) cold liquid, (b) liquid at its bubble point (saturated-liquid), (c) partially vaporised (partly vapour and partly liquid), (d) saturated vapour at its dew point and (e) superheated vapour. The condition of feed introduced on the feed plate alters the phase flow rates. Introduction of the feed as a cold liquid and a liquid at its bubble point increases the liquid flow rate in stripping section. Feed - partially vaporised increases the vapour flow rate in the rectifying section and also the liquid flow rate in the stripping section. The feed as a saturated vapour and a superheated vapour increases vapour flow rate in rectifying section.

Phase flow rates into and out of the feed plate for the various feed conditions are shown diagrammatically in Fig. 8.14.

(a) Feed - cold liquid   **(b) Feed – saturated liquid**

(c) Feed-partially vaporised   **(d) Feed-saturated vapour**

(e) Feed-superheated vapour
Fig. 8.14 : Flow through feed plate for various feed conditions

The phase flow rates shown are based on the fact that the column liquid is always at its bubble point and vapour is always at its dew point. To calculate the change in phase flow rates by the introduction of feed, a factor 'q' is introduced. **The 'q' is a measure of the thermal condition of the feed** and is defined as the *number of moles of saturated liquid resulting in the stripping section for each mole of feed introduced*. Thus for a feed F, we get :

$$L' = L + qF \quad \ldots (8.58)$$

and

$$V = V' + (1 - q) F \quad \ldots (8.59)$$

The values of 'q' for the various thermal conditions of feed are :
(a) Cold liquid : $q > 1$
(b) Saturated liquid : $q = 1$
(c) Feed partially vapour (partially flashed, i.e., a vapour-liquid mixture) : $0 < q < 1$
(d) Saturated vapour feed (feed at a dew point) : $q = 0$, and
(e) Superheated vapour feed : $q < 0$.

The value of q for any particular feed condition can be calculated from :

$$q = \frac{\text{Energy to convert 1 mole of feed to saturated vapour}}{\text{Molal latent heat of vaporisation}}$$

The liquid flow in the stripping section is :

$$L' = L + qF \quad \ldots (8.60)$$

$$\therefore \quad L' - L = qF \quad \ldots (8.61)$$

Similarly, the vapour flow in the rectifying section is :

$$V = V' + (1 - q) F \quad \ldots (8.62)$$

$$\therefore \quad V - V' = (1 - q) F \quad \ldots (8.63)$$

$$V = L + D - \text{(overall balance-upper section)} \quad \ldots (8.64)$$

$$\therefore \quad Vy = Lx + Dx_D - \text{(material balance of 'A')} \quad \ldots (8.65)$$

and

$$V' = L' - W - \text{(overall balance-lower section)} \quad \ldots (8.66)$$

$$V'y = L'x - Wx_W - \text{(material balance of A)} \quad \ldots (8.67)$$

Subtracting equation (8.67) from equation (8.65)

$$\therefore \quad y (V - V') = x (L - L') + D x_D + W x_W \quad \ldots (8.68)$$

But we know that :

$$x_F \cdot F = D \cdot x_D + W x_W \quad \ldots (8.69)$$

$\therefore$ Equation (8.68) becomes :

$$y (V - V') = x (L - L') + x_F \cdot F \quad \ldots (8.70)$$

Putting the values of V – V' and L – L' from equ. (8.63) and (8.61) into equation (8.70)

$$y (1 - q) F = x (- qF) + x_F \cdot F \quad \ldots (8.71)$$

$$\therefore \quad y = \frac{-q}{1-q} x + \frac{x_F}{1-q} \quad \ldots (8.72)$$

Equation (8.72) is known as the **feed line or q-line** (q-line equation).

The point of intersection of the feed line and the diagonal (x = y) is :

$$y = x = \frac{-q}{1-q} x + \frac{x_F}{1-q}$$

$$\therefore \quad x = x_F$$

and $\quad y = x_F$

The feed line passes through the point (x_F, x_F) on the diagonal and has the slope of $\frac{-q}{1-q}$.

For q = 1, slope = × and hence feed line is parallel to y-axis through point (x_F, x_F) on the diagonal.

For q = 0, slope = 0 and hence feed line is parallel to the x-axis through the point (x_F, x_F) on the diagonal.

Typical feed line or q-line constructions for the various values of 'q' are shown in Fig. 8.15.

Fig. 8.15 : Effect of feed condition on feed line

Draw (1) the feed line on the equilibrium diagram, (2) the operating line of the rectifying section as usual, it will cut the feed line at a certain point then (3) operating line of the stripping section can be easily plotted. This line is to be plotted through point (x_W, x_W) on the diagonal and it will pass through the point of intersection of feed line with operating line of the rectifying section.

The point of intersection of 1, 2 and 3 falls in a triangle which represents a feed plate. The triangle representing the feed plate has one corner on the rectifying section operating line and one on the stripping section operating line. Feed should be introduced at any point between 'A'

Fig. 8.16 : Plotting feed line and operating lines on x–y diagram for calculating number of theoretical plates

and 'B' but at the same time we have to keep in mind maximum enrichment and minimum number of plates. Introduction of feed near 'A' or 'B' unnecessarily results into large number of plates in the rectifying or stripping section. The optimum location will be the one at which the liquid phase composition value crosses the feed composition value x_F.

Fig. 8.17 : Feed plate location

Referring Fig. 8.17 we have :

Theoretical plates including reboiler = n = 6.

Theoretical plates in column = n – 1 = 6 – 1 = 5

Feed plate - third from top.

Reflux Ratio :

1. Infinite reflux ratio or total reflux ratio, $R_\times$:

The total reflux operation is necessary only to know the minimum number of plates required and is not a practical method of operation as at total reflux the product rate is zero.

A column operating under total reflux is shown in Fig. 8.18. In this case, enough material is charged to the distillation assembly and column is operated under total reflux. During the operation of the column, the vapour issuing from the top is condensed and all the condensed stream is fed back to the column as reflux. Also all the liquid going to the reboiler is vaporised and is fed to the column. Since $F = 0$, $D = 0$ and $W = 0$ at total reflux, $V_{n+1} = L_n$ throughout the column. The slope (L/V) of the operating lines of both sections becomes unity and hence the operating lines of both sections coincide with the diagonal and the minimum number of stages are then required for a desired degree of separation ($x_D - x_W$). The total reflux operation corresponds to a maximum reboiler heat supply and condenser cooling capacity for the separation.

Fig. 8.18 : Operation under total reflux

2. Minimum Reflux Ratio – R_m :

At total reflux, operating lines coincide with the diagonal and to effect a desired separation, number of stages required are minimum. As the reflux ratio is reduced, operating lines move towards the equilibrium curve along the feed line and the number of stages increases. Ultimately, further reduction in reflux ratio results into a condition wherein the top operating line touches the equilibrium curve as shown in Fig. 8.19. The point of intersection of operating lines lies on the equilibrium curve and at this point step become very close together, so that a zone of nearly constant composition is formed near the feed plate and an infinite number of plates are then required. This represents a condition of the minimum reflux. Thus, the minimum reflux ratio is *that reflux ratio at which an infinite number of plates are required for a desired separation*. At the minimum reflux ratio, required heat supply for reboiler and coolant supply for condenser are minimum.

Fig. 8.19 : Minimum Reflux ratio

Calculation of minimum reflux ratio (R_m) :

For liquid at its bubble point, the feed line is vertical (parallel to y-axis) and point 'C' lies on the equilibrium curve and has co-ordinates (x_F, y_F).

Draw the equilibrium curve and diagonal and draw the feed line, a vertical through the point (x_F, x_F) on the diagonal. The point of intersection of the feed line with the equilibrium curve is also a point of intersection of the operating lines at minimum reflux.

Fig. 8.20 : Method of obtaining R_m

Slope of operating line AC is given as :

$$\frac{R_m}{R_m + 1} = \frac{x_D - y_F}{x_D - x_F} \qquad \ldots (8.73)$$

$$R_m (x_D - x_F) = (R_m + 1)(x_D - y_F)$$

$$R_m \cdot x_D - R_m \cdot x_F = R_m x_D - R_m y_F + x_D - y_F$$

$$\therefore \quad R_m (y_F - x_F) = x_D - y_F$$

$$R_m = \frac{x_D - y_F}{y_F - x_F} \qquad \ldots (8.74)$$

Similarly for feed as a saturated vapour, the feed line is horizontal.

Slope of line AC is given as :

$$\frac{R_m}{R_m + 1} = \frac{x_D - y'}{x_D - x'} \qquad \ldots (8.75)$$

$$\therefore \quad R_m = \frac{x_D - y'}{y' - x'}$$

$$= \frac{x_D - x_F}{x_F - x'} \text{ (as } y' = x_F\text{)} \qquad \ldots (8.76)$$

Fig. 8.21 : R_m for saturated vapour

For feed as a cold liquid, i.e., for 'q' values greater than one :

$$R_m = \frac{x_D - y'}{y' - x'} \quad \ldots (8.77)$$

Fig. 8.22 : 'R_m' for cold liquid

For 'q' values less than one and greater than zero :

$$\text{Slope} = \frac{R_m}{R_{m+1}} = \frac{x_D - y'}{x_D - x'}$$

$$\therefore \quad R_m = \frac{x_D - y'}{y' - x'} \quad \ldots (8.78)$$

Fig. 8.23 : 'R_m' for feed-partially vapour

3. Optimum Reflux Ratio :

Any reflux ratio between infinite reflux ratio requiring a minimum number of plates and minimum reflux ratio requiring an infinite number of plates is a workable system which requires finite stages for the desired degree of separation. At minimum reflux ratio as infinite number of plates are required, the fixed cost is also infinite while the cost of heat supply to the reboiler and condenser coolant is minimum. As the reflux ratio is increased, the number of plates decreases and the fixed cost decreases at first, passes through a minimum and then increases as with higher reflux ratio the diameter of the column and sizes of reboiler and condenser increases. The operating cost increases continuously with reflux ratio as it is directly proportional to $(R + 1)$. At total reflux, though the number of plates are minimum, the cost of heat supply to reboiler and condenser coolant is maximum and also large capacity

Fig. 8.24 : Relation between reflux ratio and number of stages for distillation

reboiler and condenser are needed. The total cost which is the sum of the fixed cost and the operating cost also decreases to a minimum and then increases with reflux ratio. The optimum reflux ratio occurs at a point where the sum of the fixed cost and operating cost is minimum. As a rough approximation, **the optimum reflux ratio usually lies in the range of 1.1 to 1.5 times the minimum reflux ratio.**

Fig. 8.25 : Optimum reflux ratio for distillation

Batch Distillation :

Batch distillation is used extensively in small scale production units where the same piece of equipment is to be used for many different mixtures and where small quantities of liquid mixtures are to be handled. It is useful when more than one product is to be obtained (i.e. different quality products) and when the liquid mixture to be separated are high in solid content, tar etc. as it keeps the solids separated (in reboiler/still) which are removed at the termination of the process.

In batch distillation, the specific quantity of a liquid mixture is charged to a reboiler/still, heating is applied, vapour generated flow upward through a fractionating column and a part of the liquid from a condenser runs down the column as reflux. The entire fractionating column acts as a enriching section. As the distillate will be rich in more volatile component, the liquid in the reboiler becomes steadily weaker in the more volatile component as the operation proceeds and hence the purity of the product will steadily fall.

Batch distillation operation may be carried by varying the reflux ratio so as to get a constant overhead composition. In this case, initially column is operated under total reflux and then some value of the reflux ratio is adjusted. But as the distillation proceeds, the top product quality may fall. Thus, to keep the top product quality to be constant, the reflux ratio is increased. Reflux ratio is continually increased till it reaches a maximum value and then it is reduced and the cut is taken into a separate receiver. It may be charged in a next batch.

Another method of operating batch distillation unit is to operate column under a constant reflux ratio. Column is operated under total reflux initially and then reflux is set to a predetermined value. As the distillation proceeds, top products quality will steadily fall but distillate is collected in the same receiver until the average distillate composition is reached at the desired value and then overhead product is collected in a second receiver till the termination of operation and the same may be charged in the next batch.

Fig. 8.26 : Batch distillation unit

Still another way to operate the unit is to adopt the practice of cycling procedure wherein the column is operated at total reflux till the desired top temperature is achieved (which is indication of top product purity) and then all the overhead product is withdrawn at once, distillate removal valve is closed and again column is operated under total reflux.

Azeotropes :

An azeotrope is a *liquid mixture with an equilibrium vapour of the same composition as the liquid*. The dew point and bubble point are identical at azeotropic composition and the mixture vaporises at a single temperature, so azeotropes are called constant boiling mixtures. Close boiling components showing small deviations from ideality may form an azeotrope. An azeotrope exhibits a maximum or a minimum boiling point relative to the boiling points of pure liquids, thus are classified as maximum boiling and minimum boiling azeotropes. Minimum boiling azeotrope will boil at a temperature lower than the boiling points of pure components and maximum boiling azeotrope will boil at higher temperature than the boiling points of pure components. The temperature–composition diagrams and equilibrium diagrams for liquid mixtures forming azeotropes at constant pressure are shown in Fig. 8.27. Here we will see that the equilibrium curve crosses the diagonal - which is an indication of the existence of an azeotrope, i.e., y = x and the mixture will not be separated by ordinary distillation.

Fig. 8.27 : Minimum boiling azeotrope system carbon disulfide – acetone at one atmosphere

Fig. 8.28 : Maximum boiling azeotrope system chloroform – acetone at one atmosphere pressure

Refer to Fig. 8.27. For all the mixtures of composition less than P, the equilibrium vapour is richer in more volatile component than the liquid, while for all mixtures of composition greater than 'P', the equilibrium vapour is less rich in more volatile component than the liquid. The mixture of composition 'P' gives the vapour of composition identical with the liquid.

In such cases, complete separation by ordinary fractionation may not be possible. The constituents of a binary azeotrope are separated completely by - (1) adding a third component to the binary mixture and (2) changing the system pressure.

The third component (which is relatively volatile) added to a binary azeotrope usually forms a low boiling azeotrope with one of the feed constituents and withdrawn as the overhead product/distillate. *The third component added to break the binary azeotrope to effect its separation into pure components* is called as the **entrainer/azeotrope breaker**.

The process of distillation wherein a third component is added to a binary azeotrope to effect the complete separation is called as azeotropic distillation.

In this process, the component added forms an azeotrope with one of the feed components and that the azeotrope is withdrawn as either the overhead or bottom product.

A binary azeotrope system containing ethanol and water forms a minimum boiling azeotrope at 96% by weight ethanol and thus blocks the production of pure components by ordinary distillation. The separation into almost pure form is effected by adding benzene as an entrainer to this binary azeotrope. In the azeotropic distillation technique of this system, alcohol-water mixture containing 96% alcohol is fed to a first column, benzene used as an entrainer forms a low boiling ternary azeotrope (containing benzene, alcohol and water) which is removed as a top product and nearly pure alcohol is taken out as a bottom product. The overhead from the first column is condensed, phase separation is achieved in a decanter. The benzene rich phase is returned to the first distillation column and the water rich phase is sent to a second distillation column. The overhead from the second column containing benzene in major proportion is fed back to the first column while aqueous solution of alcohol is withdrawn as a bottom product. It is then fed to a third distillation column which gives alcohol-water azeotrope as an overhead product (to be mixed with the feed) and pure water as the bottom product.

Steam Distillation :

Steam distillation (It is a distillation process with open steam) is used : (i) for separating a high boiling component from the non-volatile impurities, (ii) for separating a high boiling mixture into different fractions wherein the decomposition of material might occur if direct distillation were employed, (iii) in cases where vaporisation temperature cannot be reached by steam heat.

Steam distillation is especially adopted in cases where substances involved cannot withstand temperature of distillation and decompose (i.e., for heat sensitive materials). Substances of this kind can be separated by reducing the partial pressure of the volatile component. This can be done by making use of an inert vapour that decreases the temperature of distillation. The inert vapour used should be practically immiscible with components to be distilled. Steam is generally used for this purpose and operation is called as steam distillation. Steam is widely used as : it is immiscible with many organic compounds, it provides required heat for vaporisation and it is readily available at low cost.

In steam distillation, steam is directly admitted into the liquid in the still (steam directly admitted in a pool of the liquid is called as live or open steam). The mixed vapour containing a desired component is taken as an overhead, condensed and the desired component is separated from the water phase by gravity while the non-volatile material remains behind in the still. The necessary condition for employing steam distillation is that the solubility of steam in the liquid must be very low i.e. product must be practically immiscible with water.

The process of steam distillation may make use of superheated steam which provide sufficient heat to vaporise the desired component without self condensing or it may make use of saturated steam which provide sufficient heat to vaporise the desired component by partly condensing. In the latter case, the liquid (water) phase is produced in the still. In either case, when the sum of the partial pressure of steam and desired component reaches the total pressure, both substances pass over (as a vapour) in the molecular ratio of their partial pressures. The mass relationship is :

$$\frac{\frac{m_A}{M_A}}{\frac{m_B}{M_B}} = \frac{p_A}{y_B}$$

$$= \frac{p_A}{P - p_A} \qquad \ldots (8.79)$$

$$\frac{m_A}{m_B} = \frac{p_A \cdot M_A}{p_B \cdot M_B}$$

$$= \frac{p_A M_A}{(P - p_A) M_B} \qquad \ldots (8.80)$$

where M_A, M_B are molecular weights of desired component and steam respectively. p_B, p_B and P are the partial pressure of desired component, steam (called as carrier) and total pressure respectively.

m_A, m_B are the masses of desired component and steam in the vapour respectively. When water phase is present and effect of a non-volatile material on vaporisation is neglected then for the system under consideration there will be two components and three phases. According to the phase rule, $F = C - P + 2$, there is only one variable that can be varied independently and setting the temperature or pressure fixes the system. Thus, if the pressure is atmospheric, temperature adjust itself so that the sum of the partial pressures of two components equals to one atmosphere. The temperature so reached is less than the boiling points of pure components. Thus if the pressure is atmospheric then it is possible to steam distill the material at a temperature lower than 100°C thus blocking/avoiding the destructive temperatures.

Distillation and Absorption Towers/Columns :

Distillation (fractionation) and Absorption are the most widely used mass transfer operations in the chemical industry. In case of these two operations, the gas-liquid contacting devices for mass transfer are the same-such as plate columns and packed columns.

A distillation (and absorption column) is also known as a tower. It is essentially a tall vertical cylindrical shell with number of nozzles. The internals of the column consist of a series of plates or trays or a variety of packings.

Based upon the contacting devices used for mass transfer to take place, the towers/columns are divided into two types namely, plate or tray columns and packed columns.

Plate Columns :

Distillation with rectification makes use of either plate (tray) column or packed towers, for intimate phase contacting, the former being more common. In plate columns, the process of mass transfer is stage wise and in packed towers/columns, the process of mass transfer is continuous.

Each plate in a vertical column represents a stage as on each plate, the phases (gas and liquid) are brought into intimate contact, mass is transferred from one phase to another, and finally phases are separated and leave the plate/tray. A plate column is a vertical column which consists of a number of plates. In this column, liquid enters from the top, flows over every plate and from plate to plate via down comers.

A certain height of a liquid pool is maintained on each plate with the help of an outlet weir. Gas/vapour enters in the column from the bottom inlet and flows upward through the openings in the plate, it bubbles through the pool of liquid on the plate, disengages from the liquid and passes to the plate above. In this way, vapour and liquid are brought into intimate contact on every plate.

Various plates used for phase contacting are :
1. Bubble cap plate/tray
2. Sieve plate and
3. Valve plate.

In plate columns, the minimum tray spacing is 300 mm. For columns of diameter 1.5 m or more, spacing of 450 or 600 mm is used for easier tray access.

In plate columns, each plate is provided with a **downcomer** and **weirs**. The function of the downcomer is to provide a passage for the downward flow of the liquid from a tray above to the tray below. The downcomer area for each plate is limited to 10 % of the total area of the plate. Pipe downcomer, segmental downcomer and chord type downcomer are various types of downcomers used. The depth of liquid on the tray required for gas contacting is maintained by an overflow (outlet) weir. An inlet weir helps to distribute liquid as it enters the tray from the downcomer and prevents impingement of liquid on contacting device.

1. Bubble cap tray/plate :

In case of bubble cap plate, gas/vapour flows through a riser, reverses flow under the cap,

Fig. 8.29 : Bubble cap

moves downward through the annular space between the riser and the cap, and finally it bubbles into a pool of liquid through a series of slots (openings) provided along the periphery of the cap in its lower portion. The slots may be circular, rectangular or trapezoidal in shape.

Bubble cap disperses the gas phase into liquid as fine bubbles, it prevents liquid drainage through the gas passage at low gas rates. It directs the gas flow first in the horizontal direction and then gas flows vertically upward through a pool of liquid in the form of bubbles. The bubble cap columns can be operated with high and constant stage efficiencies over a wide range of vapour and liquid flow rates.

Bubble cap plates are now rarely used for new installations because of (i) their relatively high cost and (ii) high pressure drop.

2. Sieve tray/plate :

Very common plates in use in recent years are the perforated plates because of their simplicity and of low cost. A sieve plate is a perforated plate that employs perforations for dispersing a gas into a liquid on the plate. It is a metal sheet having hundreds of round perforations in it of the size ranging between 3 to 12 mm. The total area of holes range from 5 to 15 % of the plate area. In sieve plate, liquid flows across the plate and gas passes vertically upward through the holes, in the form of bubbles into the liquid on the plate. Gas flow through the perforations prevents down-flow of the liquid through perforations in

Fig. 8.30 : Sieve plate disperser

the plate but at low gas rates **weeping** (draining of liquid through the perforations in the plate) is severe which in turn reduces stage efficiencies, and this is a limitation of the sieve plate. Gas-liquid contact is poor with the sieve plate as compared to that with the bubble cap plate because in the sieve plate, gas is directed vertically and in the bubble cap plate, gas is first directed horizontally and then moves vertically upward. The pressure drop with a sieve plate is low as compared to it with a bubble cap plate. It is usually operated over a wide range of flow rates between the weeping and flooding points.

Valve plate :

It is the recent development in perforated plates. A valve plate is nothing but a perforated metal sheet wherein the perforations are covered with liftable caps (valves). The valves are

Fig. 8.31 : Valve Plate Dispersers

metal discs upto about 38 mm diameter and are held in the plate by means of legs which restrict the upward motion of the caps. The valve provides variable orifices (areas) for gas flow, i.e., opening will be small at low gas rate and large at high gas rate. Thus, weeping will be greatly reduced with this plate at low gas rates. Valve plates can be operated over a wide range of phase flow rates. Gas-liquid contact with the valve plate is much better than it with the sieve plate as liftable caps direct the gas horizontally into liquid on the plate while with the sieve plate gas passes vertically upward through liquid. The cost of the valve plate is in between that of the bubble cap and the sieve plate (approximately twenty per cent higher than that of the sieve plate).

Liquid flow patterns over tray/plate :

The type of liquid flow pattern over a plate depends upon liquid to gas flow ratio.

Various flow patterns are :

1. **Cross flow :** It is most frequently used. Provides good length of liquid path.
2. **Reverse flow :** Provides a very long liquid path especially suitable for low liquid to gas ratios.
3. **Split flow :** Especially suitable for handling high liquid to gas ratios.

Fig. 8.32 : Arrangement for liquid flow over a tray

Downcomer and weir :

A downcomer is the passage for liquid flow from a plate above to the plate below. The

Fig. 8.33 : Downcomer - weir seal plot

downcomers may be in the form of circular pipes or segments of the tower (column) cross-section set aside for liquid flow by vertical plates (shaped like segments of a circle). The discharge end of the downcomer is generally projected far enough into the liquid on a plate so as to avoid gas from rising up the downcomer to short-circuit the plate above. To avoid this inlet weir may be used. A exit weir or outlet weir is used for maintaining a certain depth of liquid on each plate needed for gas contacting. Straight or rectangular weirs with length equal to 60 to 80% of the tower diameter are frequently used.

Entrainment :

As gas bubbles through a pool of liquid on a plate, a large amount of turbulence is set up, and liquid particles can be entrained by the rising gas. *Carry over of liquid particles by the rising gas from a plate below to plate above* is known as **entrainment**. It is much more pronounced at high gas flow rates. Entrainment reduces the concentration change per plate and hence, decreases the efficiency. Tray/plate spacing, vapour flow rate, depth of liquid on plate are the factors on which the amount of entrainment depends.

PACKED COLUMNS FOR DISTILLATION :

Details regarding packed columns are given in Ch. 9 : Gas Absorption.

Packed columns are useful for distillation especially whenever we have to carry out operation at low pressure (vacuum distillation) and whenever we are dealing with heat-sensitive materials. Packings are usually cheaper than plates for columns less than 600 mm diameter.

A packed column consists of a cylindrical shell containing a support plate and a liquid distributor. The cylindrical shell is filled with some sort of packings that rest on the support plate. The packing material offers large interfacial area for mass transfer. The liquid distributor is designed for effective irrigation of the packings.

The ability of a given packing to effect the desired mass transfer between gas and liquid phases is usually expressed (in an empirical form) as the height equivalent to one theoretical plate (HETP). In plate columns, wherein a process of enrichment is stage wise, the vapour leaving the plate is richer with respect to more volatile component than the vapour entering the plate by one equilibrium stage. In packed column, the same enrichment of the vapour will occur in a certain height of packing and is termed as the height equivalent to one theoretical plate. Thus in packed columns, one equilibrium step is represented by a certain height of packed bed and the required height of packing for the desired degree of separation is given by : HETP × number of ideal plates required.

Fig. 8.34 : Packed column for continuous distillation

HETP can be estimated with the help of the following empirical equation :

$$\text{HETP} = k_1 \cdot G^{k_2} \cdot D_t^{k_3} \cdot Z^{1/3} \cdot \alpha \cdot \mu_L/\rho_L$$

where k_1, k_2 and k_3 are empirical constants for packing and are function of type and size the packings

        G – Superfacial gas mass velocity
        D_t – Tower diameter
        Z – Height of packing
        α – Relative volatility

μ_L and ρ_L are the viscosity and density of liquid respectively.

Plate Efficiencies :

The relationship between the performance of theoretical/ideal and actual plates is expressed in terms of plate efficiency. The types of plate efficiency are :

1. Overall plate efficiency/overall column efficiency.
2. Murphree plate efficiency and
3. Point/local efficiency.

Overall plate efficiency is the ratio of the number of ideal or theoretical plates (stages) required to produce a given separation in the entire column to the number of actual plates required to effect the same separation.

If the overall efficiency is 60% and 12 ideal plates are called for, then the actual plates needed are 12/0.60 = 20

Murphree plate efficiency :

It applies to a individual plate in a column and is defined as the *actual change in average composition accomplished by a given plate divided by the change in average composition if the vapour leaving the plate were in equilibrium with the liquid leaving the plate.*

Point efficiency is defined in the same manner as the murphree plate efficiency but it applies to a single location on a given plate.

Unit Operations – II   8.39   Distillation

SOLVED EXAMPLES

Ex. 8.1 : A mixture of benzene and toluene boils at 368 K (95° C) under a pressure of 101.325 kPa. Determine the composition of the boiling liquid assuming that mixture obeys Raoult's law.

At 368 K (95° C), the vapour pressure of benzene is 155.56 kPa and that of toluene is 63.98 kPa.

Solution : Let x_A be the mole fraction of benzene in liquid.

$$x_A = \frac{P - p_B^o}{p_A^o - p_B^o}$$

where
$P = 101.325$ kPa
$p_B^o = 63.98$ kPa
$p_A^o = 155.56$ kPa

$$x_A = \frac{101.325 - 63.98}{155.56 - 63.98} = 0.408$$

Mole % of benzene in boiling liquid $= 0.408 \times 100 = 40.8$ ... **Ans.**

Ex. 8.2 : Calculate the equilibrium compositions of the liquid and the vapour phases for a mixture of methyl alcohol and water at a temperature of 323 K (50° C) and under a pressure of 40 kPa. Assume that both liquid and vapour behave ideally.

Data : V.P. of methanol at 323 K (50° C) = 53.32 kPa
V.P. of water at 323 K (50° C) = 12.33 kPa.

Solution : Let x_A and y_A be the mole fraction of methyl alcohol in the liquid and vapour.

p_A = partial pressure of methyl alcohol
$= p_A^o \, x_A = 53.32 \, x_A$

p_B = partial pressure of water
$= p_B^o \, x_B = 12.33 \, (1 - x_A)$

$P = p_A + p_B$
$40 = 53.32 \, x_A + 12.33 \, (1 - x_A)$
$x_A = 0.675$

$$y_A = p_A/P = \frac{p_A^o \cdot x_A}{P} = \frac{53.32 \times 0.675}{40}$$

$y_A = 0.90$

Equilibrium composition :

Liquid phase = 0.675 mole fraction of methyl alcohol
Vapour phase = 0.90 mole fraction of methyl alcohol   ... **Ans.**

Ex. 8.3 : The vapour pressures of n-heptane (A) and n-octane (B) are given in the following table. Assume that Raoult's and Dalton's laws apply, compute vapour-liquid equilibria at constant pressure of 101.325 kPa

Boiling point of n-heptane (A) = 371.4 K (98.4° C)

Boiling point of n-octane (B) = 398.6 K (125.6° C)

Data :

T, °C	98.4	105	110	115	120	125.6
T, K	371.4	378	383	388	393	398.6
p_A^o, kPa	101.325	125.323	139.988	159.987	179.985	205.316
p_B^o, kPa	44.396	55.595	64.528	74.795	86.659	101.325

Solution : n-heptane is more volatile component.

$x = x_A$ = mole fraction of n-heptane in liquid

$y = y_A$ = mole fraction of n-heptane in vapour

Here we have to compute vapour-liquid equilibrium composition at different temperatures.

$$x = \frac{P - p_B^o}{p_A^o - p_B^o} \quad \text{and} \quad y = \frac{p_A^o \cdot x}{P}$$

where P is pressure of system (101.325 kPa), p_A^o and p_B^o are vapour pressure of n-hetane and n-octane respectively.

T = 371.4 K (98.4° C)

P = 101.325 kPa, p_A^o = 101.325 kPa and p_B^o = 44.396 kPa

$$x = \frac{P - p_B^o}{p_A^o - p_B^o} = \frac{101.325 - 44.396}{101.325 - 44.396} = 1.0$$

$$y = \frac{p_A^o \, x}{P} = \frac{101.325 \times 1}{101.325} = 1.0$$

$$\alpha = p_A^o / p_B^o = 101.325 / 44.396 = 2.28$$

∴ At T = 371.4, x = 1.0, y = 1.0 and α = 2.28

2. At T = 378 K (105° C)

P = 101.325 kPa, p_A^o = 125.323 kPa and p_B^o = 55.595 kPa

$$x = \frac{101.325 - 55.595}{125.323 - 55.595} = 0.656 \text{ mole fraction of heptane in liquid}$$

$$y = \frac{125.323 \times 0.655}{101.325} = 0.810 \text{ mole fraction of heptane in vapour}$$

Unit Operations – II — 8.41 — Distillation

and $\alpha = 125.323 / 55.595 = 2.25$

Similarly calculate values x, y and α at other given temperatures.

T, °C	T, K	x	y	α
98.4	371.4	1.0	1.0	2.28
105	378	0.656	0.810	2.25
110	383	0.487	0.673	2.17
115	388	0.312	0.492	2.14
120	393	0.157	0.280	2.08
125.6	398.6	0.0	0.0	2.03

Average value of 'α' = 2.16

We know that $y = \dfrac{\alpha x}{1 + (\alpha - 1) x}$ $\quad \therefore \quad \alpha = \dfrac{2.16\, x}{1 + 1.16\, x}$

This provides a relation between y and x at 101.325 kPa.

Ex. 8.4 : The vapour pressure of n-heptane (A) and n-octane (B) are given in the following table at 101.325 kPa pressure. Assume that Raoult's and Dalton's laws apply, calculate the value of average relative volatility, generate x – y data and construct x – y plot. (equilibrium / distribution diagram)

Data :

T, °C	98.4	105	110	115	120	125.6
T, K	371.4	378	383	388	393	398.6
p_A^o, kPa	101.325	125.323	139.988	159.987	179.985	205.316
p_B^o, kPa	44.396	55.595	64.528	74.795	86.659	101.325

Boiling point of n-heptane (A) = 371.4 K (98.4° C).

Boiling point of n-octane (B) = 125.6° C (398.6 K)

Solution : n-heptane is the more volatile component.

x is the mole fraction of n-heptane in liquid.

y is the mole fraction of n-octane in vapour.

α is the relative volatility of n-heptane with respect to n-octane.

$$\alpha = \dfrac{p_A^o}{p_B^o}$$

where p_A^o is the vapour pressure of n-heptane and p_B^o is the vapour pressure of n-octane.

At T = 371.4 K

p_A^o = 101.325 kPa and p_B^o = 44.396 kPa

∴ α = 101.325 / 44.396 = 2.28

At T = 378 K

p_A^o = 125.323 kPa and p_B^o = 55.595 kPa

∴ α = 125.323 / 55.595 = 2.25

Similarly evaluate value of α at different temperatures.

T, K	371.4	378	383	388	393	398.6
α	2.28	2.25	2.17	2.14	2.08	2.03

$$\text{Average value of } \alpha = \frac{2.28 + 2.25 + 2.17 + 2.14 + 2.08 + 2.03}{6} = 2.16$$

We know that,

$$y = \frac{\alpha x}{1 + (\alpha - 1) x}$$

where x is mole fraction of n-heptane in liquid and y is the mole fraction of n-heptane in vapour.

$$y = \frac{2.16 \, x}{1 + (2.16 - 1) x} = \frac{2.16 \, x}{1 + 1.16 \, x}$$

With the help of above equation, generate x–y data.

(i.e. vapour-liquid equilibrium data)

Take x = 0.0, $y = \dfrac{2.16 \times 0.0}{1 + 1.16 \times 0} = 0$

Take x = 0.10

$$y = \frac{2.16 \times 0.10}{1 + 1.16 \times 0.1} = 0.193 \approx 0.19$$

Take x = 0.20

$$y = \frac{2.16 \times 0.20}{1 + 1.16 \times 0.20} = 0.351$$

Similarly, take x = 0.30, 0.40, 0.50 ... 1.0 and evaluate corresponding values of y.

x	0	0.10	0.20	0.30	0.40	0.50	0.60	0.70	0.8	0.90	1.0
y	0	0.19	0.35	0.48	0.59	0.68	0.76	0.83	0.90	0.95	1.0

Fig. 8.35 [Ex. 8.4]

Ex. 8.5 : For the system n-heptane and n-octane given in exercise 8.3, construct T-x and T-y plot.

Solution : Boiling point of n-heptane (A) = 371.4 K (98.4° C)

Boiling point of n-octane (B) = 398.6 K (125.6° C)

On ordinate through x = 0, y = 0 mark boiling point of n-octane (398.6 K)

On ordinate through x = 1, y = 1 mark boiling point of n-heptane (371.4 K)

Fig. 8.36 (Ex. 8.5) : T-x and T-y plot

Ex. 8.6 : The vapour pressures of n-hexane and n-octane are given below. Obtain an empirical relation between y and x for this system at constant pressure of 101.3 kPa.

T, °C	68.7	79.4	93.3	107.2	121.1	125.6
T, K	341.7	352.4	366.3	380.2	394.1	398.6
p^o_{Hexane}, kPa	101.3	136.6	197.3	283.9	399.9	455.9
p^o_{Octane}, kPa	16.1	23.1	37.1	57.8	87.2	101.3

With the help of empirical equation generate vapour-liquid equilibrium data and construct x-y plot.

Solution : Hexane is more volatile component.

α = relative volatility of hexane with respect to octane

$$\alpha = \frac{p^o_{Hexane}}{p^o_{Octane}} = \frac{p^o_A}{p^o_B}$$

At 341.7 K, $p^o_A = 101.3$ kPa and $p^o_B = 16.1$ kPa

$\therefore \quad \alpha = \dfrac{101.3}{16.1} = 6.29$

At 352.4 K, $p_A^o = 136.6$ kPa and $p_B^o = 23.1$ kPa

∴ $\alpha = 136.6/23.1 = 5.91$

Similarly, evaluate α at other data

At 366.3 K, $\alpha = 5.32$
At 380.2 K, $\alpha = 4.91$
At 394.1 K, $\alpha = 4.59$
At 398.6 K, $\alpha = 4.50$

Average value of $\alpha = \dfrac{6.29 + 5.91 + 5.32 + 4.91 + 4.59 + 4.50}{6} = 5.25$

We know that,

$$y = \dfrac{\alpha x}{1 + (\alpha - 1) x}$$

where x and y are the mole fraction of hexane in liquid and vapour.

$$y = \dfrac{5.25\, x}{1 + (5.25 - 1) x}$$

$$y = \dfrac{5.25\, x}{1 + 4.25\, x} \qquad \text{... Ans.}$$

Above is the desired empirical relation between y and x. Take x = 0, 0.10, 0.20 ... 1.0 and evaluate corresponding values of y from above relation.

e.g. Take $x = 0.20$

$$y = \dfrac{5.25 \times (0.20)}{1 + 4.25\,(0.20)} = 0.57$$

x	0.0	0.10	0.20	0.30	0.40	0.50	0.60	0.70	0.80	0.90	1.0
y	0.0	0.37	0.57	0.69	0.78	0.84	0.89	0.92	0.95	0.98	1.0

Fig. 8.37 (Ex. 8.6) : Distribution diagram

Ex. 8.7 : The vapour pressures of n-hexane and n-octane are given in the following table. n-hexane and n-octane may be expected to form ideal solutions. Compute the vapour-liquid equilibrium compositions and construct T – x – y plot for the system at total pressure of 101.3 kPa.

T, °C	68.7	79.4	93.3	107.2	121.1	125.6
T, K	341.7	352.4	366.3	380.2	394.1	398.6
p_H^o, kPa	101.3	136.6	197.3	283.9	399.9	455.9
p_O^o, kPa	16.1	23.1	37.1	57.8	87.2	101.3

Solution :

Hexane is the more volatile component (A).

Octane is the less volatile component (B).

$$P = 101.3 \text{ kPa}$$

p_A^o = vapour pressure of A (i.e. hexane)

and p_B^o is the vapour pressure of B (i.e. octane)

$$x = x_A = \frac{P - p_B^o}{p_A^o - p_B^o} \text{ and } y = y_A = \frac{p_A^o \cdot x_A}{P}$$

At $\quad T = 341.7$ K, $\quad p_A^o = 101.3$ kPa $\quad$ and $\quad p_B^o = 16.1$ kPa

∴ $\quad x = \dfrac{101.3 - 16.1}{101.3 - 16.1} = 1.0, \quad y = \dfrac{101.3 \times 1}{101.3} = 1.0$

At $\quad T = 352.4$ K, $\quad p_A^o = 136.6$ kPa $\quad$ and $\quad p_B^o = 23.1$ kPa

∴ $\quad x = \dfrac{101.3 - 23.1}{136.6 - 23.1} = 0.689 \approx 0.69$

$$y = \frac{136.6 \times 0.69}{101.3} = 0.93$$

Similarly, get x and y at other temperatures.

| T, K | 341.7 | 352.4 | 366.3 | 380.2 | 394.1 | 398.6 |

x	1.0	0.69	0.40	0.19	0.045	0
y	1.0	0.93	0.78	0.54	0.18	0

Fig. 8.38 (Ex. 8.7) : Constant-pressure vapour-liquid equilibria

Ex. 8.8 : Compute the vapour-liquid equilibrium at constant pressure of 101.325 kPa absolute for mixtures of benzene with toluene which obey Raoult's and Dalton's laws. Also find empirical relation between liquid and vapour phase composition. Vapour pressure data :

Temperature	Vapour pressure of Benzene, kPa	Vapour pressure of Toluene, kPa

353 K (80° C)	101.325	–
355.9 K (82.9° C)	108.12	41.863
358 K (85° C)	117.6	45.996
360 K (87° C)	127.6	50.396
363.5 K (90.5° C)	138.25	55.195
366.4 K (93.3° C)	149.72	60.262
369.1 K (96.1° C)	161.85	65.861
372 K (99° C)	174.65	71.727
374.6 K (101.6° C)	188.251	77.993
377.5 K (104.5° C)	202.65	84.66
380.2 K (107.2° C)	216.65	91.859
383 K (110.0° C)	234.11	99.592
383.1 K (110.1° C)	–	101.325

Solution : In a mixture of benzene - toluene boiling point of pure benzene (A) is 353 K (80° C) and that of pure toluene (B) is 383.1 K (110.1° C). Benzene is thus more volatile component. Let p_A^o, p_B^o and P be the vapour pressure of benzene, toluene and constant total pressure. Let x and y be the equilibrium liquid phase and vapour phase compositions.

i.e. x – mole fraction of benzene (more volatile component) in liquid

y – mole fraction of benzene (more volatile component) in vapour.

We have,

$$x = \frac{P - p_B^o}{p_A^o - p_B^o}$$

and

$$y = \frac{p_A^o \cdot x}{P}$$

$$P = 101.325 \text{ kPa}$$

With the help of above two relations find out the values of x and y at each temperature given in data. For example

At temperature = 358 K (85° C)

$$p_A^o = 117.6 \text{ kPa and } p_B^o = 45.996 \text{ kPa}$$

$$x = \frac{P - p_B^o}{p_A^o - p_B^o}$$

$$x = \frac{101.325 - 45.996}{117.6 - 45.996} = 0.773$$

$$y = \frac{p_A^o \cdot x}{P} = \frac{117.6\,(0.773)}{101.325} = 0.897$$

At temperature = 355.9 K

$$p_A^o = 108.12 \text{ kPa}$$

and $\quad p_B^o = 41.863 \text{ kPa}$

$$x = \frac{101.325 - 41.863}{108.12 - 41.863} = 0.897$$

and $\quad y = \dfrac{108.12 \times 0.897}{101.325} = 0.958$

At temperature = 353 K

$$p_A = 101.325 \text{ kPa}$$

$$x = \frac{P - p_B^o}{p_A^o - p_B^o}$$

$$x = \frac{101.325 - p_B^o}{101.325 - p_B^o} = 1.0$$

and $\quad y = \dfrac{p_A^o \cdot x}{P} = \dfrac{760 \times 1}{760} = 1.0$

Similarly, find out x and y at other values of temperature and tabulate them.

Find α_{AB} at each temperature with the help of relation :

$$\alpha_{AB} = \text{Relative volatility} = \frac{p_A^o}{p_B^o}$$

At temperature 355.9 K

$$p_A^o = 108.12 \text{ kPa}$$

and $\quad p_B^o = 41.863 \text{ kPa}$

$$\alpha_{AB} = \frac{p_A^o}{p_B^o} = \frac{108.12}{41.863} = 2.58$$

At temperature 358 K

$$\alpha_{AB} = \frac{117.6}{145.996} = 2.56$$

Find out the average value of α_{AB} :

Temperature	x	y	α_{AB} or α

353 K (80° C)	1	1	–
355.9 K (82.9° C)	0.897	0.958	2.58
358 K (85° C)	0.773	0.897	2.56
360 K (87° C)	0.659	0.831	2.53
363.5 K (90.5° C)	0.555	0.757	2.50
366.3 K (93.3° C)	0.459	0.657	2.48
369.1 K (96.1° C)	0.370	0.591	2.46
372 K (99° C)	0.288	0.496	2.43
374.6 K (101.6° C)	0.211	0.393	2.41
377.5 K (104.5° C)	0.141	0.281	2.39
380.2 K (107.2° C)	0.075	0.161	2.36
383 K (110° C)	0.013	0.031	2.35
383.1 K (110.1° C)	0	0	–

Ans.

Average value of $\quad \alpha_{AB} = \alpha = 2.46$

α_{AB} can also be written as α:

The relationship between vapour phase and liquid phase compositions for generating the equilibrium data is:

$$y = \frac{\alpha x}{1 + (\alpha - 1) x}$$

$$y = \frac{2.46 x}{1 + (2.46 - 1) x} = \frac{2.46 x}{1 + 1.46 x} \quad \text{... Ans.}$$

With the help of the above equation, equilibrium data can be generated by taking x equal to: 0, 0.1, 0.2 ... 1.0 and finding corresponding values of 'y'.

Ex. 8.9 : A liquid mixture containing 40 mole % benzene and 60 mole % toluene is subjected to flash distillation at a separator pressure of 101.325 kPa to vaporise 50 mole % of feed. What will be the equilibrium composition of vapour and liquid?

Data :

x	0	0.05	0.1	0.2	0.3	0.4	0.5	0.6	0.7	0.8	0.9	1.0
y	0.	0.13	0.21	0.375	0.5	0.6	0.7	0.77	0.83	0.9	0.95	1.0

Solution :

Basis : Feed containing 40 mole % benzene

$$x_F = \text{mole fraction of benzene in feed}$$
$$= \text{mole \% benzene} / 100$$

$$x_F = \frac{40}{100} = 0.4$$

50 mole % of the feed is vaporised

f = molal fraction of feed that is vaporised

$$= \frac{50}{100} = 0.5$$

Slope of operating line for flash distillation $= -\frac{(1-f)}{f}$

$$\text{Slope} = \frac{-(1-0.5)}{0.5} = -1.0$$

Draw the equilibrium diagram with the help of data given.

The point of intersection of the operating line and the diagonal is (x_F, x_F) i.e. (0.4, 0.4).

Mark the point (0.4, 0.4) on the diagonal and draw the operating line through it with slope equal to -1.0 ($\theta = -45°$) which will cut the equilibrium curve at point say P. Through 'P' read the equilibrium liquid phase and vapour phase compositions from x-axis and y-axis respectively.

Answer : From graph – [Refer to Fig. 8.39]

Equilibrium : Liquid phase composition = 0.3 mole fraction of benzene

Equilibrium : Vapour phase composition = 0.5 mole fraction of benzene

Ex. 8.10 : For the system and data given in Ex. 8.9, find the temperature in the separator for an equilibrium stage.

Temperature - composition (liquid) data :

T, °C	80	82.9	85	87	90.5	93.3	96.1	99	101.6	104.5	107.2	110	110.1
T, K	353	355.9	358	360	363.5	366.3	369.1	372	374.6	377.5	380.2	383	383.1
x	1.0	0.9	0.77	0.66	0.55	0.46	0.37	0.29	0.21	0.14	0.075	0.013	0

Refer to Fig. 8.39.

Fig. 8.39 : (Examples 8.9 and 8.10)

Construct a plot of temperature (bubble point) v/s liquid phase composition, equilibrium diagram and draw the operating line through the point (0.4, 0.4) on the diagonal with slope equal to minus one which will cut the equilibrium curve at point 'P'. Through point 'P', draw a vertical to cut the bubble point curve at point Q and then read the corresponding temperature on y-axis.

Temperature in separator (from graph) = 371 K (98 °C)   ... **Ans.**

Ex. 8.11 : A liquid mixture containing 40 mole % methanol and 60 mole % water is fed to the differential distillation at atmospheric pressure with 60 mole % of the liquid is distilled. Find the composition of the composited distillate and the residue.

Equilibrium data :

x	0.05	0.1	0.2	0.3	0.4	0.5
y	0.27	0.42	0.57	0.66	0.73	0.78

Solution :

Basis : 100 kmol of feed

Let F, D, W be the kmol of feed, distillate and residue respectively.

Given : 60 mole % of feed is distilled

∴ $\quad$ D = 60 kmol

We know $\quad$ F = D + W

$\quad$ 100 = 60 + W

∴ $\quad$ W = 40 kmol

$\quad$ x_F = mole fraction of methanol in feed

$\quad$ $x_F = \dfrac{40}{100} = 0.4$

x_W = mole fraction of methanol in residue left in still

Rayleigh equation is :

$$\ln\left(\frac{F}{W}\right) = \int_{x_W}^{x_F} \frac{dx}{y-x}$$

R.H.S. of this equation is evaluated graphically by plotting graph of $1/y-x$ v/s x and measuring the area under the curve between the limits $x = x_F$ and $x = x_W$.

L.H.S. of equation $= \ln\left(\frac{F}{W}\right) = \ln\left(\frac{100}{40}\right) = 0.916$

Plot $1/(y - x)$ v/s x and measure the area under the curve from $x_F = 0.50$ till the area equals 0.916 and the corresponding value of x represents x_W (composition of residue).

x	0.05	0.1	0.2	0.3	0.4	0.5
y	0.27	0.42	0.57	0.66	0.73	0.78
1/y – x	4.54	3.12	2.7	2.8	3.0	3.6

From Fig. 8.40, x_W = 0.075 mole fraction of methanol in residue.   ... **Ans.**

y_{Davg} – composited distillate composition.

Methanol material balance :

$$x_F \cdot F = y_{D,\,avg.} \cdot D + x_W \cdot W$$

$$0.40 \times 100 = y_{D,\,avg.} (60) + 0.075 \times 40$$

$$y_{D,\,avg.} = 0.62 \qquad \text{... \textbf{Ans.}}$$

Scale : Refer Fig. 8.40.

x-axis : 20 mm = 0.1 units
y-axis : 20 mm = 1.0 units

$$\ln\frac{F}{W} = \int_{x_F}^{x_W} \frac{dx}{y-x}$$

0.916 = Area (x-axis scale) (y-axis scale)

0.96 = Area $\left(\frac{0.1}{2}\right)\left(\frac{1}{2}\right)$

Area = 36.64 cm²

Measure the area under the curve from

x_F = 0.4 till we get : area = 36.64 cm²

and read x_W on x-axis.

∴ From Fig. 8.40 x_W = 0.075 mole fraction of methanol in residue.
x_W = 0.075   ... **Ans.**

Fig. 8.40

Ex. 8.12 : 100 kmol/h of a feed containing 35 mole % methanol is to be continuously distilled in fractionating column to get 96.5 mole % methanol as a distillate and 10 mole % methanol as a bottom product. Find the molal flow rates of distillate and bottoms.

Solution :

Basis : 100 kmol/h of feed to distillation column

x_F = mole fraction of methanol in feed

$= \dfrac{36}{100} = 0.36$

x_D = mole fraction of methanol in distillate

$= \dfrac{96.5}{100} = 0.965$

x_W = mole fraction of methanol in bottoms

$= \dfrac{10}{100} = 0.1$

Let F, D and W be the molal flow rates, in kmol/h, of feed, distillate and bottom product.

Overall material balance :

F = D + W

Material balance of methanol :

$x_F \cdot F = x_D \cdot D + x_W \cdot W$

Putting the values of F, x_D, x_W, and x_F in above equations

100 = D + W

$$D = 100 - W$$
$$\therefore \quad 0.36 \times 100 = 0.965\,D + 0.1\,W$$
$$36 = 0.965\,(100 - W) + 0.1\,W$$
$$\therefore \quad W = 69.95 \text{ kmol/h}$$
and $\quad D = 30.05 \text{ kmol/h}$ ... **Ans.**

Ex. 8.13 : A feed containing 40 mole % benzene and 60 mole % toluene is to be distilled in a fractionating column to get top product (distillate) containing 90 mole % benzene and bottoms containing not more than 10 mole % benzene. The reflux ratio of 3 kmol per kmol of product is used. Assuming feed to be a liquid at its bubble point (saturated liquid), find the number of theoretical plates required and the position of the feed plate by Lewis-Sorel method.

Equilibrium data :

x	0	0.05	0.1	0.2	0.3	0.4	0.5	0.6	0.7	0.8	0.9	1
y	0	0.13	0.21	0.375	0.5	0.6	0.7	0.77	0.83	0.9	0.95	1

Solution : Basis : 100 kmol of feed to column

$$F = D + W \text{ (overall material balance)}$$
$$F = 100 = D + W \quad \ldots (A)$$

Mole fraction of benzene in feed $= \dfrac{\text{mole \% benzene in feed}}{100}$

$$x_F = 0.4$$
$$x_D = 0.9 \text{ and } x_W = 0.1$$

Material balance of benzene :
$$x_F \cdot F = x_D \cdot D + x_W \cdot W$$
$$0.4 \times 100 = 0.9\,D + 0.1\,W$$
$$40 = 0.9\,D + 0.1\,W$$

From equation (A), $\quad D = 100 - W$

$$\therefore \quad 40 = 0.9\,(100 - W) + 0.1\,W$$

Solving, we get $\quad W = 62.5 \text{ kmol}$
and $\quad D = 37.5 \text{ kmol}$

$$R = \text{Reflux ratio} = 3 = \frac{L}{D}$$

but $L \quad = L_n$

$\therefore \quad L_n = 3\,D$
$$L_n = 3\,(37.5)$$
$$= 112.5 \text{ kmol}$$

$L_n + D = 112.5 + 37.5 = 150$ kmol

The rectifying section operating line is :

$$x_{n+1} = \frac{L_n}{L_n + D} x_n + \frac{D \cdot x_D}{L_n + D}$$

$\therefore \quad y_{n+1} = \frac{112.5 \, x_n}{150} + \frac{37.5 \times 0.9}{150}$ ... (B)

$y_{n+1} = 0.75 \, x_n + 0.225$

As feed is a liquid at its bubble point :

$L_m = L_n + F$

$= 112.5 + 100 = 212.5$ kmol

and $\quad L_m - W = 212.5 - 62.5 = 150$ kmol

The operating line of stripping section is :

$$y_{m+1} = \frac{L_m}{L_m - W} x_m - \frac{W}{L_m - W} x_W$$

$y_{m+1} = \frac{212.5}{150} x_m - \frac{62.5}{150} \times 0.1$

$y_{m+1} = 1.415 \, x_m - 0.042$ ... (C)

Distillate composition = $x_D = 0.9$

$\therefore \quad y_n = x_D = 0.9$

Corresponding x_n value from the equilibrium diagram Fig. 8.41 is 0.79

$y_{n+1} = 0.75 \, x_n + 0.225$

$= 0.75 \times 0.79 + 0.225$

$= 0.818$

Obtain the value of x_{n+1} from the equilibrium diagram corresponding to y_{n+1}

$x_{n+1} = 0.644$

$y_{n+2} = 0.75 \, x_{n+1} + 0.225$

$y_{n+2} = 0.75 \times 0.644 + 0.225 = 0.708$

x_{n+2} from the equilibrium diagram corresponding to y_{n+2} is 0.492

$y_{n+3} = 0.75 \times 0.492 + 0.225 = 0.594$

x_{n+3} from the equilibrium diagram corresponding to y_{n+3} is 0.382

x_{n+3} is near to x_F, so that feed should be introduced on plate n + 3 from top (4th plate).

For the stripping section, operating line is :

$y_{m+1} = 1.415 \, x_m - 0.042$

Writing n for m for convenience

$$y_{n+4} = 1.415\, x_{n+3} - 0.042$$
$$y_{n+4} = 1.415 \times 0.382 - 0.042$$
$$= 0.498$$

x_{n+4} from the equilibrium diagram corresponding to y_{n+4} is 0.298

$$y_{n+5} = 1.415 \times 0.298 - 0.042 = 0.379$$

Fig. 8.41 : Equilibrium diagram for benzene - toluene system

x_{n+5} from the equilibrium diagram is 0.208

$$y_{n+6} = 1.4165 \times 0.208 - 0.042 = 0.252$$

x_{n+6} from the equilibrium diagram is equal to 0.120

$$y_{n+7} = 1.415 \times 0.120 - 0.042 = 0.127$$

x_{n+7} from the equilibrium diagram is equal to 0.048.

[As $x_{n+6} = 0.12$ greater than $x_W = 0.1$, one more step is incorporated so that the liquid phase composition obtained at any case should not be more than x_W.]

Hence, there will be 7 plates in the column. ... **Ans.**

Ex. 8.14 : A mixture of benzene and toluene containing 60 mole % benzene is to be separated to give a product of 95 mole % benzene and bottom product containing 10 mole % benzene. The feed enters a column at its bubble point. It is proposed to operate the column with reflux ratio of 2.5. It is required to find the number of theoretical plates needed and position of feed plate. The vapour-liquid equilibrium data are given as below :

x	0	0.05	0.1	0.2	0.3	0.4	0.5	0.6	0.7	0.8	0.9	1.0
y	0	0.13	0.21	0.375	0.5	0.6	0.7	0.77	0.83	0.9	0.95	1.0

Solution : Basis : Feed containing 60 mole % benzene

x_F = mole fraction of benzene in feed

= mole % benzene / 100

= $\dfrac{60}{100}$ = 0.60

x_D = mole fraction of benzene in top product

= $\dfrac{95}{100}$ = 0.95

x_W = mole fraction of benzene in bottom product

= $\dfrac{10}{100}$ = 0.1

McCabe-Thiele method is adopted.

The operating line of the rectification section is having slope of R/R + 1, and intercept on y-axis equal to x_D/R + 1. The point of intersection of the operating line of the rectification section and the diagonal is – (x_D, x_D).

Slope of operating line = R/R + 1

where R = Reflux ratio = 2.5

∴ Slope = $\dfrac{2.5}{2.5 + 1}$ = 0.714

Intercept = $\dfrac{x_D}{R + 1}$

= $\dfrac{0.95}{(2.5 + 1)}$ = 0.271

With the help of given vapour-liquid equilibrium data, plot the equilibrium diagram.

Point of intersection of this operating line with diagonal

= (0.95, 0.95)

Draw the operating line of the rectification section through the point (0.95, 0.95) on the diagonal and with intercept on y-axis equal to 0.271.

As the liquid is at its bubble point, the feed line is parallel to y-axis through the point on the diagonal – (x_F, x_F).

Draw the feed line through the point (0.6, 0.6) on the diagonal and parallel to y-axis.

(For feed at its bubble point, q = 1, thus slope of feed line is infinity.)

Fig. 8.42 : Equilibrium diagram

The point of intersection of the operating line of stripping section with the diagonal is (x_W, x_W) and it also passes through the intersection of the operating line of the rectification section and feed line.

So draw the operating line of the stripping section through the point (0.1, 0.1) on the diagonal which will pass through the intersection of the feed line with the operating line of the rectification section.

Construct the stages step by step and count them. Refer to Fig. 8.42.

Number of ideal stages including reboiler (from graph) = n = 10

Number of ideal/theoretical stages required in column

$$= n - 1$$
$$= 10 - 1 = 9 \quad \text{... Ans.}$$

The point of intersection of the operating lines of the stripping and rectification section lies in a triangle which represents the feed plate.

Position of the feed plate (from graph) = 5th from top   ... **Ans.**

Ex. 8.15 : A mixture of benzene and toluene containing 40 per cent benzene and 60 per cent toluene is to be separated in a fractionating column to give a product (distillate) containing 96 per cent benzene and a bottom product containing 95 per cent toluene. Feed is a mixture of two third vapour and one third liquid. Find out the number of theoretical stages required if reflux ratio of 1.5 times the minimum is used and if relative volatility is 2.5.

Solution : Basis : Feed containing 40% benzene and 60% toluene (by wt.)

Molecular weight of benzene = 78

Molecular weight of toluene = 92

$$x_F = \text{mole fraction of benzene in feed}$$

$$= \frac{\frac{40}{78}}{\frac{40}{78} + \frac{60}{92}} \quad \begin{pmatrix} \text{in 100 kg mixture, benzene is 40 kg} \\ \text{and toluene is 60 kg} \end{pmatrix}$$

= 0.44

Similarly,

x_D = mole fraction of benzene in distillate

$$= \frac{\frac{96}{78}}{\frac{96}{78} + \frac{4}{92}} = 0.966$$

x_W = mole fraction of benzene in bottoms

$$= \frac{\frac{5}{78}}{\frac{5}{78} + \frac{95}{92}} = 0.058$$

Relative volatility = α = 2.5

With the help of relative volatility, generate x–y data and plot the equilibrium diagram.

For generating x-y data assume,

x = 0, 0.1, 0.2 … 1 and find corresponding values of y from relation :

$$y = \frac{\alpha x}{1 + (\alpha - 1) x}$$

x = 0

$$y = \frac{2.5 (0)}{1 + (2.5 - 1) 0} = 0$$

x = 0.1

$$y = \frac{2.5 \times 0.1}{1 + (2.5 - 1) 0.1} = 0.22$$

Similarly, evaluate other values of y for remaining values of x.

x	0	0.1	0.2	0.3	0.4	0.5	0.6	0.7	0.8	0.9	1.0
y	0	0.22	0.385	0.52	0.625	0.714	0.79	0.85	0.91	0.96	1.0

Procedure for finding out minimum reflux ratio :

q = fraction of the feed that is liquid

Feed is 2/3rd vapour and 1/3rd liquid

$$q = \frac{1}{3} = 0.333$$

or $\quad$ q = 1 – f, where f - fraction of feed that is vaporised

$$q = 1 - \frac{2}{3} = 1 - 0.667 = 0.333$$

$$\text{Slope of feed line} = -\left(\frac{q}{1-q}\right)$$

$$= \frac{(-0.333)}{(1-0.333)} = -0.5$$

$$\text{Slope} = \tan\theta = -0.5$$

$$\theta = -26.56°$$

$$\text{Intercept on y-axis} = \frac{x_F}{1-q}$$

$$= \frac{0.44}{(1-0.333)}$$

$$= 0.66$$

Draw the feed line through the point (0.44, 0.44) on the diagonal with slope equal to -0.5 (with angle equal to $-26.56°$) or with intercept equal to 0.66 which will cut the equilibrium curve at point 'P'. Through the point A (0.966, 0.966) on the diagonal, draw the operating line A – P of the rectification section (dotted line) and read y' and x' on y-axis and x-axis respectively. [Which represents condition for minimum reflux].

$$\text{Minimum reflux ratio} = R_m = \frac{x_D - y'}{y' - x'}$$

from graph, $y' = 0.515$, $x' = 0.3$

$$R_m = \frac{0.966 - 0.515}{0.515 - 0.3} = 2.1$$

$$\text{Operating reflux ratio} = R = 1.5\, R_m$$

$$= 1.5 \times 2.1 = 3.14$$

Operating line of rectification section :

Point A (0.966, 0.966) on the diagonal.

Intercept of rectifying section operating line is :

$$= \frac{x_D}{R+1}$$

$$= \frac{0.966}{3.14 + 1} = 0.232$$

Draw the operating line of rectifying section on the x-y diagram through point A (0.966, 0.966) with intercept on y-axis equal to 0.232. Draw operating line of stripping section with the point (0.0581, 0.058) on the diagonal passing through the point 'Q'.

Do step by step construction between equilibrium curve and operating lines from point A upto point B and count the number of stages.

From graph (Fig. 8.43) :

Number of theoretical stages required including reboiler = n = 10

Number of theoretical stages required in column = n − 1 = 10 − 1 = 9 ... **Ans.**

Fig. 8.43 : Equilibrium Diagram (Ex. 8.15)

Ex. 8.16 : A methanol (A) − water (B) solution containing 50 % by weight methanol at 300 K (27° C) is to be continuously rectified at 101.325 kPa at a rate of 5000 kg/h to provide a distillate containing 95 % methanol and a residue containing 1.0 % methanol (by weight). Calculate the flow rates of distillate and residue on (i) weight basis and (ii) mole basis.

Solution : Basis : (i) 5000 kg/h of methanol-water solution.

Let x_F', x_D' and x_W' be the weight fractions of methanol in feed, distillate and residue respectively. Let F', D' and W' be the kg/h of feed, distillate and residue respectively.

Overall material balance :

$$F' = D' + W'$$
$$5000 = D' + W' \quad \therefore \quad W' = 5000 - D'$$

Material balance of methanol :

$$x_F' \, F' = x_D' \, D' + x_W' \, W'$$
$$0.5 \times 5000 = 0.95 \, D' + 0.01 \, W'$$
$$2500 = 0.95 \, D' + 0.01 \, (5000 - D')$$

$$D' = 2606 \text{ kg/h}$$
$$W' = 5000 - D' = 5000 - 2606 = 2394 \text{ kg/h}$$

Flow rate of distillate on weight basis = 2600 kg/h
Flow rate of residue on weight basis = 2394 kg/h ... **Ans. (i)**

(ii) Distillate contain 95 % by wt. methanol.

∴ $M_{avg.}$ of distillate $= 0.95 \times 32 + 0.05 \times 18 = 31.3$ kg/kmol

Residue contain 1% by wt. methanol.

∴ $M_{avg.}$ of residue $= 0.01 \times 32 + 0.99 \times 18 = 18.14$ kg/kmol

Flow rate of distillate on mole basis $= \dfrac{2606}{31.3} = 83.26$ kmol/h

Flow rate of residue on mole basis $= \dfrac{2394}{18.14} = 131.97$ kmol/h ... **Ans. (ii)**

Ex. 8.17 : A feed containing 50 mole % hexane and 50 mole % octane is fed to a pipe still through a pressure reducing valve and then into a flash disengaging chamber. The vapour and liquid leaving the chamber are assumed to be in equilibrium. If the fraction of the feed converted to vapour is 0.5, find the composition of the top and bottom products. Equilibrium data for system is given below.

Mole fraction of hexane in liquid (x)	1	0.69	0.4	0.192	0.045	0
Mole fraction of hexane in vapour (y)	1	0.932	0.78	0.538	0.1775	0

Solution : Basis : 1 mol of feed.

Material balance line for flash distillation is –

$$y = -\dfrac{1-f}{f} x + \dfrac{1}{f} x_F$$

$$x_F = \dfrac{50}{100} = 0.5$$

f = fraction of feed converted to vapour = 0.5

$$y = -\dfrac{(1-0.5)}{0.5} x + \dfrac{0.5}{0.5}$$

$$y = (-1) x + 1$$

Material balance line has a slope of – 1 and passes through the point $x = y = x_F = 0.5$ on the diagonal.

Draw the equilibrium diagram and diagonal. Draw the material balance line with point (0.5, 0.5) on the diagonal and slope equal to – 1. This line cuts the equilibrium curve at point say P. Through P, draw a horizontal line (dotted) to cut y-axis to get the vapour composition y_D. Through P, drop a vertical (dotted) on x-axis to get the equilibrium liquid phase composition x_W. [Point P represents the equilibrium vapour and liquid phase composition].

Composition of vapour and liquid from flash chamber or drum :

Composition of top product (vapour) = $0.69 \times 100 = 69$ mole % hexane.

Composition of bottom product (liquid) = 0.31 × 100 = 31 mole % hexane.

Fig. 8.44

Ex. 8.18 : A feed of 60 mole % hexane and 40 mole % octane is fed to a pipe still through a pressure reducing valve into a flash disengaging chamber. The vapour and liquid leaving the chamber are assumed to be in equilibrium. If 50 mole % of feed is vaporised, find the composition of the top and bottom products. Equilibrium data is given below :

x, mole fraction of hexane in liquid	1.0	0.69	0.40	0.192	0.045	0
y, mole fraction of hexane in vapour	1.0	0.932	0.78	0.538	0.1775	0

Solution : Basis : 1 kmol of feed.

$$x_F = \text{mole fraction of n-hexane in feed} = \frac{60}{100} = 0.60$$

Feed is 50 mole % vaporised

∴ $$f = \frac{50}{100} = 0.5$$

f-fraction of feed converted to vapour $= \frac{0.5}{1} = 0.5$

Operating line for flash distillation –

$$y = \frac{-(1-f)}{f} x + \frac{x_F}{f}$$

$$\text{slope} = -(1-f)/f$$
$$= -(1.0 - 0.5)/0.5 = -1$$

The point of intersection of the operating line with the diagonal is (0.6, 0.6).

Draw the equilibrium diagram and draw the operating line with slope equal to – 1 passing through (0.6, 0.6) on the diagonal. It intersects the equilibrium curve at P which gives us the equilibrium liquid and vapour compositions as 0.41 and 0.79 molefraction hexane respectively.

Fig. 8.45

Composition of top product = 79 mole % hexane i.e. vapour (y_D)

Composition of bottom product = 41 mole % hexane i.e. liquid (x_W).

Ex. 8.19 : 100 kmol of a mixture containing 50 mole % n-heptane (more volatile) and 50 mole % n-octane is subjected to a differential distillation at atmospheric pressure; with 60 mole % of liquid distilled. Compute the composition of the composited distillate and the residue using Rayleigh equation.

Equilibrium data :

x	0.5	0.46	0.42	0.38	0.34	0.32
y	0.689	0.648	0.608	0.567	0.523	0.497

Solution : Basis : 100 kmol of feed

$$F = 100 \text{ kmol}$$
$$D = 0.60 \times 100 = 60 \text{ kmol}$$
∴
$$W = 100 - 60 = 40 \text{ kmol}$$
$$x_F = \frac{50}{100} = 0.50$$

Rayleigh equation is :

$$\ln F/W = \int_{x_W}^{x_F} \frac{dx}{y-x}$$

L.H.S. = ln F/W = ln (100/40) = 0.916 R.H.S. of this equation is evaluated graphically by plotting 1/(y – x) v/s x and measuring the area under the curve between limits : x = x_F and x = x_W.

x	0.5	0.46	0.42	0.38	0.34	0.32
y	0.689	0.648	0.608	0.567	0.523	0.497
1/(y – x)	5.3	5.32	5.32	5.35	5.465	5.65

Fig. 8.46

$$0.916 = \text{Area} \times \text{Scale x-axis} \times \text{Scale y-axis}$$

$$0.916 = \text{Area} \times \frac{0.1}{2} \times \frac{1}{1}$$

$$\text{Area} = 18.32 \text{ cm}^2$$

Measure the area under the curve from x_F = 0.5 till area equals 18.32 cm² and read corresponding value of x_W from x-axis.

From graph, x_W = 0.325

Overall material balance

$$x_F F = D y_{Davg} + W x_W$$
$$0.5 (100) = 60 \, y_{Davg} + 40 \times 0.325$$
$$y_{Davg.} = 0.6167$$

Bottom product / Residue composition = 0.325 mole fraction of n-heptane
Composited distillate composition = 0.6167 mole fraction of h-heptane.

Ex. 8.20 : A fractionating column is designed to separate 15000 kg/h of a feed containing 60% toluene and 40% benzene into overhead product containing 97% benzene and a waste containing 98% toluene. All % are by weight. Calculate the weight of product and waste product per hour.

Solution : Basis : 15000 kg/h of feed to distillation column. Feed contains 40% by benzene.

$F' = 15000$ kg/h
$D' = $ product, kg/h
$W' = $ waste product, kg/h
$x'_F = $ wt. fraction of benzene in feed $= \dfrac{40}{100} = 0.40$
$x'_D = $ wt. fraction of benzene in product $= \dfrac{97}{100} = 0.97$
$x'_W = $ wt. fraction of benzene in waste product $= \dfrac{2}{100} = 0.02$

Overall material balance :

$$F' = W' + D'$$
$$30{,}000 = W' + D'$$
$$W' = 15000 - D'$$

Material balance of benzene :

$$x'_F F = x'_D D' + x'_W W'$$
$$0.4\,(15000) = 0.97\,D' + 0.02\,W'$$
$$6000 = 0.97\,D' + 0.02\,(15000 - D')$$

∴ $D' = 6000$
$W' = 15000 - 6000 = 9000$ kg/h

Distillate/Product flow rate $= 6000$ kg/h
Bottom/Waste product flow rate $= 9000$ kg/h ... **Ans.**

Ex. 8.21 : A liquid mixture has a relative volatility of 2.5. Compute the vapour-liquid equilibria for the liquid mixture.

The above mentioned liquid mixture is fed to a distillation column for separation purpose. Feed is a liquid at its bubble point with 50 mole % of more volatile component. The product/distillate is to contain 95 mole % of more volatile component and residue is to contain 10 mole % of more volatile component. Reflux ratio used is 2.5. Calculate the number of ideal plates required and position of feed plate.

Solution : Relative Volatility $= \alpha = 2.5$

$$y = \dfrac{\alpha x}{1 + (\alpha - 1)\,x}$$

Take
$$y = \frac{2.5 x}{1 + (2.5 - 1) x} = \frac{2.5 x}{1 + 1.5 x}$$

$x = 0$ ∴ $y = 0$

$x = 0.10$

$$y = \frac{2.5 \times 0.1}{1 + 1.5 \times 0.1} = 0.217$$

Take $x = 0.2, 0.3, 0.4, \ldots 1$ and evaluate values of y,

x	0	0.1	0.2	0.3	0.4	0.5	0.6	0.7	0.8	0.9	1
y	0	0.217	0.385	0.52	0.62	0.714	0.79	0.85	0.91	0.96	1

x_F = mole fraction of more volatile = 50/100 = 0.50
component in feed

$$x_D = \frac{95}{100} = 0.95$$

$$x_W = \frac{10}{100} = 0.10$$

Draw the equilibrium diagram. Draw the operating lines. The operating line of the rectification section has a point (x_D, x_D) on the diagonal.

$$\text{Intercept of operating line of rectification section} = \frac{x_D}{R + 1}$$

$$= \frac{0.95}{2.5 + 1} = 0.2714$$

The point of intersection of the feed line with the diagonal is (x_F, x_F) i.e. (0.5, 0.5) and the line is parallel to y-axis through it.

Point of intersection of the operating line for the stripping section with the diagonal is (x_W, x_W) i.e. (0.1, 0.1). First draw the operating line of the rectifying section through the point (0.95, 0.95) on the diagonal and with intercept on y-axis equal to 0.2714, then draw the feed line through the point (0.5, 0.5) on the diagonal and parallel to y-axis. Then draw the operating line of stripping section through the point (0.1, 0.1) on the diagonal and passing through the intersection of line for rectification section and feed line. Construct the triangles representing ideal plates between operating lines and equilibrium curve starting from (0.95, 0.95) till we reach or cover point (0.1, 0.1). Count number of ideal plates.

Fig. 8.47

Number of ideal plates including reboiler = n = 8

Number of ideal plates in column = n − 1 = 7.

Position of feed plate = 5th from top.

Ex. 8.22 : A rectification column is fed with 100 kmol/h of a mixture containing 50 mole % hexane and 50 mole % octane at 101.325 kPa absolute pressure. The feed is at its boiling point. The distillate is to contain 90 mole % hexane and the bottoms 10 mole % hexane. The reflux ratio is 3 : 1. Calculate the kmol/h distillate and kmol/h bottoms, and the number of theoretical trays needed for this separation. The equilibrium data for this system is given below.

Mole fraction of hexane in liquid, x	1.0	0.69	0.4	0.192	0.045	0
Mole fraction of hexane in vapour, y	1.0	0.932	0.78	0.538	0.1775	0

Solution : Basis : 100 kmol/h of feed mixture

$$F = 100 \text{ kmol/h}$$
$$x_F = 0.5 \text{ mole fraction of hexane in feed}$$
$$x_D = 0.90$$
$$x_W = 0.10$$

Overall material balance :

$$F = D + W$$

Material balance of hexane :

$$x_F F = x_D D + x_W W$$
$$0.5 \times 100 = 0.9 D + 0.1 W$$
$$100 = D + W$$
$$W = 100 - D$$
$$50 = 0.9 D + 0.1 (100 - D)$$
$$D = 50 \text{ kmol/h}$$

∴ $\quad W = 100 - 50 = 50 \text{ kmol/h}$

Distillate = 50 kmol/h
Bottom product = 50 kmol/h

Construct the equilibrium diagram

x_F = 0.5 mole fraction of hexane.

As feed is at its bubble point, feed line is parallel to y-axis through (0.5, 0.5) on the diagonal.

x_D = 0.90

$$\text{Intercept of rectification line on y-axis} = \frac{x_D}{R+1}$$

$$= \frac{0.9}{3+1} = 0.225$$

The operating line of the rectification section has the point (x_D, x_D) i.e. (0.9, 0.9) on the diagonal.

We have x_W = 0.1

The operating line of the stripping section has point (0.1, 0.1) on the diagonal and passes through the point of intersection of feed line and operating line for the rectification section.

Locate the lines on the equilibrium diagram and construct triangles representing plates between operating lines and equilibrium curve starting from (0.9, 0.9) till we cover point (0.1, 0.1).

Fig. 8.48

Number of theoretical plate including reboiler = 4

Theoretical plates in column = 4 − 1 = 3

Feed plate – 2nd from top

Ex. 8.23 : 100 kmol/h of a feed containing 40 mole % hexane and 60 mole % octane is to be distilled in a column consisting of a still pot, plate and condenser. The feed is a liquid at its boiling point and is fed into the reboiler from which a residue is continuously withdrawn and the ratio of liquid reflux flow to distillate flow is 2. The distillate contains 80 mole % hexane.

(i) Using the McCabe – Thiele procedure, calculate the bottom composition and moles of distillate per hour.

Equilibrium data :

| y (mole fraction of hexane) | 1.0 | 0.69 | 0.40 | 0.192 | 0.045 | 0 |
| y (mole fraction of hexane) | 1.0 | 0.932 | 0.78 | 0.538 | 0.1775 | 0 |

Solution : Basis : 100 kmol/h of feed containing 40 mole % hexane.

Plot : x-y diagram, draw : diagonal x = y.

The rectification section operating line is :

$$y = \frac{R}{R+1} x + \frac{x_D}{R+1}$$

x_D = composition of distillate

= mole fraction of hexane in distillate = 0.80

Reflux ratio = R = 2 (given)

Slope of operating line = $\frac{R}{R+1} = \frac{2}{2+1} = \frac{2}{3} = 0.67$

Intercept of operating line = $\frac{x_D}{R+1} = \frac{0.8}{3} = 0.267$

The point of intersection of the operating line with the diagonal is (x_D, y_D) i.e. (0.8, 0.8). Locate the point (0.8, 0.8) on the diagonal and draw the operating line through it with slope equal to 0.67 or intercept on y-axis 0.267.

Step off the theoretical stages and read the bottom composition. Theoretical stages including reboiler = 3.

Bottom product composition = x_W = 0.135 ... **Ans.**

Overall material balance :

$$F = D + W$$
$$W = F - D = 100 - D$$

Material balance for hexane :

$$x_F \cdot F = D \cdot x_D + W x_W$$
$$0.4 (100) = 0.8 D + 0.135 (100 - D)$$

Fig. 8.49

∴   D = 39.85 kmol/h

Distillate flow rate = 39.85 kmol/h   ... **Ans.**

Ex. 8.24 : A liquid mixture containing 40 mole % n-heptane and 60 mole % n-octane is subjected to differential distillation at atmospheric pressure, with 60 mole % of the liquid distilled. Compute the composition of the composited distillate and the residue.

Data : Relative volatility for the given system is 2.16

Solution : Basis : 100 mol of feed.

$$x_F = 40/100 = 0.4$$

Distillate :   D = 0.60 × 100 = 60 mol

Residue :   W = 100 – 60 = 40 mol

Rayleighs equation

$$\ln \frac{F}{W} = \int_{x_W}^{x_F} \frac{dx}{y - x}$$

Relative volatility = α = 2.16

$$y = \frac{\alpha x}{1 + \alpha(1 - x)}$$

Generate the equilibrium data taking x = 0, 0.1, ... 0.9, 1.0.

x	0.1	0.2	0.25	0.3	0.35	0.4	0.45
y	0.194	0.35	0.42	0.48	0.54	0.59	0.64

Calculate y–x, 1/(y – x) and tabulate.

y–x	0.094	0.15	0.17	0.18	0.19	0.19	0.19
1/(y – x)	10.63	6.66	5.88	5.56	5.26	5.26	5.26

Data is generated upto x = 0.45 as x_F = 0.40

$$\ln \frac{100}{40} = 0.916 = \int_{x_W}^{0.4} \frac{dx}{y-x}$$

Plot a graph of 1/(y – x) v/s x. The value of integral on RHS between x = x_F = 0.4 and x = x_W is 0.916. So measure the area under the curve from x = x_F = 0.4 till we get area = 9.16 cm² and read the value of x_W.

$$0.916 = \text{Area} \times \text{Scale x-axis} \times \text{Scale y-axis}$$

Fig. 8.50

From Fig. 8.50 : x_W = 0.22

Material balance for n-heptane :

$$F\, x_F = W\, x_W + D\, y_{Davg.}$$
$$100 \times 0.40 = 40 \times 0.22 + 60\, y_{Davg.}$$
$$y_{Davg.} = \frac{40 - 8.8}{60}$$
$$= 3.12/60 = 0.52$$

Therefore, composition of composited distillate = 0.52 mole fraction of heptane.
Composition of residue = 0.22 mole fraction of heptane. ... **Ans.**

Ex. 8.25 : A mixture of benzene and toluene containing 40 mole % benzene is to be separated to give a product of 90 mole % of benzene at a top and a bottom product with not more than 10 mole % benzene. Using an average value of 2.4 for the volatility of benzene relative to toluene, calculate the number of theoretical plates required at total reflux.

Also calculate the minimum reflux ratio, if the feed is liquid at its bubble point.

Solution :

Relative volatility $= \alpha = 2.4$

$$y = \frac{\alpha x}{1 + (\alpha - 1) x} = \frac{2.4 x}{1 + 1.4 x}$$

For x = 0, 0.1, 0.2 ... 1.0 obtain corresponding values of y and plot the equilibrium diagram.

x	0	0.1	0.2	0.3	0.4	0.5	0.6	0.7	0.8	0.9	1.0
y	0	0.21	0.375	0.507	0.615	0.706	0.783	0.850	0.906	0.95	1.0

Fig. 8.51

$$x_F = \frac{40}{100} = 0.40$$

$$x_D = \frac{90}{100} = 0.90$$

$$x_W = \frac{10}{100} = 0.10$$

At total reflux for finding plates start constructing the triangles representing stages from the point (0.9, 0.9) till we cover the point (0.1, 0.1) on the diagonal between diagonal and equilibrium curve.

Number of plates including reboiler = n = 6

Number of plates in column = n − 1 = 6 − 1 = 5

Feed is a liquid at its bubble point. So draw a feed line through the point (0.4, 0.4) on the diagonal and parallel to y-axis.

Feed line cuts the equilibrium curve at point P (x_F, y_F)

$$x_F = 0.4, \quad y_F = 0.615$$

Minimum reflux ratio = R_m

$$R_m = \frac{x_D - y_F}{y_F - x_F}$$

$$= \frac{0.90 - 0.615}{0.615 - 0.40} = 1.325 \quad \ldots \text{Ans.}$$

Ex. 8.26 : 1000 kmol/h of an ethanol–propanol mixture containing 65 mole percent ethanol is to be separated in a continuous plate column operating at 101.325 kPa total pressure. The desired terminal composition in terms of mole fraction of ethanol are –

$$x_D = 0.92 \text{ and } x_W = 0.07$$

The feed is saturated vapour and total condenser is used. When the reflux flow rate is four times the amount of top product, find the number of theoretical plates required for the separation.

Relative volatility of ethanol-propanol system may be taken as 2.10.

Solution : $\alpha = 2.10$

$$y = \frac{\alpha x}{1 + (\alpha - 1)x}$$

$$y = \frac{2.1 x}{1 + 1.1 x}$$

Take x = 0, 0.1, 0.2 ... 1.0 and find corresponding values of y.

x	0	0.1	0.2	0.3	0.4	0.5	0.6	0.7	0.8	0.9	1.0
y	0	0.19	0.34	0.47	0.58	0.67	0.76	0.83	0.89	0.95	1.0

$$x_F = \frac{65}{100} = 0.65$$

$$x_D = 0.92, \quad x_W = 0.07$$

The operating line of the rectification section has point (0.92, 0.92) on the diagonal.

Intercept of this line = $\dfrac{x_D}{R + 1}$

L = reflux fow rate = 4D

∴ $\quad$ L/D = R = 4

$$\text{Intercept} = \frac{0.92}{4+1} = 0.184$$

Draw this line on the equilibrium diagram. Feed is a saturated vapour, therefore a feed line is parallel to x-axis and the point of intersection of it with the diagonal is (0.65, 0.65). Draw the feed line.

The operating line of stripping section passes through the point of intersection of feed line and operating line of rectification section. It has the point (0.07, 0.07) on the diagonal. Draw this operating line.

Starting from the point (0.92, 0.92), construct the triangles which represent ideal plates between equilibrium diagram and operating lines till we cover the point (0.07, 0.07) on the diagonal.

Fig. 8.52

From graph,

Number of theoretical plates including reboiler = n = 9

Number of theoretical plates in column = n – 1 = 9 – 1 = 8

Location of feed plate = 4th from top. ... **Ans.**

Ex. 8.27 : A methanol-water solution contains 50% by wt. methanol. It is to be continuously rectified in a column operating at atmospheric pressure (101.325 kPa) to obtain a distillate containing 95% methanol and a residue containing 5% methanol (by weight). The feed enters the column at its bubble point. It is proposed to operate the column at a reflux ratio of 1.5. Find graphically the number of theoretical plates required to effect a given separation and the position of the feed plate.

x	0	0.05	0.1	0.2	0.3	0.4	0.5	0.6	0.7	0.8	0.9	1.0
y	0.	0.27	0.42	0.57	0.66	0.73	0.78	0.83	0.87	0.93	0.96	1.0

Solution :

Feed contains 50% methanol by wt.
Distillate contains 95% methanol by wt.
Residue contains 5% methanol by wt.
1 kg of solution contains 0.5 kg of methanol and 0.5 kg of water.

$$x_F = \text{mole fraction of methanol in feed} = \frac{0.50/32}{0.50/32 + 0.50/18}$$
$$= 0.36$$

$$x_D = \text{mole fraction of methanol in distillate} = \frac{0.95/32}{0.95/32 + 0.05/18}$$
$$= 0.914$$

$$x_W = \text{mole fraction of methanol in residue} = \frac{0.05/32}{0.05/32 + 0.95/18}$$
$$= 0.03$$

1. Construct a x-y plot.
2. Locate a feed line. As feed is at its bubble point, the feed line is parallel to y-axis and has the point ($x_F = 0.36$, $x_F = 0.36$) on the diagonal. Operating line of the rectifying section has intercept on y-axis given by :

$$\text{Intercept} = \frac{x_D}{R+1} = \frac{0.914}{1.5+1} = 0.366$$

Draw the operating line of the rectification section on the equilibrium diagram. It has the point ($x_D = 0.914$, $x_D = 0.914$) on the diagonal and has intercept on y-axis of 0.366. Draw the operating line of the stripping section through ($x_W = 0.03$, $x_W = 0.03$) on the diagonal and passing through the point of intersection of feed line and top operating line of rectification section. Construct the stages by usual method and count them.

Fig. 8.53

From graph, total plates including reboiler = n = 6

Number of plates in column = n − 1 = 6 − 1 = 5

Feed plate = 4th from top ... **Ans.**

Ex. 8.28 : A liquid mixture containing 35 mole % n-heptane and 65 mole % n-octane (average relative volatility is 2.16) is subjected to differential distillation at atmospheric pressure (101.325 kPa), with 65 mole % of the liquid distilled. Estimate the composition of the composited distillate and residue. Heptane is the more volatile component.

Solution : Basis : 100 kmol of feed.

Given : 65% of feed distilled.

$\therefore$ $\quad$ D = 0.65 × 100 = 65 kmol

$\quad$ F = D + W

$\therefore$ $\quad$ W = 100 − 65 = 35 kmol

$\quad$ x_F = mole fraction of heptane in feed = 0.35

$\quad$ x_W = mole fraction of heptane in residue

$\quad$ $y_{D, avg.}$ = mole fraction of heptane in distillate

$$\ln\left(\frac{F}{W}\right) = \int_{x_W}^{x_F} \frac{dx}{y - x}$$

$$\text{LHS} = \ln\left(\frac{F}{W}\right) = \ln\left(\frac{100}{35}\right) = 1.05$$

Generate : x-y data with the help of α = 2.16

$$y = \frac{\alpha x}{1 + (\alpha - 1) x} = \frac{2.16\, x}{1 + (2.16 - 1) x} = \frac{2.16\, x}{1 + 1.16\, x}$$

As x_F = 0.35, generate data upto x = 0.5.

Take x = 0.05, 0.10, 0.2 ... 0.5 and evaluate corresponding values of y.

RHS of the Rayleigh equation is to be evaluated graphically by plotting $1/(y-x)$ against x.

x	0.05	0.10	0.20	0.30	0.40	0.50
y	0.10	0.190	0.35	0.48	0.59	0.68
$1/(y-x)$	20	11.11	6.67	5.55	5.26	5.55

$$\ln\left(\frac{F}{W}\right) = \int_{x_W}^{x_F} \frac{dx}{(y-x)}$$

1.05 = Area × (x-axis scale) × (y-axis scale)

= Area × $\left(\frac{0.1 \text{ units}}{2 \text{ cm}^2}\right)\left(\frac{2 \text{ units}}{1 \text{ cm}^2}\right)$

Area = 10.5 cm²

So measure the area under the curve from $x_F = 0.35$ till we get the area = 10.5 cm² and then read x_W on the x-axis.

∴ From graph, $x_W = 0.18$

Fig. 8.54

Material balance of heptane :

$$x_F \cdot F = x_W W + y_{D, avg.} D$$
$$0.35 \times 100 = 0.18 \times 35 + y_{D, avg.} \times 65$$
$$y_{Davg.} = 0.44$$

∴ Composition of composited distillate = 0.44 mole fraction of heptane
= 44 mole % heptane
Composition of residue = 0.18 mole fraction of heptane
= 18 mole % heptane ... **Ans.**

EXERCISES

Ex. 1. Fill in the blanks :

1.1 Separation by distillation is not possible when relative volatility is equal to ....
Ans. one

1.2 In distillation operation mass ..... takes place in both the directions. **Ans.** transfer

1.3 The ratio of vapour pressure of A to vapour pressure of B is called as .... of A with respect to B. **Ans.** relative volatility

1.4 Relative volatility is the measure of separation by .... **Ans.** distillation

1.5 Distillation utilises the differences in .... of different components to effect separation. **Ans.** vapour pressures

1.6 .... diagrams are used to see how equilibrium vapour phase and liquid phase compositions changes with temperature. **Ans.** Boiling point

1.7 In boiling point diagram, the saturated vapour curve is called as .... curve.
Ans. dew point

1.8 Fractionating column is divided into two section, one is called as rectifying section and other is called as .... section. **Ans.** stripping

1.9 In case of fractionation, the plate on which the feed is introduced is called as .... plate. **Ans.** feed

1.10 In case of rectification, the portion of the condensed liquid that is returned to column is called .... **Ans.** reflux

1.11 Plate column is a stage wise gas-liquid contactor whereas .... is a differential or continuous gas-liquid contactor. **Ans.** packed column

1.12 In case of fractionating column, the liquid from tray above to tray below, flows via ...... comer. **Ans.** down

2. Define following terms :
   (1) Distillation (2) Relative volatility (3) Reflux ratio (4) Volatility
   (5) Rectifying section (6) Azeotrope.

3. Write in brief on two principal methods of distillation.

4. State Raoult's law and Dalton's law.

5. Explain briefly boiling point diagram.
6. Define reflux ratio and write in brief on optimum reflux ratio.
7. Write a note on steam distillation.
8. What do you mean by azeotrope and azeotropic distillation ?
9. Write in brief with sketch on fractionating column.
10. Explain in brief McCabe-Thiele method used for obtaining theoretical plates required for given degree of separation.
11. Explain in brief Lewis-Sorel method used to obtain theoretical plates required for given degree of separation.
12. What do you mean by H.E.T.P ?
13. Write in brief on flash distillation and draw its sketch.
14. Draw the neat sketch of differential distillation and explain it in brief.
15. Draw a x–y plot and show on it the operating lines in case of flash distillation for f = 0 f = 1 and 0 < f < 1.0.
16. Draw the feed line on equilibrium diagram for various values of 'q', q = 0, q = 1, q > 1 and 0 < q < 1.
17. Derive the equation of q-line $y = [-q/(1-q)] \cdot x + x_F/(1-q)$.
18. Write in brief on
    (a) bubble cap tray/plate and (ii) sieve plate
19. In case of differential distillation derive Rayleighs equation.
20. Explain in brief-rectification on ideal plate.

CHAPTER NINE

GAS ABSORPTION

In gas absorption, a gas phase contacts a liquid phase and mass is transferred from the gas phase to the liquid phase (liquid solvent).

Gas absorption refers to an operation in which a gas mixture is contacted with a liquid to preferentially dissolve one or more soluble components of the gas mixture in the liquid. This unit operation is sometimes also termed as scrubbing. The differences in solubility of gases in a given solvent are exploited to effect such a separation. Gas absorption is the second most important mass transfer operation encountered in the chemical industry and is used for the recovery or removal of the solute gas.

In absorption, the soluble component of a gas mixture is called as the solute gas, the insoluble component is called as the inert gas or carrier gas and the liquid used for absorption purpose is called as the solvent or absorbent. Under a given set of operating conditions, the volatility of the solvent used is very low, so it is essentially immiscible in the gas phase. A typical example of gas absorption is the removal of ammonia from a mixture of ammonia and air by means of water. Here, since ammonia is soluble in water, air is almost insoluble and water does not vapourise to an appreciable extent in the gas mixture at ambinent temperature, the only transfer is of ammonia from the gas phase to the liquid phase.

The reverse of absorption is called as desorption or stripping. It is an operation in which a dissolved gas from a solution (a liquid) is removed from the liquid by contacting it with an inert gas (i.e., a stripping medium). So the removal of sulfur dioxide from flue gases by alkaline solutions is an example of absorption, whereas the removal of the volatile components of oil by steam is an example of stripping.

The absorption may be a purely physical phenomenon - physical absorption, e.g., absorption of ammonia from a mixture of ammonia and air by water or it may be accompanied by a chemical reaction (the transfer of a solute component to the liquid phase and then reaction of this solute with a constituent of the liquid), e.g., absorption of NO_2 in water to produce nitric acid. Gas absorption is exothermic in nature, so this operation demands a cooling provision and is normally carried out at low temperatures (the solubility of solute gas in a given solvent is high at low temperatures).

Comparison of gas absorption and distillation :

Absorption	Distillation

1. Gas absorption is related with the separation of the constituents of a gas mixture.	1. Distillation is related with the separation of the constituents of a liquid mixture.
2. In gas absorption, the constituents of a gas mixture are separated by using liquid solvent.	2. In distillation, the constituents of a liquid mixture are seperated by using thermal energy.
3. Liquid solvent used in gas absorption is below its boiling point.	3. Liquid in distillation operation is at its bubble point.
4. In gas absorption, a gas phase contacts a liquid phase and mass (solute) is transferred from the gas phase to liquid phase-mass transfer takes place in one direction. It is a case of steady state diffusion of A through non-diffusing B. [e.g., A is NH_3 and B is air in absorption of NH_3 from an ammonia-air mixture in water.	4. In distillation, a vapour phase contacts a liquid phase and mass is transferred both from the liquid phase to the vapour phase and from the vapour phase to the liquid phase-mass transfer takes place in both the directions simultaneously. It is a case of steady state equimolar counter diffusion.
5. Gas absorption does not give pure product. It needs further processing for the recovery of the solute/solvent (by distillation).	5. Distillation gives almost pure product in single processing step.
6. In gas absorption, heat effects are attributed to the heat of solution of the dissolved gas.	6. In distillation, heat effects are attributed to the latent heats of vaporisation and condensation.
7. Gas in absorption operation is well below its dew point.	7. Vapour in distillation is always at its dew point.
8. Example – the removal of SO_2 from flue gases by alkaline solutions.	8. Example – separation of petroleum crude into gasoline, kerosene, fuel oil, etc.
9. Packed towers are widely used for absorption operation.	9. Plate towers are widely used for distillation operation.
10. Differences in solubility of gases in a selective solvent are exploited to effect the separation by absorption.	10. Differences in volatility of constituents of a liquid mixture at the same temperature solution are exploited to effect the separation by distillation.

Both the gas absorption and distillation operations are carried out in plate or packed columns with higher liquid to gas ratios (flow rate) in absorption as compared to it in distillation and with higher liquid flow rates, packed columns are very common.

Condition of Equilibrium : Liquid-Gas :

The degree to which a gas is absorbed from a gaseous mixture by a liquid solvent is determined by its partial pressure. Each dissolved gas exerts a definite partial pressure at a given temperature and concentration. The gas is said to be slightly soluble when the partial pressure exerted by the dissolved gas from the solution is higher, while it is said to be more soluble when the partial pressure exerted by the dissolved gas from the solution of given concentration is lower. With oxygen, large partial pressures are exerted by the solution while with ammonia very low partial pressures are exerted by the solution of a given concentration. Thus, oxygen is slightly soluble while ammonia is highly soluble in water. With water as the solvent, ammonia is very soluble gas, sulphur dioxide is moderately soluble gas and oxygen is slightly soluble gas.

A given quantity of liquid will dissolve any amount of slightly or more soluble gas depending upon the partial pressure of dissolved gas in the gas phase in contact with the liquid. A slightly soluble (insoluble gas) gas requires a higher partial pressure of the gas in contact with the liquid to yield the solution of desired concentration while a very soluble gas requires very low partial pressure to give the solution of same concentration.

Equilibrium condition will be reached when the partial pressure of solute gas in the gas phase is equal to its partial pressure from the liquid phase. The equilibrium condition thus fixes the upper limit for operation of an absorption unit.

The solubility of gas (the concentration of dissolved gas in liquid at given temperature and pressure) is not substantially affected by the total pressure over a system but gets influenced by the temperature. Generally, the solubility of gas in a given solvent decreases with increase in temperature.

In a majority of cases, the gas absorption results with the evolution of heat and solubility falls off if provisions are not made to remove the evolved heat. Usually adequate cooling arrangements are provided to keep the temperature sufficiently low to achieve a good rate of absorption.

For dilute solutions of most gases, the equilibrium relationship is given by Henry's law :

$$p_A = H \cdot x_A \qquad \ldots (9.1)$$

where
p_A = partial pressure of the solute gas A in the gas phase

x_A = mole fraction of the solute gas A in the liquid phase (the concentration of A in terms of mole fraction)

H is Henry's constant.

Please refer to Equilibrium - chapter 7 – page 7.18 for Equilibrium in gas absorption.

Selection criteria for solvent in gas absorption :

While selecting a particular solvent for absorption operation, the following properties of the solvent are considered :

1. Gas solubility :

The solubility of a solute gas in a solvent should be high, i.e., the solvent should have high capacity for dissolving the desired solute gas so that the less amount of the solvent will be then required for a given absorption duty. In general, for good solubility a solvent of chemical nature similar to that of the solute to be absorbed must be searched out and used.

The solvent selected should have high solubility for the solute to be absorbed.

2. Volatility :

As the gas leaving an absorption unit is generally saturated with the solvent, there will be a loss of the solvent with the gas leaving the unit operation. Hence, to minimise the solvent loss (in the gas leaving), the solvent should be as far as possible less volatile, i.e., should have a low vapour pressure under the given operating conditions.

3. Corrosive nature :

The solvent should not be corrosive (as far as possible) towards common materials of construction so that the construction material for an absorption equipment will not be too expensive.

4. Viscosity :

The solvent should have low viscosity for rapid absorption rates, low pumping cost and better heat transfer. The solvent should be non-viscous.

5. Cost and availability :

The solvent should be cheap and readily available. Losses are less costly with cheap solvent.

6. Miscellaneous :

The solvent should be non-toxic, non-flammable, non-foaming, and chemically stable from a handling and storage point of view.

Material balances – One Component Transferred :

Consider a packed column as shown in Fig. 9.1. Let V_1, V_2 and V be the molal flow rates of the total gas at the inlet (rich gas), outlet (lean gas) and at an arbitrary section in the column. Let y_1, y_2 and y be the mole fractions of the solute gas at the respective stations.

Fig. 9.1 : Material balance diagram for Absorption tower

Let L_1, L_2 and L be the molal flow rates of liquid (as a whole) at the outlet, inlet and at an arbitrary sections respectively and x_1, x_2 and x be the mole fractions of the solute gas in the liquid at the respective stations. Also let V' and L' be the molal flow rates of an inert (insoluble) gas and the non-volatile solvent (solute free solvent) respectively through the column.

The overall material balance over the control surface 'A' of Fig. 9.1 gives

$$V_1 + L = L_1 + V \qquad \ldots (9.2)$$

Material balance of the solute component :

$$V_1 y_1 + L x = L_1 x_1 + V y \qquad \ldots (9.3)$$

The overall material balance over the entire column is

$$V_1 + L_2 = V_2 + L_1 \qquad \ldots (9.4)$$

For the solute component, the material balance over the entire column is :

$$V_1 y_1 + L_2 x_2 = L_1 x_1 + V_2 y_2 \qquad \ldots (9.5)$$

y = the mole fraction of the solute in the gas phase

∴ (1 − y) = the mole fraction of an inert gas in the gas phase

So $\quad V' = V(1-y) = V_1(1-y_1) = V_2(1-y_2) \qquad \ldots (9.6)$

Similarly, (1 − x) be the mole fraction of the solute free solvent in the liquid phase.

∴ $\quad L' = L(1-x) = L_1(1-x_1) = L_2(1-x_2) \qquad \ldots (9.7)$

Equation (9.3) becomes

$$V'\left(\frac{y_1}{1-y_1}\right) + L'\left(\frac{x}{1-x}\right) = L'\left(\frac{x_1}{1-x_1}\right) + V'\left(\frac{y}{1-y}\right) \qquad \ldots (9.8)$$

∴ $\quad V'\left[\frac{y_1}{1-y_1} - \frac{y}{1-y}\right] = L'\left(\frac{x_1}{1-x_1} - \frac{x}{1-x}\right) \qquad \ldots (9.9)$

Let Y and X be the mole ratio defined as :

$$Y = \frac{y}{1-y}$$

= moles solute per mole of solute-free gas (inert gas)

$$X = \frac{x}{1-x} \text{ moles solute per mole of solute-free solvent.}$$

(As in 1 mole of a gas mixture, there will be y moles of the solute gas and (1 − y) moles of the inert (insoluble gas).

Equation (9.9) is the equation of the operating line for absorption operation in terms of mole fraction and is curve on x, y - co-ordinates.

Equation (9.9) in terms of mole ratio is :

$$V' [Y_1 - Y] = L' [X_1 - X] \qquad \ldots (9.10)$$

The above equation represents the equation of the operating line for absorption operation and is a straight line on x, y co-ordinates with a slope equal to L'/V' and passes through the points (X_1, Y_1). The line also passes through the points (X_2, Y_2).

Material balance of the solute gas component over the entire tower/column in terms of L', V' and mole ratios is :

$$V' [Y_1 - Y_2] = L' [X_1 - X_2] \qquad \ldots (9.11)$$

If the solvent used is pure/fresh, $x_2 = 0$ and $X_2 = 0$, then the above equation becomes :

$$V' [Y_1 - Y_2] = L' (X_1) \qquad \ldots (9.12)$$

Minimum Liquid Gas Ratio :

Consider that the values of the terms V', Y_1, Y_2 and X_2 are fixed by a process requirement and the value of L' is decreased through the absorption tower. The operating line on X, Y coordinates passes through the point (X_2, Y_2) and has a slope equal to L'/V'. As liquid flow rate is decreased, the slope of the operating line decreases (operating line shifts toward the equilibrium curve) and the exist liquid composition (with respect to the solute) increases from X_1' to X_1'' as indicated by the line AC. A reduction in liquid flow rate reduces the driving force for mass transfer and absorption becomes more and more difficult. Further reduction in the liquid flow rate leads to a situation wherein the upper end of the operating line touches the equilibrium curve as indicated by the line AD and the exist liquid composition is then in equilibrium with the inlet gas. Thus, the driving force for mass transfer becomes zero at the bottom of the tower, required time of contact for the desired concentration change becomes infinite, and an infinitely tall tower results. The value of L'/V' corresponding to this situation (corresponding to the line AD) represents a minimum liquid-gas ratio. If tower is to operate practically, the liquid flow rate should be greater than that corresponding to the minimum L'/V' ratio.

Low values of L'/V' ratio result into taller tower and hence there is an increase in the fixed cost but the recovery cost of the solute will be low (due to small quantities of liquid). High values of L'/V' ratio result into small tower due to favourable driving force, and hence there is decrease in the fixed cost but the recovery cost of the solute will be higher. So while selecting L'/V' ratio, a balance must be made between the rate fixed and the recovery costs. In general, the operating liquid flow rate for the absorber is usually 1.1 to 1.5 times the minimum.

Fig. 9.2 : Minimum liquid-gas ratio for absorption

Pressure drop in packed columns :

In packed columns operated in a counter current fashion, the liquid fed at the top flows downward under the influence of gravity/gravitational force and the gas fed at the bottom of the column is moved upward by a fluid moving machinery such as a blower or fan. So as to maintain the upward flow of gas, pressure at the top must be less than at the bottom. In packed columns since the same channels are available for liquid downflow and gas upflow, the gas pressure drop is a function of both the phase flow rates and further its knowledge is must as it is a important factor in the design of packed towers.

In randomly packed towers, the dependency of a gas pressure drop on the gas and liquid flow rates is similar to that shown in Fig. 9.3 wherein the pressure drop per unit height of packed bed is plotted against the superficial gas mass velocity (mass flow rate per unit empty tower cross-section) on logarithmic co-ordinates.

In case of dry packing (L = 0), the relationship between pressure drop and gas mass velocity is represented by a straight line A indicating that the pressure drop is proportional to $(V/A)^{1.8-2}$ which is consistent with a usual law of fluid friction in turbulent flow. For wet packing, the relationship is indicated by a straight line B similar to line A (for dry packing) but for a given velocity, the pressure drop will be more than that for dry packing. If in addition to gas flow, liquid flows down the tower at a fixed gas velocity, the pressure drop increases with increased liquid flow rate (see lines C and D) as most of the free space in the packed bed gets occupied by the liquid, i.e., the free cross-section available for gas flow becomes smaller and smaller as liquid flow increases.

Fig. 9.3 : Pressure drop characteristics of packed column (logarithmic axes)

With liquid flow down the tower at low and moderate gas velocities, the pressure drop is proportional to 1.8 th power of the gas velocity but is greater than that for wet packing as liquid flow occupies the part of free cross-section available for gas flow. Upto point 'X' the amount of liquid held in packings is constant. At point 'X', the gas flow begins to impede the downflow of liquid and the local accumulation of liquid appears here and there in packings.

As the gas velocity increases further (beyond X upto Y), the liquid hold up progressively increases due to which the free area for gas flow becomes smaller and the pressure drop rises much more quickly (pressure drop is proportional to 2.5 th power of the gas mass velocity over the X-Y section). At gas flow rates beyond Y, the pressure drop rises very steeply for a given liquid flow rate. Point X is called as the loading point and point Y is called as the flooding point. At a given liquid flow rate at point Y, a layer of liquid may appear at the top of packings or inversion of phases may occur (the liquid becomes the continuous phase and the gas becomes the dispersed phase) and the entrainment of liquid by the gas leaving the top of the tower increases rapidly and tower is then said to be flooded. The gas velocity corresponding to the flooding conditions is called as the flooding velocity.

The point at which the liquid hold up in the column starts to increase, as indicated by a change in the slope of the pressure drop line, it is called the loading point.

From this point onward the present drop increases more rapidly with an increase in gas velocity.

If tower is to operate practically, the operating gas mass velocity must, obviously be lower than the flooding velocity. For safe operations, the packed towers are designed using gas velocities of about 50 to 70 per cent of the flooding velocity at the expected liquid rate. This value corresponds to the one somewhere below the loading point and thus ensures stable operating conditions.

Gas Absorption Equipments :

Various gas absorption equipments used are :
1. Mechanically agitated vessels.
2. Packed Columns/towers.
3. Plate Columns.

1. Mechanically agitated vessel :

Fig. 9.4 : Standard Mechanically agitated vessel

Fig. 9.5 : Multiple impeller for deep vessels

It is usually used in a small scale industry. This unit gives performance equivalent to one theoretical stage. It consists of a baffled vessel usually incorporating an open or disc flat blade turbine type agitator as it maintains very large discharge velocities normal to the gas flow. Solvent liquid with a depth equal to the vessel diameter is taken in the vessel and gas is introduced below the impeller through a ring shaped sparger under agitation. Adequate free board is provided over the liquid level for the gas hold up during gas flow and ultimately the unabsorbed gas leaves the top of the vessel. For high absorption capacity, the operation is carried out at low temperature and for maintaining it, a cooling coil is incorporated in the vessel. The diameter of sparger is equal to or slightly less than that of the impeller and is arranged with holes (3 to 6.5 mm in diameter) on top.

Deep vessels with usually two impellers are used when the time of contact required is relatively large wherein a large interfacial area is maintained by redispersing the gas bubble coalesced.

2. Packed Columns/Towers :

Packed columns are most frequently used for gas absorption (and are used to a limited extent for distillation) wherein the liquid is dispersed in the form of film and the gas flows as a continuous phase. These are continuous contact equipments generally operated in a counter current fashion. A packed column consists of a vertical cylindrical shell constructed out of metal, plastic, ceramic, etc. and filled with suitable packings which offer a large interfacial area for gas-liquid contact for mass transfer between the phases. A bed of the packing rests on a support plate which offers very low resistance to gas flow. It is provided with a gas inlet and distributing space at the bottom, a liquid inlet and a liquid distributor at the top and gas and liquid outlets at the top and bottom. A liquid solvent is introduced from the top through the liquid distributor (which distributes the liquid on the packing), which

Fig. 9.6 : Packed Tower / column for absorption

irrigates/wets the surface of packing uniformly, liquid trickles down the bed, and finally the liquid enriched in solute called a strong liquor (solute + solvent) leaves the bottom of the column. The liquid flow rate should be sufficient for good wetting of packing. A solute-containing gas (rich gas) is introduced from the bottom of the tower and rise upward through the interstices/open spaces in the packing counter current to the flow of the liquid. The lean gas (dilute gas) leaves the column from the top of the tower. In case of tall columns/towers, liquid redistributors are used to redistribute liquid to avoid channeling of the same (flow the liquid along the wall).

Advantages of packed columns :

(i) Minimum structure (ii) low pressure drop (iii) low liquid hold-up (iv) handle corrosive liquids and liquids that tends to foam (v) low initial investment and (vi) high liquid to gas ratios.

Disadvantages of packed columns :

(i) Relatively inflexible (ii) can not operate over wide ranges of either vapour or liquid rates per unit cross section (iii) distribution of liquid is difficult (iv) can not handle dirty fluids that tends to deposits a sediment (v) can not be used where large temperature changes are encountered.

Packed columns are well suited for :
1. Small diameters
2. Handling highly corrosive fluids.
3. Handling liquids that tend to foam.
4. Operations where it is important to have a low pressure drop and low liquid hold up.

Tower Packings :

Many types of packings are in use ranging from simple to complex geometric shapes. Packings are made of ceramics, metals and plastics and vary in size from 6 to 75 mm.

Characteristics of a Tower Packing :

1. It should provide a large interfacial area for phase contacting., i.e., it should have a large wetted surface area per unit volume of packed space for high efficiencies.

2. It should provide a large void volume or empty space in the packed bed so that reasonable throughputs of the phases are handled without excessive pressure drop.

3. It should possess good wetting characteristic.

4. It should have high corrosion resistance.

5. It should be relatively cheap/inexpensive.

6. It should have a low bulk density so that the weight of the entire packed bed is low which thereby reduces serious support problems.

7. It should possess enough structural strength.

8. It should be chemically inert to the fluids handled in the tower.

Types of packings :

For obtaining efficient gas-liquid contact, many different types of packings are available ranging from simple to complex geometrical shapes but are generally classified as random packings and regular packings. If the packings are simply dumped into the tower during installation and fall of random (the individual pieces are not arranged in any particular pattern), they are called as **random packings**. The packings arranged in a particular pattern are called **stacked packings**.

In case of randomly packed installations for obtaining high and uniform voidage and preventing breakage, tower is first filled with liquid (water) and packings are then dumped into it. Most common random packings used in industrial towers are Raschig rings, Pall rings, Hy-pak, Berl saddles, Intalox saddles, Super intalox saddles, etc. As Pall rings, and Intalox saddles permit a more economical tower design they are replacing older Raschig rings and Berl saddles. Pall rings are made out of metal or plastic (poly propylene) and have the same general form as Raschig rings with height equal to diameter, however portions of the original cylinder wall are cut with the projections bent inward leaving holes in the wall. They are generally available in sizes ranging from 16 to 50 mm (5/8 to 2 in).

Berl saddles and Intalox saddles are available in range 6 to 50 mm and are formed out of plastic or ceramics. They provide more gas-liquid contacting area than Raschig rings.

Raschig rings are hollow cylinders with their length equal to outside diameter and usually formed out of ceramic, carbon and metal. They are generally available in a size range – 6 to 100 mm $\left(\frac{1}{4} \text{ to 4 in}\right)$. They are simple in construction and relatively cheap as compared to other packings. When a single web is added to the inside of the Raschig ring, the packing is called as Lessing ring and when a cross web is added to the Raschig ring then the packing

Fig. 9.7 : Tower Packings

formed is called as cross partition ring. Added web's provide additional active surface. They are normally available in a size range – 75 to 150 mm (3 to 6 in) and usually used as stacked packings. Stacked packings offer lower pressure drops for the gas than random packing for equivalent phase flow rates.

Channeling in Packed Columns :

The tendency of the liquid to segregate towards the walls of a packed column and to flow along the walls (region of greatest void space) is termed as **channeling** which leads to low mass transfer efficiencies. Thus, with good initial liquid distribution in randomly packed columns channeling can be minimised by providing tower diameter to packing size ratio greater than 8 i.e. the diameter of the tower should be at least eight times the packing size (or the packing size smaller than at least one-eighth of the tower diameter).

In packed columns, the region of greatest void space is the region near the wall of the column since the packing material cannot nest tightly with the plane wall as it does with itself. It is a natural tendency for the fluid to move toward the region of greatest void space during its flow.

Height Equivalent to an Equilibrium stage (Theoretical Plate) :

The height equivalent to a theoretical plate (HETP) is the *height of a section of packing that will give the same separation as that achieved with one theoretical plate*. The HETP is determined experimentally and is characteristic of each packing. It depends upon the type and size of the packing, flow rates of fluids and concentration. The height of a packed column
(i.e., the height of packing) required to effect a given degree separation is calculated by multiplying the number of theoretical plates required to achieve the same degree of separation by HETP.

Liquid distribution :

For maximum active surface area, the packing should be wetted completely by the descending liquid and this can be achieved by its proper distribution. For efficient column operation, uniform distribution of liquid at the top of the packed bed is essential. A liquid distributor is a device that spreads the liquid uniformly across the top of the packing. Several types of liquid distributors used are : (1) Perforated pipe distributor; (2) Orifice-type distributor; (3) Trough-type distributor; and (4) Weir-riser distributor.

Support Plate :

       (a) Liquid distributor   **(b) Support plate for packed towers**

Fig. 9.8

In packed columns, the packing support must be sufficiently strong as it carries the weight of the entire packed bed and at the same time it must have a large free area for passage of gas and liquid phases so as to offer a very low resistance to gas and liquid flow.

Relative merits of plate and packed towers :

The selection of a particular kind of contactor-plate or packed tower for a given mass transfer operation, generally rests on the cost and profit considerations but in many cases the choice can be made on the basis of quantitative analysis of relative merits and demerits of the plate or packed tower. For selecting the right type of the contactor for a given mass transfer duty, following merits and demerits should be considered.

    1. Plate columns operate over a wide range of liquid flow rates without flooding.

2. Plate columns by repeated mixing and separation provide more positive contact between fluid phases whereas packed columns may lead to backmixing or by passing.
3. Because of difficulties arising in dispersion of liquid in packed tower, plate tower is more reliable and needs less safety factors at low liquid to gas mass velocity ratios.
4. Side streams are very easily taken out from plate towers.
5. For plate towers, design information is generally more readily available and it is more reliable than it for packed towers.
6. Whenever liquid mixtures containing dispersed solids are to be handled, plate towers should be preferred as cleaning of the plate is very easy.
7. Whenever intermediate cooling arrangement is required to remove the heat of a solution or reaction, plate towers are preferred. Cooling coils are easily incorporated in plate towers.
8. For a given duty, the total weight of a dry plate tower is normally less than the weight of a packed tower but weight of both towers is approximately the same if the liquid holdup in the plate tower during operation is taken into account.
9. For a column diameter more than 1200 mm, packed towers are seldom designed and for a column diameter less than 600 mm, packings are cheaper than plates.
10. For liquids having tendency to foam, packed towers are usually preferred.
11. High values of liquid-gas ratio are best handled in packed towers.
12. The liquid hold-up is considerably low in packed towers so they are used in cases where the liquid deterioration might occur with high temperatures (for handling heat-sensitive liquids).
13. The pressure drop through a packed tower is usually low which makes the packed tower particularly desirable for vacuum distillation operations.
14. Packed towers may be more economical than plate towers when highly corrosive fluids are to be handled, because of corrosion resistant ceramic/plastic packings.
15. Plate towers are often preferred when large temperature changes are involved, as in distillation, thermal expansion or contraction of the equipment component may crush the packing.

Packed columns and plate columns are the commonly used equipments for gas-liquid operations such as distillation and gas absorption. They are also used for liquid extraction.

Comparison of packed column and plate column :

Packed columns are differential contactors wherein mass transfer occurs throughout the length of the contactor and equilibrium is not reached at any point between the phases in contact whereas **plate columns** are stagewise contactors wherein mass transfer occurs intermittently and equilibrium is established between the phases at a number of discrete stages. In **packed columns**, packings are used as gas-liquid contacting devices whereas in **plate columns**, plates are used as gas-liquid containing devices. Design of a **packed column** mainly involves the calculation of the height of transfer unit and number of transfer units for a given separation whereas design of a **plate column** requires the calculation of the number of theoretical stages required to effect a given separation Constructionwise-**packed columns** are simple in construction whereas **plate columns** are complex in construction. Raschig rings, pall rings, berl saddles, intalox saddles are the various types of packings used in **packed columns** whereas bubble cap plate, sieve plate and valve plate are the various types of plates used in **plate columns**.

The selection of a particular type of equipment for gas-liquid operation in particular situation will depend upon many factors such as : efficiency, capacity, pressure drop, corrosion, hold up, cost, etc.

SOLVED EXAMPLES

Ex. 9.1 : Ammonia from ammonia-air mixture is to be absorbed in an absorption tower using water as a solvent. Data for absorption system is as follows :

Air flow rate – 200 kg/h

Liquid phase compositions :

At the top of packing – 0.000013 kg NH_3/kg H_2O

At the bottom of packing – 0.0006 kg NH_3/kg H_2O

Gas phase compositions :

At the bottom of packing – 0.0084 kg NH_3/kg inert gas

At the top of packing – 0.0044 kg NH_3/kg inert gas.

Calculate flow rate of water entering the absorption tower.

Solution : Basis : 200 kg/h of air flow to absorption tower.

Fig. 9.9

X_1' = NH_3 composition at bottom (in liquid leaving tower)
 = 0.0006 kg NH_3/kg H_2O

X_2' = NH_3 composition at top (in solvent entering the tower)
 = 0.000013 kg NH_3/kg H_2O

Y_1 = NH_3 composition in inlet gas to tower
 = 0.0084 kg NH_3/kg air

Y_2 = NH$_3$ composition in outlet gas from tower
= 0.0044 kg NH$_3$/kg air

L' = Mass flow rate of solute free solvent in kg/h

V' = Mass flow rate of solute free gas or air in kg/h

$$V'[Y_1 - Y_2] = L'[X_1 - X_2]$$
$$200\,[0.0084 - 0.0044] = L'\,[0.0006 - 0.000013]$$
$$L' = 1362.86 \text{ kg/h}$$

Mass flow rate of water (solute free) = **1362.86 kg/h** ... **Ans.**

Ex. 9.2 : Gas containing 2 % by volume solute A is fed to an absorption tower at a rate of 0.35 m³/s at 299 K (26° C) and 106.658 kPa pressure, and 95 % of original solute is removed by absorbing it in solvent B. Solvent containing 0.005 mole fraction of solute enters the tower at top and exist liquid streams from absorption tower contains 0.12 mole A per mole B. Find out the flow rate of liquid solvent entering the absorption tower on solute free basis.

Solution : Basis : 0.35 m³/s of gas entering the tower.

$$P = \text{pressure} = 106.658 \text{ kPa}$$
$$T = 299 \text{ K}$$

Assume ideal gas law holds good, we have :

$$PV = nRT$$

where
R = 8.31451 (m³ · kPa)/ (kmol · K)

n = molal flow rate of gas in kmol/s

V = volumetric flow rate of gas = 0.35 m³/s

Fig. 9.10

$$n = \frac{PV}{RT} = \frac{106.658 \times 0.35}{8.31451 \times 299} = 0.015 \text{ kmol/s} = 15 \text{ mol/s}$$

Solute A in inlet gas = 2 %

y_1 = Mole fraction of A in gas

$$= \frac{2}{100} = 0.02$$

Mole fraction of inert gas in inlet gas = $1 - y_1$
$$= 1 - 0.02 = 0.98$$

$Y_1 = \dfrac{\text{Moles solute}}{\text{Moles inert gas (solute free gas)}}$

= Mole ratio at inlet

$Y_1 = \dfrac{y_1}{1 - y_1} = \dfrac{0.02}{1 - 0.02} = 0.020408$

V' = Molal flow rate of solute free gas (inert gas)
$= 15(1 - y_1) = 15(1 - 0.02) = 14.7$ mol/s

Solute A in inlet gas per second $= 15 \times 0.02 = 0.3$ mol

95% of solute is absorbed i.e. 5% of solute leaves the tower with inert gas.

Unabsorbed solute appearing in gas leaving tower
$$= 0.3 \times 0.05 = 0.0015 \text{ mol/s}$$

Inert gas leaving the tower = Inert gas entering the tower
$$= 14.7 \text{ mol/s}$$

Y_2 = mole ratio at outlet (gas phase)

$= \dfrac{\text{moles solute}}{\text{moles inert gas}}$

$= \dfrac{0.015}{14.7} = 0.0010204$

x_2 = mole fraction of solute A in liquid entering tower
$= 0.005$

$X_2 = \dfrac{\text{moles solute A}}{\text{mole solute free solvent B}} = \dfrac{x_2}{1 - x_2}$

∴ X_2 = mole ratio at liquid inlet

$= \dfrac{0.005}{1 - 0.005} = 0.005025$

$X_1 = 0.12 \dfrac{\text{moles solute A in exit liquid}}{\text{moles solute free solvent}}$

L' = molal form rate of solute free solvent to tower in mol/s

Material balance of solute over tower :
$$V'[Y_1 - Y_2] = L'[X_1 - X_2]$$

∴ $14.7[0.020408 - 0.0010204] = L'[0.12 - 0.005025]$

∴ $L' = 2.48$ mol/s ... **Ans.**

Ex. 9.3 : 1000 m³/h of a gas mixture containing 10 mole % solute and rest inert enters the absorber at 300 K temperature and 106.658 kPa pressure 90% of the original solute is removed. Solute free water used for absorption contains 5 mole % solute when it leaves the tower at the bottom. Calculate the solvent flow rate to tower.

Solution : Basis : 1000 m³/h of gas mixture.

Molal flow rate of gas, n, is given by

$$n = \frac{PV}{RT}$$

where,
- R = 8.31451 (m³·kPa) / (kmol·K)
- P = 106.658 kPa
- T = 300 K, V = 1000 m³/h

$$n = \frac{(106.658) \times 1000}{8.31451 \times 300} = 42.76 \text{ kmol/h}$$

Mole fraction of solute in gas mixture $= y_1 = \frac{10}{100} = 0.10$

$$Y_1 = \frac{\text{moles solute}}{\text{moles inert gas}} = \frac{y_1}{1-y_1}$$

$$= \frac{0.10}{1-0.10} = 0.111$$

Solute in gas entering = 0.10 × 42.76 = 4.276 kmol/h
V' = Inert gas at inlet = 42.76 − 4.276 = 38.484 kmol/h
90% of the solute is absorbed.
Amount of solute absorbed = 0.90 × 4.276 = 3.848 kmol/h

At outlet,
$$Y_2 = \frac{\text{moles solute in gas outlet}}{\text{moles inert gas at outlet}}$$

$$= \frac{0.428}{38.484} = 0.0111$$

For solute free solvent
$$X_2 = 0$$

Solvent leaving absorption tower contains 5 mole % solute

x_1 = mole fraction of solute in solvent leaving absorption tower = $\frac{5}{100} = 0.05$.

At exit,
$$X_1 = \frac{\text{moles solute}}{\text{moles solute free solvent}}$$

$$= \frac{x_1}{1-x_1} = \frac{0.05}{1-0.05} = 0.0526$$

Material balance for solute –

$$V'(Y_1 - Y_2) = L'(X_1 - X_2)$$
$$38.484 \,(0.111 - 0.0111) = L'\,(0.0526 - 0)$$
$$L' = 73.09 \text{ kmol/h}$$

Molar flow rate of solute free water (solvent) to absorption tower = 73.09 kmol/h ... **Ans.**

Ex. 9.4 : Benzene is to be recovered from cool gas by scrubbing it with wash oil as an absorbent. 855 m³ of coal gas containing 2 % by volume of benzene are to be handled per hour, and a 95 % removal is required. The operating temperature and pressure are 299.7 K (26.7° C) and 106.658 kPa. The wash oil has an average molecular weight of 260 and contains 0.005 mole fraction benzene as it enters the absorber. Calculate the minimum oil circulation rate. Equilibrium data is given by –

$$\frac{Y}{1+Y} = 0.125 \frac{X}{1+X}$$

where, Y – moles benzene/mole dry coal gas.

X – moles benzene/mole benzene free wash oil.

Solution : Basis : 855 m³/h of coal gas.

Assuming ideal gas behaviour

$$n = \frac{PV}{RT}$$

$P = 106.658$ kPa,

$T = 299.7$ K, $V = 855$ m³/h

$R = 8.31451 \dfrac{m^3 \cdot kPa}{kmol \cdot K}$

$$n = \frac{(106.658) \times 855}{8.31451 \times 299.7}$$

$= 36.59$ kmol/h

Molal flow rate of gas at inlet = $V_1 = n = 36.59$ kmol/h

y_1 = mole fraction of benzene in coal gas = 2/100 = 0.02

$V' = V_1 (1 - y_1)$

$= 36.59 (1 - 0.02) = 35.86$ kmol/h

Molal flow rate of benzene free coal gas = 35.86 kmol/h

At inlet, $Y_1 = \dfrac{\text{moles benzene}}{\text{moles dry coal gas}}$

$= \dfrac{y_1}{1 - y_1} = \dfrac{0.02}{1 - 0.02} = 0.0204$

95% of benzene is removed by absorption.

At outlet, $Y_2 = (1 - 0.95) Y_1$

$= 0.05\ Y_1 = 0.05 \times 0.0204$

$$= 0.00102 \; \frac{\text{moles benzene}}{\text{moles benzene free gas}}$$

Benzene in coal gas inlet $= 0.02 \times 36.59 = 0.7318$ kmol/h

Benzene removed by wash oil $= 0.95 \times 0.7318 = 0.6952$ kmol/h

Benzene in coal gas leaving absorber $= 0.7318 - 0.6952 = 0.0366$ kmol/h

$$Y_2 = \frac{0.0366}{35.86} = 0.00102$$

x_2 = mole fraction of benzene in wash oil (solvent inlet) = 0.005

$$X_2 = \frac{x_2}{1 - x_2}$$

$$= \frac{0.005}{1 - 0.005} = 0.00503 \; \frac{\text{moles benzene}}{\text{moles benzene free oil}}$$

When L' (mole flow rate of benzene free wash oil) is minimum

$$\frac{Y_1}{1 + Y_1} = 0.125 \; \frac{X_1}{1 + X_1}$$

$$\frac{0.0204}{1 + 0.0204} = 0.125 \; \frac{X_1}{1 + X_1}$$

Solving $\quad X_1 = 0.1904$

Material balance of benzene:

$$V'(Y_1 - Y_2) = L'_{min} (X_1 - X_2)$$

$$35.86 \, (0.0204 - 0.00102) = L'_{min} \, (0.1904 - 0.00503)$$

Solving $\quad L'_{min} = 3.75$ kmol/h

Flow rate (minimum) of benzene free wash oil $= 3.75 \times 260 = 975$ kg/h ... **Ans.**

Ex. 9.5 : Benzene is to be recovered from coal gas by scrubbing it with wash oil as an absorbent. Absorber handles 900 m³/h of coal containing 2% by volume benzene. Coal gas enters at a temperature at 300 K (27° C) and 107.324 kPa pressure. 95% of the benzene should be recovered by the solvent. The solvent enters at 300 K (30° C) containing 0.005 mole fraction of benzene and has an average molecular weight of 260. Calculate the circulation rate of oil (solvent) per hour if the column is to be operated at 1.5 times the minimum oil circulation rate.

Equilibrium data is:

$$\frac{Y}{1+Y} = 0.125 \; \frac{X}{1+X}$$

where,   Y is mole ratio of benzene to dry coal gas

X is mole ratio of benzene to benzene free solvent.

Solution : Basis : 900 m³/h

Assuming ideal gas behaviour

$$n = \frac{PV}{RT}$$

$$P = 107.324 \text{ kPa}$$

$$R = 8.31451 \frac{(m^3 \cdot kPa)}{(kmol \cdot K)}$$

$$T = 300 \text{ K}$$

$$V = 900 \text{ m}^3/\text{h}$$

$$n = \frac{(107.324) \times 900}{8.31451 \times 300} = 38.72 \text{ kmol/h}$$

Molal flow rate of coal gas = V_1 = n = 38.72 kmol/h

$$V' = \frac{\text{molal flow rate of benzene}}{\text{free coal gas (inert/dry gas)}} = 0.98 \times 38.72 = 37.95 \text{ kmol/h}$$

y_1 = mole fraction of benzene in coal gas

$$= \frac{2}{100} = 0.02$$

$$V' = (1 - y_1) V_1 = (1 - 0.02)\, 38.72 = 37.95 \text{ kmol/h}$$

At inlet $\quad Y_1 = \dfrac{\text{moles benzene}}{\text{moles benzene free coal gas}}$

$$= \frac{y_1}{1 - y_1} = \frac{0.02}{1 - 0.02} = 0.0204$$

95% of the benzene is recovered by absorption

At outlet ∴ $\quad Y_2 = (1 - 0.95)\, Y_1$

$$Y_2 = 0.05 \times 0.0204$$

$$= 0.00102 \ \frac{\text{moles benzene}}{\text{moles benzene free coal gas}}$$

x_2 = mole fraction of benzene in solvent (wash oil) at inlet

$$= 0.005$$

At inlet $\quad X_2 = \dfrac{x_2}{1 - x_2} = \dfrac{0.005}{1 - 0.005} = 0.005025$

$$X_2 = \frac{\text{moles benzene}}{\text{moles benzene free coal gas}} = 0.005025$$

Let $\quad X_1$ = mole ratio of benzene to benzene free wash oil at the exit.

When, L' (molal flow rate of benzene free wash oil/solvent) is minimum,

$$\frac{Y_1}{1 + Y_1} = 0.125 \ \frac{X_1}{1 + X_1}$$

$$\frac{0.0204}{1+0.0204} = 0.125 \frac{X_1}{1+X_1}$$

Solving $X_1 = 0.1904$

Material balance of benzene :

$$V'(Y_1 - Y_2) = L'_{min} (X_1 - X_2)$$

$$37.95 (0.0204 - 0.00102) = L'_{min} (0.1904 - 0.005025)$$

$$L'_{min} = 3.97 \text{ kmol/h}$$

Minimum flow rate of benzene free wash oil (solvent) : L'_{min}

$$L' \text{ actual} = 1.5 \, L'_{min}$$
$$= 1.5 \times 3.97 = 5.96 \text{ kmol/h}$$

Actual flow rate of benzene free solvent $= 5.96 \times 260 = 1549.6$ kg/h ... **Ans.**
(circulation rate of wash oil)

Ex. 9.6 : Benzene is to be recovered from coal gas by scrubbing it with wash oil as an absorbent 1000 m³/h of coal gas containing 2% by volume benzene enters column at a temperature of 300 K (27° C) and 106.658 kPa pressure. 95% of benzene should be recovered by the solvent. The solvent (wash oil) enters at 300 K (27° C) containing 0.005 mole fraction of benzene and has an average molecular weight of 260. Calculate the circulation rate of solvent per hour if the column is to be operated at 1.5 times the minimum solute free solvent flow to absorber.

Assume that the wash oil-benzene obeys Raoult's law and the vapour pressure of benzene at 300 K (27° C) is 13.33 kPa.

Solution : **Basis :** 1000 m³/h of coal gas.

Assuming ideal gas behaviour,

$$n = \frac{PV}{RT}$$

where, $P = 106.658$ kPa,

$T = 300$ K

$V = 1000$ m³/h

$R = 8.31451 \, \frac{(m^3 \cdot kPa)}{(kmol \cdot K)}$

$$n = \frac{(106.658) \times 1000}{8.31451 \times 300} = 42.76 \text{ kmol/h}$$

Molal flow rate of coal gas $= V_1 = n = 42.76$ kmol/h

y_1 = mole fraction of benzene in coal gas at inlet = $\frac{2}{100}$ = 0.02

V' = molal flow rate of dry coal gas to absorber.
= $V_1(1 - y_1)$
= 42.76 (1 – 0.02) = 41.90 kmol/h

Y_1 = mole ratio of benzene to dry coal gas at inlet to absorber
= $\frac{y_1}{1 - y_1} = \frac{0.02}{1 - 0.02} = 0.0204$

95% of benzene is removed by absorption.

∴ $Y_2 = (1 - 0.95) \, Y_1 = 0.05 \times 0.024 = 0.00120 \, \frac{\text{moles benzene}}{\text{moles dry coal gas}}$

x_2 = mole fraction of benzene in wash oil in let.
= 0.005

$X_2 = \frac{\text{moles benzene}}{\text{moles benzene free wash oil}}$

= $\frac{x_2}{1 - x_2} = \frac{0.005}{1 - 0.005} = 0.005025$

At total pressure of 106.658 kPa and a temperature of 300 K, the equilibrium relationship is given by

$$p^* = p^o \, x$$

$$y = \frac{p^*}{P} = \left(\frac{p^o}{P}\right) x$$

$$y = \frac{13.33}{106.658} \, x$$

$$y = 0.125 \, x$$

∴ $\frac{Y}{1 + Y} = 0.125 \, \frac{X}{1 + X}$

as $Y = \frac{y}{1 - y}$

$1 + Y = \frac{y}{1-y} + 1 = \frac{1}{1-y}$

∴ $\frac{Y}{1+Y} = \frac{y}{(1-y) \times \frac{1}{(1-y)}} = y$

when, L'_{min}, molal flow rate of benzene free wash oil that is minimum,

$$\frac{Y_1}{1+Y_1} = 0.125 \frac{X_1}{1+X_1}$$

$$\frac{0.0204}{1+0.0204} = 0.125 \frac{X_1}{1+X_1}$$

$$\therefore \quad X_1 = 0.1904$$

Material balance of benzene yields –

$$V'(Y_1 - Y_2) = L'_{min}(X_1 - X_2)$$

$$41.90\,(0.00204 - 0.00102) = L'_{min}\,(0.1904 - 0.005025)$$

$$L'_{min} = 4.38 \text{ kmol/h}$$

Actual benzene free wash oil flow rate $= 1.5 \times L'_{min} = 1.5 \times 4.38$
$= 6.57$ kmol/h

Mass flow rate of benzene free wash oil $= 6.57 \times$ Avg. Mol. Wt. of wash oil
$= 6.57 \times 260 = 1708.2$ kg/h ... **Ans.**

Ex. 9.7 : A packed tower is designed to recover 98% CO_2 from a gas mixture containing 10% CO_2 and 90% by volume air using water. A relation $y' = 14\,x'$ can be used for equilibrium conditions where,

y' is $\frac{\text{kg } CO_2}{\text{kg dry air}}$ and x' is $\frac{\text{kg } CO_2}{\text{kg water}}$

The water to gas rate is kept 30% more than the minimum value. Calculate actual mole ratio of water to solute free gas.

Solution : Gas mixture contains 10% CO_2 and 90% air by volume (i.e. by mole)

$$y_1 = \text{mole fraction of } CO_2 = \frac{10}{100} = 0.1$$

$$Y_1 = \frac{\text{moles } CO_2}{\text{moles dry air}} = \frac{y_1}{1-y_1} = \frac{0.1}{1-0.1} = 0.1111$$

$$Y_2 = (1 - 0.98)\,Y_1 = 0.02 \times 0.1111 = 0.0022$$

For pure water as a solvent

$$X_2 = 0$$

$$\therefore \quad x_2 = 0$$

Equilibrium relationship is

$$y' = 14\,x'$$

$$\frac{Y/44}{1/29} = \frac{X/44}{1/18}$$

$$0.66\,Y = 14\,(0.409\,X)$$

$$Y = 8.676\, X$$

For minimum liquid rate,

$$X_1 = Y_1/8.676 = \frac{0.1111}{8.676} = 0.0128$$

Material balance of CO_2:

$$V'(Y_1 - Y_2) = L'_{min}(X_1 - X_2)$$

$$\frac{L'_{min}}{V'} = \frac{Y_1 - Y_2}{X_1}$$

as $\quad X_2 = 0$

$$\frac{L'_{min}}{V'} = \frac{0.1111 - 0.0022}{0.0128} = 8.5$$

$$\left(\frac{L'}{V'}\right) = 1.3 \left(\frac{L'_{min}}{V'}\right)$$

$$= 1.3 \times 8.5$$

$$= \mathbf{11.05} \qquad \ldots \textbf{Ans.}$$

Ex. 9.8 : An air-ammonia mixture containing 5% ammonia by volume is absorbed in water in a packed column operated at 293 K (20° C) and 101.325 kPa pressure so as to recover 98 % ammonia. If the inert gas mass velocity to column is 1200 kg (m²·h), calculate the mass velocity of water to this column if column is operated at 1.25 times the minimum liquid rate to column. Also calculate the composition of liquid leaving column corresponding to this condition.

Equilibrium relationship is $y = 1.154\, x$, where x and y are mole fractions.

Solution : Basis : 1200 kg/(m²·h) of inert gas to column.

Mol. Wt. of air = 29

$$V' = \text{inert gas (air) to column} = 1200/29 = 41.38\ \text{kmol/(m}^2\text{·h)}$$

$$y_1 = \begin{array}{l}\text{mole fraction of ammonia}\\\text{at inlet to column}\end{array} = \frac{5}{100}$$

At inlet, $\quad Y_1 = \dfrac{\text{moles ammonia}}{\text{moles air}} = \dfrac{y_1}{1 - y_1} = \dfrac{0.05}{1 - 0.05}$

$$Y_1 = 0.0526$$

At outlet, $\quad Y_2 = \dfrac{\text{moles ammonia}}{\text{moles air}} = (1 - 0.98)\, Y_1$

$$= (1 - 0.98) \times 0.0526 = 0.001$$

Equilibrium relationship is $\quad y = 1.154\, x$

$\therefore \quad \dfrac{Y}{1+Y} = 1.154 \dfrac{X}{1+X}$

At inlet to column as water is pure $X_2 = 0$

At minimum liquid rate

$$\dfrac{Y_1}{1+Y_1} = 1.154 \dfrac{X_1}{1+X_1}$$

$$\dfrac{0.0526}{1+0.0526} = 1.154 \dfrac{X_1}{1+X_1}$$

$$X_1 = 0.0453$$

Material balance of ammonia :

$$V'(Y_1 - Y_2) = L'_{min}(X_1 - X_2)$$

$$41.38\,(0.0526 - 0.001) = L'_{min}\,(0.0453 - 0)$$

$\therefore \quad L'_{min} = 41.73 \text{ kmol/(m}^2\cdot\text{h)}$

L' actual $= 1.25\, L'_{min}$

$\qquad = 1.25 \times 41.73 = 58.9 \text{ kmol/(m}^2\cdot\text{h)}$

Actual mass velocity of $\;= 58.9 \times 18$

water to column $= 938.92 \text{ kg/(m}^2\cdot\text{h)}$

Let X'_1 be the liquid composition corresponding to this condition.

Hence, $\quad 41.38\,(0.0526 - 0.001) = 58.9\, X'_1$

Solving $\qquad X'_1 = 0.0363$

Composition of liquid leaving column in terms of mole ratio $= 0.0363$

Ex. 9.9 : A mixture of acetone vapour and air containing 5% by volume of acetone is to be freed of its acetone content by scrubbing it with water in a packed bed absorber. The flow rate of the gas mixture 700 m³/h of acetone free air measured at N.T.P., and that of water is 1500 kg/h. The absorber operates at an average temperature of 293 K (20 °C) and a pressure of 101 kPa. The scrubber absorbs 98% of the acetone.

The equilibrium relationship for the acetone vapour-water system is given by $-Y^* = 1.68\, X$.

where $\qquad Y^* =$ kg mole acetone/kg mole dry air

$\qquad X =$ kg mole acetone/kg mole water.

Calculate the mean driving force for absorption.

Hint : $\Delta Ylm = \dfrac{\Delta Y_1 - \Delta Y_2}{\ln(\Delta Y_1/\Delta Y_2)}$

ΔY_1 and ΔY_2 are driving forces at the top and bottom of the tower. $\Delta Y = Y - Y^*$

Solution : Flow rate of acetone free air
$$= 700 \text{ m}^3/\text{h N.T.P.}$$
$$= 700/22.4 = 31.25 \text{ kmol/h}$$

Flow rate of acetone free water
$$= 1500 \text{ kg/h}$$
$$= 1500/18 = 83.33 \text{ kmol/h}$$
$$y_1 = 5/100 = 0.05$$
$$Y_1 = y_1/(1 - y_1) = \dfrac{0.05}{1 - 0.05} = 0.0526$$

98% of the acetone is scrubbed.
$$Y_2 = (1 - 0.98)\, Y_1 = 0.02\, Y_1 = 0.02 \times 0.0526$$
$$Y_2 = 0.00105$$

Water entering absorber is pure, therefore
$$X_2 = 0.0$$

Solute material balance over absorber :
$$V'(Y_1 - Y_2) = L'(X_1 - X_2)$$
$$X_1 = \dfrac{V'}{L'}(Y_1 - Y_2)$$
$$= \dfrac{31.25}{83.33}(0.0526 - 0.00505) = 0.0193$$

The quantity of acetone absorbed $= V'(Y_1 - Y_2)$
$$= 31.25\,(0.0526 - 0.00105)$$
$$= 1.611 \text{ kmol/h}$$

The driving force for absorption process is at the bottom of the tower.
$$\Delta Y_1 = Y_1 - Y_1^* = Y_1 - 1.68\, X_1$$
$$= 0.0526 - 1.68 \times 0.0193 = 0.0202$$

At the top of the tower :
$$\Delta Y_2 = Y_2 - Y_2^* = Y_2 - 1.68\, X_2$$
$$= 0.00105 - 1.68 \times 0$$
$$= 0.00105$$

The mean driving force is

$$\Delta Ylm = \frac{\Delta Y_1 - \Delta Y_2}{\ln(\Delta Y_1 / \Delta Y_2)}$$

$$= \frac{0.0202 - 0.00105}{\ln \frac{0.0202}{0.00105}}$$

$$= 0.0065 \text{ kg mol acetone/kg mol dry air} \quad \ldots \text{Ans.}$$

Ex. 9.10 : In case of exercise 9.9, estimate the number of transfer units (NTU) and height of column required if height of transfer unit (HTU) is 2 m.

Height of column = NTU × HTU

and

$$NTU = \frac{Y_1 - Y_2}{\frac{(Y_1 - Y_1^*) - (Y_2 - Y_2^*)}{\ln (Y_1 - Y_1^*)/(Y_2 - Y_2^*)}} = \frac{Y_1 - Y_2}{\Delta Ylm}$$

Solution : $Y_1 = 0.0526$, $Y_2 = 0.00105$

Equilibrium relationship is :

$$Y^* = 1.68 \, X$$

∴ $Y_1^* = 1.68 \, X_1 = 1.68 \times 0.0193 = 0.0324$

$Y_2^* = 1.68 \, X_2 = 1.68 \times 0 = 0.0$

$$NTU = \frac{(0.0526 - 0.00105)}{\frac{(0.0526 - 0.0324) - (0.00105 - 0)}{\ln (0.0526 - 0.0324)/(0.00105)}}$$

$$= 7.95 \approx 8$$

Height of packed column = NTU × HTU = 8 × 2 = 16 m ... **Ans.**

EXERCISES

1. Fill in the blanks :
1.1 In gas absorption, mass transfer takes place from ...... phase to liquid phase. **Ans.** gas
1.2 .... used for gas absorption should be less volatile to avoid its loss in lean gas.

Ans. Solvent

1.3 .... are continuous gas-liquid contactors and .... are stage-wise contactors. **Ans.** Packed columns, plate columns
1.4 Operating velocity in packed columns should be 50 to 70% of the .... velocity.

Ans. flooding

1.5 Packing size should not be more than 1/8th of column .... **Ans.** diameter
1.6 Absorption of NO_2 in water to produce nitric acid is example of absorption with .... **Ans.** chemical reaction.

1.7 The tendency of the liquid to segregate towards the walls and to flow along the walls is termed as .... **Ans.** channeling

2. Define gas absorption. What for it is carried out industrially ? Give suitable examples.

3. What factors should be considered while selecting solvent for gas absorption ?

4. State the desirable characteristics of packings.

5. List various types of packings used in industry and state their materials of construction.

6. Write in brief on packing used in industry.

7. Explain briefly hydrodynamics / press drop characteristics of packed column.

8. Compare plate and packed columns for merits and demerits.

9. Draw the neat sketch of packed column and write its construction and functioning.

10. What do you mean by HETP ? State the factors on HETP depends.

11. Compare gas absorption and distillation.

12. Compare plate column with packed column.

13. State the advantages and disadvantages of packed column.

14. State the situations in which the packed columns are well suited.

15. What do you mean by channeling ? How it can be avoided/minimised ?

16. Write briefly on mechanically agitated vessels used for gas absorption.

CHAPTER TEN

LIQUID-LIQUID EXTRACTION

The techniques of removing one component from a solid or liquid by means of a liquid solvent fall into two categories, the first one is called as leaching or solid extraction and the second as liquid extraction. **Leaching** is used to dissolve soluble matter from its mixture with an insoluble solid [Leaching is an operation in which a particular component of the solid is leached out with the help of a solvent] whereas **liquid extraction** is used to separate two miscible liquids by the use of a solvent which preferentially dissolves one of them. In this chapter, our discussion is restricted to liquid extraction – the extraction of the liquid phase with a solvent.

When a mixture of liquids is not easily separable by distillation, i.e., when separation by distillation is ineffective or very difficult, liquid extraction is employed. Close boiling mixtures or substances that cannot withstand the temperature of distillation, even under vacuum [i.e., substances that are thermally unstable (heat sensitive)] may often be separated by extraction. In this operation, a solvent is added to the liquid-mixture. As a result, two immiscible layers are formed, both containing varying amounts of different components. The isolated layers are then separated using density difference as extract phase and raffinate phase using density difference. For the recovery of the solvent for re-use, extraction is followed often by distillation or evaporation.

Liquid-liquid extraction (liquid extraction) refers to an operation in which the constituents of a liquid mixture are separated by contacting it with a suitable insoluble liquid solvent, which preferentially dissolves one or more constituents. This operation is sometimes also termed as solvent extraction. Extraction utilises the differences in solubility of the constituents/components to effect a separation. In this operation, a solute in a liquid solution is removed by contacting the solution with another liquid solvent. The solvent is relatively immiscible with the solution. In liquid extraction, the feed solution to be handled represents one phase and the solvent to be used to effect separation represents the second phase. In this operation, the two immiscible phases in contact are both liquid and so is a liquid-liquid operation. The mass transfer of the solute (liquid) takes place from the feed solution to the solvent phase.

Distillation and extraction both are used for separation of the constituents of a liquid mixture based on relative merits/demerits of the individual methods.

Difference between distillation and extraction.

Distillation	Extraction

1. Distillation/fractionation is an operation in which the constituents of a liquid mixture are separated by using thermal energy.	1. Extraction is an operation in which the constituents of a liquid mixture are separated by using an insoluble liquid solvent.
2. Distillation utilises differences in vapour pressure of different components at the same temperature to effect a separation.	2. Extraction utilises differences in solubility of components to effect a separation.
3. In distillation, relative volatility is used as a measure of the degree of separation.	3. In extraction, selectivity is used as a measure of the degree of separation.
4. In distillation, a new phase is created by addition of heat.	4. In extraction, a new insoluble liquid phase is created by addition of solvent to the original mixture.
5. In distillation, mixing and separation of phases is easy and rapid.	5. In extraction, phases are hard to mix and harder to separate.
6. Distillation/fractionation gives almost pure products.	6. Extraction itself does not give pure products and needs further processing.
7. It does not offer more flexibility in the choice of operating conditions.	7. It does offer more flexibility in the choice of operating conditions.
8. It requires thermal energy.	8. It requires mechanical energy (for mixing and separation).
9. It needs heating and cooling provisions.	9. It does not need heating and cooling provisions.
10. It is a primary choice for separation of the components of a liquid mixture.	10. It is a secondary choice for separation of the components of a liquid mixture.
11. Extractive distillation is the extraction of the vapour phase with solvent.	11. Liquid extraction is the extraction of the liquid phase with solvent.

Field of application of Liquid Extraction :

Whenever separation by both distillation and extraction is possible, the choice is usually distillation irrespective of heating and cooling requirements. In extraction, the solvent should be recovered for reuse and hence extraction is usually followed by distillation for the recovery of the solvent. This combined operation is more complicated and more expensive than ordinary distillation. But whenever separation of the components of a liquid mixture is very difficult or ineffective by distillation, extraction can be thought of as an alternate process (alternative) to it (distillation).

Thus, (i) whenever very large amount of latent heats are required (as in the case with very dilute solutions where water must be vaporised, the latent heats of organic liquids are substantially lower than that of water), (ii) whenever we are dealing with a liquid mixture forming an azeotrope / close boiling mixtures and (iii) whenever we are dealing with substances that are thermally unstable/heat sensitive, separation by distillation is expensive, ineffective and difficult. In such cases, extraction is attractive and preferred. For example,
(i) Recovery of acetic acid from dilute aqueous solutions is done more economically by extraction followed by distillation than distillation alone because of high latent heat of

vaporisation of water (distillation would be possible but extraction reduces substantially the amount of water to be vaporised) (ii) Long chain fatty acids can be removed from vegetable oils economically by extraction with liquid propane than by a high vacuum distillation technique. (iii) Separation of petroleum products that have about the same boiling range. The separation of aromatics from lube oil fractions using furfural as a solvent and (iv) Recovery of penicillin from the fermentation broth using butyl acetate.

A typical liquid-liquid extraction utilising the differences in the solubilities of the components of a liquid mixture may be described as consisting of the following steps :

1. Contacting the feed with a solvent.
2. Separation of the resulting phases, and
3. Removal / Recovery of solvent (s) from each phase.

In liquid-liquid extraction operation, the liquid solution and a insoluble solvent are brought into intimate contact, the constituents of the liquid mixture are distributed between the phases resulting into some degree of separation (which can be improved by a multistage contact), and then the phases are separated from one another based on density difference. For example, acetone may be preferentially extracted from a solution in water with the help of chloroform and the resulting chloroform phase is found to contain large part of acetone, but little water.

In extraction operation, the solution which is to be extracted is called the **feed** and the liquid with which the feed is contacted for the extraction of solute (i.e., to bring about the extraction) is called as the **solvent**. The solvent lean, residual liquid solution from which solute is removed is called as the **raffinate** (also termed as the raffinate phase/layer) and the solvent-rich product of the operation, containing the extracted solute, is called as the **extract** (also termed as the extract phase/layer). The extract phase contains the desired product in a larger proportion.

Thus, if we contact a solution of acetic acid in water with a solvent such as ethylacetate then the two phases/layers will result. The extract (ester layer/organic layer) will contain most of the acetic acid in ethylacetate with some water. While the raffinate (aqueous layer) will contain weaker acetic acid solution with a small amount of ethylacetate. The amount of water in the extract and ethyl acetate in the raffinate depends upon their solubilities into one another.

Distribution coefficient :

In dilute solutions at equilibrium, *the ratio of the concentrations of a solute in the two phases* is called as the distribution coefficient or distribution constant K. Thus,

$$K = C_E / C_R$$

where C_E and C_R are the concentrations of the solute in the extract and the raffinate phases respectively.

The distribution coefficient can also be given in terms of weight fraction of the solute in the two phases in contact at equilibrium.

$$K' = x_E/x_R$$

where x_E is the weight fraction of the solute in the extract and x_R is the weight fraction of the solute in the raffinate.

Ternary System :

The addition of a new solvent to a binary liquid mixture (of a solute in a solvent) yields different types of mixture :

(i) The solvent may be completely immiscible with the feed solvent. This is the ideal case.

(ii) The solvent may be partially miscible with the feed solvent, forming one pair of partially miscible liquid. If A is the feed solvent, C is the solute and B is the extracting solvent, then C dissolves in A and B completely while A and B dissolve only to a limited extent in each other. This is the most common type of system.

(iii) A homogeneous solution may be formed, then the solvent selected is not suitable and should be rejected.

(iv) The solvent may lead to the formation of two or three partially miscible liquids. A and C are completely soluble, while A and B, and B and C dissolve only to a limited extent in each other (two pairs partially miscible). It is observed occasionally and not desired.

Triangular Diagrams :

In liquid-liquid extraction, when the solvent is partially miscible with the original solvent (diluent), the solubility and equilibrium relations are often shown on a triangular diagram. The composition of ternary systems can be shown by a point lying inside an equilateral triangle.

Consider a system C (acetone), A (water) and B (methyl isobutyl ketone) at 25° C wherein acetone is the solute, water is the diluent and methyl isobutyl ketone is the solvent for extracting the solute. This system is shown in Fig. 10.1. In this system, the (acetone) solute 'C' is completely miscible with the two solvents A(water) and B(MIK) and the two solvents A - B are partially miscible with each other. Apex C represents 100% acetone and apexes A and B represent 100% water and 100% Methyl Isobutyl Ketone respectively. Along line BC, concentration of A is zero and the same is true for B and C along AC and AB. The ternary system represented by point 'P' consists of three components C, A and B in the ratio of perpendiculars PL, PJ and PK respectively. The distances AD and BE represent the solubility of solvent B in A and that of A in B respectively. Every mixture of MIK and water of composition lying between points D and E forms two liquid layers, and for calculating mass ratio of these two-layers, centre of gravity principle is applicable. When acetone is added to the two phase/layer mixture of MIK and water, acetone gets distributed between the phases/layers, and compositions of phases/layers follow the raffinate phase and extract phase solubility curves. The curved line ERF indicates composition of saturated MIK layer and the curved line DQF indicates the composition of saturated water layer. The area under binodal solubility curve represented by the curved line DQFRE represents a two - phase region that will split up into two layers in equilibrium with each other. Equilibrium composition of the two phases lie on this curve. These two layers have composition represented by points Q and R and QR is a tie - line. The tie-line is the one which connects together the two phases in equilibrium with each other (it shows equilibria in triangular diagrams) and points of tie - lines must be found by experiment. The point F on the binodal solubility curve represents a single phase which does not split into two phases (i.e. at this point, phases become identical) and corresponds to a tie line of zero length and is known as a plait point. The plait point must be found by experiment and at a given temperature and pressure it is fixed. It is not necessary that the plait point be at the peak of the binodal curve and tie-lines be parallel. In the system under consideration wherein C is the solute and B is the extraction solvent, the separation will increase as the plait point approaches A and tie-lines increase in slope. All points outside the binodal curve represent single phase mixtures.

If a solution of composition X is mixed with another solution of composition Y, then the mixture obtained will have a composition represented by point Z on a line XY such that :

$$\frac{XZ}{ZY} = \frac{\text{Amount of Y}}{\text{Amount of X}}$$

Fig. 10.1 : Equilibrium relationship of distribution of acetone between Water and MIK

The percentage of the solute in the extract phase (B - phase) may be plotted against the percentage of solute in the raffinate phase (A - phase), which is in equilibrium with it over the entire composition range. Such a plot is shown in Fig. 10.2.

This type of plot is very useful in selecting the solvent and determining the number of stages required.

Fig. 10.2 : Equilibrium distribution of solute A in B and C phases

One of the important factors in selecting a solvent is the selectivity of the solvent and is given by –

$$\beta = [x_C/x_A]_E / [x_C/x_A]_R$$

where x_A and x_B are weight fractions/mole fractions of C and A in the extract and the raffinate phase.

The selectivity has the same significance in extraction as the relative volatility has in distillation. So it is a measure of the degree of separation by extraction. When selectivity is equal to one, separation by extraction is not possible. For all practical operations, the selectivity should be greater than one.

Selection of Solvent for Extraction :

Any particular liquid to be used as a solvent for extraction will not possess all the properties considered desirable for extraction and hence compromise is usually necessary of selecting the best solvent out of various possible liquid solvents available.

While selecting a solvent for extraction, the qualities such as selectivity, recoverability, distribution coefficient, density, etc. must be considered.

1. Selectivity : The *ratio of the concentration ratio of solute to feed solvent in the extract phase to that in the raffinate phase* is called the selectivity or separation factor. It is a measure of the effectiveness of solvent for separating the constituents of a solution. The selectivity should be greater than one for all useful extraction operation and if it is equal to one, separation by extraction is not possible.

If B is the solvent, feed contains A and C, where C is the solute, and E and R are the equilibrium phases then selectivity, β is given as –

$$\beta = \frac{[\text{Wt. fraction of C/Wt. fraction of A}]_E}{[\text{Wt. fraction of C/Wt. fraction of A}]_R}$$

The selectivity (β) is analogous to the relative volatility (α) in distillation.

2. Recoverability : As the solvent should be recovered for reuse frequently by distillation, it should not form an azeotrope with the extracted solute and for low cost recovery, the relative volatility should be high.

The latent heat of vaporisation of a solvent should be small whenever the solvent is to be volatilised.

3. Distribution coefficient : Higher values (>1) of the distribution coefficient are generally desirable as less solvent will then be required for a given extraction duty.

4. Density : The difference in densities of the saturated liquid phases should be larger for physical separation.

5. Insolubility of solvent : The solvent insoluble in the original liquid solvent should be preferred. It should have a high solubility for the solute to be extracted as then small amounts of the solvent are required.

6. Interfacial tension : Interfacial tension should be high for coalescence of emulsions to occur more readily, as the same is of a greater importance than dispersion.

7. The solvent should be stable chemically. It should be inert towards the components of the system.

8. It should not be corrosive towards common materials of construction.

9. The solvent should be cheap.

10. The solvent should be non-toxic and non-flammable.

11. The solvent should have a low viscosity, freezing point, vapour pressure for ease in handling and storage.

Extraction Equipments :

In liquid-liquid extraction operation, the two phases must be brought into intimate contact for mass transfer to occur and then the phases are separated. This operation may be carried out batchwise or continuously. Whenever we are dealing with simple systems and quantities to be handled are small, batchwise procedure is adopted and when large quantities are to be handled and several contacts are required, continuous operation becomes economical.

Most of the extraction equipments are operated continuously with either successive stage contacts (stagewise contactors) or differential contacts (differential contactors).

Industrial extraction equipments are classified as :

1. Stage-type extractors and
2. Differential (continuous contact) extractors.

Mixer-settler (single and multistage), plate column, pulsed sieve plate column, etc. are examples of stage-type extractor.

Packed column, spray column, pulsed packed column, rotating disc contactors, etc. are examples of differential extractor.

In stage-type extractors, the two phases are allowed to mix together so as to reach equilibrium and then the phases are separated before they passed countercurrent to each other. Advantages of stage-type contactors include simplicity of design, no axial mixing, high stage efficiency, etc. These units are large and bulky owing to the requirement of a separator for the phase separation after each stage.

In differential extractors, the two phases are always in continuous contact. These are compact for a given throughput and require a small floor space.

In plate columns, packed columns, spray columns used for extraction operation, the phase interdispersion and countercurrent flow are produced by the force of gravity (acting on the density difference between the phases). In mixer settlers, rotating disc contactors, the phase interdispersion is produced by mechanical agitation and countercurrent flow is produced by gravity.

Mixer-Settlers :

A mixer-settle is a single stage extraction device comprising of a mixture for contacting the two liquid phases to effect mass transfer and a settler for mechanical separation of the phases.

For extraction operations carried out in a batchwise fashion/manner, the mixer and settler may be the same unit (i.e., mixing and settling is carried out in the same piece of equipment). [Fig. 10.3 (a)]. It consists of a vertical vessel incorporating a turbine or propeller agitator. It is provided with charging nozzles at the top and a discharge connection provided with a sight glass at the bottom. The feed solution to be extracted is taken into the agitated vessel, required amount of the solvent is added, and whole mass is agitated for predetermined time. At the end of mixing cycle, agitation is stopped and settling is applied for the phase separation. Afterwards, the raffinate and extract phases are withdrawn from the bottom discharge connection into separate receivers.

(a) : **Mixer settler for batch operation** (Mechanically agitated vessel)

(b) : **Continuous single-stage** Mixer-settler

Fig. 10.3

For continuous extraction operation, the mixer and settler are separate units. [Fig. 10.3 (b)]. The mixer is a small baffled-agitated tank provided with inlet-outlet connections and the settler is often a continuous gravity decanter (simple or settler with coalescer for emulsifying liquids).

In this extractor, the two phases are continuously in contact with each other in the mixer under thorough agitation before flowing to the settler for the phase separation.

One phase is usually dispersed into the other in the form of small droplets so as to produce large interfacial areas resulting in faster extraction.

When **several contacts** are required, a **battery/train of mixer settlers** operated in a counter

Fig. 10.4 : Mixer settler battery for counter current extraction

current fashion is used. Generally the liquids are pumped from one stage to the next, but if sufficient headroom is available gravity flow is arranged. A feed solution is introduced in the first mixer and a fresh solvent is fed to the last mixer so that the raffinate from each settler becomes the feed to the next settler, and the extract from the last settler acts as the solvent to the second last mixer and so on. Final extract leaves the first settler while final raffinate is taken out from the last settler.

Fig. 10.5 : Gravity settlers (a) simple and (b) with coalescer

In case of liquids which emulsify easily and having nearly the same density it is necessary to pass a mixer discharge through a pad of glass fibre to coalesce the droplets of the dispersed phase before gravity settling is practicable.

Since pumps and piping systems are involved in the installation of a train of mixer-settlers, initial investment on equipment is high.

Advantages of mixer-settlers :

(i) High stage efficiency (ii) good flexibility (iii) capacity to handle liquids of high viscosity and (iv) high capacity.

These units are employed in industries such as petrochemical, fertilisers, metallurgical, etc.

Perforated plate/Sieve Tray Tower/Column :

These are multistage, counter current contactors wherein the axial mixing of the continuous phase is confined to the region between trays, and redispersion occurs at each tray resulting into effective mass transfer. These are very effective, especially for systems of low interfacial tension both with respect to the liquid handling capacity and extraction efficiency. The perforations in the plates are about 1.5 to 4.5 mm in diameter and the plate/tray spacings are usually 150 to 600 mm.

Fig. 10.6 shows a perforated plate tower wherein the light liquid is dispersed. General arrangement of plates and downcomers is the same as that used for the gas-liquid contact except that no weir is needed. Light liquid (dispersed phase) is introduced at the bottom, passes through the perforations in the plate in the form of fine droplets, which rise through the heavy continuous phase, coalesce into layer beneath the plate, and again redisperses through the plate above. The heavy continuous phase liquid is introduced at the top, passes across each plate and flows downward from a plate above to a plate below via downcomer. The principal interface is maintained at the top, the light liquid is removed from the top and the heavy liquid from the bottom. The heavy liquid can be dispersed in which case, the tower is turned so that the downcomer of each plate becomes the upcomer.

**Fig. 10.6 : Perforated plate tower for continuous counter current extraction
(light liquid dispersed)**

Spray Tower/Column :

Spray towers are the simplest of differential contactors. In its simplest form, it consists of an empty tower provided with inlet and outlet connections at the top and bottom, for introducing and removing the heavy and light liquid phases. Due to maximum freedom for liquid movement, as the shell is empty, there will be severe axial mixing in these extractors and hence it is practically very difficult to obtain the equivalent of more than one or two theoretical stages even with tall towers. In these towers, mixing and settling proceeds simultaneously, and there is a continuous transfer of material between phases and composition of each phase changes as it flows through the tower/column. Either light or heavy phase may be dispersed (i.e., introduced in the tower in the form of fine drops), but generally the phase with high flow rate and the phase of which the viscosity is high should be dispersed.

Spray towers are operated into two distinct ways - Either light phase or heavy phase may be dispersed. When the light phase is to be dispersed, it is introduced through a nozzle from the bottom, droplets rise through the heavy phase and finally coalesce to form a liquid-liquid interface at the top. In operation, where the heavy phase is dispersed, it enters the tower from the top, droplets fall through the light-phase and finally coalesce to form a liquid-liquid interface at the bottom of the tower and then leaves the tower in the form of stream through the bottom outlet. In this case, the light phase introduced at the bottom flows as a continuous phase and ultimately leaves the tower from the top. Fig. 10.7 shows both the methods of operating spray towers.

Though the spray tower is simple to construct, its performance is poor because of considerable recirculation of the continuous phase (axial mixing) and little turbulence in it.

In spray towers, the droplets of dispersed phase rise or fall through the continuous phase under the influence of gravity, thus there is a limit for the amount of dispersed phase that can pass through the tower for any given flow rate of the continuous phase. Additional light phase fed to the bottom of the tower (wherein the light liquid is dispersed) in excess of that flows upwards under the influence of gravity will be rejected through the bottom of the tower and the tower is then said to be flooded.

Fig. 10.7 : Spray towers (a) for light liquid dispersed and (b) for heavy liquid dispersed

It is simple in construction and does not contain any internal structures like plate, packings etc., so gives high throughputs per unit cross-sectional area.

Disadvantages of the spray column include – low efficiency due to axial mixing in the continuous phase and necessity for a tall tower to effect a given degree of separation.

Packed tower/Column :

Randomly packed towers used for gas-liquid contact are also adopted for liquid-liquid extraction. As packing provides large interfacial area for the phase contacting and causes the drops to coalesce and reform, the mass transfer rates in packed towers are very high than those obtained with spray towers as packings cut down the recirculation of the continuous phase. Packed towers are used in the petroleum industry. Packed towers are unsuitable to handle dirty liquids, suspensions or high viscosity liquids.

Packed tower shown in Fig. 10.8 is arranged for the light phase dispersed. It consists of a cylindrical shell filled with packings, packings rest on a support plate, and the shell is provided with inlet-outlet connections at the top and the bottom for the introduction and withdrawal of liquid phases. The heavy liquid phase is fed from the top and the light liquid (dispersed through a distributor) is fed from the bottom. A large portion of the void space in packings is filled by the continuous phase which flows downward and the remainder of the void space is filled with the drops of the light liquid which rise through the continuous phase and finally coalesce to form a liquid-liquid interface at the top. The light liquid leaves the tower from the top and heavy liquid leaves from the bottom. There is a continuous transfer of material between phases, and the composition of each phase changes as it flows through the tower/column. Usually, the packing material should be such that it should preferentially get wetted by the continuous phase.

Fig. 10.8 : Packed tower for light phase dispersed

Carbon and plastic packings get preferentially wetted by organic liquids and ceramic by aqueous solutions. The packing size should not be greater than one-eighth the tower diameter. A dispersed phase distributor is always embedded in the packing whenever the dispersed phase droplets do not wet the material of a packing support to avoid premature flooding (drops will have difficulty in entering).

Packed columns are easy to construct. They can be made to handle corrosive liquids at a reasonable cost. Their performance is better than spray columns. The chief disadvantage of packed columns is that the solids tend to collect in the packing and cause channeling.

Rotating Disk Contactor (R.D.C.) :

For systems of high interfacial tension, good dispersion is achieved by mechanical agitation of the liquids which in turn results in good mass transfer rates.

Rotating disk contactor is a mechanically agitated countercurrent extractor wherein an agitation is brought with the help of rotating disks which usually run at much higher speed than turbine type impellers.

Fig. 10.9 : Rotating disc contactor for light phase dispersed

It consists of a cylindrical column that is divided into a number of compartments formed by a series of stator rings. Each compartment contains a rotating, centrally located horizontal rotor disk that create a high degree of turbulence inside the column. The diameter of the rotor disk is less than the opening in the stationary stator rings, usually the disk diameter is 33 to 66 % of the column diameter. The recommended compartment height for a column of diameter 2 m is 200 to 300 mm. The tower is provided with inlet and outlet connections at the top and the bottom for light and heavy phases. Fig. 10.9 shows a rotating-disk contactor for light phase dispersed. In these units, disks disperse the liquids and impel them outward toward the tower wall, where stator rings create quiet zones wherein the two phases can separate.

It has reasonable capacity, low operating cost and high efficiency. With corrosive liquids it is very difficult to maintain the internal moving parts (maintenance problem - a major disadvantage).

It is commonly used in the petroleum industry for furfural extraction (of lubricating oils), separation of aromatics from aliphatics, desulphurisation of gasoline, recovery of phenol from waste waters, etc.

Pulse Column :

A pulse column may contain ordinary packings or sieve plates without downcomers. The application of an oscillating pulse to the contents of such columns increases the efficiency because the pulse increases both turbulence and interfacial areas.

A reciprocating pump is a common mechanically pulsing device which pulses the entire contents of the column at a frequent intervals, owing to which a rapid reciprocating motion of relatively small amplitude is superimposed on usual flow of the liquid phases. Bellows or diaphrams of steel, teflon, etc. are also used as pulsing devices.

A pulsed sieve plate column consists of a vertical column with a large number of sieve plates without downcomers. The perforations in the plates of such columns are smaller than nonpulsing columns (1.5 to 3 mm diameter). Pulsing amplitudes of 5 to 25 mm are generally recommended with frequencies of 100 to 260 cycles/minute. The pulsation causes the light liquid to be dispersed into the heavy phase on the upward stroke and the heavy liquid phase to jet into the light phase on the downward stroke. The column has no moving parts, low axial mixing and high extraction efficiency.

A pulsed packed column consists of a vertical column filled with packings.

In pulse columns (either sieve plate or packed) the height required for a given number of theoretical contacts is often less than one-third that needed in a nonpulsing column.

Fig. 10.10 : Pulse column (sieve plate)

Pulse columns are extensively used for processing radioactive solutions in atomic-energy work.

Ex. 10.1 : The picric acid is to be extracted with benzene. If the aqueous solution contains 0.2 mol of picric acid 1 per litre, calculate the volume of benzene with which 1 litre of the solution must be extracted in order to form a benzene solution containing 0.02 mol of picric acid per litre (Neglect the difference between the volume of a solution and that of pure solvent). Also calculate the percent recovery of picric acid from the aqueous solution.

$$K = \text{distribution coefficient} = C_E/C_R = 0.505$$

where C_E = concentration of picric acid in benzene, mol per litre of solution
C_R = concentration of picric acid in water, mol per litre of solution

Solution : Basis : 1 litre of original aqueous solution. It contains 0.2 mol of picric acid.

$$K = 0.505 = C_E/C_R$$

Final concentration of picric acid in aqueous solution $= C_R = C_E/K = \dfrac{0.02}{0.505}$

$$= 0.0396 \text{ mol}/l$$

Picric acid in final benzene solution $= 0.20 - 0.0396$

$$= 0.16 \text{ mol}$$

$$\text{Benzene required} = \frac{0.16}{0.02}$$

$$= 8 \ l \text{ per } l \text{ of aqueous solution} \quad \ldots \textbf{Ans.}$$

$$\% \text{ extraction of picric acid} = \frac{0.16}{0.20} \times 100$$

$$= 80 \% \quad \ldots \textbf{Ans.}$$

Ex. 10.2 : The picric acid is to be extracted with benzene as extraction solvent. Aqueous solution contains 0.2 mol of picric acid per litre. Calculate the quantity of benzene required to be contacted with 5 litres of aqueous solution in order to form a benzene solution containing 0.02 mol of picric acid per litre. Also calculate the percent extraction of picric acid.

$$K = C_E/C_R = 0.505$$

where, C_E = concentration of picric acid in benzene in mol/l

C_R = concentration of picric acid in water, in mol/l

Solution : Basis : 5 litres of aqueous solution of picric acid. It contains 0.2 mol/l of picric acid.

∴ Amount of picric acid in aqueous solution = 0.2×5

$$= 1.0 \text{ mol}$$

$$K = 0.505 \text{ in final system} = C_E/C_R$$

C_E = concentration of picric acid in benzene = 0.02 mol/l

Final concentration of picric acid aqueous solution = $C_R = C_E/K$

$$= \frac{0.02}{0.505}$$

$$= 0.0396 \text{ mol}/l$$

Picric acid in aqueous solution = 0.0396×5

$$= 0.198 \text{ mol}$$

Amount of picric acid extracted in benzene = $1 - 0.198$

$$= 0.802 \text{ mol}$$

Amount of Benzene required = $\frac{0.802}{0.02} = 40.1 \ l$ \quad \ldots **Ans.**

$$= 80.2 \quad \ldots \textbf{Ans.}$$

Ex. 10.3 : A solution of picric acid in benzene contains 30 grams of picric acid per litre. Calculate the quantity of water with which 1 litre of this solution must be shaken at 291 K (18° C) in order to reduce the picric acid concentration to 4 g/l in the benzene phases.

Molecular weight of picric acid is 229, and the distribution coefficient K is given as –

$$C_E/C_R = 0.548$$

where, C_R = concentration of picric acid in water, mol/l
               C_E = concentration of picric acid in benzene, mol/l

Solution : Basis : 1 litre of solution of picric acid in benzene.

Initial picric acid = 30 g
Final picric acid = 4 g
Picric acid extracted = 30 − 4 = 26 g
$$= \frac{26}{229} = 0.1135 \text{ mol}$$
Picric acid in benzene = 4 g/l
$$= \frac{4}{229} = 0.01746 \text{ mol}$$
C_E = 0.01746 mol/l
$$K = \frac{C_E}{C_R} = 0.548$$
$$C_R = \frac{C_E}{0.548} = \frac{0.01746}{0.548}$$
$$= 0.03186 \text{ mol}/l$$
Quantity of water required = $\frac{0.1135}{0.03186}$ = 3.56 l   **... Ans.**

Ex. 10.4 : A solution of picric acid in benzene contains 40 grams of picric acid per litre. Calculate the quantity of water with which 2 litre of this solution must be shaken at 291 K (18° C) in order to reduce the picric acid concentration to 5 g/l in the benzene phase.

Molecular weight of picric acid is 229, and the distribution coefficient K is given as $C_E/C_R = 0.548$.

where, C_R = concentration of picric acid in water, mol/l
               C_E = concentration of picric acid in benzene, mol/l

Solution : Basis : 2 litre of solution of picric acid in benzene.

Initial picric acid = 40 × 2 = 80 g
Final picric acid = 5 × 2 = 10 g
Picric acid extracted = 80 − 10 = 70 g
$$= 70/229 = 0.3057 \text{ mol}$$
Picric acid in benzene = 5 g/l
$$= 5 \times 2 = 10 \text{ g}$$
$$= 10/229 = 0.0437 \text{ mol}$$
Picric acid in benzene = 0.0437/2 = 0.02185 mol/l
C_E = 0.02185 mol/l

$$C_E/C_R = 0.548$$
$$C_R = C_E/0.548$$
$$= 0.02185/0.548 = 0.03987 \text{ mol}/l$$
$$\text{Quantity water required} = \frac{0.3057}{0.03987} = \mathbf{7.67\ l} \quad \ldots \text{Ans.}$$

Ex. 10.5 : Carbon disulphide is used to extract iodine from its saturated aqueous solution. The distribution of iodine between carbon disulphide and water at equilibrium may be expressed as

$$K = \frac{y^*}{x} = \frac{\text{grams iodine/litre of carbon disulphide}}{\text{grams iodine/litre of water}} = 588.2$$

(i) Calculate the concentration of iodine in the aqueous phase when 1 litre of a saturated aqueous solution at 293 K (20° C) containing 0.3 grams of iodine per 1 litre of water is stirred with 50 ml of carbon disulphide.

(ii) Repeat for two ideal extractions using 25 ml of solvent each time.

Solution : Basis : 1 litre of saturated solution. It contains 0.3 g iodine.

$$\frac{\text{grams iodine/litre of CS}_2}{\text{grams iodine/litre water}} = 588.2$$

Let x be grams iodine/litre of water at equilibrium

$$\text{grams iodine/litre of CS}_2 = 588.2\ x$$
$$= 588.2\ x$$

Material balance of iodine in aq. phase :

$$= \text{iodine in CS}_2 + \text{iodine in water phase}$$
$$0.3 = 588.2\ x \times \frac{50}{1000} + x = 30.41\ x$$
$$x = 0.009865 \text{ g}/l \quad \ldots \text{Ans.}$$

Case II :
$$0.3 = 488.2\ x_1 \left(\frac{25}{1000}\right) + x_1$$

Concentration of iodine in aqueous solution for second stage.

$$x_1 = 0.191 \text{ g}/l$$
$$0.0191 = 588.2\ x_2 \left(\frac{25}{1000}\right) + x_2$$
$$x_2 = \mathbf{0.001268 \text{ g}/l}$$

Ex. 10.6 : 150 kg of a nicotine-water solution containing 1% nicotine is to be extracted with 250 kg of kerosene at 293 K (20° C). Water and Kerosene are essentially immiscible in each other. Determine the percentage extraction of nicotine after single stage. At the dilute end of the system the equilibrium relationship is

$$Y^* = 0.798\ X$$

where Y and X are expressed as kg nicotine/kg kerosene and kg nicotine/kg water, respectively.

Solution : Basis : 150 kg of nicotine-water solution.

X_0 is the kg nicotine/kg water in original solution. Nicotine content is 1% by weight. Weight fraction of nicotine is $1/100 = 0.01$

$$x_0 = 0.01$$

$$X_0 = \frac{x_0}{1-x_0}$$

$$X_0 = \frac{\text{kg nicotine}}{\text{kg water}} = \frac{0.01}{1-0.01} = 0.0101$$

kg original solvent (kg water in aqueous solution) =

$$A_0 = 150(1-0.01)$$
$$= 148.5 \text{ kg}$$
$$B_0 = \text{kg of kerosene solvent} = 250 \text{ kg}$$

Material balance of Nicotine :

$$\begin{matrix}\text{kg nicotine} \\ \text{in original solution}\end{matrix} = \begin{matrix}\text{kg nicotine} \\ \text{in water phase}\end{matrix} + \begin{matrix}\text{kg nicotine in} \\ \text{kerosene phase}\end{matrix}$$

$$A_0 X_0 = A_0 X_1 + B_0 Y_1$$

where, X_1 and Y_1 are equilibrium values of weight ratio of solute to solvent in raffinate and extract phases.

X_1 = kg nicotine/kg water in aqueous solution after one stage

We have, $Y^* = 0.798\, X$

$\therefore \qquad Y_1 = 0.798\, X_1$

So, $\qquad A_0 X_0 = A_0 X_1 + B_0 \times 0.798\, X_1$

$$148.5 \times 0.0101 = 148.5\, X_1 + 250 \times 0.798\, X_1$$
$$1.49985 = 348\, X_1$$
$$X_1 = 0.0043$$

Nicotine removed/extracted from water $= A_0 (X_0 - X_1)$
$$= 148.5\,(0.0101 - 0.0043)$$
$$= 0.8613 \text{ kg}$$

Nicotine (original) present in water $= 0.01 \times 150 = 1.5$ kg

$$\%\text{ extraction of nicotine} = \frac{0.8613}{1.5} \times 100$$
$$= \mathbf{57.42} \qquad \text{... Ans.}$$

Ex. 10.7 : The picric acid is to be extracted with benzene. If the aqueous solution contains 0.20 mol of picric acid per litre, calculate the volume of benzene with which 1 litre of this solution must be extracted in order to form a benzene solution containing 0.01 mol of picric acid per litre. Also calculate the percentage recovery of picric acid from the aqueous solution.

K = distribution coefficient at 288 K (15 °C)

$$K = C_E/C_R = 0.705$$

where, C_R = concentration of picric acid in water in mol/l
C_E = concentration of picric acid in benzene in mol/l

Solution : Basis : 1 litre of original aqueous solution. It contains 0.2 mol of picric acid.

$$K = 0.705 \text{ in final system} = C_E/C_R$$
$$C_E = \text{concentration of picric acid in benzene} = 0.01 \text{ mol}/l$$

Final concentration of picric acid in aqueous solution $= \dfrac{0.01}{0.705}$

$$= 0.01418 \text{ mol}/l$$
$$[C_R = C_E/K]$$

Picric acid in final benzene solution $= 0.20 - 0.01418$
$$= 0.18582 \text{ mol}$$

Benzene required $= \dfrac{0.18582}{0.01}$

$$= 18.582 \; l \text{ per } l \text{ of aqueous solution}$$

% extraction of picric acid $= \dfrac{0.18582}{0.2} \times 100$

$$= \mathbf{92.91}$$

Equilateral Triangular Coordinates/Equilateral Triangular Diagram : The equilateral triangular diagrams are extensively used for graphical presentation of the compositions of ternary systems/mixture. In the case of an equilateral triangle, we know that the sum of the perpendicular distances from any point inside the triangle to its three sides is equal to the altitude of the triangle, so we can assume here that the altitude represents 100 percent composition and the perpendicular distances to the three sides represent the percentages or fractions of the three components.

(i)   (ii)

Fig. 10.11 : Equilateral triangular coordinates/diagram

Here we are considering a ternary system comprising of components A, C and B, so in Fig. 10.11, the apexes of the triangle are marked with 100 % A, 100 % C and 100 % B (each apex representing the pure component). Any point on a side of the triangle represents the locus of all possible mixtures of two of any three components, i.e., it represents a binary mixture and any point inside the triangle represents a mixture of all three components. Therefore,

a side AC represents the locus of all possible mixtures of A and C only, i.e., it represents a binary mixture of A and C. Similarly, a side AB represents a binary mixture of A and B, and a side BC, a binary mixture of C and B. For example, point D marked on the side AB represents a binary mixture containing 80 % A and 20 % B.

Any point within the triangle represents a mixture consisting of all three components. If the two components are marked with their compositions then the third one is fixed because of the property of the triangle. The mixture indicated by point P consists of the three components A, B and C in the ratio of the perpendiculars PN, PM, PQ. The perpendicular distance from point P to the base AB, i.e., PQ represents the composition of C in the mixture at P. Similarly, the perpendicular distances PM (to the base AC) and PN (to the base BC) represent the compositions of B and A in the mixture at P respectively. So $x_p = 0.40$.

If R kg of a mixture at point R is added to E kg of a mixture at point E, then the new mixture resulted (M kg) is shown on the straight line RE at point M, such that :

$$\frac{R}{E} = \frac{\text{line ME}}{\text{line RM}} = \frac{x_E - x_M}{x_M - x_R} \qquad \ldots (10.1)$$

where x_R is the weight fraction of C in R

x_E is the weight fraction of C in E

x_M is the weight fraction of C in M

Systems of three liquids – One pair partially miscible :

(a)   (b)

Fig. 10.12 : Equilibrium relationship of distribution of acetone (C) between water (A) and MIK (B)

(System of three liquids, A and B partially miscible)

Consider a system C (acetone), A (water) and B (methyl isobutyl ketone, MIK) at 298 K (25°) wherein acetone is the solute, water is the diluent (feed solvent) and methyl isobutyl ketone is the solvent used to extract acetone, i.e., extracting solvent. Acetone and water are completely miscible, and acetone and MIK are completely miscible while water and MIK are partially miscible with each other. Water (A) and MIK (B) dissolve to a limited extent in each other to give rise to the saturated liquid solutions (A - rich) at D and (B - rich) at G. Apex C represents 100 % acetone, and apexes A and B represent 100 % water and 100 % MIK respectively. Along a side AB the concentration of C is zero and same is true for A and B along BC and AC respectively. Every mixture of MIK and water (binary mixture) of composition lying between points D and G say at H forms two liquid phases (layers) of compositions at D and G and the relative amounts of phases depend upon the position of H according to the mixture rule Equation (10.1). When acetone is added to the two phase mixture of MIK and water, acetone gets distributed between the phases (layers) and compositions of the phases follow the raffinate phase and extract phase solubility curves. The curved line GEP indicates the composition of saturated MIK layer-extract phase and the curved line DRP indicates the composition of saturated water layer-raffinate phase. The area under the binodal solubility curve represented by curved line DRPEG represents a two phase region that will split into two phases/layers in equilibrium with each other. Any mixture outside this curve will be a homogeneous solution of one liquid phase. The equilibrium compositions of two phases will lie on this curve. Any mixture underneath the curve at point M will split into two saturated liquid phases of equilibrium compositions indicated by points R and E. The line joining the equilibrium compositions of two phases (raffinate and extract) i.e. line RE is called as a tie line. The tie line is one which connects together two phases in equilibrium with each other. The points of a tie line must be found by experiment. The point P on the binodal solubility curve represents a single phase which does not split into two phases (i.e., at this point, phases become identical) and at this point A-rich and B-rich curves merge; so the point P corresponds to a tie line of zero length and is known as a plait point. At a given temperature and pressure point P is fixed. It is not necessary that the plait point be at the peak of the binodal solubility curve and tie lines be parallel. In the system under consideration wherein C is the solute and B is the extraction solvent, the separation will increase as the plait point approaches A and tie lines increase in slope.

From Fig. 10.12, it is clear that % of C in E (extract) is greater than in R (raffinate) and so in this case the distribution of C favours the B-rich phase (extract phase). This is shown on the distribution diagram wherein composition of C in extract phase is plotted against the composition of C in the raffinate phase (composition expressed in terms of weight fraction). In Fig. 10.12 (b), the point E, R lies above the diagonal $y = x$ indicating that y^* is always greater than x.

So in this case the distribution coefficient y^*/x is greater than unity. When the concentration of C at the ends of tie lines are plotted on the x - y diagram, we get the distribution curve as shown.

For the ternary systems of the type described above, the mutual solubility of A and B increases with increase in temperature and at one particular critical solution temperature they get dissolved completely. So liquid extraction operations that depend upon formation of insoluble liquid phases must be carried below such temperature.

EXERCISES

1. Define liquid extraction and state briefly the field of application of extraction.
2. Define the following terms with reference to extraction
   (i) feed, (ii) solvent (iii) raffinate and (iv) extract.
3. Explain in briefly the selection criteria for solvent to be used for liquid-liquid extraction.
4. Define selectivity and state what it indicates ?
5. Explain in brief, triangular diagram for system with one pair partially miscible.
6. Give the construction and working of batch operated mixer-settler with neat sketch.
7. Explain briefly the mixer-settler assembly operated in counter current fashion with sketch. Give advantages of mixer-settlers.
8. Explain in brief the construction and operation of sieve plate column for extraction.
9. Write briefly on classification of extraction equipments.
10. Write a short note with neat sketch on the following equipments used for liquid-liquid extraction.
    (a) packed column (b) spray column (c) pulse column
11. Write in brief on rotating-disk contactors.
12. Differentiate between distillation and extraction.

CHAPTER ELEVEN

LIQUID-LIQUID EXTRACTION

In this chapter, our discussion is restricted to crystallisation from solution.

Crystallisation is an operation in which solid particles are formed from a liquid solution.

It is a solid-liquid operation used to separate solutes from solution in the form of crystals. In this operation, mass is transferred from the liquid phase (solution) to the solid phase/the crystal surface.

Crystallisation is an important operation in the chemical industry because of the number of soluble products (from plants) have to be in the form of crystals (solid particles). This operation gives almost pure product in the form of crystals of the desired size range from relatively impure solutions in a single processing step. From the energy point of view, crystallisation requires much less energy for separation as compared to other purification methods (e.g., distillation). It may be carried out at relatively low temperatures and on a scale ranging from a few grams to thousands of tons per day.

Crystallisation usually involves : (i) concentration of solution (by evaporating a part of the solvent) and (ii) cooling of solution until the concentration of the solute becomes higher than its solubility at the prevailing temperature. The solute then comes out of the solution (i.e., precipitates) in the form of pure crystals.

The performance of crystallisation process is evaluated in terms of size, shape, structure, yield and purity of crystals. So in commercial crystallisation, the size and shape of crystals are as important as the yield and purity of crystals.

Solubility :

The solubility of a solute in a given solvent is the *concentration of the solute in a saturated solution at a given temperature.*

The concentration of a solute in a saturated solution is called the solubility of the solute in the solvent.

The solubility of a solute in a given solvent depends on the nature of the solute, the nature of the solvent and the prevailing temperature (solubility mainly depends on temperature). Solubility data are generally given as parts by weight of anhydrous solute material per 100 parts by weight of the solvent, e.g., the solubility of $MgSO_4$ in water at

293 K (20° C) is 35.5 kg MgSO$_4$ per 100 kg water. Solubility data are plotted as solubility curves-curves wherein solubilities are plotted against temperature.

The solubility of the solute in a given solvent is different at different temperatures and it forms the basis of crystallisation by cooling.

Saturation :

Consider a process of dissolving copper sulphate in water (solvent) at a given temperature. Initially, when some amount of copper sulphate is added, all of it goes in the solution. Additional amount can be dissolved further till a stage comes when no more copper sulphate can be dissolved in a given amount (i.e. a fixed amount) of the solvent. At this stage, the solution is called as a saturated solution.

A saturated solution is defined as the *one which is in equilibrium with an excess of solid solute at a given temperature.*

If the temperature of the solution is increased, more solute [CuSO$_4$] can be dissolved. Therefore, a saturated solution will contain different amounts of solute dissolved in it at different temperatures. When a saturated solution at higher temperature (say at T$_1$) is cooled to say T$_2$ (T$_1$ > T$_2$) then theoretically the amount of the solute corresponding to the difference in solubilities at these two temperatures will come out of the solution in the form of crystals.

Solubility Curves :

A graphical relationship between the solubility and temperature is termed as the solubility curve.

The concentration necessary for crystal formation and chemical species that separate can be determined from solubility curves. Such curves are obtained by plotting the solubility of a solute as a function of temperature (solubilities against temperature). It shows the effect of temperature on the solubility of the solute substance. The solubility of solutes in a given solvent may increase, decrease, or more or less remains constant with temperature. Solubility curves have no general shape or slope.

Fig. 11.1 : Solubility curves : Solubilities of salts in water

Solubility curves of potassium chlorate, sodium chloride are continuous solubility curves as they show no sharp breaks any where. Sometime, the solubility curve exhibit sudden changes of direction and these curves are therefore referred to as discontinuous solubility curves, e.g., that of $FeSO_4$, Na_2SO_4 etc.

For some substances, their solubility decreases with increase in temperature and in such cases their solubility curves are called as inverted solubility curves (e.g., that of $MnSO_4 \cdot H_2O$ in H_2O).

Usually, increase in the temperature of the solution increases the solubility of the solute when no true compounds are formed between the solute and solvent, e.g., $KClO_3$, KNO_3 in H_2O. In case of a hydrated salt, the solubility increases with increase in temperature over a certain temperature range and then decreases. Fig. 11.1 shows solubility curves for a number of salts in water. In case of potassium chlorate, the solubility increases with temperature so it can be readily crystallised by cooling a saturated solution. The solubility of NaCl in water is almost independent of temperature (a slight increase in the solubility results by a large increase in temperature), so for crystallisation to occur, some of the solvent should be evaporated.

Supersaturation :

Consider an equilibrium solution (solid solute + liquid solvent). If we disturb this equilibrium either by cooling the solution or evaporating a portion of the solvent then the quantity of solute will exceed the equilibrium concentration and the system will try to attain a new state of equilibrium by expelling (precipitating) excess solute present in it in the form of crystals. This process of forming crystals is called crystallisation from solution and the concentration difference driving force is called supersaturation.

Supersaturation : It is the *quantity of solute present in solution (in which crystals are growing) compared with the quantity of solute that is in equilibrium with the solution (i.e., the equilibrium solubility at the temperature under consideration).* The supersaturation is expressed as a coefficient, given as

$$s = \frac{\text{(Parts solute / 100 parts solvent) at prevailing condition}}{\text{(Parts solute / 100 parts solvent) at equilibrium}} \geq 1.0$$

Crystallisation cannot take place/occur (i.e., crystals can neither form nor grow) unless a solution is supersaturated. The amount of crystals formed however depend upon the difference in saturation concentration since once the crystallisation begins the extra solute held in the solution due to supersaturation also comes out of the solution in the form of crystals.

Mechanism of crystallisation / crystal formation :

A knowledge of the mechanism by which crystals form and grow is required in the design and operation of equipment used for crystallisation. The formation of a crystal from a solution is a two-step process.

The first step is called nucleation (the birth of new small particles or nuclei) and the second one is called crystal growth (growth of crystals to macroscopic size).

The generation of a new solid phase (i.e., new small particles) either on an inert material in the solution or in the solution itself is called **nucleation**. *The increase in size of these nuclei with a layer-by-layer addition of solute is called crystal growth.* Supersaturation is the common driving force for nucleation and crystal growth. Crystals can neither form nor grow unless a solution is supersaturated.

The number of nuclei and rate of growth of crystals does depend upon the temperature of operation. The number of nuclei and growth rate of crystals increase with increase in temperature upto a certain point and then decreases. The temperature corresponding to a maximum number of nuclei formation is different than the temperature at which a growth rate is maximum.

If initially a large number of nuclei is formed, then the yield of the process contains many small or tiny crystals and if a few nuclei are formed initially (at the start), then the yield of the process contains large size crystals. Slow cooling results in the formation of a less number of nuclei and hence large size crystals are formed (as the material deposits on a relatively few nuclei), whereas rapid cooling results in the/leads to the formation of a large number of nuclei, giving the yield containing a large number of tiny crystals.

Methods of Supersaturation :

Unless a solution is supersaturated, neither nucleation nor crystal growth occurs (i.e., crystals can neither form nor grow). Thus, for crystallisation to occur, supersaturation can be generated by any one of the following methods :

(a) By cooling a concentrated, hot solution through indirect heat exchange.

(b) By evaporating a part of the solvent/By evaporating a solution.

(c) By adiabatic evaporation and cooling (i.e., by vacuum cooling) : by flashing of a feed solution adiabatically to a lower temperature and inducing/causing crystallisation by simultaneous cooling and evaporation of the solvent.

(d) By adding a new substance (i.e., a third substance) which reduces the solubility of the original solute, i.e., by salting.

(e) By chemical reaction with a third substance.

When the solubility of the solute increases with increase in temperature, a saturated solution becomes supersaturated, i.e., supersaturation is generated by cooling and temperature reduction. This is the case with many inorganic salts and organic substances (e.g. potassium nitrate, potassium chlorate, oxalic acid, etc.). When the solubility of the solute is relatively independent of temperature (as is the case with common salt (NaCl) in H_2O), supersaturation is generated by evaporating a part of the solvent. When the solubility of the solute is very high then neither cooling nor evaporation helps and supersaturation may be generated by adding a new substance (a third component). The added component may get mixed physically with the original solvent to form a mixed solvent in which the solubility of the solute is reduced. This technique is called salting. The third component added may react with the original solute and form an insoluble substance. This technique is called precipitation. The methods employed in wet quantitative analysis are prime examples of precipitation. The rapid creation of very large supersaturations is possible by the addition of a third component but it is not common in industry.

Miers' Supersaturation theory :

According to Miers' theory there is a definite relationship between the concentration and temperature at which crystals will spontaneously form in a pure solution. This relationship is represented by the supersolubility curve which is approximately parallel to the solubility curve. Both the curves are shown in Fig. 11.2. The curve AB is the solubility curve and the curve PQ is the supersolubility curve. The curve AB represents the maximum concentration of solutions which can be achieved by bringing solid solute into equilibrium with liquid solvent. If a solution having the composition and temperature indicated by the point C is cooled in the direction shown by the arrow it first crosses the solubility curve AB and we would expect here crystallisation to start. Actually if we start with initially unseeded solutions, crystal formation will not begin until the solution is super cooled considerably past the curve AB. According to the Miers' theory, crystallisation will start in the neighbourhood of the point D and the concentration of the solution then follows roughly along the curve DE. For an initially unseeded solution, the curve PQ represents the limit at which spontaneous nuclei formation begin and consequently, crystallisation can start. According to Miers' theory, under normal conditions, nuclei cannot form and crystallisation cannot then occur in area between the solubility curve and the supersolubility curve i.e. at any position short of point D along line CD.

Miers' theory is useful in discussion of qualitative aspects of nucleation from seeded and unseeded solutions.

Fig. 11.2 : The Miers' Supersaturation Theory

Yield of crystallisation process :

Usually, crystallisation processes are carried out slowly and the mother liquor is in contact with sufficiently large crystals so that at the end of the process, the mother liquor is saturated at the final temperature. In such cases, the yield of crystallization process is calculated from the initial solution composition and the solubility of the solute material at the final temperature. If appreciable evaporation of the solvent occurs during the crystallisation process, the solvent evaporated must be taken into account in determining the yield. Whenever crystals are anhydrous, the yield is obtained by taking the difference between the initial composition of the solution and the solubility of the solute corresponding the final temperature of the process. In cases where material precipitates as a hydrated salt, we have to take into account the water of crystallisation (in crystals), as this water is not available for retaining solute in solution. Under these circumstances, the key to calculations of yields is to express all compositions in terms of hydrated salt and excess water (free water), as excess water remains constant during crystallisation operation and compositions or amounts thus expressed on the basis of excess water can be deducted in order to obtain the correct results.

The percentage yield of a crystallisation process is the amount of solute crystallised/ expressed as a percentage of the amount of solute originally present.

Crystal form :

The constituent particles of a crystal are arranged in an orderly and repetitive manner. The constituent particles may be atoms, molecules or ions. They are arranged in orderly three dimensional arrays called space lattices. Crystals are classified according to the angle between the faces and this is the area of the science of crystallography. Different forms of crystals based upon the angle between faces and lengths of axes are : cubic, tetragonal, orthorhombic, hexagonal, monoclinic, triclinic and trigonal.

Caking of Crystals :

Caking of crystalline materials is caused by to a small amount of dissolution occuring at the surface of crystals and subsequent re-evaporation of the solvent. Due to caking, the crystals can get very tightly bonded together.

Since the vapour pressure of a saturated solution of a crystalline solid is less than that of pure water at a given temperature, condensation can take place on the surface of the crystals even though the atmospheric relative humidity is less than 100 percent. The solution thus formed enters into/penetrates into the pack of crystals as a result of capillary action of the small gaps between the crystals and caking can result due to subsequent evaporation of moisture when the atmospheric humidity falls. Crystalline materials can also cake at a constant relative humidity, as the vapour pressure of a solution is less in a small capillary as compared to it in a large capillary as a result of temperature effect. As condensation occurs, the small particles get first dissolved and therefore average size of capillaries increases and the vapour pressure of the solution may increase sufficiently for evaporation to take place. When the particle size is non-uniform, a crystalline material will cake more rapidly since the porosity of a bed of particles of mixed sizes is less and fine particles are more readily soluble. Thus, the tendency of crystalline materials to cake can be reduced by forming crystals of relatively large and uniform sizes or by adding a water repellent agent, such as stearic acid.

Magma : It is a two-phase mixture of mother liquor and crystals that occupies the crystalliser and withdrawn as product.

In order to reduce the load on a crystalliser, evaporation may be carried out to remove the excess solvent. Crystallisation is generally followed by filtration for the separation of crystals from mother liquor.

Effect of impurities on crystal formation :

(i) Soluble impurities may get adsorbed on the surface of the nuclei or crystals nucleation sites and retard the rate of nucleation and crystal growth.

(ii) The shape of crystal may get modified as adsorption of impurities may occur preferentially on a particular face.

The impurities may decrease the rate of crystal growth. In some cases it is desirable e.g. addition of a small quantity of glue or tannin to boiler feed water prevents nucleation and growth of calcium carbonate crystals and thus reduces scaling.

Classification of Crystallisers :

Crystallisers may be classified on the basis of mode of operation. These may be operated batch wise or continuously.

1. Batch crystalliser : stir-tank crystalliser
2. Continuous crystalliser : Swenson-Walker crystalliser.

Crystallisers may also be classified according to the method by which supersaturation achieved adopted in the actual practice. Thus, agitated tank crystalliser, Swenson Walker crystalliser are examples of crystallisers wherein supersaturation is achieved by cooling (or temperature reduction) which is a usual practice for materials of which the solubility decreases with decrease in temperature. Krystal crystalliser is an example of evaporative crystalliser wherein supersaturation is achieved by evaporating a part of the solvent and is a usual practice for materials whose solubility remains almost constant with variation in temperature. Vacuum crystalliser is an example of crystalliser wherein supersaturation is achieved by adiabatic evaporation and cooling which is most suitable for heat sensitive materials. This is used for large scale production in which supersaturation is achieved by introducing the hot solution into a vacuum in which pressure is less than the vapour pressure of the solvent at the temperature at which it is fed, the solvent thus flashes or evaporates and the solution is cooled adiabatically. Salting out with the help of a third substance is not often in use. An indirect application of salting method is found out in the evaporation of glycerin soap lyes. In this case, the presence of glycerin in high concentration reduces the solubility of the solute, so that as the concentration of very soluble component increases, the solubility of the less soluble component (in this case sodium chloride) decreases to a point where it crystallises out. At present, deliberate introduction of a foreign substance to decrease the solubility is rarely found.

Classification based on the method of achieving supersaturation :

1. Supersaturation by cooling alone :
    (a) Batch – Agitated tank crystallisers
    (b) Continuous – Swenson-Walker crystalliser
2. Supersaturation by adiabatic evaporation and cooling :
    (a) Vacuum crystallisers with and without external classifying seed bed
3. Supersaturation by evaporation :
    (1) Krystal crystallisers
    (2) Draft-tube crystallisers.

Crystallisers may also be classified according to the method of suspending the growing product crystals, as (a) where suspension is agitated in a tank, (b) it is circulated through a heat exchanger (c) it is circulated through a scraped surface exchanger.

Agitated Tank Crystalliser :

It is also known as stir-tank crystalliser or agitated batch crystalliser. This is the simplest and perhaps the most economical unit. In this crystalliser, supersaturation is generated by cooling so it is a cooling crystalliser.

This type of crystalliser is commonly employed in small scale production or batch processing due to several advantages, such as low initial cost, simple in construction and flexibility. These are having capacities more than tank crystallisers.

Construction : Agitated tank crystalliser consists of a cylindrical tank provided with a low speed agitator and a cooling coil. The tank is having a conical bottom through which the product is withdrawn. The agitator improves the heat transfer rate, keeps the temperature of the solution uniform and keeps the fine crystals in suspension which is essential for uniform growth of the crystals, simplicity of operation.

Fig. 11.3 : Agitated tank crystalliser

Working : A known quantity of hot solution is charged to the crystalliser, cooling is applied by circulating a coolant through the coil and agitator is started. The mass in the crystalliser cools due to heat transfer to the circulated coolant and as the temperature decreases, crystals are formed due to decrease in the solubility of the solute. The mass is cooled to a predecided temperature and finally a product stream containing crystals plus mother liquor is withdrawn from the bottom of the crystalliser.

One of the drawbacks of this crystalliser is that the solids deposited on the surface of the coil add resistance to heat transfer so that it ceases to function efficiently. High supersaturation at a cooling surface is unavoidable and because of which the cooling surface get rapidly fouled with adhering crystals so the surface might therefore require frequent washing and scrapping. Other disadvantages include difficulty in controlling nucleation and size of crystals and high labour costs.

This type of crystalliser is used to produce fine chemicals, pharmaceutical products and dye intermediates.

Scrapped surface crystalliser :

(i) Swenson-Walker crystalliser and (ii) Double pipe crystalliser.

Swenson-Walker Crystalliser :

The Swenson-Walker crystalliser is a cooling type, continuous, jacketed trough crystalliser. It is an example of the scrapped surface crystalliser and is probably the most widely used crystalliser.

Construction :

It consists of a long open rectangular trough with a semi-cylindrical bottom, i.e., U-shaped trough, of width 0.6 m and length 3 to 6 m. The trough is jacketed externally for circulating the coolant during operation. A spiral agitator rotating at about 7 rpm is incorporated in the trough in such a way that it is as close to the bottom of the trough as possible. The capacity of this crystalliser can be increased by use of a number of units in a series (four troughs of 3 metre length each may be arranged). At one end of the crystalliser, an inlet for the hot solution is provided and at the other end of the crystalliser, an overflow gate for the crystals and mother liquor discharge is provided. The functions of the spiral agitator include : (i) to scrap the crystals for the cooling surface (i.e., to prevent accumulation of the crystals on the heat transfer surface), (ii) to lift and shower the crystals through the solution so that the crystals will be held in suspension and thereby the crystals of uniform size can be obtained (as deposition occurs mainly by build up on previously formed crystals) and (iii) to convey the crystals from one end of equipment to the other end.

The trough is formed out of metal sheets welded to an angle-iron frame at the top. A jacket is usually made of mild steel. The spiral agitator is supported at either end outside the trough. A stuffing box assembly is attached to the cover on either end that prevents leakage of the liquor from the opening provided for a shaft. The shaft is driven by belt, etc.

Fig. 11.4 : Swenson – Walker Crystalliser

Working :

The hot, concentrated solution is fed at one end of the open trough and flows slowly towards the other end of the trough. Water is fed to the jacket in such a way that it flows in a counter current fashion with respect to the solution. The solution while flowing through the trough cools by heat transfer to water. Once the solution becomes supersaturated crystals starts forming and building. A spiral agitator keeps the crystals in suspension so that previously formed crystals grow instead of formation of new crystals and ultimately the two phase mixture of crystals and liquor leaves the crystalliser through an overflow gate.

Advantages of this crystalliser include : saving in floor space, in material in process and saving in labour.

This crystalliser is suitable only when supersaturation can be achieved by cooling alone.

Double pipe scrapped surface crystalliser :

Less common type of continuous scrapped surface crystalliser that is some what similar to the jacketed trough crystalliser, i.e., Swenson-Walker crystalliser is a double pipe crystalliser. It consists of a concentric double pipe, the outer pipe acting as a jacket. Cooling water flows through the annular space between the two pipes and a long pitch spiral agitator rotates in the inner pipe at 5 to 30 rpm. These are also arranged in a series (3 pipes each of 3 m long). Other constructional features and the method of operation is the same as in the Swenson-Walker crystalliser.

It is used in crystallising ice cream and plasticizing margarine.

Vacuum Crystalliser :

In this crystallizer, supersaturation is achieved by adiabatic evaporative cooling. A hot solution (feed) is introduced into a vessel wherein a vacuum is maintained that corresponds to the boiling point of the solution lower than the temperature of the feed solution. Evaporation will result due to flashing. The energy needed for vaporisation is taken from the feed (sensible heat), so that the temperature of a liquor-vapour mixture after flashing becomes much lower than the temperature of the liquor before flashing.

Vacuum crystallisers often operated continuously but they can also be operated batch-wise. These crystallisers are very simple and contain no moving parts so they can be constructed out of corrosion resistant materials or lead-or rubber lined mild steel.

Construction :

A continuous vacuum crystalliser consists of a tall vertical cylindrical vessel with a conical bottom, a circulating pump (screw pump) of low head and a vertical tubular heater on the shell side of which, steam is condensing. A low pressure (i.e., vacuum) in the vertical cylindrical vessel (crystallising body) is maintained by a condenser, usually with the help of a steam jet ejector. A tangential inlet is provided on the cylindrical vessel for introducing a hot solution into it and a vapour outlet is provided on the top. A discharge connection for mother liquor and crystal is provided on a down-pipe just above the feed connection.

Fig. 11.5 : Continuous Vacuum Crystalliser / Circulating magma vacuum crystalliser

Working :

The magma from the bottom of a cylindrical vessel goes to a pump via a down-pipe and is pumped through a vertical tubular heater where it is heated by means of condensing steam and finally a hot stream enters the cylindrical vessel tangentially just below the level of the magma surface. Flash evaporation of the solution takes place and produces rapid cooling, resulting into supersaturation, which is the driving force for nucleation and growth. Fresh solution enters the down pipe just before the suction of the circulating pump and a suspension of crystals is continuously taken out from a discharge pipe located above the feed inlet in the down pipe. The suspension of crystals is fed to a centrifuge machine, the crystals are taken out as a product, and the mother liquor is recycled to the down-pipe with small part of it continuously bled.

It is used for the production of large crystals.

Krystal or Oslo Crystalliser :

It is widely used whenever large quantities of crystals of controlled size are to be produced.

In this crystalliser, a supersaturated solution is passed upward through a bed of crystals which are maintained in a fluidised state whereby uniform temperature is maintained and the crystals segregate in the bed with large ones at the bottom and small ones at the top.

Oslo Cooler Crystalliser :

In this crystalliser, supersaturation is generated by indirect cooling. It consists of a crystallising chamber, a circulating pump, and a external cooler for cooling the solution. It is a circulating liquid cooling crystalliser.

The solution to be crystallised is fed from the top. Mother liquor from a crystallising chamber is withdrawn near a feed point 'A' with the help of a circulating pump and it is then admitted to a cooler (E) wherein supersaturation is achieved by cooling. The supersaturated solution from the cooler is finally fed back to the bottom of the crystallising chamber through a central pipe (P). Usually, nucleation takes place in the bed of crystals in the crystallising chamber. The nuclei formed circulate with mother liquor and once they grow sufficiently large, they will be retained in the fluidised bed. Once the crystals grow to a required size, they are removed as product from the bottom of the crystallising chamber through a valve 'V' as these cannot be retained in the fluidised bed by the circulation velocity.

Fig. 11.6 : Oslo / Krystal Cooling Crystalliser

Oslo Evaporative Crystalliser :

In this crystalliser, supersaturation is generated/achieved by evaporation. It is a circulating liquid evaporative crystalliser.

It consists of a crystallising chamber containing a bed of forming and growing crystals, a circulating pump, an external heater for heating the solution with the help of condensing steam and a vapour - head wherein reduced pressure is maintained by a vacuum generating equipment. The heater is maintained under sufficient hydrostatic head to avoid the boiling on the heating surface.

Fig. 11.7 : Oslo/Krystal Evaporative Crystalliser

The solution from the crystallising chamber is pumped by a circulating pump on the suction side of which the feed solution forming a small part of the total circulating liquid is introduced into a heater, where it is heated by means of condensing steam (on the shell side of the heater) and then fed to a vapour head wherein some of the solution flashes into vapour resulting into some degree of supersaturation. The supersaturated solution is then returned to the bottom of the crystallising chamber through a central duct prolonged from the vapour head into the crystallising chamber. Nucleation takes place in the crystal bed which is maintained in a fluidised state by means of a upward flowing stream of liquid through the duct. The nuclei formed circulate with the mother liquor and once they grow sufficiently large they will be retained in the fluidised bed. When the crystals grow to a required size, they will be withdrawn as product from the bottom of the crystallising chamber as they will not be maintained in the fluidised bed by the circulation velocity.

Material balances of crystalliser

Material balances are used to calculate the yield of the crystallisation operation which is the mass of crystals obtained from a given mass of solution.

Fig. 11.8

Consider the crystallisation process carried out under steady state shown in Fig. 11.8.
Let

    F be the mass flow rate of feed solution in kg/h

    X_F' be the weight fraction of anhydrous solute in the feed solution

    C be the kg/h of crystals obtained

    V be the mass flow rate of evaporated solvent in kg/h

    X' be the solubility of the solute at the final temperature of operation expressed as a weight ratio of anhydrous salt to solvent

    M_1 be the molecular weight of anhydrous solute salt

    M_2 be the molecular weight of hydrated salt

    L' be the kg/h of solvent in the mother liquor

    L be the kg/h of mother liquor leaving the crystalliser

Overall material balance :

$$F = C + L + V \qquad \ldots (11.1)$$

Material balance of solvent :

Solvent in feed = Solvent evaporated + Solvent in mother liquor
+ Solvent in hydrated crystals

$$\therefore \quad F(1 - X_F') = V + L' + \left(\frac{M_2 - M_1}{M_2}\right) C \qquad \ldots (11.2)$$

Rearranging the above equation, we get :

$$L' = F(1 - X_F') - V - \left(\frac{M_2 - M_1}{M_2}\right) C \qquad \ldots (11.3)$$

Material balance of solute :

Solute in feed = Solute in product crystals + Solute in mother liquor

$$F \cdot X_F' = C \cdot \frac{M_1}{M_2} + \left[F(1 - X_F') - V - \left(\frac{M_2 - M_1}{M_2}\right) C\right] X' \qquad \ldots (11.4)$$

If the crystals obtained are anhydrous then above equation takes the following form :

$$F X_F' = C + [F(1 - X_F') - V] X' \qquad \ldots (11.5)$$

If no evaporation takes place and anhydrous salts are crystallised then :

    V = 0 and equation (10.5) becomes :

$$F \cdot X'_F = C + [F(1 - X'_F)] X' \qquad \ldots (11.6)$$

C – kg/h of crystal obtained (anhydrous/hydrated) and is the yield of the process.

$$\% \text{ yield crystals} = \frac{\text{Amount of solute crystallised}}{\text{Amount of solute in feed solution}} \times 100$$

Energy balances :

Energy balance calculations in a crystallisation process are essential to determine the cooling requirements or to determine the final conditions. In these calculations, heat of crystallisation is important and it is the latent heat evolved when a solid (crystal) forms from a solution. Ordinarily, the crystallisation process is exothermic and heat of crystallisation varies with temperature and concentration. Heats of crystallisation are not available, but heat of solution data are available. The process of crystallisation is the reverse of dissolution. Therefore, the heat of solution (i.e., the heat of dissolution) with a reverse sign is taken as heat of crystallisation (heat of crystallisation = –heat of solution). In case of a cooling crystalliser with no evaporation the heat balance is :

Heat to be removed = $Q = F C_{p_F} \Delta T + C \lambda_c$

When specific heat data are available for the initial feed solution over a range of temperature then the heat to be removed is equal to the heat to be removed to cool the feed from the initial temperature (T_1) to the final temperature $(T_2$, such that $T_1 > T_2)$ without any crystal precipitating plus the heat liberated/evolved due to formation of crystals from the supersaturated solution at the final temperature.

Heat with solution at T_1 + Heat liberated due to crystallisation =

$$= \text{Heat with solution at } T_2 + \text{Heat to be removed}$$

$$F C_p T_1 + C \lambda_c = F C_p T_2 + Q$$

$\therefore \qquad Q = FC_pT_1 - FC_pT_2 + C\lambda_C = FC_p\Delta T + C\lambda_C$

(valid for crystallisation by cooling alone - no evaporation)

where, $\quad \Delta T$ = cooling range $(T_1 - T_2)$, where $T_1 > T_2$

C_{p_F} = specified heat of feed solution, kJ/(kg·K)

F = feed or feed rate, kg/h

C = crystal formed, kg or kg/h

λ_C = heat of crystallisation, kJ/kg

$$Q = U A \Delta T lm = \dot{m}_c \cdot C_{p_c} (t_2 - t_1)$$

where $\dot{m}_c$ is the mass flow rate of coolant and C_{p_c} is the specific heat of the coolant

t_1 and t_2 = inlet and outlet temperatures of coolent

$$\Delta Tlm = \frac{(T_1 - t_2) - (T_2 - t_1)}{\ln\left[(T_1 - t_2)/(T_2 - t_1)\right]}$$

SOLVED EXAMPLES

Ex. 11.1 : A solution of sodium nitrate in water contains 48 % $NaNO_3$ by weight at 313 K (40° C) temperature. Calculate the percentage yield of $NaNO_3$ crystals that may be obtained when temperature is reduced to 283 K (10° C). Also calculate the yield of $NaNO_3$ crystals from 100 kg of solution.

Data : Solubility of $NaNO_3$ in water at 283 K (10° C) is 80.18 kg $NaNO_3$ per 100 kg water.

Solution : Basis : 100 kg of feed solution.

$F = 100$ kg

$X'_F = \dfrac{48}{100} = 0.48$ weight fraction of $NaNO_3$ in feed

$C = $ yield of crystals (kg of $NaNO_3$ crystals obtained)

$X' = $ solubility of $NaNO_3$ at 283 K

$\quad = 80.18$ kg/100 kg water

$L' = $ kg of solvent in mother liquor

Water (solvent) balance :

Solvent in feed = Solvent in mother liquor

$F(1 - X'_F) = L'$

$100(1 - 0.48) = L'$

$\therefore \quad L' = 52$ kg

$NaNO_3$ balance – (Anhydrous salt as crystal) :

$NaNO_3$ in feed = $NaNO_3$ obtained as crystals + $NaNO_3$ in mother liquor

$X'_F \cdot F = C + L' \cdot X'$

$X'_F \cdot F = C + [F(1 - X'_F)] X'$

$0.48 \times 100 = C + [100(1 - 0.48)]\left(\dfrac{80.18}{100}\right)$

$C = $ yield of crystals

$\quad = 6.3$ kg ... Ans.

% yield of crystals $= \dfrac{\text{kg of } NaNO_3 \text{ crystallised}}{\text{kg of } NaNO_3 \text{ in feed solution}} \times 100$

$\quad = \dfrac{6.3}{48} \times 100$

$\quad = 13.12$ % ... Ans.

Ex. 11.2 : What will be the yield of $Na_2S_2O_3 \cdot 5H_2O$ crystals when 100 kg of 48% $Na_2S_2O_3$ solution is cooled to 293 K (20° C). Also calculate percentage yield of the hydrated crystals.

(At. Wt. : Na = 23, S = 32, O = 16, H = 1)

Data : Solubility of $Na_2S_2O_3$ is 70 parts per 100 parts water at 293 K (20° C).

Solution : Basis : 100 kg of feed solution.

It contains 48 kg of $Na_2S_2O_3$ and 52 kg of water. Let 'C' be the yield of crystals.

M_1 = Molecular weight of $Na_2S_2O_3$ = 158

M_2 = Molecular weight of $Na_2S_2O_3 \cdot 5 H_2O$ = 248

X'_F = weight fraction of solute in feed

$= \dfrac{\text{weight \%}}{100} = \dfrac{48}{100} = 0.48$

Material balance of water :

Water in feed = Water of crystallisation in crystals + Water in mother liquor

$52 = C \cdot \dfrac{M_2 - M_1}{M_2} + L'$

$L' = 52 - \dfrac{C[248 - 158]}{248}$

Material balance of solute :

Solute in feed = Solute in crystals produced + Solute in mother liquor

$0.48 \times 100 = C\left(\dfrac{158}{248}\right) + \left[52 - \left(\dfrac{248 - 158}{248}\right)C\right] X'$

X' –Solubility expressed as weight ratio of solute to solvent at 293 K.

$48 = 0.637\,C + [52 - 0.363\,C] \times \left(\dfrac{70}{100}\right)$

$= 0.637\,C + 36.4 - 0.254\,C$

∴ $C = 30.3$ kg

Yield of $Na_2S_2O_3 \cdot 5 H_2O$ crystal = 30.3 kg ... **Ans.**

$Na_2S_2O_3 \cdot 5 H_2O$ in feed solution $= 48 \times \dfrac{248}{158} = 73.34$ kg

% yield of hydrated crystals $= \dfrac{30.3}{73.34} \times 100$

$= \mathbf{41.31}$ ... **Ans.**

Ex. 11.3 : Calculate the yield of $MgSO_4 \cdot 7 H_2O$ crystals when 1000 kg saturated solution of $MgSO_4$ at 353 K (80° C) is cooled to 303 K (30° C) assuming 10 % of the water is lost by evaporation during cooling.

Data : Solubility of $MgSO_4$ at 353 K (80° C) = 64.2 kg/100 kg water

Solubility of $MgSO_4$ at 303 K (30° C) = 40.8 kg/100 kg water

At. Wt. : Mg = 24, S = 32, H = 1 and O = 16

Solution : Basis : 1000 kg of solution at 353 K (80° C)

$F = 1000$ kg

X'_F = weight fraction of $MgSO_4$ in feed

$= \dfrac{64.2}{164.2} = 0.391$

Water in feed solution = $F(1 - X'_F)$

$= 1000 (1 - 0.391) = 609$ kg

V = kg of water evaporated during cooling

$= 609 \times 0.1 = 60.9$ kg

X' = solubility of $MgSO_4$ at 303 K = 40.8 kg/100 kg water

M_1 = Molecular weight of $MgSO_4$ = 120

M_2 = Molecular weight of $MgSO_4, 7 H_2O$ = 246

C = Yield of $MgSO_4 \cdot 7 H_2O$ crystals from feed solution

$M_2 - M_1$ = water of crystallisation

$= 246 - 120 = 126$ kg

Material balance of $MgSO_4$:

$$X'_F F = C \cdot \dfrac{M_1}{M_2} + \left[F(1 - X'_F) - V - C \left(\dfrac{M_2 - M_1}{M_2} \right) \right] X'$$

$MgSO_4$ in feed = $MgSO_4$ in hydrated crystal

+ $MgSO_4$ in mother liquor at 303 K

$\therefore \quad 0.391 (1000) = C \left(\dfrac{120}{246} \right) + \left[1000 (1 - 0.391) - 60.9 - \dfrac{C(126)}{246} \right] \dfrac{40.8}{100}$

$391 = 0.488 C + [609 - 60.9 - 0.512 C] (0.408)$

$MgSO_4 \cdot 7 H_2O$ yield = $C = 599.7$ kg ... **Ans.**

Ex. 11.4 : A hot solution containing 5000 kg of Na_2CO_3 and water with a concentration of 25 % by weight. Na_2CO_3 is cooled to 293 K (20 °C) and crystals of $Na_2CO_3 \cdot 10 H_2O$ are precipitated. At 293 K (20 °C), the solubility is 21.5 kg anhydrous Na_2CO_3 per 100 kg of total

Unit Operations – II   11.19   Crystallisation

water. Calculate the yield of hydrated Na_2CO_3 crystals obtained if 5 % of the original water in the system evaporates on cooling. Also calculate the quantity of mother liquor.

At. Wt. : Na = 23, C = 12, O = 16, H = 1.

Solution : Basis : 5000 kg of hot solution of Na_2CO_3.

It contains :

$$Na_2CO_3 = 0.25 \times 5000 = 1250 \text{ kg}$$
$$\text{Water} = 0.75 \times 5000 = 3750 \text{ kg}$$
$$M_1 = \text{Mol. Wt. of } Na_2CO_3 = 106$$
$$M_2 = \text{Mol. Wt. of } Na_2CO_3 \cdot 10 H_2O = 286$$
$$M_2 - M_1 = \text{water of crystallisation} = 10 H_2O = 180$$
$$F = 5000 \text{ kg}$$
$$X_F' = \text{weight fraction of } Na_2CO_3 \text{ in feed}$$
$$= \frac{25}{100} = 0.25$$
$$V = \text{kg of water evaporated during cooling}$$
$$= 0.05 \times 3750 = 187.5 \text{ kg}$$

Material balance of water :

Water in feed = Water of crystallisation
+ Water in mother liquor + Water evaporated

$$0.75 \, (5000) = C \left(\frac{M_2 - M_1}{M_2} \right) + L' + 187.5$$

$$3750 = C \left(\frac{286 - 106}{286} \right) + L' + 187.5$$

$$3562.5 = C \left(\frac{180}{286} \right) + L'$$

$$L' = 3562.5 - C \left(\frac{180}{286} \right)$$

Material balance of solute :

Solute in feed = Solute in crystals produced + Solute in mother liquor

$$X_F' F = C \frac{M_1}{M_2} + L' X'$$

where,   C = yield of hydrated crystals
L' = kg of solvent water in mother liquor
X' = solubility of anhydrous solute as kg solute/kg solvent.

$$X'_F \, F = C\frac{M_1}{M_2} + \left[3562.5 - C\left(\frac{180}{286}\right)\right] \times X'$$

$$0.25 \times 5000 = C\frac{106}{286} + \left[3562.5 - C\left(\frac{180}{286}\right)\right]\frac{21.5}{100}$$

$$1250 = 0.37\,C + [3562.5 - 0.629\,C]\,0.215$$

$$1250 = 0.37\,C + 765.94 - 0.135\,C$$

$$0.235\,C = 484.06$$

$$C = 2059.83 \text{ kg}$$

∴ yield of $Na_2CO_3 \cdot 10\,H_2O$ crystals = 2059.83 kg ... **Ans.**

Quantity of mother liquor obtained = kg of feed – kg of crystals – kg water evaporated
= 5000 – [2059.83 + 187.5]
= **2752.67 kg** ... **Ans.**

Ex. 11.5 : A hot solution containing 2000 kg of $MgSO_4$ and water at 330 K (57 °C) and with a concentration of 30 wt. % $MgSO_4$ is cooled to 293 K (30 °C) and $MgSO_4 \cdot 7H_2O$ crystals are removed. The solubility at 293 K (30 °C) is 35.5 kg $MgSO_4$ per 100 kg water. Calculate the yield of crystals. Assume that no water is vaporised.

At. Wt. : Mg = 24, S = 32, O = 16, H = 1.

Solution : Basis : 2000 kg of hot solution

$$F = 2000 \text{ kg}$$

$$X'_F = \frac{30}{100} = 0.30$$

$$M_1 = \text{Mol. Wt. of } MgSO_4 = 120$$

$$M_2 = \text{Mol. Wt. of } MgSO_4 \cdot 7\,H_2O = 246$$

Material balance of water :

Water in feed = Water of crystallisation + Water in mother liquor

$$(1 - X'_F)\,F = C\left(\frac{M_2 - M_1}{M_2}\right) + L'$$

$$(1 - 0.30)\,2000 = C\left(\frac{246 - 120}{246}\right) + L'$$

$$L' = 1400 - \frac{126}{246}\,C = 1400 - 0.5122\,C$$

where C is the yield of hydrated crystals.

Material balance of solute :

$MgSO_4$ in feed = $MgSO_4$ in crystals produced + $MgSO_4$ in mother liquor

$$X'_F F = C\frac{M_1}{M_2} + L'X'$$

where X' = solubility of $MgSO_4$ as kg $MgSO_4$/kg solvent

$$= \frac{35.5}{100} = 0.355$$

M_1 = 120
M_2 = 246
X'_F = 0.3   F = 2000 kg

$$0.3(2000) = C\left(\frac{120}{246}\right) + [1400 - 0.5122\,C]\,0.355$$

$600 = 0.488\,C + 497 - 0.182\,C$
$C = 336.6$ kg

Yield of $MgSO_4 \cdot 7\,H_2O$ crystal = **336.6 kg**   ... Ans.

Ex. 11.6 : What will be the per cent yield of Glauber salt ($Na_2SO_4 \cdot 10\,H_2O$) if a pure 32 % solution is cooled to 293 K (20° C) without any loss due to evaporation ?

Data : Solubility of Na_2SO_4 in water at 293 K (20° C) is 19.4 g per 100 g water.

At. Wt. : Na = 23, S = 32, O = 16, H = 1.

Solution : Basis : 100 kg of original solution

It contains 32 kg of Na_2SO_4 and 68 kg of water

F = 100 kg
X'_F = weight fraction of Na_2SO_4 in feed
     = 32/100 = 0.32
M_1 = Mol. Wt. of Na_2SO_4 = 142
M_2 = Mol. Wt. of $Na_2SO_4 \cdot 10\,H_2O$ = 322

Material balance of water :

Water in feed = Water of crystallisation + Water in mother liquor

$$0.68 \times 100 = C\frac{(M_2 - M_1)}{M_2} + L'$$

$$68 = C\left(\frac{322 - 142}{322}\right) + L'$$

$68 = 0.559\,C + L'$
$L' = 68 - 0.559$

Material balance of solute :

Solute in feed = Solute in crystals produced + Solute in mother liquor

$$X'_F F = C \frac{M_1}{M_2} + L' X'$$

C = yield of hydrated solute
L' = kg of solvent in mother liquor
X' = solubility of anhydrous solute as kg solute/kg solvent
$= \frac{19.4}{100} = 0.194$

$$0.32 \times 100 = C \left(\frac{142}{322}\right) + L' \times 0.194$$

$$32 = 0.441 C + 0.194 L'$$

We have, $L' = 68 - 0.559 C$

$$32 = 0.441 C + 0.194 (68 - 0.559 C)$$
$$32 = 0.441 C + 13.192 - 0.1084 C$$
$$0.3326 C = 18.808$$
$$C = 56.55$$

$Na_2SO_4 \cdot 10 H_2O$ in feed solution $= 32 \times \frac{322}{142} = 72.56$

% yield of Glauber salt $= \frac{56.55}{72.56} \times 100 = 77.93$ ... **Ans.**

Alternate method :

Basis : 100 kg of free water

100 kg of original solution contain 32 kg Na_2SO_4 and 68 kg water.

Water associated with
32 kg Na_2SO_4 in 100 kg solution $= \frac{\text{Mol. Wt. of 10 H}_2\text{O}}{\text{Mol. Wt. of Na}_2\text{SO}_4} \times 32$

$= \frac{(10 \infty 18)}{142} \times 32 = 40.56$ kg

Free water in 100 kg original solution $= 68 - 40.56 = 27.44$ kg

Glauber salt ($Na_2SO_4 \cdot 10 H_2O$)
present in 100 kg of free water $= (32 + 40.56) \times \frac{100}{27.44}$

At 293 K, the final liquor contains 19.4 kg Na_2SO_4 in 100 kg water.

Water associated with Na_2SO_4
in final solution $= \frac{180}{142} \times 19.4 = 24.6$ kg

Free water in final solution $= 100 - 24.6 = 75.4$ kg

Glauber salt present in 100 kg water $= \frac{(19.4 + 24.6)}{75.4} \times 100$

Yield of Glauber salt per 100 kg free water = 264.43 − 58.35

= 206.08 kg $Na_2SO_4 \cdot 10 H_2O$

% yield of Glauber salt = $\frac{206.08}{264.43} \times 100$ = 77.93 ... **Ans.**

Ex. 11.7 : A crystalliser is charged with 7500 kg of an aqueous solution at 377 K (104° C), 29.6 % by weight of which is anhydrous sodium sulphate. The solution is cooled. During the cooling operation, 5 % of the initial water is lost by evaporation. As a result, crystals of $Na_2SO_4 \cdot 10 H_2O$ crystallises out. If the mother liquor is found to contain 18.3 % by weight anhydrous Na_2SO_4, calculate the yield of crystals and the quantity of mother liquor.

At. Wt. : Na = 23, S = 32, O = 16, H = 1.

Solution : Basis : 7500 kg of aqueous solution

M_1 = Mol. Wt. of Na_2SO_4 = 142

M_2 = Mol. Wt. of $Na_2SO_4 \cdot 10 H_2O$ = 322

F = 7500 kg

Amount of $MgSO_4$ in feed = $X'_F F$

= $\frac{29.6}{100} \times 7500$ = 2220 kg

Amount of water in feed = $(1 - X'_F) F$

= (1 − 0.296) 7500 = 5280 kg

V = Amount of water lost by evaporation = $\frac{5}{100} \times 5280$ = 264 kg

Material balance of water :

$(1 - X'_F) F = C \left(\frac{M_2 - M_1}{M_2} \right) + L' + V$

$5280 = C \left(\frac{322 - 142}{322} \right) + L' + 264$

$5016 = 0.56 C + L'$

$L' = 5016 - 0.56 C$

where C is the yield of hydrated crystals.

Mother liquor contains 18.3 % by weight Na_2SO_4

X' = kg Na_2SO_4/kg water (solvent) = $\frac{0.183}{1 - 0.183}$ = 0.224

Material balance of Na_2SO_4 :

$$X'_F F = C\frac{M_1}{M_2} + L' X'$$

$$2220 = \frac{142}{322} C + 0.224 L'$$

$$2220 = 0.441 C + 0.224 L'$$

We have $L' = 5016 - 0.56 C$

∴ $\quad 2220 = 0.441 C + 0.224 (5016 - 0.56 C)$

Solving $\quad C = 3474.5$ kg

Overall material balance :

Feed = Hydrated crystals + Mother liquor + Water evaporated

$7500 = 3474.5$ + Mother liquor + 264

∴ Amount of mother liquor = 3761.5 kg

Yield of $Na_2SO_4 \cdot 10 H_2O$ crystals = 3474.5 kg ... **Ans.**

Ex. 11.8 : A saturated solution of $MgSO_4$ at 353 K (80° C) is cooled to 303 K (30° C) in a crystalliser. During cooling, 4 % solution is lost by evaporation of water. Estimate the quantity of the original saturated solution to be fed to the crystalliser per 1000 kg of $MgSO_4 \cdot 7 H_2O$ crystals.

Data : Solubility of $MgSO_4$ at 303 K (30° C) = 40.8 kg/100 kg water

Solubility of $MgSO_4$ at 353 K (80° C) = 64.2 kg/100 kg water

At. Wt. : Mg = 24, S = 32, O = 16, and H = 1.0

Solution : Basis : 100 kg of feed solution

M_1 = Mol. Wt. of $MgSO_4$ = 120

M_2 = Mol. Wt. of $Mg SO_4 \cdot 7 H_2O$ = 246

$M_2 - M_1$ = Mol. Wt. of $7 H_2O$ = 126

Solubility of $MgSO_4$ at 353 K = 64.2 kg/100 kg water

Solubility of $MgSO_4$ at 303 K = 40.8 kg/100 kg water

$MgSO_4$ in feed solution = $\frac{64.2}{164.2} \times 100 = 39.1$ kg

Loss of solution by evaporation = $0.04 \times 100 = 4$ kg

Solute balance equation for hydrated salt :

$$F \cdot X'_F = C \cdot \frac{M_1}{M_2} + \left[F(1 - X'_F) - V - \left(\frac{M_2 - M_1}{M_2}\right) C \right] X'$$

where $\quad F = 100$ kg

$X'_F = 39.1/100 = 0.391$

Unit Operations – II   11.25   Crystallisation

$$V = 4 \text{ kg}$$
$$X' = \frac{40.8}{100} = 0.408$$
$$100 \times 0.391 = \frac{120}{246} C + \left[100(1-0.391) - 4 - \left(\frac{246-120}{246}\right)C\right] \times 0.408$$
$$39.1 = 0.4878 C + [60.9 - 4 - 0.512 C] \times 0.408$$
$$0.2788 C = 15.89$$
$$C = 56.99 \text{ kg yield of crystals}$$

C is the kg of hydrated crystals obtained.

For 56.99 kg of crystals 100 kg of feed solution is required.

$$\therefore \text{For a yield of 1000 kg crystals, the charge to the crystalliser} = \frac{100}{56.99} \times 1000$$

(i.e. quantity of feed solution) = **1754.56 kg**   ... **Ans.**

Ex. 11.9 : A solution of sodium nitrate in water contains 48% $NaNO_3$ by weight at 313 K temperature. Calculate the percentage yield of $NaNO_3$ crystals that may be obtained when temperature is reduced to 283 K. Solubility of $NaNO_3$ at 283 K is 80.18 kg/100 kg water.

Solution : Basis : 100 kg of feed solution.

Instead of using notations for various streams and other terms, we will solve the problem by writing material balances and solving them simultaneously.

Let x be the kg of $NaNO_3$ crystals obtained and y be the kg of mother liquor obtained.

Overall material balance :

$$\text{Feed solution} = \text{crystals} + \text{mother liquor}$$
$$100 = x + y \qquad \ldots (1)$$

Feed solution contains 48% by weight $NaNO_3$.

The solubility of $NaNO_3$ at 283 K is 80.18 kg per 100 kg water.

It means 180.18 kg (100 + 80.18) mother liquor contains 80.18 kg $NaNO_3$.

Material balance of $NaNO_3$:

$$NaNO_3 \text{ in feed solution} = NaNO_3 \text{ crystals} + NaNO_3 \text{ in mother liquor}$$
$$0.48 \times 100 = x + \frac{80.18}{180.18} y$$
$$48 = x + 0.445 y \qquad \ldots (2)$$

Solve equations (1) and (2) simultaneously to get x and y known.

$$x + y = 100$$
$$x = 100 - y$$
$$48 = x + 0.445 y$$

$$48 = (100 - y) + 0.445\, y$$
$$\therefore \quad 0.555\, y = 52$$
$$y = 93.7 \text{ kg}$$
$$x + 93.7 = 100$$
$$x = 6.3 \text{ kg}$$

Yield of $NaNO_3$ crystals from 100 kg solution = 6.3 kg

$NaNO_3$ in feed solution = 48 kg

% yield of $NaNO_3$ crystals = $\dfrac{6.3}{48} \times 100$

= 13.12 ... **Ans.**

You can adopt this method to solve remaining problems also.

Ex. 11.10 : Calculate the yield of $MgSO_4 \cdot 7H_2O$ crystals when 1000 kg saturated solution of $MgSO_4$ at 353 K is cooled to 303 K assuming 10% of water is lost by evaporation during cooling.

Data : Solubility of $MgSO_4$ at 353 K = 64.2 kg/100 kg water

Solubility of $MgSO_4$ at 303 K = 40.8 kg/100 kg water

Mol. Wt. of $MgSO_4$ = 120, Mol. Wt. of $MgSO_4 \cdot 7\,H_2O$ = 246

Solution : Basis : 1000 kg of saturated solution at 353 K.

Let us solve this problem without using notations.

Let x be the kg of $MgSO_4 \cdot 7\,H_2O$ crystals obtained, y be the kg of mother liquor obtained.

Saturated solution = 1000 kg

Solubility at 353 K = 64.2 kg/100 kg water

i.e. 164.2 kg (100 + 64.2) of saturated solution contains 64.2 kg of $MgSO_4$ and 100 kg of water.

Water in saturated solution = $\dfrac{100}{164.2} \times 1000$

= 609 kg

$MgSO_4$ in saturated solution = 1000 − 609 = 391 kg

Water lost by evaporation = 10% of original water

Water lost by evaporation = 0.10 (609) = 60.9 kg

Overall material balance :

Feed solution = crystals + mother liquor + water lost by evaporation

1000 = x + y + 60.9

x + y = 939.1 ... (1)

Solubility of $MgSO_4$ at 303 K = 40.8 kg/100 kg water

i.e. 140.8 kg of mother liquor contains 40.8 kg of $MgSO_4$ and 100 kg water.

We have :

1 kmol $MgSO_4 \cdot 7H_2O$ + 1 kmol $MgSO_4$

246 kg $MgSO_4 \cdot 7H_2O$ + 120 kg $MgSO_4$

Material balance of $MgSO_4$:

$MgSO_4$ in feed solution = $MgSO_4$ in crystals + $MgSO_4$ in mother liquor

$$391 = \frac{120}{246} \times x + \frac{40.8}{140.8} y$$

$$391 = 0.488 x + 0.2898 y \quad \ldots (2)$$

Solve equations (1) and (2) simultaneously.

$$x + y = 939.1$$
$$y = 939.1 - x$$
$$391 = 0.488 x + 0.2898 (939.1 - x)$$

$\therefore \quad x = 599.64$ kg (crystals obtained)

$599.64 + y = 939.1 \quad \therefore y = 339.46$ kg

Yield of $MgSO_4 \cdot 7H_2O$ crystals = 599.64 kg ... **Ans.**

EXERCISE

1. Fill in the blanks :

1.1 .... and .... are the phases involved in crystallisation. **Ans.** Liquid, solid

1.2 In crystallisation from solution simultaneous .... and mass transfer takes place.

1.3 In crystallisation, mass transfer occurs from solution to .... phase. **Ans.** solid

1.4 .... is the driving force for crystallisation. **Ans. supersaturation**

1.5 For common salt (NaCl) ...... is independent of variation in temperature.

Ans. solubility

1.6 Solubility is generally expressed as parts by weight .... per .... parts by weight solvent. **Ans.** solute, 100

1.7 For solutes whose solubility increases within increase in temperature, supersaturation is achieved by .... alone. **Ans.** cooling

1.8 For solutes whose solubility remains more or less constant with temperature, supersaturation is achieved by .... of a part of solvent. **Ans.** evaporation

1.9 Vacuum crystalliser is used for .... sensitive materials. **Ans.** heat

1.10 .... and crystal growth are the two basic steps in the overall process of crystallisation. **Ans.** Nucleation.

2. Define the following terms :
   (a) crystallisation (b) solubility (c) nucleation
   (d) crystal growth (e) supersaturation.

3. Explain in brief solubility curves.

4. State various methods of generating supersaturation.

5. Explain briefly the classification of crystallisers.

6. Discuss in brief crystal formation.

7. Explain in brief with neat sketch Swenson-Walker crystalliser.

8. Write in brief on Oslo-cooling crystalliser.

9. Write a short note on agitated tank crystalliser.

10. With neat sketch explain construction and working of vacuum crystalliser.

CHAPTER TWELVE

DRYING

Drying refers to an operation in which the moisture of a substance (usually solid) is removed by thermal means (i.e., with the help of thermal energy).

Drying usually refers to the removal of relatively small amounts of water from a solid or nearly solid material. It involves the transfer of liquid from a wet solid into an unsaturated gas phase (drying medium).

During drying operation, mass and heat transfer occur simultaneously. Heat is transferred from the the bulk of the gas phase (drying medium) to the solid phase and mass is transferred from the solid phase to the gas phase in the form of liquid and vapour through various resistances. The material (liquid) that is transferred is the solute and transfer takes place as the gas phase is always unsaturated with respect to the solute material.

In drying, relatively small amounts of water or other liquid is removed from a solid or semi-solid material (using thermal energy), whereas in evaporation, relatively large amount of water is removed from the solutions. Drying involves the removal of water at a temperature below the boiling point, while evaporation involves the removal of water as a vapour at its boiling point. Drying involves circulation of a hot air or other gas over a solid material for the removal of water while in evaporation use of steam heat is done for the removal of water
(i.e., for evaporator). To obtain the products almost in the dried form is the purpose of drying operation, whereas the concentration of solution is the main purpose of evaporation.

As the removal of moisture by thermal means is more costly than mechanical means (e.g., filtration), the moisture content of the solids must be reduced to the minimum possible level by the latter means before the material is fed to drying equipments.

In most of the drying operations, the heat (required to evaporate water) is provided by hot air or any other gas-drying medium.

Drying is frequently the last operation in manufacturing process and is usually carried after evaporation, filtration, or crystallisation.

Drying operations are mostly encountered in food, chemical, agricultural, pharmaceutical and textile industries.

Drying operation is carried out for number of reasons given below :

(i) For reducing the transport cost.

(ii) For purifying a crystalline product so that the solvent adhering to the crystals is removed.

(iii) For making a material more suitable for handling and storage. Handling and storage of dry solids is easy.

(iv) To meet the market specifications of solid products set by the customers.

(v) For providing definite properties to materials.

(vi) In some cases for preventing corrosion arising due to the presence of moisture. Dry chlorine gas is not corrosive but traces of moisture make it very corrosive.

(vii) Sometimes it is an essential part of the process (e.g., drying of paper in paper making).

General Definitions :

Moisture content, wet basis : It is expressed as the *ratio of the weight of the moisture to the weight of the wet feed material*. If X is the kg moisture associated with one kg of dry solids then

$$\text{Moisture content on wet basis} : \frac{X}{1+X}$$

Percent moisture on a wet basis is the moisture associated with a feed material, expressed as a percentage of the weight of the feed material (i.e. wet solids).

$$\text{Weight \% moisture content (on wet basis)} = \frac{\text{kg moisture}}{\text{kg wet solid}} \times 100 = 100 \left[\frac{X}{1+X}\right]$$

Moisture content, dry basis : It is expressed as the *ratio of the weight of the moisture to the weight of the dry solids present in a wet feed material*. If the feed material contains X kg moisture and 1 kg of dry solids then

$$\text{Moisture content (on dry basis)} = \frac{\text{kg moisture}}{\text{kg dry solid}} = \frac{X}{1} = X$$

Percentage moisture content on dry basis = 100 X

Equilibrium moisture content (X^*) : *The moisture content of a solid material that is in thermodynamic equilibrium with its vapour (given partial pressure of vapour) in the gas phase under the specified humidity and temperature of the hot gas or air is termed as equilibrium moisture content.* It represents the limiting moisture content to which a given material can be dried under constant drying conditions.

Bound Moisture content :

It is that *moisture in a solid material which exerts a vapour pressure less than that of the pure liquid at the same temperature.*

Unbound moisture content :

It is the *moisture held by a solid material in excess of the equilibrium moisture content corresponding to saturation humidity.* It is primarily held in the voids of solid.

It is that *moisture in a solid material which exerts an equilibrium vapour pressure equal to that of the pure liquid at the given temperature.*

Free moisture content : It is the *moisture contained by a solid material in excess of the equilibrium moisture content $(X - X^*)$.* At a given temperature and humidity, it is the moisture content of a material that can be removed by drying. It may include bound and unbound moisture.

Critical moisture content :

The moisture content of a material at which the constant rate period ends and the falling rate period starts is called as critical moisture content. It is a function of the constant drying rate, material properties and particle size.

Constant rate period :

It is that part of the *drying process during which the rate of drying expressed as the moisture evaporated per unit time, per unit area of drying surface remains constant.*

Falling rate period :

It is that part of the *drying process during which the rate of drying varies with time and the instantaneous drying rate (expressed as the amount of moisture evaporated per unit time, per unit area of drying surface) continuously decreases.*

Properties of air-water system :

The moisture removed (from a wet solid) during drying operation gets added in the hot gas or air which in turn depends upon the temperature and humidity of the gas or air. Usually, in drying operation the hot air is used as a drying medium, so it is essential to know some of the properties of the air-water system.

Relative humidity (R.H.) :

It is defined as the *ratio of the partial pressure of water vapour in the air water-vapour mixture to the vapour pressure of pure water at the temperature of the mixture.*

$$\% \text{ R.H.} = (p_A/p_A^o) \times 100$$

where p_A = partial pressure of water-vapour in the mixture

p_A^o = vapour pressure of pure water

when $p_A = p_A^o$, air is said to be saturated with water vapour.

Humidity (H)/Absolute humidity :

It is the *ratio of the mass of water vapour to the mass of dry air present, in the air-water vapour mixture under any given set of conditions.*

$$H = \frac{\text{kg of water vapour}}{\text{kg of dry air}} = \frac{18}{29}\left(\frac{p_A}{P - p_A}\right) = 0.62\, H_m$$

H_m is the molal humidity.

Dry bulb temperature :

The temperature of the vapour-gas mixture recorded by a thermometer whose bulb is kept dry, is called as the dry bulb temperature.

Wet bulb temperature :

The temperature recorded by a thermometer whose bulb is kept wet by wrapping a wet cloth in the open air is called as the wet bulb temperature.

The temperature of the bulb goes down as the latent heat of vaporisation required for natural evaporation of water from the cloth will be supplied from the bulb. The evaporation is continued until the air surrounding the bulb becomes saturated. Some of the heat will flow from the surrounding air to the bulb by temperature difference, even then the temperature of bulb will not rise as that heat is consumed in evaporation of water. At one particular point, the temperature becomes constant and is recorded as a wet bulb temperature.

When the air is more unsaturated, then the difference between dry bulb temperature and wet bulb temperature is more and is less for a more humid air. The relative humidity of the air is found out from a psychrometric chart knowing wet bulb and dry bulb temperatures.

Saturation humidity :

It is the *humidity of air when saturated with water vapour* and is denoted by the symbol – H_s.

$$H_s = \frac{18}{29} \left(p_A^o / P - p_A^o \right)$$

Percentage humidity :

It is the *ratio of the actual humidity of air (H) to the humidity of saturated air (H_s).*

$$\text{Percentage humidity} = p_A (P - p_A^o) / p_A^o (P - p_A)$$

Dew point :

When the air-water vapour mixture is cooled, at some temperature it becomes saturated and further cooling results in the condensation of water vapour. The *temperature at which the condensation will first occur* is known as the dew point. For saturated air, the dew point, wet bulb and dry bulb temperatures are identical.

Equilibrium :

The moisture of wet solids exerts a definite vapour pressure depending upon the temperature and the nature of solid and the moisture. Consider that the wet solids containing liquid which exerts a vapour pressure of p_m^o are exposed to a continuous supply of fresh gas (usually air) with a fixed partial pressure of the vapour (p_A). If p_m^o is greater than p_A, then the solids will lose moisture (reverse is true for $p_m^o < p_A$) by evaporation till the vapour pressure of the moisture of the solids equals the partial pressure of the vapour in the gas. The solid and the gas are then said to be in equilibrium with each other and the corresponding moisture content is referred to as equilibrium moisture content. The equilibrium data in case of drying operations are given as the *relationship between the moisture content of a solid (expressed on a dry basis) and the relative humidity of a gas in contact with the solid.*

Fig. 12.1 : Equilibrium Moisture Curve

When the humidity of air is less as compared with the moisture content of the solid, then the solid will lose moisture by evaporation and dry to equilibrium and if the air is more humid than the solids, then solids will gain moisture until the equilibrium is attained. A typical equilibrium curve for drying of a certain wet solid is shown in Fig. 12.1 where the ordinate is the relative humidity of the gas and the abscissa is the moisture content on dry basis. When solids having very high initial moisture content (X) are exposed to a continuous supply of gas with relative humidity of (RH_1), the solids will lose moisture by evaporation and thus go on drying until the moisture content corresponding to the point A is reached. (Which is equilibrium moisture content X^*).

Beyond this, no drying takes place even if the solids are exposed to this air for infinitely long periods. The moisture content of solids can be reduced below X^* (below that corresponding to point A) only by exposing the solids to air of lower humidity and to obtain bone-dry solids, we have to expose it to perfect dry air which corresponds to the origin of curve.

Constant drying conditions :

These conditions mean the *conditions under which the temperature, humidity, velocity and direction of flow of the hot air or gas across the drying surface are constant during drying operation.*

Rate-of-drying curve :

The drying characteristics of wet solids are generally described by the drying rate curves obtained under constant drying conditions. These curves : moisture content v/s time and drying rate v/s moisture content are shown in Figs. 12.2 and 12.3. Generally, the experimental evaluation of these curves is done before design calculations.

Consider that the wet solids with an initial moisture content (X_1) are exposed to air of constant temperature and humidity. If we then measure the moisture content as a function of time (i.e., moisture content of the material is measured at various values of time), then a curve as shown in Fig. 12.2 (a) is obtained from the collected data. The curve relates the such moisture content on dry basis with time. It is clear from the curve that the moisture content of solids decreases with time and after sometime it remains constant at X^*, which is the equilibrium moisture content.

(a) (b)

Fig. 12.2

From this curve, we can draw another type of curve which is known as the rate of drying curve. This curve is much more descriptive of the drying process. The rate of drying curve gives relationship between the rate of drying, expressed as, the moisture evaporated per unit time per unit area of the drying surface and the moisture content on a dry basis. This curve can be constructed by measuring the slopes of tangents drawn to the curve of Fig. 12.2 (a) at various values of the moisture content and then calculating rate as $R = -W' \frac{dX}{dt} \times \frac{1}{A}$, where W' is the weight of dry solids and A is the drying area/surface.

Fig. 12.3 shows the **rate of drying curve**. The section AB of the curve represents the warming up period during which the temperature of the solid is becoming equal to the temperature of drying air. From B to C, the curve is a straight line parallel to X-axis

Fig. 12.3 : Typical rate of drying curve under constant drying conditions

representing the constant rate of drying, thus the section BC is called the **constant rate period** during which the layer of water on the surface of solid is being evaporated. The rate of drying is constant from B to C as the drying takes place from a saturated surface. The section (CE) of the curve represents the **falling rate period** composed of the first falling rate period (CD) and the second falling rate period (DE). From point 'C' onwards some dry patches have started forming on the surface of the solid. The rate of drying decreases for the unsaturated portion and hence the rate for total surface decreases. The section CD of the curve represents the period corresponding to the zone of unsaturated surface drying. The moisture content at which the constant rate period ends and the drying rate starts to fall (i.e. at which unsaturated surface drying starts) is known as the **critical moisture content**. After point D, the surface of the solid is completely dry and now the internal moment of moisture starts coming to the surface and this is continued upto the point E, where the equilibrium is attained. The rate of drying over section DE is governed by the rate of internal moisture movement. The second falling rate period (DE) represents zone where the internal moisture movement controls.

The rate of drying curve consists of two parts : (i) a period of constant rate/a constant rate period, wherein the rate of drying is constant and (ii) a period of falling rate/a falling rate period, wherein the rate of drying is falling.

The rate of drying as a function of time is given in Fig. 12.4, which indicates how long each drying period lasts.

Fig. 12.4 : Drying rate v/s time

Factors on which the rate of drying depends :

(a) **Gas velocity :** When the velocity of the gas or air is high, the rate of drying will also be high.

(b) **Humidity of gas :** Lesser the relative humidity, the more will be the rate of drying.

(c) **Area of drying surface :** If the area of the wet surface exposed to the gas or air is more, the rate of drying will also be more.

(d) **Temperature :** If the temperature of the gas is increased, its relative humidity decreases (i.e., gas becomes more unsaturated) and thus increases a driving force (i.e., the concentration difference of moisture between the solid and gas) and so the rate of drying increases.

Time of drying under constant drying conditions :

Consider that the wet solids are to be dried by passing the hot air over them under constant drying conditions. The time of drying required to dry the material from the initial moisture to the final moisture content of solids, is the sum of the time required during the constant rate period and time required during the falling rate period (when the final moisture is less than the critical).

(a) Constant rate period :

Let X_1 be the initial moisture content of the wet solids and X_2 be the final moisture content of the wet solids during the constant rate period. Let X_c be the critical moisture content of the wet solids. [$X_1, X_2 > X_c$]

The rate of drying is given as :

$$R = -\frac{W'}{A} \times \frac{dX}{dt} \qquad \ldots (12.1\ a)$$

$R = R_c$ = rate during constant rate period

$$R_c = -\frac{W'}{A} \times \frac{dX}{dt} \qquad \ldots (12.1\ b)$$

where W' = mass of dry solids in kg
 A = area of drying surface in m²
 R_c = rate in kg/(m²·hr)
 t = time in hours

Rearranging equation (12.1 b), we get

$$dt = \frac{-W'}{A \cdot R_c}\ dX \qquad \ldots (12.2)$$

Integrating equation (12.2) between the limits :
 $t = 0, \quad X = X_1$
and $t = t, \quad X = X_2$, we get

$$\int_0^t dt = \left[\frac{-W'}{AR_c}\right] \int_{X_1}^{X_2} dX \qquad \ldots (12.3)$$

$$t = \frac{-W'}{A \cdot R_c}\ [X_2 - X_1] \qquad \ldots (12.4)$$

$$t = \frac{W'}{A \cdot R_c}\ [X_1 - X_2] \qquad \ldots (12.5)$$

Equation (12.5) gives the time of drying for drying the material from X_1 to X_2 in the constant rate period.

If the material is to be dried to the moisture content of X_c, then the time required during the entire constant rate period is given by :

$$t_c = \frac{W'}{A\ R_c}\ [X_1 - X_c] \qquad \ldots (12.6)$$

(b) Falling rate period :

During this period, the rate of drying is proportional to the free moisture content.

$$\frac{-W'}{A} \times \frac{dX}{dt} = m\ [X - X^*] \qquad \ldots (12.7)$$

where X^* is the equilibrium moisture content and X is the moisture content of wet solids less than critical moisture content.

Let X_1 be the initial moisture content and X_2 be the final moisture content such that $X_1, X_2 < X_c$.

Fig. 12.5 : Rate v/s moisture content

Assume that entire falling rate period is represented by a straight line CE, then :

$$m = \frac{R_c}{[X_c - X^*]} \qquad \ldots (12.8)$$

$$m = \text{slope of line CE}$$

Equation (12.1) then becomes :

$$\frac{-W'}{A} \frac{dX}{dt} = \frac{R_c}{[X_c - X^*]} [X - X^*] \qquad \ldots (12.9)$$

$$\frac{-dX}{[X - X^*]} = \frac{R_c A}{[X_c - X^*] W'} dt \qquad \ldots (12.10)$$

Integrating equation (12.10) between the limits

$$X = X_1$$
$$X = X_2 \; [X_1, X_2 < X_c], \text{ we get}$$

$$-\int_{X_1}^{X_2} \frac{dX}{[X - X^*]} = \frac{R_c A}{[X_c - X^*] W'} \int_0^t dt \qquad \ldots (12.11)$$

$$t = \frac{W'(X_c - X^*)}{R_c A} \ln\left[\frac{X_1 - X^*}{X_2 - X^*}\right] \qquad \ldots (12.12)$$

Equation (12.12) gives the time of drying during the falling rate period to dry the material from X_1 to X_2.

If the material is to be dried from the critical moisture content X_c to the final moisture content $X_2 (X_2 < X_c)$ then the time required for drying during the entire falling rate period is given by t_f as :

$$t_f = \frac{W'(X_c - X^*)}{R_c \cdot A} \ln\left[\frac{X_c - X^*}{X_2 - X^*}\right] \qquad \ldots (12.13)$$

[As X_1 becomes X_c]

t_f – drying time during entire falling rate period.

Total time of drying = $t_c + t_f$

Appropriate equations and values of X_1, X_2 and X_c are to be used for the calculation of the time required during a particular period.

DRYING EQUIPMENTS :

Dryers used in industry may be classified on the basis of (a) mode of operation (b) physical properties and handling characteristics of the material and (c) the method of supplying heat to the material to be dried, i.e., method of heat transfer.

(i) Mode of operation :

On basis of mode of operation that is based on the production schedule there are two types of drying equipments – (i) batch dryers and (ii) continuous dryers.

In case of batch dryer, a definite size of batch of the wet feed is charged to the dryer and drying is carried out over a given time period. These dryers operate under unsteady state conditions.

Drying in batches is relatively expensive operation and consequently batch dryers are preferred for small-scale production, pilot plant and for drying valuable materials.

In case of continuous dryer, the material flows in and out continuously and drying is carried out under steady state conditions continuously. These are generally used for large scale production.

Advantages of continuous drying include :

Equipment necessary is small relative to the quantity of product.

Product has more uniform moisture content.

Cost of drying per unit of product is relatively small.

(ii) Physical properties and handling characteristics of material :

The wet feed material may be a liquid solution, a slurry, a paste, a sludge, free flowing powder, granular, crystalline or fibrous solid. The design of dryer depends upon the physical properties of the wet feed material and therefore dryer handling similar feeds may have many common design characteristics.

(iii) Method of heat transfer :

On the basis of method of heat transfer, dryers are classified as (a) direct dryers, and (b) indirect dryers.

Direct dryers :

In such dryers, heat transfer is accomplished by direct contact between the wet wet feed material and hot gases. The heat of evaporation is supplied by the sensible heat of a gas in contact with the material to be dried (adiabatic dryer). The moisture evaporated from the wet feed is carried by hot gases.

Indirect dryers :

In such dryer, heat necessary for drying is transferred to the wet feed by conduction through a metal surface/wall in contact with the feed material to be dried (non-adiabatic dryer). The moisture evaporated from the wet feed is carried by the air or other gas independently of a heating medium.

Production rates of 5000 kg per day are best handled by batch dryers and rates over 50000 kg in a continuous dryer.

Tray Dryer :

Construction : It is the simplest of batch dryers and also known as a cabinet or compartment dryer. The tray dryer shown in Fig. 12.6 is a batch operated direct dryer. It consists of an enclosed insulated cabinet or a large compartment into which the material to be dried is placed on a number of removable trays. The trays may either be fabricated from sheets or from screens. The trays may be stacked on racks or loaded on trucks. It is provided with inlet and outlet connections for air. A heating coil either electrical or steam-heating is incorporated in it. In these dryers, steam, gas or electrically heated air is used as the drying medium. The air is circulated in the dryer over the trays by means of a fan fitted at the top (on one of the sides, opposite to the coil).

Working : The material to be dried is spread over the trays and put into the cabinet and then it is closed. Steam is continuously passed through the coil and fan is started. Air is heated by heating coils, its relative humidity decreases (i.e., its capacity to evaporate the moisture is increased) and the hot air then passes over the trays.

Fig. 12.6 : Tray Dryer

The moisture is evaporated from the wet feed, gets added in the air and finally the air leaves the dryer through the outlet. The process is continued until the solids are dried. The cabinet is opened, dried material is removed from the trays and a fresh batch is charged.

For getting good drying, the air after drying should be thrown out completely but by this way, a large portion of heat associated with the hot gas will be lost and the operation will become costly. To avoid this heat loss (i.e., to conserve heat), about 80 – 95 % of the air is recirculated by adjusting a damper provided at the outlet, and the remaining portion is exhausted out, and the same amount of fresh air is taken in through the inlet.

The overall rate of drying of such a dryer is 0.2 to 2.0 kg water/(m²·h) material surface and the thermal efficiency is of the order of 20 – 25 %.

The trays are generally 600 mm wide, 900 to 1500 mm long and 30 to 40 mm deep. They are made of mild steel, stainless steel, enamelled iron, etc. and are fabricated from sheets of 3 mm to 6 mm thick.

Advantages :

– Relatively cheap and easy to construct/build.
– Low space requirement.
– Ease in cleaning.
– Requires low maintenance (low maintenance cost).
– No loss of product during drying.

Disadvantages :

– Expensive to operate due to high labour requirements for loading and unloading (high labour costs and low heat economy).
– Long drying cycles (4 to 48 h per batch).
– Small quantities are handled.

Applications :

Tray dryer is well suited for small scale production (i.e., for small production rate) and drying valuable materials like dyes and pharmaceuticals. It is especially useful for drying wet lumpy solids and wet filter cakes which must be spread over the trays.

These dryers may be operated under vacuum, in many cases with indirect heating. In such dryers, all joints must be air-tight. The trays may rest on hollow metal plates supplied with steam vapour from the wet solid is removed by a vacuum pump. Vacuum tray dryers are suited for heat sensitive materials. (i.e., thermally unstable materials).

Dryer control :

Refer to Fig. 12.7. Fresh air is taken through value 'A' by means of a blower or fan and then it enters a heater. Before entering the heater, the air is divided into two parts, one part of it goes to the heater through a valve 'B' and the part of it is by-passed through a valve 'C'. The valves 'B' and 'C' are connected together by mechanical links in such a way that if one starts closing, other will start opening. Both the valves are operated by a diaphragm control valve which is getting signals from a dry and wet bulb recorder and controller. The hot air from heater and cold by-passed air are mixed together and sent to the dryer for drying. For heat economy, a major part of the air leaving the dryer (moist air) can be recirculated in the system through valve 'D' and the remaining air is vented to atmosphere through a valve 'E'. The valves 'A', 'D' and 'E' are connected together by mechanical links in such a way that if valve 'E' starts opening, valve D will start closing, and valve 'A' will start opening. All three valves are operated by a diaphragm control valve which is getting signals from the dry and wet bulb recorder and controller. The dry and wet bulb thermometer assembly is kept in the outlet line from the dryer.

(control valves instead of operating valve stem they operate a lever that actuates dampers)

Fig. 12.7 : Instrumentation diagram for dryer

When the temperature of the outgoing air from the dryer increases beyond a certain limit then the controller will give a signal to the valves B and C through the control valve which is actuated by the dry bulb thermometer in such a way that valve 'B' starts opening and valve 'C' starts closing so that less hot air is going to the dryer and vice versa. When the humidity of the outgoing air from the dryer increases, wet bulb temperature will increases. Controller will detect this increase in the wet-bulb temperature and accordingly will give a signal to the control valve which operates valves 'A', 'D' and 'E' in such a way that when valve 'E' starts opening, 'D' starts closing and 'A' starts opening, so that more fresh air is taken into the system and moist air is thrown out and recirculation is also reduced. Because of this action, the humidity is lowered. The dryer control of this type can be used for batch as well as for continuous dryers.

Rotary Dryer :

This type of dryer (that may be directly or indirectly heated) is adopted for the continuous drying of free-flowing granular materials on a large scale. Fig. 12.8 shows one form of a rotary dryer. It consists of a relatively long cylindrical shell (having a diameter of 1 m to 3 m and length 3 m to 30 m), set with its axis at a slight angle to the horizontal (slightly inclined towards the outlet), so that material fed is consequently advanced through the dryer (under gravity) from one end to the other end (from where it is discharged).

(a) : Direct heat counter current flow Rotary dryer

(b) : Rotary dryer, side view

(c) : Schematic view of rotary dryer
Fig. 12.8

The shell is mounted on rollers so that it can be rotated. To avoid its slipping over the rollers, it is fitted with thrust wheels. It is fitted inside with flights which lift the material upward and shower it down from the top. A few spiral flights are fitted near the feed end which help in giving the initial forward motion to the material before principle flights are reached. The material to be dried (feed) is fed at the high end of the dryer by a hopper and the product is taken out from the lower end of the dryer. The material moves through the dryer by virtue of rotation, heat effect and slope (inclination) of cylindrical shell.

The cylindrical shell is rotated by a gear mechanism at a speed of 2 to 25 r.p.m. Air is taken into the dryer from the product end, it is heated in a heater, and then moves through the dryer in a counter current fashion with respect to the material to be dried. The moisture of the feed evaporates and gets added into the drying medium, and finally the moist air leaves the dryer at the feed end. Generally, an exhaust moist air leaves the dryer at the feed end. Generally, an exhaust fan is used to pull the air through the dryer. The air leaving the dryer will contain some dust particles which are removed by interposing a cyclone separator between the dryer and the exhaust fan as shown in Fig. 12.9.

Fig. 12.9 : Rotary dryer with dust collector (cyclone)

The mode of operation is usually continuous. In case of direct contact, the hot gas is passed over the material in a counter-current fashion. In case of indirect contact, heat is transferred through the wall of the cylindrical shell.

The thermal efficiency of rotary dryers is about 50 – 80 % and the drying rate ranges between 10 – 50 kg/(h·m³ of shell volume).

Advantages :
– Good gas contacting
– moderate drying time
– low capital cost
– drying and calcining in the same unit
– high thermal efficiency
– greater flexibility of control of the gas velocity.

Disadvantages :

- difficulty of sealing
- product build-up on interior walls
- high structural load
- non-uniform residence time.

Rotary dryers are grouped into four categories :

1. Direct heat counter current flow :

This type of dryer is shown in Fig. 12.8 and employed for the materials which may be heated to a high temperature like minerals, sand clays, etc. Hot flue gas is usually used as the drying medium. It is also used for products like ammonium sulphate and cane sugar wherein the hot air is used as a drying medium.

2. Direct heat parallel flow :

In this type both the material and hot gas/air move in the same direction through the dryer. It is used for drying materials like gypsum, iron pyrites, etc., which should not be heated to destructive temperatures.

3. Indirect heat counter current flow :

It is used for materials which can be heated to high temperatures out of contact with flue gas such as white pigments, etc. It is shown in Fig. 12.10.

Fig. 12.10 : Indirect-Counter flow rotary dryer

4. Direct-indirect type dryer :

This type of dryer is used for solids, which may be heated to very high temperatures by flue gas, such as lignite, coal, and coke. It is shown in Fig. 12.11.

It contains an inner hollow tube through which the flue gas passes from a combustion chamber to the lower end of the dryer. At this end, the direction of flue gas is reversed and made to pass through hollow flights, through an annular space and leaves the dryer from the feed end. The central tube is provided with longitudinal fins to increase the outer area of heat

Fig. 12.11 : Direct - Indirect type dryer

transfer. The wet material is admitted at the high end of the dryer and travels down to the lower end and taken out as dried product. Air enters from the product end and travels over the solid in the reverse direction. The moisture gets added in the air and finally leaves the dryer from the feed end. The material is heated indirectly by the flue gas by conduction and radiation and the moisture is taken out by air, flowing in a counter current fashion with respect to the feed. Another type of indirect dryer is the steam tube dryer employing a number of tubes and finds application where material must not be heated to a high temperature, e.g., drying of cattle feed, etc.

Fig. 12.12 : Indirect steam-tube dryer

Drum Dryer

Construction :

Fig. 12.13 : Single drum dryer

A drum dryer consists of one or more metal rolls (drums) that are heated internally by steam and rotate at about 1 to 10 revolutions per minute. The rolls of the drum dryer are usually 0.6 to 3.5 m in diameter and 0.6 to 5 m in length (may be fabricated from plates). The drum is submerged into a pool of solution or slurry contained in a trough. For an agitation purpose, i.e., to avoid the setting of solids, an agitator is incorporated in the trough. A spreader is provided on one side to regulate the thickness of the film of substance on the outside of the drum and a knife is provided on the other end to scrap the dried material from the slowly revolving roll/drum. A vapour-hood is provided at the top of the drum for collection and removal of vaporised moisture. Fig. 12.13 shows such a dryer.

Working :

A slowly revolving internally steam heated drum continuously dips into a trough and picks up the feed which retains on the drum surface as a thin film. The thickness of this film of material is regulated by means of a spreader. During the course of revolution of the drum, the material is dried due to heat transfer from condensing steam through the metal wall of the drum and large surface area. As it reaches the other end, the dried product (in the form of flakes) of operation is scrapped by a knife. The moisture evaporated from the feed material is collected and removed through a vapour-hood provided above the drum(s).

Drum dryers are usually made of cast iron but where contamination of the product must be avoided, for example, in case of pharmaceuticals or food products, chromium plated steel or alloy steel is used as a material of construction. The capacity of the drum dryers is less as compared to the spray dryer but their operating cost is low.

Drum dryers are suitable for handling fluid and semifluid materials such as slurries, pastes of solids in fine suspension and dilute or concentrated solutions of highly soluble materials. These units are not suited for solution of salts with limited solubility and for slurries of abrasive solids that have the tendency to settle-out.

Cylindrical dryers are drum dryers which are commonly employed for handling material in the continuous sheet form, such as paper and cloth. The wet material is fed continuously over the revolving drum or a series of drums each heated internally by steam.

Spray Dryer :

It is a continuous direct contact dryer employed for drying of solutions, slurries, and pastes. In this dryer, a liquid solution or slurry is introduced in the form of very fine droplets into a stream of hot gas inside a large drying chamber, thereby a large contact area becomes available for perfect drying. The moisture of feed is evaporated and gets added into the hot gas.

Construction : Fig. 12.14 shows a typical spray dryer. The essential components of the dryer are : a drying chamber (a vertical cylindrical chamber with a short conical bottom), where the feed material is contacted with a hot gas (air), a heater for heating the fresh air sucked by a fan or blower, cyclone separators for dust separation and collection, a pneumatic conveying duct and blowers, which are assembled as shown in Fig. 12.14. The material is usually spread in the form of a mist of fine droplets by spray nozzles or high speed rotating spray discs into a hot gas stream inside the chamber as shown in Fig. 12.14.

Working : The feed is pumped to the top of the dryer (drying chamber) where it is disintegrated into small droplets by an atomiser. The large quantity of fresh air is taken in by a fan, it is heated in a heater and finally fed below the atomiser in the drying chamber. As the surface area of drops is very large, the liquid portion of these drops rapidly evaporates and before they touch the bottom of the drying chamber they are completely dried. This dried product (in the form of dry powder) is taken out and conveyed to a cyclone dust collector - 2 by a stream of air. The major portion of the air is taken out through the air outlet duct which mostly contains dust and is sent to a cyclone -1. The solids collected by the cyclone -1 are fed to a pneumatic conveying duct. The air leaving the cyclone - 2 may contain some dust and therefore it is sent to the cyclone - 1, for further separation, by the fan. The air from the cyclone -1 is thrown out to the atmosphere by a blower. The dried product from the cyclone - 2 is collected in a dry product collector.

An atomiser is a device which causes the liquid to be disintegrated into the fine drops. The atomisers commonly employed are :

1. Pressure nozzles which make use of pressure energy for atomisation.

2. Two fluid nozzles wherein air or steam at a certain pressure is used to tear a liquid into droplets, i.e., they make use of gas energy and

3. Rotating discs which make use of centrifugal energy for atomisation. Spray nozzles (type -1 and type - 2) are relatively inflexible in operation and also subject to erosion and tear. The rotating discs (may be plane, vaned or cup-shaped) rotate at a speed of about 3000 to 12000 r.p.m. The feed introduced at the centre of disc is centrifugally accelerated to the periphery and ultimately thrown in an umbrella-shaped spray. The rotating discs are very flexible in their operating characteristics and can handle thick slurries without danger of clogging.

Fig. 12.14 : Spray Dryer

In this dryer care must be taken to ensure that the droplets or wet particles of solids do not strike and stick to solid surfaces before complete drying. So as to avoid this, large drying chambers are used.

Advantages :

very short drying times (2 – 20 s)

handle heat sensitive products

control of a product particle size

rapid dehydration.

relatively low operating costs, particularly in large capacity units.

Disadvantages :

low solids content

relatively large units

maintenance of atomiser

inefficient in (its) energy use

product built-up on interior walls.

These dryers are popular in dairy industry, food industry, detergent industry, chemical and dyes industry.

Spray dryers are extensively used for products such as milk powder, detergents, dyes, coffee, pharmaceuticals, etc.

Fluidised Bed Dryer :

It is also known as a fluid bed dryer. Fluid bed drying systems are becoming popular because of the following reasons :

(i) absence of moving parts-results in ease of maintenance

(ii) high heat transfer rates

(iii) rapid mixing indicating more or less an isothermal operation leading to the uniform drying.

In this dryer, a hot gas / air is passed through a wet material at a velocity sufficiently high to fluidise the wet material but not too high enough to cause pneumatic conveying.

Typical gas/air velocities are :

Particle size (μm)	Velocity (m/s)
300 – 800	0.4 to 0.8
800 – 2000	0.8 to 1.2

Fig. 12.15 : Fluidised Bed Dryer

A fluidised bed system in addition to a fluidising chamber also needs an air blower, a hot air generator, a feed conveyor, a cyclone separator and a product conveyor.

In this dryer, hot air is used to keep the wet feed in a fluidised state. In the dryer shown in Fig. 12.15 the wet material is dried and cooled in the same bed. Wet feed material is admitted to the top of the bed through a hopper via a rotary valve and hot air is distributed at the bottom of the bed through a diffuser plate and dry product is taken out from the side or near the bottom. Heat and mass transfer coefficients are high because of turbulence created in the bed. The material to be dried and hot air are in cross flow with respect to the direction of flow of each other. The residence time can be controlled from seconds to hours. The moist air from the dryer containing fines is admitted to a cyclone separator for the recovery of fines.

It is used for drying very fine size free flowing materials. It is well suited for temperature / heat sensitive materials.

These dryers may also be operated batchwise. A charge of wet feed material in a perforated container attached to the bottom of the fluidising chamber is fluidised, heated until dry and then discharged. Such units have replaced tray dryers in many processes.

Tunnel Dryer :

The continuously operated direct type tunnel dryer is shown in Fig. 12.16. This dryer is built in the form of a long tunnel. It is provided with inlet and outlet for air. The fan and heating coils are incorporated in the tunnel as shown in Fig. 12.16. The material to be dried is filled in trays and trucks loaded with these trays move progressively through the tunnel in contact with a current hot gas to evaporate the moisture. Air flow in the tunnel dryer can be totally concurrent, counter current or a combination of both with respect to the material flow. The wet material enters at one end and dried product leaves at the other end. For relatively low temperature operation, steam heated air is used as the drying medium, while for high temperatures, flue gas is used as the drying medium (where contamination is permissible).

These dryers are generally employed for drying of all forms of particulate solids and large solid objects, on a large scale.

Fig. 12.16 : Tunnel Dryer

It is often used for drying of pottery, ceramic products, paraffin wax, etc. which require slow rate of drying.

Pneumatic (flash) Dryer :

In a flash dryer, drying is carried out in a very short span of time-0.5 to 3 seconds. Pneumatic conveying duct is the heart of the system wherein drying operation is carried out. Hot gas is the conveying medium-flowing rapidly with velocity of the order ~ 25 m/s in which the granular free flowing solids are dispersed.

Fig. 12.17 : Pneumatic (Flash) dryer

1 : drying duct 2 : Heater 3; 6 : blower, 4 : cyclone and 5 : bag filter

Finely powdered wet material is introduced into the hot gas (air stream) with the help of a screw conveyor. The material is pneumatically conveyed through the duct and during its conveyance moisture is removed. The dried material is separated from the air stream in a cyclone and a bag filter. The product from the bottom of the collecting equipments (cyclone and bag filter) is transported to a silo via a screw conveyor (not shown).

Due to very short residence time it is used for drying of heat sensitive materials.

SOLVED EXAMPLES

Ex. 12.1 : A wet solid is to be dried from 80 % to 5 % moisture on wet basis. Calculate the amount of moisture to be evaporated per 100 kg of dried product.

Solution : Basis : 100 kg of dried product

dry solids in product = $0.95 \times 100 = 95$ kg

moisture in product = $0.05 \times 100 = 5$ kg

Let x be the kg of wet solids,

moisture in wet solid = 80 %

Material balance of solids :

$$0.20 \, x = 95$$
$$x = 475 \text{ kg}$$

Moisture in wet solid = $0.80 \times 475 = 380$ kg

Amount of moisture to be evaporated per 100 kg of dried product :

$$= 380 - 5 = 375 \text{ kg} \quad \ldots \textbf{Ans.}$$

Ex. 12.2 : Find out the rate of drying and moisture content from the following data :

Weight of wet saw dust	Weight of saw dust after drying	Time (h)
250 g	230 g	0.5
250 g	215 g	0.75

Dimension of tray = 10 cm × 10 cm

Weight of dry saw dust on tray = 150 g

Solution :

$$A = \text{Area of tray} = \text{Area of drying surface}$$
$$A = 0.1 \times 0.1 = 0.01 \text{ m}^2$$
$$W' = \text{weight of dry solids (saw dust)}$$
$$W' = 150 \text{ g} = \frac{150}{1000} = 0.15 \text{ kg}$$

Moisture in saw dust initially = $250 - 150 = 100$ g

$$X_1 = \text{Initial moisture content}$$
$$X_1 = \frac{100}{150} = 0.666 \text{ kg/kg dry solid}$$

Moisture after 0.5 h in wet saw dust = $230 - 150 = 80$ g

$$X_2 = \text{Final moisture content (after 0.5 h)}$$

$$X_2 = \frac{80}{150} = 0.533 \quad \text{... Ans.}$$

Time of drying $= t = \dfrac{W'}{A}\left[\dfrac{X_1 - X_2}{R}\right]$

where R is rate of drying in kg/(m²·h)

Rearranging the above equation :

$$R = \frac{W'}{A \cdot t}[X_1 - X_2]$$

$$= \frac{0.15}{0.01 \times 0.5}[0.666 - 0.533]$$

$$= 3.99 \text{ kg/(m}^2\cdot\text{h)} \quad \text{... Ans. (1)}$$

Weight of wet sample after 0.75 h = 215 g

Weight of moisture in wet solids after 0.75 h

$$= 215 - 150 = 65 \text{ g}$$

$X_3 =$ Moisture content after 0.75 h

$$= \frac{65}{150} = 0.433 \quad \text{... Ans. (2)}$$

Rate of drying $= \dfrac{W'(X_1 - X_3)}{A \cdot t}$

$$= \frac{0.15\,[0.666 - 0.433]}{0.01 \times 0.75}$$

$$= 4.194 \text{ kg/(m}^2\cdot\text{h)} \quad \text{... Ans. (3)}$$

Ex. 12.3 : A wet solid is to be dried from 35 % to 10 % moisture under the constant drying conditions in five hours. If the equilibrium moisture content is 4 % and the critical moisture content is 14 %, how long it will take to dry solids to 6 % moisture under the same conditions ?

Solution :

Data given for first case :

Initial moisture = 35 %

Final moisture = 10 %

Critical moisture = 14 %

and Equilibrium moisture = 4 %

Time required for drying solids from 35 % to 10 % moisture = 5 h

It is clear from values of the moisture content given above (final moisture and critical moisture) that the period of five hours will be the time required during the constant rate period plus the time required during the falling rate period.

Let x = wt. fraction of moisture in solid = (wt. %)/100

X_1 = Initial moisture content

$$= \frac{x_1}{1-x_1} = \frac{0.35}{1-0.35} = 0.5385$$

X_c = Critical moisture content

$$= \frac{x_c}{1-x_c} = \frac{0.14}{1-0.14} = 0.1628$$

X^* = Equilibrium moisture content

$$= \frac{x^*}{1-x^*} = \frac{0.04}{1-0.04} = 0.0417$$

X_2 = Final moisture content (in falling rate period)

$$= \frac{x_2}{1-x_2} = \frac{0.1}{1-0.1} = 0.111$$

t = Time of drying
$$= t_c + t_f$$

$$t = \frac{W'}{A \cdot R_c}[X_1 - X_c] + \frac{W'(X_c - X^*)}{R_c \cdot A} \ln\left[\frac{X_c - X^*}{X_2 - X^*}\right]$$

where R_c = rate of drying in constant rate period
  W' = kg of dry solids
  A = area of drying surface.

The above equation can be written as

$$t = \frac{W'}{A \cdot R_c}\left[(X_1 - X_c) + (X_c - X^*) \ln\left(\frac{X_c - X^*}{X_2 - X^*}\right)\right]$$

Putting the values of t, X_1, X_2, X_c and X^*

$$5 = \frac{W'}{R_c \cdot A}\left[(0.5385 - 0.1628) + (0.1628 - 0.0417) \ln\left(\frac{0.1628 - 0.0417}{0.111 - 0.0417}\right)\right]$$

$$\therefore \quad \frac{W'}{R_c \cdot A} = 11.28$$

For the second case, the final moisture is given as 6 %

X_2 = Final moisture content for second case

$$= \frac{0.06}{1-0.06} = 0.0638$$

Using the above equation and putting the value of various terms to get time of drying from 35 % to 6 % moisture

$$t = \frac{W'}{R_c \cdot A}\left[(X_1 - X_c) + (X_c - X^*) \ln\left(\frac{X_c - X^*}{X_2 - X^*}\right)\right]$$

$$t = (11.28)\left[(0.5385 - 0.1628) + (0.1628 - 0.0417) \ln\left(\frac{0.1628 - 0.0417}{0.0638 - 0.0417}\right)\right]$$

$$t = 6.56 \text{ h} \qquad \text{... Ans.}$$

Ex. 12.4 : A 100 kg bath of granular solids containing 30 % moisture is to be dried in a tray dryer to 16 % moisture by passing a current of air at 350 K across its surface at a velocity of 1.8 m/s. If the constant rate of drying under these conditions is 0.7×10^{-3} kg/(m²·s) and the critical moisture content is 15 %, calculate the drying time.

Drying surface = 0.03 m²/kg dry weight.

Solution :

Moisture content data from constant rate period is :

Initial moisture = 30 %

Final moisture = 16 %

Critical moisture = 15 %

As the final moisture is greater than the critical moisture, we are in the constant rate period. The equation for calculating time of drying during the constant rate period is :

$$t = \frac{W'}{A}\left[\frac{X_1 - X_2}{R_c}\right]$$

where W' = weight of dry solids

A = Area of drying surface

and X_1 and X_2 are initial and final moisture contents respectively.

X_1 = Initial moisture content (dry basis)

$$= \frac{0.3}{1 - 0.3} = 0.428$$

X_2 = Final moisture content

$$= \frac{0.16}{1 - 0.16}$$

$$= 0.19 \frac{\text{kg moisture}}{\text{kg dry solid}}$$

Surface of drying is given as :

= 0.03 m² per kg dry solid weight, therefore

$$\frac{A}{W'} = 0.03$$

$$\frac{W'}{A} = \frac{1}{0.03} = 33.33$$

R_c = Rate of drying during constant rate period

$= 0.7 \times 10^{-3}$ kg/(m²·s)

$= 0.7 \times 10^{-3} \times 3600$ kg/(m²·h)

$= 2.52$ kg/(m²·h)

$$t = \frac{W'}{A} \times \left[\frac{X_1 - X_2}{R_c}\right]$$

Putting the values of X_1, X_2, R_c and $\frac{W'}{A}$ in the above equation

$$t = 33.33 \times \left[\frac{0.428 - 0.19}{2.52}\right] = 3.15 \text{ h}$$

Time of drying = 3.15 h ... **Ans.**

Ex. 12.5 : A 50 kg batch of granular solids containing 25 % moisture is to be dried in a tray dryer to 12 % moisture by passing a stream of air at 363 K (90 °C) tangentially across its surface at a velocity of 1.8 m/s. If the constant rate of drying under these condition is 0.0008 kg moisture/(m²·s) and the critical moisture content is 10 %, calculate the drying time. The surface area available for drying is 1.0 m².

Solution : Basis : 50 kg of batch of granular solids.

Moisture content data for constant rate period as :

Initial moisture – 25 %

Final moisture – 12 %

Critical moisture – 10 %

As the final moisture is greater than critical moisture, we are in constant rate period. Equation for calculating time of drying during constant rate period is :

$$t = \frac{W'}{A}\left[\frac{X_1 - X_2}{R_c}\right]$$

where, W' – Weight of dry solids

         A – Area of drying surface

X_1 and X_2 are initial and final moisture content respectively.

X_1 = Initial moisture content (dry basis)

$= \dfrac{0.25}{1 - 0.25} = 0.333$

X_2 = Final moisture content

$= \dfrac{0.12}{1 - 0.12} = 0.1364$ kg moisture/kg dry solid

$A = 1$ m²

kg of dry solids in batch $= 0.75 \times 50 = 37.5$ kg

R_c = rate of drying during constant rate period
= 0.0008 kg/(m²·s)
= 0.0008 × 3600
R_c = 2.88 kg/(m²·h)

$$t = \frac{W'}{A}\left[\frac{X_1 - X_2}{R_c}\right]$$

$$= \frac{37.5}{1.0}\left[\frac{0.333 - 0.1364}{2.88}\right] = 2.56 \text{ h} \quad \ldots \text{Ans.}$$

Ex. 12.6 : 1400 kg (bone dry) of granular solid is to be dried under the constant drying conditions from a moisture content of 0.2 kg/kg dry solid to a final moisture content of 0.02 kg/kg dry solid. The drying surface is given as 0.0615 m²/(kg). Under the same conditions, the following rates were previously known. Calculate the time required for drying.

Moisture content :

X, kg/kg dry solid	0.3	0.2	0.14	0.096	0.056	0.046	0.026	0.016
Rate, R, kg/(m²·h)	1.71	1.71	1.71	1.46	1.29	0.88	0.54	0.376

Solution : Construct a plot of rate v/s X [Fig. (A)]. It is evident that the falling rate period is not a straight line. Hence, the time for it is to be calculated by the graphical integration.

W' — kg dry solid = 1400 kg
X_1 — Initial moisture content = 0.2 kg/kg dry solid
X_2 — Final moisture content = 0.02 kg/kg dry solid
Drying surface = A = 0.0615 × 1400 = 86.1 m²
Constant drying rate = 1.71 kg/(m²·h)
Drying time = $t = t_c + t_f$

$$t_c = \frac{W'}{A R_c}[X_1 - X_c]$$

where
W' = 1400 kg
A = 86.1 m²
R_c = 1.71 kg/(m²·h)
X_c = 0.14

$$t_c = \frac{1400}{86.1 \times 1.71}[0.20 - 0.14] = 0.57 \text{ h}$$

For falling rate period :

$$t_f = \frac{-W'}{A} \int_{X_c}^{X_2} \frac{dX}{R} = \frac{W'}{A} \int_{X_2}^{X_c} \frac{dX}{R}$$

X	0.140	0.096	0.056	0.046	0.026	0.02	0.016
R	1.71	1.46	1.29	0.88	0.54	0.50	0.376
1/R	0.585	0.685	0.775	1.136	1.852	2.0	2.66

Fig. (A)

Plot 1/R v/s X and measure the area under the curve. The area under the curve between $X_c = 0.14$ and $X_2 = 0.02$ will give the value of integration.

$$\int_{X_2}^{X_c} \frac{dX}{R} = \text{Area under curve} \times \text{Scale of x-axis} \times \text{Scale of y-axis}$$

$$= 0.104$$

$$t_f = \frac{W'}{A} \int_{X_2}^{X_c} \frac{dX}{R}$$

$$= \frac{1400}{86.1} \times 0.104 = 1.69 \text{ h}$$

Total drying time = 0.57 + 1.69 = 2.26 h ... **Ans.**

Ex. 12.7 : Solids are to dried under the constant drying conditions from 67 % to 25 % moisture. The value of equilibrium moisture for material is 1 %. If the critical moisture content is 40 % and rate of drying in constant rate period is 1.5 kg/(m²·h), calculate the drying time

Drying surface = 0.5 m²/kg dry solid

Solution : X_1 = Initial moisture content. x = wt. fraction of moisture in solid.

$$= \frac{0.67}{1 - 0.67} = 2.03, \quad \left[= \frac{x_1}{1 - x_1}, \quad x_1 = 67/100 = 0.67 \right]$$

X_2 = Final moisture content

$$= \frac{0.25}{1-0.25}, \left[=\frac{x_2}{1-x_2} \text{ with } x_2 = 25/100 = 0.25\right]$$

$$= 0.333$$

X^* = Equilibrium moisture content

$$X^* = \frac{0.01}{1-0.01} = 0.0101, \left[=\frac{x^*}{1-x^*} \text{ with } x^* = 1/100 = 0.01\right]$$

$$X_c = \frac{0.40}{1-0.40} = 0.67$$

R_c = 1.5 kg/(m²·h)

$$\frac{A}{W'} = 0.5$$

$$\frac{W'}{A} = 2.0$$

$$t = \frac{W'}{A \cdot R_c}\left[(X_1 - X_c) + (X_c - X^*) \ln \frac{X_c - X^*}{X_2 - X^*}\right]$$

$$t = \frac{2}{1.5}\left[(2.03 - 0.67) + (0.67 - 0.0101)\ln\left[\frac{0.67 - 0.0101}{0.333 - 0.0101}\right]\right]$$

$$t = 2.44 \text{ h} \qquad \ldots \text{ Ans.}$$

Ex. 12.8 : Slabs of paper pulp 100 cm × 100 cm × 1.5 cm is to be dried under constant drying conditions from 67 % to 30 % moisture. The value of equilibrium moisture for the material is 0.5 %. If the critical moisture content is 60 % and rate of drying at the critical point is
1.5 kg/(m²·h), calculate the drying time. The dry weight of each slab is 2.5 kg. All moisture contents are on weight basis.

Solution : Considering drying from the two big faces,

A = 1 × 1 × 2 = 2 m²
W' = dry weight of slab = 2.5 kg
x = wt. fraction of moisture in solid.

$$\text{Initial moisture content} = X_1 = \frac{0.67}{1-0.67}, \left[=\frac{x_1}{1-x_1} \text{ with } x_1 = \frac{67}{100} = 0.67\right]$$

$$= 2.03 \frac{\text{kg moisture}}{\text{kg dry solid}}$$

$$\text{Final moisture content} = X_2 = \frac{0.30}{1-0.30} = 0.428, \left[=\frac{x_2}{1-x_2} \text{ with } x_2 = \frac{30}{100} = 0.30\right]$$

$$\text{Equilibrium moisture content} = X^* = \frac{0.005}{1-0.005} = 0.005025$$

$$\text{Critical moisture content} = X_C = \frac{0.60}{1-0.60} = 1.5$$

R_c = Constant rate of drying
  = 1.5 kg/(m²·h)

Total time of drying = t = $t_c + t_f$

$$t = \frac{W'}{A \cdot R_c} \left[(X_1 - X_c) + (X_c - X^*) \ln \left(\frac{X_c - X^*}{X_2 - X^*} \right) \right]$$

$$= \frac{2.5}{2 \times 1.5} \left[(2.03 - 1.5) + (1.5 - 0.005025) \ln \frac{(1.5 - 0.005025)}{(0.428 - 0.005025)} \right] = 2.01 \text{ h}$$

Time of drying = 2.01 h ... **Ans.**

EXERCISE

1. Fill in the blanks.
   (i) .... refers to the removal of moisture of a substance by thermal means. **Ans.** Drying
   (ii) Removal of moisture by .... means is more costly than mechanical means. **Ans.** thermal
   (iii) The moisture content in excess of equilibrium moisture content is called as .... moisture content. **Ans.** free
   (iv) At .... moisture content constant rate period ends and falling rate period starts. **Ans.** critical
   (v) Rotating discs make use of .... energy for atomisation. **Ans.** centrifugal
   (vi) For producing milk powder .... dryer is used. **Ans.** spray
   (vii) .... dryer is commonly used for wet filter cakes and wet lumpy solids. **Ans.** Tray
   (viii) Drying operation involves the transfer of solute material from .... phase to gas phase. **Ans.** solid

2. Define the following terms :
   (i) critical moisture content (ii) equilibrium moisture content (iii) bound moisture content and (iv) drying.

3. State what for the drying is carried out industrially ?

4. What do you mean by constant drying conditions ?

5. Draw a rate of drying curve and mention various zone on it.

6. Explain in brief rate of drying curve.

7. Draw the plot of (i) relative humidity v/s moisture content and moisture content v/s time.

8. What do you mean by constant rate period and falling rate period ?

9. State the factors on which the rate of drying depends. Explain in brief.

10. Draw a neat sketch of tray dryer and explain its construction.

11. Give the advantages, disadvantages and applications of
    (i) Tray dryer (ii) Spray dryer.
12. Write in brief on rotary dryer with respect to its construction and working.
13. Draw the sketch of spray dryer and explain its working.
14. Write in brief on classification of the dryers.
15. Write in brief on fluidised bed dryer.
16. Write in brief on pneumatic (flash) dryer.

APPENDIX – I
TRY YOURSELF

1. The materials A and B have thermal conductivities as k_1 and k_2 respectively where k_1 is greater than k_2, state which material has higher resistance to heat transfer for a given thickness?
2. State the units of thermal conductivity in SI system.
3. Is thermal conductivity a function of temperature?
4. Heat flow is inversely proportional to temperature difference. State whether this statement is correct or not and if not, correct it.
5. Is there temperature variation with time at steady state in brick walled furnace at any location?
6. The pipe has inside diameter of D_1 and outside diameter of D_2. What will be the value of log mean radius in terms of D_1 and D_2?
7. In forced convection, heat transfer coefficients are higher than those in natural convection. State whether this statement is true or false.
8. Name the three resistances in series in case of heat transfer from hot fluid to cold fluid separated by metal wall.
9. What will happen to the value of heat transfer coefficient, if velocity of flowing fluid is increased from u_1 to u_2 ($u_2 > u_1$).
10. Coolants with specific heats of C_{P_A} and C_{P_B} are available where $C_{P_A} > C_{P_B}$. For a given duty and for same terminal temperatures of coolants, state which fluid needs higher mass flow rate through exchanger.
11. If heat exchanger is put into service for long time, which is designed without taking into account fouling what will be the effect on temperatures of hot and cold fluids?
12. If heat exchanger is put into service for long time which is designed based on clean overall coefficient, will it transfer required amount of heat and if not. Justify your answer.
13. In heat exchange process if one of fluids is viscous, state whether it should be directed, on shell side or tube side.
14. In heat exchange process if one of fluids is corrosive, state whether it should be directed on shell side or tube side of shell and tube heat exchanger.
15. For which heat duty condenser and cooler are used?
16. What for baffles are incorporated in shell and tube heat exchanger?
17. Why the heat transfer coefficients are low in case of film wise condensation?
18. Which type of surface leads to condensation to proceed in dropwise manner?

19. State which of the following apparatus has more ability to recover heat:
    (1) Parallel flow apparatus.
    (2) Counter current flow apparatus.
20. Is it possible in parallel flow for hot fluid temperature to fall below the outlet temperature of the cold fluid. If not, state the type of flow in which it is possible.
21. In parallel flow, theoretically, the lowest temperature attainable by hot fluid is that of outlet temperature of the cold fluid. If this were obtained what do you think of heat transfer surface requirement and its feasibility ?
22. What do you understand by nucleate boiling and film boiling ?
23. Why film boiling is not desired in commercial equipment ?
24. Mention whether film heat transfer coefficient is higher in nucleate boiling or in film boiling ?
25. Which type of pitch arrangement will offer larger heat transfer surface in a given shell diameter ?
26. If frequent cleaning is required, which type of pitch arrangement should be adopted for laying tubes in tubesheet ?
27. Which type of flow arrangement do you suggest to limit the maximum temperature of cooler fluid ?
28. Why the steam carrying pipes are insulated ?
29. State whether cleaning of the tubes from inside or from outside is easy ?
30. State with which of the following exchanger, the heat recovery will be maximum ?
    (1) 1 –1 shell and tube exchanger,
    (2) 1 – 2 shell and tube exchanger,
    (3) 2 – 4 shell and tube exchanger.
31. What do you mean by term "fins" ?
32. In heating of gases or oil say by condensing steam, finned tube units are employed. Why ?
33. In finned tube units, state whether the fluid having very low heat transfer coefficient as compared to other should be directed on fin side or other side.
34. Is it possible to take out tube bundle outside of shell and clean it in case of
    (i) fixed tube sheet exchanger
    (ii) U-tube exchanger
    (iii) floating head heat exchanger.
35. The problem of differential expansion is eliminated in floating head heat exchangers. State whether this statement is correct or not ?
36. Does the presence of non condensable gas in condensing vapour decrease the film heat transfer coefficient ?
37. State the two methods of increasing the steam economy of evaporation system.

38. If condensate formed does not wet the surface, which type condensation do you expect to occur ?
39. Unlike conduction and convection, energy transfer by radiation does not need physical contact. State whether this statement is true or false.
40. At high temperature levels, heat loss by radiation from unlagged steam pipe is very high as compared heat loss by conduction and convection. State whether this statement is true or false.
41. Driving force for heat transfer is temperature difference or gradient. What is the driving force in case of mass transfer ?
42. Boiling point of solution is 380 K (107º C) at atmospheric pressure in vapour space. What is the boiling point elevation of the solution ?
43. State the operation in which equimolal counter diffusion takes place.
44. Mention the law for mass transport like Fourier's law for heat transport.
45. What happens to the product purity if boil-up rate is suddenly increased ?
46. Why actual stages are more than theoretical stages ?
47. State whether a packed column is a continuous contactor or stage wise contactor.
48. Mention the condition which limits the mass transfer.
49. What is the effect of increasing the total pressure on separation by distillation ?
50. State whether bubble point and dew point are identical for pure component or not.
51. State the phases involved in case of
    (i) distillation, (ii) crystallization and (iii) drying.
52. State direction of solute transfer in gas absorption.
53. Which factor is a measure of separation by distillation ?
54. What will happen to the boiling point temperature if pressure starts building in simple distillation still ?
55. What will happen if vaporisation rate is increased above that for which the condenser is designed in case of distillation. The vent is provided on condenser.
56. What is the upper limit for bubble point of binary mixture at given pressure ?
57. State whether plate or packed column is usually preferred for batch distillation operation.
58. What is the upper limit for packing size in case of packed column.
59. In dealing with liquid mixtures containing solids, whether we should go for continuous process or batch process of distillation to keep the solids separated.
60. Whether cleaning is easy with plate or packing ?
61. What is the common driving force for nucleation and growth of crystals ?
62. Whether cooling should be fast or slow for obtaining large size crystals ?
63. Suggest suitable dryer for

(i) milk powder
(ii) wet lumpy solids
(iii) free flowing materials.

64. State whether fluidised bed dryers can be used for heat sensitive materials or not.
65. The solvent used for gas absorption should be non-volatile. Why?
66. To conserve the heat energy, major portion of hot air is recirculated in the tray dryer. State whether this statement is true or false?
67. What for flights are incorporated in rotary dryer?
68. State the two unit-operations involving simultaneous heat and mass transfer.
69. Why the orifices should be cleaned from time to time in case of spray dryers using pressure nozzles?
70. What happens if dryers are not insulated?
71. Suppose in drying operation, wet bulb temperature of the outgoing air increases. State what it indicates and state whether outgoing flow should be increased or not?
72. Like relative volatility in distillation, state the factor which is a measure of separation by liquid-liquid extraction.
73. What do you mean by azeotrope.
74. Extraction followed by distillation can be thought more economical than distillation alone in case of dilute solution of acetic acid. State whether this statement is true or false?
75. State the method of achieving supersaturation in case of solutes of which solubility increases with increase in temperature.
76. Why dispersed phase distributor should be embedded in packings in case of extraction in packed column?
77. State the nature of solutions for which forced circulation evaporators are commonly employed.
78. In spray tower used for extraction, true counter current is not observed. State whether it is true or false.
79. In Swenson-Walker crystalliser. What is the role of spiral agitator?
80. In case of steam distillation, if the pressure is atmospheric boiling temperature is always less than 373 K (100° C). State whether it is true or false.

ANSWERS (TRY YOURSELF)

1. Material B of thermal conductivity k_2.
2. W/(m·K).
3. Yes.
4. No. Heat flow is directly proportional to the temperature difference.
5. No.

6. $\dfrac{1}{2} \dfrac{(D_2 - D_1)}{\ln\left(\dfrac{D_2}{D_1}\right)}$

7. True.
8. Resistance of hot fluid film, resistance of metal wall, and resistance of cold fluid film.
9. Film heat transfer coefficients will increase form h_1 to h_2 ($h_2 > h_1$, h_2 corresponds to u_2).
10. Coolant having specific heat of C_{P_B}.
11. Temperature of hot fluid increases and that of cold fluid falls.
12. No. After long time in service scale or dirt deposits on heat transfer surface which will add to thermal resistance, value of U will be reduced and required amount of heat will be no longer transferred.
13. Viscous fluid should be directed on shell side.
14. Corrosive fluid should be directed through tubes.
15. Condensers are employed to remove latent heat and coolers are employed to remove sensible heat.
16. Baffles reduce the flow area and direct the fluid across tube bundle which leads to generation of turbulence in shell side fluid, thus increasing shell side heat transfer coefficient.
17. Due to the resistance of condensate film to the heat passing through it, film heat transfer coefficients are low.
18. Oily and greasy surface, surface on which dirt is present.
19. Counter current flow apparatus.
20. No. Counter current flow.
21. LMTD would be zero and as Q and U are finite, surface required would be infinite, and it is not feasible practically.
22. When vaporisation takes place directly from surface, it is called nucleate boiling and when vaporisation takes place through blanketing a film of gas, it is called as film boiling.
23. Heat transfer rate is much low for large temperature drop and temperature drop is not utilised effectively.
24. Film heat transfer coefficient is higher in nucleate boiling.
25. Triangular pitch arrangement.
26. Square pitch arrangement.
27. Parallel flow arrangement
28. To avoid heat loss by radiation, convection and conduction through pipe i.e. to conserve heat.
29. Cleaning of the tubes from inside is easy.

30. 2 – 4 shell and tube exchanger.
31. The metal pieces attached to ordinary tube or pipe to extend (or increase) the heat transfer surface are called fins.
32. In case of heating of gas or oil by condensing steam, gas or oil heat transfer coefficient is very small. In comparison with it, for steam and heat transfer will be controlled by it so as to make h ∞ A on gas side approximately equal to h ∞ A on condensing steam side, gas or oil surface should be extended with fins. In finned tube units, gas or oil side surface is extended by fins, hence finned tube units are used for heating of gas or oil by condensing steam.
33. Fluid having very low film transfer coefficient should be directed on fin side.
34. (i) No. (ii) Yes. (iii) Yes.
35. This statement is correct.
36. Yes.
37. (i) Multiple effect evaporation (ii) Vapour recompression.
38. Dropwise condensation.
39. This statement is True.
40. This statement is True.
41. Concentration difference.
42. 380 – 373 = 10 K = boiling point elevation of the solution.
43. Distillation.
44. Fick's law.
45. Product purity goes down.
46. While calculating the ideal stages according to the definition of ideal stage, it is assumed that equilibrium exists between the vapour and liquid, leaving the each stage which is not generally achieved in actual practice, so actual stages are more than ideal stages.
47. Packed column is a continuous contactor.
48. Equilibrium condition.
49. As the total pressure is increased, the relative volatility decreases and separation becomes difficult.
50. Bubble point and dew point are identical for pure component, and are equal to boiling point of pure component at given pressure.
51. (1) Vapour - liquid (2) Solid - liquid (3) Solid - gas.
52. From gas phase to liquid solvent phase.
53. Relative volatility.
54. Boiling point increases.
55. Vapour loss through vent provided on condenser.

56. Boiling point of a less volatile component at given system pressure.
57. Packed column (due to low liquid hold-up).
58. Packing size should not be greater than one - eighth of the column diameter.
59. Batch distillation process.
60. Cleaning is easy with plate.
61. Supersaturation.
62. Cooling should be slow.
63. (i) Spray dryer. (ii) Tray dryer. (iii) Rotary dryer.
64. Yes.
65. The gas leaving the absorption tower is usually saturated with solvent, so to minimise the loss of solvent with gas, the solvent should be non- volatile (i.e. solvent should have low vapour pressure).
66. True.
67. Flights lift the material and shower it down through the current of hot air, otherwise material to be dried may only slip or roll over the dryer shell.
68. (i) Crystallization (ii) Drying.
69. To avoid clogging.
70. Dryers are insulated to conserve heat and if not insulated, dew may form from inside of dryer and it may fall on the dried product.
71. Increase in humidity of outgoing air. The air flow should be increased.
72. Selectivity.
73. An azeotrope is a liquid mixture with vapour of same composition as that of liquid.
74. True.
75. Supersaturation by cooling.
76. If the material of the packing support does not get wet by dispersed phase droplet and if distributor is placed outside the packing, the drop will face difficulty in entering packing and premature flooding results. For this reason distributor is embedded packing.
77. For viscous, scale forming and salting solutions, forced circulation evaporators are commonly employed.
78. True.
80. The spiral agitator prevents the deposition of crystals on cooling surface, keeps the crystals in suspension (by lifting and showering) to yield crystals of uniformed size and conveys the crystals from one end to other end of crystallizer.
80. True.

APPENDIX – II
THERMAL CONDUCTIVITIES OF VARIOUS MATERIALS

Material	Temp (K)	k, W/(m·K)
Metals :		
Silver	373	412
Copper	373	377
Aluminium	373	230
Nickel	373	57
Iron (cast)	326	48
Lead	373	35
Carbon steel, 1% C	373	43
Stainless steel (18% Cr, 8% Ni)	373	16.3
Bronze	–	189
Non metallic solids :		
Diamond		2300
Asbestos	373	0.19
Asbestos	473	0.21
Bricks (Alumina)	703	3.1
Bricks (Building)	293	0.69
Mica	323	0.43
Cotton wool	303	0.05
Glass wool	–	0.041
Saw dust	293	0.052
Cork	303	0.043
Graphite	273	151
Liquids :		
Water	303	0.62
Water	333	0.66
Gases :		
Air	273	0.024
Air	273	0.031
CO_2	273	0.015

APPENDIX – III
STEAM TABLES

STEAM TABLES NOTATION

p = Absolute pressure in mm Hg, kPa or MPa
t = Saturation temperture in °C
T = Sautration temperature in K
h = Specific enthalpy of saturated or compressed water in kJ/kg
H = Specific enthalpy of saturated steam in kJ/kg
λ = Latent heat of vaporization of saturated water in kJ/kg

Table 1 : Properteis of saturated water and saturated steam up to atmospheric pressure

p mm Hg	p kPa	t °C	T K	h kJ/kg	H kJ/kg	λ kJ/kg
1	0.133	– 19.302	253.848	– 82.56	2466.0	2548.6
2	0.267	– 10.902	262.248	– 46.30	2481.5	2527.8
3	0.400	– 5.693	267.457	– 24.12	2491.1	2515.2
4	0.533	– 1.854	271.296	– 7.87	2498.1	2506.0
5	0.667	1.210	274.360	5.06	2503.8	2498.7
6	0.800	3.772	276.922	15.84	2508.5	2492.6
7	0.933	5.980	279.130	25.13	2512.5	2487.4
8	1.067	7.926	281.076	33.29	2516.1	2482.8
9	1.200	9.667	282.817	40.60	2619.3	2478.7
10	1.333	11.246	284.396	47.22	2522.2	2475.0
11	1.467	12.691	285.841	53.27	2524.8	2471.6
12	1.600	14.025	287.175	58.86	2527.3	2468.4
13	1.733	15.265	288.415	64.05	2529.5	2465.4
14	1.867	16.423	289.573	68.90	2531.7	2462.8
15	2.000	17.511	290.661	73.45	2533.6	2460.2
16	2.133	18.538	291.688	77.74	2535.5	2457.8
17	2.266	19.509	292.659	81.81	2537.3	2455.5
18	2.400	20.432	293.582	85.67	2539.0	2453.3
19	2.533	21.311	294.461	89.34	2540.6	2451.2
20	2.666	22.150	295.300	92.85	2542.1	2449.2
21	2.800	22.954	296.104	96.21	2543.6	2447.4
22	2.933	23.724	296.874	99.43	2545.0	2445.5

p mm Hg	p kPa	t °C	T K	h kJ/kg	H kJ/kg	λ kJ/kg
23	3.066	24.465	297.615	102.53	2546.3	2443.8
24	3.200	25.178	298.328	105.51	2547.6	2442.1
25	3.333	25.866	299.016	108.38	2548.9	2440.5
26	3.466	26.530	299.680	111.16	2550.1	2438.9
27	3.600	27.172	300.322	113.84	2551.2	2437.4
28	3.733	27.794	300.944	116.44	2552.4	2435.9
29	3.866	28.396	301.546	118.96	2553.4	2434.5
30	4.000	28.981	301.131	121.41	2554.5	2433.1
31	4.133	29.549	302.699	123.78	2555.5	2431.8
32	4.266	30.102	303.252	126.09	2556.5	2430.4
33	4.400	30.639	303.789	128.34	2557.5	2429.2
34	4.533	31.163	304.313	130.52	2558.5	2427.9
35	4.666	31.673	304.823	132.66	2559.4	2426.7
36	4.800	32.171	305.321	134.74	2560.3	2425.5
37	4.933	32.657	305.807	136.77	2561.2	2424.4
38	5.066	33.132	306.282	138.75	2562.0	2423.3
39	5.200	33.596	306.746	140.69	2562.9	2422.2
40	5.333	34.050	307.200	142.59	2563.7	2421.1
41	5.466	34.494	307.644	144.44	2564.5	2420.0
42	5.600	34.929	308.079	146.26	2565.3	2419.0
43	5.733	35.355	308.505	148.04	2566.0	2418.0
44	5.866	35.772	308.922	149.79	2566.8	2417.0
45	5.999	36.182	309.332	151.50	2567.5	2416.0
46	6.133	36.583	309.733	153.17	2568.2	2415.1
47	6.266	36.977	310.127	154.82	2568.9	2414.1
48	6.399	37.364	310.514	156.44	2569.6	2413.2
49	6.533	37.744	310.894	158.02	2570.3	2412.3
50	6.666	38.117	311.267	159.58	2571.0	2411.4
55	7.333	39.892	313.042	167.00	2574.2	2407.2
60	7.999	41.533	314.683	173.86	2577.1	2403.3
65	8.666	43.059	316.209	180.24	2579.8	2399.6
70	9.333	44.488	317.638	186.21	2582.4	2396.2
75	9.999	45.831	318.981	191.83	2584.8	2393.0
80	10.666	47.099	320.249	197.13	2587.0	2389.9
85	11.332	48.301	321.451	202.15	2589.2	2387.0
90	11.999	49.444	322.594	206.93	2591.2	2384.3
95	12.666	50.534	323.684	211.49	2593.1	2381.6
100	13.332	51.575	324.725	215.84	2595.0	2379.1
120	15.999	55.339	328.489	231.59	2601.6	2370.0
140	18.665	58.601	331.751	245.23	2607.3	2362.0

p mm Hg	p kPa	t °C	T K	h kJ/kg	H kJ/kg	λ kJ/kg
160	21.332	61.486	334.636	257.31	2612.3	2355.0
180	23.998	64.080	337.230	268.17	2616.8	2348.6
200	26.664	66.439	339.589	278.05	2620.8	2342.7
220	29.331	68.606	341.756	287.13	2624.5	2337.4
240	31.997	70.613	343.763	295.54	2628.0	2332.4
260	34.664	72.482	345.632	303.38	2631.1	2327.8
280	37.330	74.234	347.384	310.72	2634.1	2323.4
300	39.997	75.884	349.034	317.64	2636.9	2319.2
320	42.663	77.443	350.593	324.18	2639.5	2315.3
340	45.329	78.922	352.072	330.39	2642.0	2311.6
360	47.996	80.330	353.480	336.30	2644.3	2308.0
380	50.662	81.673	354.823	341.94	2646.5	2304.6
400	53.329	82.959	356.109	347.34	2648.7	2301.3
420	55.995	84.192	357.342	352.52	2650.7	2298.2
440	58.662	85.376	358.526	357.50	2652.6	2295.1
460	61.328	86.517	359.667	362.29	2654.5	2292.2
480	63.995	87.616	360.766	366.91	2656.3	2289.4
500	66.661	88.678	361.828	371.38	2658.0	2286.6
520	69.327	89.705	362.855	375.70	2659.7	2284.0
540	71.994	90.700	363.850	389.88	2661.3	2281.4
560	64.660	91.664	364.814	383.94	2662.8	2278.9
580	77.327	92.600	365.650	387.88	2664.3	2276.4
600	79.993	93.510	366.660	391.71	2665.8	2274.1
620	82.660	94.395	367.545	395.44	2667.2	2271.7
640	85.326	95.256	368.406	399.07	2668.5	2269.5
660	87.993	96.095	369.245	402.60	2669.9	2267.3
680	90.659	96.914	370.064	406.05	2671.2	2265.1
700	93.325	97.712	370.862	409.42	2672.4	2263.0
720	95.992	98.492	371.642	412.71	2673.7	2260.9
740	98.658	99.255	372.405	415.92	2674.8	2258.9
760	**101.325**	**100.000**	**373.150**	**419.06**	**2676.0**	**2256.9**
780	103.991	100.729	373.897	422.14	2677.1	2255.0
800	106.658	101.443	374.593	425.15	2678.3	2253.1

Table 2 : Properties of saturated water and Dry steam from 0.10 to 14 MPa a

P MPa	t °C	T K	h kJ/kg	H kJ/kg	λ kJ/kg
0.10	99.63	372.78	417.51	2675.4	2257.9
0.11	102.32	375.47	428.84	2679.6	2250.9
0.12	104.81	377.96	439.36	2683.4	2244.1
0.13	107.13	380.28	449.19	2687.0	2237.8
0.14	109.32	382.47	458.42	2690.3	2231.9
0.15	111.37	384.52	467.13	2693.4	2226.2
0.16	113.32	386.47	475.38	2696.2	2220.9
0.17	115.17	388.32	483.22	2699.0	2215.7
0.18	116.93	390.08	490.70	2701.5	2210.8
0.19	118.62	391.77	497.85	2704.0	2206.1
0.20	120.23	393.38	504.70	2706.3	2201.6
0.21	121.78	394.93	511.28	2708.5	2197.2
0.22	123.27	396.42	517.62	2710.6	2193.0
0.23	124.71	397.86	523.73	2712.6	2188.9
0.24	126.09	399.24	529.63	2714.5	2184.9
0.25	127.43	400.58	535.34	2716.4	2181.0
0.26	128.73	401.88	540.87	2718.2	2177.3
0.27	129.98	403.13	546.24	2719.9	2173.6
0.28	131.20	404.35	551.44	2721.5	2170.1
0.29	132.39	405.54	556.50	2723.1	2166.6
0.30	133.54	406.69	561.43	2724.7	2163.2
0.31	134.66	407.81	566.23	2726.1	2159.9
0.32	135.75	408.90	570.90	2727.6	2156.7
0.33	136.82	409.97	575.46	2729.0	2153.5
0.34	137.86	411.01	579.92	2730.3	2150.4
0.35	138.87	412.02	584.27	2731.6	2147.4
0.36	139.86	413.01	588.53	2732.9	2144.4
0.37	140.83	413.98	592.69	2734.1	2141.4
0.38	141.78	414.93	596.76	2735.3	2138.6
0.39	142.71	415.86	600.76	2736.5	2135.7
0.40	143.62	416.77	604.67	2737.6	2133.0
0.41	144.52	417.67	608.51	2738.7	2130.2
0.42	145.39	418.54	612.27	2739.8	2127.5
0.43	146.25	419.40	615.97	2740.9	2124.9
0.44	147.09	420.24	619.60	2741.9	2122.3
0.45	147.92	421.07	623.16	2742.9	2119.7
0.46	148.73	421.88	626.67	2743.9	2117.2
0.47	149.53	422.68	630.11	2744.8	2114.7
0.48	150.31	423.46	633.50	2745.7	2112.2
0.49	151.08	424.23	636.83	2746.6	2109.8

P MPa	t °C	T K	h kJ/kg	H kJ/kg	λ kJ/kg
0.50	151.84	424.99	640.12	2747.5	2107.4
0.52	153.33	426.48	646.53	2749.3	2102.7
0.54	154.76	427.91	652.76	2750.9	2098.1
0.56	156.16	429.31	658.81	2752.5	2093.7
0.58	157.52	430.67	664.69	2754.0	2089.3
0.60	158.84	431.99	670.42	2755.5	2085.0
0.62	160.12	433.27	676.01	2756.9	2080.9
0.64	161.38	434.53	681.46	2758.2	2076.8
0.66	162.60	435.75	686.78	2759.5	2072.7
0.68	163.79	436.94	691.98	2760.8	2068.8
0.70	164.96	438.11	697.06	2762.0	2064.9
0.72	166.10	439.25	702.03	2763.2	2061.1
0.74	167.21	440.36	706.90	2764.3	2057.4
0.76	168.30	441.45	711.67	2765.4	2053.7
0.78	169.37	442.52	716.35	2766.4	2050.1
0.80	170.41	443.56	720.94	2767.5	2046.5
0.82	171.44	444.59	725.43	2768.5	2043.0
0.84	172.45	445.60	729.85	2769.4	2039.6
0.86	173.44	446.59	734.19	2770.4	2036.2
0.88	174.41	447.56	738.45	2771.3	2032.8
0.90	175.36	448.51	742.64	2772.1	2029.5
0.92	176.29	449.44	746.76	2773.0	2026.2
0.94	177.21	450.36	750.82	2773.8	2023.0
0.96	178.12	451.27	754.81	2774.6	2019.8
0.98	179.01	452.16	758.74	2775.4	2016.7
1.00	179.88	453.03	762.61	2776.2	2013.6
1.05	182.02	455.17	772.03	2778.0	2005.9
1.10	184.07	457.22	781.12	2779.7	1998.5
1.15	186.05	459.20	789.92	2781.3	1991.3
1.20	187.96	461.11	798.43	2782.7	1984.3
1.25	189.81	462.96	806.69	2784.1	1977.4
1.30	191.61	464.76	814.70	2785.4	1970.7
1.35	193.35	466.50	822.49	2786.6	1964.2
1.40	195.04	468.19	830.07	2787.8	1957.7
1.45	196.69	469.84	837.46	2788.9	1951.4
1.50	198.29	471.44	844.66	2789.9	1945.2
1.55	199.85	473.00	851.69	2790.8	1939.2
1.60	201.37	474.52	858.56	2791.7	1933.2
1.65	202.86	476.01	865.28	2792.6	1927.3
1.70	204.31	477.46	871.84	2793.4	1921.5

P MPa	t °C	T K	h kJ/kg	H kJ/kg	λ kJ/kg
1.75	205.72	478.87	878.27	2794.1	1915.9
1.80	207.11	480.26	884.57	2794.8	1910.3
1.85	208.47	481.62	890.75	2795.5	1904.7
1.90	209.80	482.95	896.81	2796.1	1899.3
1.95	211.10	484.25	902.75	2796.7	1893.9
2.00	212.37	485.52	908.59	2797.2	1888.6
2.05	213.63	486.78	914.32	2797.7	1883.4
2.10	214.63	488.00	919.96	2798.2	1878.2
2.15	216.06	489.21	925.50	2798.6	1873.1
2.20	217.24	490.39	930.95	2799.1	1868.1
2.25	218.41	491.56	936.32	1799.4	1863.1
2.30	219.55	492.70	941.60	2799.8	1858.2
2.35	220.68	493.83	946.80	2800.1	1853.3
2.40	221.78	494.93	951.93	2800.4	1848.5
2.45	222.87	496.02	956.98	2800.7	1843.7
2.50	223.94	497.09	961.96	2800.9	1839.0
2.55	225.00	498.15	966.87	2801.2	1834.3
2.60	226.04	499.19	971.72	2801.4	1829.6
2.65	227.06	500.21	976.50	2801.6	1825.1
2.70	228.07	501.22	981.22	2801.7	1820.5
2.75	229.07	502.22	985.88	2801.9	1816.0
2.80	230.05	503.20	990.48	2802.0	1811.5
2.85	231.01	504.16	995.03	2802.1	1807.1
2.90	231.97	505.12	999.52	2802.2	1802.6
2.95	232.91	506.06	1003.96	2802.2	1798.3
3.00	233.84	506.99	1008.35	2802.3	1793.9
3.10	235.67	508.82	1016.99	2802.3	1785.4
3.20	237.45	510.60	1025.43	2802.3	1776.9
3.30	239.18	512.33	1033.70	2802.3	1768.6
3.40	240.88	514.03	1041.81	2802.1	1760.3
3.50	242.54	515.69	1049.76	2802.0	1752.2
3.60	244.16	517.31	1057.56	2801.7	1744.2
3.70	245.75	518.90	1065.21	2801.4	1736.2
3.80	247.31	520.46	1072.74	2801.1	1728.4
3.90	248.84	521.99	1080.13	2800.8	1720.6
4.00	250.33	523.48	1087.40	2800.3	1712.9
4.20	253.24	526.39	1101.60	2799.4	1697.8
4.40	256.05	529.20	1115.38	2798.3	1682.9
4.60	258.75	531.90	1128.76	2797.0	1668.3
4.80	261.37	534.52	1141.78	2795.7	1653.9

P MPa	t °C	T K	h kJ/kg	H kJ/kg	λ kJ/kg
5.00	263.91	537.06	1154.47	2794.2	1639.7
5.50	269.93	543.08	1184.89	2789.9	1605.0
6.00	275.55	548.70	1213.69	2785.0	1571.3
6.50	280.82	553.97	1241.14	2779.5	1538.4
7.00	285.79	558.94	1267.42	2773.5	1506.0
7.50	290.50	563.65	1292.69	2766.9	1474.2
8.00	294.97	568.12	1317.10	2759.9	1442.8
8.50	299.23	572.38	1340.75	2752.5	1411.7
9.00	303.31	576.46	1363.73	2744.6	1380.9
9.50	307.21	580.36	1386.14	2736.4	1350.2
10.00	310.96	584.11	1408.04	2727.7	1319.7
11.00	318.05	591.20	1450.57	2709.3	1258.7
12.00	324.65	597.80	1491.77	2689.2	1197.4
13.00	330.83	603.98	1532.01	2667.0	1135.0
14.00	336.64	609.79	1571.64	2642.4	1070.8

❑❑❑

www.ingramcontent.com/pod-product-compliance
Lightning Source LLC
Chambersburg PA
CBHW060504300426
44112CB00017B/2542